NEGOTIATION:
THEORY AND
PRACTICE

SECOND EDITION

(REVISED AND EXPANDED EDITION.
ORIGINALLY PUBLISHED AS UNDERSTANDING NEGOTIATION.)

MELISSA L. NELKEN
Professor of Law
Faculty Chair, Center for Negotiation and Dispute Resolution
University of California
Hastings College of the Law

Library of Congress Cataloging-in-Publication Data

Nelken, Melissa L.

Negotiation: theory and practice / Melissa L. Nelken — 2nd ed.

   p. cm.

Includes index.

ISBN 1-4224-1162-1 (soft cover)

1. Negotiation — United States. 2. Dispute resolution (law) — United States

   3. Mediation — United States. 4. Attorney and Client — United States.

KF9084.N45 2007

347.73'9 — dc22   2007009922

Editorial Offices
744 Broad Street, Newark, NJ 07102 (973) 820-2000
201 Mission St., San Francisco, CA 94105-1831 (415) 908-3200
701 East Water Street, Charlottesville, VA 22902-7587 (434) 972-7600
www.lexis.com

(Pub.3571)

DEDICATION

To Ron, who makes it all worthwhile.

PREFACE TO SECOND EDITION

In addition to revising and updating the existing chapters from the first edition (originally published as *Understanding Negotiation*), I have added two new chapters to this edition, one on culture and gender in negotiation and one on multiparty negotiation. Although the first edition dealt with issues of culture and gender in limited ways, I decided that the challenge of teaching about them in a negotiation class would be better addressed in a separate chapter. In addition, many negotiation teachers include a multiparty or team negotiation at the end of an introductory class, as an example of the next level of challenges in learning about the subject. To incorporate such an exercise into the book's coverage, I have added a chapter that focuses on some distinguishing characteristics of multiparty negotiations, including coalition formation and dissolution; teams; representing groups; and common procedural issues that arise in the multiparty context.

My thanks again to my students at Hastings, who teach me new things about negotiation every semester; to my colleague and Center for Negotiation and Dispute Resolution Director Chris Knowlton for her willingness to read drafts and to talk about important issues for negotiation teachers; to Beverly Taylor for secretarial assistance; and to Jolynn Jones of CNDR for making a completed manuscript a reality in record time. A sabbatical leave and a summer research grant from Hastings enabled me to complete this project, for which I am grateful.

PREFACE TO FIRST EDITION

This is a book about negotiation for law students and lawyers. In addition to covering general negotiation topics such as distributive and integrative bargaining, it focuses on issues of special importance to lawyers, including the lawyer-client relationship and ethical issues that arise in negotiations. It also pays particular attention to the psychology of negotiation, from both a cognitive and a psychodynamic viewpoint. By combining introductory explanatory material with selections from a wide range of authors in each chapter, I have designed the book to be used as the primary text in a law school negotiation course, or as a reference for lawyers interested in learning more about negotiation from a variety of perspectives. I have tried to include excerpts from articles and books that are excellent but not widely known to lawyers, as well as from standards in the field. I have omitted certain other works, such as Fisher, Ury and Patton's *Getting to YES*, because they are already so familiar and easily found in inexpensive paperback editions.

When law students think about negotiations, they often imagine a scenario in which adversaries compete: Who will get the contract to supply XYZ Corporation's widgets? How much will Defendant pay Plaintiff to settle his employment discrimination lawsuit? Such scenarios fit the standard case law model of law school instruction, which assumes an adversary system in which each side hires a zealous advocate to fight for it. But does this model actually fit the reality of lawyers' negotiations? In one sense, all too well, since law-trained advocates tend to carry over the "win/lose" mentality of the classroom and the courtroom to negotiations. In another sense, a singular focus on "besting" the other lawyer in a negotiation may result in losing sight of larger goals of the parties, such as maintaining long-term working relationships. It may also damage a lawyer's ability to work effectively with other lawyers in resolving disputes.

Much of the negotiation literature of the last twenty years has focused on the relative merits of a "win/lose" versus a "win/win" orientation in negotiation, what I refer to in this book as distributive versus integrative bargaining. In reality, few negotiations fit neatly into one or the other category. Much of the skill of negotiation lies in assessing the nature of a particular conflict, the interests of the parties, and the personalities of their representatives in order to select the most productive approach to resolving that dispute. I use the word "select" to suggest that as a negotiator, you can and should develop a flexible style that will vary depending on the situation you find yourself in. How to start developing such flexibility is the subject of this book.

The book is organized in much the same way as the course I teach on negotiation. The first chapter, on the background and context of legal negotiations, can be used as an introduction to the subject or, towards the end of the class, as a vehicle for encouraging critical thinking about dispute resolution systems in general; the special characteristics of lawyers' negotiations; and cultural aspects of negotiating and of American negotiation theory. The next three chapters introduce distributive and integrative bargaining and analyze the tension between them. I then turn to psychological aspects of negotiation; lawyer-client issues; and ethical dilemmas. These three topics, of course, permeate any consideration of negotiation. I have put them in separate chapters for purposes of analysis; but the materials covered in them could certainly be introduced at an earlier stage, as specific issues come up for discussion in class. The final chapter focuses on mediation as a form of facilitated negotiation — one that lawyers can learn from in order to improve their own negotiating skills, as well as a resource that they can turn to in the event of an insuperable impasse in negotiations. In addition, as court-annexed alternative dispute resolution becomes more common, lawyers will be more regularly exposed to mediation as an extension of and an adjunct to private settlement negotiations.

In the chapters that follow, I have adopted one simplifying convention based on my own teaching experience. I treat negotiations as two-sided, rather than multi-sided, and do not discuss group negotiations and the complex dynamics of coalition-building and coalition-breaking that characterize them. Although I often include a group negotiation at the end of my four-unit beginning negotiation course, I do so primarily to call the students' attention to their next big challenge in learning about negotiations. To my mind, the topic is one that can be addressed adequately only after mastering the basic material covered here.

I want to thank my hundreds of negotiation students, law students and lawyers alike, who have helped me refine my thinking about negotiation over the past twenty years. They have been generous with their reflections and insights about the ways they approach, avoid, and deal with conflict in negotiation, and they have taught me a great deal about the intricate interweaving of the personal and the professional in the experience of negotiating for a client. A sabbatical leave and a summer research grant from Hastings gave me the time I needed to complete this project. Beverly Taylor provided superb secretarial assistance from beginning to end; and John Borden of the Hastings Law Library and Adrienne Leight, Hastings class of 2003, researched and helped clean up loose ends during the final months. I am grateful for their assistance. My negotiation colleagues Chris Knowlton, Howard Herman, Bea Moulton, and Maude Pervere read and commented on early drafts of several chapters. Their thoughtful suggestions have certainly improved the final version; and I appreciate their input.

TABLE OF CONTENTS

Chapter 1
LEGAL NEGOTIATIONS: BACKGROUND AND CONTEXT

Everyone negotiates. Anytime you deal with someone else, seeking to reach agreement on some matter, you are involved in a negotiation. Teenagers negotiate with parents about how late they can stay out on Friday night; spouses negotiate about what car to buy or when to have children; students negotiate with professors about paper deadlines. These daily negotiations are part and parcel of all human interaction, averting or resolving more or less open conflicts between individuals or among groups. How you conduct them reflects your fundamental beliefs about the importance of self-assertion and autonomy versus preserving ties with others; about how to get what you want; about right and wrong behavior. These negotiations are just as real as the movie deal, class action settlement, or peace agreement that you might more readily think of as negotiations. Indeed, your lifetime of ordinary negotiating experiences will inevitably affect the way you approach negotiations as a lawyer. Whether these experiences will be a help or a hindrance to you in a professional context will depend to a large extent on your ability to become aware of your underlying assumptions about negotiations and to put that awareness to use as you develop negotiating skills as a lawyer.

A. NEGOTIATING FOR A LIVING

Everyone negotiates, and lawyers negotiate for a living. Acting as agents, lawyers work on behalf of other people to reach a mutually agreeable resolution — a sale, a settlement, a development deal — for the parties involved. Even those lawyers who specialize in litigation are primarily negotiators, since fewer than 10% of lawsuits are actually tried to verdict. Lawyers negotiate the details of their professional daily life — when depositions and meetings will take place; whether and when a particular motion will be filed or set for hearing; which documents will be produced without a judge's order — as well as the large and small elements of a long-term supply contract or of a settlement in a major case.

When they negotiate for their clients, lawyers are governed not only by the general principles of agency law, but also by the rules of legal ethics, which reinforce the ideal of duty to the client as a primary professional obligation. This ideal is used to justify behavior in negotiations — puffing, bluffing, and other forms of deception short of affirmative misrepresentation — that many lawyers find difficult to square with their personal convictions about how to deal with other people or about appropriate

1

professional conduct. At the same time, the realities of negotiation do not readily conform to the ideal in other respects. Lawyers have many clients, and in negotiations they face conflicts between what is in one client's interest today and what will be in another client's interest next week, especially when they negotiate repeatedly with the same opponents. The lawyer's own interests may also conflict with the client's, in terms of the time and effort required to negotiate an optimal agreement for the client and the lawyer's need to make a living. These ethical dilemmas are an inherent part of the negotiation context within which lawyers operate, and the stresses they create can never be fully resolved.

B. NEGOTIATING TO STAY OUT OF COURT

Despite the centrality of negotiation to law practice, courses in negotiation were a rarity in American law schools as recently as twenty-five years ago. The few skills courses offered focused primarily on advocacy at the trial and appellate levels. Since then, concerns about the rigidity of the adjudicatory system and about a litigation "explosion" that some believed was swamping the courts, among other factors, have led to increased scholarly and practitioner focus on alternative methods of dispute resolution (ADR), including negotiation. Courses on negotiation, mediation, and arbitration have become more common, and both private practitioners and many court systems have made ADR widely available to clients and litigants.

Scholars have drawn on research in economics, game theory, and social and cognitive psychology to think systematically about how lawyers and others negotiate and about the strengths and weaknesses of various approaches to negotiation. As Mnookin and Kornhauser discuss below in the case of divorce, lawyers' negotiations take place "in the shadow of the law." Unlike negotiators in other fields, lawyers operate within a specialized dispute resolution framework, namely that created by laws and the courts that enforce them. Legal rules and the uncertainties of judicial decision-making, as well as the parties' attitudes toward the risks entailed in going to court, have a powerful influence on the private agreements that lawyers construct through negotiation. At the same time, lawyers approach negotiation knowing that a litigated resolution is often the primary alternative to private settlement. The adversary system is thus both background and context when lawyers negotiate, even when their goal is to keep their clients out of court.

C. NEGOTIATING NORMS

As a form of conflict resolution, negotiation is less formal and less hierarchical than adjudication, the dispute resolution system most familiar to American lawyers. Instead of leaving the decision in the hands of a stranger, negotiation participants try to come up with a mutually satisfactory agreement on their own, or through representatives of their choosing. Compared to litigation, negotiation is also flexible and open. There are no hard and fast rules (of civil procedure or evidence) that govern what the parties can say or what information they can consider during the process, nor are there any fixed standards (laws) that control its outcome. That is not to say, however, that negotiation is unprincipled. As Eisenberg discusses in the excerpt below, the norms that govern negotiation are simply different from those that govern adjudication, partly because of the absence of a judge.

Resolving a dispute by negotiation, rather than by adjudication, makes it possible for the participants to decide not only what the outcome will be, but also what the process will be for reaching that outcome. Even when lawyers conduct the negotiations, parties can instruct them to keep in mind the importance of maintaining a good relationship with the other side, or to compromise rather than to insist on the sort of "win/lose" distributive outcome that would result from a court trial. Often enough, however, lawyers trained in the adversary system view negotiation, like litigation, as war, and they fail to explore integrative opportunities for both parties to benefit in the process. Both distributive and integrative approaches have a place in legal negotiations, and they are considered in detail in the next three chapters.

If the norms governing the process of negotiation are different from those that characterize adjudication, are the effects of a negotiated resolution on the parties also different? Building on the work of authors writing about so-called transformative mediation, Williams has suggested that negotiations have the possibility of radically altering the way parties experience conflict. In the excerpt below, he argues that when a person is able to take steps in a negotiation that challenge his comfortable view of himself as an aggrieved party, and to accept responsibility for his own role in creating the dispute he finds himself in, he may not only reach an acceptable resolution, but also may experience a healing "change of heart" in the process.

D. CULTURE AS CONTEXT

This book looks at negotiation through the lens of an American lawyer trained by the case law method and working in an adversary system. Law students are routinely told that law school will teach them to "think like lawyers", that is, it will initiate them into a professional culture and a new way of viewing the world and their role in it. Until relatively recently, members of this group have also been predominantly white, male, middle-class European Americans. These salient educational and personal characteristics have had a profound impact on American legal culture, on the profession's understanding of conflict and conflict resolution through negotiation, and on its success in incorporating women and people of color into the profession.

Although the cultural dimensions of legal negotiations will be discussed in greater depth in Chapter Six, it is worth highlighting in this introductory chapter that every dispute and every negotiation takes place within a cultural context that the negotiator ignores at his or her peril. There is, first, the culture of the parties and the meaning that the particular dispute has in the context of their lives. In addition, when the parties are represented by lawyers, there is the superimposed context of legal culture, with its own understandings of the goals of negotiation and the role of the negotiator. Finally, the process of negotiation itself, especially if negotiations are lengthy and complex, may create a new cultural context of its own. Attention to the cultural context of a negotiation is imperative in the humanitarian negotiations discussed below by Avruch. It is also important in many other negotiations, where differing cultural understandings of the situation may be less obvious, but no less critical to reaching workable solutions to a particular dispute.

Melvin Aron Eisenberg,[*] *Private Ordering Through Negotiation: Dispute-Settlement and Rulemaking*
89 HARV. L. REV. 637, 638, 642-45, 654-60 (1976)[**]

* * *

Nowhere does the contrast between official processes and their private counterparts appear greater than between adjudication and negotiation. Adjudication is conventionally perceived as a norm-bound process centered on the establishment of facts and the determination and application of principles, rules, and precedents. Negotiation, on the other hand, is conventionally perceived as a relatively norm-free process centered on the transmutation of underlying bargaining strength into agreement by the exercise of power, horse-trading, threat, and bluff.

* * *

To explore the limitations of this view it is necessary to compare the universe and operation of norms in dispute-negotiation, on the one hand, and adjudication, on the other. At this point, three differences may be identified, having to do with the problems presented by *conflicting, colliding, and person-oriented* norms.

> *First*, norms may be said to *conflict* when they are mutually inconsistent across the entire spectrum of their applicability. For example, the doctrine of contributory negligence is inconsistent with the

---

* Melvin A. Eisenberg is Koret Professor of Law at University of California at Berkeley. His article explores the norms that govern dispute negotiation and that make it often more flexible than adjudicative decision making.

doctrine of comparative negligence. Typically, when two norms conflict one becomes dominant, in the sense that it is generally accepted as the "better" or "valid" norm. The other norm, while subordinate, may, however, be given some degree of continued recognition.

Second, norms may be said to *collide* where each has a sphere of action within which it is admittedly valid, but they point in opposing directions in cases in which their respective spheres of applicability intersect. For example, in a number of recent cases involving suits for damages against media of various sorts, the principle of right to privacy has pointed to a verdict for the plaintiff, while the principle of freedom of speech has pointed to a verdict for the defendant.

Third, norms may be said to be *person-* rather than *act-oriented* where their applicability depends on the personal characteristics of the disputants rather than on the nature of their acts. For example, in a society that does not recognize testamentary disposition, the norm "sons inherit" is act-oriented; its applicability does not usually depend on the personal characteristics of a particular father and son. In contrast, a norm such as "brothers should help each other" might be described as person-oriented, because, despite its apparent generality, its application depends almost entirely on the personal characteristics of the individual parties — a wealthy brother should not seek economic help from a poor one; an unkind brother may not be entitled to any help at all.

In adjudication (or, at least, that style of adjudication prevalent in complex Western cultures) the universe and operation of norms is highly stylized and tightly controlled. Where norms conflict, a court will characteristically treat one norm as not only subordinate but totally invalid — so that a court which adopts the doctrine of contributory negligence will deny the validity of comparative negligence. Where norms collide, a court will characteristically select one as determinative of the outcome of the case and reject the other as inapplicable — so that in a case to which the norms of privacy and free speech might be applicable, a court will typically hold that the outcome is controlled by one or the other, but not both. Finally, courts tend to treat person-oriented norms as either invalid or irrelevant — so that in the United States the socially recognized principle that brothers owe each other special obligations will typically give rise to neither a cause of action nor a defense.

In contrast, the universe and operation of norms in dispute-negotiation is typically open-ended. Thus it is characteristic of dispute-negotiation that when norms collide account is taken of both, although the eventual settlement may reflect an adjustment for relative applicability and weight. Similarly, the parties in dispute-negotiation may accord partial or even full recognition to a norm that is generally deemed subordinate or even legally invalid, so that a negligent plaintiff who has no "right" to prevail in a tort action because of the doctrine of contributory negligence may nevertheless make a favorable settlement by reason of the legally invalid but socially real principle of comparative negligence. Finally, parties to dispute-negotiation can and frequently do take person-oriented norms into account as freely as act-oriented norms.

Because adjudication is often regarded as the paradigm of principled decisionmaking, dispute-settlement processes in which the universe and operation of norms differ sharply from adjudication are often perceived as not turning heavily on principle for that reason alone. But whether a process turns heavily on principle depends on the extent to which principles determine the outcome, not on the nature of the principles nor the precise manner in which they determine the outcome. A process that accommodates colliding norms, and freely recognizes subordinate, legally invalid, and person-oriented norms, is not intrinsically less principled than a process that selects between colliding norms, treats subordinate norms as invalid, and focuses on acts rather than personal characteristics.

* * *

1. The Binary Character of Adjudication. The classical model of adjudication, at least in complex Western cultures, is characterized by the dominant role of an official, neutral third party who is vested with formal power to impose a settlement after affording the disputants an opportunity to make arguments and present proofs. For convenience, I shall refer to this model as traditional adjudication. It is sometimes suggested, directly or by inference, that this form of adjudication is distinguishable from negotiation (and other forms of dispute-settlement) because it is a zero-sum game. But zero-sum outcomes are characteristic of all dispute-settlement processes, including dispute-negotiation. If B damages A's car, and A claims the cost of repairs, A's gain in dispute settlement can only come at the expense of B's loss, whether the dispute is settled by traditional adjudication, dispute-negotiation, or other means.

There is, however, a closely related factor, bearing both on outcomes and on the manner in which the outcomes are rationalized, that does tend to distinguish the two processes. Dispute-negotiation has a *graduated* and *accommodative* character: In reaching and rationalizing outcomes, any given norm or any given factual proposition can be taken into account according to the degree of its authoritativeness and applicability (in the case of a norm) or probability (in the case of a factual proposition). In contrast, traditional adjudication tends to have a *binary* character: In reaching, and even more clearly in rationalizing outcomes, any given proposition of fact is normally found to be either true or false, colliding norms are generally treated as if only the more compelling norm were applicable, conflicting norms are generally treated as if only the dominant norm were applicable, and each disputant is generally determined to be either "right" or "wrong." One cause of this binary character is that the very purpose of resorting to adjudication may be to achieve a clear-cut determination of which disputant is right. The binary character of traditional adjudication also reflects a second deep cleavage between that process and dispute-negotiation. While dispute-negotiation is usually controlled by the disputants themselves, and is therefore characterized by its *intimacy*, traditional adjudication is characterized by the central role given to a *stranger*. The impact of the stranger's role makes itself felt dramatically across every element of the two processes: selection and application of norms; determination of facts; choice of remedy; and, perhaps most dramatically, the emotional effect of participation.

2. *The Impact of the Stranger. (a) The selection and application of norms.* — It has been shown that in social relations a broad spectrum of norms can be taken into account in a wide variety of ways, while in traditional adjudication the selection and application of governing norms is highly stylized. The insertion into the dispute of' a stranger is a major cause of this stylization. Since the stranger typically draws his authority from the principle of objectivity, in reaching, and particularly in rationalizing, his decision, he is likely to stress his compliance with that principle and to downplay the amount of his discretion. One way in which the stranger can achieve that end is by treating norms in a binary fashion, rather than attempting to assign appropriate degrees of weight. Furthermore, a decision that is rationalized on the basis of the norms advanced by one of the two disputants requires a smaller commitment of resources by the stranger than an accommodative solution, and involves less risk that the stranger will settle the dispute on the basis of norms that neither party deems relevant.

The impact of a stranger is even more pervasive in the area of person-oriented norms. Since such norms tend to be intimate in nature, a stranger typically has little standing to dictate behavior on their basis. Furthermore, a stranger is typically not in position to determine the applicability of such norms, which usually depends upon intimate familiarity with the parties. To determine whether the norm "One who takes care of an aging relative should share in his estate" is applicable, an adjudicator would have to determine not only the texture of the relationship between the decedent and the claimant, but that between the decedent and other potential claimants to his estate — no easy task even for an intimate, but a herculean one for a stranger. For both these reasons, a stranger is usually much readier to invoke act-oriented than person-oriented norms.

* * *

Thus, the stranger-adjudicator is likely to treat as irrelevant some principles the disputants themselves regard as relevant, and consequently to have at his command less than the sum total of principles potentially applicable to a dispute. In a real sense, therefore, traditional adjudication may actually be a less principled process than dispute-negotiation.

(b) Fact-determination. Just as the universe and operation of norms is more constricted in adjudication than in dispute-negotiation, so is the uni-

verse of techniques for fact-determination. In dispute-negotiation most factual issues can be determined by explicit or tacit agreement, since the participants in the process will have personal knowledge of most of the material facts. Where the disputants do not have personal knowledge, they can often agree on the truth of a proposition on the basis of their mutual acceptance of a realtor's credibility. If agreement on a factual proposition cannot be reached, a further cluster of techniques is available. The disputants can assume the truth of the proposition provisionally, and proceed to develop and examine its implications; they can bypass the proposition provisionally, to determine whether a settlement can be reached if its truth is left open; or they can make a settlement whose terms accommodate, in an appropriate way, conflicting versions of the proposition or doubt as to its validity. Finally, if none of these techniques proves effective, the disputants can terminate negotiation entirely.

The insertion of a stranger into a dispute, coupled with the binary character of traditional adjudication, entails radical changes in the modes of fact-determination. Propositions of fact that could be quickly agreed to in dispute-negotiation must be laboriously reconstructed to the stranger's satisfaction. The linear nature of the process may make it difficult or impossible to develop and test hypotheses on a provisional basis or provisionally to bypass contested propositions. The compulsion to reach a decision may preclude the adjudicator from declining to render judgment when he is genuinely undecided. Exclusionary rules, necessitated by the role of the stranger, may prevent consideration of relevant evidence, and thereby the establishment of important facts. The binary character of the process may force the adjudicator to treat as unquestionably true propositions he regards as only probably true. In sum, the modes of fact-determination associated with traditional adjudication may be not only less efficient but actually less reliable than those associated with dispute-negotiation.

(c) Choice of remedy. In choice of remedy, too, dispute-negotiation is considerably more flexible than adjudication, and for the same reasons. Just as the stranger is ill-equipped either to select or to apply person-oriented principles, so he is ill-equipped to determine whether a person-oriented remedy — an apology, a handshake, an invitation — would be either appropriate or effective; and just as a stranger typically lacks the moral authority to invoke person-oriented norms even when he believes himself capable of selecting and applying them, so he typically lacks the moral authority to order a person-oriented remedy even when he believes it would be efficacious. Similarly, a stranger-adjudicator cannot easily decree a remedy logically unrelated to the claim before him, such as topping off a tree to improve the claimant's view in lieu of paying damages for defamation.

(d) Emotional effect of participation. The elements considered so far concern the manner in which outcomes are reached and rationalized in adjudication and dispute-negotiation. A second set of elements concerns the emotional effect of participation in each of these processes. The major dis-

continuities in this area relate to the disputant's sense of control, and of being judged.

In dispute-negotiation, the settlement is made by the parties themselves. Each party therefore controls the process, or at least shares jointly in its control. As a consequence, the disputant must be treated with dignity, at the risk of a breaking-off; may participate freely and directly, unless he voluntarily chooses to negotiate through affiliates; and may have his full say, although some of what he says may seem rambling or irrelevant. Correspondingly, dispute-negotiation does not entail a passing of judgment upon the disputant by a superordinate party. Indeed, it may not involve any definitive judgment at all. Since a negotiated settlement can take account of competing norms, the disputants can recognize the validity of the norms invoked by the claimant and still accord a degree of recognition to those relied on by the respondent to justify his actions. In some cases it may suffice that the respondent admits either that he *might* have been wrong, or that the claimant's belief that he was wrong is held in good faith. Thus, participation in the process need not be overly threatening, and a reasonable degree of harmony between the parties can be maintained both during and after resolution of the dispute * * *.

Where, on the other hand, the dispute is settled by a stranger-adjudicator, each disputant is by posture a supplicant and by role an inferior. He must tacitly admit that he cannot handle his own affairs. He must appear at times and places which may be decidedly and expensively inconvenient. He must bend his thought and expressions, perhaps his very body, in ways that will move the adjudicator. He must show various signs of obeisance — speak only when permitted, be orderly, and act respectfully if not deferentially. He not only has little or no control over the process, but may be sharply limited in both the content and form of his say and the extent of his participation. Indeed, because of the superstructure necessitated by the role of the stranger — particularly limitations on cognizable evidence and norms — the proceeding is likely to be conducted in a manner so technical that each disputant can participate only through an intermediary who himself assumes a large degree of control over the disputant by virtue of his technical mastery. Finally, the settlement is not fashioned by the disputants themselves, but comes down in the form of a judgment by a superordinate, while the binary nature of the process so structures the dispute that the judgment must recognize one party as "right" and brand the other as "wrong." The prospect of subjection to such a judgment, coupled with the lack of control over the process leading up to the judgment, tends both to generate a state of tension and to drive the disputants irreconcilably apart, whatever the outcome.

* * *

Robert H. Mnookin & Lewis Kornhauser,[*] *Bargaining in the Shadow of the Law: The Case of Divorce*
88 YALE L.J. 950, 950-56, 966-77 (1979)[**]

* * *

This article suggests an alternative way of thinking about the role of law at the time of divorce. It is concerned primarily with the impact of the legal system on negotiations and bargaining that occur *outside* the courtroom. We see the primary function of contemporary divorce law not as imposing order from above, but rather as providing a framework within which divorcing couples can themselves determine their postdissolution rights and responsibilities. This process by which parties to a marriage are empowered to create their own legally enforceable commitments is a form of "private ordering."

Available evidence concerning how divorce proceedings actually work suggests that a reexamination from the perspective of private ordering is timely. "Typically, the parties do not go to court at all, until they have worked matters out and are ready for the rubber stamp." Both in the United States and in England, the overwhelming majority of divorcing couples resolve distributional questions concerning marital property, alimony, child support, and custody without bringing any contested issue to court for adjudication.

This new perspective and the use of the term "private ordering" are not meant to suggest an absence of important social interests in how the process works or in the fairness of its outcomes. The implicit policy questions are ones of emphasis and degree: to what extent should the law permit and encourage divorcing couples to work out their own arrangements? Within what limits should parties be empowered to make their own law by private agreement? What procedural or substantive safeguards are necessary to protect various social interests?

Nor is this perspective meant to imply that law and the legal system are unimportant. To divorcing spouses and their children, family law is inescapably relevant. The legal system affects *when* a divorce may occur, *how* a divorce must be procured, and *what* the consequences of divorce will be. Our primary purpose is to develop a framework within which to consider how the rules and procedures used in court for adjudicating disputes affect the bargaining process that occurs between divorcing couples *outside* the courtroom.

---

[*] Robert H. Mnookin is Samuel Williston Professor of Law at Harvard University. Lewis Kornhauser is Alfred B. Engelberg Professor of Law at New York University. This classic article examines how law and the legal system affect private negotiation decision making in the case of divorce.

* * *

Dramatic changes in divorce law during the past decade now permit a substantial degree of private ordering. The "no-fault revolution" has made divorce largely a matter of private concern. Parties to a marriage can now explicitly create circumstances that will allow divorce. Indeed, agreement between spouses is not necessary in most states; either spouse can unilaterally create the grounds for dissolution simply by separation for a sufficient period of time.

The parties' power to determine the consequences of divorce depends on the presence of children. When the divorcing couple has no children, the law generally recognizes the power of the parties upon separation or divorce to make their own arrangements concerning marital property and alimony. A spousal agreement may be subject to some sort of judicial proceeding — or, in England, submission to a Registrar — but on both sides of the Atlantic the official review appears to be largely perfunctory. In some American states a couple may make its agreement binding and final — *i.e.*, not subject to later modification by a court.

In families with minor children, existing law imposes substantial doctrinal constraints. For those allocational decisions that directly affect children — that is, child support, custody, and visitation — parents lack the formal power to make their own law. Judges, exercising the state's *parens patriae* power, are said to have responsibility to determine who should have custody and on what conditions. Private agreements concerning these matters are possible and common, but agreements cannot bind the court, which, as a matter of official dogma, is said to have an independent responsibility for determining what arrangement best serves the child's welfare. Thus, the court has the power to reject a parental agreement and order some other level of child support or some other custodial arrangement it believes to be more desirable. Moreover, even if the parties' initial agreement is accepted by the court, it lacks finality. A court may at any time during the child's minority reopen and modify the initial decree in light of any subsequent change in circumstances. The parties entirely lack the power to deprive the court of this jurisdiction.

On the other hand, available evidence on how the legal system processes undisputed divorce cases involving minor children suggests that parents actually have broad powers to make their own deals. Typically, separation agreements are rubber stamped even in cases involving children. A study of custody in England suggests, for example, that courts rarely set aside an arrangement acceptable to the parents. Anecdotal evidence in America suggests that the same is true here.

The parents' broad discretion is not surprising for several reasons. First, getting information is difficult when there is no dispute. The state usually has very limited resources for a thorough and independent investigation of the family's circumstances. Furthermore, parents may be unwilling to provide damaging information that may upset their agreed arrangements. Second, the applicable legal standards are extremely vague and give judges very little guidance as to what circumstances justify overriding a parental decision. Finally, there are obvious limitations on a court's practical power to control the parents once they leave the courtroom. For all these reasons, it is not surprising that most courts behave as if their function in the divorce process is *dispute settlement*, not child protection. When there is no dispute, busy judges or registrars are typically quite willing to rubber stamp a private agreement, in order to conserve resources for disputed cases.

* * *

B. Toward a Theory of Divorce Bargaining

Ideally, a bargaining theory would allow us to predict how alternative legal rules would affect negotiations between particular spouses and the deal, if any, they would strike. Such a theory might be combined with knowledge of how the characteristics that determine bargaining behavior are distributed among divorcing couples. Alternative rules and procedures could then be compared by evaluating the patterns of bargains that would result under each. Unfortunately, no existing theory of bargaining allows confident prediction of how different legal rules and procedures would influence outcomes; nor is there much information about current patterns and outcomes of the bargaining process.

What follows is not a complete theory. Instead, we identify five factors that seem to be important influences or determinants of the outcomes of bargaining, and then offer some observations on the bargaining process. The factors are (1) the preferences of the divorcing parents; (2) the bargaining endowments created by legal rules that indicate the particular allocation a court will impose if the parties fail to reach agreement; (3) the degree of uncertainty concerning the legal outcome if the parties go to court, which is linked to the parties' attitudes towards risk; (4) transaction costs and the parties' respective abilities to bear them; and (5) strategic behavior.

1. Parental Preferences

Parental preferences vary with regard to money and child-rearing responsibilities. Ordinarily, economists assume that a person's tastes for most goods and services are insatiable: no matter how much a person has, he will see himself as better off with more. This is certainly a reasonably apt description of most people's taste for money; other things being equal, nearly everyone would prefer having more money to having less. This is not to say, of course, that people view the relative importance of money in the same way.

Preferences with regard to custody, however, probably vary a great deal more from person to person. Many individuals like spending time with their children and are willing to sacrifice a great deal in order to have child-rearing responsibilities. Sadly, some parents might pay a great deal to avoid

child-rearing tasks altogether. There are also a wide variety of prerogatives and duties associated with child rearing, and parental preferences
may vary among them. A parent may value very highly some tasks, like
reading the child a bedtime story, and place negative value on others, like
shopping for school clothes. Preferences may vary depending on how much
custody a parent has; a parent will not necessarily prefer more. Some parents with limited child-rearing responsibilities may be willing to sacrifice
money for additional custody up to a certain point; but once they have
"enough" custody, they may be willing to give up money to avoid additional
responsibility. For other parents, no amount of money can adequately compensate for a reduction in custody below a certain minimum level. Above
that point, however, trade-offs between money and custody would be consistent with their tastes.

Informed bargaining requires a parent to assess accurately his or her own
preferences concerning custodial alternatives. Yet the assessments are difficult and complicated. The information each parent has relates to the
actual division of child-rearing tasks in an ongoing family. Dissolution or
divorce inevitably alters this division, and the parent may discover new
advantages or disadvantages to child-rearing responsibilities. Moreover,
the parents' own needs may alter drastically after divorce. A parent interested in dating may find the child an intrusion in a way that the child
never was during marriage. Additionally, a parent's interest in children
may vary according to their age. Because children and parents both change,
and changes may be unpredictable, projecting parental preferences for custody ten years into the future is a formidable task. Nevertheless, most parents have some self-awareness, however imperfect, and no third party (such
as a judge) is likely to have better information about a parent's tastes, present or future.

Parental preferences, of course, will not generally be determined solely by
self-interested judgments; a bargaining theory must take note of possible
altruism or spite. One hopes that parental preferences reflect a desire for
their children's happiness and well-being, quite apart from any parental
advantage.

For example, a father may commit himself to child-support payments
beyond what he predicts a court would require, simply because he does not
want his children to suffer economic detriment from a divorce. A mother may
agree to substantial visitation for the father because she thinks this is good
for the children, even though she personally despises the father and wants
nothing more to do with him. Similarly, either or both spouses may have
preferences that attach great weight to the happiness and desires of their
former spouse.

At the other extreme, one can easily imagine preferences that reflect
spite and envy. A spouse may simply have a strong wish to punish the other
spouse, regardless of the detriment to himself or to the children. An angry
parent may engage in a protracted and largely hopeless custody fight,

exhausting his financial reserves and bringing emotional torment to the children, simply to punish his spouse.

2. How Legal Rules Create Bargaining Endowments

Divorcing parents do not bargain over the division of family wealth and custodial prerogatives in a vacuum; they bargain in the shadow of the law. The legal rules governing alimony, child support, marital property, and custody give each parent certain claims based on what each would get if the case went to trial. In other words, the outcome that the law will impose if no agreement is reached gives each parent certain bargaining chips — an endowment of sorts.

A simplified example may be illustrative. Assume that in disputed custody cases the law flatly provided that all mothers had the right to custody of minor children and that all fathers only had the right to visitation two weekends a month. Absent some contrary agreement acceptable to both parents, a court would order this arrangement. Assume further that the legal rules relating to marital property, alimony, and child support gave the mother some determinate share of the family's economic resources. In negotiations under this regime, neither spouse would ever consent to a division that left him or her worse off than if he or she insisted on going to court. The range of negotiated outcomes would be limited to those that leave both parents as well off as they would be in the absence of a bargain.

If private ordering were allowed, we would not necessarily expect parents to split custody and money the way a judge would if they failed to agree. The father might well negotiate for more child-time and the mother for less. This result might occur either because the father made the mother better off by giving her additional money to compensate her for accepting less child-time, or because the mother found custody burdensome and considered herself better off with less custody. Indeed, she might agree to accept less money, or even to pay the father, if he agreed to relieve her of some child-rearing responsibilities. In all events, because the parents' tastes with regard to the trade-offs between money and child-time may differ, it will often be possible for the parties to negotiate some outcome that makes both better off than they would be if they simply accepted the result a court would impose.

3. Private Ordering Against a Backdrop of Uncertainty

Legal rules are generally not as simple or straightforward as is suggested by the last example. Often, the outcome in court is far from certain, with any number of outcomes possible. Indeed, existing legal standards governing custody, alimony, child support, and marital property are all striking for their lack of precision and thus provide a bargaining backdrop clouded by uncertainty. The almost universal judicial standard for resolving custody disputes is the "best interests of the child." Except in situations when one parent poses a substantial threat to the child's well-being, predicting who will get custody under this standard is difficult indeed, especially given the increasing pressure to reject any presumption in favor of maternal custody. Similarly, standards governing alimony and child support are also extraordinarily vague and allow courts broad discretion in disputed cases.

Analyzing the effects of uncertainty on bargaining is an extremely complicated task. It is apparent, however, that the effects in any particular case will depend in part on the attitudes of the two spouses toward risk — what economists call "risk preferences." This can be illustrated by considering a mechanism suggested in *Beyond the Best Interests of the Child* for resolving custody disputes between equally acceptable spouses: they would draw straws, with the winner getting full custodial rights and the loser none.

Because drawing straws, like flipping a coin, gives each parent a fifty percent chance of receiving full custody, economic theory suggests that for each parent the "expected" outcome is half-custody. We cannot, however, simply assume that each parent will bargain as if receiving half of the child's time were certain. Attitudes toward risk may be defined by asking a parent to compare two alternatives: (1) a certainty of having one-half of the child's time; or (2) a gamble in which the "expected" or average outcome is one-half of the child's time. By definition, a parent who treats these alternatives as equally desirable is risk-neutral. A parent who would accept a certain outcome of less than half-custody in order to avoid the gamble — the chance of losing the coin flip and receiving no custody — is risk-averse. Other parents may be risk preferrers: they would rather take the gamble and have a fifty percent chance of winning full custody than accept the certain outcome of split custody.

The reality of custody litigation is more complicated, and the knowledge of the parties much less complete, than in our hypothetical. The parties in the example know the standard for decision and the odds of winning custody in court. But in real situations, the exact odds of various possible outcomes are not known by the parties; often they do not even know what information or criteria the judge will use in deciding.

4. Transaction Costs

Costs are involved in resolving the distributional consequences of separation or divorce, and in securing the divorce itself. The transaction costs that the parties must bear may take many forms, some financial and some emotional. The most obvious and tangible involve the expenditure of money. Professional fees — particularly for lawyers — must be paid by one or both parties. In addition, there are filing fees and court costs. More difficult to measure, but also important, are the emotional and psychological costs involved in the dispute-settlement process. Lawsuits generally are emotionally burdensome; the psychological costs imposed by bargaining (and still more by litigation) are particularly acute in divorce.

The magnitude of these transaction costs, both actual and expected, can influence negotiations and the outcome of bargaining. In the dissolution process, one spouse, and that spouse's attorney, can substantially affect the magnitude of the transaction costs that must be borne by the other spouse. As is generally the case, the party better able to bear the transaction costs, whether financial or emotional, will have an advantage in divorce bargaining.

In divorce, transaction costs will generally tend to be (1) higher if there are minor children involved, because of the additional and intensely emotional allocational issues to be determined; (2) an increasing function of the amount of property and income the spouses have, since it is rational to spend more on negotiation when the possible rewards are higher; and (3) higher when there is a broad range of possible outcomes in court.

5. Strategic Behavior

The actual bargain that is struck through negotiations — indeed, whether a bargain is struck at all — depends on the negotiation process. During this process, each party transmits information about his or her own preferences to the other. This information may be accurate or intentionally inaccurate; each party may promise, threaten, or bluff. Parties may intentionally exaggerate their chances of winning in court in the hope of persuading the other side to accept less. Or they may threaten to impose substantial transaction costs — economic or psychological — on the other side. In short, there are a variety of ways in which the parties may engage in strategic behavior during the bargaining process.

Opportunities for strategic behavior exist because the parties often will not know with certainty (1) the other side's true preferences with regard to the allocational outcomes; (2) the other spouse's preferences or attitudes towards risk; and (3) what the outcome in court will be, or even what the actual odds in court are. Although parents may know a great deal about each other's preferences for money and children, complete knowledge of the other spouse's attitudes is unlikely.

How do parties and their representatives actually behave during the process? Two alternative models are suggested by the literature: (1) a *Strategic Model*, which would characterize the process as "a relatively norm-free process centered on the transmutation of underlying bargaining strength into agreement by the exercise of power, horse-trading, threat, and bluff"; and (2) a *Norm-Centered Model*, which would characterize the process by elements normally associated with adjudication — the parties and their representatives would invoke rules, cite precedents, and engage in reasoned elaboration. Anecdotal observation suggests that each model captures part of the flavor of the process. The parties and their representatives do make appeals to legal and social norms in negotiation, but they frequently threaten and bluff as well.

C. The Task Facing the Spouses and the Process of Negotiation

The task facing divorcing spouses can be summarized, based on the preceding analysis, as one of attempting through bargaining to divide money and child-rearing responsibilities to reflect personal preferences. Even though the interests of the two parents may substantially conflict, opportunities for making both parents better off through a negotiated agreement will exist to the extent that parental preferences differ.

This analysis suggests why most divorcing couples never require adjudication for dispute settlement. The parties gain substantial advantages when they can reach an agreement concerning the distributional consequences of divorce. They can minimize the transaction costs involved in adjudication. They can avoid its risks and uncertainties, and negotiate an agreement that may better reflect their individual preferences.

Furthermore, divorcing spouses usually have no incentive to take cases to court for their precedential value. Unlike insurance companies, public-interest organizations, and other "repeat players," a divorcing spouse will generally have no expectation that an adjudicated case will create precedent, or that any precedent created will be of personal benefit in future litigation.

Given the advantages of negotiated settlements, why do divorcing spouses ever require courtroom adjudication of their disputes? There are a variety of reasons why some divorce cases will be litigated:

1. Spite. One or both parties may be motivated in substantial measure by a desire to punish the other spouse, rather than simply to increase their own net worth.

2. Distaste for Negotiation. Even though it costs more, one or both parties may prefer the adjudicative process (with third-party decision) to any process that requires a voluntary agreement with the other spouse. Face-to-face contact may be extremely distasteful, and the parties may not be able to negotiate — even with lawyers acting as intermediaries — because of distrust or distaste.

3. Calling the Bluff — The Breakdown of Negotiations. If the parties get heavily engaged in strategic behavior and get carried away with making threats, a courtroom battle may result, despite both parties' preference for a settlement. Negotiations may resemble a game of "chicken" in which two teenagers set their cars on a collision course to see who turns first. Some crack-ups may result.

4. Uncertainty and Risk Preferences. The exact odds for any given outcome in court are unknown, and it has been suggested that litigants typically overestimate their chances of winning. To the extent that one or both of the parties typically overestimate their chances of winning, more cases will be litigated than in a world in which the outcome is uncertain but the odds are known. In any event, when the outcome is uncertain, settlement prospects depend on the risk preferences of the two spouses.

5. No Middle Ground. If the object of dispute cannot be divided into small enough increments — whether because of the law, the practical circumstances, or the nature of the subject at issue — there may be no middle ground on which to strike a feasible compromise. Optimal bargaining occurs when, in economic terminology, nothing is indivisible.

These points can be illustrated through a simple example. Assume a divorcing couple has no children and the only issue is how they will divide 100 shares of stock worth $10,000. Let us further assume that it would cost each spouse $1,000 to have a court decide this issue, and that each spouse must pay his own litigation costs.

If the outcome in court were entirely certain, would the parties ever litigate? Suppose it were clear that a court would inevitably award one-half of the stock to each spouse because it would be characterized as community property. If the issue were litigated, each spouse would end up with only $4,000. A spouse would therefore never accept a settlement offer of less than $4,000. One might expect that the parties would normally simply settle for $5,000, and save the costs of litigation. Taking the issue to court would substitute an expensive mode of dispute resolution — adjudication — for a cheaper mode — negotiation.

Even when the outcome in court is certain, litigation is still possible. A spouse might engage in strategic behavior and threaten to litigate in order to get more than half. Suppose the husband threatened to litigate unless the wife agreed to accept a settlement of $4,500. The wife might accept $4,500 but only if she believed the threat. She would know with proper legal advice that her husband would only end up with $4,000 if he litigated. Therefore the threat ordinarily would not be credible. She might call his bluff and tell him to sue. If the wife were convinced, however, that her husband was motivated by spite and in fact preferred to litigate rather than accept less than $5,500, she might accept $4,500. If the outcome in court is certain, then, absent spite, strategic behavior, or a distaste for negotiations, adjudication should not generally occur; litigation would impose an expensive mode of dispute settlement when a less expensive alternative could achieve the same result.

What about cases in which the result in court is uncertain? Assume, for example, that there is a fifty percent chance that the husband will get all $10,000, and a fifty percent chance that the wife will get all $10,000. Settlement in these circumstances obviously depends on the risk preferences of the two spouses. If both are risk-neutral, then both will negotiate the same way as they would if they knew for certain that a court would award each of them $5,000 — the "expected" value of the litigation in this case.

To the extent that the parties are both risk-averse — each is prepared to accept less than $5,000 to avoid the risks of litigation — the parties have a broader range of possible settlements that both would prefer to the risks of litigation. This may facilitate agreement.

Conversely, if both parties are risk preferrers — each prefers the gamble to an offer of the expected value of $5,000 — all cases are likely to be litigated. When one party is a risk preferrer and the other is risk-averse, it is difficult to predict the effect on the rate of litigation. In any negotiated outcome, a risk preferrer will have an advantage over the party who is risk-averse.

* * *

Gerald R. Williams,[*] *Negotiation as a Healing Process*
1996 J. DISP. RESOL. 1, 25-37, 42-56[**]

* * *

II. NEGOTIATION AS A RITUAL PROCESS

In an earlier portion of this article, we saw that metaphors can give us insight about one thing by comparing it to something else. Examples are *negotiation is war* and *negotiation is problem-solving for mutual gain*. At this point, I would like to introduce a third metaphor for negotiation that I hope will broaden our understanding of the reason why negotiation is so important and from whence it derives power. The metaphor is that, in many respects, *negotiation is a ritual process*. Since this metaphor may be unfamiliar to some readers, I would like to begin the discussion by suggesting three aspects of ritual that come most readily to mind.

A. Negotiation is a Stylized Form of Interaction

* * *

If we accept the proposition that negotiation is a necessary means to the end sought, we can see that the ritual of negotiation is an *indirect* means for accomplishing something that cannot be obtained more *directly*. This aspect of negotiation is frustrating for Americans, with our Yankee can-do directness, who want to cut through the preliminaries and get the matter resolved. We are impatient with *delay*, or it makes us feel we are *wasting time*. We seem to be guided by the metaphor that *time is money*, and we do not permit ourselves to *waste* it. This attitude reduces our effectiveness in doing business in many countries of the world, where meaningful interpersonal relationships are necessary preconditions for *doing business together*. As Nancy Adler so aptly puts it:

> Americans need to increase their emphasis on building relationships with bargaining partners. They need to discuss topics other than business, including the arts, history, culture, and current eco-

---

[*] Gerald R. Williams is Professor of Law, Brigham Young University. His article explores ritual aspects of negotiation and its potential to transform how parties deal with conflict.

[**] Copyright © 1996 Journal of Dispute Resolution. Reprinted with permission.

nomic conditions of the countries involved. Effective negotiators must view luncheon, dinner, reception, ceremony, and tour invitations as times for interpersonal relationship building, and therefore as key to the negotiating process. When American negotiators, often frustrated by the seemingly endless formalities, ceremonies, and "small talk," ask how long they must wait before beginning to "do business," the answer is simple: wait until your opponents bring up business (and they will). Realize that the work of conducting a successful negotiation has already begun, even if business has yet to be mentioned.

In the United States and other industrialized countries, we tend to think the give-and-take of bargaining is a hazard we encounter abroad, but not something we must deal with at home. As to consumer transactions, it is true that shoppers have come to expect "fixed prices." But even here, there are many settings in which bargaining is virtually unavoidable, as on new or used car lots, or where bargaining, if it is not *required*, is at least *permissible*, as in flea markets, garage sales, or responding to classified ads in the newspaper. In fact, even in mainstream retail outlets the concept of fixed prices is illusory in the sense that essentially all retailers conduct seasonal or other periodic "sales" in which prices are reduced below the usual sticker price on some pretense (pre-inventory sale, post-inventory sale, inventory reduction sale, pre-season sale, post-season sale, and so forth). Some high volume retailers of consumer goods take this notion a step further by advertising "we will not be undersold," so that, regardless of the current selling price of their goods, if a customer brings an ad or other evidence of a lower price offered by a competitor in the relevant geographic area, they will match it. Some stores go even further by offering to beat any competitors' price by, say, five percent. Add to these the use of coupons, rebates, and other sales devices, and we begin to see that all of these mechanisms are forms of bargaining. They manage to introduce price breaks without spoiling the apparent simplicity and efficiency of fixed prices. But they also force us to admit that so-called fixed prices are actually highly fluid and variable, if not wholly illusory. In actuality, fixed prices are nothing more than statements of the retailers' initial position. Shoppers who need the item immediately, or who do not have the patience or time to play the game, are required to pay full price. Shoppers interested in better terms must be willing to devote some time and energy to the process. They must watch the newspaper for a sale, or find a coupon or rebate offer, or drive across town to a discount outlet. In our consumer economy, then, the form of discipline required of shoppers is not a willingness to devote time and energy to the *inter*personal give-and-take of traditional marketplace bargaining, but the capacity to delay gratification while seeking some "objective" justification for receiving a lower price. Thus, the skills demanded of modern consumers are not the skills of human interaction; they are the *impersonal* skills of information processing, storage, and retrieval; the ability to scan the media for announcements of sales, to collect and organize coupons and rebate offers, and to make the rounds of stores to take advantage of items on sale.

Most importantly, as a matter of practice, the give-and-take of negotiation has always been a characteristic of the negotiating process among lawyers. * * *

B. The Negotiation Process is Highly Predictable

In law school we learn that no two cases are alike, and in our culture we assume that no two people are alike. We might surmise from this that no two negotiations are alike. Fortunately, this is only partially true. One of the defining characteristics of a ritual, including the ritual of negotiation, is that it provides an accepted structure for and sequencing of events. As a general proposition, then, we can say *the ritual of negotiation unfolds in predictable stages over time*. The predictability helps explain why so many lawyers lose patience with the process; it is highly repetitive, and thus not as stimulating as new adventures would be. This aspect of ritual is well captured by W. John Smith when he says, "*ritual* connotes . . . behavior that is formally organized into repeatable patterns. Perhaps the fundamental and pervasive function of these patterns is to facilitate orderly interactions between individuals." The point could not be more clear. Negotiation is a highly repetitive process. Without predictable patterns, the negotiators could not hope to achieve orderly interaction with each other. As Smith explains: "Ritual behavior facilitates interactions because it makes available information about the nature of events, and about the participants in them, that each participating individual must have to interact without generating chaos."

* * *

For our purposes, the most helpful elaboration of the negotiation process is by Gulliver. In his processual model of negotiation, he sees two interrelated dynamics simultaneously in operation. One is iterative and cyclical; the other is linear and developmental. He compares these two processes to an automobile. The iterative, cyclical aspects are analogous to the movement of the wheels, driveshaft, pistons, and valves. Their motion is continual and infinitely repetitive, yet they provide the energy which propels the car forward. The more linear development process is compared to the actual progress of the car from its point of origin to its final destination. Both of these processes are highly predictable, in the sense they typically occur over the course of each negotiation.

In summary, then, while negotiation *outcomes* are not predictable, the stages are. There are several advantages to being aware of these developmental stages. They tell negotiators what to expect at each stage, give them guidance in planning their own strategy and a basis for interpreting the strategies of their opponents, facilitate coordination of the negotiation process with the litigation process, and prevent the embarrassment and harmful effects of mistakes in timing.

* * *

C. Negotiation Can Transform Peoples' Lives

The final aspect of negotiation as a ritual process is that, if you do it right, something sacred may happen. I do not mean *sacred* in a narrowly religious or theological sense. Perhaps the better word is transcendent, suggesting that negotiation is also a healing process, and something transformative can happen to the parties involved as the process unfolds and comes to an appropriate resolution.

* * *

To illustrate what is involved in a healing perspective on negotiation, let us assume a typical lawsuit in which both sides have hired lawyers to represent them, the plaintiff has filed a complaint, the defendant has filed an answer, discovery is proceeding apace, and a trial date has been set. By definition, the parties are now *in conflict*. Once they are fully engaged in the conflict, they confront a far more fateful and hazardous problem, *how to get out of that conflict*.

Once the case has been filed in court, we might say metaphorically that the legal system itself constitutes a kind of vessel or container which holds the two contestants in an uncomfortable relationship with each other until they have resolved their problem. This is a highly paradoxical situation. On the one hand, they see the legal system as the vehicle for obtaining their will over the other party. On the other hand, at the same time, the legal system constitutes a metaphorical vessel which holds the protagonist and antagonist together in the same vessel in a forced relationship with each other until they resolve their conflict or it is resolved for them. By the very act of engaging the legal system, they condemn themselves to be in the legal vessel with the person against whom they hold the hardest of feelings, and to staying together in the heat and discomfort of that vessel until their conflict is resolved.

* * *

IV. THE FIVE STEPS FOR RECOVERING FROM CONFLICT

To articulate more specifically the kinds of changes the negotiation ritual is intended to encourage in disputants, I would like to propose a preliminary five-step model of the stages clients must generally move through in order to shift from being *in* a state of conflict to being healed from the conflict. The stages are: *denial, acceptance, sacrifice, leaps of faith*, and *renewal*. Just as researchers have found that getting *into* a conflict is a multi-step process that typically involves naming, blaming, claiming, rejection, and a decision to go public, even so, the task of getting *out of* a conflict requires the disputants to work their way through a multistage process.

A. Denial

As a preliminary model of the process of recovering from conflict, the first stage is typically a condition of *denial*. As James Hall explains, there is in each of us "a deep-seated human desire *not* to be the one at fault, *not* to be the one who must change." This resistance to being the one at fault, to being the one who must change, is part of what makes conflict so painful and its resolution so difficult. Most conflicts are a story of two parties, both of whom contributed to the problem, and neither of whom wants to admit his or her role in it. In the literature on grieving we gain a broader sense of what is meant by the term *denial* and some of the risks it poses to the parties and others: "The person will strongly deny the reality of what has happened, or search for reasons why it has happened, and take revenge on themselves and others."

Properly understood, then, conflicts serve as . . . a mirror. They expose the disputants' weaknesses; the areas in which they have been too much the victim, or too much the exploiter; their complexes, their unresolved angers, and their feelings of specialness and entitlement. Because it is so painful for disputants to see these parts of themselves exposed by their own involvement in the conflict, they need the protection and reinforcement, the containment and channeling, that the lawyer-client relationship provides, and they need the benefit of the full play of the negotiation process to help them gradually face what they see in the mirror and to come to terms with it.

This is why the negotiation ritual must be performed with such understanding and care. It is intended to help the disputants through an extremely painful and threatening process.

Seen in this light, conflicts are opportunities to increase in self-knowledge and in an empathetic understanding of the world around us. But it is extremely difficult for disputants to learn from this painful experience without the assistance of experienced, knowledgeable, ritual leaders. In our secular society, it seems as though law is one of the few authentic mediating structures left.

* * *

B. Acceptance

The next step is *acceptance*. It may take time, but at some point the parties need to move beyond denial and to *accept the possibility that they themselves are part of the problem*. They do not yet need to *do* anything about it, just to accept the possibility that the problem does not begin and end with the other side, that they themselves may have some complicity in the problem. In some cases, however, it may be that one side actually is wholly innocent and the other wholly to blame for the problem. But even when parties are wholly innocent, they still need to accept the possibility there is *something they could do now to move the situation in the direction of an appropriate resolution*. Again, they don't need to actually take action, they simply need to register a change in attitude that opens them to the possibility of movement in the direction of an appropriate solution.

C. Sacrifice

Assuming the parties have accepted the possibility they are part of the problem, or the possibility there is something they could do now to move in the direction of a resolution, the next step is to consider what they might be willing to do about it. In its starkest form, the principle is that, for the conflict to be resolved, the parties must be willing to make a sacrifice. From a judge's point of view, the minimum sacrifice required for a valid settlement agreement is a *compromise* by each side, meaning that both parties must make some concession, must move from their original position. But as a general matter, mere concessions or compromises do not require a change of heart. It has been observed that people usually are not willing to make a sacrifice until they have been brought to a more humble attitude. Anthropologists say it without varnish: the way people move from denial and to acceptance and willingness to sacrifice is by means of *ritual mortification*. Because power leads to abuses of power, and *ritual mortification* sounds like an abuse of power, it is good if we feel some discomfort with the idea that part of the lawyers' task is to lead their clients through a ritually mortifying process. Assuming, for the sake of argument, that the experience of ritual mortification is a necessary part of the process, is it possible to identify the elements that produce it? The first element that comes to mind is the lawyers' monthly billing statement. It is, and ought to be, painful for clients to pay their lawyers to pursue this conflict. Another means of mortification is to involve the client in the preparation of the case, for example, helping to answer the written interrogatories, and other tasks. If this is not sufficient to bring about the needed broadening of perspective, then perhaps it is time for oral depositions. One can see that, from a ritual perspective, there is symbiosis here; the things that lawyers do, on one level, to prepare the case for trial should trial become necessary, are the very things that, on another level, are most likely to help the clients see their own role in the conflict more clearly and open up the possibility of an appropriate, mutually agreeable resolution.

Assuming that sacrifices need to be made, what should they be? This is an extremely delicate question. We know, for example, that some people have a history of being *too compliant*, of giving away too much, whether motivated by a need for affection and approval, by fear of reprisals, or for some other reason. For those who are too compliant, the sacrifice called for would probably *not* be to make more concessions to their antagonist, but rather to forebear from giving, to reverse themselves, to give up the part of themselves that always wants to please others. For other people, the problem may be just the opposite. They may be exploiters who are too good at looking out for themselves at others' expense. For them, the sacrifice may be to recognize their exploitive patterns and become more conscious of the interests and needs of other people. There are many other possibilities.

The answer will depend on the personalities involved and the particularities of their situations. In some situations, parties may need to sacrifice — to let go of — such things as a desire for a total victory, or an impulse for revenge, a mistaken belief that they themselves are faultless and the other side totally to blame, their pride, their unwillingness to acknowledge or appreciate another's point of view, or their unwillingness to forgive another for his or her mistake. In other situations, parties may need to give up the belief that they can get away with exploiting others, their belief that they are better or more deserving than others, or their excessive opinions of their own abilities, worth, privileged status, etc. There may be situations in which parties need to give up their hope of obtaining a windfall or other unearned benefit, or give up their envy or spite or jealousy with respect to possessions, luck and social position.

Before proceeding to the fourth step, there is one final consideration. Is it mandatory that parties make a sacrifice? The answer is a firm "no." There can be no *requirement* that the client have a change of heart. It is fundamental that, as lawyers, we implicitly and explicitly declare to our clients that they can stay just the way they are, and so long as they do not expect us to do that which is illegal or unethical, we will stand by them. Our willingness to represent our clients should not depend upon their willingness to change, much less to move in directions *we* think right. As Shaffer and Elkins remind us, "[t]he client has to be free to be wrong." The negotiation process, then, is not intended for lawyers to impose our values upon our clients, but for us to help contain and channel our clients' energies in appropriate ways until they have had enough time to see their own situations more clearly and to discover for themselves what steps they may be willing to make.

D. Leap of Faith

The fourth stage refers to action or movement, what might be called the *leap of faith*. It is a leap of faith, for example, to admit to the other side that you might be *willing* to make a sacrifice to resolve the case. Practicing lawyers recognize it as the moment when their client looks them in the eye and asks, "[I]f I do this, can you guarantee it will work?" And the lawyer has to reply, "[N]o, I can't guarantee that, because I don't know that. But the trial is coming up really soon, and we haven't thought of anything better to do, but you decide." And the client must decide.

A leap of faith is an expressed willingness to make a sacrifice in the hope of moving a conflict toward a meaningful and appropriate resolution. One of the most powerful is an apology sincerely given. The wrongdoer says to the aggrieved person, "I am truly sorry for the trouble I have caused you." In our rights-oriented society, we are quick to justify our own harmful acts, and we are slow to recognize how healing it can be to the injured person for us to acknowledge our fault, to offer an appropriate apology, and, if the situation warrants, to offer to make reparation. Similarly, we usually think the lawyers' role, when representing defendants, is to *protect their clients from having to admit wrongdoing or having to make legal compensation for the harms they cause.* But as Macaulay and Walster remind us, just as there are negative psychological consequences to people who are harmed, there are also psychological consequences to those who do the harming, whether purposefully or not.

* * *

Other leaps of faith are to admit one's part in causing the conflict or in making the problem more difficult to resolve. Here are examples: I acknowledge that I was really angry at myself, but I was shouting at you; I can see that made the problem much worse; I am sorry that I was so accusatory when I talked with you; I was wrong to say you were completely at fault; I see now that I really misunderstood your intentions; it was at least half my fault that we got so angry at each other; I was wrong to blame you so strongly; or I'm sorry I overreacted; I can see now that it made things worse. At a more fundamental level, at the appropriate time (after receiving an apology, for example) it is a leap of faith to explicitly forgive the other side, and perhaps to add the hope of someday also being forgiven by the other.

Leaps of faith are inherently risky. This is what gives them their healing power. They open people to danger, exploitation, and ridicule. Admissions can be used in court as evidence against us. When one side to a conflict takes a step downward, in the direction of a less demanding or more understanding attitude, the other side has a choice: they may choose to reciprocate with a downward movement of their own, or they may use it as a pretext for stepping up their own demands. Because lawyers have seen the latter response many times before, they are understandably wary about encouraging clients to take steps downward, and often try to shield their clients from this essential part of the healing process. This is good and bad. It is good that lawyers help clients avoid making concessions when those concessions will be used against them. It is bad because, unless both sides are willing to take some risks, there is no chance for mutual agreement and reconciliation. So the question is not *whether* to permit or encourage the client to make leaps of faith, but *when* and *under what circumstances*. To understand *when* to make concessions, lawyers need to be well attuned to the people involved, the stages of the negotiation process, and their own inner dynamics. It is actually at this point, in my opinion, that the work of Roger Fisher, William Ury, and their colleagues becomes especially relevant, because they describe a method that helps attorneys and clients step safely through in this particularly risky and difficult stage of the negotiation process. Use of neutral third parties as go-betweens is also a highly effective method for reducing the risk involved in leaps of faith, which may be one reason why healing has emerged more clearly as a potential byproduct of mediation while it remains largely ignored in the negotiation literature. The same may be true for such leaps of faith as forgiveness and apology.

E. Renewal or Healing from Conflict

If the process works well enough, and both parties are willing to move by incremental leaps of faith in the direction of agreement, and if they seek in the process to fathom the underlying problems and address them along the way, the effect can be two-fold: they may reach a mutually acceptable solution and, in the best of circumstances, they may also experience a change of heart, be reconciled to one another and healed and feel renewed as human beings. This is the transformation objective; it is the goal or purpose of all ritual processes, whether it be theater or court trial or graduation exercise or religious rite or negotiated settlement. Rituals are to help prepare the participants, those on whose behalf the ceremony is enacted, to move forward in a new condition, to a new phase of life. *Renewal* or transformation in this context means not simply they are as good as they were before the conflict, but they are better — they are more whole, or more compassionate, or less greedy, or otherwise changed in an important way from their attitude or condition before the crisis began. Certainly, when people experience such a fundamental change through the process of conflict resolution, they will be far less likely to find themselves in a similar conflict again. On the other hand, if they fail at this process, then to the extent the conflict was a product of their own developmental shortcomings, it is likely they will find themselves in similar conflicts in the future, returning again and again until the party acknowledges and addresses the underlying developmental need.

* * *

Kevin Avruch,* *Culture as Context, Culture as Communication: Considerations for Humanitarian Negotiators*
9 HARV. NEGOT. L. REV. 391, 392-99 (2004)**

* * *

In his memoirs, former United Nations Under Secretary General Sir Brian Urquhart tells the story of the first night in 1957 that a contingent of the United Nations Emergency Force (UNEF) was deployed to Gaza. That evening, upon hearing from the minarets the muezzin's call to prayers, but not understanding Arabic or the meaning of the act, the U.N. troops believed it to be a call to civil disorder and fired in panic on the mosque.

---

* Kevin Avruch is Professor of Anthropology at George Mason University, and Associate Director of the Institute for Conflict Analysis and Resolution, based at the University. In this article he discusses "culture" as it gives meaning to an individual's experience of the world around him.

Today, it is hard to imagine such a complete lack of fundamental and substantive knowledge about the "host" society and its culture by the majority of international participants in a complex humanitarian intervention. Yet the level of culture-specific pre-deployment training in most IOs, NGOs, and militaries is far from sufficient. Typically, humanitarian agents learn about their host society's culture by committing to memory a standardized list of "do's and don'ts" (e.g., "don't offer your left hand to an Arab"; "don't pat a Buddhist on the head;" "don't expect the Latin Americans to be on time for the meeting"). This practice conceives of cultures as collections of static traits and customs. What gets left out is the dynamism —the conflicts, change, and quality of emergence that characterize cultures. To try to learn about another culture from lists of traits and custom is akin to trying to learn English by memorizing the Oxford English Dictionary — all vocabulary, no grammar. This method is particularly illsuited for those trying to master a dynamic process like negotiation in a foreign cultural context.

There are numerous definitions of culture and they continue to proliferate. For our purposes, culture refers to the socially transmitted values, beliefs and symbols that are more or less shared by members of a social group. These constitute the framework through which members interpret and attribute meaning to both their own and others' experiences and behavior. One key assumption implicit in this definition is that culture is a quality of social groups and perhaps communities, and that members may belong to multiple such groups. Therefore, an individual may "carry" several cultures, for example, ethnic or national, religious, and occupational affiliations. Thus, for any given individual, culture always comes "in the plural," and therefore every interaction (including negotiation) between individuals is likely to be multicultural on several levels. Another assumption is that culture is rarely, if ever, perfectly shared by all members of a group or community. Intracultural variation is likely to be present, perhaps considerable, and this should caution us against ascribing value, belief, or behavioral uniformity to members of a group — against stereotyping. These assumptions suggest that socialization is the aggregate of numerous social interactions where culture is transmitted. It therefore becomes crucial to understand the different sources of culture and their different modes of transmission.

These assumptions militate against using lists of traits and do's and don'ts to learn about another culture. Rather, as specialists in intercultural communication put it, a more sophisticated approach is necessary to become "culturally competent." For humanitarian workers, who routinely find themselves working under difficult conditions in unfamiliar cultural settings, the attainment of such cultural competence is especially important — it might mean the difference between the success or failure of the mission. Certainly, it lies at the core of the broader concept of "communicational competence," which in turn is a prerequisite for social interaction generally, and in particular, for the kind of interaction called negotiation.

One popular model of culture is the "iceberg," commonly depicted as a triangle or pyramid. In this model, the top level visible above the surface is comprised of behavior, artifacts, and institutions. Underlying this level, just beneath the surface but fairly easily accessible to sensitive observers, are norms, beliefs, values and attitudes. At the deepest level, all but invisible even to members of a cultural group, lie the fundamental assumptions and presuppositions, the sense-and-meaning-making schemas and symbols, the ontology, about the world and individuals' experience in it. While a useful heuristic, the iceberg concept tends unhelpfully to assume a homogeneity of cultural sharing among individuals (this is never the case), and it lacks dynamism. Much more goes on "inside" the iceberg than the simple model implies; furthermore, icebergs frequently move about, often with disastrous results for shipping.

* * *

Of the many different ways to conceive of the role of culture in humanitarian negotiation, two deserve special discussion: culture as context and culture as communication. "Context" refers to culture in its broadest, framework-defining, worldview-constituting sense. Here culture includes deep presuppositions and presumptions about how the world works, which give contour to how individuals meaningfully experience and act in their worlds.

Consider the domain of social conflict — culture frames the context in which conflict occurs. Culture determines what manners of things are subjects for competition or objects of dispute, often by postulating their value and relative (or absolute) scarcity: for example, notions of honor or purity, or accumulation of capital and profits. Culture also stipulates rules, sometimes precise, usually less so, for how contests should be pursued, including when they begin and how to end them. Finally, returning to our earlier definition, culture provides individuals with cognitive and affective frameworks for interpreting the behavior and motives of self and others. With respect to conflict, to see culture as context is to understand that culture per se, and even cultural differences, are rarely if ever the main "cause" of conflict (Samuel Huntington's "clash of civilizations" notwithstanding). Culture, however, is always the lens that refracts the causes of conflict. With respect to negotiation, to see culture as context is to understand that even before parties meet and converse for the first time, their most fundamental comprehensions of their respective positions, interests, and values have been set and circumscribed by the very language (i.e. culture) with which they bring them to expression.

UNICEF representative Daniel Toole provides two examples of the role of "deep" cultural context — the base parts of the iceberg — in humanitarian negotiations. While not addressing culture specifically, he first describes the deep divide between U.N. negotiators and the Taliban in Afghanistan over fundamental conceptions of human rights, such as treatment of girls and women. The lack of shared values and norms respecting gender equality made any discussion across the cultural divide on these issues next to impossible. "As a consequence," Toole writes, "negotiation of numerous issues was very difficult and made little headway." Many humanitarian programs in Afghanistan were subsequently suspended.

Toole's second example relates to the different principles of action that distinguish the U.N. from many humanitarian organizations. Such principles underlying action are sometimes called "strategic culture." In difficult cases, the UN's strategic culture employs a principle of "conditionality" — using a combination of carrots and sticks to induce change in recalcitrant negotiation partners. For many humanitarians, however, who remain committed to providing aid to people in need regardless of political considerations, such conditionality appears ethically unsound and unacceptable.

The debate over conditionality raises concerns about the viability of traditional negotiation concepts when applied in humanitarian contexts. In classical negotiation theory, parties must always bear in mind their "reservation prices" (the point at which each will not "sell" or "buy"), and what Roger Fisher and his collaborators famously called the BATNA, or "best alternative to a negotiated agreement[.]" This is the imagined best-case scenario should negotiations break down, and correlates to "the point at which a negotiator is prepared to walk away from the negotiation table." If a party has not settled on a reservation price or thought through his BATNA, he is seriously disadvantaged in subsequent negotiation. Consider what the lack of conditionality implies for humanitarian negotiators — especially if the other party learns of that deficiency. The principle that one gives aid or renders protection to those in need, irrespective of identity, past actions, or "politics," means that there is no "reservation price" available to humanitarians, save in the field an operational withdrawal point if the situation becomes too dangerous. Also, in humanitarian negotiation there is no real BATNA for access or aid or protection — all the alternatives are bad ones, and inaction becomes unthinkable. Humanitarians thus face ethically precarious options of negotiating how many sacks of rice a warlord takes for allowing the convoy through, or (even more unsavory) of allowing militias or genocidaires to distribute the food in a refugee camp so that any is distributed at all.

In both cases described by Toole, any negotiations that take place will be framed from the start by the different cultural constructions of the world brought to the table by the parties. In this sense, the parties never wholly define the negotiating situation; it comes to them, as they come to it, partly predefined. Such predefinition may create an obstacle for negotiations. For instance, should one negotiating party's construction of the world be based upon a universal human rights discourse not shared by other parties, an impasse may result. Such is the power of cultural context.

Notice that Toole's two examples draw from different sites of cultural difference. In the U.N.-Taliban case, parties deal across a "civilizational" divide à la Huntington, separating the familiar categories of Western and fundamentalist Islamic cultures. In the U.N.-humanitarian divergence over the issue of conditionality, the locus of strategic culture appeared to reside in organizations or institutional settings. Culture then is not merely a property of racial, ethnic, religious, or national groups — the usual "containers" for culture depicted in the negotiation literature. Organizations, institutions, professions and occupations are also containers for culture and sites of cultural difference. Each may serve to delimit its own context.

* * *

For example, in a multicultural arena an American military officer and an American civilian aid worker may share many of the same understandings and perceptions of the world based upon their shared American culture, and easily communicate about many matters (though they may still have much to disagree about, of course). However, on matters relating to security, force protection, command-and-control, or rules of engagement, the American military officer may share more cultural commonality with an Indian, Pakistani, or Nigerian military colleague; the mutual premises of a transnational "military culture" will facilitate communication between them. This may be the case even when language differences necessitate the services of an interpreter. On the other hand, within the NGO community, even the English-speaking one, conflicts may arise in the field because of differences in the organizational or strategic cultures of relief or humanitarian workers focused on quick response, immediate access to populations in need, and crisis problem solving; those of workers representing sustainable development organizations who have longer term or infrastructural concerns; and those of a U.N. official focused on political or diplomatic issues.

* * *

Chapter 2
DISTRIBUTIVE BARGAINING

Suppose you represent the plaintiff in a personal injury suit. Your client was injured when the defendant skidded into her car on a rainy day. If you take the case to court and win at trial, she will receive a sum of money intended to compensate her for the losses she suffered as a result of the collision. If you negotiate a settlement out of court, she will also receive a sum of money. Your client does not know and will probably never encounter the defendant again. Although the suit is against the defendant as an individual, his insurance company will pay any judgment or settlement. There is no pre-existing relationship between the parties, nor is there any interest in a long-term relationship. The only issue, then, is money. Your goal as the plaintiff's lawyer is to obtain the largest sum possible to compensate her — to "claim value"[1] so that the maximum amount is transferred from the defendant's insurance company to the plaintiff. This is a classic example of a distributive, or zero-sum, bargaining situation. The parties deal with each other at arm's length, and every dollar you gain is a dollar less for the other side. Faced with such a situation, how do you maximize your client's gain through a negotiated settlement?

A. BARGAINING RANGE AND RESISTANCE POINTS

Assuming that there is some overlap between what your client is willing to settle for and what the insurance company is willing to pay, a *bargaining range* can be said to exist; and a negotiated agreement is theoretically possible. If there is no overlap, then settlement will be impossible, no matter how long the parties negotiate. For example, if your client says she will accept any offer over $123,000 (plaintiff's *resistance point*), and the insurance company will pay up to $175,000 (defendant's *resistance point*) to settle the case, agreement is possible at any point between those two figures:

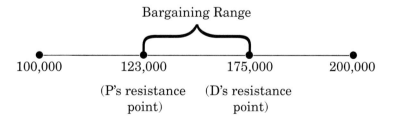

Bargaining Range

100,000   123,000   175,000   200,000

(P's resistance   (D's resistance
point)   point)

---

[1] *See* DAVID A. LAX & JAMES K. SEBENIUS, THE MANAGER AS NEGOTIATOR (1986).

If the insurance company will pay only $100,000, though, your client will not agree to settle; if she demands $200,000, the insurance company will not pay it. Thus, any settlement must occur in the range bracketed by your client's "bottom line" and the insurance company's maximum payout. How these figures are arrived at will be discussed later. For the time being what is important is to recognize that such resistance points or "walkaway" points exist in every negotiation. "Resistance" point, "walkaway" point, and "bottom line" are interchangeable phrases used to indicate the point beyond which a party to a negotiation will not agree to a proposed settlement. A plaintiff's or seller's walkaway point is the *least* that party will agree to accept in settlement; a defendant's or buyer's walkaway point is the *most* the party will agree to pay. For a lawyer, the client's walkaway point also marks the outer limit of the lawyer's *authority* to reach a negotiated agreement on behalf of her client. The plaintiff's lawyer in our example thus lacks present authority to accept an offer of $122,999, even if she is convinced that the defendant will not pay a dollar more to settle the case.

Given the parties' resistance points, the heart of the negotiation will be over *where* in the bargaining range a final settlement will fall. Who will claim the larger share of the available surplus (the $52,000 difference between $123,000 and $175,000)? In a distributive bargaining situation, where your goal is to maximize your client's gain, the single most useful piece of information you could have about your opponent would be to know her walkaway point. With this information, the insurance company's lawyer in our example could offer the plaintiff $123,001, thereby exceeding her minimum acceptable figure and making settlement desirable from her point of view, while retaining virtually all the available surplus for his client. For obvious reasons, negotiating parties do not readily share accurate information about resistance points in a distributive bargaining situation. Indeed, one way to describe the negotiator's task is to say that she should attempt to learn as much as she can about the other party's resistance point while revealing as little as possible about her own. Each lawyer will actively engage in what the sociologist Erving Goffman[2] called "impression management" in an effort to claim as much of the bargaining surplus as possible. In addition to various forms of puffing and bluffing, lawyers also use normative arguments to support their claims, as the excerpt below from Lax and Sebenius illustrates.

What is the point of all this subterfuge? Remember that neither lawyer knows what the bargaining range actually is, and each wants to capture as much of it as possible for his client. The jockeying that goes on through offers and counter-offers is designed, first, to deal with the reality that both lawyers begin with only imperfect and partial information about the subject of the negotiation. As a result, either may overestimate the strength of the other side's position and set a walkaway point that is too low (for a plain-

---

[2] *See* ERVING GOFFMAN, THE PRESENTATION OF SELF IN EVERYDAY LIFE (1959).

tiff/seller) or too high (for a defendant/buyer). The plaintiff knows the extent of her own injuries, and she may have learned through discovery that the defendant had been drinking before the collision occurred. However, other factors affecting liability may not have come out, for example, that he had also had a fight with his wife, or that he was taking a prescription medication that contributed to his erratic driving.

Second, concealing your true bottom line makes allowances for the parties' differences in valuing both the subject of the negotiation and settlement itself. A collection of old lighting fixtures may not bring a high price if the buyer is interested only in finding something to cover the naked light bulbs in his house. If, however, he wants to use them to restore his home to its period splendor, he may be willing to pay a much higher price for the particular fixtures you are selling. Until you begin gathering information in the course of the negotiation, you will not know which kind of buyer you are dealing with, and thus cannot know whether the "junk" you are clearing out of your garage might represent a treasure trove to the buyer and thus command a high price. Similarly, if the defendant in our personal injury example is interested in running for political office, he may be willing to pay a premium to get the case settled quickly with no publicity, regardless of the merits.

Finally, when you are interested only in maximizing your own client's gain, it will be to your advantage for the other side to think that your settlement requirements are higher than they actually are. To return to the personal injury example, the plaintiff's lawyer will seek to persuade the defense lawyer that her client must have *more* than $123,000 to settle; and the defendant's lawyer, conversely, will maintain that his client is only willing to pay *less* than the $175,000 he is actually authorized to offer. If the plaintiff's lawyer convinces her opponent that her client will not seriously consider any settlement offer under $150,000, she will have captured more than half of the original bargaining range of $123,000-$175,000. The focus of the negotiation will then shift to how the remaining $25,000 (between $150,000 and $175,000) will be split between the parties. Schelling's classic essay below on the use of commitments in bargaining illustrates one way a negotiator might try to convince her counterpart that she has little room to move in a negotiation.

B. TARGET POINT

The fact that our plaintiff's walkaway point is $123,000 does not mean that her lawyer will go into the negotiations asking for $123,001, for all the reasons discussed above. Although the lawyer knows that, in the end, she will accept such an offer if she can't do any better, she expects to do better. In the course of preparing for the negotiation, she sets a *target* for herself that is a high, but reasonable, settlement figure based on her evaluation of the case and her client's walkaway point. Whereas the walkaway number represents the point beyond which there will not be a settlement, the target is a flexible number that reflects the lawyer's optimistic assessment of how *well* she can do in the negotiation. It will be based on the strongest case the lawyer can make for her client under the facts and will take into account any known or anticipated weaknesses on the other side.

Given the uncertainties inherent in any negotiation, a high target is often the best predictor of success — in part because it tends to resolve doubts about the bargaining range in favor of the person setting the target, and in part because a confident, optimistic attitude about a negotiation can be a self-fulfilling prophecy. An inexperienced negotiator, however, is more likely to focus on the weaknesses of her own case and the strengths of her opponent's case and to set overly conservative targets. In doing so, she effectively contracts the bargaining range so that she never has the opportunity to negotiate over the entire range. If our plaintiff's lawyer's target is only $130,000, for example, she is not likely to make a persuasive case for a settlement in the upper end of the bargaining range:

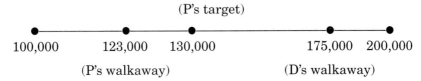

Conversely, if her target is $165,000, she will structure her arguments to justify a high recovery for her client and will not easily accept a lower figure proposed by the other side. A high target will also require a high opening demand, which serves to anchor the negotiation at a favorable point. If the plaintiff starts by asking for over $200,000, the defendant may end up feeling lucky to reach a settlement close to his maximum of $175,000.

Viewed from the outside, then, a distributive bargaining situation can be represented as a series of points on a line. Each side has a walkaway point, beyond which no settlement is possible. The parties' walkaway points define the zone of possible agreements between them, or bargaining range. In addition, each negotiator will have a target point, or estimated best deal-figure, different from the walkaway point. After the fact, all this information could be plotted out, as has been done above. When the negotiation begins, though, each negotiator knows only her own target and walkaway points, and thus cannot know what the actual bargaining range is:

Plaintiff knows:

```
         ●                              ●
       123,000                        165,000
    (P's walkaway)                  (P's target)
```

but does not know where along the line defendant's walkaway point lies ($120,000? $150,000? $180,000?).

Defendant knows:

140,000   175,000

(D's target)   (D's walkaway)

but does not know what plaintiff's walkaway point is ($185,000? $150,000? $120,000?).

Given each side's initial uncertainty about the other's walkaway point, the actual process of negotiation between them will revolve around their efforts to assess where that walkaway point lies and to settle as close to it as possible. Since a distributive bargaining scenario assumes a fixed quantity of resources, usually money, to be divided between the parties, the interaction will be a competitive one, with each lawyer attempting to capture as much of the bargaining range as possible for her own client. How do you prepare for and carry out such a negotiation?

C. PREPARATION

Thorough preparation is essential to success in negotiation. A lawyer who is well prepared will be more confident that she can obtain what her client wants and needs from the negotiation, will be less likely to be caught off guard during the negotiation by something the other negotiator does or says, and will be more able to respond productively to the unexpected when it does happen. Preparation is the surest way to build your confidence as a negotiator and to improve your performance.

1. Determining Walkaway and Target Points

In a distributive bargaining situation, preparing means, first, determining your walkaway and target points and deciding, relative to them, what your opening offer or demand will be. The lawyer-client skills of interviewing and counseling are essential to effective negotiation and will be discussed in more detail in Chapter Seven. In order to set the walkaway point, you must assess with your client what her options are if you do not reach a settlement. On the one hand, if widgets are readily available and your client is interested in buying them only at a very good price, her walkaway figure will be low. On the other hand, if only one seller can supply them and her business is likely to go under if you do not make a deal, her walkaway price will be high. According to Korobkin in the article below, the source of your power in any negotiation is your ability to walk away from the table (or, at least, to make the other party *believe* that you can do so). What Fisher, Ury and Patton[3] call the "Best Alternative To a Negotiated Agreement," or BATNA, has to be taken into account: you have to know when to *stop* nego-

---

[3] *See* ROGER FISHER, ET AL., GETTING TO YES (2d ed. 1991).

tiating and to exercise your other options instead. A rational negotiator will accept any deal that is better than a client's BATNA and refuse any deal that is not. A bad deal is worse than no deal, and you need to know your client's situation thoroughly in order to help her figure out what is a "good enough" deal in a particular case.In a lawsuit negotiation, where your BATNA is to go to trial, you have to calculate the likely recovery at trial, based on the evidence and verdicts in similar cases. You then have to weigh the expected verdict against your client's ability to wait for it (the time-value of money), her preference for a certain recovery now versus an uncertain one in the future, and the additional costs of going to trial.

Once you have established your walkaway point, or minimum accept-able settlement, you need to establish a target for the negotiation: what you would consider not merely a "good enough" result for your client, but a very good result. As a beginning negotiator, you may find it difficult to stray far from your walkaway point in setting a target point. Lack of confidence leads you to feel that you will be lucky to get any acceptable settlement, and you focus on the weaknesses of the case rather than its strengths. As you prepare to negotiate, it may be helpful to keep in mind that you are not responsible for the facts your client presents you with, only for making the best case possible based on those facts. The defendant's lawyer in our per-sonal injury example might wish his client hadn't been drinking before the collision, but he can't change that fact. What he can do is to minimize its impact on the outcome of the negotiation, as he would do at trial, by point-ing out that the drinking occurred several hours before the accident, or that his client also ate a full meal at the same time, and so on. In setting a target, the lawyer looks at a best case scenario, but still a realistic one. There is little point in setting a target based on favorable circumstances sur-rounding the defendant's drinking if there are reliable witnesses who will say that he downed four double scotches before climbing into his car.

When it comes to setting high and obtainable targets, as in many other aspects of negotiation, the biggest hurdles are often internal. If you fear overreaching by asking for an amount well above the minimum your client will accept, or if you feel guilty not offering all your client is prepared to pay an injured party, it is worth examining the sources of such feelings. Unex-plored, they are likely to result in your consistently bargaining against yourself in negotiations by undervaluing your client's case. Becoming aware of and understanding the ways in which you regularly undercut your own success, both in preparing for and in conducting negotiations, is an impor-tant part of developing and increasing your skill in bargaining with others. If you are not optimistic by nature, you can develop optimism by experi-menting in your negotiations. Set a target for yourself that is just outside of your comfort zone. If you do that and succeed, as most people do, you will become more confident in your ability to choose and meet a target that cap-tures more of the bargaining range for your client. You may not get every-thing you ask for, but you will certainly get more than if you never ask for much of anything. The article below by Schneider addresses the importance of optimistic aspirations in negotiation and the obstacles you may encounter in setting them.

2. Opening Offers/Demands

Once you have figured out your walkaway and target points, you have to decide what *opening offer/demand* to make, that is, what number to put on the table first. Assuming that you will have to make some concessions in the course of the negotiation, you want to leave room to do so and still meet your target. In our personal injury example, the parties' preparations might leave them with the following points mapped out:

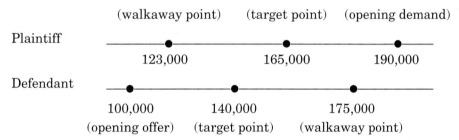

In choosing an opening figure, each party must pick a number that can be justified based on the facts of the case. If the plaintiff's opening demand is too high (in our example, say, $280,000), the defendant may conclude that she is not serious about reaching settlement and may terminate the negotiation. If it is too low, however, (say $135,000) she will have foreclosed the possibility of settling for a higher figure within the bargaining range. Since preparation can only take you so far in the absence of relevant information from the other party, negotiators should always be ready to adjust their planned opening figures based on information gained in the early stages of a negotiation.

Indeed, gathering information before making *any* offer or demand is essential. You have to make assumptions about the other side and their willingness to settle in preparing for the negotiation, but you also have to test those assumptions once the negotiation begins to make sure you are not off base. If the plaintiff's lawyer in our example simply walks into the room and says "My client wants $190,000 to settle," she misses the opportunity to assess whether she has set her target, and hence her opening demand, too low. Too much emphasis on "cutting to the chase" in negotiations, rather than being a sign of skill and a businesslike attitude, only results in cutting off the flow of information you need to adjust your initial figures appropriately. A quick deal may well prove to be a poor deal.

3. Concessions

Having your walkaway point, your target, and your opening demand clearly in mind, you need also to prepare for what concessions you will be willing to make, if necessary, and how you will make them. Throwing out numbers at random in an effort to get the other side to agree to a settlement is not likely to lead to good results. You need to have reasons for the positions you take, and for the concessions you make in response to the arguments of the other side. Compare the following interchanges in terms of credibility:

A: My client wants $150,000 to settle.

B: That's ridiculous. This case isn't worth even half that!

A: Well, she might be willing to accept $120,000.

* * *

A: Based on my client's injuries and the amount of time she lost from work, as well as the long period of painful recovery she went through, $150,000 is a reasonable settlement figure if we can resolve this without going to trial.

B: I understand that your client did have medical bills and some lost income; but in light of the fact that her injuries, and her claimed pain and suffering, would have been mitigated if she had sought medical attention sooner, a settlement of $70,000 is fair.

A: Given your client's drinking and erratic driving, a jury is not likely to reduce my client's recovery for pain and suffering by more than 5-10% because of the short delay in treating her injuries. If we can settle this now for $140,000, both of our clients will be satisfied with the result.

If you have thought ahead about the concessions you are willing to make, and the reasons for those concessions, you are unlikely to get caught up in the heat of the negotiation and to give up things that you will regret later. Planning your concessions will help you keep your target firmly in mind and will better enable you to achieve it. You will also be more credible in the positions you take, even when you are making concessions, if those positions are supported by reasons that relate to specific aspects of the negotiation, as the second example above illustrates.

When planning concessions, you need to look objectively at the strengths and weaknesses of your case. Often, what at first appears to be a weakness can be turned into a strength, or less of a weakness, if you think carefully about how to present it to the other side. Just as experienced trial lawyers know that a bad fact brought out inconspicuously on direct examination has far less negative impact on a jury than the same fact brought out resoundingly on cross-examination, skilled negotiators learn how to present troublesome aspects of a case in a way that serves their clients' interests. To do this, you have to be willing to look at your bad facts rather than hoping that they will magically disappear or that the other lawyer will not be aware of them. First, assume that your counterpart will be as well prepared as you are. Second, think about how you will respond to minimize the impact of bad facts when he brings them up, or even about how you might raise them yourself in order to dispose of them effectively. If you have planned in this way, you will not flounder when a problem surfaces. A prepared response is less likely to betray your concern than something you say when you are caught off guard.

4. Anticipating the Other Side's Case

A related aspect of planning is anticipating what the other side's target and walkaway points will be, based on the information available to you before the negotiation begins. Depending on the amount of information you have, these estimates may be rough, indeed; but it will be a useful check on your own planning to spend time thinking about what positions the other side may take and what reasons they may give for those positions. Putting yourself in the opposing party's shoes will help you pinpoint difficulties in your own case and will give you insight into his strengths and weaknesses and the arguments his lawyer is likely to make during the negotiation. It may also alert you to concessions that are potentially valuable to him, and relatively costless to you.

5. Managing Information

In the course of the negotiation, you will try to learn things about the other party's case, and about his perception of your case, that you don't know when the negotiation starts. He, of course, will do the same with you. Another important aspect of preparation, then, is deciding what you need to find out before you actually make a deal. Without considering what information you need to gather in the early stages of the negotiation, you will not be able to gauge how well the actual situation fits the assumptions you have made in preparing to negotiate. You may have overestimated how much the other party needs a deal with you, or underestimated the value he places on what you are selling. Only careful attention to gathering information will enable you to adjust your goals appropriately. In addition to what you want to learn, you also have to decide what information you are willing, or even eager, to divulge to the other party — for example, the large number of offers you have already received for the subject property — and what information you want to conceal — for example, the fact that none of those offers exceeds the price you paid for the property originally. Managing information is a central feature of distributive bargaining, and you have to plan to do it well.

A beginning negotiator often feels that she has to conceal as much as possible, that virtually anything she reveals will hurt her or be used against her. As discussed above in connection with planning concessions, you are more likely to feel this way if you have not thought through your case and prepared how to present it in the best light that you realistically can. If you choose when and how you will reveal information, rather than anxiously concealing as much as possible, you gain a degree of control over the negotiation that you lack when you merely react to what your counterpart says or does. Increasing the amount of information you are prepared to reveal, and reducing the amount you feel you absolutely must conceal, will help you make a stronger case for your client. In addition, the more willing you are to share information that the other party considers useful, the more likely you are to learn what you need to know from your counterpart before you make a deal.

6. Using Outside Sources

As part of your preparation, you need to consult outside sources of information to help you understand the context of a given negotiation. You will need data about the subject of the negotiation — market prices, alternate sources of supply, industry standards, market factors affecting the company you are dealing with, and so on. In addition, information about the parties and their representatives from others who have negotiated with them in the past will be helpful in planning your strategy. You will also want to learn about any relevant negotiation conventions, for example, the convention in personal injury litigation that the plaintiff makes the first demand.

While it may seem stilted to plan so many steps in the negotiation before it even starts, planning will actually make it easier to act spontaneously as the negotiation develops and will enable you to make better judgments about how to respond to new information or unexpected arguments in the course of the negotiation. At the same time, you must not be so wedded to your plan that you carry it out regardless of anything the other side says to suggest that your initial assumptions were inaccurate. A main point of planning is to free you up to listen during the negotiation itself and to use what you hear to adjust your approach.

D. DISTRIBUTIVE BARGAINING TACTICS

Distributive bargaining theory assumes an arms-length transaction between parties who both seek to maximize gain in a zero-sum situation. The quality of the relationship between the parties or their representatives is not taken into account; each encounter is like a one-shot deal. Tactics aim generally at accumulating as much information and as many concessions as possible from the other side, while revealing little and making minimal concessions yourself. For lawyers conducting negotiations on behalf of clients, ethical rules place some limitations on what tactics are acceptable. These rules and their implications for distributive bargaining tactics are considered at length in Chapter Eight.

1. Bargaining for Information

A central aspect of distributive bargaining is bargaining for information. In the course of planning, you have to make certain working assumptions about the motives and wishes of the other side, as well as about the factual context of the negotiation. In addition, we all have a tendency to "fill in" missing information in order to create a coherent picture of a situation. For a negotiator, it is imperative to separate out what you know to be true from what you merely believe to be true. If you do not test your assumptions during the early stages of the negotiation, you risk making decisions based on inaccurate information and misunderstanding what the other side actually tells you.

A simple demonstration of the power of assumptions is a silent negotiation, in which the parties must negotiate the sale of widgets that will retail for a certain price. They are allowed to communicate only by exchanging slips of paper with dollar figures on them. Most pairs will reach an agreement, despite their lack of information about what exactly they are agreeing to. When asked the basis for the deal, it turns out that each negotiator has *assumed* a certain set of facts about the condition and location of the goods, the standard retail markup, who pays shipping costs, and so on. It also turns out that within pairs there are widely differing assumptions operating, so that the widgets A thought she was buying may be quite different from the widgets that B thought he was selling. When parties fail to recognize and then to test their assumptions about each other, the same thing can happen in negotiations where the parties are free to communicate verbally.

Many negotiators forget that they start with only a partial picture of the situation, and they push to "get down to numbers" before learning anything about the other side's point of view. Yet the relevant facts of a situation are not immutable; they are often dependent on your perspective. Knowing the other side's perspective is a valuable source of information about possibilities for settlement. The most obvious way to gather that information is by asking questions, especially about the reasons behind positions taken by the other party. Why does a deal have to be made today? How good are her alternatives to settlement with you? What is the basis for a particular offer? Asking questions allows you to test the assumptions that you bring to the negotiation about both parties' situations. Questions also permit you to gauge the firmness of stated positions by learning how well supported they are by facts. In addition, the information you gather can alert you to issues that are important (or unimportant) to your counterpart, opening up possibilities for an advantageous settlement if you value those issues differently.

In addition to asking questions, you have to learn to listen carefully to what the other party says, to look for verbal and non-verbal cues that either reinforce or contradict the surface message conveyed. If someone tells you that he wants $40,000-50,000 to settle, you can be sure that he will settle for $40,000, or less. If he starts a sentence by saying, "I'll be perfectly frank with you. . .", take whatever follows with a large grain of salt and test it against other things you've heard. Asking questions is only one way to gather information, and not always the most informative one. You also have to listen for what someone omits from an answer, for answers that are not answers or that deflect the question, for hesitations and vagueness in the responses that you get. There is no simple formula for what such things mean, but the more alert you are for ways in which you are not getting information in a straightforward way, the better able you will be to sort through the information that you get. Paying attention to patterns that develop in the negotiation can also be useful. For example, a negotiator who says she wants $250,000 to settle, then drops down to $200,000, then to $160,000 is indicating that there is a lot of air in her demands, so you should not be too quick to close a deal. Conversely, as her concessions become smaller and smaller, she may be nearing her walkaway point, and you will have to begin considering whether the available deal is good enough for you.

One of the most effective and underutilized methods of bargaining for information is silence. Many inexperienced negotiators, especially lawyer-negotiators, think that they are paid to talk and are not comfortable sitting quietly. If you can teach yourself to do so, you will find that you often learn things that would never be revealed in response to a direct question. When silences occur, people tend to fill them in; and because the silence is unstructured, what they say is often more spontaneous than any answer to a question would be. Since you are interested in gathering new information in the course of the negotiation, it is useful to keep in mind that if *you* are talking, you probably aren't hearing anything you do not already know. Therefore, silence is truly golden.

2. Positional Bargaining

The language of distributive bargaining is competitive and self-centered. Parties talk in terms of what they *want,* they make *demands* of each other, they take *positions*, and they are prepared to *walk away* if they do not get what they came for. They are either indifferent to the outcome for the other side, or positively interested in besting them, often as an outgrowth of the fundamentally competitive atmosphere. While "false statements of material fact" are prohibited by the rules of legal ethics (see Model Rule 4.1 in Chapter Eight), puffing and bluffing are common practices in negotiations, legal and otherwise. If your goal is to maximize your own gain, the positions you take will be *designed* to exaggerate what you must get in order to make a deal and, at the same time, to persuade the other negotiator that he must substantially compromise what he is seeking in order to get any deal at all.

The ethical rules, rather than setting a higher standard for lawyers acting in a representative capacity, essentially accept these aspects of negotiation. The Comment to Model Rule 4.1 explicitly notes that "under generally accepted conventions in negotiation," statements about value ("This truck is worth at least $18,000") and about a party's willingness to settle ("My client wants $50,000 to settle this case" when she actually will take anything over $30,000) are not considered to be statements of material fact.

Given the circumstances of positional bargaining, you must be prepared to recognize and meet, if not to engage in, any number of tactics designed to contribute to the goal of maximizing gain. Some of the most common ones include: good cop/bad cop, where a pair of negotiators take differing roles, with one being tough and hard-nosed about every issue and the other acting as if he is trying to help bring the negotiation to a successful conclusion by persuading his partner to agree to *something*; bringing up new issues at the last minute and pressing to have them included in what had appeared to be a final agreement; negotiating an agreement and then declaring that you lack the authority to close the deal without taking it back to a superior for approval; and using anger or threats to intimidate the other side. While some of these tactics are questionable, they can be quite effective unless you recognize them for what they are when they are used against you. Often, the most useful response to such tactics is to name them. Once you make clear that you know what game is being played and that you are not going to be taken in, they lose their value. Goodpaster's article below on competitive bargaining contains an extensive catalogue of commonly used distributive bargaining tactics, and Lowenthal's piece examines how arguments and threats are used to gain advantage in negotiation.

Since you do not want to reveal what your true bottom line is, it is important to learn not to react overtly to anything the other side says or does, however surprising or disappointing it may be. It is not easy to teach yourself not to respond spontaneously to what you hear. But in this respect, a negotiation is a performance, both in terms of what you reveal to the other lawyer about your own case and in terms of what you convey about your evaluation of his positions, your willingness to settle, and so on. Part of your role as a lawyer is to speak and to listen without "leaking" your feelings and reactions to the other side through facial expressions, tone of voice, word choice, and other verbal and nonverbal cues. What counts in the end is not just the actual strengths or weaknesses of your case, but the other side's perceptions of those strengths and weaknesses. Thorough preparation is a significant aid in developing the capacity to affect those perceptions. The better prepared you are, the less likely you are to be surprised by something that happens in the negotiation. In addition, if you have already thought through what you will say, for example, if the other side turns out to know your worst fact and attempts to use it against you, your reaction will be a far more confident and measured one than if you actually are caught unawares and have to come up with a response on the spot. Some people are better at thinking on their feet than others, but most people who appear good at it have actually done a lot of thinking in advance, in order not to have to do it all on their feet.

3. Bargaining in a Litigation Context

Many negotiations that lawyers handle take place in the context of pending or potential litigation. As discussed above in the section on planning, in a litigated case your walkaway point will be largely determined by the expected recovery at trial, since that is the alternative to a negotiated settlement. There are also other, less direct, ways that the adversary system, with its emphasis on partisan advocacy and judicial resolution of disputes according to law, influences legal negotiations. As Menkel-Meadow discusses below, it colors participants' attitudes towards the negotiation process, privileges distributive approaches to bargaining that produce a winner and a loser like at trial, and often limits ideas for possible resolutions to those that a court could impose. Litigation itself is also used strategically to gain certain ends in negotiation, for example, when a party seeks to force a settlement by initiating suit or by imposing extensive discovery costs on the other side. Goodpaster's second article below explores how litigation decisions affect the likelihood of a negotiated resolution to a dispute and also how they can be viewed as moves in a negotiation process leading either to trial or to settlement.

4. Dealing with Conflict

Every negotiation involves a certain level of conflict between the parties, and a search for a mutually agreeable resolution of that conflict. The conflict is most marked in a true distributive bargaining situation, where the resources are assumed to be fixed and each party cares only about getting the largest possible share for itself. In such a situation a competitive approach to dividing the resources is most likely to achieve the goal of maximizing gain. It does so, however, at the possible cost of friction and antagonism between the negotiators, who have no reason to trust each other in the process. The level of conflict involved in such negotiations can be uncomfortable, and that discomfort can lead to less than optimal results for clients.

The lack of trust between parties in a distributive bargaining situation means that each is forced to act independently of the other and to remain skeptical of anything the other says or does. The negotiation is largely an exercise in convincing your counterpart that you are committed to your positions, that you have viable alternatives to settlement, that a jury will believe your version of the facts if the case goes to trial. For many negotiators the discomfort engendered by such a contest is hard to tolerate, and they end up behaving in ways that minimize the differences between the two parties. For example, someone who feels bad about pushing to maximize his client's gain may try instead to reach a result that is "fair" to both sides, without realizing that he is motivated as much by wanting to avoid conflict as by any other goal. Fairness, like value, is highly subjective; and trying to reach a fair result often means using the lawyer's notion of what is fair instead of what the client would consider an optimal outcome. Similarly, "splitting the difference" with the other side — accepting an outcome midway between your two positions — ends the negotiation quickly and relatively painlessly for the lawyer. It does not necessarily serve the client's purposes, however, since it substitutes an arbitrary figure for a reasoned position favorable to the client. At the other end of the spectrum is the negotiator who gets so caught up in the conflict that tensions mount and a stalemate results. Such a negotiator may also lose sight of his client's interests altogether in the heat of battle and walk away from an adequate agreement rather than "give in" to the other side.

If you repeatedly find yourself responding to negotiation conflict in these or similar ways, you are probably getting in the way of your own (and your client's) success. You would do well to try to understand what triggers these responses and to think about how else you might handle such situations in the future. Do you generally tend to back down when challenged? Do you feel that it is your job to keep things smooth between people? Do you respond aggressively when your position is questioned? When you negotiate, you are often acting on longstanding beliefs about interpersonal conflict. The more you can understand about what you bring to conflict situations and what your automatic responses are likely to be, the more you will be able to *choose* how to act and to tailor your behavior to the negotiation and to the needs of your client. The materials in Chapter Five deal extensively with psychological aspects of negotiation and address how what you bring to the negotiation table affects the results you achieve.

5. Disarming the Opposition

The literature on competitive bargaining emphasizes the arms-length nature of such negotiations and the tense and even hostile atmosphere that distributive tactics can foster and exploit. While some distributive bargainers do use threats and intimidation to get what they want, such tactics have the disadvantage of being completely obvious and providing an explicit warning to an opponent to protect himself as best he can. It is also possible, and often more successful, to bargain competitively without attacking or alienating the other negotiator. A low-key, cordial negotiation style is completely compatible with a firm focus on maximizing your client's gain. Such a style also has the advantage of not encouraging an aggressive response, thus reducing the likelihood of stalemate. By not damaging working relationships, an amicable competitive negotiator leaves open opportunities to seek joint gain (see Chapter Three) that might be lost to a more hard-nosed distributive bargainer.

6. Pros and Cons of a Distributive Bargaining Approach

A strong positional bargainer is focused on the goal of maximizing her client's gain. Whatever tactics she adopts are designed to implement that goal; and that single-mindedness itself will often contribute to her ultimate success, especially against negotiators who are more ambivalent about their goals or less skilled in achieving them. To many law students, the competitive atmosphere of distributive negotiations mirrors the adversary system that is the basis for most law school instruction, and seems to fit with the ethical requirement of zealous advocacy for one's client.

Since most negotiations will have distributive aspects, lawyers who are comfortable being competitive will do well when it comes to claiming the last dollar, and in true one-shot deals they will often do very well indeed.

The focus that is the hallmark of such a negotiator can also be a liability, however. When two competitive negotiators meet, the risk of stalemate is increased by the potential for intransigence on both sides. The clients' concerns may get lost in the shuffle if their representatives get caught up in efforts to best each other. In addition, few actual negotiations fit the single-issue, fixed pie model of distributive bargaining theory. Most negotiations involve multiple issues, if not multiple parties; and ongoing relationships are often more valuable to clients than obtaining the last dollar in any single negotiation. A hard distributive bargainer is often blind to possibilities other than winning: opportunities for mutual gain, or even for trade-offs, such as in the timing of payments or delivery, that might produce a more satisfactory result for both parties. Much of the development in negotiation theory over the last twenty-five years has focused on these integrative, or problem-solving, aspects of negotiation, and they are the subject of the following chapter.

Thomas Schelling,[*] *An Essay on Bargaining*
in STRATEGY OF CONFLICT 22–28 (1963)[**]

* * *

Bargaining Power: The Power to Bind Oneself

"Bargaining power," "bargaining strength," "bargaining skill" suggest that the advantage goes to the powerful, the strong, or the skillful. It does, of course, if those qualities are defined to mean only that negotiations are

---

[*] Thomas Schelling, a pioneer in game theory, is Distinguished Professor at University of Maryland School of Public Policy. This excerpt from his classic book analyzes the power of commitments in negotiation.

won by those who win. But, if the terms imply that it is an advantage to be more intelligent or more skilled in debate, or to have more financial resources, more physical strength, more military potency, or more ability to withstand losses, then the term does a disservice. These qualities are by no means universal advantages in bargaining situations; they often have a contrary value.

The sophisticated negotiator may find it difficult to seem as obstinate as a truly obstinate man. If a man knocks at a door and says that he will stab himself on the porch unless given $10, he is more likely to get the $10 if his eyes are bloodshot. The threat of mutual destruction cannot be used to deter an adversary who is too unintelligent to comprehend it or too weak to enforce his will on those he represents. The government that cannot control its balance of payments, or collect taxes, or muster the political unity to defend itself, may enjoy assistance that would be denied it if it could control its own resources. And, to cite an example familiar from economic theory, "price leadership" in oligopoly may be an unprofitable distinction evaded by the small firms and assumed perforce by the large one.

Bargaining power has also been described as the power to fool and bluff, "the ability to set the best price for yourself and fool the other man into thinking this was your maximum offer." Fooling and bluffing are certainly involved; but there are two kinds of fooling. One is deceiving about the facts; a buyer may lie about his income or misrepresent the size of his family. The other is purely tactical. Suppose each knows everything about the other, and each knows what the other knows. What is there to fool about? The buyer may say that, though he'd really pay up to twenty and the seller knows it, he is firmly resolved as a tactical matter not to budge above sixteen. If the seller capitulates, was he fooled? Or was he convinced of the truth? Or did the buyer really not know what he would do next if the tactic failed? If the buyer really "feels" himself firmly resolved, and bases his resolve on the conviction that the seller will capitulate, and the seller does, the buyer may say afterwards that he was "not fooling." Whatever has occurred, it is not adequately conveyed by the notions of bluffing and fooling.

How does one person make another believe something? The answer depends importantly on the factual question, "Is it true?" It is easier to prove the truth of something that is true than of something false. To prove the truth about our health we can call on a reputable doctor; to prove the truth about our costs or income we may let the person look at books that have been audited by a reputable firm or the Bureau of Internal Revenue. But to persuade him of something false we may have no such convincing evidence.

When one wishes to persuade someone that he would not pay more than $16,000 for a house that is really worth $20,000 to him, what can he do to take advantage of the usually superior credibility of the truth over a false assertion? Answer: make it true. How can a buyer make it true? If he likes the house because it is near his business, he might move his business, persuading the seller that the house is really now worth only $16,000 to him. This would be unprofitable; he is no better off than if he had paid the higher price.

But suppose the buyer could make an irrevocable and enforceable bet with some third party, duly recorded and certified, according to which he would pay for the house no more than $16,000, or forfeit $5,000. The seller has lost; the buyer need simply present the truth. Unless the seller is enraged and withholds the house in sheer spite, the situation has been rigged against him; the "objective" situation — the buyer's true incentive — has been voluntarily, conspicuously, and irreversibly changed. The seller can take it or leave it. This example demonstrates that if the buyer can accept an irrevocable *commitment*, in a way that is unambiguously visible to the seller, he can squeeze the range of indeterminacy down to the point most favorable to him. It also suggests, by its artificiality, that the tactic is one that may or may not be available; whether the buyer can find an effective device for committing himself may depend on who he is, who the seller is, where they live, and a number of legal and institutional arrangements (including, in our artificial example, whether bets are legally enforceable).

If both men live in a culture where "cross my heart" is universally accepted as potent, all the buyer has to do is allege that he will pay no more than $16,000, using this invocation of penalty, and he wins — or at least he wins if the seller does not beat him to it by shouting "$19,000, cross my heart." If the buyer is an agent authorized by a board of directors to buy at $16,000 but not a cent more, and the directors cannot constitutionally meet again for several months and the buyer cannot exceed his authority, and if all this can be made known to the seller, then the buyer "wins" — if, again, the seller has not tied himself up with a commitment to $19,000. Or, if the buyer can assert that he will pay no more than $16,000 so firmly that he would suffer intolerable loss of personal prestige or bargaining reputation by paying more, and if the fact of his paying more would necessarily be known, and if the seller appreciates all this, then a loud declaration by itself may provide the commitment. The device, of course, is a needless surrender of flexibility unless it can be made fully evident and understandable to the seller.

Incidentally, some of the more contractual kinds of commitments are not as effective as they at first seem. In the example of the self-inflicted penalty through the bet, it remains possible for the seller to seek out the third party and offer a modest sum in consideration of the latter's releasing the buyer from the bet, threatening to sell the house for $16,000 if the release is not forthcoming. The effect of the bet — as of most such contractual commitments — is to shift the locus and personnel of the negotiation, in the hope that the third party will be less available for negotiation or less subject to an incentive to concede. To put it differently, a *contractual* commitment is usually the assumption of a contingent "transfer cost," not a "real cost"; and if all interested parties can be brought into the negotiation the range of indeterminacy remains as it was. But if the third party were available only at substantial transportation cost, to that extent a truly irrevocable commitment would have been assumed. (If bets were made with a number of people, the "real costs" of bringing them into the negotiation might be made prohibitive.)

The most interesting parts of our topic concern whether and how commitments can be taken; but it is worthwhile to consider briefly a model in which practical problems are absent — a world in which absolute commitments are freely available. Consider a culture in which "cross my heart" is universally recognized as absolutely binding. Any offer accompanied by this invocation is a final offer, and is so recognized. If each party knows the other's true reservation price, the object is to be first with a firm offer. Complete responsibility for the outcome then rests with the other, who can take it or leave it as he chooses (and who chooses to take it).Bargaining is all over; the commitment (that is, the first offer) wins.

Interpose some communication difficulty. They must bargain by letter; the invocation becomes effective when signed but cannot be known to the other until its arrival. Now when one party writes such a letter the other may already have signed his own, or may yet do so before the letter of the first arrives. There is then no sale; both are bound to incompatible positions. Each must now recognize this possibility of stalemate and take into account the likelihood that the other already has, or will have, signed his own commitment.

An asymmetry in communication may well favor the one who is (and is known to be) unavailable for the receipt of messages, for he is the one who cannot be deterred from his own commitment by receipt of the other's. (On the other hand, if the one who cannot communicate can feign ignorance of his own inability, the other too may be deterred from his own commitment by fear of the first's unwitting commitment.) If the commitments depend not just on words but on special forms or ceremonies, ignorance of the other party's commitment ceremonies may be an advantage if the ignorance is fully appreciated, since it makes the other aware that only his own restraint can avert stalemate.

Suppose only part of the population belongs to the cult in which "cross my heart" is (or is believed to be) absolutely binding. If everyone knows (and is known to know) everyone else's affiliation, those belonging to this particular cult have the advantage. They can commit themselves, the others cannot. If the buyer says "$16,000, cross my heart" his offer is final; if the seller says "$19,000" he is (and is known to be) only "bargaining."

If each does not know the other's true reservation price there is an initial stage in which each tries to discover the other's and misrepresent his own, as in ordinary bargaining. But the process of discovery and revelation becomes quickly merged with the process of creating and discovering commitments; the commitments permanently change, for all practical purposes, the "true" reservation prices. If one party has, and the other has not, the belief in a binding ceremony, the latter pursues the "ordinary" bargaining technique of *asserting* his reservation price, while the former proceeds to *make* his.

The foregoing discussion has tried to suggest both the plausibility and the logic of self-commitment. Some examples may suggest the relevance of the tactic, although an observer can seldom distinguish with confidence the consciously logical, the intuitive, or the inadvertent use of a visible tactic. First, it has not been uncommon for union officials to stir up excitement and determination on the part of the membership during or prior to a wage negotiation. If the union is going to insist on $2 and expects the management to counter with $1.60, an effort is made to persuade the membership not only that the management could pay $2 but even perhaps that the negotiators themselves are incompetent if they fail to obtain close to $2. The purpose — or, rather, a plausible purpose suggested by our analysis — is to make clear to the management that the negotiators could not accept less than $2 *even if they wished to* because they no longer control the members or because they would lose their own positions if they tried. In other words, the negotiators reduce the scope of their own authority and confront the management with the threat of a strike that the union itself cannot avert, even though it was the union's own action that eliminated its power to prevent the strike.

Something similar occurs when the United States Government negotiates with other governments on, say, the uses to which foreign assistance will be put, or tariff reduction. If the executive branch is free to negotiate the best arrangement it can, it may be unable to make any position stick and may end by conceding controversial points because its partners know, or believe obstinately, that the United States would rather concede than terminate the negotiations. But, if the executive branch negotiates under legislative authority, with its position constrained by law, and it is evident that Congress will not be reconvened to change the law within the necessary time period, then the executive branch has a firm position that is visible to its negotiating partners.

When national representatives go to international negotiations knowing that there is a wide range of potential agreement within which the outcome will depend on bargaining, they seem often to create a bargaining position by public statements, statements calculated to arouse a public opinion that permits no concessions to be made. If a binding public opinion can be cultivated and made evident to the other side, the initial position can thereby be made visibly "final."

These examples have certain characteristics in common. First, they clearly depend not only on incurring a commitment but on communicating it persuasively to the other party. Second, it is by no means easy to estab-

lish the commitment, nor is it entirely clear to either of the parties concerned just how strong the commitment is. Third, similar activity may be
available to the parties on both sides. Fourth, the possibility of commitment,
though perhaps available to both sides, is by no means equally available; the
ability of a democratic government to get itself tied by public opinion may
be different from the ability of a totalitarian government to incur such a
commitment. Fifth, they all run the risk of establishing an immovable position that goes beyond the ability of the other to concede, and thereby provoke the likelihood of stalemate or breakdown.

* * *

David A. Lax & James K. Sebenius,[*]
The Language of Claiming
in THE MANAGER AS NEGOTIATOR: BARGAINING FOR COOPERATION
AND COMPETITIVE GAIN 141-43 (1986)[**]

* * *

The Language of Claiming

Although the object of tactical action may be an opponent's perception of
the bargaining set, the language by which value is claimed often has a
moral ring. In many negotiations, positions are advanced and justified not
by arguing that the negotiator desires them but rather that they are "right,"
morally, socially, or scientifically. Distributive negotiations over who will get
more are often carried out by a proxy discussion over who is more morally
or factually correct. To argue for advantageous outcomes, negotiators draw
on norms of justice and equity, institutional rules, consistency with past
promises and performance, and appropriate social behavior.

Sometimes, the forceful assertion of a norm is sufficient to gain agreement: "It is only right that I pay you what the others are getting, not more."
Even when one does not place intrinsic value on acting in accord with a certain norm, one may bear social costs for rejecting it outright. For example,
in response to an appeal to a widely accepted standard of fairness in dividing benefits, one may argue that the proposed rule is not applicable and propose another, more favorable one. By contrast, the response that "I do not
want to be fair, I want the biggest slice of the pie," can be costly. Thus, a
negotiator is more likely to acknowledge the norm but argue that it is inappropriate to the situation at hand or that it has been applied incorrectly.

[*] David A. Lax is a principal in Lax Sebenius LLC and co-head of Summa Capital Management. James K. Sebenius is Gordon Donaldson Professor at Harvard University Business
School. This excerpt from their influential book examines how negotiators use normative
arguments to claim value.

Applied correctly, with the real facts about the real situation, the outcome would be quite different (and advantageous to the opponent). "Yes, fifty-fifty would be the right way to go, but I put in more work and am more senior."

Pressures to do the "right" thing can be applied not merely to the outcome but to behavior during the negotiation as well. For example, consider a restaurant chain owner who sought to expand her business in two new regions (the South and Southwest). She hoped to share the returns from the South with an early investor but retain for herself the profits from the more promising Southwest. The investor argued that because he invested early in the life of the chain, he deserved the same treatment from all of the chain's ventures. Accepting the norm in the discussion, she responded that she wanted to treat him in this way, but laid out the "insuperable" practical problems that prevented her from acting in this way. (In fact, she did not want to act in accord with the norm of equal treatment, but found baldly rejecting it hard; hence rejecting the "practical" aspects was her way to the same end.) When the investor suggested a way around these practical difficulties — which he had in fact had in the back of his mind from the start — the restaurateur found herself in a tricky position. Rather than violate a norm of consistency with her earlier statement in the negotiation — that equal treatment was the "right way to go" — she felt "morally" forced to accede even at a likely cost of several million dollars. Though this whole negotiation was carried out in terms of right and wrong, its effects were purely distributive.

The role of norms and normative argument goes well beyond cynical self-serving uses. As we have mentioned before, negotiators frequently derive value from acting in accord with social norms; this can be understood as an interest. The post-negotiation desire to justify the agreement to oneself and to explain the agreement to others also makes agreement in accord with norms desirable. At the same time, norms can also serve as the basis for nonantagonizing commitments and as focal points.

Because negotiators frequently find it costly to reject the suggestion that they should act consistently with norms of the group, introducing normative argument can limit the bargaining set to those outcomes that are "socially acceptable." Egregious demands that cannot find strong normative support can sometimes be ruled out.

In short, the language in which much negotiation is carried out and with which much value is claimed can be normative. Carefully working out normative arguments and counter-arguments can be an important part of preparing for a negotiation.

* * *

Russell Korobkin,[*] *Bargaining Power as Threat of Impasse*
87 Marq. L. Rev. 867 (2004)[**]

In an ideal world, all negotiators would have what are sometimes called "common interests." The old chandelier that to me is clutter in the basement would be an antique to you, and your pleasure in receiving it would be outweighed only by my joy in getting rid of it. In most bargaining situations, however, negotiators' interests are in conflict. You might like the chandelier more than I do, which makes a mutually advantageous bargain possible, but it is currently lighting my dining room and I would prefer to keep it rather than give it away. You are interested in buying the chandelier from me, but you want to pay a low price. I will consider selling it to you, but I want a high price. Who will succeed in achieving his goal will most likely depend on who has more bargaining power, defined as the ability to convince the other negotiator to give us what we want even when the other would prefer not to do so.

The source of bargaining power is misunderstood by many negotiators, who wrongly assume that the indicia of success in other realms of life are directly related to power at the negotiating table. Wealth, brains, beauty, political power, prestige, and social influence are nice to have, but none of these items guarantee you the ability to exercise power in any particular negotiation. Bargaining power is situational, not personal. In some labor disputes, unions have more power than management; in others, management has more power than unions. In some merger negotiations, the target company enjoys more power than the suitor; in others, the dynamic is reversed. In some litigation settlement negotiations, the plaintiff has more power than the defendant; in others, the defendant enjoys the advantage. An employee seeking a raise from his boss might enjoy a relative power advantage, or he might not.

In each of these situations, relative bargaining power stems entirely from the negotiator's ability to, explicitly or implicitly, make a single threat credibly: "*I will walk away from the negotiating table without agreeing to a deal if you do not give me what I demand.*" The source of the ability to make such a threat, and therefore the source of bargaining power, is the ability to project that he has a desirable alternative to reaching an agreement, often referred to as a "BATNA." This essay elaborates on this claim.

I. BATNA STRENGTH

What you will do in the case of impasse determines your relative power in the negotiation. In market situations with fungible buyers and sellers,

---

[*] Russell Korobkin is Professor of Law, University of California Los Angeles. This article argues that power in negotiation depends solely on the strength of your alternatives.

[**] Copyright © 2004 Marquette Law Review. Reprinted by permission.

your BATNA is to enter into a similar transaction with someone other than your negotiating counterpart and, thus, your power depends implicitly on the forces of supply and demand. Imagine that you arrive at an automobile dealership hoping to pay "dealer invoice" for the car of your choice and begin to negotiate with a dealer who hopes to charge the "sticker price." Your BATNA is to buy the same car from another dealer. The dealer's BATNA is to wait for the next customer to enter the showroom and attempt to sell the car to that customer. If the model you have selected is in short supply and all of the other dealers in town have a waiting list of purchasers, your BATNA is relatively weak (you will have to wait for a car and probably pay a premium) and the dealer's BATNA is relatively strong (he is confident that another customer will be willing to pay the sticker price). The dealer enjoys substantial power because he can threaten impasse if you do not agree to pay the sticker price, and that threat would be credible because impasse would be in his best interest. In contrast, if all dealers are over-stocked and the new year's models are soon to arrive, you will enjoy power. You can credibly threaten to walk away if the dealer will not agree to a handsome discount because the chances are good that another dealer anxious to reduce inventory would likely agree to a discount, meaning that impasse would be in your best interest if you do not receive the price that you demand.

If the negotiation situation has an element of bilateral monopoly — that is, comparable transactions are unavailable to the parties — your bargaining power will depend on the relative quality of the substitute transaction you would enter into in the case of impasse. In litigation bargaining, a plaintiff and defendant who fail to reach agreement do not have the option of settling with different parties. Instead, both have the BATNA of submitting to adjudication of the dispute. Bargaining power depends on whether that BATNA is more desirable for the plaintiff or the defendant. If the plaintiff's case is strong on the legal merits and provable damages are high, the plaintiff will enjoy bargaining power because she can credibly threaten to end negotiations and proceed to adjudication if she does not receive the high settlement price that she demands. The defendant, of course, can make the same threat if the plaintiff will not accept a low settlement offer, but the threat would not be credible because it would not be in the defendant's best interest to take a weak case to court and face the likelihood of a large verdict rather than agree to pay a higher settlement price.

II. PERCEPTION IS REALITY

Strictly speaking, it is not the actual, objective quality of the negotiator's BATNA that determines his degree of bargaining power, but what the counterpart believes that the negotiator believes about the quality of his BATNA. For example, when an employee receives a job offer from a competing firm and asks his boss for a raise, whether the employee has power depends on whether the boss believes that the employee believes it is in the employee's best interest to accept the competing offer if the demand for a raise is not met. The credibility of the employee's threat to walk away from the negotiation and accept the competing offer if his demand is not met is unaffected by the fact that neither the boss nor any of the employee's colleagues would prefer the competing offer to the employee's current job at his current salary. Where power is concerned, the beauty of a BATNA is in the eye of the beholder, and eccentricity is not penalized as long as it is perceived to be genuine. The employee's threat of impasse will be credible to the boss, thus giving the employee power, even if the employee himself actually would not prefer the competing offer, so long as the boss thinks that the employee would prefer that offer.

An objectively strong BATNA is helpful, of course, because a BATNA that appears strong renders the negotiator's claim that he *believes* his BATNA is strong more credible. The employee's threat of impasse will more likely translate into bargaining power if his competing job offer is a $300,000 per year CEO position than if it is a $15,000 per year mailroom attendant position. But either a phantom BATNA (i.e., a nonexistent alternative) or a real BATNA with phantom *value* (i.e., an existent but undesirable alternative) can be a source of power in the hands of a persuasive negotiator.

III. PATIENCE AND POWER

In many bargaining contexts, especially those involving bilateral monopoly, the BATNA of both parties, at least in the short term, will be to continue to negotiate not to pursue a substitute transaction. In this situation, a negotiator's threat not to agree unless her demands are met is in essence a threat of *temporary* rather than permanent impasse. When both parties have a BATNA of temporary impasse, the negotiator for whom temporary impasse is less costly has the strongest BATNA and thus the lion's share of bargaining power. If you have a low cost of temporary impasse, you have the ability to be patient in the negotiations. Thus, it follows that patience translates into bargaining power.

When a union and management meet to attempt to negotiate a settlement of a strike, union members rarely threaten to find substitute employment, and management is precluded by law from firing the striking workers. The union's threat is that if management does not meet its demands, it will continue to strike. Management's threat is that, if the union does not accede to its terms, it will continue to permit the strike to go on. If the union has a large strike fund and if management cannot fill its orders with the labor of replacement workers, the union can be more patient in reaching an agreement and will enjoy superior bargaining power. In contrast, if the union's strike fund is empty and its members cannot pay their rents while management has a large quantity of inventory in storage, temporary impasse will be relatively more costly to the union, giving management power.

IV. THE RISKS OF POWER

In a world in which opposing negotiators had perfect information about the other's alternatives and preferences and both made all negotiating decisions with cold rationality, attempts to exercise bargaining power would never cause impasse. In any situation in which a mutually beneficial agreement were possible, the party with relatively less power would yield to the party with relatively more.

Few negotiations, however, are characterized by perfect information and lack of emotion. If both negotiators believe that they have a strong BATNA but that their counterpart does not, each might try to exercise power while neither yields. Thus, lawsuits go to trial, labor strikes drag on, and ethnic warfare continues, even when agreements that would make both sides better off are feasible. Alternatively, or in addition, the less powerful party might resent the sense of coercion or inequity inherent in the more powerful negotiator's demands and refuse to yield, even knowing that this course of action will cause harm to both sides. These twin possibilities make the exercise of bargaining power as potentially risky as it is potentially rewarding.

Andrea Kupfer Schneider,[*] *Aspirations in Negotiation*
87 MARQ. L. REV. 675, 676-80 (2004)[**]

* * *

Negotiators should establish optimistic aspirations because empirical evidence has shown that negotiators with higher aspirations tend to achieve better bargaining results. The classic study demonstrating this proposition was run by psychologists Sidney Siegel and Lawrence Fouraker in 1960. One set of negotiators were given a modest goal of $2.10 profit in a buy-sell negotiation and the other set were given the "high aspirations" of $6.10. Both sets were told that they could keep any profits they made and could qualify for a second, "double-their-money" round if they met or exceeded their specified bargaining goals. The negotiators with the more ambitious $6.10 goal achieved a mean profit of $6.25, far outperforming the median profit of $3.35 achieved by those with the modest $2.10 goal. More recently, Sally Blount White and Margaret Neale set up an experiment in house buying where buyers and sellers were each given reservation prices in addition to aspirational goals for the house price. Again, those buyers with high aspirations (to buy the house at a low price) did better than those buyers with low aspirations (as did the sellers with high aspirations).

---

[*] Andrea Kupfer Schneider is Professor of Law at Marquette University Law School. Her article discusses the importance of high aspirations in negotiation.

There are different explanations for this effect. First, a negotiator's aspirations help to determine the outer limit of what she will request. Because a negotiator will almost never achieve more than what she asks for, setting relatively high goals is important so that the negotiator makes suitably aggressive demands.

Second, optimistic aspirations can cause negotiators to work harder at bargaining than they otherwise might, increasing the likelihood of achieving a desirable outcome. Professor Jennifer Brown hypothesizes that when negotiators set an aspiration level, they gain more utility as offers increase toward that level versus the utility gained as offers proceed beyond that level. In other words, the marginal utility associated with each improvement beyond one's aspirations is less than the marginal utility associated with movement toward the aspirations. This theory implies that negotiators will care relatively more about achieving their aspirations than exceeding them.

Professor Russell Korobkin writes that one effect of negotiators working harder is that negotiators with high aspirations will also exhibit more patience at the bargaining table than those with low aspirations. Rather than getting frustrated and either walking away or giving in, the negotiator with high aspirations will be more willing to tolerate a longer give-and-take in order to reach her aspirations. As more patient negotiators achieve a greater share of the gains of negotiation than less patient negotiators, high aspirations can lead to better outcomes.

Aspirations should be specific. A general goal of "doing well" or "let's see what they say" is insufficient to trigger the positive behavioral benefits of setting aspirations discussed earlier. Much in the same way that negotiators learn to define their BATNA and then use it to determine their bottom line, negotiators should take vague aspirations and turn them into specific goals for the negotiation — either monetary or actions or both.

In addition specific goals for the negotiation can keep the negotiator more focused on his or her interests than on the game of negotiation. If a negotiator enters the negotiation with an ambiguous "let's see what happens" agenda, it is far easier to become entangled in debilitating negotiation mistakes such as getting anchored on the counterpart's numbers, assuming a fixed pie, or getting one's ego trapped in a game of chicken.

* * *

The availability of objective criteria makes it easier for the negotiator to justify a refusal to make concessions. Demands that are not objectively grounded are harder to hold onto during the bargaining process. Imagine a scenario where a seller would like to get $500,000 for her house because it is a nice round number and she could use it to buy another house, versus a scenario in which the seller lists her house for $500,000, based on the fair market value of the house in comparison to other houses in the neighborhood. In the latter case, the seller has fair and convincing arguments for why she will not accept less.

Demands that lack an objective justification also encourage the opposing negotiator to make unprincipled counter demands. If financial desire is the justification for the seller's list price, then the buyer could just as easily respond with their financial capacity of the $100,000 in their bank account. The seller's justifiable list price of $500,000 instead should lead to the more appropriate counteroffer of $450,000 based on the objective criteria that the roof needs to be replaced or that the kitchen should be updated.

* * *

Negotiators often fail to follow the "optimistic but justifiable" approach to setting aspirations, instead setting vague goals such as "achieving a good deal" or aspiring to relatively low, easy-to-achieve results. Why? One reason is that specific, optimistic aspirations can result in disappointment when they are not achieved. Setting low or non-specific goals — what Shell calls a "wimp-win" approach — maximizes the likelihood of success and protects self-esteem. If a negotiator sets his goals low, as in a car buyer who is willing to pay up to list price for a car, this "low aspirations" negotiator is more likely to accomplish his goals. After all, it is a rare car dealer who is not happy to accept list price! On the other hand, if a negotiator sets his goal high, as in a car buyer who is aiming to pay up to $500 over the dealer's invoice for a particular car, that "high aspirations" negotiator may be disappointed in himself when he can only negotiate a deal at $1000 over the dealer's invoice — $500 over his original goal. The "high aspirations" car buyer may well have paid $2000 less than the "low aspirations" car buyer, but he may be more focused on his perceived aspirations-based loss of $500. In order to avoid this disappointment, negotiators often set low goals. A related risk is that this disappointment from one negotiation can lead negotiators to set lower goals in future negotiations, again in a self-protective response.

Another circumstance in which negotiators set low aspirations is when the negotiator feels that she lacks enough information about the other side's interests and bottom line to confidently predict what results are possible. A negotiator may assume that she needs the deal more than her counterpart or may not understand why reaching a settlement is important to the other side. Without this information, she may set her goals lower than the goals should be from an objective perspective. For example, if a house seller receives an offer that is $20,000 below the listed price after the house has been on the market for several weeks without any interest, the seller's response depends, to a great extent, on the information the seller has about the buyer. Without any information, the seller might be so excited to get an offer that she accepts the offer immediately. On the other hand, if the seller learns that the buyer needs to move next month or has told his realtor that this was his favorite house, the seller may be more willing to hold onto high aspirations. Just as setting aspirations takes preparation and the appropriate criteria, it also requires preparation about the other side.

Finally, a negotiator may set low goals when she is relatively uninterested in the result or wants to avoid conflict with another person who seems more concerned than she is about the money, power, or other issues at stake. These low goals may be appropriate as long as the negotiator makes a rational decision about this.

* * *

Gary Goodpaster,[*] *A Primer on Competitive Bargaining*
1996 J. DISP. RESOL. 325, 349-68[**]

* * *

V. Competitive Negotiation Tactics

A. *Commonly Used Ploys and Tactics*

In addition to using basic hard bargaining strategy, a competitive negotiator may also use a variety of ploys and tactics to persuade or induce the other party to settle at a point as favorable as possible to the competitor. Not all competitors use these devices. Some manage quite well with just the basic *high demand, small concession, firmness* strategy. Even those who use such devices do not use them all, nor any standard set of them all the time. Nonetheless, some are commonly used, and some are a part of standard practice in some negotiating arenas.

* * *

"Precondition" demands. Sometimes a party will refuse to negotiate unless some condition or demand is satisfied prior to beginning the negotiation. Actually, setting a precondition is a way of obtaining a concession without giving any in return and, in effect, is the price paid to get the other party to bargain. Demanding satisfaction of a precondition may not only gain a concession without cost, it may also reveal how eager the other party is to secure a deal. If the other party meets the demand, it signals, intentionally or not, that it is willing to compromise, that its positions may be soft, and that it may possibly be successfully pushed hard during the negotiation.

Simply understanding that precondition demands actually are, and should be, a part of the principal negotiation dictates the appropriate response. Essentially that response is simply to make clear that you consider the precondition issues to be a part of the negotiation. Then, you should either demand reciprocal concessions in return for any concessions you

---

[*] Gary Goodpaster is Professor Emeritus at University of California Davis School of Law. His article catalogues a multitude of tactics commonly used in distributive bargaining situations.

[**] Copyright © 1996 Journal of Dispute Resolution. Reprinted with permission.

make or delay consideration of the demands until the full negotiation begins.

Your move, or you first. If competitive negotiation is an information game, the party that has the most and best information regarding the underlying issues and the real desires of the other party positions itself to maximize its gains. A competitor thus seeks to gain as much information as possible while disclosing as little as possible. One way to do this, often disguised as simple politeness, is to convince the other party to make the first offer. Whatever information is received allows the negotiator to set her own first offer advantageously by adjusting the offer for maximum, ultimate gain.

First offer — large demand. For a first offer, which was ideally made only after the other party made its offer, the competitive negotiator states an extreme demand, which is beyond or at the far margin of the range of credible or reasonable offers. This has the effect of setting the perceived or apparent bargaining range. When combined with the tactic of splitting the difference, it allows the user to manipulate the other party for maximum gain.

A variation on the first offer-large demand tactic is the *extreme demand-small demand* ploy. The negotiator first makes an extreme demand which she knows the other party certainly will refuse. On refusal, the negotiator then makes a "smaller" demand. The smaller demand looks reasonable by contrast, and the other party, "indebted" from withdrawal of the extreme demand, may more readily accept the smaller demand.

If the other party's initial demand is extreme or high in this fashion, it is a good indicator it is hard-bargaining. In dealing with such an opening, you can either ignore it by tactfully stating that it is extreme, and you will not use it as a basis of bargaining; or counter with an equally extreme demand in the other direction. Both of these moves have the effect of nullifying the initial claim.

Anchoring. Anchoring is fixing or establishing the focus of discussion around a certain point, whether it be a figure, a range, an issue, and the like, simply by asserting it. As a technique, anchoring plays on human suggestibility, that is, on the human tendency to fix attention on, and be influenced by, what someone says.

Psychologists sometimes demonstrate the phenomenon of anchoring in the following way. A psychologist will divide a group into two smaller groups, say groups A and B. She will then ask the members of group B to close their eyes while she writes a number on a blackboard, for example, 4,000,000, on the blackboard [sic] so group A can see it. She then erases the figure and has the groups switch roles, group A members now closing their eyes and group B members watching. She writes another number on the board, for example, 30,000,000, and then erases it. After this, she tells the entire group that she will now ask them a question whose answer is unrelated to the number they saw on the board. She asks everyone to estimate the correct number for the population of Nepal. When the results are tallied, estimates from group A members are consistently lower than those from group B members. Evidently, the figure the psychologist wrote on the board influenced the subsequent estimates of those who saw it, notwithstanding its asserted irrelevance to the actual figure for the population of Nepal. In other words, the simple assertion of an item sets it as an anchor, holding the recipient's mind in its vicinity.

False demand, false concession. In using the false issue or false demand-false concession tactic, a negotiator attempts to convince the other party that an issue, which she actually cares little about, is very important. The negotiator makes it appear that she will concede the issue only if the other party makes either a great concession or a particular concession which, perhaps unknown to the other party, has great value to the negotiator. When the concession is finally made, the negotiator reluctantly gives up or concedes the false demand. In effect, the negotiator obtains an important concession with an *asserted*, but not *real*, exchange of value.

A variation on false concession is *reverse false concession*. In this ploy, the negotiator inflates the significance of an issue which she actually considers minor, but she knows is important to the other party. After intense bargaining, the negotiator then concedes the issue. Later, however, the negotiator demands a large concession on an issue she truly deems important in return for the earlier concession on the minor issue.

The false demand-false concession tactic is difficult to deal with because our ideas of what is important to the other party usually come from information the other party provides. This makes it difficult to discount the party's claims that some issue has great importance to it. Obtaining outside information, assessing probabilities, and probing questions aimed at establishing convincing justifications for the other party's claims are the major defenses.

Escalation. Escalation involves raising demands, in some way, either before or during a negotiation. Escalation before a negotiation can take the form of adding conditions to be met before the negotiation occurs. During a negotiation, escalating demands is another way of finding the limits of what the other party is willing to give to effect an agreement. It is particularly effective when used against conciliatory or naively cooperative negotiators.

A negotiator can also escalate demands as the first move in a negotiation. Suppose, for example, two parties are meeting to discuss a proposed contract for sale of real property for an offered price of $650,000. When the negotiation begins, the seller could state that he was sorry, but he must raise the asking price to $750,000 for a variety of reasons. The buyer, who was originally prepared to try and whittle down the $650,000 figure, now must struggle to even reach that figure. This tactic makes $650,000 look awfully good.

Escalation taking the form of precondition demands should be dealt with as such. First move escalations change the parameters of the negotiation you prepared to enter and provide a sufficient reason to call off the negotiation so that you can coolly consider whether you want to negotiate on the new terms. Such an escalation also invites the counter that you are not willing to negotiate on the basis of the change since all your preparation was based on other assumptions. This may induce the other party to return to the original proposal.

A party counters escalations during a negotiation by calling attention to them, by indicating that counter escalations are possible and by refusing to agree to any escalated terms.

Nibble or late hit. The nibble or late hit is a form of escalation which comes at the end of a negotiation after the parties have invested time and energy and the major matters have been resolved. The nibbler then raises a relatively small, but yet undiscussed, item and indicates that it "must have" the item or the negotiation may otherwise fail; in other words, it may be a "deal-breaker." Usually, the other party will concede because of the large psychological investment in the potential agreement and the apparent risk of loss. Importantly, this type of escalation can also involve significant matters.

The nibble is really a test of firmness or resolve that plays on possible impatience and frustration, on "sunk costs" and on deal momentum concerns. In dealing with a nibble, it helps to recognize that both parties can play the game of threatening a final agreement. Expressing a willingness to accept the fact that the deal may fail and refusing to succumb to these demands may cause the nibbler to retreat from these demands.

Low-balling. A difficult point in many transactions and negotiations is getting a party to make a decision. Once a party makes a decision and has committed to it in some way, however, he is unlikely to back out of it. Low-balling plays on this psychological phenomenon. In low-balling, one party induces another to make a decision or to commit to a particular choice. The inducer then confirms that commitment and then changes the original terms which induced it. Automobile salesmen, for example, often use low-balling. They offer an automobile on very favorable terms and induce the buyer to purchase on that basis. They have the buyer sign papers and perhaps even permit the buyer to use the car prior to any money changing hands. They then claim that some mistake has been made or that the manager will not approve the original deal and ask for more money. Since the buyer has committed to buying the car, he is likely to accept the new demands and pay the additional money, assuming he is unaware of the ploy. Generalizing, it is easy to see that low-balling is a method of baiting a party and it is a different form of "nibble." The way to deal with low-balling is to protest the changed terms and express a willingness to walk away from the deal proposed on terms other than the original terms.

Linkage. Negotiators sometimes attempt to expand the scope of a negotiation by bringing in issues which, while not clearly related, a party can make a plausible case for. Successful linkage may change bargaining power and leverage, the focus and character of the dispute, or the set of gains and opportunities the parties are attempting to divide.

* * *

Salami. Eventually, as one slices thin rounds from a salami, it disappears. The salami tactic involves making a series of small demands, which, if all are conceded, add up to something considerable. Psychologically and practically speaking, small demands may be easier to tolerate and concede than large demands. Salami plays on this tolerance in order to make significant gains from small, consecutive, and perhaps seemingly inconsequential requests. Note, too, that a negotiator could use salami as a concession tactic as well as a demand tactic. Using it as a concession tactic might result in the negotiator giving up less overall.

Boulewarism. Boulewarism is, in effect, a single offer approach to reaching an agreement. It is the antithesis of genuine bargaining aimed at resolving issues. It is named after Lemuel Bouleware, a General Electric Vice-President and negotiator, who used this technique. It involves making a single, firm offer, usually based on a unilateral idea of what is fair or right under the circumstances, and, in effect, tells the other party to "take it or leave it." The offeror may act quite sincerely and believe that he is making the most reasonable offer possible. There is a certain arrogance in this as the posture does not permit the other party's input and, therefore, does not treat the other party as a bargaining equal. Aside from any question of the substantive position taken, this tactic will likely create resistance and anger.

If genuine, the Boulewarism posture tells the other party that there is nothing to bargain. This posture is a way to assert an upper hand or make clear where a party firmly stands. Of course, this approach could be used as a tactic to mislead the other party into thinking there is no give when in fact there can be. While Boulewarism may be inimical to developing good relationships, it wears a cloak of righteousness and could be effective with weak or dependent parties. In this sense, it is a kind of authoritarian paternalism as much concerned with maintaining authority and future freedom of action for the offeror as it is with maintaining the substantive merits of a proposal.

Split the difference. Splitting the difference is a common phenomenon in negotiations. The parties reach a point where they are close to an agreement but remain some distance apart. Each party lacks compelling reasons to convince the other party to accept its position, and each is unwilling to give up its position. In these circumstances, the parties often agree to settle by splitting the difference. This approach seems fair, appears to involve equal concessions, and saves face for the parties. Aware that parties close to agreement are likely to split the difference, a party who may already have everything it wants in a negotiation can consciously use it as a tactic to exact a further gain. The tactic is often effectively used in conjunction with the first offer-large demand tactic.

Splitting the difference is not a bad method to employ, unless, of course, the other party has so manipulated the game that it gets an unwarranted gain when the difference is split. It is important to remember, however, that although splitting the difference seems fair, it is not necessarily so. Fairness depends on where the parties start. Splitting the difference is not the only "fair" formula to use to close the gap when the parties are some distance apart. You should seek other formulas which might divide the difference more advantageously.

Other offer. To test the other party's willingness to reach an agreement or to extract concessions, a negotiator can state he has another offer or possibility and either specify what it is or deliberately leave it vague. If true, the other offer gives a baseline to judge the superiority of any pending agreement. If untrue, this is simply a tactic used to gain information or secure an advantage from the other party. Direct lies in negotiations carry considerable risks, however, particularly when the parties will have future dealings. When there is this kind of risk, those using this tactic may merely hint or imply they have another offer. This vagueness allows them to claim a misunderstanding if the other party discovers that another offer did not exist. Therefore, never accept vague assertions of the existence of other offers. You can deal most effectively with claims of other offers by demanding detailed information about them. This allows you to assess the reality and firmness of the "other offers" and compare their terms concretely with your own offer.

False scarcity. Psychologically, people generally tend to respond to the scarcity of some item or commodity by valuing it higher. In addition, psychological reactance theory holds that when opportunities which were once open are now limited, e.g., items become scarcer or some authority imposes restrictions on conduct, people react by wanting the opportunity *more* than when it was more openly available. Negotiators sometimes use this psychology. They try to induce the other party into agreeing to certain positions or terms by suggesting that the opportunities to get those terms are somehow quite limited.

Induced competitiveness. Induced competitiveness is a distinctive form of *false scarcity* which combines aspects of the *other offer* ploy. It involves converting what would ordinarily be a two party negotiation into a multi-party negotiation where all the parties interested in a particular good are forced to compete with each other for it. The competition makes the item more desirable, therefore driving up its price. For example, suppose that someone wishes to sell some item, and instead of dealing with prospective buyers one at a time, he invites them all to meet with him simultaneously. The appearance of a number of persons apparently interested in the item will likely make it appear more desirable and incline some party to want it more. (A particularly duplicitous form of this ploy involves using confederates or "shills" to act as competitors.) An alternative way of inducing a similar effect is to create an auction for the item. In one reported case, when a Hollywood movie was auctioned to broadcasting companies rather than sold through ordinary two party bargaining, the movie went for more than $1 million higher than the highest price ever previously paid for a similar broadcast showing.

Final offer. "Final offer" is just a statement that the negotiator has reached her final position and will concede no further. This could be true or false. If the statement is false, then the final offer is just a tactic used to mislead the other party into thinking the stated position is firm. In some ways, this is a risky tactic to use because a party must be prepared to terminate negotiations if the other party rejects the final offer. To claim "final offer" and then concede when the offer is rejected discloses that the offer was not actually final and creates a "cry wolf" reaction to subsequent final offer claims. A party could evade this consequence by linking a retreat from the asserted final offer to the receipt of some significant concession. If consciously used this way, the final offer tactic is similar to a false demand.

Misleading concession pattern. In win-lose or distributive negotiations, each side uses all available information and attempts to figure out the other party's bottom line in order to extract all possible gains. Reading the concession pattern is one way to do that. In theory at least, a party will make smaller and smaller concessions as the bargaining converges on his bottom line or reservation point. Knowing that this is a common view, a negotiator can mislead the other party by planning a concession pattern which converges at a point above or below his actual bottom line. While "reading" the concession pattern, the other party may then extrapolate it to that point and mistakenly conclude the conceder has reached his bottom line.

Red herring. A red herring is essentially a false, yet highly distracting, issue which a party can use to bring pressure to bear on the other party in a negotiation. Red herring is often used in politics, where politicians play off easily manipulated public fears to attack opponents regarding their stands, or lack of them, on red herring issues. The American communist or "red scare" in the late 1950s and the early 1960s is a good example. While red herrings may be most useful in negotiations where the parties represent outside constituencies which can be manipulated to bring pressure to bear on a recalcitrant party, negotiators sometimes use them tactically in ordinary negotiations. The *false issue-false demand* tactic, for example, is one version of red herring brought into ordinary negotiations.

Threats, anger, and aggression. The use of threats, angry displays, and aggressive tactics in a negotiation may evidence personality, frustration, or calculation. If the threat is real and the party making it can carry it out, the threat is an exercise of power and poses to the recipient the adverse consequences of a wrong choice. Negotiators, however, sometimes deliberately use such tactics simply to intimidate, disturb, and confuse the other party. As the psychological assault can unnerve and incline the victim to seek to mollify or conciliate the tantrum-thrower, negotiators using such tactics are attempting to create and to play on vulnerability in order to induce appeasement and exact concessions.

Blaming or fault-finding. Perhaps most common in negotiations involving interpersonal issues, blaming, or assigning of fault is an aggressive tactic possibly having several aims. This tactic may invoke conciliatory behavior as a result of induced guilt feelings or a sensed need to mollify. It may distract by focusing the negotiation on a substantively irrelevant, but psychologically volatile or conflictual relationship issue. "Winning" the relationship issue may result in concessions on the substantive issue. Note, however, that a person can use the tactic even in arms-length transactions where the parties do not have a psychologically invested relationship. For example, the department store claims-adjuster could parry a customer claim by asking, "Do you have a receipt?" If a receipt is not actually necessary, the question implies that a receipt is necessary. Thus, the customer is *at fault* for failing to have one, and the store cannot process the claim *for that reason*.

Sudden change of mood. Sometimes, either during a single negotiation session or over the course of several sessions, a negotiator will shift radically from a reasonable, friendly tone to an angry, abusive, hostile tone, or vice-versa. Such a shift may reflect the conscious use of psychological tactics designed to confuse the other party, place it off-balance, and create vulnerability. One who is the target of another's anger often assumes, many times mistakenly, that he has somehow caused it. A natural human reaction then occurs to attempt to placate the angry person in order to smooth the situation and save the relationship. Response in kind or *tit-for-tat* is an effective way of dealing with such tactics.

Intransigence and entrenchment. Negotiators sometimes just dig in their heels and refuse to budge from a position. They may offer all sorts of reasons for not moving and skillfully counter arguments offered to persuade them to move. The refusal to move can be a ploy aimed at testing the other party's firmness and discovering just how much concession room exists.

Sowing doubts; dismissals out-of-hand; or put-downs. Sowing doubts about proposals; curt dismissals of offers, positions, and concessions; and various other kinds of put-downs and denigrations are ways of shaping the other party's perceptions of its own bargaining position and its expectations of what it can get out of the negotiation. Unless the other party enters the negotiation reasonably well-informed, prepared, and fairly hard-skinned, this kind of devaluation can undermine its confidence and cause it to make faulty judgments about the relative merits of its bargaining position.

Playing to fears or assumptions. Sometimes negotiators can advantageously manipulate the other party's fears or assumptions. Suppose, for example, a buyer who wants an item badly and fears others may be interested volunteers to the seller, "I suppose there are a lot of people interested in that." This reveals a concern for competition. The seller might respond truthfully by stating, "Well, you might say that." This suggests, without affirming, that the buyer's statement is true. The buyer might take the remark as confirming that others were interested in buying the same item, and the buyer may decide to buy the item while the opportunity still exists.

In general, whenever a party discloses in some way that it has made an assumption favorable to the other party's bargaining position, the other party can use that knowledge to its advantage. It can take advantage, even where the assumption is not true, simply by not disconfirming the assumption or disabusing the party of its mistake. In order to do this, however, a negotiator has to draw the other party out, getting a sense of its thought processes as it approaches the negotiation.

Deadlock and walkout. A deadlock occurs when the parties assert they are, or seem to be, hopelessly unable to agree. A walkout is a unilateral termination of negotiation, usually expressed by actually walking out of the negotiating room, often in a righteous huff. Negotiations sometimes become stymied, and the proceedings and lack of progress upset the parties so much that they feel they must leave the negotiations.

Deadlocking is risky behavior because it may mean there will be no negotiated settlement. Deadlocking likely results when a party is concerned with what it may lose through a negotiation. Psychological "prospect" theory is helpful in understanding this concern. This theory holds that persons will act to conserve current wealth, and that they have a risk-averse orientation toward seeking gains and a risk-accepting orientation toward preventing losses. In other words, persons will take risks rather than face a loss but will not take equal risks in order to secure gains. Consequently, parties who enter negotiations concerned with what they may lose are likely to engage in behaviors which risk deadlock, such as escalation tactics.

Whether or not people can articulate the prospect theory, they instinctively understand it. They interpret a party declaring a deadlock to mean that the negotiation proposals under discussion, if accepted, will impose an unbearable loss on it. Knowing that this is the likely conclusion to be drawn, negotiators sometimes consciously use deadlock and walkout as tactics. When used as tactics, they are simply threatening pretenses designed to mislead the other party into thinking the deadlocking party's bottom line has been reached, to test the other party's resolve, and to impel the other party to make major concessions. Such risky and high stakes tactics, however, make credible retreat difficult unless the other side does make a large concession. Consequently, to permit a return to the table without concession and to save face, negotiators often hedge deadlock and walkout threats with language providing an escape if they need it.

Deadlock and concede. In deadlock and concede, the negotiator sets the agenda and organizes her issues so that she raises her least important issue first and her most important issue second. The remaining issues are handled similarly, alternating less important with more important issues. As the negotiator bargains, she deadlocks on the first issue but then concedes. Continuing to bargain, she also deadlocks on the most important issue, but then demands that the other party concede the issue because she conceded on the first issue and there has not yet been a reciprocal concession, and so on.

Friendliness. People are generally well-disposed to those who are friendly and more easily persuaded to give or concede them at least some of what they desire. Friendliness can be genuine, reflect good-will, or be a tactic used to mask an underlying aim to gain advantage. Friendliness elicits friendliness; but, unless a negotiator's aim is to build a relationship, he should not concede simply out of friendliness. This is not to suggest that one should be hostile, but rather, to note that it is important to distinguish between a friendly demeanor and what is a good deal. In hard-bargaining, a negotiator should make concessions only for return concessions of equivalent value.

Mutt and Jeff, good guy-bad guy, black hat-white hat. Mutt and Jeff, also called good guy-bad guy or black hat-white hat, is a well-known negotiation tactic combining anger, threats, hostility, and friendliness. In this tactic, two negotiators work together to off-balance the other party psychologically. One negotiator is hard, aggressive, angry, while the other negotiator is soft, friendly, well-disposed, and reasonable. Disconcerted and perhaps threatened by the attacking Mutt, the party being worked on turns to the friendly and reasonable Jeff, whom he or she feels may be an ally of a kind. Softened in this way, the target is more likely to make important information or position concessions to the friendly negotiator.

Negotiator without authority. Persons negotiating for others may or may not have authority to agree to the resolution of any or all issues concerned in the negotiation. A negotiator who does not have authority will have to clear proposed settlements with his or her principal. The negotiator-without-authority device, however, can also be used for tactical advantage in a negotiation, particularly where the other side is misled into thinking there is apparent authority to settle or is unaware authority is lacking. The negotiator who lacks authority or who pretends he lacks authority can explore the other party's positions and even gain concessions without making any real commitments or corresponding concessions of his own. Essentially, it is a way to obtain full information while reserving time to make careful, calculated decisions.

* * *

Representative cloak or phantom player. Sometimes negotiators will assert that they are acting in a representative capacity and must take the stance of their principal despite being personally sympathetic to the other party's position. Such statements can be genuine or ploys. As a ploy, the assertion of representative status is a subtle combination of negotiator without authority and the Mutt and Jeff approach and effectively allows a negotiator using it to adopt two postures at the same time, one of sympathy and friendliness, the other of toughness and arms-length dealing, and to play on both. We can also think of this as a phantom player phenomenon. Depending on how the competitor plays it, he may proceed as though there was a third party at the table; a party who can make demands but cannot be questioned.

Status, authority, association and credentialing. Although not commonly acknowledged, there are significant wealth, class, and status differences and distinctions in the United States. Most people are aware of them on at least an unconscious level. Wealth, class, and status distinctions and their trappings can sometimes influence negotiations. This occurs when one party is consciously or unconsciously impressed by the status, stature, or authority of the other side and either defers for that reason or makes unwarranted assumptions about the other side's power, strength, or resolve. One inoculates oneself from such influence by being aware of the phenomenon. If bitten, there are the antidotes of carefully considering the relevance of the displayed array, adopting a "show me" attitude and resisting persuasions based on a relative social position alone.

* * *

Principle. Appeals to principle are often highly persuasive. On the other hand, negotiators and others, including politicians, sometimes use principles in unprincipled ways as tools to manipulate. Unless simply horse-trading or haggling, most bargainers invoke principles as a justification for positions they take. Indeed, one good way to prepare for negotiations is to develop arguments of principle for the positions one takes. There is a difference, however, between deriving positions from principles and finding principled arguments to support a position taken for other reasons. The latter may be simply rationalizing or seeking to find a high moral gloss for what is actually a calculation for private advantage. One should not be easily taken in by arguments of principle but should seek close, reasoned justifications supported by evidence.

Time, timing and end-game. Time is important in negotiations and can be used in many ways. Usually, the party that is more patient or less pressed for time has an advantage. The need to come to agreement within a specified time may force one to make concessions one would not otherwise make.

A negotiator can also pretend that time is important when it is not, forcing the other party to a speedy agreement or to hasty concessions.

Cunning negotiators who know that the other party is under some time deadline or pressure to conclude negotiations can use time to their advantage. As the time deadline approaches, they may begin to stall, to raise new issues or resurrect old ones, to inject new complications, to produce documents containing already rejected agreement language, or generally to appear to unravel what once appeared already settled. The hope is that the need to reach an agreement by a certain time will force the needy party to make significant concessions. It may even force the needy party to concede points already won. Not having a deadline, not announcing a deadline, patience, and a willingness to walk away are ways to deal with such tactics.

Deadline. When both sides bargain competitively but also want a deal, most concessions will likely occur toward the end of the negotiation when the deadline approaches. In the initial stages of a competitive negotiation, the parties mutually explore each other's position and test each other's firmness and resolve. If both parties are competitive, they will both follow the firmness strategy. When they do, the negotiation becomes a contest of respective resolve. As a result, neither party is likely to move much until it appears absolutely necessary. Deadlines under urgency, especially externally imposed deadlines that preclude or seriously inhibit further negotiations bring the parties to the very brink of the consequences of non-agreement. Examples of such deadlines include the beginning of a trial, a company's need for a certain product to meet its own manufacturing deadline or other contractual obligation. Indeed, it is as the deadline approaches that competitors are most likely to attempt to outwait the other party so that the need to settle and related time pressures cause them to concede.

Setting a deadline to accept or refuse an offer or position can also be a tactic, although it may be dangerous and risky. A deadline may succeed where the side imposing the deadline is committed to accepting the consequences of no agreement and the other side has less resolve. Where the consequences of no agreement are severe for the side refusing to agree, the approach of the deadline enhances psychological pressure and concentrates the mind on the downsides of refusing to agree. Certainly, if the side refusing to agree is simply bluffing, then the deadline calls the bluff and changes the contest to a test of resolve.

Draftsman or single negotiating text. Sometimes a party to a negotiation will bring to the table a document it has already drafted and offer it as a basic text to set the agenda or to work from in moving toward a final agreement. While this is often a useful technique to advance negotiations, it is also a powerful tactic because a document tends almost irresistibly to set the agenda and focus the parties, not only on particular issues, but also on a prescribed resolution of those issues. It is really a way to take the initiative in negotiations. The other party's choices include either working with the document, ignoring it, offering a counter-document, or using enormous self-discipline in dealing with the document for selective advantage.

Backtracking or unraveling. Backtracking or unraveling can occur when the parties negotiate a number of issues separately and sequentially during a single negotiation. After a few issues appear to have been settled, a negotiator may threaten to undo the earlier agreements in order to succeed on a new issue under discussion. Note that a negotiator can use this ploy as a means to gain leverage over the issue currently under discussion or use intransigence over the current issue to force reopening apparently settled issues in order to obtain more gain on them.

Irrevocable commitment. One problem a negotiator may have is persuading the other party that the negotiator has reached his bottom line, particularly when he has not. One way to accomplish this is to apparently commit oneself to a course of action which shows the other party that the negotiator cannot budge. For example, union negotiators could propose a negotiating position to the union and ask the union to vote on it. If the membership adopts it, then the negotiators can claim to management that they cannot agree to a less advantageous settlement position because the union would dismiss the negotiators and strike.

Reinforcement and reward. In reinforcement and reward, the negotiator, in effect, applies principles of operant conditioning theory and treats concessions as rewards for desired concession behavior of the other party. The concession follows the other party's concession and is a greater than equivalent concession with the excess or "unearned" portion of the reciprocal concession being the reward. This tactic apparently produces more concessions and even stimulates concessions to continue even when the negotiator stops making reciprocal concessions.

* * *

C. Competitive Communication Tactics for Managing Information and Party Perceptions

Masking intentions. A negotiator may conceal his actual goals in a negotiation and minimize the giving of any clues regarding his real intentions. The aim is either to manipulate the other party or to protect the negotiator from the risk of disclosing information the other party will use to his disadvantage. For example, a negotiator may not disclose that he has no other alternatives to getting what he wants other than dealing with the other party. He may pretend he has other alternatives in order to persuade the other party that he has bargaining power or to prevent the other party from taking advantage of him because he has nowhere else to turn.

Bluffing. Bluffing is a form of pretense in which the bluffer either shows strength to mask weakness and to convince the other party that there is no weakness, or he shows and simulates weakness in order to hide strength and tempt the other party to make some move that the bluffer knows he can beat. In a negotiation, for example, the bluffing negotiator may attempt to show strength by confident assertions of claims or by using false threats and promises. Similarly, to avoid giving information and to entice the other party to make some disclosing move, the negotiator may feign ignorance or engage in "calculated incompetence."

Predictions. Negotiators sometimes make claims which in the quick and often animated exchanges of a negotiation seem to be factual assertions but are actually only predictions. Predictions are not true or false, but rather, they are claims about the future. A prediction about one's own behavior is really only a promise or a threat.

Repeated claims or assertions of "fact." Parties to short negotiations or to negotiations with an impending deadline rarely recess to investigate claims or assertions of fact. In these situations, negotiators, particularly inexperienced negotiators, oftentimes fail to challenge factual claims by asking for proof or support. When a negotiator repeatedly asserts something as a "fact," the negotiation dynamic tends to induce the other parties to treat it as fact and, thus, fail to explore the claim more deeply. For example, a negotiator representing a company in a negotiation says to the other side, "We can't do X," and repeats this position several times as the negotiation progresses. Unless alert and aware of the repetition phenomenon, the other party will likely accept the statement as fact, even though it may be no more than a refusal to concede. This is just another form of anchoring.

Opinions of value or worth. Persons negotiating often make exaggerated claims of value or worth. Of course, opinions can be informed or uninformed and can be correct or incorrect. When one makes a claim of value, however, there is generally some referent or standard of value implicit in the claim which supports it. For example, when the diamond dealer says, "This diamond is worth $5,000," the prospective purchaser tends to assume that the dealer means the diamond would bring $5,000 if offered on the open retail diamond market. But the dealer could really be saying that *he* places a $5,000 value on the diamond or that he thinks that he might induce someone to buy it for $5,000. Consequently, in making claims of value or worth, negotiators sometimes play off the assumptions the hearer makes about the objectivity of the claim. Note also that the repeated assertion of the unchallenged value claim tends to make it an operative negotiating fact.

Disinformation. Disinformation consists of either untrue statements made to deceive or mislead or of technically true statements which raise false impressions. In the latter case, the statements are not actually false respecting any material facts, but they are misleading because of a faulty assumption the hearer makes. Some of the tactics and claims described previously have this character. Suppose a negotiator says, "In the past, I've made it a practice never to come back to the negotiating table after I've made a final offer and it was refused." The implication is that the speaker will continue this practice during this negotiation even though, in fact, he may not. The hearer concludes that the negotiator will behave in the future as he said he has behaved in the past. The speaker, however, does not actually say that he will behave in the same manner and he could later credibly claim that he did not say he would. The other party might still feel misled but, nonetheless, be uncertain whether a lack of shrewdness or attention to detail resulted in the misunderstanding.

Misrepresentations of position. There is no law of negotiation which requires bargainers to state their actual position on issues. Indeed, during the negotiation, negotiating parties tend to assume that each party will move away from its initial, and possibly subsequent, positions. Consequently, for the most part, statements of position are simply bargaining points. Although not truthful in accurately reporting the party's reservation point or bottom line, negotiators view positions taken as moves and not as factual statements within the context of the negotiating game.

Withholding information — general failures to disclose. Even given the general norm that one should not lie, there is an important difference between lying and failing to provide information. Rather than lie or provide false information, negotiators often fail to provide requested information or they provide only partial information which results in a misleading effect. Although debatable, there appears to be a customary norm that unless the negotiating parties have some sort of trust or fiduciary relationship, negotiators may treat negotiations as arms-length transactions in which each party must take care of itself. Generally, this means that negotiators need not disclose information useful to the other party in the negotiation.

Withholding information provides advantages when the other party acts on factual assumptions favorable to the withholding party. Suppose, for example, that a manufacturer who is under a contract to produce a certain product by a certain date has had an equipment failure but has found a supplier of the same product. Unknown to the manufacturer, the supplier has an oversupply of the product and eagerly wants to dispose of its supply. The supplier could withhold information of its overstock and possibly even claim that to meet the manufacturer's order on short notice, the manufacturer would have to pay a premium or rush-order price. Here, the supplier has no obligation to disclose its actual position. Unless a good business reason, such as the development of a good, longer-term relationship suggests otherwise, the supplier could exact a greater gain by simply failing to disclose.

Failures to disclose specific requested information. Sometimes negotiators deliberately refuse to provide known information which the other party specifically requests. There is a difference between a refusal to disclose information on one's own initiative and a refusal to disclose information following a specific request for information. One may properly ignore general requests for information because they are open-ended requests to reveal one's hand. Practically, however, it is more difficult to avoid requests for specific information because there are few ways, short of lying, to avoid answering. Sometimes a refusal to respond will provide the very information the negotiator seeks to withhold. Unless very artfully stated, falsely denying that one has knowledge is a lie. If the other party relies to its detriment on the misrepresentation of no-knowledge, the negotiator has, in effect, provided materially false information. To avoid this, negotiators often prefer to evade the question or to provide some plausible excuse for a refusal to provide the requested information.

Providing false factual information. Providing materially false factual information is simply lying. It is more than a sharp practice and can amount to fraud. People do lie in negotiations, but no one would assert that it is a proper tactic.

D. Avoidance Tactics

Negotiators avoid lying and answering information-seeking questions in a number of ways. They sometimes combine them to divert the other party and to take the initiative in maneuvering the discussion.

Shifting or diverting attention. Rather than answer a direct question, the negotiator ignores it and shifts the subject. One common way to do this is to "answer" the question with a question. Since many people react unconsciously by feeling a need to answer questions, this shift returns the initiative to the second questioner.

Answering unresponsively. Answering unresponsively occurs when the negotiator answers vaguely or answers a different question. He can answer a different question by simply being unresponsive or by restating the question as a different question and then answering the restated question. The psychology involved in this move is interesting. The response may simply dupe the questioner into not noticing that his original question went unanswered by distracting him with the reply. On the other hand, the questioner may notice but think the other party misunderstood. Out of politeness, the questioner may choose not to pursue the matter.

Answering partially. The negotiator answers incompletely, usually at some length, so that the questioner fails to notice that the question was not answered.

Promising. The negotiator promises to answer at a proper time but never does so. Instead, the negotiator takes the initiative and begins talking on a point he wants to make. This often results in diverting the questioner's attention to the matter the negotiator is pressing.

Tactfully refusing. The negotiator refuses to answer and gives some explanation such as, "I'm not at liberty to tell you that" or "I'm not prepared to answer at this time." Such statements are disingenuous and "artful." Note that the lack of freedom to respond or lack of preparation may be matters completely within the speaker's control. If so, the speaker is really saying that she does not give herself permission to answer now or that she is not ready to answer; however, the other party may conclude differently.

Subtle or ambiguous qualifying. In order to avoid giving the requested information, the negotiator may add a qualification to his statement. The qualification, usually unnoticed unless the other party listens carefully and is attuned to subtlety and nuance, makes the statement technically true. For example, if a negotiator says, "I can't offer you more at this time," the phrase "at this time" qualifies the statement. The statement could mean that the negotiator truly cannot raise the offer; or it could mean that the negotiator has decided that he would be better off in the negotiation if he did not immediately offer more. The statement is true either way. Indeed, the negotiator in this example may mean the latter, but hope that the other party interprets the statement as the former.

Bargaining. The negotiator treats giving an answer as a concession and requires reciprocal equivalent disclosure. For example, "I will answer your question if you will tell me. . . . "

Listening. The negotiator generally avoids the information disclosure dilemma by asking open-ended questions and adopting the tactic of listening much and saying little.

* * *

Gary T. Lowenthal,* *A General Theory of Negotiation Process, Strategy, and Behavior*
31 U. KAN L. REV. 69, 83-88 (1982) **

* * *

C. Modes of Communication

A principal objective of the competitive negotiator in communicating with an opponent is to persuade the opponent that three propositions are true: (1) The competitor will not make concessions (or substantial concessions) from the position of commitment that she has taken; (2) The benefits of settlement on the competitor's terms are greater for the opponent than the opponent previously has been willing to acknowledge; and (3) The costs to the opponent of nonsettlement are greater than the opponent previously has realized. In other words, the competitive negotiator's objective is to convince the opposition that settlement must be according to the competitor's terms and that this settlement is in the opponent's best interest. Effective persuasion on these issues is essential to avoid either deadlock or one's own capitulation.

The competitor has several modes of communication to implement a persuasion strategy. For instance, the competitor may make *promises* that bind the competitor herself, in return for reciprocal concessions from the adversary. An enforceable promise is similar to a commitment that limits

---

* Gary T. Lowenthal is Professor at Arizona State University Sandra Day O'Connor College of Law. This excerpt focuses on the use of arguments and threats in distributive bargaining.

flexibility because it obligates the person making it to follow a prescribed course of action. Unlike a commitment, however, a promise in negotiation is made to the other party, and the other party has the power to release the promisor from her obligation. Therefore, a negotiator's promise does not have the competitive effect of limiting her flexibility, and, as a result, promises are appropriate modes of communication in collaborative negotiation as well as competitive bargaining. On the other hand, two modes of persuasive communication that distinguish competitive negotiation from problem solving are the "argument" and the "threat."

The word "argument" may be defined as a communication designed to persuade an audience by drawing logical inferences from known data, just as a lawyer would attempt to persuade a trier of fact at the conclusion of a trial or hearing. In negotiation, argument is focused on such matters as the likelihood of a defendant being found liable by a prospective trier of fact, the ability of a union to survive a lengthy strike, or the difficulty a buyer might experience in locating a product of comparable quality from another source. Such arguments may be useful in problem solving negotiation as well as in competitive bargaining, but the competitive negotiator uses argument for purposes other than persuasion.

When two competitive negotiators engage in argument, their words often seem to have little effect on one another. This may occur because an important objective of a competitor is the creation of the *appearance* that the opponent's arguments are not having a persuasive effect. A competitor who reveals to an opponent that the opponent's communications have convinced her to consider seriously the opponent's settlement terms weakens, if not destroys, the competitor's own committed position. For this reason, competitive negotiators often seem irrational in rejecting out of hand the persuasive arguments of their adversaries. By seeming irrational, the competitor gains a major tactical advantage over an objective opponent, so long as the competitive negotiator's settlement terms are less undesirable to the opponent than are the costs of deadlock.

Arguments directed at a competitive negotiator may still serve an essential purpose. When one competitor negotiates against another, the respective opponents' arguments are of critical importance in justifying concessions. . . . As trial approaches, exchanges of threats and arguments seemingly have had no effect on the two negotiators. Each negotiator wants a settlement, however, if she can "get out of" a rigidly committed position without losing hard earned credibility. An exchange of well timed arguments at this point in the negotiation permits a corresponding exchange of concessions and breaks the impasse. For this reason, truly skilled negotiators know the strategic importance of "saving" a strong argument; the argument is presented not to "convince" an opponent, but instead to allow a competitive adversary to save face.

The second predominant mode of persuasive communication in competitive bargaining is the "threat." A threat is a communication from one party to a second indicating that, if the second party does not settle according to terms acceptable to the first party, the first party will take action unpleasant or detrimental to the second party. A union's strike vote on the eve of contract negotiations and a prosecutor's statement to defense counsel that if the defendant does not plead guilty the prosecutor will seek a lengthy prison sentence are classic examples of bargaining threats. Similarly, when a party in a civil action submits a long list of prospective witnesses to testify at trial, even though the amount in controversy is relatively small, the list may serve more as a threat of the consequences of nonsettlement than as a reflection of the intricacies of proof in the case.

A threat is an effective negotiation tactic only if the threatened consequence of nonsettlement appears credible to the other party, since the second party's "tendency to comply with or defy the threatener, other things being equal, depends on his estimates of the probability of being punished for noncompliance." In other words, the prosecutor's threat of a lengthy prison sentence is not persuasive if the defendant is a first time offender, the offense is not serious, and the judge is a firm believer in probation. Several factors influence the credibility of threats, including the proportionality of a threatened consequence, the events on which the threat is contingent, and the threatener's previous behavior in carrying out similar threats.

First, credible threats must be reasonably proportionate to the action they are deterring, since "small threats are ignored and large threats are not believed." A buyer's statement that she will take her business elsewhere unless the seller lowers her price is a small threat in a "seller's market," and therefore is not likely to be an effective tactic. Similarly, a threat of incarceration for overtime parking will not deter a potential parking violator if she considers the punishment too awful to be real. Particularly when the threatener herself will suffer along with the other party if the threat is carried out, the negative consequences cannot be disproportionately large and still retain credibility. For example, if defense counsel submits a list of twenty-five prospective trial witnesses in a small damage action to induce plaintiff's counsel to settle, the lawyer for the plaintiff may conclude that the trial will be just as time consuming and expensive for the defense as for the plaintiff, and that the list is probably a bluff. As a result, the threat does not have its intended persuasive effect.

A second factor influencing the credibility of threats is the threatened party's perception of contingencies that must occur before the threatened action takes place. Assume that a labor union's negotiating team threatens a strike unless management agrees to a 12% across-the-board wage increase. If the union negotiators can state, "We have taken a vote of our membership and have a unanimous mandate to strike unless we get a 12% agreement by next Wednesday," the threat is unambiguous and not subject to any apparent major contingencies, other than management's failure to meet the demand within the specified time frame. On the other hand, if the union team states, "If you do not agree to a 12% increase by next Wednesday, we will take a vote of our membership for strike authorization," the threatened consequences are one step further removed by the membership vote, which may or may not provide the "unanimous mandate" of the first example. As a result, management may conclude fairly that the strike is not an *automatic* consequence of a failure to settle at 12%, and the threat loses some of its effectiveness.

The competitive negotiator's history of making and carrying out threats also influences the credibility of a particular threat. " lawyer with a reputation of never going to trial is unlikely to obtain an excellent settlement for a client in an action with triable issues, since the trial threat is not credible to counsel for the other party. On the other hand, carrying out a threat in one case may be an effective means of making other threats credible in future cases. In *Bordenkircher v. Hayes*, for example, a criminal defendant with two prior felony convictions was charged with presenting a forged instrument in the amount of $88.30, an offense punishable by a term of two to ten years in prison. During plea negotiation the prosecutor offered to recommend a sentence of five years in prison if the defendant pleaded guilty to the forgery charge. The prosecutor also indicated that if the accused did not plead guilty, the prosecutor would return to the grand jury and seek an indictment charging the defendant as a habitual offender, a charge which, if it resulted in conviction, would subject him to a mandatory sentence of life imprisonment because of his two prior felony convictions. The defendant refused to plead guilty, the prosecutor followed through on the threat, and the defendant received a sentence of life imprisonment. The United States Supreme Court affirmed the conviction and sentence over a claim of prosecutorial vindictiveness, thereby signaling to prosecutors that they may use such tactics to establish the credibility of their charging and trial threats in order to maintain firmness in future negotiations with other defense counsel.

* * *

Carrie Menkel-Meadow,[*] *Toward Another View of Legal Negotiations: The Structure of Problem Solving*
31 UCLA L. REV. 754, 780-83, 789-94 (1984)[**]

* * *

The one strategic exhortation that seems to dominate most descriptions of adversarial negotiation is the admonition that the negotiator should never reveal what is really desired. Thus, the process of exaggerated offers

[*] Carrie Menkel-Meadow is the A.B. Chettle, Jr. Professor of Law, Dispute Resolution, and Civil Procedure at Georgetown University Law Center. This excerpt deals with the central role of the lawyer in distributive negotiations and the influence of the adjudication alternative on the process of negotiation.

is designed to cloak real preferences so that one negotiator cannot obtain unfair advantage over another by knowing what the other really wants.

> In any negotiation, and particularly in lawsuit settlement negotiation, the opposing negotiators may have widely different views of the same case. . . . The logical corollary to the foregoing principle is that one should not reveal his own settling point. . . . Presumably in the optimal negotiation, one will determine his opponent's settling point without revealing his own.

The assumption here, of course, is that in every negotiation each side will attempt to thwart what the other really wants, and therefore the negotiator does well to refuse the adversary such leverage.

The principle that one should hide information about one's real preferences is based on unexplored assumptions of human behavior that negotiators are manipulative, competitive and adversarial. The danger of acting on such assumptions is that opportunities for better solutions may be lost . . . and that when one party behaves in this way, the other side may be more likely to reciprocate with competitive and manipulative conduct of its own. Like many of the other assumptions of the adversarial model, the notion that one should hide information is based on a conception of the court outcome. Trial lawyers may fear releasing information in pre-trial negotiations because of the presumed loss of advantage at trial. In this era of discovery, however, this fear may be misplaced. Although thoughtless revelation of "all the facts" may not lead to satisfactory solutions either, failure to disclose real preferences has been shown to foreclose some of the most efficient and mutually satisfactory solutions. Moreover, revealing preferences or needs is not the same thing as revealing "evidence."

Competitive descriptions of negotiations foster a perception of the negotiator as the principal actor in legal negotiations. Because legal negotiations are so stylized and are based on understanding of a special culture, the lawyer becomes the provider of what the court would order if the case went to trial, or what the law allows in transaction planning. The client, intimidated by these adversarial and specialized proceedings, depends on the lawyer to structure solutions that are "legal" rather than what the client might desire if the client had free rein to determine objectives. The client may also assume that the lawyer knows the only "right" way to accomplish the result and may therefore be hesitant to suggest other alternatives. Although clients generally engage lawyers to do what they cannot do themselves, they do not necessarily wish to relinquish all control over either the desired outcomes or the process by which they are achieved. This is especially true where the negotiation involves parties who will have to continue a relationship with one another, such as partnership or post-dissolution custody relationships. The client may also have an interest in how the negotiation is pursued because, if competitive processes are used, the client may have trouble enforcing the agreement or in continuing a relationship with the other party.

* * *

2. *Negotiating in the Shadow of the Court: Assumptions of Polarized Results and Limited Solutions*

The assumption that only limited items are available in dispute resolution occurs because negotiation takes place in the shadow of the courts. Negotiators too often conclude that they are limited to what would be available if the court entered a judgment. To the extent that court resolution of problems results in awards of money damages and injunctions, negotiators are likely to limit their crafting of solutions to those remedies. To the extent that a court would not allow a particular remedy such as barter, exchange, apology, or retributory action, negotiators may reject or not even conceive of these solutions.

Similarly, because courts often declare one party a winner and the other a loser, negotiators often conceive of themselves as winners and losers, and in court games, the result is usually "winner take all." Although some have argued that courts do or should compromise, the more common structure of court resolution of disputes, such as "plaintiff wins $25,000" or "defendant acquitted," tends to narrow the conceptions of negotiation solutions since all solutions are judged against what the court is likely to do. Negotiations, therefore, proceed as an earlier version of court resolution, without the judge.

A clear example of how this court model affects negotiation can be found in the literature which suggests that negotiators set "goals, minimum/maximum dispositions, target points, reservation points and aspiration levels" at levels which are based on assessments of what the court might do if the case goes to trial. This is especially true in the personal injury literature which suggests numerical formulas for setting goals at such values as "three times the specials" or "midway between the maximum recovery potential and minimum recovery expectation." Thus, even though the eventual solution may be one of compromise within the bargaining range, this settlement is based on the presumed limits set by the court. To the extent that courts do "compromise" through doctrines such as comparative negligence, even parties' "split the difference" solutions may be based, at least in part, on what the court would do.

One of the strengths of the legal system — definitive, precedential rulings to promote clarity, certainty, and order — may actually be dysfunctional for the creation of innovative and idiosyncratic solutions to problems that may never reach judicial resolution. To the extent that negotiations in the shadow of the court are limited by conceptions of what the court would do, negotiation may present no real, substantive alternative to trial. Lawyers may prefer this limited conception because it makes evaluation of possible outcomes clearer and easier, especially when discussing alternatives with clients. If this is so, then the large number of settlements can only be explained by the lower cost and relative speed of completion, rather than the superior substantive justice that is done. The limited remedial imagination of courts, when extended to negotiation, narrows not only what items might be distributed but also how those items might be apportioned.

The process described above is strongly influenced by a court conception of dispute resolution. Although there is no third party adjudicator present in most negotiations, the negotiators will frequently adopt adversarial postures, engaging in debate with the hope that they will persuade the other party that it will lose in court, and thus should concede now, without further ado or expense. While debate and some exaggeration may be tolerable in a trial with a third party to "mediate" the truth, such forms may be dysfunctional for achieving the best results in a situation where two parties negotiate voluntarily, without a third party to evaluate their relative claims. If adversarial processes limit one's ability to conceive of creative solutions then it may be unwise to have trial lawyers conduct pretrial negotiations. In effect, the ten percent of cases which are tried control the types of solutions which are achieved in the other ninety percent of cases.

Transactional negotiations may be similarly limited in the types of solutions considered plausible due to previous litigation about particular clauses, or because of "industry practices" or form provisions which are common in usage and seldom questioned by successive negotiators. Thus, although the use of form terms can be likened to precedent in the guidance and efficiency it offers the parties, it can also produce a limiting or "channeling" effect. The parties to a commercial lease, for example, may adopt the convention of a percentage of gross sales for rent, though they might both be better off with a more secure and stable fixed rent. "Although, as Eisenberg suggests, these form terms are most likely to be used in the subsidiary terms which are not crucial to the transaction, their use even in this capacity may limit the possible trade-offs of more creative solutions between and among subsidiary terms and "deal points." Thus, in the commercial lease example above, a subsidiary term allocating property maintenance costs could have some bearing on the possible rent terms. Finally, as the theme of this Article should make clear, differing needs or values of the parties may make one party's subsidiary term another party's crucial term. Thus, the choice of use of common terms may itself become an important aspect of the negotiation, requiring less limited conceptions of what might be possible.

C. Consequences of the Adversarial Assumptions: The Limits of Linearity

When negotiators adopt zero-sum conceptions of the problems or transactions they seek to resolve or plan, they unnecessarily limit themselves in a number of ways. First, by assuming single-issue negotiations in which parties value the single item equivalently, they may fail to consider whether the parties have other needs or issues that consequently may go unresolved. Second, by focusing on maximizing immediate, individual gain, negotiators may fail to appreciate long-term consequences of a particular solution. . . . Third, zero-sum, single-issue conceptions of negotiation problems often fail to consider transaction costs, both in terms of process costs to the client in the use of an adversarial approach and the costs of a less than optimal solution. The adversarial negotiation conception narrowly limits potential solutions by encouraging negotiators to develop mind-sets about possible solutions which include only court solutions or commonly used solutions that may not meet the parties' needs.

The adversarial model can lead to stalemate or no agreement by failing to exploit differences in values that could broaden the range of possible solutions or even increase the gain to one party without decreasing the gain to another. By focusing too exclusively on how only one side can gain, the parties may miss opportunities to expand what they must divide or to trade off unequally valued items.

Seeing negotiation as an arena with only one victor may result in withdrawal, submission, dependence, and, ultimately, resentment on the part of the party which perceives itself as the weaker. Enforcement of agreements made under such circumstances may be impaired by failure to comply, causing forced compliance costs or new negotiations about compliance.

Adversarial orientations lead to competitive strategies, and thus may produce inefficiencies by taking more time and costing more money. Escalation in negotiation strategies may not only intensify the conflicts in the situation by increasing rigidity of positions, but also may prevent the creation and realization of solutions which more closely meet the needs of the client.

* * *

Gary Goodpaster,[*] *Lawsuits as Negotiations*
8 NEGOT. J. 221, 229-34 (1992)[**]

* * *

Litigation as bargaining power equalizer. Litigation is combative, expensive, and, compared with some other ways of reaching agreements or decisions, highly inefficient, distracting, time and resource consumptive. Viewed simply as a form of competitive bargaining, those are some of its virtues. The power to litigate is the power to force the situation, the power to require another party to attend to one's claims seriously. It is also a way to impose costs — time, money, administrative, psychological, and reputational costs — on another. The ability to impose costs — through forcing a need for legal services, requiring responses to discovery requests, and appearances at hearings and depositions — changes the bargaining power relationships

---

[*] Gary Goodpaster is Professor Emeritus at University of California Davis School of Law. This article looks at the use of litigation in negotiation strategy and technique.

[**] Copyright © 1992 Negotiation Journal. Reprinted with permission of Blackwell Publishing, Inc. and the Program on Negotiation at Harvard Law School.

between the parties. Further, the litigation dynamic creates situations of perceived stalemate and deadlock, but under substantial threats of possible trial loss. Stalemated disputes often settle just prior to a deadline, and in a lawsuit, trial is the deadline. Litigation, therefore, is a way — a potent, albeit painful way — of initiating a process leading to a negotiated agreement.

Litigating parties bargain strategically not only in the unusual, unpredictable case, but in ordinary cases as well. Where the facts of a case appear to fail within some norm for similar cases, it is predictable. Predictability of outcome, however, only assures that a case will probably settle, not *where* it will settle. A predictable verdict does not entail a predictable damage award, which remains negotiable. Litigants often are likely to have strong disagreements over where to settle — different attorneys assessing the same case give widely discrepant estimates of its worth. When opposing parties are far apart on case value, they will likely use litigation tactics and the continued threat of trial as means to gain concessions.

Where a case is unusual and therefore unpredictable (or an attorney can make it appear to be so), it also poses the serious prospect that there will be a trial. Whether a case goes to trial because it is unusual or because the parties are far apart on damages, the litigants will likely have significant uncertainties about possible outcomes. The adjudication will turn on many variables that, try as they might, the parties cannot control. These variables include the respective skills of the parties' attorneys, the state of the provable evidence, the availability and credibility of witnesses, and the composition of the jury. In addition, such factors as the trial judge, the character of the complaint or causes of action and the state of the law, and who the parties are and how they present themselves can also affect the trial outcome. The resources the parties have to devote to discovery and trial preparation can also certainly affect the trial result. All these uncertainties serve, in some respects, to equalize the parties' bargaining power because neither can predict who is likely to prevail, thus placing a party's alternative to negotiation in doubt. In such cases, an attorney might gamble that the other side will make a substantial concession to avoid trial. In effect, the attorney believes the other side is more risk-averse than his own, and forces the issue.

Strategic Bargaining and Structural Bargaining Factors

A party using a negotiation strategy based on the other party's risk-aversion might reason as follows: I will take a calculated risk to minimize losses. If I go to trial, I risk a major loss. If my opponent, however, is risk-averse, perhaps I can impose increasing risk of loss on her. That will diminish her prospects of gain, and she will likely prefer settlement to trial. I will suffer the least loss from a negotiated settlement when I negotiate from a position of maximum power. My power is maximal when it convincingly appears I will elect my alternative to try the case rather than negotiate a settlement close to the eve of trial.

Litigators often do follow this combined strategy of doing everything possible to appear committed to trial while secretly preferring and looking for settlement. Attorneys do use litigation tactics and the threat of trial as hard-bargaining tools to extract concessions. Of course, it is exceptionally difficult for a litigator to *pretend* she is going to try a case, for she may *have* to try it. The litigator therefore has no real alternative than to prepare for trial. This conveys the right message to the other side, yet also may increase the risk of going to trial.

If both attorneys so reason, they put in play a game of chicken. In an attempt to gain maximum advantage for a possible settlement, each lawyer, while pretending to wish to go to trial, chooses to defer entering settlement negotiations until the last possible minute. In such showdowns, lawyers test the resolve of their opponents to litigate, hoping to pressure them into favorable settlements

"Sunk cost" psychology and nonrational processes of escalation also play a role in this phenomenon of negotiation standoff, commitment to trial, and trial eve settlement. Parties who have already invested significantly in a particular course of action are likely to invest more when faced with a choice of investing more or changing course. Similarly, when a party faces losses stemming from a lack of agreement, which is always the case in an ongoing lawsuit, it may be likely to *increase* rather than *decrease* its commitment to its position. Thus, the litigants may incline toward pursuing the lawsuit rather than seeking a negotiated settlement, at least until the threat of impending loss forces them to reconsider negotiation seriously.

Risk-aversion and lawsuit bargaining strategies. Persons act conservatively when faced with the prospect of significant loss or gain. They have a risk-averse orientation toward seeking gains and a loss-averse or risk-positive orientation in taking action to prevent losses. Or, put another way, persons will take a risk to prevent a loss but will not take equal risks to secure a gain. In the context of a lawsuit, this suggests that defendants will more likely engage in strategic or hard bargaining, than plaintiffs. For a defendant, a settlement is a loss, and she should be willing to take a risk to avoid it. All trials, where there is any uncertainty of outcome at all, carry a significant risk of loss. Plaintiffs, by definition parties seeking gains, often should be more risk-averse and more willing to settle. These generalizations are but rough guides, however. Other factors, such as the opposing parties' relative stakes in the litigation, whether a party faces similar litigation with others, and attorney-fee and lawsuit-financing arrangements deeply affect how risk-tolerant a party is.

Asymmetric stakes. Opposing parties in lawsuits sometimes have different stakes in a litigation. The character of these stakes will in part determine whether the party is risk-averse or risk-neutral in a given lawsuit. For example, suppose a single plaintiff, disturbed by the noise level coming from a factory near his home, sues to enjoin the factory from producing noise above a certain level. If the factory had to curtail manufacturing to comply, it might lose more from the suit than the plaintiff gains from a lowered noise level. Similarly, a defendant might worry that a particular lawsuit, if litigated through appeal, could establish an adverse precedent that would damage his position in future cases. The plaintiff, by contrast, might want a recovery, and care nothing about making law.

In these examples, the defendant would want to settle. On the other hand, a doctor sued for medical malpractice might wish to go to trial, having a concern that settlement will negatively affect her reputation and future career. Thus, one litigating party's greater relative stake in a litigation could incline it either to hard bargain or to compromise. Which it would elect to do depends on which strategy best serves its overall set of interests, as implicated in the litigation.

Repeat players and claim discounting. An important subclass of lawsuits involves business or other parties seeking to minimize settlement losses over an aggregate of cases. The parties include such repeat players as insurance companies or other businesses handling or facing a large number of claims. For them, whether to resist claims to the point of suit, when claims go to suit, and when and how they should settle them essentially become business questions. In risk-aversion terms, they are willing to hard bargain and run the risk of trial in individual cases because their experience tells them that most of these cases will settle on advantageous terms. This is particularly true where the plaintiff's litigation transaction costs are high relative to stakes.

Where the guiding rule is profit, it is rational to treat claim resolution, including trial, as just another aspect of business. One obvious and commonly adopted strategy to maximize gain over an aggregate of cases is hardballing. Hardballing involves resisting a claim until there is a credible threat of suit, or even a continuing refusal to negotiate in spite of a pending litigation. A party can impose significant financial, psychological, and opportunity costs on a claimant by forcing it to pursue litigation. Hardballing, or ignoring or resisting claims, requires the claimant to bear all the costs of filing and prosecuting a lawsuit to force the respondent into a position where it must address the claim. Many claimants will not cross that threshold, and their claims will either fall away or the respondent can negotiate them quite advantageously.

By forcing claimants to resort to law, the nonresponder creates a claims clearing-and-discount system. Even where a claimant does file a lawsuit, however, continued hardballing can bring discount benefits. Prosecuting a lawsuit involves additional expense, delay, uncertainty, and perhaps anxiety. Any or all of these may either cause a claimant to give up or to compromise its demands. Thus, even when a resisting party knows its claimant is in the right and can succeed, it may nonetheless use litigation to impose litigation transaction costs and erode the asserted value of the claim.

Particularly in situations where a business faces repetitive "garden variety" claims, business judgment might follow this kind of claim resolution policy. That policy, while perhaps occasionally costly in those cases where the strategy results in a trial that the business loses, might be least costly in the aggregate of all cases. Thus, repeat player parties sometimes ignore or resist even meritorious individual cases. They treat them as instances of a class of cases to be hardballed to ensure discounting. Similarly, in some cases a repeater will prefer trial to negotiation because settling the claim may encourage similar claims by others.

In more unusual cases, business calculation will take into account the possible precedential value of the case. Then the decision whether to settle or litigate will turn partly on an assessment of which process will lead to the best prospects for future cases. For example, cigarette companies now generally choose to litigate rather than settle cancer-from-smoking claims. They do so because the cases are not clear cases of liability, because plaintiffs demand large settlements, and the companies can afford expensive litigation. What is more important, however, notwithstanding the great expense of these trials, the company's investment in winning the trial has a large potential payoff for its possible future liabilities.

For these reasons, repeat players, such as insurance companies, are relatively risk-neutral. They have a present interest in a settlement's effect on future cases, that is, the message the settlement sends to future claimants. They therefore factor potential future loss into their bargaining equation and have an incentive to hard-bargain.

Litigation fee and financing arrangements. An attorney handling a case on a contingent-fee basis receives a percentage, usually a third but sometimes more, of the settlement or trial recovery. In addition, contingent fee attorneys usually finance the litigation, that is, they advance the costs necessary to move the case to litigation. Contingent fee attorneys who finance the litigation have a direct personal interest in it and any possible settlements. That personal stake may affect the lawyer's assessments of trial or settlement prospects and may also induce a lawyer to shape his client's perceptions in ways that favor the lawyer's, rather than the client's, interests. Notwithstanding rules of professional ethics, one would expect contingent fee attorneys to exert a greater say in litigation and settlement decisions than attorneys lacking such an interest. The lawsuit is a joint venture, and the attorney acts much as a general partner managing the investment.

Litigation sponsors. A party who can, without risk, shift trial costs and risks of loss onto someone else is more likely to litigate than to settle. When a litigant has a litigation sponsor, such as occurs in attorney-financed contingent fee cases or cases where insurance companies bear defense costs, he can afford to hard-bargain. On the other hand, where the litigant pays her own litigation costs, she is more likely to settle, except in those cases where she is reasonably certain of trial victory.

Sponsored litigation does not by any means always result in hard bargaining. Whether a sponsored litigant will force a case trial depends on the litigant's relationship to its sponsor and who controls the decision whether to litigate. For example, in ordinary litigation involving relatively small sums, neither hard bargaining, nor integrative bargaining, nor trial makes much sense. Negotiation and trial transaction costs are high relative to stakes, and the lawyer needs to value the claim in dollars, rather than engage in creative problem solving, in order to collect a fee. When the case is relatively small, the lawyer's interest is to invest relatively little and settle rapidly.

Empirical evidence indicates this is what occurs: Most small, ordinary litigation cases settle in only one or two rounds of bargaining, and the lawyers do not engage in strategic bargaining to maximize gains. Indeed, in a case of this sort, the lawyer's predominant bargaining aim apparently is "to locate a case within a set of norms and expectations" and to settle it for the "going-rate" for that kind of case. Attempting to maximize results for individual clients would impose additional costs on the attorney, and might lead to trials risking no gain at all. When a lawyer can turn over many small cases rapidly, however, it makes for a steady income with minimal investment. Thus, in small, garden-variety cases, attorneys apparently deal both to obtain satisfying results for clients in individual cases and maximize their own aggregate gain (effective hourly rate) over all their cases.

In high-stakes, contingent fee cases, the pattern is different. The contingent fee attorney may gamble on going to trial in hope of obtaining a large judgment. Viewed as financial investors in litigation, contingent fee attorneys carry a portfolio of cases in which they have invested. If they win some big cases, they can afford to lose others, for it is the overall return on overall investment that counts. Thus in high-stakes cases, contingent fee lawyers are both more likely to engage in hard bargaining and go to trial. Trial may result either from a gamble on trial results or a bargaining miscalculation.

Ally effects. While most lawsuits have only two sides, represented by the plaintiff and the defendant, lawsuit negotiations are only superficially two-party negotiations. The parties themselves are not unitary, but litigating teams composed of client and attorney. The litigating team may involve other participants as well. For example, as in the sponsored litigation mentioned earlier, an insurance company may stand in the background in a defendant's case, sometimes supplying and controlling the defendant's lawyer, sometimes not. In any case, allies comprise litigating teams, and this means that lawsuit negotiations are multi-party negotiations. It also means that each lawsuit team has its own internal negotiations — regarding relationships, decision making, and control — to conduct.

The allies on each side in a lawsuit negotiation do not always have completely congruent interests. Instead, they have some interests that are compatible and some that are divergent. This is particularly true in contingent fee and insurance defense cases where the litigant's ally is the litigation sponsor. For example, a contingent fee attorney in a high-stakes case sometimes has a greater interest in gambling on a trial than her client, who may be more risk-averse. Similarly, an insurance company might prefer to settle a libel case in which going to trial risks a high award. In the same case, the named defendant might prefer trial for vindication that he had done no wrong. As a further complication in the same case, the defense attorney, usually paid on an hourly basis by the insurance company, may have an interest in drawing out the litigation to enhance his fee.

There is no rule to apply to determine how litigation allies will sort out relationship and litigation control issues. It is reasonable to claim that where litigation ally interests diverge, the interests of the ally having practical control of the litigation will determine whether the parties settle or try the case.

* * *

Chapter 3
INTEGRATIVE BARGAINING

The negotiation model presented in the preceding chapter assumes that the parties have mutually exclusive goals — each seeking to maximize his share of a fixed good. While some negotiations, such as the personal injury case used as an example in Chapter Two, fit the distributive bargaining model fairly well, most negotiations — even lawsuit negotiations — that lawyers handle present more complicated situations of mixed independence and interdependence of the parties. A seller may be concerned not only about the results of today's negotiation, but also about next week's and next year's market for widgets. If a distributive "win" today means that the other party never wants to do business with your client again, it will be against your client's self-interest for you to push for the last dollar in a competitive pursuit of maximum gain. When continuing business relationships are important, a lawyer cannot afford to be indifferent to the other party's satisfaction with the outcome of a negotiation. In addition, the parties may value different aspects of the negotiation differently — one may care more about quick delivery and the other more about price, for example — and they are likely to reach a more mutually satisfactory result if they share sufficient information to reveal their dissimilar preferences. Negotiation theorists have argued that less distributive approaches to negotiation can produce better agreements, in the economic sense of optimizing results (reaching the "efficient" or "Pareto optimal" frontier[1]), as well as more lasting ones, in terms of the parties' commitment to the agreement reached.

The literature on integrative approaches to negotiation has burgeoned over the last twenty-five years,[2] although many of the ideas on which it is based have been around since the early twentieth century.[3] Their basic premise is that a negotiator can often do better by working together with other parties rather than by assuming that the parties' interests are necessarily antagonistic. Such approaches are variously referred to as principled, integrative, collaborative, or problem-solving negotiation. All are distinguished from the self-centered, dominating orientation of the distributive bargainer. The discussion that follows uses the terms "integrative"

---

[1] *See* HOWARD RAIFFA, THE ART AND SCIENCE OF NEGOTIATION (1982).

[2] *See* ROGER FISHER & WILLIAM URY, GETTING TO YES (1981); ROGER FISHER, ET AL., GETTING TO YES (2d ed. 1991); DAVID A. LAX & JAMES K. SEBENIUS, THE MANAGER AS NEGOTIATOR (1986); WILLIAM URY, GETTING PAST NO (1991, 1993); Carrie Menkel-Meadow, *Toward Another View of Legal Negotiations: The Structure of Problem-Solving*, 31 UCLA L. REV. 754 (1984).

[3] *See* MARY P. FOLLETT, THE NEW STATE (1918); MARY P. FOLLETT, CREATIVE EXPERIENCE (1924); MARY P. FOLLETT, DYNAMIC ADMINISTRATION (1942).

or "collaborative" bargaining to refer to the main features of these related methods of negotiation, and it focuses on their differences from distributive bargaining. While such a sharp distinction between the two is artificial, since most negotiations have both distributive and integrative elements — and good negotiators employ both approaches — it is a helpful way to understand their distinguishing features.

A. COLLABORATION, NOT COMPETITION

An integrative bargainer has a collaborative, rather than a competitive, orientation. Instead of focusing exclusively on maximizing her own gain, she looks first for ways to improve outcomes for both parties — what Fisher, Ury, and Patton[4] term "inventing options for mutual gain" and Lax and Sebenius[5] call "creating value". The idea is to look for ways to enlarge the negotiation pie before dividing it, so that each party comes out ahead. For example, a divorcing couple might agree to treat payments from one spouse to the other as either child support or alimony, depending on which designation results in the most favorable tax consequences overall. The excerpt below from Menkel-Meadow discusses some of the ways parties can enhance the results for both by treating their dispute as a problem to be solved jointly rather than a war to be won by one side or the other. Such an approach is frequently referred to as "win-win" negotiation, to contrast it with the "win-lose" orientation of the distributive bargainer, although some authors like Greenhalgh, below, have questioned the usefulness of the "winning" metaphor in the context of integrative bargaining.

Many lawyers are initially suspicious of an approach to negotiation that does not proceed from an adversary model. They worry that taking the other side's interests and concerns into account will lead to their being taken advantage of and will undermine the ethical duty of zealous representation. However, a collaborative negotiator is not simply trying to get along with the other party and thus to reduce the level of tension often present in a distributive negotiation. Adopting a collaborative approach can be an act of enlightened self-interest in a situation where the relationship of the parties or the nature of the negotiation suggests that you may be able to improve the outcome for your client by helping the other side achieve its goals as well. A collaborative negotiator, as Follett[6] put it almost 60 years ago, has "just as great a respect for [her] own view as for that of others." She does not cooperate for the sake of soothing others or of making the negotiation go smoothly, as some negotiators do, but in order to achieve her own goals by enlisting the involvement and participation of her counterparts to find an optimal resolution for both.

---

[4] ROGER FISHER, ET AL., GETTING TO YES (2d ed. 1991).

[5] DAVID A. LAX & JAMES K. SEBENIUS, THE MANAGER AS NEGOTIATOR (1986).

[6] MARY P. FOLLETT, DYNAMIC ADMINISTRATION 48 (1942).

B. OPEN DISCUSSION

One way that negotiators seek to improve results through collaboration is by encouraging wide-ranging discussion of the problems at hand before trying to come up with potential solutions. Instead of starting with a fixed idea of a desired result, a collaborative negotiator tries to utilize her counterpart's knowledge of his client's situation to come up with unanticipated or creative ways to satisfy both parties. The parties explore possibilities together before committing themselves to any particular outcome. Being willing to discuss a proposal is not the same as agreeing to it, and you may learn something in the process that improves your own ideas. By taking both overlapping and divergent interests of the parties into account, the negotiators may be able to fashion an agreement that maximizes joint gain rather than benefits one at the other's expense.

A collaborative approach to negotiation requires more openness on the part of all participants than is common in a distributive bargaining setting, since it presumes that a better result will be possible if the parties start with better information about each other's needs and preferences. For example, a first-time novelist may care more about the publicity effort made to sell her book than about the amount of her advance, since she thinks the publicity will do more for her career in the long run. The publisher wants the book to sell well, so spending money on publicity makes sense from its point of view, too. If the parties take a distributive approach to the negotiation, they may never see this opportunity for joint gain: instead, each will focus on the amount of the advance and seek to maximize individual gain. If, however, they are more forthcoming about what really matters to them under the circumstances, they may reach an agreement in which the publisher spends more on publicity and somewhat less on the writer's advance, to the advantage of both.

C. MOTIVATION TO NEGOTIATE

In integrative bargaining, the focus is not on the fixed positions of each side — the target, walkaway, and concession points of the distributive negotiator — but on what actually motivates each party to participate in the negotiation. The writer in the example above is interested not only in the financial security represented by an advance, but also in the enhanced reputation that publicity might generate. An agreement that addresses both of these concerns will be more satisfactory to her than one that deals with only one of them. In addition, understanding the underlying motivations of the parties may enable you to come up with a variety of ways of meeting their needs within the context of a negotiated settlement, increasing the possibilities for joint gain. When parties lock horns over how much money is going to change hands, it is difficult for them to be creative about solutions to their conflict other than "if you get more, then I get less." If they can figure out what the money represents to each party in the context of the negotiation, and what other issues matter to each of them, they may be able to put together a better deal than either of them could think up alone. A frequently used example illustrates the potential benefits of moving beyond a purely distributive approach to negotiation. If two children argue over a single orange, the most likely outcome is that they will split it and each take half. If, instead, they explore what use each has for the orange, it may turn out that one wants the peel to use in baking and the other wants the juice to drink. In this case, they can both end up better off by dividing the orange accordingly and maximizing their joint gain.

Focusing on the parties' motivations means looking past the positions they take to get at what underlies them. Why does the other party insist that she has to have $150,000 to settle? Does she need the money now to pay for current expenses, or is she more concerned about the future? If the former, is there some way your client can provide her with necessary services for less than they would cost on the open market? If the latter, perhaps an annuity to provide a reliable stream of future income could satisfy her needs at a lower cost to your client than a lump-sum settlement. Without an understanding of the parties' motivations, it is difficult to come up with concrete proposals that can benefit both and that are tailored to their particular situations.

D. RELATIONSHIP BETWEEN THE PARTIES

When the parties have or want to establish an ongoing relationship, an integrative approach to bargaining will be more appropriate than the purely self-interested stance of the distributive bargainer. If parties are going to be partners in a business venture, their individual success will be bound up with their joint success; and it will be in their mutual interest to negotiate an agreement that is not one-sided, either in terms of obligations or of rewards. If the parties anticipate dealing with each other repeatedly, that fact itself will curb extreme distributive approaches to negotiation, since hard-nosed tactics will not foster good relations and flat-out misrepresentations will be difficult to hide over time. A supposedly long-term relationship that is not based on some foundation of trust, however hard earned, is not likely to endure. A buyer and seller may each want to get the best price they can, but they will also recognize the value of a steady supply of reliable quality goods or of repeat orders that are promptly paid for. An ongoing business relationship is seldom based on one party's consistently forcing agreement at the other's expense.

Even if the relationship between the parties is not a paramount concern in and of itself, a negotiation process that focuses on exploiting opportunities for joint gain makes sense from the point of view of self-interest alone, as discussed in the example of the newly-published writer above. Ignoring such opportunities risks leaving money on the table and ending up with an inferior agreement. Taking advantage of them requires that the parties have sufficient trust in each other to reveal their needs and preferences in a straightforward way and to engage in open discussion of the issues. Creating a negotiation atmosphere in which this can happen presumes a different relationship between the negotiators than in the typical distributive bargaining situation. They must start from the premise that both can benefit from exchanging information and that they are to some extent interdependent, rather than wholly independent, actors. The conflict between them is a problem to be solved, rather than a contest to be won; and each of them possesses information necessary to an optimal resolution.

E. PREPARATION

Although flexibility is one key to success in integrative negotiations, thorough preparation is just as essential as it is in distributive negotiations. You cannot be open as to the means of achieving your client's goals without a clear understanding of what those goals are and what the alternatives are to a negotiated agreement. Since you can anticipate a wide-ranging discussion of potential solutions and a premium on creative methods of maximizing joint gain, you will have to assess carefully the information available to you in advance, in order to be both flexible and firm in pursuing your client's interests during the negotiation.

1. Exploring Your Client's Motivations

To prepare for negotiation when the relationship between the parties or the nature of the conflict suggests that an integrative approach is appropriate, you have to have a thorough understanding of your client's needs and priorities. While it may be enough for the distributive bargainer to know *what* a client wants, usually translated into a dollar figure, to do a good job as an integrative bargainer, you also have to know *why* she wants it — what it means to her and what she plans to do with it if she can get it. Without an understanding of your client's motivations to negotiate, you will not be able to evaluate the other side's proposals adequately, nor will you be able to make proposals that serve your client's interests well. Only a detailed interview with the client will give you the information you need to understand her perspective on the subject of the negotiation and what alternatives might reasonably meet her needs.

The lawyer-client relationship in the context of negotiations will be discussed in more detail in Chapter Seven. For the moment, it is worth noting that many of the aspects of integrative bargaining discussed here will be useful in preparing with your client: open discussion of a wide range of potential outcomes; brainstorming ideas for enlarging the pie as well as for possible solutions to the conflict; looking for possibilities for joint gain, and so on. Your client will probably know more about the other party to the negotiation than you do initially and can be a valuable resource as you try to develop ideas in advance about the other side's goals. If your aim is to explore opportunities for joint gain, thinking about the other side's needs and ways to satisfy them that also work for your client will be an essential part of your preparation. The more you can anticipate what will be important to the other party and are prepared with concrete proposals that further his goals, too, the more quickly a productive, collaborative atmosphere can be established in the negotiation.

2. Exploring Alternatives

In the process of establishing your client's needs and her priorities in the negotiation, you also have to consider what she will do if the negotiation fails. What alternatives does she have to reaching a deal here? As in a distributive bargaining situation, your client will have a walkaway point — a point at which her "best alternative to a negotiated agreement" or "BATNA"[7] is preferable to the deal on the table. You are not engaging in integrative bargaining in order to make *some* deal, no matter what. If you are not clear about what your client's alternatives are, you will not be able to evaluate proposals made during the negotiation. Suppose your client needs 25,000 widgets within 30 days in order to complete a product that is due to ship in 45 days. She already has an offer from Seller A of 10,000 widgets next week and another 15,000 a month after that, at market price. Unless Seller B can somehow improve on that offer, your client has no reason to reach an agreement with him. But there might be a number of ways in which Seller B could offer a more desirable alternative: he might be able to provide more widgets sooner; or all the widgets for a better price, but with the same time constraints; or a guaranteed future supply of widgets in addition to filling this order. Your understanding of your client's needs and alternatives will allow you to weigh the various possible deals with Seller B and to decide which, if any, of them will suit your client.

3. Using Outside Sources

Since you do not want the negotiation to degenerate into a battle of personalities, but rather to focus on the problem at hand, your preparation should include looking to outside sources for information about how similar situations have been handled: industry standards, market price, external factors affecting the subject of the negotiation, and so on. If your proposals can be justified based on credible external sources, they are less likely to evoke a competitive response from the other party. Instead of relying on bending the other party to your will, you can introduce an objective basis for

---

[7] *See* ROGER FISHER, ET AL., GETTING TO YES (2d ed. 1991).

agreement that both parties can accept. For example, compare the following exchanges:

A: I can't sell you this first edition for less than $50,000.

B: $50,000! That's highway robbery! What makes you think it's worth anything close to that?

A: That's my price! Take it or leave it!

* * *

A: In trying to come up with a price for this first edition of X, I've looked into what other copies have sold for recently. Dealer prices have ranged between $40,000 and $55,000. Since the binding on mine is in particularly good condition and it is the only one currently on the market, I think a price of $50,000 is reasonable.

B: That's more than I can afford to pay for it, as much as I'd like to own it.

A: Well, I've had my eye out for a copy of Y, and I know you have one. Perhaps you'd be interested in selling that to me and paying only the difference in cash in order to get X.

Outside sources can also be useful in learning about the other negotiators and the parties they represent, both in terms of what their goals are likely to be and in terms of how receptive they will be to a collaborative approach to the negotiation itself. If you learn as much as you can about them in advance, it will be easier during the negotiation to present proposals that take their needs into account as well as yours.

F. COLLABORATIVE BARGAINING TECHNIQUES

Collaborative bargaining assumes that the parties will both get better results by maximizing opportunities for joint gain. The relationship between the parties is often expected to continue in the future, and its stability may be of considerable importance to them. The conduct of the negotiation is intended to foster any existing or desired relationship; and it does so by relying on open communications, sharing of information, and a respectful process that aims at the parties' mutual satisfaction with the outcome.

1. Establish a Basis for Collaboration

Just as it takes two to tango, you cannot collaborate alone. Unless the lawyer you are negotiating with sees or can be helped to see the benefits of collaboration, you risk giving more than you get in the process and ending up with a poor agreement for your client. If you do not have prior experience negotiating with the other lawyer, the first thing you will have to do is to negotiate the process itself. That is, you will have to establish a mutually agreeable process that allows and fosters collaboration between you. Rather than taking an adversarial stance that assumes that the other negotiator is an opponent, you have to treat him as a potential partner in solving the problem that has brought you both to the table. Making this shift can be difficult. On the one hand, if you treat him as an enemy, you will be likely to defend yourself to the utmost, but you will have a hard time collaborating. On the other hand, if you simply assume that you can work as partners, you may not defend yourself enough.

A cautiously optimistic attitude will allow you to test the potential for collaboration, without plunging ahead regardless of the other side's response. You can start by expressing your view that the parties share certain interests and that, by exploiting those, you may both be able to benefit. Unless the other lawyer has independently reached the same conclusion, you may have to demonstrate that this is so. You can point out what you believe the parties' overlapping interests to be and attempt to engage your counterpart in clarifying and enlarging upon his client's needs. By starting off with a discussion of both parties' motivations to negotiate, you discourage taking positions and leave for a later time any concrete proposals for resolving the conflict. Fisher, Ury, and Patton refer to the process of converting a reluctant or skeptical opponent as using "negotiation jujitsu". They suggest various tactics for handling opposition without responding in kind, such as trying to figure out the interests behind stated positions; inviting comment on your own proposals rather than defending them; treating personal attacks as communications about the subject of the negotiation; asking questions instead of making pronouncements; and using silence both as a comment on what has been said and as an encouragement to say more. Ury refined and extended many of these ideas for "getting past no" with difficult people by proposing specific techniques for overcoming the barriers to successful collaboration, as the excerpt that follows illustrates.

One successful technique to encourage collaboration is to brainstorm with the other side about the subject of the negotiation. Rather than seeing the negotiation as a contest in which one of you will prevail, you work together to come up with ideas about the problem itself and potential solutions. The goal in brainstorming is to generate as many ideas as possible, without judging their feasability or desirability or committing yourself to any one of them in advance. Maintaining a non-judgmental attitude during brainstorming allows negotiators to think creatively and to build on each other's ideas in a way that seldom happens if they take an adversarial stance. Since each lawyer knows her own client's situation best, their joint efforts may produce better ideas than either of them could come up with alone. Brainstorming gives both sides time to assess a number of alternatives before coming up with possible solutions to the conflict. What they learn from each other in the process will also help them later, when they begin to evaluate and choose among the various options they have developed. The article below by Brown discusses brainstorming and other creative approaches to negotiation.

Even if you are successful initially in establishing a collaborative atmosphere for the negotiation, you cannot simply assume that the process will thereafter take care of itself. At any point where conflict increases, negotiators tend to retreat to a more self-protective, positional bargaining stance. When this happens, the most productive response is often to break off substantive discussions and to go back to negotiating the process. You may be able to get the negotiation back on a collaborative track by stressing your clients' shared interests and the progress already made in finding mutually beneficial solutions. A renewed focus on common ground and on gains achieved will help to reduce interpersonal tensions and to remind all parties of the benefits of working together.

2. Negotiating Power

If you are going to share information with the other side and work to maintain a collaborative and collegial atmosphere during the negotiation, what power will you be able to wield to accomplish your client's goals? Lawyers often feel that concealment, bluff, threats and even intimidation are likely to be the most reliable ways of influencing others in the give and take of negotiation. While a commitment to use force if the other party does not do what you want can be effective in getting your way, it can also be costly if you have to carry through on your threat or if you ever need to deal with the same person again. What other sources of power are there? Roger Fisher, in the article excerpted below, has described a number of them and shown how they are compatible with an integrative approach to bargaining. He discusses the power of skill and knowledge; the power of a good relationship; the power of a good alternative to negotiating; the power of an elegant solution; the power of legitimacy; and the power of commitment. Fundamentally, all the forms of power he discusses derive from doing your own job well, rather than relying on your ability to compel the other side to capitulate. Being well prepared for a negotiation, coming up with creative solutions, understanding your client's goals, and being firm in pursuing them are all consistent with establishing and maintaining a good working relationship with your negotiation counterparts. How does Fisher's discussion of power in negotiation compare to Korobkin's in Chapter Two?

3. Dealing with Conflict

In order to explore opportunities for joint gain, negotiating parties must be able to manage the conflict between them in such a way that it does not take over and turn the negotiation into a distributive standoff. At the same time, integrative negotiation requires far more than that the parties simply resolve to be easy on each other. Unless each party has a clear and comprehensive understanding of its own needs, and is firmly committed to meeting as many of them as possible, there is no way that an optimal agreement can be reached. The merits of integrative bargaining rest not on its being "nice," compared to distributive bargaining, but on its ability to produce better results by focusing on the parties' underlying motivation to negotiate, as the article below by Friedman and Shapiro discusses.

What is required is a recognition that the parties' interests are likely to overlap in some respects and to diverge in others, and a willingness to tolerate that ambiguity in seeking opportunities for joint gain. A more one-sided approach — treating the negotiation only as a competitive struggle with a winner and a loser — has the advantage of being simpler, in that it casts the situation in black and white terms. It is also far more likely to lead to a stalemate or a sub-optimal result if both parties compete, or to resentment and an unstable agreement if one side gives in to competitive pressure from the other. It is the capacity to work toward a mutually satisfactory outcome while recognizing that some of the parties' needs will be incompatible that characterizes successful collaborative bargaining.

Unlike the distributive bargainer, who may use and manipulate the tension inherent in negotiation to pressure the other side to give in, a collaborative negotiator seeks ways to diffuse that tension, emphasizing the value of joint efforts rather than an adversarial stance. The momentum of collaboration, however, is always threatened by the reality that at some point all possible joint gains will have been realized and the remaining gains will have to be divided between the parties. In order to maintain collaborative momentum and to reduce conflict, it helps to build in successes as early and as often as possible. Small points of agreement set the stage for larger ones. Since the parties are likely to have different needs and preferences, finding ways to trade these off against each other is one way to create value for both. For example, if one business person wants to be able to count on a certain minimum monthly return, she may be willing to trade a guaranteed sum against a higher percentage of the remaining profits going to her partner, who is less risk-averse and has less immediate need of money. The fact that both get something of value (a sum certain versus higher upside gain) increases each side's investment in maintaining a collaborative approach going forward and also increases the likelihood of their uncovering further opportunities for joint gain that may exist. Similarly, finding ways to make satisfying one party less costly to the other, for example, by purchasing an annuity to provide a future income stream, will help counter the tendency to revert to more self-protective and competitive negotiation techniques.

4. Dealing with Communication Obstacles

The advent of the internet and the widespread use of e-mail have increased the difficulty of establishing a collaborative relationship between

negotiators. Face to face negotiations are sometimes impossible if the negotiators are on opposite sides of the world, and even telephone conversations can be difficult to arrange across time zones. As a result, more and
more negotiations are conducted by e-mail, sometimes by lawyers who have
never seen or spoken to each other. Because e-mail lacks the visual and audi-
tory cues we typically rely on to pick up information about people, it is a particularly opaque medium through which to establish the sort of positive
relationship that fosters collaboration and integrative bargaining. The article below by Nadler identifies some methods that have been successful in
establishing rapport and a collaborative atmosphere between negotiators
who do not meet face to face.

5. Sharing Information

All that has been said so far about integrative bargaining suggests that
lawyers will only be able to do a good job if they share substantive information about their clients' needs and preferences and look for ways to make
their differences work for them in the negotiation. According to Follett,[8] "the
first rule for obtaining integration is to put your cards on the table, face the
real issue, uncover the conflict, bring the whole thing into the open." This
is a far cry from the bargaining for information that characterizes distributive negotiations, where each side seeks to learn as much as possible about
the other while revealing as little as it can. The more straightforward and
clear the negotiators' communications are, the fewer obstacles there will be
to recognizing and capitalizing on opportunities for mutual gain. This
means, first, that they must be clear about their clients' goals, even if they
are open as to the means of reaching those goals. In addition, there must be
sufficient trust between them so that both are willing to reveal their clients'
true motivations. Such trust may be based on past experience, but it may
also be developed in the course of a negotiation, as the negotiators exchange
information and evaluate the information they have received. It does not
have to be based on an assumption that the other side has your best interests at heart, but only that he is as interested as you are in uncovering ways
that you can both do better through your negotiation. Self-interest can keep
both sides honest in the process, even where there might be a short-term
gain from misrepresentation. Of course, the need to share information in
order to optimize results creates risks for the negotiators as well, as will be
discussed in the next chapter.

Flexibility, rather than rigid positions, is key to integrative bargaining,
since the outcome will depend on fitting together the parties' needs as much
as possible. When the negotiators share adequate information, they may
even end up redefining the conflict they are trying to resolve. For example,
what seemed a specific problem about failure to fulfill the terms of a contract may turn out to be a more fundamental difficulty with the structure

---

[8] MARY P. FOLLETT, DYNAMIC ADMINISTRATION 36 (1942).

of the contract itself. A better outcome for both sides may result if the contract is renegotiated. As mentioned before, the parties need to be open to the means by which a particular negotiation goal will be achieved. In this regard, open discussion of problems and possible solutions in the early stages of the negotiation will help the negotiators develop a range of options from which to choose. Rather than being committed to positions, they must be committed to a process that allows creative ideas to develop and to be analyzed without rushing to reach a resolution. All too often, however, negotiators succumb to the pressure to "get the deal done" and cut off discussion prematurely, which can lead to decidedly inferior results.

6. Leveraging Disparate Interests

One advantage of focusing on the parties' motivations to negotiate is that it allows their lawyers to craft a solution that exploits the clients' differences as well as satisfies their overlapping interests. Parties may differ in their attitudes toward risk, in their priorities, in their immediate need for money, and so on. Knowing about these dissimilarities enables negotiators to trade off issues purposefully, taking into account what matters most to each client and leaving both better off than if the trade-offs occurred randomly. For example, the parties can enter into a contingent agreement based on their differing views of how likely a future event is, such as a flat salary with specified bonuses for various levels of performance. The more information the negotiators have to work with, the more flexible and tailored to their clients' specific situation the final contract can be. The article below by Moffitt discusses how contingent contracts can add value in negotiations.

G. PROS AND CONS OF INTEGRATIVE BARGAINING

A collaborative approach to negotiation allows negotiators to explore and take advantage of whatever possibilities may exist for joint gain. When successfully implemented, it can result in both parties doing better than either would have done in a purely distributive negotiation. It also creates a solid basis for future negotiations or an ongoing relationship between the parties. The possibilities for creative solutions are increased when the negotiators focus on the conflict as a common problem to be solved, rather than on each other as adversaries. The negotiation process itself may lead them to shift their priorities or to clarify needs that had not been considered before. It will certainly produce new ideas about how to resolve the conflict, as they build on each other's suggestions and on their increased understanding of their respective clients' needs. The process will be an iterative one, with considerable back and forth and fine tuning as they seek the optimal agreement for both parties. All of this takes time; and sometimes, time itself is of the essence. If what your client needs is a speedy resolution —

widgets tomorrow, no matter what — his short-term need may dictate quick closure. In other circumstances the time invested in developing an integrative agreement can pay off in the long run, because both parties' interests will be taken into account on the best terms possible.

For the negotiator herself, a collaborative negotiation will be less contentious than a distributive one. Interpersonal tensions will not be exploited in order to maximize gain, and the negotiators' communications are less likely to involve arguments and threats. At the same time, engaging in integrative bargaining requires a high tolerance for ambiguity. You have to keep both your client's point of view and the other party's in mind. You also have to seek solutions that benefit both without losing sight of your ethical duty to your client. In the context of integrative bargaining, the lawyer's duty of zealous advocacy requires an ability to be responsive to the other side's interests, rather than reflexively adversarial, and to work toward joint gains for both parties, while recognizing that at some point the parties' interests will diverge and become adverse. The duty to your client is not contrary to an effort to increase the size of the negotiation pie, but it does impose a partisan duty when the time comes to divide the jointly created pie.

Critics of integrative bargaining, such as White in his book review of *Getting to YES*, below, have argued that its advocates focus on what is essentially only one aspect of negotiation — how to make the most of opportunities for joint gain — to the exclusion of distributive issues, and that the result is a naive description of the challenges of negotiation. In his comment to that review, Fisher articulates what he see as principled approaches even to distributional questions, and why he believes them to be preferable to arguing over positions. The next chapter takes up the tension between integrative and distributive bargaining.

Carrie Menkel-Meadow,[*] *Toward Another View of Legal Negotiations: The Structure of Problem Solving*
31 UCLA L. Rev. 754, 798-801; 809-13; 818-23 (1984)[**]

* * *

Understanding that the other party's needs are not necessarily as assumed may present an opportunity for arriving at creative solutions. Traditionally, lawyers approaching negotiations from the adversarial model view the other side as an enemy to be defeated. By examining the underlying needs of the other side, the lawyer may instead see opportunities for

---

[*] Carrie Menkel-Meadow is the A.B. Chettle, Jr. Professor of Law, Dispute Resolution, and Civil Procedure at Georgetown University Law Center. This excerpt discusses some of the principles of what she calls "problem-solving" negotiation.

[**] Copyright © 1984 Regents of the University of California. Reprinted by permission of the UCLA Law Review.

solutions that would not have existed before based upon the recognition of different, but not conflicting, preferences.

An example from the psychological literature illustrates this point. Suppose that a husband and wife have two weeks in which to take their vacation. The husband prefers the mountains and the wife prefers the seaside. If vacation time is limited and thus a scarce resource, the couple may engage in adversarial negotiation about where they should go. The simple compromise situation, if they engage in distributive bargaining, would be to split the two weeks of vacation time spending one week in the mountains and one week at the ocean. This solution is not likely to be satisfying, however, because of the lost time and money in moving from place to place and in getting used to a new hotel room and locale. In addition to being happy only half of the time, each party to the negotiation has incurred transaction costs associated with this solution. Other "compromise" solutions might include alternating preferences on a year to year basis, taking separate vacations, or taking a longer vacation at a loss of pay. Assuming that husband and wife want to vacation together, all of these solutions may leave something to be desired by at least one of the parties.

By examining their underlying preferences, however, the parties might find additional solutions that could make both happy at less cost. Perhaps the husband prefers the mountains because he likes to hike and engage in stream fishing. Perhaps the wife enjoys swimming, sunbathing and seafood. By exploring these underlying preferences the couple might find vacation spots that permit all of these activities: a mountain resort on a large lake, or a seaside resort at the foot of mountains. By examining their underlying needs the parties can see solutions that satisfy many more of their preferences, and the "sum of the utilities" to the couple as a whole is greater than what they would have achieved by compromising.

In addition, by exploring whether they attach different values to their preferences they may be able to arrive at other solutions by trading items. The wife in our example might be willing to give up ocean fresh seafood if she can have fresh stream or lake trout, and so, with very little cost to her, the couple can choose another waterspot where the hikes might be better for the husband. By examining the weight or value given to certain preferences the parties may realize that some desires are easily attainable because they are not of equal importance to the other side. Thus, one party can increase its utilities without reducing the other's. This differs from a zero-sum conception of negotiation because of the recognition that preferences may be totally different and are, therefore, neither scarce nor in competition with each other. In addition, if a preference is not used to "force" a concession from the other party (which as the example shows is not necessary), there are none of the forced reciprocal concessions of adversarial negotiation.

The exploitation of complementary interests occurs frequently in the legal context. For example, in a child custody case the lawyers may learn that both parties desire to have the children some of the time and neither of the parties wishes to have the children all of the time. It will be easy, therefore, to arrange for a joint custody agreement that satisfies the needs of both parties. Similarly, in a commercial matter, the defendant may want to make payment over time and the plaintiff, for tax purposes or to increase interest income, may desire deferred income.

* * *

b. *Expanding the Resources Available.* Of course, the parties' needs will not be sufficiently complementary in all cases to permit direct solutions. Needs may conflict or there may be conflict over the material required to satisfy the needs. In addition to focusing on the parties' needs as a source of solutions, negotiators can attempt to expand the resources that the parties may eventually have to divide. In essence, this aspect of problem-solving negotiation seeks wherever possible to convert zero-sum games into non-zero-sum or positive-sum games. By expanding resources or the material available for division, more of the parties' total set of needs may be satisfied. Indeed, as the literature on legal transactions and the economic efficiency of such transactions makes clear, the parties come together to transact business precisely because their joint action is likely to increase the wealth available to both. To the extent that principles of wealth creation and resource expansion from transactional negotiation can be assimilated to dispute negotiation, the parties to a negotiation have the opportunity to help each other by looking for ways to expand what is available to them.

Various substantive strategies may increase the material available for distribution. Resources can be expanded by exploring *what* could be distributed, *when* it could be distributed, *by whom* it would be distributed, *how* it could be distributed and *how much* of it could be distributed. The following examples are illustrative. In [a] personal injury [case] resources can be expanded by providing the plaintiff with a job, rather than money *(what)*, and money payments over time which would result in tax savings for both parties *(when)*. In exploring the *what* for distribution it is often useful to determine whether the defendant can satisfy the plaintiff's needs more directly and at less expense than with a money payment which the plaintiff must use to purchase an item on the open market. As in the above example, it may be less costly for the defendant to provide the plaintiff with a job, and thus earnings, to satisfy rehabilitation needs than if the defendant simply pays the plaintiff to purchase these items. Also, in exploring the *what* of distribution the parties should examine whether there are substitute goods or other forms of exchange that could be used to expand what is available for division.

By whom and *when* solutions can be illustrated by the following solution drawn from an actual legal negotiation. In the settlement of a large antitrust case against drug manufacturers an original settlement figure of $100 million was considered inadequate when a group of drug wholesalers and retailers requested more than the $3 million originally allocated to them. A change in the distribution of the settlement fund would have been a time consuming and costly process given the nature of the classes of litigants. The settlement terms required that no one receive payment until the time for appeal had run. A solution was devised whereby the defendant drug companies placed a large portion of the total settlement in a bank account in trust for the plaintiffs. Thus, the defendants were able to take a corporate tax deduction in one year and by accruing interest the plaintiffs received an augmented settlement award one year later. In this solution, the bank, as a third party, increased the resources by paying interest to the plaintiff. The use of third parties to expand resources available to the negotiating parties is a common device for solving problems. In real estate transactions, for example, a buyer and seller can expand the material of their negotiation by persuading the broker to take a reduced commission.

Variations on the *how* and *how much* of distribution are illustrated by the types of creative sharing arrangements discussed above, such as joint custody, shared ownership, and preservation of items with geographic or other integrity.

In addition to these devices the growing negotiation literature is replete with other suggestions for expanding resources or exploiting trade-offs between the parties so that more solutions will be available on the "efficient frontier." For example, in a one item pricing problem, the parties can both be made better off by aggregating items. In one of the classic negotiation problems in the literature a tourist enters a grocery store with the intention of buying a single can of beans. By focusing on the low price the tourist wants to pay for one can and the seemingly high price the grocer wishes to charge, the parties discern no range of agreement. But by buying more than one can of beans, the tourist is able to get a lower unit price and the grocer a reasonable profit. This is a simple case of producing a better or more economically efficient result by searching for ways to increase each party's gain without hurting the other side. Aggregating units may also be seen as taking advantage of a long-term conception of needs. While at the moment the tourist is concerned with buying only one can and the seller with the short-term profit, the parties can meet their long-term needs by buying a larger quantity of food for the future and taking a long-term rather than short-term profit. As a corollary, in some cases where the parties are focused on larger units in the negotiation, disaggregation may also lead to a greater number of items or solutions.

As another device for broadening the conception of a problem and expanding resources, Fisher and Ury have recently suggested that negotiators examine how problems would be solved by those with expertise in another field. For example, hotly contested public interest litigation against public agencies such as departments of welfare, prisons, and schools focuses not only on liability but also on the availability of funds to accomplish institutional changes. One of the major issues in such cases is to look at the problems from the perspective of financiers or legislators who must find a source of funds to pay for a particular project.

This device can be used productively by examining the checklist of needs and seeing how fundraisers, tax lawyers, and economists might solve the economic problems, psychologists the psychological problems, and so on. The approach requires lawyers to step out of their own worlds of expertise and control and may lead to additional expense. Although learning to break through the paradigms of professional training and ways of looking at the world may be difficult, there is a rapidly growing literature on increasing creativity by exploring new or different paradigms.

* * *

1. Planning

As the discussion thus far should indicate, the crux of the problem-solving approach is the conceptualization and planning which precede any execution of the negotiation. A problem-solving conception of negotiation should be distinguished from cooperative or collaborative negotiation. The latter refers to particular behaviors engaged in during the negotiation, such as "being flexible, disclosing information and establishing good relationships with the other negotiator." These behaviors may be useful in problem-solving negotiations, but they can also be used as tactics in adversarial negotiations where their purpose is to achieve greater individual gain. The conceptualization used in planning problem-solving negotiation is useful in all negotiation, regardless of the particular behaviors chosen in the executory stages. Planning may indicate that needs are truly incompatible and call for the use of adversarial strategies to maximize individual gain, or that resort to adjudication is necessary.

Although economic evaluation of the case and some prediction of how a court would rule in a dispute resolution will still be appropriate, potential solutions need not be limited to some prediction of the mid-point compromise between estimated first offers. Instead, the planning stages of a problem-solving negotiation resemble the brainstorming process described by Fisher & Ury in *Getting to Yes*. The process emphasizes exploring and considering both parties' underlying needs and objectives and the devices suggested earlier in this Article for expanding resources. The problem solver who has engaged in a brainstorming planning session is likely to approach a negotiation with a number of possible proposals which can be offered for two-sided brainstorming with the other party. While the planning stages of an adversarial negotiation may narrow and make the offers more precise, the problem solving planning stages are more likely to result in a broadening of solutions. As Fisher & Ury point out, the key to creative problem solving is to separate the creative stages of planning from the necessarily more rigid judgment stages. The more potential solutions a negotiator is able to bring to the bargaining table, the more probable it is that agreement will be reached; stalemate and rejection are less likely to occur. In the legal context these brainstorming sessions should include the client, as she may have some solutions of her own, as well as important insights into what the other party desires.

The planning discussed above is primarily substantive planning focused on potential solutions rather than strategic planning focused on what positions to take in the negotiation. Strategic planning may depend on how willing the other party is to depart from the more familiar adversarial negotiation process. At the intersection of substantive and strategic planning are considerations of what information about the other party's needs is necessary to plan for solutions acceptable to the other party. An example best illustrates this point.

Suppose that in a lawsuit based on concealment of a leaky roof in the sale of a residence, the plaintiff has sued for $10,000, the cost of repairing the roof. However, a more extensive portion of the roof was repaired than that which seemed necessary to prevent leaks. The plaintiff has been forced to take out a bank loan in order to repair the roof. This is a further encumbrance on the property, and the plaintiff is having a great deal of difficulty making all of the payments on the house. In addition, the plaintiff is concerned that her parents will learn she bought the house without following their advice to have an inspection made. The defendant seller of the house needs to make payments on her own house and is worried about the possibility of rescission. A bona fide dispute about the facts is whether the defendant misrepresented the facts, and if so, whether he did so negligently or intentionally. The seller holds a second mortgage on the house and the plaintiff now threatens to withhold payment. The plaintiff has taken the deposition of the defendant's former housekeeper who does remember a leaky roof when the defendant was in possession.

Assuming that we represent the plaintiff in this case, there are a number of needs that can be identified. Economically, the plaintiff would like to recover the cost of the roof repair, probably with a minimum of transaction costs. Depending on her dealings and relationship with the defendant, the plaintiff might wish to have the defendant's actions declared legally fraudulent. Recall, however, that in this example the defendant holds a second mortgage on the house so that the plaintiff and the defendant will have a continuing relationship if the plaintiff remains in the house. The plaintiff's social needs may include preventing her parents from discovering that she bought the house without an inspection. Psychologically, it is possible that the plaintiff feels both foolish for not discovering the leak and angry because it was hidden. Furthermore, the plaintiff may feel that the defendant's deception was morally wrong and she may want an apology, payment as punishment, and/or an assurance that this is the only undisclosed defect.

At this point all we know of the defendant's needs may be what we learned from our client, the plaintiff. We know, for example, that the defendant needs the money from the second mortgage to pay the mortgage on her own new home. We may know that the defendant would prefer not to have a legal judgment of fraud entered against her because it will damage her credit rating. Similarly, the defendant may not want a lawsuit for fraud to become public because it could damage her relationship with business associates or her reputation in the community. Finally, it is possible that because the housekeeper has already given testimony against her, the defendant fears losing a lawsuit and may feel regretful or guilty about what she has done. Note that many of the assumptions or speculations about the defendant's needs have to be more fully discovered, either in pretrial discovery or in informal investigation, or tested in the negotiation.

Having identified the parties' needs, we can now begin to consider a number of general solutions. These may include such things as settling the case privately because both parties fear publicity, an apology and new promise that nothing else is defective, and perhaps a delayed or installment payment from defendant to plaintiff, or a reduction on the plaintiff's obligation on the second mortgage. The one remaining issue which is likely to result in conflicting views, the amount of the settlement, can be made less difficult either by having an independent determination of the proper amount to repair the original damage or by expanding the resources through time payments and tax structures that may permit the plaintiff to realize more dollars than the defendant actually pays out.

The structure of this example may not work in all cases, but it illustrates how the analysis of both parties' needs may lead to a number of possible solutions.

2. Execution

To the extent that both parties engage in a problem-solving negotiation structure, the negotiation is likely to resemble a fluid brainstorming session. Even if only one party has engaged in a problem-solving planning process, the negotiation need not be reduced to an adversarial exercise. First, the parties may begin with a greater number of possible solutions simply because two heads are better than one. In addition, as empirical research has demonstrated, when both parties approach negotiation with the objective of working collaboratively, more of the information reflecting the parties' needs may be revealed, facilitating the search for solutions. Thus, in the case of the leaky roof, the amount of damages might be easier to determine if both parties approached the problem by looking for ways to reach agreement than if one approached the problem as simply maximizing or minimizing payment, using litigation as a threat. On the other hand, even a single problem solver can propose alternative ways of measuring liability that may eventually be successful, if she has accurately determined the other party's needs.

When the problem solver is able to present a number of different solutions which potentially satisfy at least some of the other party's needs, it is more likely that the adversarial concession and argumentation pattern can be avoided than if she presents a single demand. The parties can consider variations of each of the proposals using the techniques of game theorists who simply alter the coordinates slightly at each play to see if a more efficient solution can be achieved. Thus, the negotiation game may be played on a multi-dimensional field rather than on one that is linear, or two dimensional. In the leaky roof case one party may suggest a number of different methods of payment, such as reduction of the second mortgage, lump-sum, or installment payments at different discount factors, rather than simply demanding $10,000.

In addition to the different offer structure, problem-solving negotiations are likely to have different information sharing processes. As discussed above, many conventional works on negotiation urge the negotiator not to reveal information. The problem solver recognizes that he is more likely to develop solutions which meet the parties' needs by revealing his own needs or objectives, while at the same time trying to learn about the other party's. In short, there is no incentive to dissemble. When this is the goal, the process consists of asking questions in search of clarification and information, rather than making statements or arguments designed to persuade the other party to accept one's own world view.

On the other hand, totally uninhibited information sharing may be as dysfunctional as withholding information. In experimental simulations Pruitt & Lewis found that there was not necessarily a correlation between free information exchange and joint profit. Instead, joint profit was associated with information processing — that is, the ability to listen to, receive, and understand the information and how it related concretely to the problem. Furthermore, information sharing in a thoughtless and unrestricted fashion may lead to the sharpening of conflict as value differences are revealed in competing goals and needs. In problem-solving negotiation it is crucial to understand the usefulness and function of particular pieces of information — such as exploring how strongly one party desires something — because each piece is related to possible solutions. Problem solvers must determine what information is needed and why, and must be able to absorb information from the other side to test assumptions about needs, goals or objectives.

An example taken from my negotiation course can illustrate. In negotiating a partnership agreement, students are given information about each of the prospective partners. One partner has an immediate need for a relatively high salary because he must provide for a disabled child. The other partner would also like a high salary, but is more concerned about creating the partnership because he is excited about entering a new business. Students, who in my experience are more likely to be adversarial negotiators, have tended to approach the salary negotiation as a conventional zero-sum negotiation. When, as happens occasionally, one side reveals why the salary

is needed, a greater variety of solutions seem to come unlocked, such as slid-
ing scales, deferred versus immediate compensation, special provisions for
the child, and salary trade-offs for other items. In this situation the party
who learns of the disabled child either may be moved by sympathy or by the
more instrumental realization that if this is of concern to his future partner it should be dealt with now so it is not a future drain on the partnership.
Whatever the motivation, the new information can serve as a source of new
solutions ending an otherwise stalemated salary negotiation. Obviously,
not all negotiation problems will contain such useful information, but the
problem solver is willing to share information about needs that may facilitate such solutions. Thus, problem solving produces a more sophisticated
calculus concerning what information should be revealed.

* * *

Leonard Greenhalgh,[*] *The Case Against Winning in Negotiations*
3 NEGOT. J. 167, 168-73 (1987)[**]

* * *

Prevalence of Win-Lose Metaphors

Because of the prevalence of sports metaphors in the United States and
in other Western cultures, winning comes up often as a theme in describing
negotiations. Sports metaphors are somewhat interchangeable with military
metaphors, as is evident from the prevalence of hybrid metaphors. We
speak of war games, the arms race, tennis volleys, shots on goal, knocking
out a machine gun emplacement, and designation of players as lines, for-
wards, captains, guards, and so on. Thus it is not always possible to tell precisely when someone using win-lose metaphors is visualizing sports or war,
and harder still to tell what imagery those metaphors evoke in the listener
or reader. Either way, the win-lose metaphor is limiting when used uncritically to characterize negotiations.

Win-lose metaphors are pressed into service to characterize a wide variety of interaction situations, especially those in which there is some incompatibility of wills or interests. Sometimes win-lose metaphors are
appropriate, such as when describing the relationship between two businesses attempting to gain sales among a limited set of customers. Indeed,
it is difficult to avoid describing firms in such circumstances as "competing."

---

[*] Leonard Greenhalgh is Professor of Management at Tuck School of Business, Dartmouth
College. This article discusses the difficulties created by negotiation metaphors drawn from
sports and games that have "winners" and "losers."

[**] Copyright © 1987 Negotiation Journal. Reprinted with permission of Blackwell Publishing, Inc. and the Program on Negotiation at Harvard Law School.

However, more often than not, the application of the win-lose metaphor is inappropriate to describe the interaction situation.

* * *

Pitfalls of Win-Lose Metaphors

The most obvious disadvantage of win-lose metaphors is their inherent zero-sum quality. Sports contests, like battles, are meant to be won. The common norm is for players to strive to the best of their ability, strength, and stamina to defeat the other player (or team). In fact, to do less is "unsportsmanlike"; nobody wants to beat or even be narrowly defeated by a player who wasn't trying very hard. Instead, the losing player is supposed to *escalate* the attack to make the other player's victory as difficult as possible. The emphasis on winning is so heavy that even a tie score is undesirable. In fact, many sports have rules that preclude ties or have mechanisms to eliminate them such as "sudden death overtime." As a result of these connotations, when the sports metaphor is applied to negotiation situations, there is little room for compromise, or even mercy.

Furthermore, the notion of a "win-win solution" in this context makes no sense. The metaphor cannot be stretched to accommodate a win-win outcome without violating the essence of sports contests or military engagements. It seems more advisable to abandon the inescapably zero-sum winning metaphor, therefore, when discussing nonzero-sum outcomes. It is better to talk about mutual advantage, because the focus is on the benefits of cooperation rather than on winning; the latter focus tends to portray the other negotiator as an opponent and implies that the benefit has to come at someone else's expense. Simply, the "win-win" notion, besides being illogical, conjures up all the wrong images.

* * *

Winning-oriented sports metaphors have several disadvantages beyond fostering a zero-sum perspective. One of these is the emphasis on rules rather than relationships. In sports contests, it is generally acceptable for players to stretch rules to the limit; the norms tolerate almost any tactic that can be used in pursuit of victory, so long as it doesn't violate explicit rules. Innovations within the rules that give the contestant an advantage make heroes of the rule-benders.

Knute Rockne, for instance, became a legend when he discovered that there was nothing in the rules of football that precluded a forward pass. This invention revolutionized football strategy. Similarly, race car designer Jim Hall discovered that the rules of road racing were silent on the topic of aerodynamic devices. So he added an "upside-down" wing to his Chaparral cars to force the tires against the pavement and thereby increase the grip necessary for high cornering speeds. This innovation, and the ground-effects cars he subsequently pioneered, changed the shape of automobiles. Other sports have seen analogous breakthroughs by people who violated the spirit of the rules. The important point here is that the "unfair advantage" they thereby gained was usually idolized rather than condemned.

Despite our admiration for those who sought the maximum advantage over competitors within the limits of the explicit rules of the game, we have to be critical of such behavior in negotiations. In fact, we need to examine carefully the effects of focusing on rules rather than relationships.

It appears, first of all, that a focus on rules easily can lead to attempts to exploit rather than negotiate fairly. The tactics of the sports-oriented negotiator are constrained by explicit rules rather than being motivated by the good of all the parties involved. In other words, rather than devise creative solutions to mutual problems, negotiators often spend valuable time and energy trying to figure out how much they can get away with. Even worse, ethical considerations tend to become subordinated to the rules applied to the situation; this has a profound impact on trust.

Consider, for instance, two close friends playing poker. In the game, they have no qualms about deceiving each other. In fact, the poker game would be no fun if both people were open and honest about the cards they held. Now, visualize the same two friends negotiating, with one trying to sell a major appliance to the other. Suppose the seller has found out that the manufacturer of the appliance is on the verge of going out of business, and, consequently, the value of the appliance will plummet because the guarantee will be worthless and spare parts will be difficult to obtain. The seller who defines this situation as a game might say nothing about the risks of buying the appliance. By contrast, the seller who focused on the relationship is more likely to make a full disclosure of information to the friend, or will sell the appliance to a stranger instead.

A more subtle rules-oriented effect can occur in collective bargaining. The National Labor Relations Act specifies that the parties must "bargain in good faith." If management conceives of the interaction as a rules-bounded game, management's tactics may be to cooperate as little as possible without violating "the letter of the law"; there will be little emphasis on mutual accommodation and the development of goodwill. This situation actually happens with surprising frequency. Almost inevitably, management's relationship with the union suffers as a result of such treatment, and managers subsequently blame the union for not cooperating for the good of all, as if their own behavior had nothing to do with the outcome.

* * *

Another disadvantage of having one's thinking shaped by sports metaphors is that they induce disputants to focus on the immediate conflict episode rather than take a longer-term perspective. Sports contests are discrete, independent events. Irrespective of who won or lost the last game, the scores are set at zero at the beginning of the next game. Furthermore, sports norms would not permit players to let one team win this week in exchange for reciprocal leniency by the other team the next week. Thus, the history and future of the ongoing relationship between contestants is irrelevant in sports.

When this same short-term perspective is applied to negotiation situations, the conflict becomes much more difficult to deal with than it would be otherwise. Negotiators with a short-term perspective can choose harsh or exploitative tactics without fear of repercussions, because they view any future interaction as "a new game." Likewise, there is nothing to gain in the future from being accommodating in the current interaction, since anything "given up" is perceived as forever lost. From this standpoint, intransigence — and even aggression — is rational.

For instance, imagine a salesman with a short-term perspective engaged in a dispute over the interpretation of ambiguous terms in a sales contract. Let's say, furthermore, that the purchasing agent is predisposed to avoid conflicts. The salesman acts on his belief that he can "win" the dispute by applying pressure: browbeating, ad hominem attacks, threats, withholding or distorting information, and other aggressive behaviors. This approach does indeed result in the predicted concessions from the purchasing agent. However, any winning in this scenario is likely to be a Pyrrhic victory: The purchasing agent will subsequently go to great lengths to avoid doing business with this abrasive salesman, and will no doubt tell other purchasing agents — and possibly the salesman's superior — about the experience. Thus the long-term cost in terms of relationships and reputation offsets the short-term gain.

A final disadvantage of the win-lose metaphor is that it induces negotiators to try to fractionate the other party. The rationale is that if the opposing group can be thrown into disarray, that group is easier to defeat.

Fractionating the other party has the advantage of weakening coalitions; however, this practice also may subsequently make the conflict more difficult to resolve, simply because there is no clear leader or unified group that can agree to a comprehensive settlement. The Palestine Liberation Organization, the Organization of Petroleum Exporting Companies, and the Afghan resistance movement are familiar examples of parties to a conflict whose fractionation makes them difficult to negotiate with successfully. What happens is that some subgroups agree to a settlement, while others resist, engaging in passive resistance, subtle sabotage, wildcat strikes, outright defiance, or turning on the subgroups who have agreed.

A Better Metaphor?

What makes the win-lose metaphor particularly insidious in negotiations is its invisibility: It is so innocuous to most people that it goes unnoticed and, therefore, its usefulness and disadvantages are not evaluated. The metaphor is innocuous because it seems superficially compatible with the ways companies compete in the marketplace, but this apparent compatibility is actually spurious. Relationships between people are qualitatively different from relationships between organizations; therefore, people need to assess the metaphor's advantages and limitations for each application.

Sometimes a negotiator will encounter a zero-sum situation that is truly a single transaction unaffected by a past relationship or a potential future relationship. When this happens, a competitive approach is useful, and making sense of the situation in terms of winning and losing is appropriate. These situations, however, are rare.

The more typical situation involves an ongoing relationship and has some positive-sum possibilities. In these circumstances, awareness of how the win-lose metaphor can affect a person's thinking about a dispute and its settlement alerts the negotiator to be aware of the other party's frame of reference. When the other party is trying to "win" a negotiation, a negotiator might try to make the other party aware of the shortcomings of a win-lose approach. If such persuasion is to no avail, then the negotiator should also attempt to win, otherwise he or she is destined to lose.

* * *

WILLIAM URY,[*] GETTING PAST NO
7-13 (Rev. ed. 1993)[**]

* * *

The Goal:		Strategy:
Joint Problem-solving	Barriers to Cooperation	Breakthrough Negotiation
• People Sitting Side by Side	• Your Reaction • Their Emotion	• Go to the Balcony • Step to Their Side
• Facing the Problem	• Their Position	• Reframe
• Reaching a Mutually Satisfactory Agreement	• Their Dissatisfaction • Their Power	• Build Them a Golden Bridge • Use Power to Educate

* * *

At the start, you may try to get your opponent to tackle the problem jointly, but instead you may find yourselves in a face-to-face confrontation.

---

[*] William L. Ury is Co-Founder of the Program on Negotiation, Harvard University, and the Director of the Global Negotiation Project. This excerpt outlines an approach to difficult negotiations that he calls "breakthrough" negotiating.

[**] Copyright © 1991, 1993 by William Ury. Used by permission of Bantam Books, a division of Random House, Inc.

It is all too easy to get drawn into a ferocious emotional battle, to fall back into the familiar routine of adopting rigid positions, or to let the other side take advantage of you.

There are real-world barriers that get in the way of cooperation. The five most common ones are:

Your reaction. The first barrier lies within you. Human beings are reaction machines. When you're under stress, or when you encounter a NO, or feel you are being attacked, you naturally feel like striking back. Usually this just perpetuates the action-reaction cycle that leaves both sides losers. Or, alternatively, you may react by impulsively giving in just to end the negotiation and preserve the relationship. You lose and, having demonstrated your weakness, you expose yourself to exploitation by others. The problem you thus face in negotiation is not only the other side's difficult behavior but your own reaction, which can easily perpetuate that behavior.

Their emotion. The next barrier is the other side's negative emotions. Behind their attacks may lie anger and hostility. Behind their rigid positions may lie fear and distrust. Convinced they are right and you are wrong, they may refuse to listen. Seeing the world as eat-or-be-eaten, they may feel justified in using nasty tactics.

Their position. In joint problem-solving, you face the problem and attack it together. The barrier in the way is the other side's positional behavior: their habit of digging into a position and trying to get you to give in. Often they know no other way to negotiate. They are merely using the conventional negotiating tactics they first learned in the sandbox. In their eyes, the only alternative is for *them* to give in — and they certainly don't want to do that.

Their dissatisfaction. Your goal may be to reach a mutually satisfactory agreement, but you may find the other side not at all interested in such an outcome. They may not see *how* it will benefit them. Even if you can satisfy their interests, they may fear losing face if they have to back down. And if it is *your* idea, they may reject it for that reason alone.

Their power. Finally, if the other side sees the negotiation as a win-lose proposition, they will be determined to beat you. They may be guided by the precept "What's mine is mine. What's yours is negotiable." If they can get what they want by power plays, why should they cooperate with you?

Getting past no requires breaking through each of these five barriers to cooperation: your reaction, their emotion, their position, their dissatisfaction, and their power. It is easy to believe that stonewalling, attacks, and tricks are just part of the other side's basic nature, and that there is little you can do to change such difficult behavior. But you *can* affect this behavior if you can deal successfully with its underlying motivations.

The Breakthrough Strategy

This book lays out a five-step strategy for breaking through each of these five barriers — the strategy of *breakthrough negotiation*.

An analogy from sailing will help explain this strategy. In sailing, you rarely if ever get to your destination by heading straight for it. In between you and your goal are strong winds and tides, reefs and shoals, not to speak of storms and squalls. To get where you want to go, you need to tack — to zigzag your way toward your destination.

The same is true in the world of negotiation. Your desired destination is a mutually satisfactory agreement. The direct route — focusing first on interests and then developing options that satisfy those interests — seems straightforward and easy. But in the real world of strong reactions and emotions, rigid positions, powerful dissatisfactions and aggressions, you often cannot get to a mutually satisfactory agreement by the direct route. Instead, you need to navigate past no by tacking — taking an indirect route.

The essence of the breakthrough strategy is *indirect action*. It requires you to do the opposite of what you naturally feel like doing in difficult situations. When the other side stonewalls or attacks, you may feel like responding in kind. Confronted with hostility, you may argue. Confronted with unreasonable positions, you may reject. Confronted with intransigence, you may push. Confronted with aggression, you may escalate. But this just leaves you frustrated, playing the other side's game by *their* rules.

Your single greatest opportunity as a negotiator is to *change the game*. Instead of playing their way, let them have *your* way — the way of joint problem-solving. The great home-run hitter Sadahara Oh, the Japanese equivalent of Babe Ruth, once explained his batting secret. Oh said that he looked on the opposing pitcher as his *partner*, who with every pitch was serving up an *opportunity* for him to hit a home run. Breakthrough negotiators do the same: They treat their opponents as negotiating partners who are presenting an opportunity to reach a mutually satisfactory agreement.

As in the Japanese martial arts of judo, jujitsu, and aikido, you need to avoid pitting your strength directly against your opponent's. Since efforts to break down the other side's resistance usually only increase it, you try to go around their resistance. That is the way to break through.

Breakthrough negotiation is the opposite of imposing your position on the other side. Rather than pounding in a new idea from the outside, you encourage them to reach for it from within. Rather than telling them what to do, you let them figure it out. Rather than pressuring them to change their mind, you create an environment in which they can learn. Only *they* can break through their own resistance; *your* job is to *help* them.

Their resistance to joint problem-solving stems from the five barriers described above. Your job as a breakthrough negotiator is to clear away the barriers that lie between their NO and the YES of a mutually satisfactory agreement. For each of the five barriers, there is a corresponding step in the strategy:

Step One. Since the first barrier is your natural reaction, the first step involves suspending that reaction. To engage in joint problem-solving, you need to regain your mental balance and stay focused on achieving what you want. A useful image for getting perspective on the situation is to imagine yourself standing on a balcony looking down on your negotiation. The first step in the breakthrough strategy is to *Go to the Balcony.*

Step Two. The next barrier for you to overcome is the other side's negative emotions — their defensiveness, fear, suspicion, and hostility. It is all too easy to get drawn into an argument, but you need to resist this temptation. Just as you've regained your mental balance, you need to help the other side regain *theirs.* To create the right climate for joint problem-solving, you need to defuse their negative emotions. To do this, you need to do the opposite of what they expect. They expect you to behave like an adversary. Instead, you should take their side by listening to them, acknowledging their points and their feelings, agreeing with them, and showing them respect. If you want to sit side by side facing the problem, you will need to *Step to Their Side.*

Step Three. Now you want to tackle the problem together. This is hard to do, however, when the other side digs into their position and tries to get you to give in. It's natural to feel like rejecting their position, but this will only lead them to dig in further. So do the opposite. Accept whatever they say and reframe it as an attempt to deal with the problem. For example, take their position and probe behind it: "Tell me more. Help me understand *why* you want that." Act as if they were your partners genuinely interested in solving the problem. The third step in the breakthrough strategy is to *Reframe.*

Step Four. While you may now have engaged the other side in joint problem-solving, you may still be far from reaching a mutually satisfactory agreement. The other side may be dissatisfied, unconvinced of the benefits of agreement. You may feel like pushing them, but this will only make them more resistant. So do the opposite. In the words of the Chinese sage, "build a golden bridge" from their position to a mutually satisfactory solution. You need to bridge the gap between their interests and yours. You need to help them save face and make the outcome look like a victory for them. The fourth step is to *Build Them a Golden Bridge.*

Step Five. Despite your best efforts, the other side may still refuse to cooperate, believing they can beat you at the power game. You may be tempted at this point to escalate. Threats and coercion often backfire, however, and lead to costly and futile battles. The alternative is to use power not to escalate, but to educate. Enhance your negotiating power and use it to bring them back to the table. Show them that they cannot win by themselves but only together with you. The fifth step is to *Use Power to Educate.*

* * *

Jennifer Gerarda Brown,* *Creativity and Problem-Solving*
87 MARQ. L. REV. 697, 698-706 (2004)**

* * *

Most teachers and trainers of interest-based negotiation will spend some time teaching creative thinking. Following the template set forth in *Getting to YES*, they will encourage their students to "brainstorm." Brainstorming, as most readers of this essay know, is a somewhat formalized process in which participants work together to generate ideas. I say that it is formalized because it proceeds according to two important ground rules: participants agree not to evaluate the ideas while they are brainstorming, and they agree not to take "ownership" of the ideas. They strive to generate options and put them on the table, no matter how wacky or far-fetched they may seem. The "no evaluation" rule encourages participants to suspend their natural urge to criticize, edit, or censor the ideas. Evaluation can come later, but the notion here is that solutions will flow more easily if people are not assessing even as they articulate them. The "no ownership" rule also facilitates innovation because participants are encouraged to feel free to propose an idea or solution without endorsing it — no one can later attribute the idea to the person who proposed it, or try to hold it against that person. People can therefore propose ideas that might actually disadvantage them and benefit their counterparts without conceding that they would actually agree to such proposals in the final analysis. The ground rules for brainstorming constrain the natural inclination to criticize, so that participants are free to imagine, envision, and play with ideas, even though these processes come less easily to them. Why is brainstorming so popular, both in practice and in negotiation training? Perhaps the answer lies not so much in what it activates, but in what it disables. What I mean is that it may be easier to teach people what *not* to do — rather than what to do affirmatively — in order to enhance their creative thinking. We may not know much about how to unleash new sources of creativity for negotiators, but we are pretty sure about some things that impede creative thinking. Theory and practice suggest that creative thinking is difficult when people jump to conclusions, close off discussion, or seize upon an answer prematurely. Indeed, the very heuristics that make decision-making possible — those pathways that permit people to make positive and sometimes normative judgments — can also lead people astray. One of the ways they may be led astray is that the heuristic prompts them to decide too quickly what something is or should be. Once judgment has occurred, it is tough to justify the expenditure of additional energy that creative thinking would

---

* Jennifer Gerarda Brown is Professor of Law and Director, Center on Dispute Resolution, Quinnipiac University School of Law. Her article discusses various techniques for encouraging creative problem solving.

require. Creativity could be considered the "anti-heuristic"; it keeps multiple pathways of perception and decision-making open, even when people are tempted to choose a single, one-way route to a solution. If we do nothing else, we can attempt to delay this kind of judgment until negotiators have considered multiple options. Brainstorming provides the structure for this kind of delay.

But is brainstorming the only technique for enhancing creativity? The answer would seem to be an easy "no." Psychologists and other specialists in creative thinking have much to teach us beyond brainstorming. . . .

* * *

A. Wordplay

Once an issue or problem is articulated, it is possible to play with the words expressing that problem in order to improve understanding and sometimes to yield new solutions.

1. Shifting Emphasis

To take a fairly simple example, suppose that two neighbors are in a dispute because cigarette butts and other small pieces of trash, deposited by Mr. Smith in his own front yard, are blowing into Mr. Jones's yard, and those that remain in Mr. Smith's yard are detracting from the appearance of the neighborhood (at least as Mr. Jones sees it). Mr. Jones might ask himself (or a mediator at the neighborhood justice center), "How can I get Mr. Smith to stop littering in his yard?" Shifting the emphasis in this sentence brings into focus various aspects of the problem and suggests possible solutions addressing those specific aspects. Consider the different meanings of the following sentences:

"How can I get Mr. Smith to stop littering in his yard?"

"How can I get *Mr. Smith* to stop littering in his yard?"

"How can I get Mr. Smith to stop *littering* in his yard?"

"How can I get Mr. Smith to stop littering in *his* yard?"

"How can I get Mr. Smith to stop littering in his *yard*?"

As the focus of the problem shifts, so too different potential solutions might emerge to address the problem as specifically articulated.

2. Changing a Word

Sometimes changing a word in the sentence helps to reformulate the problem in a way that suggests new solutions. In the example above, Mr. Jones might change the phrase "littering in his yard" to something else, such as "neglecting his yard" or "hanging out in his yard." It may be that something besides littering lies at the root of the problem, and a solution will be found, for example, not in stopping the littering, but in more regularized yard work.

3. Deleting a Word

Through word play, parties can delete words or phrases to see whether broadening the statement of the problem more accurately or helpfully captures its essence. Mr. Jones might delete the phrase "Mr. Smith" from his formulation of the problem, and thereby discover that it is not just Mr. Smith's yard, but the entire street, that is looking bad. Focusing on Mr. Smith as the source of the problem may be counterproductive; Mr. Jones might discover that he needs to organize all of the homeowners on his block to battle littering in order to make a difference. Deleting words sometimes spurs creativity by removing an overly restrictive focus on the issue or problem.

4. Adding a New Word

A final form of word play that can spur creative thinking is sometimes called "random word association." Through this process, participants choose a word randomly and then think of ways to associate it with the problem. "Suppose Mr. Jones and Mr. Smith were given the word 'work', and asked how it might relate to their dispute." Here are some possible results:

> *Work (time, effort)*: Mr. Smith will try to work harder to keep his yard looking nice, and he will check Mr. Jones's yard every Saturday to make sure there are no cigarette butts or other pieces of trash in it.

> *Work (being operational or functional)*: What the neighborhood needs is a sense of cohesion; Mr. Jones and Mr. Smith will organize a neighborhood beautification project to try to instill a sense of community among their neighbors.

> *Work (job)*: Although Mr. Smith's odd working hours sometimes lead him to smoke on his front porch and chat with his friends or family late at night (after Mr. Jones has gone to bed), Mr. Smith will stay in the back of his house after 10 p.m., further from Mr. Jones's bedroom window.

As the different meanings and resulting associations of "work" are explored by the parties, they discover new ways to solve their shared problem. Other seemingly unrelated words might trigger still more associations and more potential solutions.

Adding words can also be helpful if participants insert adjectives that narrow the problem so it appears more manageable. Mr. Jones might ask, "How can I get Mr. Smith to stop littering in his *front* yard?" Narrowing the problem from all of Mr. Smith's property to the front yard might suggest agreements that could keep Mr. Smith's front yard looking nice but still permit him to use other parts of his property (such as a side or back yard) as he wishes. This approach to word play builds upon the insight that many creative solutions are incremental. The problem will not seem so daunting to the parties when it is narrowed, and they can address the larger issues step by step.

These techniques of word play (especially random word association) are designed to "force the mind to 'jump across' its usual pathways (mental ruts), or make new connections between old pathways in order to create a new idea out of two seemingly disparate ideas." The exercises might feel mechanical to the parties at first, but if adopted with some energy and good faith, they could help the parties to enhance the creativity of their thinking.

B. Mind-Mapping/Word Clustering

Weinstein and Morton also describe a form of word association called "Word Clustering" or "Mind Mapping," in which participants:

> write the problem out and then write down words that come to mind, randomly, as related to the problem. The words are written without any particular order all over a paper, and once that aspect is completed, lines are drawn connecting the words as connections come to mind.

This technique, they explain, can help participants discover the inner pathways by which their brains are connecting aspects of the problem in hidden ways. These connections can then lead parties to creative ideas about the problem.

C. De Bono's "Six Hats" Technique

Edward de Bono has proposed a technique he calls "Six Thinking Hats," in which six aspects of a problem are assessed independently. As problem solvers symbolically don each of six differently colored hats, they focus on an aspect of the problem associated with each color: red for emotions, white for facts, yellow for positive aspects of the situation, green for future implications, black for critique, and blue for process. As Weinstein and Morton point out, the technique of isolating the black/critique hat may be especially important for lawyers, whose tendency to move quickly into a critical mode may prevent them from seeing other important aspects of a problem. If the black hat is worn at or near the end of the process, the Six Hats technique displays a characteristic shared by brainstorming: it delays critique and judgment until other approaches can be tried. And shutting down judgment may enable creativity, as suggested above. By forcing themselves to address separately the emotional, factual, and process issues at stake in a problem, parties may discover room for creative solutions. Similarly, creative solutions are sometimes found in the terms of a future relationship between the parties. Wearing the green hat may force participants to come to terms with a future they would rather ignore.

The prospect of changing hats, even (perhaps especially) if it is done symbolically, could make some participants uncomfortable. Negotiators and neutrals should bear in mind that age, sex, ethnicity and other cultural specifics may create dignitary interests for some participants that would be threatened or compromised by some techniques for boosting creative thought. Some people would feel embarrassed or humiliated if they were asked to engage in the theatrics required by some of these exercises. For others, the chance to pretend or play might be just the prod they need to open new avenues of thought. In a spirit of flexibility (surely a necessary condition for creativity), therefore, one should be thinking of ways to modify these techniques to fit other needs of the parties.

D. Atlas of Approaches

Another technique for stimulating creative ideas about a problem from a variety of perspectives is called the "Atlas of Approaches." Roger Fisher, Elizabeth Kopelman and Andrea Kupfer Schneider propose this approach in *Beyond Machiavelli*, their book on international negotiation. Using the Atlas of Approaches technique, participants adopt the perspectives of professionals from a variety of fields. By asking themselves, for example, "What would a journalist do?", "What would an economist do?", "How would a psychologist view this?", and so on, negotiators are able to form a more interdisciplinary view of their problem. With this more complete picture of the issues and potential outcomes, they might be able to connect disciplines in ways that give rise to creative solutions.

E. Visualization

When parties use the visualization technique, they take time to imagine the situation they desire, one in which their problem is solved. What do they see? What specific conditions exist, and how might each of those conditions be achieved? Weinstein and Morton suggest that parties can engage in visualization simply by closing their eyes and thinking about the problem in terms that are visual rather than abstract. Another approach is to "look at the problem from above, and see things otherwise invisible." The goal is to deploy a variety of the brain's cognitive pathways (verbal, visual, spatial and abstract), the better to make connections that give rise to creative solutions.

* * *

G. "Feel My Pain"

Sometimes people reach creative solutions by focusing sharply on the specific sorts of harm caused by the problem. When one person's decision-making has negative spillover effects on others, economists say that the person's decision or activity is creating "negative externalities." Nalebuff and Ayres argue that "there can be great payoffs to asking whether you're feeling other people's pain," because "[i]gnoring others' interests leads to inefficient decisions." Solutions to this call for the parties to design "incentives so that all parties more fully feel the impacts that their decisions have on each other."

H. Flipping or Reversal

With this technique, one asks whether flipping or reversing a given situation will work. As Edward de Bono explains:

> In the reversal method, one takes things as they are and then turns them round, inside out, upside down, back to front. Then one sees what happens . . . one is not looking for the right answer but for a different arrangement of information which will provoke a different way of looking at the situation.

Chris Honeyman sometimes uses this technique in his work as a neutral when he asks the parties to put forward some really *bad* ideas for resolving the conflict. When people offer ideas in response to a call for "bad" ideas, they may free themselves to offer the ideas they partially or secretly support; again, as in brainstorming, they disclaim ownership of the ideas. It is also possible that the instruction to offer bad ideas stimulates creative thinking because it can seem *funny* to people. Humor is a good stimulant for creativity.

Chris Honeyman's theory is that bad ideas are easy to come by (they can often be found in abundance), and in many bad ideas there resides the kernel of a good idea. Framing them as "bad" ideas effects a sort of reversal or flipping; in de Bono's words, the participants produce a "different arrangement of information." Carrie Menkel-Meadow suggests that negotiators or parties to mediation use another form of reversal when they engage in "perspective-taking" or "role-reversal" exercises.

Most conflicts are multidimensional, giving rise to multiple sites at which elements could be reversed. Once the parties have broken down the situation into component parts, they can try reversing or flipping some elements to see whether this yields superior solutions.

* * *

Roger Fisher,[*] *Negotiating Power: Getting and Using Influence*
27 Am. Behav. Sci. 149, 150-65 (1983)[**]

* * *

How Should We Define Negotiating Power?

It seems best to define "negotiation" as including all cases in which two or more parties are communicating, each for the purpose of influencing the

---

[*] Roger Fisher is Samuel Williston Professor of Law, Emeritus, at Harvard University. This article deals with sources and types of power in negotiations.

[**] Copyright © 1983 American Behavioral Scientist. Reprinted with permission of Sage Publications, Inc.

other's decision. Nothing seems to be gained by limiting the concept to formal negotiations taking place at a table, and much to be gained by defining the subject broadly. Many actions taken away from a table — ranging from making political speeches to building nuclear missiles — are taken for the purpose of "sending a message" to affect decisions of the other side.

The concept of "negotiating power" is more difficult. If I have negotiating power, I have the ability to affect favorably someone else's decision. This being so, one can argue that my power depends upon someone else's perception of my strength, so it is what they *think* that matters, not what I actually have. The other side may be as much influenced by a row of cardboard tanks as by a battalion of real tanks. One can then say that negotiating power is all a matter of perception.

A general who commands a real tank battalion, however, is in a far stronger position than one in charge of a row of cardboard tanks. A false impression of power is extremely vulnerable, capable of being destroyed by a word. In order to avoid focusing our attention on how to deceive other people, it seems best at the outset to identify what constitutes "real" negotiating power — an ability to influence the decisions of others assuming they know the truth. We can then go on to recognize that, in addition, it will be possible at times to influence others through deception, through creating an illusion of power. Even for that purpose, we will need to know what illusion we wish to create. If we are bluffing, what are we bluffing about?

What Kind of Theory Are We Looking For?

An infinite number of truths exist about the negotiation process, just as an infinite number of maps can be drawn of a city. It is easy to conclude that negotiators who are more powerful fare better in negotiations. By and large, negotiators who have more wealth, more friends and connections, good jobs, and more time will fare better in negotiations than will those who are penniless, friendless, unemployed, and in a hurry. Such statements, like the statement that women live longer than men, are true — but they are of little help to someone who wants to negotiate, or to someone who wants to live longer. Similarly, the statement that power plays an important role in negotiation is true — but irrelevant.

As negotiators we want to understand power in some way that helps us. We want diagnostic truths that point toward prescriptive action. The statement that women live longer than men points toward no remedial action. I am unable to live longer by choosing to become a woman. On the other hand, the statement that people who don't smoke live longer than people who do smoke is no truer, but it is far more helpful since I can decide not to smoke.

Thus a lively interplay exists between descriptive and prescriptive theory. The pure scientist may not care whether his truths have any relevance to the world of action; he leaves that to others. But those of us who are primarily concerned with change (one hopes, for the better) are searching for descriptive categories that have prescriptive significance. We are looking for ideas that will help us make better choices. We are not simply trying to describe accurately what happens in a negotiation; we are trying to produce advice of use to negotiators, advice that will help them negotiate better. We need to say something other than that powerful princes tend to dominate less powerful princes, as true as that may be. We are looking for the kind of theory that will help a prince. He, presumably, has two key questions with respect to negotiating power; how to enhance negotiating power and how to use such power as he may have.

Mistaken Views of Negotiating Power

(1) "Physical Force " Negotiating Power"

It is widely believed that in order to enhance our negotiating power we should acquire those assets like a strike-fund, a band of terrorists, or 100 MX missiles, which convey an implicit or explicit threat to harm the other side physically if it fails to agree with us. This belief is based on the assumption that, since threats of physical force undoubtedly exert influence, the ability to make such threats is the essence of negotiating power. Force is seen as the necessary and sufficient element of negotiating power.

Negotiating power is the ability to influence others. The pain that we threaten to inflict if the other side does not decide as we like is simply one factor among many. And as I have written elsewhere, making threats is a particularly expensive and dangerous way of trying to exert influence.

Total negotiating power depends upon many factors. Enhancing negotiating power means building up the combined potential of them all. Exercising negotiating power effectively means orchestrating them in a way that maximizes their cumulative impact. And this is where a second, widely held assumption about negotiating power appears to be mistaken and dangerous.

(2) "Start tough, you can always get soft later."

There is a widespread belief that the best way to start a negotiation is with a hard time. "Let them know early who's in charge." The thought is that since, in the last analysis, physical power may be the decisive factor, the entire negotiation should take place governed by its shadow. Conventional wisdom insists that it is easier to soften one's position than to harden it. A negotiator is encouraged to start off flexing his muscles.

* * *

The notion that it is best to start off a negotiation with a warning or threat of the consequences of nonagreement may result from a false analogy. Other things being equal, it is true that in purely positional bargaining the more extreme one's initial position (the higher a price one demands or the lower a price one offers), the more favorable an agreed result is likely to be. But opening with a very low substantive offer is quite different from opening with a threat of painful consequences if that offer is not accepted. The more firmly one is committed at an early stage to carrying out a threat, the more damaging that threat is to one's negotiating power.

If these two propositions are wrong, how should someone enhance and exercise negotiating power?

Categories of Power

My ability to exert influence depends upon the combined total of a number of different factors. As a first approximation, the following six kinds of power appear to provide useful categories for generating prescriptive advice:

(1) The power of skill and knowledge

(2) The power of a good relationship

(3) The power of a good alternative to negotiating

(4) The power of an elegant solution

(5) The power of legitimacy

(6) The power of commitment

Here is a checklist for would-be negotiators of what they can do in advance of any particular negotiation to enhance their negotiating power. The sequence in which these elements of power are listed is also important.

1. The Power of Skill and Knowledge

All things being equal, a skilled negotiator is better able to influence the decision of others than is an unskilled negotiator. Strong evidence suggests that negotiating skills can be both learned and taught. One way to become a more powerful negotiator is to become a more skillful one. Some of these skills are those of dealing with people: the ability to listen, to become aware of the emotions and psychological concerns of others, to empathize, to be sensitive to their feelings and one's own, to speak different languages, to communicate clearly and effectively, to become integrated so that one's words and nonverbal behavior are congruent and reenforce each other, and so forth.

Other skills are those of analysis, logic, quantitative assessment, and the organization of ideas. The more skill one acquires, the more power one will have as a negotiator. These skills can be acquired at any time, often far in advance of any particular negotiation.

Knowledge also is power. Some knowledge is general and of use in many negotiations, such as familiarity with a wide range of procedural options and awareness of national negotiating styles and cultural differences. A repertoire of examples, precedents, and illustrations can also add to one's persuasive abilities.

Knowledge relevant to a particular negotiation in which one is about to engage is even more powerful. The more information one can gather about the parties and issues in an upcoming negotiation, the stronger one's entering posture. The following categories of knowledge, for example, are likely to strengthen one's ability to exert influence:

Knowledge about the people involved. What are the other negotiators' personal concerns, backgrounds, interests, prejudices, values, habits, career hopes, and so forth? How would we answer the same questions with respect to those on our side?

Knowledge about the interests involved. In addition to the personal concerns of the negotiators, what additional interests are involved on the other side? What are their hopes, their fears, their needs? And what are the interests on our side?

Knowledge about the facts. It is impossible to appreciate the importance of unknown facts. Time permitting, it is usually worthwhile to gather a great deal of unnecessary information about the subject under negotiation in order to gather a few highly relevant facts. The more one knows about the history, geography, economics, and scientific background of a problem, as well as its legal, social, and political implications, the more likely it is that one can invent creative solutions.

It takes time and resources to acquire skill and knowledge; it also takes initiative and hard work. Lawyers who would never think of walking into a trial without weeks of preparation will walk into a negotiation with almost none: "Let's see what they have to say." Yet the lawyer would help his client more in persuading the other side next week than in persuading a judge next year. The first way to enhance one's negotiating power is to acquire in advance all the skill and knowledge that one reasonably can.

2. The Power of a Good Relationship

The better a working relationship I establish in advance with those with whom I will be negotiating, the more powerful I am. A good working relationship does not necessarily imply approval of each other's conduct, though mutual respect and even mutual affection — when it exists — may help. The two most critical elements of a working relationship are, first, trust, and second, the ability to communicate easily and effectively.

Trust. Although I am likely to focus my attention in a given negotiation on the question of whether or not I can trust those on the other side, my power depends upon whether they can trust me. If over time I have been able to establish a well-deserved reputation for candor, honesty, integrity, and commitment to any promise I make, my capacity to exert influence is significantly enhanced.

Communication. The negotiation process is one of communication. If I am trying to persuade seem people to change their minds, I want to know where their minds are; otherwise, I am shooting in the dark. If my messages are going to have their intended impact, they need to be understood as I would have them understood. At best, interpersonal communication is difficult and often generates misunderstanding. When the parties see each other as adversaries, the risk of miscommunication and misunderstanding is greatly increased. The longer two people have known each other, the more broadly and deeply each understands the point of view and context from which the other is operating, the more likely they can communicate with each other easily and with a minimum of misunderstanding.

Each side benefits from this ability to communicate. We may have interests that conflict, but our ability to deal with those conflicting interests at minimum risk and minimum cost is enhanced by a good working relationship. Two men in a lifeboat at sea quarreling over limited rations have sharply conflicting interests. But the longer they have known each other, the more dealings they have had, and the more they speak the same language, the more likely they are to be able to divide the rations without tipping over the boat. The ability of each to affect favorably the other's decision is enhanced by an ability to communicate. More power for one is consistent with more power for the other.

A good working relationship is so helpful to the negotiation of satisfactory outcomes that it is often more important than any particular outcome itself. A banker, for example, is often like a person courting. The prospect of a satisfactory relationship is far more important than the terms of a particular loan or a particular date. A relationship, which provides a means for happily resolving one transaction after another, becomes an end in itself. Particular substantive negotiations become opportunities for cooperative activity that builds the relationship.

* * *

3. The Power of a Good Alternative to Negotiation

To a significant extent, my power in a negotiation depends upon how well I can do for myself if I walk away. In *Getting to YES*, we urge a negotiator to develop and improve his "BATNA" — his Best Alternative To a Negotiated Agreement. One kind of preparation for negotiation that enhances one's negotiating power is to consider the alternatives to reaching agreement with this particular negotiating partner, to select the most promising, and to improve it to the extent possible. This alternative sets a floor. If I follow this practice, every negotiation will lead to a successful outcome in the sense that any result I accept is bound to be better than anything else I could do.

In the case of buying or selling, my best alternative is likely to result from dealing with a competitor. Obtaining a firm offer from such a competitor in advance of a proposed negotiation strengthens my hand in that negotiation. The better the competing offer, the more my hand is strengthened.

In other cases, my best alternative may be self-help. What is the best I can do on my own? If the two boys offering to shovel the snow off the front walk are asking an exorbitant price, my best alternative may be to shovel the walk myself. To think about that option, and to have a snow shovel in the basement, strengthens my hand in trying to negotiate a fair price with the boys.

The less attractive the other side's BATNA is to them, the stronger my negotiating position. In negotiating with my son to cut the lawn, I may discover that he lacks interest in earning a little pocket money: "Dad," he says, "you leave your wallet on your bureau and if I need a little money I always borrow some." My son's best alternative to a negotiated agreement to cut the lawn is to get the same amount or even more for doing nothing. To enhance my negotiating power, I will want to make his BATNA less attractive by removing that alternative. With my wallet elsewhere, he may be induced to earn some money by cutting the lawn.

Conventional military weapons typically enhance a country's negotiating power by making a nonnegotiated solution less attractive to a hostile neighbor. With adequate defense forces, Country A can say to Country B: "Let's settle our boundary dispute by negotiation; if you try to settle it by military force, you will fail." With sufficient military force, Country A may be able to improve its alternative to negotiation enough that it will be in an extremely strong negotiation position: "We hope you will agree through negotiation to withdraw your forces to the boundary which has been recommended by impartial experts; if you do not agree to withdraw your forces voluntarily, we may force them to withdraw."

The better an alternative one can develop outside the negotiation, the greater one's power to affect favorably a negotiated outcome.

4. The Power of an Elegant Solution

In any negotiation, there is a mélange of shared and conflicting interests. The parties face a problem. One way to influence the other side in a negotiation is to invent a good solution to that problem. The more complex the problem, the more influential an elegant answer. Too often, negotiators battle like litigators in court. Each side advances arguments for a result that would take care of its interests but would do nothing for the other side. The power of a mediator often comes from working out an ingenious solution that reconciles reasonably well the legitimate interests of both sides. Either negotiator has similar power to effect an agreement that takes care of his or her interests by generating an option that also takes care of some or most of the interests on the other side.

A wise negotiator includes in his or her preparatory work the generation of many options designed to meet as well as possible the legitimate interests of both sides. Brainstorming enhances my negotiating power by enhancing the chance that I will be able to devise a solution that amply satisfies my interests and also meets enough of your interests to be acceptable to you.

* * *

5. The Power of Legitimacy

Each of us is subject to being persuaded by becoming convinced that a particular result *ought* to be accepted because it is fair; because the law requires it; because it is consistent with precedent, industry practice, or sound policy considerations; or because it is legitimate as measured by some other objective standard. I can substantially enhance my negotiating power by searching for and developing various objective criteria and potential standards of legitimacy, and by shaping proposed solutions so that they are legitimate in the eyes of the other side.

Every negotiator is both a partisan and one of those who must be persuaded if any agreement is to be reached. To be persuasive, a good negotiator should speak like an advocate who is seeking to convince an able and honest arbitrator, and should listen like such an arbitrator, always open to being persuaded by reason. Being open to persuasion is itself persuasive.

Like a lawyer preparing a case, a negotiator will discover quite a few different principles of fairness for which plausible arguments can be advanced, and often quite a few different ways of interpreting or applying each principle. A tension exists between advancing a highly favorable principle that appears less legitimate to the other side and a less favorable principle that appears more legitimate. Typically, there is a range within which reasonable people could differ. To retain his power, a wise negotiator avoids advancing a proposition that is so extreme that it damages his credibility. He also avoids so locking himself into the first principle he advances that he will lose face in disentangling himself from that principle and moving on to one that has a greater chance of persuading the other side. In advance of this process, a negotiator will want to have researched precedents, expert opinion, and other objective criteria, and to have worked on various theories of what ought to be done, so as to harness the power of legitimacy — a power to which each of us is vulnerable.

6. The Power of Commitment

The five kinds of power previously mentioned can each be enhanced by work undertaken in advance of formal negotiations. The planning of commitments and making arrangements for them can also be undertaken in advance, but making commitments takes place only during what everyone thinks of as negotiation itself.

There are two quite different kinds of commitments — affirmative and negative:

(a) Affirmative commitments

(1) An offer of what I am willing to agree to.

(2) An offer of what, failing agreement, I am willing to do under certain conditions.

(b) Negative commitments   *threats*

(1) A commitment that I am unwilling to make certain agreements (even though they would be better for me than no agreement).

(2) A commitment or threat that, failing agreement, I will engage in certain negative conduct (even though to do so would be worse for me than a simple absence of agreement).

Every commitment involves a decision. Let's first look at affirmative commitments. An affirmative commitment is a decision about what one is willing to do. It is an offer. Every offer ties the negotiator's hands to some extent. It says, "This, I am willing to do." The offer may expire or later be withdrawn, but while open it carries some persuasive power. It is no longer just an idea or a possibility that the parties are discussing. Like a proposal of marriage or a job offer, it is operational. It says, "I am willing to do this. If you agree, we have a deal."

We have all felt the power of a positive commitment — the power of an invitation. (We are not here concerned with the degree of commitment, or with various techniques for making a constraint more binding, but only with the content of the commitment itself. Advance planning can enhance my power by enabling me to demonstrate convincingly that a commitment is unbreakable. This subject, like all of those concerned with the difference between appearance and reality, is left for another day.) The one who makes the offer takes a risk. If he had waited, he might have gotten better terms. But in exchange for taking that risk, he has increased his chance of affecting the outcome.

A wise negotiator will formulate an offer in ways that maximize the cumulative impact of the different categories of negotiating power. The terms of an affirmative commitment will benefit from all the skill and knowledge that has been developed; the commitment benefits from the relationship and is consistent with it; it takes into account the walk-away alternatives each side has; the offer will constitute a reasonably elegant solution to the problem of reconciling conflicting interests; and the offer will be legitimate — it will take into account considerations of legitimacy.

With all this power in its favor, there is a chance the offer will be accepted. No other form of negotiating power may be needed. But as a last resort the negotiator has one other form of power: that of a negative commitment, or threat.

A negative commitment is the most controversial and troublesome element of negotiating power. No doubt, by tying my own hands I may be able to influence you to accept something more favorable to me than you otherwise would. The theory is simple. For almost every potential agreement, there is a range within which each of us is better off having an agreement than walking away. Suppose that you would be willing to pay $75,000 for my house if you had to; but for a price above that figure you would rather buy a different house. The best offer I have received from someone else is $62,000, and I will accept that offer unless you give me a better one. At any price between $62,000 and $75,000 we are both better off than if no agreement is reached. If you offer me $62,100, and so tie your hands by a negative commitment that you cannot raise your offer, presumably, I will accept it since it is better than $62,000. On the other hand, if I can commit myself not to drop the price below $75,000, you presumably will buy the house at that price. This logic may lead us to engage in a battle of negative commitments. Logic suggests that "victory" goes to the one who first and most convincingly ties his own hands at an appropriate figure. Other things being equal, an early and rigid negative commitment at the right point should prove persuasive.

Other things, however, are not likely to be equal.

The earlier I make a negative commitment — the earlier I announce a take-it-or-leave-it position — the less likely I am to have maximized the cumulative total of the various elements of my negotiating power.

The power of knowledge. I probably acted before knowing as much as I could have learned. The longer I postpone making a negative commitment, the more likely I am to know the best proposition to which to commit myself.

The power of a good relationship. Being quick to advance a take-it-or-leave-it position is likely to prejudice a good working relationship and to damage the trust you might otherwise place in what I say. The more quickly I confront you with a rigid position on my part, the more likely I am to make you so angry that you will refuse an agreement you might otherwise accept.

The power of a good alternative. There is a subtle but significant difference between communicating a warning of the course of action that I believe it will be in my interest to take should we fail to reach agreement (my BATNA), and locking myself in to precise terms that you must accept in order to avoid my taking that course of action. Extending a warning is not the same as making a negative commitment. If the United States honestly believes that deploying one hundred MX missiles is a vital part of its national security, then letting the Soviet Union know that in the absence of a negotiated agreement we intend to deploy them would appear to be a sound way to exerting influence. In these circumstances, the United States remains open to considering any negotiated agreement that would be better for us than the MX deployment.

* * *

The second kind of negative commitment is illustrated by the MX case if one assumes, as many of us believe, that deploying one hundred MX missiles does not really enhance U.S. security but rather damages it. The proposed deployment is bad for us; perhaps worse for the Soviet Union. On this assumption, the threat to deploy the MX missiles is like my trying to influence a fellow passenger by threatening to tip over a boat whether or not I am the better swimmer. Tipping over the boat will be bad for both of us, perhaps worse for him. I am committing myself to do something negative to both of us in the hope of exerting influence. If I make such a commitment, it is because I hope that by precluding myself from acting in some ways that would be in my interest, I will be able to achieve a result that is even more favorable.

To make either kind of negative commitment at an early state of the negotiation is likely to reduce the negotiating power of a good BATNA. It shifts the other side's attention from the objective reality of my most attractive alternative to a subjective statement that I won't do things that (except for my having made the commitment) would be in my interest to do. Such negative commitments invite the other side to engage in a contest of will by making commitments that are even more negative, and even more difficult to get out of. Whatever negotiating impact my BATNA may have, it is likely to be lessened by clouding it with negative commitments.

* * *

The power of an elegant solution. The early use of a negative commitment reduces the likelihood that the choice being considered by the other side is one that best meets its interests consistent with any given degree of meeting our interests. If we announce early in the negotiation process that we will accept no agreement other than Plan X, Plan X probably takes care of most of our interests. But it is quite likely that Plan X could be improved. With further study and time, it may be possible to modify Plan X so that it serves our interests even better at little or no cost to the interests of the other side.

Second, it may be possible to modify Plan X in ways that make it more attractive to the other side without in any way making it less attractive to us. To do so would not serve merely the other side but would serve us also by making it more likely that the other side will accept a plan that so well serves our interests.

Third, it may be possible to modify Plan X in ways that make it much more attractive to the other side at a cost of making it only slightly less attractive to us. The increase in total benefits and the increased likelihood of quickly reaching agreement may outweigh the modest cost involved.

Premature closure on an option is almost certain to reduce our ability to exert the influence that comes from having an option well crafted to reconcile, to the extent possible, the conflicting interests of the two sides. In multilateral negotiations it is even less likely that an early option will be well designed to take into account the plurality of divergent interests involved.

The power of legitimacy. The most serious damage to negotiating power that results from an early negative commitment is likely to result from its damage to the influence that comes from legitimacy. Legitimacy depends upon both process and substance. As with an arbitrator, the legitimacy of a negotiator's decision depends upon having accorded the other side "due process." The persuasive power of my decision depends in part on my having fully heard your views, your suggestions, and your notions of what is fair before committing myself. And my decision will have increased persuasiveness for you to the extent that I am able to justify it by reference to objective standards of fairness that you have indicated you consider appropriate. That factor, again, urges me to withhold making any negative commitment until I fully understand your views on fairness.

The power of an affirmative commitment. Negative commitments are often made when no affirmative commitment is on the table. The Iranian holders of the hostages in Tehran said for months that they would not release the hostages until the United States had adequately atoned for its sins and had met an ambiguous set of additional demands. No clear offer was given by Iran, and the United States, accordingly, was under no great pressure to do any particular thing. During the Vietnam War, the United States similarly failed to offer those on the other side any clear proposition. We would not leave, we said, until North Vietnam agreed "to leave its neighbors alone" — but no terms were on the table; no offer, no affirmative commitment was given.

Once an affirmative commitment is on the table, the negotiator must make sure that the varied elements of the communication are consistent with each other. No matter what the magnitude of a threat, it will have little effect unless it is constructed so that the sum total of the consequences of acceptance are more beneficial to the other side than is the sum total of the consequences of rejection. While negotiators frequently try to increase power by increasing the magnitude of a threat, they often overlook the fact that increasing the favorable consequences of acceptance can be equally important.

But no matter how favorable the consequence of acceptance are to the other side, and how distasteful the consequences of rejection, the proposition will carry little impact if the various implications of timing have not been thought through as well. Just as my son will look at me askance if I tell him that unless he behaves next week he will not be permitted to watch television tonight, so the North Vietnamese were unable to comply when the United States said, in effect, "If over the next few weeks you haven't reduced support for opponents of South Vietnam, we will bomb you tomorrow." The grammar must parse. * * *

To make a negative commitment either as to what we will not do or to impose harsh consequences unless the other side reaches agreement with us, without having previously made a firm and clear offer, substantially lessens our ability to exert influence. An offer may not be enough, but a threat is almost certainly not enough unless there is a "yesable" proposition on the table — a clear statement of the action desired and a commitment as to the favorable consequences which would follow.

This analysis of negotiating power suggests that in most cases it is a mistake to attempt to influence the other side by making a negative commitment of any kind at the outset of the negotiations, and that it is a mistake to do so until one has first made the most of every other element of negotiating power.

This analysis also suggests that when as a last resort threats or other negative commitments are used, they should be so formulated as to complement and reinforce other elements of negotiating power, not undercut them. In particular, any statement to the effect that we have finally reached a take-it-or-leave-it position should be made in a way that is consistent with maintaining a good working relationship, and consistent with the concepts of legitimacy with which we are trying to persuade the other side. For example, I might say:

> "Bill, I appreciate your patience. We have been a long time discussing the sale of my house, and I believe that we each fully understand the other's concerns. We have devised a draft contract which elegantly reconciles my interest in a firm deal, adequate security, and reasonable restrictions to protect the neighbors, with your interest in being able to move in early, to stretch out the payments, and to have your professional office in the house. The only open issue is price. On that, we have discussed various criteria, such as market value based on recent sales, providing me a fair return on my investment, and value based on professional estimates of replacement cost depreciated for wear and tear. These criteria produce figures ranging from $73,000 down to $68,000. I have offered to sell you the house for $70,000.

> "Your response, as I understand it, is to say that you will pay no more than $100 above the best written offer I have from another potential buyer, now $62,000. Knowing that you would pay $75,000 if you had to, I am unable to understand why you should get all but $1000 of the advantage of our shared interest in my selling and your buying the house. Nor, as we have discussed, do I think it is wise practice for me to defer to what looks to me like an arbitrary commitment.

> "The transaction costs of further discussion would appear to outweigh any potential advantage. Unless you have something further you would like to say now, or unless you would like to try to convince

me that this procedure is unfair, I hereby make a final offer of $68,000, the lowest figure I believe justified by objective criteria. Let me confirm that offer now in writing and commit myself to leaving that offer open for three days. Unless something wholly unexpected comes up, I will not sell the house to you for less. Please think it over.

"In any event, let's plan to play golf on Saturday afternoon if you are free."

* * *

Raymond A. Friedman & Debra L. Shapiro,[*]
Deception and Mutual Gains Bargaining: Are They Mutually Exclusive?
11 NEGOT. J. 243, 246-51 (1995)[**]

* * *

Mutual Gains Bargaining and Ethical Claims

MGB is an approach that helps negotiators produce the greatest joint gains possible. As noted earlier, it is also called "integrative bargaining," "win-win" or "principled" negotiation, and is often contrasted with "distributive" bargaining, that is, bargaining that is zero-sum or focused on getting more for oneself by forcing the opponent to take less. As explained by Fisher and Ury, MGB is based on four principles: separating the people from the problem; focusing on interests, not positions; inventing options for mutual gain; and insisting on objective criteria.

There is nothing in these principles that directly addresses the issue of ethical behavior or deceptive tactics. However, there are several ways in which these principles can be inadvertently related to ethical behavior and trainees may come to believe that the primary reason for MGB is that it is more "honest" than traditional negotiations. It is possible that some trainers do frame MGB as the more ethical way to bargain, or that the "principled" and "mutual gains" labels themselves convey that message to trainees. More importantly, the connection between MGB and ethics may come from more deep-seated and fundamental misunderstandings of the ideas of MGB, especially the difference between interests and positions.

[*] Raymond A. Friedman is Brownlee O. Currey Professor of Management at Owen Graduate School of Management, Vanderbilt University. Debra L. Shapiro is Clarice Smith Professor of Management & Organization at University of Maryland. Their article discusses whether integrative bargaining is inherently more ethical than distributive bargaining, and therefore preferable.

MGB suggests that negotiators explain to their opponent what their *interests* are, so that the opponent can propose actions that meet one's real needs at least cost. It does not, however, say anything about revealing one's alternatives to a negotiated agreement, what one's true reservation price is, or how much money is in the bargaining budget — all of which influence what final *position* will be acceptable. The problem is that the distinction is difficult for many negotiators to understand; even for trainers, the line between the two is frequently not completely clear. In fact, the distinction represents more of a continuum than an absolute difference. For example, a "5 percent pay raise" is a position in that it is one way to achieve the interest of "a better quality of life." From another perspective, it is an interest that may be achieved in various ways (such as 3 percent base wage increase and a 2 percent lump sum or via other "positions"). Therefore, some will tend to hear the MGB prescriptions as saying "reveal everything about oneself." MGB says only that you should not deceive the other party about your core, underlying interests. And — this is worth emphasizing — the reason for this prescription is not that being honest about interests is inherently ethical. Rather, it is that being honest about one's interests can help you get more. If others do not know what really matters to you, they cannot help search for ways to meet your needs that are feasible for them.

Confusion is also likely to the degree that MGB is framed as an alternative to distributive bargaining. For pedagogical reasons it may be necessary at some stage of training to present MGB as a completely different model for negotiations, but few scholars would presume that many negotiations are wholly integrative. Rather, most negotiations are "mixed motive"; they include both opportunities for joint gain, and opportunities for grabbing more from the other side. Walton and McKersie call this the integrative and distributive dimensions of negotiation, while Lax and Sebenius write of the distinction between creating and claiming value in negotiation. There is indeed a tension between the two; strategies that are wise for creating are often opposite from those that are wise for claiming (e.g., deception about positions and power is necessary for claiming, while deception about interests is disruptive for creating). But all negotiations include both elements, and few negotiations occur where a wise negotiator would not employ at least some of each set of behaviors. Indeed, one of the more interesting challenges faced by negotiators is how to balance both of these elements.

Pruitt and Lewis have argued that the two approaches appear in the same negotiation by means of separating creating and claiming into distinct phases of the process, or by having different individuals on bargaining teams engage in creating or claiming. More recently, Friedman has argued that the two approaches coexist by having separate "stages" for each. While distributive tactics and deception occur front stage, integrative tactics and honest communication about interests occur backstage. In public, labor negotiators engage in a great deal of bravado, exaggeration, hiding, and, in general, attempts to deceive the other about what they want, what they are willing to accept, and what they are willing to fight over. But out of public view, negotiators engage in a well understood process of signaling to opponents, discounting information, and engaging in private sidebar meetings to clarify interests.

In sum, MGB does teach negotiators not to deceive the opponent — about their interests. But it makes this suggestion based on effectiveness, not ethics. And it does not presume that all parts of negotiations are integrative — there is a domain for distributive bargaining in most negotiations. This distinction can be easily lost if the interest-position distinction is not made clear, or if teachers express a preference for MGB because of its higher ethical status.

If, in these ways, ethics and MGB become conflated, several problems can occur. First, negotiators may miss the distinctions between ethical and unethical behavior that exist in traditional negotiations. Second, they may misunderstand the true benefits that MGB provides. And third, they may perceive MGB as naive and therefore avoid using it.

Ethical Conventions in Labor Negotiations

Equating MGB with ethics overlooks the fact that there are ethical constraints on deception in traditional negotiations. We can see this by looking at the example of labor negotiations. During a study of labor negotiations, the first author studied thirteen negotiations, including direct observations of eight cases and over 150 interviews, and in addition interviewed nineteen experienced labor negotiators. The negotiators in that study talked extensively about their relationships with opponents and the kinds of tactics that they used and expected others to use. From these interviews and observations, it became clear that professional labor negotiators have a definite sense, in practice, of what is appropriate and inappropriate behavior. Experienced labor negotiators expect that opponents will hide information and try to build up false perceptions about their limits and determination. Negotiators on both sides expect their opponents to have "laundry lists" of demands, put exaggerated financial offers on the table, declare that constituents will not accept less, say that they and their constituents could and would weather a strike, and even put on displays of anger and resolve to show how tough they will be in defense of these demands.

Nonetheless, some types of deception are beyond the pale. The same negotiators who expressed tolerance for some levels of deception also reported that there was a limit to what was acceptable. Overtly inaccurate statements are considered unethical (and unprofessional) by lead bargainers. It is acceptable and expected for the company to say "we cannot pay a penny more for health care," while it is unacceptable to say "adding physical therapy to the benefit package will cost us an additional $100 a year per employee" when it is known that it would only add $20 a year. The first statement is a general claim that can be readily interpreted as a bargaining stance; the latter is a factual claim that is either true or false. The first type of statement would be considered "bargaining" by experienced labor negotiators, and those who do it with cleverness and gusto are respected as savvy and skilled. The latter type of statement would be considered a lie, and the bargainer who was caught in such a lie would be deemed unprofessional and untrustworthy. In addition, for these negotiators it makes a difference if either statement is made in private between lead bargainers or in public across the main table. What is said across the table is expected to be exaggerated and not fully accurate; what is said in private is expected to be accurate. To claim inaccurately that the company cannot spend one penny more on health care across the table is expected and not deemed unethical; to make that same false claim in private would produce outrage if the lie was discovered.

Underlying this distinction is an understanding that some statements are *expected* to be untrue while others are not. When negotiators make statements that are expected to be untrue, the other negotiators are able to make appropriate adjustments, calculations, and predictions. These statements are interpreted, discounted, and treated with caution. Negotiators anticipate that these statements are made as bargaining stances, open to change, or that they are positions that need to be stated to look good to constituents and teammates. By contrast, when one negotiator makes statements that are expected to be true, the other party proceeds to act on them; this information is often represented to constituents as true, and major decisions are made based on it. The consequences of deception in those situations can be great: there might be an unnecessary strike, the negotiators could be hurt professionally if constituents find out that they were duped, and negotiators' ability to count on some truthful communication between the two sides is eliminated and their ability to manage the negotiations wisely is greatly diminished.

* * *

Putting the MGB Message in Context

If the message of mutual gains bargaining is not that integrative tactics alone should be used or that deception should be completely precluded, and if integrative tactics (including prohibitions against deception during integrative phases of negotiations) already exist in most negotiations, why have MGB training? We can identify three primary benefits to teaching MGB that do not depend on the "do-not-ever-be-deceptive" message. First, MGB training can help inexperienced trainees to discover that there is an integrative — and not only a distributive — side to bargaining. This discovery is especially likely among negotiators who may have been exposed only to the more public, high conflict aspects of bargaining.

Second, MGB can help negotiators anticipate times when their emotions make them forget what they know about integrative bargaining, and focus only on distributive bargaining. In this way, emotionally-triggered escalation traps are made less likely. Although professional bargainers usually know how to keep their emotions under control and "focus on the problem not the person," less experienced bargainers may not be as well prepared for the pressures of bargaining. And there may be times when relations between the two sides have become so difficult that even experienced bargainers have a difficult time sustaining the integrative side to bargaining that they know should exist. Third, MGB can encourage negotiators to be integrative bargainers somewhat more than they traditionally are. More specifically, MGB training may help negotiators lengthen the phase of negotiations that is more integrative, or to include more people in the backstage arena where integrative bargaining is done. While not eliminating hard bargaining, or telling negotiators to give up the deceptive tactics that are central to hard bargaining, MGB training may be able to shift the balance somewhat towards integrative bargaining.

The Dangers of Naive MGB Training

Not only is the "do-not-ever-deceive" message unnecessary in MGB training, it may also reduce the effectiveness of the training. The message "do-not-ever-deceive" does not recognize the fact that, even when integrative bargaining works well, there is still a need to engage in distributive tactics, nor the fact that being completely honest about one's fall-back positions can diminish one's power. For these distributive elements of negotiations, tactics such as hiding information and shaping impressions are often necessary and do work. To teach that negotiators should abandon all impression management tactics would be unwise from an analytic perspective, would make the teacher appear naive, and ensure that the MGB approach would be seen as damaging to one's negotiating goals.

Moreover, these costs are not necessary; practicing mutual gains bargaining does not require that negotiators make themselves vulnerable through comprehensive revelations about their situation. It says only that it makes no sense to deceive the opponent about one's *interests*. Finally, to the degree that trainers signal an ethical priority (or allow trainees to read that into the training), trainees have a more difficult time seeing that MGB helps people to negotiate *smarter* and get better results. While some may believe that MGB helps make negotiations more ethical, that is unlikely to generate among trainees a true commitment to understand and use the MGB lessons.

That is not to say, however, that there are no ethical constraints. MGB does not free negotiators to be deceptive in ways that are traditionally unacceptable. If one is found to have lied, that would be a source of distrust during negotiations, it would engender uncooperative behavior by the opponent, and make him or her less likely to engage in integrative bargaining — with or without MGB training. To the degree that we might encourage people to use MGB techniques, or at least not to do less of it, negotiators should stay within commonly understood norms of acceptable behavior. Misrepresentations that cross the line have been found to interfere with negotiators' willingness to use MGB, just as those that cross the line make backstage interactions more difficult in traditional negotiations.

* * *

Janice Nadler,[*] *Rapport in Negotiation and Conflict Resolution*
87 Marq. L. Rev. 875, 880-82 (2004)[**]

* * *

In the absence of visual access or a basis for a positive relationship, negotiators are less likely to develop the kind of rapport that promotes cooperation necessary to reach efficient agreements in mixed-motive negotiations. Can negotiators working under these circumstances take steps to develop rapport on their own initiative? Even though rapport normally develops in social interactions without social actors even being aware of it, several studies have identified methods that can be used by negotiators who wish to develop rapport to enhance negotiation processes and outcomes.

Sometimes we must negotiate with people we do not know and have never met. Moreover, the advent of communication technologies, like e-mail, means that sometimes the negotiation itself does not provide the opportunity for a face-to-face meeting with our counterpart. Negotiating with someone with whom we have no prior relationship, and using a communication medium that provides no visual access (e.g., telephone, e-mail), makes it more likely that rapport will not sufficiently develop, that cooperative information exchange will be insufficient, and that the result will be an impasse rather than a mutually beneficial agreement. How can this undesirable state of affairs be avoided in a world in which negotiation with strangers using information technology is taken as a given?

First, negotiators who make an effort to create a basis for a positive relationship by engaging in a short, get-acquainted conversation create a basis for smooth negotiation processes that follow. For example, in two studies, some negotiators who used e-mail to negotiate a transaction with a stranger were instructed to talk on the telephone and schmooze for ten minutes in an effort to get to know one another. Other negotiators were not given this opportunity. Engaging in small talk enabled negotiators who were strangers to affiliate in a fashion that did not spontaneously occur during the process of e-mail exchange. The seemingly inert act of schmoozing facilitated cooperation during the negotiation, leading to the sharing of crucial information

---

[*] Janice Nadler is Professor of Law, Northwestern University. This excerpt addresses creating rapport when negotiating electronically.

[**] Copyright © 2004 Marquette Law Review. Reprinted by permission.

with the other part, and resulting in favorable impressions of the counter-part after the negotiation.

By contrast, negotiators who did not chat with their counterpart prior to negotiation either failed to exchange the kind of information that would lead to identification of mutually beneficial solutions, or failed to recognize as beneficial the solutions which arose, leading to a greater likelihood of impasse. In the absence of the preliminary chat, the two negotiation coun-terparts were complete strangers, never having seen one another or heard one another's voice, hindering the development of rapport. By failing to reach agreement, pairs that reached an impasse settled for a result that was economically worse than any of the many possible agreements that would have resulted in a profitable outcome for each party. The prenegotiation, get-ting-to-know-you chat allowed the negotiation to proceed more smoothly by creating rapport before the negotiation began. This rapport helped nego-tiators approach the negotiation with a more cooperative mental model, thereby trusting in each others' good intentions. This mental model, in turn, led to a successful negotiation that concluded with a contract and engendered positive feelings about one another. Adopting an attitude that was more cooperative than competitive allowed negotiators to trust the other party enough to share with them relevant private information, and to expect the other party to reciprocate by sharing their own relevant private information, which, in turn, resulted in identification of and agreement to efficient solutions.

If preliminary small talk is not possible, there are other means for cre-ating the basis for a rapport-promoting positive relationship. For example, in the Moore et al. study discussed earlier, negotiators who were students at the same school (but did not necessarily know one another) were more successful at generating rapport than students at different schools. As a result, their impasse rate was lower (especially when their e-mail exchanges contained mutual self disclosures). In addition, other negotiators who exchanged pictures and personal biographical information (such as alma mater, interests, hobbies) generated more affect-based rapport. The absence of either of these factors (ingroup identification or mutual self-disclosure) led to a much higher impasse rate than when negotiators had a basis for a positive relationship. Thus, prior to negotiation, strangers who negotiate can try to create a basis for affiliation, through identification of shared interests, group memberships, and so forth. This shared affiliation will then create the basis for affect-based rapport that leads to cooperation, information exchange, and mutually beneficial agreements.

* * *

Michael Moffitt,[*] *Contingent Agreements: Agreeing to Disagree about the Future*
87 MARQ. L. REV. 691, 691-96 (2004)[**]

"That won't happen." "Yes, it will." "No, it won't." "Will too." "Will not."

Negotiators generally find no shortage of things about which to disagree. For example, negotiators seeking to resolve a dispute often have sharply differing perceptions of the past. What happened? Whose decisions and actions caused the effects in question? How does their conduct compare with expectations or duties? In some circumstances, settlement is impossible without resolution of these backward-looking questions. A significant component of classical dispute resolution theory suggests that one might overcome impasse by shifting the focus of conversations toward the future. Sometimes, however, the shift to a forward-looking exploration merely provides fertile, new grounds for disagreement. Rather than arguing about what happened, the negotiators argue about what will happen. A wholesaler asserts that demand for the product will skyrocket in the future, and the retailer suspects otherwise. A defendant points to the relatively minor and temporary injuries caused in a car crash, but the victim fears that currently undetected injuries may manifest themselves down the road. Instinct may suggest that one negotiator will need to persuade the other about the likelihood of future uncertain events. Instead, genuinely held disagreements about the future present an important opportunity for negotiators to discover an attractive trade. The vehicle for capturing this potential is the contingent agreement.

Structurally, a contingent agreement is one in which the parties identify the universe of possible future conditions and agree to take on different obligations in each of those conditions. The simplest contingent deals are those in which the future has only two possible relevant conditions. X will happen, or it will not. If X happens, the terms of our deal are ABC; otherwise, we will do DEF. If I think X is unlikely to happen, I will be happy to give you terms you prefer for ABC, in exchange for terms I favor for DEF. Believing that she will get the work finished on time, an author signs a lucrative book contract with a very harsh penalty for late completion. Buyer loves Seller's house, but really wants a property with off-street parking. Seller firmly expects that the city council will approve a variance required for construction of a new garage, but Buyer is less confident about the likelihood of getting approval. Buyer agrees to purchase the property from Seller at a reduced price, with a substantial additional payment to Seller if the City Council grants a variance within the next twelve months. Negotiators can craft attractive trades

---

[*] Michael Moffitt is Associate Professor of Law and Associate Director of the Appropriate Dispute Resolution Center, University of Oregon. His article explores the use of contingent contracts as a way of integrating parties' differing perspectives in negotiation.

[**] Copyright © 2004 Marquette Law Review. Reprinted by permission.

by establishing obligations that are contingent on a future uncertain event that affects each side's valuation of the agreement.

Contingent agreements can also include variable terms, pegged to some benchmark to be measured in the future. I think interest rates will increase over the next few months, and you think they will go down. If I am loaning you money today, we will each be happy to agree to a deal with a floating interest rate. A school board is nervous about the future level of state funding to the districts, while the teachers' union is optimistic. The teachers' union agrees to a wage and benefit increase tied to a particular line in next year's state budget. The plaintiff believes that he may suffer long-term health effects of exposure to the defendant's product, while the defendant believes no significant health risks exist. The defendant agrees to pay specified medical monitoring expenses for the plaintiff and to assume any future medical costs associated with exposure. Parties to a joint venture agree to final, binding resolution of their intellectual property dispute by an appointed arbitrator. Without the possibility of contingent agreements, uncertainty regarding future conditions can make distributive decisions (for example, who gets how much money) difficult. By linking the allocation of resources to an externally measurable variable, negotiators can sometimes overcome otherwise paralyzing disagreements about the future.

Contingent agreements also present an opportunity to create favorable incentives. Some negotiated deals involve no future relationship between the negotiators and are self-executing. Buying a trinket in a marketplace involves a simple exchange of money for goods. In more complex circumstances, however, ongoing relationships exist and implementation of the agreement takes place over time. When the negotiated deal involves more than a simple, one-time exchange, parties' behavior *after* the agreement is relevant. Contingent agreements can help to create incentives for parties to behave well after the terms of the deal are fixed. A company may agree to tie a sales executive's compensation to sales performance, thus promoting sales-maximizing behavior out of the executive after the deal is signed. The health ministry of a developing country approaches a prospective donor, seeking support for particular health sector programs. Both the prospective donor and the developing country want to see multiple sources of funding. They agree to a matching program under which the donor will contribute an amount equal to the funds the ministry secures from other sources, giving the ministry officials added incentive to garner resources. In some contingent deals, one party can affect the likelihood of the contingent trigger — the salesman can make more sales calls, the ministry officials can approach more donors. Contingent agreements can affect parties' behavior after the agreement.

Precisely because contingent agreements can affect parties' behaviors, some contingent agreements risk creating conditions of moral hazard. Moral hazard is a condition in which one party, under the terms of an agreement, may undetectably or uncontrollably behave in a way that is adverse to the other party. How quickly do you take the speed bumps when you are driving a rental car? Moral hazard suggests that many drivers will drive more cautiously over the bumps if they are driving their own cars because they consider the long-term effects of their driving behavior. Athletes' contracts often contain contingent incentive clauses. If the athlete scores a certain number of points, for example, he or she receives additional money. Moral hazard arises when, toward the end of the season, a team notices that the athlete is only a few points away from the triggering contingent event. Will the team structure its play to enable the athlete to achieve the statistical goal? If an agent's contract provides for a thirty percent commission on sales this year, but only a ten percent commission in future years, the agent will have an incentive to push deals into the current year — even if the deal he or she could have struck next year would have been on terms more favorable to the company. Negotiators crafting a contingent agreement should foresee the possibility of moral hazard and, where appropriate, structure incentives and disclosures to minimize the incentive for subsequent adverse behavior.

One challenge in crafting a contingent agreement is identifying the boundaries of future possible conditions with sufficient clarity to know what obligations attach. A married couple might agree, "If the weather is nice tomorrow, we'll hike. Otherwise, we'll go shopping." The next morning, when it is cloudy but not raining, the spouse who wants to hike is likely to declare it "nice," while the person preferring to shop will argue the opposite. Rather than peg future obligations on something difficult to define with precision — the weather, the economy, one's health, political stability — wise contingent deals depend on easily-measured external variables. Did the airport weather station register precipitation in the past twenty-four hours? Did the unemployment rate for the state increase last month? Did the lab results show a drop in the level of LDLs in your blood? Did the local elections take place on the pre-specified date? Answering such questions is relatively reliable and costless.

Challenges akin to ambiguous contingent triggers arise when the variable being measured is under the interpretive control of one party. For example, a mid-level executive may not want to have her bonus tied to the performance of the business unit as a whole if she has concerns that the company may subsequently adopt accounting methods that shift credit from her unit to another unit. Contingent agreements containing unambiguous, external triggers are less likely to produce post-agreement disagreements.

Crafting contingent deals also raises considerable questions about strategic disclosure. Without any disclosure regarding forecasts and preferences, negotiators will not spot the possibility for a contingent agreement. Such disclosures, however, inevitably produce a risk of exploitation. Assume that I am virtually certain that X will happen, and you are virtually certain that X will not happen. If I begin our negotiations by declaring that I am "virtually certain X will happen," you may have an incentive to misstate your actual forecast. Rather than tell me that you are virtually certain of the opposite, you may tell me that you think there is "a decent chance" that X will not happen. You then may have an opportunity to demand a more favorable premium for being the party to take on the apparently greater risk. Contingent agreements are not different from most other aspects of bargaining; this presents opportunities both for mutually beneficial value creation and for one-sided efforts to skew value distribution.

Contingent agreements may affect negotiators' perceptions of "winning" and "losing." Classical negotiation advice counsels negotiators to conceive of negotiations in terms other than win-lose, pointing to the risk that competitive behavior may cloud opportunities for joint gains. In one respect, contingent agreements may present an opportunity for negotiators to avoid the necessity of identifying a winner. Rather than forcing one side to concede on its forecast, contingent agreements permit (in fact, require) both sides to maintain their conflicting predictions about the future. At the time of the agreement, therefore, each side can declare "victory," to the extent such a declaration is important. On the other hand, contingent agreements have the nature of a wager or a bet. Unless one counts the sheer joy of gambling as a victory, *both* sides cannot win a wager. The contingent event either happens or it does not. Either way, one side may be disappointed. In some organizational cultures, failure is punished more harshly than success is rewarded. A negotiator fearful of identifiable failure (for example, a wager that visibly did not pay off) may forgo an elegant contingent agreement in favor of a less efficient non-contingent deal. Elegantly structured contingent deals may help to reduce the risk of visibly "losing." For example, if the plaintiff fears that a jury may award him nothing, and a defendant fears a runaway jury award of millions, the two could agree to a small guaranteed recovery in exchange for a cap on the maximum recovery. The losing party at trial will then be grateful to have made the contingent agreement, and the winner's regret will be dampened by having won a favorable verdict.

Given that two people virtually never agree entirely on the likely shape of the future, why aren't *all* deals contingent? Part of the answer lies in the transaction costs associated with identifying differences and crafting elegant contingent agreements. Two parties crafting the terms of a joint venture cannot imagine that they will plan for every possible contingency. At some point, they will agree to resolve future uncertainties when/if they arise. Even in circumstances without trust or a structural incentive for cooperation, the contingent stakes may simply be too low to justify the effort of crafting and implementing the deal. The value captured simply may not outweigh the cost of crafting a contingent deal to capture it.

A final, often overlooked, factor dissuading parties from crafting contingent deals is that parties place some value on certainty and finality. Particularly for negotiators embroiled in a dispute, achieving resolution may have an inherent value independent of the terms of the deal. Many disputants find it emotionally costly to carry around uncertainty. A contingent agreement does not represent complete finality, as at least some of the terms are yet to be determined. Uncertainty also can be costly for economic reasons. A company with an uncertain liability or benefit on its books faces considerable challenges in planning appropriate reserves of money, for example. If a company has a large collection of similar contingent agreements, it may be able to spread the risks and allocate money accurately in the aggregate. Similarly, some circumstances may permit parties to manage risks through the use of hedging instruments such as futures or options. Such allocations are not generally available to all individual negotiators, potentially making contingent agreements less attractive. For a contingent agreement to be appropriate in a given context, therefore, the perceived benefit it captures for each negotiator must exceed the transaction costs of discovering and implementing the agreement.

Negotiators arguing about the past sometimes "agree to disagree," preferring instead to focus on what they will do moving forward. Negotiators with differing perceptions of the future should similarly agree to disagree — using contingent agreements to capture the potential benefits of their differences.

James J. White,[*] *Essay Review: The Pros and Cons of GETTING TO YES*
34 J. LEGAL EDUC. 115 (1984)[**]

Getting to YES is a puzzling book. On the one hand it offers a forceful and persuasive criticism of much traditional negotiating behavior. It suggests a variety of negotiating techniques that are both clever and likely to facilitate effective negotiation. On the other hand, the authors seem to deny the existence of a significant part of the negotiation process, and to oversimplify or explain away many of the most troublesome problems inherent in the art and practice of negotiation. The book is frequently naive, occasionally self-righteous, but often helpful.

Initially, one should understand what the book is and what it is not. It is not a scholarly work on negotiation; it is not the kind of work that Schelling, Eisenberg or Bartos might write. The book is not rigorous and analytical, rather it is anecdotal and informative. It does not add fundamentally to our understanding of the negotiation process. Rather it points to a need for change in our general conception of negotiation, and points out errors of emphasis that exist in much of the thinking about negotiation.

---

[*] James J. White is Robert A. Sullivan Professor at University of Michigan Law School and co-author of one of the first law school textbooks on negotiation, THE LAWYER AS A NEGOTIATOR (West 1977). This essay reviews the then recently published book by Roger Fisher and William Ury, *GETTING TO YES*.

[**] Copyright © 1984 Journal of Legal Education. Reprinted with permission.

The book's thesis is well summarized by the following passage:

> Behind opposed positions lie shared and compatible interests, as well as conflicting ones. We tend to assume that because the other side's positions are opposed to ours, their interests must also be opposed. If we have an interest in defending ourselves, then they must want to attack us. It we have an interest in minimizing the rent, then their interest must be to maximize it. In many negotiations, however, a close examination of the underlying interests will reveal the existence of many more interests that are shared or compatible than ones that are opposed (p.43).

This point is useful for all who teach or think about negotiation. The tendency of those deeply involved in negotiation or its teaching is probably to exaggerate the importance of negotiation on issues where the parties are diametrically opposed and to ignore situations where the parties' interests are compatible. By emphasizing that fact and by making a clear articulation of the importance of cooperation, imagination, and the search for alternative solutions, the authors teach helpful lessons. The book therefore provides worthwhile reading for every professional negotiator and will make sound instruction for every tyro.

Unfortunately the book's emphasis upon mutually profitable adjustment, on the "problem solving" aspect of bargaining, is also the book's weakness. It is a weakness because emphasis of this aspect of bargaining is done to almost total exclusion of the other aspect of bargaining, "distributional bargaining," where one for me is minus one for you. Schelling, Karrass and other students of negotiation have long distinguished between that aspect of bargaining in which modification of the parties' positions can produce benefits for one without significant cost to the other, and on the other hand, cases where benefits to one come only at significant cost to the other. They have variously described the former as "exploring for mutual profitable adjustments," "the efficiency aspect of bargaining" or "problem solving." The other has been characterized as "distributional bargaining" or "share bargaining." Thus some would describe a typical negotiation as one in which the parties initially begin by cooperative or efficiency bargaining, in which each gains something with each new adjustment without the other losing any significant benefit. Eventually, however, one comes to bargaining in which added benefits to one impose corresponding significant costs on the other. For example, in a labor contract one might engage in cooperative bargaining by the modification of a medical plan so that the employer could engage a less expensive medical insurance provider, yet one that offered improved services. Each side gains by that change from the old contract. Ultimately parties in a labor negotiation will come to a raw economic exchange in which additional wage dollars for the employees will be dollars subtracted from the corporate profits, dollars that cannot be paid in dividends to the shareholders.

One can concede the authors' thesis (that too many negotiators are incapable of engaging in problem solving or in finding adequate options for mutual gain), yet still maintain that the most demanding aspect of nearly every negotiation is the distributional one in which one seeks more at the expense of the other. My principal criticism of the book is that it seems to overlook the ultimate hard bargaining. Had the authors stated that they were dividing the negotiation process in two and were dealing with only part of it, that omission would be excusable. That is not what they have done. Rather they seem to assume that a clever negotiator can make any negotiation into problem solving and thus completely avoid the difficult distribution of which Karrass and Schelling speak. To my mind this is naive. By so distorting reality, they detract from their powerful and central thesis.

Chapter 5, entitled "Insist on Objective Criteria," is a particularly naive misperception or rejection of the guts of distributive negotiation. Here, as elsewhere, the authors draw a stark distinction between a negotiator who simply takes a position without explanation and sticks to it as a matter of "will," and the negotiator who is reasonable and insists upon "objective criteria." Of course the world is hardly as simple as the authors suggest. Every party who takes a position will have some rationale for that position: every able negotiator rationalizes every position that he takes. Rarely will an effective negotiator simply assert "X" as his price and insist that the other party meet it.

The suggestion that one can find objective criteria (as opposed to persuasive rationalizations) seems quite inaccurate. As Eisenberg suggests, the distributive aspect of the negotiation often turns on the relative power of the parties. One who could sell his automobile to a particular person for $6,000 could not necessarily sell it for more than $5,000 to another person, not because of principle, but because of the need of the seller to sell and the differential need of the two buyers to buy. To say that there are objective criteria that call for a $5,000 or $6,000 price, or in the case of a personal injury suit for a million dollars or an $800,000 judgment, is to ignore the true dynamics of the situation and to exaggerate the power of objective criteria. Any lawyer who has been involved in a personal injury suit will marvel at the capacity of an effective plaintiff's lawyer to appear to do what the authors seem to think possible, namely to give the superficial appearance of certainty and objectivity to questions that are inherently imponderable. For example, an effective plaintiff's lawyer will sometimes fix a certain dollar amount per week for the pain and suffering which one might suffer. He will then multiply that amount by the number of weeks per year and the number of years in the party's life expectancy. Thus he produces a series of tables and columns full of "hard" numbers. These have the appearance of objectivity, but in fact they are subjective, based (if on anything) on a judgment about how a jury would react to the case. Every lawyer who has ever been involved in a lawsuit in which experts have been hired by each side will have a deep skepticism about the authors' appeal to scientific merit as a guide in determining a fair outcome in the negotiation of any hotly disputed problem.

In short, the authors' suggestion in Chapter 5 that one can avoid "contests of will" and thereby eliminate the exercise of raw power is at best naive and at worst misleading. Their suggestion that the parties look to objective criteria to strengthen their cases is a useful technique used by every able negotiator. Occasionally it may do what they suggest: give an obvious answer on which all can agree. Most of the time it will do no more than give the superficial appearance of reasonableness and honesty to one party's position.

The authors' consideration of "dirty tricks" in negotiation suffers from more of the same faults found in their treatment of objective criteria. At a superficial level I find their treatment of dirty tricks to be distasteful because it is so thoroughly self-righteous. The chapter is written as though there were one and only one definition of appropriate negotiating behavior handed down by the authors.

Apart from the rather trivial concern about their self-righteousness, their discussion is troublesome because it discloses an ignorance of, or a disregard for, the subtleties involved in distinguishing between appropriate and inappropriate conduct in negotiation. There is no concession to the idea that certain forms of behavior may be acceptable within certain regional or ethnic groups; that Jews may negotiate differently than Quakers, or city people differently than those in the country. There is no recognition that the setting, participants, or substance may impose a set of rules. Rather a whole host of things labeled "dirty tricks," "deliberate deception, psychological warfare, and positional pressure" are out of bounds. Consider their treatment of threats:

> Good negotiators rarely resort to threats. They do not need to; there are other ways to communicate the same information. If it seems appropriate to outline the consequences of the other side's action, suggest those that will occur independently of your will rather than those you could choose to bring about. Warnings are much more legitimate than threats and are not vulnerable to counter threats: "Should we fail to reach agreement, it seems highly probable to me that the news media would insist on publishing the whole sordid story. In a matter of this much public interest I don't see how we could legitimately suppress information. Do you?"

The statement which they approve (and label as a "warning" and not a "threat") would likely be construed as a threat. One who wishes to threaten his opponent in a negotiation is not likely to say, "If we do not reach agreement I will see to it that the information concerning your client becomes public." Rather he is likely to say what the authors suggest, "In a matter of this much public interest, I don't see how we could legitimately suppress information, do you?" In fact the authors have suggested merely a more subtle and more Machiavellian form of threat.

The question of deception is dealt with in the same facile way:

> Less than full disclosure is not the same as deception. Deliberate deception as to facts or one's intentions is quite different from not fully disclosing one's present thinking. Good faith negotiation does not require total disclosure. Perhaps the best answer to questions such as "What is the most you would be willing to pay if you had to?" would be along the following lines: "Let's not put ourselves under such a strong temptation to mislead. If you think no agreement is possible and that we may be wasting our time, perhaps we could disclose our thinking to some trustworthy third party, who can tell us whether there is a zone of potential agreement." In this way it is possible to behave with full candor about information that is not being disclosed.

The authors seem not to perceive that between "full disclosure" and "deliberate deception" lies a continuum, not a yawning chasm. They seem to ignore the fact that in one sense the negotiator's role is at least passively to mislead his opponent about his settling point while at the same time to engage in ethical behavior.

Most who have engaged in significant negotiation will concede the tension between those two responsibilities. How does one answer a question about his authority? Can one ethically allow a bumbling opponent who has drawn the incorrect inference about one's statement to continue in ignorance? Assume for example that one is a skillful negotiator representing a housing authority that is attempting to buy houses subject to condemnation. Assume that the opposing lawyer, a person of marginal competence, concludes incorrectly from a statement that you have made that you have been purchasing similar houses for $20,000, when in fact you have been paying $60,000 for them. When he says, "Now I understand that you have been buying similar houses for $20,000," can one remain silent? Can one make accurate statements concerning his position in the hope that the other party will draw incorrect inferences from those statements? "We have other offers, and we are asking $25." The other offers are in fact at $10. Can one make the foregoing statement in the hope that the other party will draw the inference that the other offers are at or near $25? Each has a different point on the continuum where he will stop. Notwithstanding superficial agreement on generalizations among lawyers, if one stimulates open discussion about lying and dissembling in negotiation, he will find large differences of position among lawyers on specific cases. To suggest that drawing the line between appropriate disclosure and inappropriate deception is easy [is] to mislead the reader.

Finally, because the book almost totally disregards distributive bargaining, it necessarily ignores a large number of factors that probably have a significant impact on the outcome of negotiations. For example, Karrass and Ross suggest that a party's aspiration level is an important factor in determining the outcome of a negotiation, other things being equal. There is evidence that the level of the first offer, and the pace and form of concessions all affect the outcome of negotiation, yet there is no consideration of those matters. Doubtless the authors can be forgiven for that. No book of 163 pages can be expected to deal with every aspect of negotiation. Yet this one suffers more than most, for implicitly if not explicitly, it seems to suggest that it is presenting the "true method."

In his recent article Marvin Mindes' identifies three prominent images of lawyers: hero, helper, and trickster. From Machiavelli onward much classical negotiating behavior could certainly be classified as trickster behavior, yet the trickster is the most pejorative of the various lawyer models. In a sense *Getting to YES* may be regarded as a plea for the recognition that a lawyer can be a good negotiator without deviating at all from his role as "helper." I believe that the authors are fundamentally mistaken about that. Anyone who would maximize his potential as a negotiator must occasionally do things that would cause others to classify him as a "trickster," whether he so classifies himself or not. To suggest that the world is otherwise is to mislead the reader.

Thus the book is more elegant and urbane than those written by Nierenberg and Cohen, but at bottom it suffers from some of the same problems. On the one hand the book promises an entirely new technique of negotiation, but it delivers only interesting techniques and insights. On the other hand the book delivers more than it promises in that its argument rests on a series of inarticulated moral premises. In sum, the book is useful; it contains interesting techniques and valid criticism of much negotiator behavior. However, its overstatement and its facile denial of some of the various difficulties involved in negotiation detract from its quality.

Comment by Roger Fisher

The editor has kindly invited me not to "respond" to Jim White's review, but rather to clarify areas of disagreement between us, and to suggest where my own thinking has changed since Bill Ury and I wrote *Getting to YES*. But for the editor's fortunate prohibition, there would be a tendency to react to a review that describes oneself or one's book as distasteful, self-righteous, not rigorous, not scholarly, distorting, and naive. Although I do not agree with those adjectives, I, too, see some inadequacies in the book. On the first day of my most recent negotiation course I tore a paperback copy in half to convince students how much work we had yet to do.

Although clearer, I believe, that most books on negotiation, concepts such as "position" and "power" are not presented as precisely as they might be, nor is it made sufficiently clear how using objective criteria to talk about fairness can be combined with being an advocate. *Getting to YES*, however, is beyond recall. With twelve foreign editions and a third of a million copies in print, the book will have to take care of itself. Far more important is jointly working to improve our collective analysis and understanding of the negotiation process.

Different purposes? To some extent, I believe, White is more concerned with the way the world is, and I am more concerned with what intelligent people ought to do. One task is to teach the truth — to tell students the unpleasant facts of life, including how people typically negotiate. But I want a student to negotiate better than his or her father. I see my task as to give the best possible prescriptive advice, taking into account the way other human beings are likely to behave as well as one's own emotions and psychological state.

Suppose a husband and wife come to an expert in negotiation asking advice on how best to negotiate the terms of a separation agreement that will involve children and jointly-held property. What is the best advice that such an expert could give to both about the process — about the manner of negotiating that would be mostly likely to produce a wise and fair outcome while maximizing their ability to deal with future problems, and minimizing their costs in terms of time, resources, and emotional stress? If one of them alone asked for such advice, in what ways would wise recommendations differ? These are the questions I am interested in.

The world is a rough place. It is also a place where, taken collectively, we are incompetent at resolving our differences in ways that efficiently and amicably serve our mutual interests. It is important that students learn about bluffing and hard bargaining, because they will certainly encounter it. It is also important that our students become more skillful and wise than most people in dealing with differences. Thus, to some extent, White and I are emphasizing different aspects of what needs to be taught.

Are distributional issues amenable to joint problem solving? The most fundamental difference between White's way of thinking and mine seem to concern the negotiation of distributional issues "where one for me is minus one for you." We agree on the importance of cooperation, imagination, and the search for creative options where the task is to reconcile substantive interests that are compatible. White, however, sees the joint problem-solving approach as limited to that area. In his view, the most demanding aspect of nearly every negotiation is the distributional one in which one seeks more at the expense of the other. Distributional matters, in his view, must be settled by the ultimate hard bargaining. He regards it as a distortion of reality to suggest that problem solving is relevant to distributional negotiation.

Here we differ. By focusing on the substantive issues (where the parties' criteria may be directly opposed), White overlooks the shared interest that the parties continue to have in the process for resolving that substantive difference. How to resolve the substantive difference is a shared problem. Both parties have an interest in identifying quickly and amicably a result acceptable to each, if one is possible. How to do so is a problem. A good solution to that process-problem requires joint action.

The guts of the negotiation problem, in my view, is not who gets the last dollar, but what is the best process for resolving that issue. It is certainly a mistake to assume that the only process available for resolving distributional questions is hard bargaining over positions. In my judgment it is also a mistake to assume that such hard bargaining is the best process for resolving differences efficiently and in the long-term interest of either side.

Two men in a lifeboat quarreling over limited rations have a distributional problem. One approach to resolving that problem is to engage in hard bargaining. *A* can insist that he will sink the boat unless he gets 60 percent of the rations. *B* can insist that he will sink the boat unless he gets 80 percent of the rations. But *A*'s and *B*'s shared problem is not just how to divide the rations; rather it is how to divide the rations without tipping over the boat and while getting the boat to safer waters. In my view, to treat the distributional issue as a shared problem is a better approach than to treat it as a contest of will in which a more deceptive, more stubborn, and less rational negotiator will tend to fare better. Treating the distributional issue as a problem to be solved ("How about dividing the rations in proportion to our respective weights?" or "How about a fixed portion of the rations for each hour that one of us rows?") is likely to be better for both than a contest over who is more willing to sink the boat.

Objective criteria. It is precisely in deciding such distributional issues that objective criteria can play their most useful role. Here is a second area of significant disagreement. White finds it useful to deny the existence of objective standards: "The suggestion that one can find objective criteria (as opposed to persuasive rationalizations) seems quite inaccurate." To his way of thinking the only approach is for a negotiator first to adopt a position and later to develop rationalizations for it: ". . . every able negotiator rationalizes every position that he takes."

No one has suggested that in most negotiations there is a single objective criterion that both parties will quickly accept as determinative. The question is rather what should be treated as the essence of the negotiation, and what attitude should be taken toward arguments advanced in the discussion. White thinks it better to treat positions of the parties as the essence of the negotiation, and objective standards advanced by either party as mere rationalizations. That is one approach. A different approach is possible and, I believe, preferable.

Two judges, in trying to reach agreement, will be looking for standards that should decide the case. They may have their predispositions and even strongly-held views, but they will jointly look for an agreed basis for decision. Each will typically advance law, precedent, and evidence not simply as rationalizations for positions adopted for other reasons, but honestly, as providing a fair basis for decision. White's example of litigation is the very one I would advance to demonstrate that however great the disagreement, the wise approach is to insist upon using objective criteria as the basis for decision. It is better for the parties in court to be advancing objective standards which they suggest ought to be determinative than to be telling the court that they won't take less (or pay more) than so many dollars. The same, I believe, is true for negotiators.

Two negotiators can be compared with two judges, trying to decide a case. There won't be a decision unless they agree. It is perfectly possible for fellow negotiators, despite their self-interest, to behave like fellow judges, in that they advance reasoned arguments seriously, and are open to persuasion by better arguments. They need not advance standards simply as rationalizations for positions, but as providing a genuine basis for joint decision.

What we are suggesting is that in general a negotiator should seek to persuade by coming up with better arguments on the merits rather than by simply trying to convince the other side that he is the more stubborn. A good guideline is for a negotiator to advance arguments as though presenting them to an impartial arbitrator, to press favorable bases for decision, but none so extreme as to damage credibility. (On the receiving side, a good guideline is for a negotiator to listen to arguments as though he were an impartial arbitrator, remaining open to persuasion despite self-interest and preconceptions.) My experience suggests that this method is often more efficient and amicable than hard positional bargaining and more often leads to satisfactory results for both parties.

Power. White seems to find the concept of "raw power" useful for a negotiator. I do not. For a negotiator, the critical questions of power are (1) how to enhance one's ability to influence favorably a negotiator on the other side, and (2) how to use such ability as one has. My ability to exert influence depends upon the cumulative impact of several factors: skill and knowledge, the state of our relationship, the legitimacy of our respective interests, the elegance of a proposed solution, my willingness and ability to commit myself, and the relative attractiveness to each side of its best alternative. In advance of a negotiation I can work to enhance each of those elements. During a negotiation I can orchestrate my use of these factors so that they reenforce and augment each other, or I can use some elements in ways that undermine others. Unless I am careful, a threat to use "raw power" will weaken rather than enhance my total ability to influence the other side, since it is likely to deprive me of knowledge, damage a relationship, and undercut my legitimacy.

Incidentally, I consider warnings (of what it will be in my interest to do, or what will happen independent of my action) to be not simply a more Machiavellian form of threat. Being more legitimate than a threat (of harm I could cause you), a warning tends to exert more influence.

Deception. White correctly calls attention to the difficult issue of ethical behavior, where disclosure of what a negotiator would be willing to do if he or she had to in order to reach agreement would be damaging to self-interest. The problem is particularly acute if the substance of the negotiation is haggling over positions — over statements or what one is willing or unwilling to do. With such positional bargaining in mind White sees the negotiator's role as being "to mislead his opponent about his settling point while at the same time to engage in ethical behavior."

I believe White fails to appreciate the extent to which the ethical problem is reduced if instead of negotiating by making a series of offers and counteroffers (each often intended to deceive the other as to what one is really willing to do), one treats negotiation as a joint search for an appropriate objective basis for decision, taking into account legitimate interest. If one tries to persuade the other side on the merits, as one would try to persuade an arbitrator, the rewards for — and need for — misleading are far less.

Changed thinking. Getting to YES says "Don't Bargain Over Positions." Students have now taught me that there are categories of negotiations where positional bargaining is the best way to proceed. On single-issue negotiations among strangers where the transaction costs of exploring interest would be high and where each side is protected by competitive opportunities, haggling over positions may work better than joint problem solving. A typical case would be negotiating a sale on the New York Stock Exchange.

Another chapter heading, "Separate the People from the Problem," also puts the matter too broadly. In some cases the people *are* the problem; negotiating a good relationship with them may be more important than the substantive outcome of any one negotiation. And good relations can ease future substantive negotiations. I still think that relationship issues and substantive issues should be separated to the following extent: One should not threaten a relationship as a means of trying to coerce a substantive concession; nor should one make an otherwise unjustified concession in hopes of buying a good relationship.

Getting to YES as a whole, I believe, blurs a desirable distinction between descriptive analysis and prescriptive advice. Descriptively, it sorts facts into useful categories: positions vs. interests; people issues vs. substantive ones; inventing vs. deciding; discussing what negotiators will or won't do vs. discussing what they ought to do. Those distinctions, like distinctions between reptiles and mammals, or between short snakes and long snakes, are objectively true and, despite possible difficulties in drawing lines, exist as facts in the real world. Whether or not they are useful is another question.

We go beyond suggesting these descriptive categories by advancing some prescriptive rules of thumb, indicated by the chapter headings in the book. These are not advanced as guidelines that will in every case produce the desired result. No such guidelines can exist, since negotiators who deal with each other often desire different results. The rules of thumb we advanced are the best we could come up with. Without knowing the particular subject matter of a negotiation or the identity of the people on the other side, what is the best advice one can give to a negotiator? People may prefer to ask different questions, but I have not yet heard better answers to the question on which we were and are working.

I am confident, however, that with the continued stimulating participation of people such as Jim White, we jointly will be able to produce both better questions and better answers.

Chapter 4

THE TENSION BETWEEN INTEGRATIVE
AND DISTRIBUTIVE BARGAINING

As you have seen in the preceding two chapters, integrative and distributive bargaining differ in many respects, in terms both of the goals of the negotiators and of the means used to achieve those goals. Moreover, since the vast majority of negotiations cannot be neatly categorized as purely distributive or purely integrative, but rather include aspects of both, the tension between the two approaches is inevitable and pervasive. In some respects, your client's interests are likely to overlap those of the other party; in others they will be different and complementary; and in others still they will be different and antagonistic. How are you to make your way through a process that demands such disparate and incompatible skills?

The fundamental paradox of negotiation is that each party is likely to be better off in some ways through collaboration and in others, through competition. Much of the literature on integrative bargaining is written as if, once mastered, its techniques obviate the need to resort to distributive tactics. There are those who believe that integrative approaches are always better because they imply a less egocentric attitude toward human interaction, a shunning of base self-interest as the motivating factor in negotiation. The article by Friedman and Shapiro in the preceding chapter discusses whether integrative, or "mutual gains" bargaining as they call it, is inherently more ethical than distributive bargaining and preferable for that reason, or if its merits lie in the results it produces. Given the mixed nature of most negotiations, every negotiator has to confront this question: if what is enlarged through collaboration must ultimately be divided, how is that dividing to be done? Does each party simply take half, because that's "fair"? Does the lawyer's ethical duty of zealous representation require the lawyer to fight for as large a share as possible? And how are the parties to be able to collaborate, with the specter of division hanging over them?

One way to begin thinking about the problem is to compare some basic tenets of each approach, as in the following chart:

DISTRIBUTIVE AND INTEGRATIVE BARGAINING COMPARED

Distributive	Integrative
Zero-sum (Fixed Pie)	Non-zero-sum (Expand the Pie)
Positional Bargaining ("I want"; demands, targets, walkaway)	Interest-based Bargaining ("I need"; motivations, options)
Bargain for Information	Wide-ranging Discussion
Minimize Concessions	Generate Many Proposals
Maximize Own Gain	Seek Joint Gain
One-shot Deal	Long-term Relationship

As you can see, the two approaches are diametrically opposed in many ways. Some writers have downplayed this conflict by describing negotiations as going through "phases": for example, an initial distributive phase, during which the parties jockey for position and test each other's resolve to see if either will capitulate; followed by an integrative phase, during which they seek opportunities for joint gain and creative solutions; followed by a final distributive phase, during which the created surplus is divided between them. In the article that follows, Lytle and her co-authors depict a cyclical process in which negotiating parties use arguments based on interests, rights, or power at different points, depending on what they are trying to accomplish and also on how the other negotiator behaves.

Such descriptions of the negotiation process are analytically useful. From a practical standpoint, however, the phases do not occur independently of each other. If you behave competitively during the early stages of a negotiation, your counterpart will be wary when you later profess interest in collaborating. Similarly, any lawyer looking for ways to "expand the pie" also has to think ahead about what will happen after that. Will the information shared early on be used against her at a later stage of the negotiation? Will taking the other side's needs into account in seeking creative solutions make her "soft" when the time for division comes?

Contemplating questions like these often leads lawyers to conclude that the only safe course is to take a closed, self-centered approach to negotiation, in which each side battles for what it wants. As you have seen in earlier chapters, such a simplification of the task, resulting in a purely distributive stance, runs the risk of not even serving self-interest well, since it foregoes opportunities for joint gain. If one party needs money soon and the other is more interested in the long-term rate of return, an agreement whereby they share profits equally will not be as good for either of them as one that takes their different preferences into account, providing the first with more money up front and the second with higher downstream revenues. How to balance moves to take as much as possible with moves to make as much as possible, and how to keep one from defeating the possibility of succeeding at the other, is an inescapable problem for negotiators. What are some of the sources of this tension, and what are some of the ways it can be mitigated in the negotiation process?

A. INSUFFICIENT INFORMATION

The limited information available to each side before the negotiation begins — about the substance of the negotiation, the characteristics of the other negotiator, the values each seeks to implement — exacerbates the tension between distributive and integrative bargaining. In addition, a lawyer always has to cope with the difficulties of knowing and putting forward accurately her client's point of view. As the first Condlin piece below points out, these inherent uncertainties usually incline lawyers to behave cautiously and strategically in negotiation. As a result, trust is hard to achieve as each party decides what steps are safe to take in the delicate dance of "mutually assessed mutual assessment" that typifies negotiation.

B. STRATEGIC USE OF INFORMATION

There is also anxiety because the amount of shared information needed for integrative bargaining to succeed may be more than a distributive bargainer wants to reveal. For example, a distributively-inclined buyer may prefer that his counterpart think that time of delivery, which he does not care much about, is very important to him, so that he can exact concessions on other aspects of the deal by "giving in" to a later delivery to accommodate the seller. Since it is hard to know in advance what issues will be most significant to the other side, it can be difficult to decide how much information to share and how to evaluate the quality of the information you receive about your counterpart's priorities. The fear of being taken advantage of often results in both sides' taking preemptive action focused on "winning" rather than on collaborating. Sometimes such strategies are effective; but they are also likely to impede or prevent what could be a fruitful search for joint gains.

C. LESSONS FROM THE PRISONERS' DILEMMA

How can a climate of collaboration develop under conditions of uncertainty? How contingent is any agreement to cooperate? Mathematical game theorists have tried to work out the optimal balance of competitive and cooperative moves in negotiation through the so-called "prisoners' dilemma" problem. Two prisoners are encouraged by the authorities to incriminate each other. If both refuse, both will go free; if both talk, each will get a short sentence. If one talks and the other is silent, the talker goes free and the other is jailed for a long time. The best strategy here is for both prisoners to refuse to talk — in effect, to cooperate with each other rather than with the authorities. However, since neither can prevent the other from talking, the most rational choice for both is to talk, for fear of a long jail sentence if the other fails to appreciate the value of cooperation.

Essentially, a good outcome for both is thwarted in a way that is familiar to every negotiator. This kind of downward spiral occurs frequently in negotiations because of the parties' failure or inability to say what they mean, because of their lack of information about or misapprehension of the other side's true intentions, and so on. The second excerpt below from Condlin's article discusses recent work on the prisoners' dilemma problem — especially Axelrod's groundbreaking research using computer tournaments to determine which negotiation strategies work best over time under the conditions of the prisoners' dilemma. Condlin also considers the implications of this research for legal negotiations.

D. IN(TER)DEPENDENCE OF THE PARTIES

The tension created by the mixed independence and interdependence of the parties — what Lax and Sebenius[1] have called the "negotiator's dilemma" — cannot be wished or willed away, as Mnookin's article below on why negotiations fail and Wetlaufer's on the limits of integrative bargaining illustrate. Korobkin, in the article excerpted below, even characterizes the negotiation process as inevitably distributive in what he calls the "zone definition" phase, although it is at least potentially integrative in the "surplus allocation" phase. The challenge, then, is to create an atmosphere in which a productive search for mutual gain can take place, without denying the reality that at some point the parties will have to divide what they have created. As in every other complex human interaction, conflict is inevitable in negotiation, but collaboration will often produce sufficient gains for both parties to warrant something other than a "fight or flight" response to the emergence of conflict.

E. THE VALUE OF CONTEXT

One reason that integrative bargaining is particularly suited to situations in which the parties have or desire a long-term relationship is that repeated dealings can help to reduce the tension between collaborating and dividing. With a history of what was said and done in the past, and with experience of what happened after earlier negotiations ended, negotiators have a better sense of what to expect both *during* and *from* the negotiation. Similarly, the use of external and objective standards as a basis for agreement can lessen concerns about one side imposing its will on the other. When both par-

---

[1] DAVID A. LAX & JAMES K. SEBENIUS, THE MANAGER AS NEGOTIATOR (1986).

ties have a stake in their relationship, the temptation to take advantage is tempered by the realization that there will be a tomorrow when they will meet again. Just as you cannot neatly isolate phases of negotiation and the appropriate behavior for each, you know in repeat negotiations that what you say and do today will be remembered and taken into account in future encounters. The mutually created context in which any given negotiation takes place helps to allay anxieties about being misled or otherwise taken advantage of and allows creative rather than rigid thinking to prevail.

F. MANAGING THE TENSION

Even when the parties do not want or expect to have an ongoing relationship, the potential for gain from collaboration argues against a combative approach to negotiation in many cases. Establishing a basis for it is not easy, however, since the context that fosters openness between parties to an ongoing relationship is absent. How do you explore the possibilities for fruitful collaboration, while at the same time protecting your client from exploitation in the event that the other side proves to be unwilling to join in the search? First, you have to recognize that simply cooperating with your counterpart is unlikely to produce the desired result. The other negotiator will either take whatever you offer, without feeling any obligation to reciprocate — a distributive response — or, if you are both cooperative types, you will quickly reach a compromise that fails to take full advantage of opportunities for joint gain.

To create a negotiation context that encourages collaboration, you have to be both optimistic about the benefits of collaborating and prepared to demonstrate to the other party how such an approach can serve both your interests, as discussed above in Chapter Three. At the same time, the reality of the negotiator's dilemma means that you have to demonstrate that you *do* expect reciprocity and will not make unilateral substantive concessions simply to keep the negotiation going. Ultimately, you cannot collaborate alone; and if you are not successful in convincing your opponent that there are joint gains to be had, you will have to revert to a more competitive posture in order to protect your client's interests. Rosenstein's article below gives practical advice on how to deal with potential obstacles to reaching agreement and how to manage some aspects of the tension between collaboration and competition in negotiation.

G. LAWYER-CLIENT CONFLICTS

A further source of tension in developing negotiation strategy stems from the potentially differing interests of lawyers and their clients. Lawyers, as repeat players in the negotiation arena, are like parties who have an ongoing business relationship: they have a history with each other and a professional context within which they will continue to work after this particular client's case is resolved. As a result, lawyers have a stake in behaving cooperatively with each other, so that colleagues do not see them as intransigent or inflexible over the long term. Conversely, any individual client may prefer that her lawyer behave purely distributively and fight for the last possible nickel from the other side in settling her case. The excerpt below from Mnookin and Gilson's article examines this conflict in the context of the lawyer's ethical duty of zealous advocacy, and it is discussed further in Chapter Eight.

Ultimately, the tension between collaborating and competing in negotiation cannot be resolved, only recognized and managed. A skillful negotiator will develop her abilities in both arenas and will employ one or the other based on a careful assessment of the subject of the negotiation and of the other parties involved. No single approach is adequate for all situations; most negotiations will provide opportunities for both to be used effectively and productively. While every negotiator will perhaps feel more comfortable with one approach than with the other, it is important to develop a range of skills in negotiation while remaining aware of where your greatest strengths lie. The following chapter, on psychological aspects of negotiating, addresses how self-observation can help you expand the skills you bring to your study of legal negotiations and how the findings of social psychologists and others can contribute to your understanding of the interpersonal dynamics of negotiating.

Robert H. Mnookin,[*] *Why Negotiations Fail: An Exploration of Barriers to the Resolution of Conflict*
8 OHIO ST. J. ON DISP. RESOL. 235, 239-42 (1993)[**]

A. Strategic Barriers

The first barrier to the negotiated resolution of conflict is inherent in a central characteristic of negotiation. Negotiation can be metaphorically compared to making a pie and then dividing it up. The process of conflict resolution affects both the size of the pie, and who gets what size slice.

The disputants' behavior may affect the size of the pie in a variety of ways. On the one hand, spending on avoidable legal fees and other process costs shrinks the pie. On the other hand, negotiators can together "create value" and make the pie bigger by discovering resolutions in which each party contributes special complementary skills that can be combined in a synergistic way, or by exploiting differences in relative preferences that permit trades that make both parties better off. Books like "Getting to Yes"

---

[*] Robert H. Mnookin is Samuel Williston Professor of Law at Harvard University. In this excerpt he discusses some of the difficulties encountered in taking a mixed distributive/integrative approach to negotiation.

[**] Copyright © 1993 Ohio State Journal on Dispute Resolution. Reprinted with permission.

and proponents of "win-win negotiation" emphasize the potential benefits of collaborative problem-solving approaches to negotiation which allow parties to maximize the size of the pie.

Negotiation also involves issues concerning the distribution of benefits, and, with respect to pure distribution, both parties cannot be made better off at the same time. Given a pie of fixed size, a larger slice for you means a smaller one for me.

Because bargaining typically entails both efficiency issues (that is, how big the pie can be made) and distributive issues (that is, who gets what size slice), negotiation involves an inherent tension — one that David Lax and James Sebenius have dubbed the "negotiator's dilemma." In order to create value, it is critically important that options be created in light of both parties' underlying interests and preferences. This suggests the importance of openness and disclosure, so that a variety of options can be analyzed and compared from the perspectives of all concerned. However, when it comes to the distributive aspects of bargaining, full disclosure — particularly if unreciprocated by the other side — can often lead to outcomes in which the more open party receives a comparatively smaller slice. To put it another way, unreciprocated approaches to creating value leave their maker vulnerable to claiming tactics. On the other hand, focusing on the distributive aspects of bargaining can often lead to unnecessary deadlocks and, more fundamentally, a failure to discover options or alternatives that make both sides better off. A simple example can expose the dilemma. The first involves what game theorists call "information asymmetry." This simply means each side to a negotiation characteristically knows some relevant facts that the other side does not know.

Suppose I have ten apples and no oranges, and Nancy Rogers has ten oranges and no apples. (Assume apples and oranges are otherwise unavailable to either of us.) I love oranges and hate apples. Nancy likes them both equally well. I suggest to Nancy that we might both be made better off through a trade. If I disclose to Nancy that I love oranges and don't eat apples, and Nancy wishes to engage in strategic bargaining, she might simply suggest that her preferences are the same as mine, although, in truth, she likes both. She might propose that I give her nine apples (which she says have little value to her) in exchange for one of her very valuable oranges. Because it is often very difficult for one party to know the underlying preferences of the other party, parties in a negotiation may puff, bluff, or lie about their underlying interests and preferences. Indeed, in many negotiations, it may never be possible to know whether the other side has honestly disclosed its interests and preferences. I have to be open to create value, but my openness may work to my disadvantage with respect to the distributive aspect of the negotiation.

Even when both parties know all the relevant information, and the potential gains may result from a negotiated deal, strategic bargaining over how to divide the pie can still lead to deadlock (with no deal at all) or protracted and expensive bargaining, thus shrinking the pie. For example, suppose Nancy has a house for sale for which she has a reservation price of $245,000. I am willing to pay up to $295,000 for the house. Any deal within a bargaining range from $245,000 to $295,000 would make both of us better off than no sale at all. Suppose we each know the other's reservation price. Will there be a deal? Not necessarily. If we disagree about how the $50,000 "surplus" should be divided (each wanting all or most of it), our negotiation may end in a deadlock. We might engage in hardball negotiation tactics in which each tried to persuade the other that he or she was committed to walking away from a beneficial deal, rather than accept less than $40,000 of the surplus. Nancy might claim that she won't take a nickel less than $285,000, or even $294,999 for that matter. Indeed, she might go so far as to give a power of attorney to an agent to sell only at that price, and then leave town in order to make her commitment credible. Of course, I could play the same type of game and the result would then be that no deal is made and that we are both worse off. In this case, the obvious tension between the distribution of the $50,000 and the value creating possibilities inherent in any sale within the bargaining range may result in no deal.

Strategic behavior — which may be rational for a self-interested party concerned with maximizing the size of his or her own slice — can often lead to inefficient outcomes. Those subjected to claiming tactics often respond in kind, and the net result typically is to push up the cost of the dispute resolution process. . . . Parties may be tempted to engage in strategic behavior, hoping to get more. Often all they do is shrink the size of the pie. Those experienced in the civil litigation process see this all the time. One or both sides often attempt to use pre-trial discovery as leverage to force the other side into agreeing to a more favorable settlement. Often the net result, however, is simply that both sides spend unnecessary money on the dispute resolution process.

Robert J. Condlin,[*] *Bargaining in the Dark: The Normative Incoherence of Lawyer Dispute Bargaining Role*
51 MD. L. REV. 1, 8-10 (1992)[**]

* * *

In this world of strategic interaction, uncertainty, thought of as incomplete and imperfect information about the factors a rational actor should take into account in deciding how to proceed, is dispute settlement's most salient attribute. Parties come to bargaining with diverse and not always compatible expectations about outcome, and often incommensurable beliefs

---

[*] Robert J. Condlin is Professor at University of Maryland School of Law. In this excerpt he discusses the centrality of uncertainty in negotiation.

[**] Copyright © 1992 Robert J. Condlin. Reprinted with permission.

about the legitimacy of their respective positions. While they know in advance that such incompatibility and incommensurability are possible, they do not know in any particular case to what extent they are present. When they enter a negotiation, therefore, bargainers do not know for certain whether they will be friends or enemies, focused on questions of efficiency or fairness, able to work together or locked intractably in combat. As a result, they must approach the negotiation prepared for all of the above.

Uncertainty results in part from the fact that in law, and in life generally, there are competing conceptions of the good, and thus no necessary consensus on how a dispute ought to be resolved, or even on the principles on which a resolution could be grounded. Not everyone believes, for example, that property rights count for as much as personal rights (or even that rights discourse is the best framework for resolving questions of resource distribution), that all values can be expressed in terms of some common denominator such as money, that proceeding forward efficiently is more important than determining responsibility for present states of affairs, that properly promulgated laws are necessarily valid, or that procedural justice is the same as justice simpliciter. Parties starting from such diverse premises often reach different conclusions about what result a bargaining interaction ought to produce, and with good reason. The effect is that bargainers usually cannot say with precision at the beginning of a negotiation what their counterparts will accept to settle the dispute. They can make predictions, and these often will come close, particularly if their past dealings involved similar disputes or were long standing. But they cannot be exact in these predictions or do more than specify a range of possible outcomes. If it were otherwise, there would be no need to bargain. Each would offer the minimum the other would take, because to offer more would be to make a gift and not a bargain.

Uncertainty is exacerbated by the fact that bargainers must make statements and describe intentions in their clients' best light, and therefore, in the strongest credible terms that the most generous or compliant (hypothetical) adversary might accept. Consequently, what is said in bargaining is usually an exaggerated version of what is meant, and known to be so. Yet, bargainers need to know whether particular adversaries are the most generous, or of what generosity consists in a given case. Therefore, they must learn during the course of the bargaining interaction what their counterparts truly believe and would be willing to do, and to do this they must interpret actions and statements of the other side as much for what they reveal as for what they say. In such a world, communication itself is another source of uncertainty. Every disclosure is viewed as (and is) potentially a concession, every argument potentially a provocation, and every proposal potentially a gift. In speaking at all, then, bargainers understandably will be cautious and circumspect, revealing as little and defending as much as possible until the other's intentions are known. While this is only prudent — one does not bare the throat until it is clear that it will not be cut — the effect is to make communication more difficult. Suspicion increases, candor diminishes, and indirect and self-protective methods of expression replace open and straightforward ones.

Uncertainty is also increased by the recursiveness of the bargaining dynamic. In the process of trying to dope out, influence, and trade favorably with one another, the state of mind each bargainer tries to understand has as one of its properties the fact that it is also trying to understand the other. Bargaining is thus a process of mutually assessed mutual assessment, in which each party makes moves that carry fateful implications and that must be chosen in light of one's thoughts about the other's thoughts about oneself, and so on. Such information is unknowable in any final sense, of course, because it changes at the moment it becomes known, by virtue of the fact that it is known. Bargainers can make assumptions about what their counterparts believe, about what they (the bargainers) believe, about what the others believe, and so on, but to the extent that they try to understand these beliefs finally, they will inevitably be trapped in an outguessing regress.

In short, the lack of perfect information about adversary wants and needs, the possibility of competing conceptions of the good, the practice of a "best lights" discourse, recursiveness, and ordinary prudence combine to cause dispute bargainers to approach a bargaining relationship cautiously and to communicate strategically. Dispute bargainers must and do learn to trust, of course, for without trust bargainers could not settle disputes. But this is an instrumental understanding of trust, as predictability, or the capacity to know when others will honor their commitments, and trust as predictability does not do much to soften the cautiousness and suspicion that is built into the structure of the bargaining conversation or to change bargaining's distinctive and identifying character as strategic interaction.

* * *

Gerald B. Wetlaufer,[*] *The Limits of Integrative Bargaining*
85 GEO. L.J. 369, 390-91 (1996)[**]

* * *

A final claim that can now be evaluated is that opportunities for integrative bargaining necessarily imply that it is in a negotiator's immediate pecuniary self-interest to engage in the tactics of cooperation, openness, truthtelling, honesty, and trust. First, I have demonstrated that opportunities for integrative bargaining, especially meaningful opportunities for integrative bargaining (e.g., where the pie may be made to expand and to

---

[*] Gerald B. Wetlaufer is Professor at University of Iowa College of Law. His article challenges the notion that many negotiations involve opportunities for true integrative bargaining.

[**] Copyright © 1996 Georgetown Law Journal. Reprinted with permission.

stay expanded), exist within a narrower range of circumstances than sometimes has been claimed. Some of the differences cited by Lax and Sebenius simply do not create opportunities for integrative bargaining. Others, namely those involving different assessments regarding future events, create opportunities to expand the pie only if the parties are willing to bet on their projections. And even when the parties are willing to bet, there will be opportunities for integrative bargaining only some of the time and only in ways that will sometimes prove self-defeating in the sense that the pie may eventually return to its original size. If the pie shrinks back, one or both of the parties will be worse off than they had expected to be and, potentially, worse off than they would have been had they not entered the agreement. Other circumstances named by Lax and Sebenius — multiple issues differently valued, differing projections concerning future events, differing time preferences, differing levels of risk aversion — sometimes offer opportunities for integrative bargaining but sometimes do not. Although the general claim is made that opportunities for integrative bargaining provide a reason, based solely on immediate pecuniary self-interest, to engage in openness and truthtelling, those opportunities are considerably less pervasive than has been announced. Thus, this argument for openness and truthtelling is, in that degree, narrower and less persuasive.

Second, even within the range of circumstances in which there are significant opportunities for integrative bargaining, the bargainer must almost always engage in distributive bargaining as well. Therefore, it is in the bargainer's self-interest not just to adopt the tactics of openness and truthtelling that are said to be appropriate to integrative bargaining, but somehow also to adopt the tactics of truth-hiding and dissimulation that are said to be appropriate to distributive bargaining. However we might manage these incompatible tactics, this situation presents at most a weak and highly qualified argument for openness and truthtelling. Moreover, the argument for openness and truthtelling is not an argument for openness and truthtelling with respect to everything, but instead, is limited to information useful in identifying and exploiting opportunities for integrative bargaining. Thus, an opportunity for integrative bargaining will present an occasion for a certain amount of truthtelling with respect to one's relative interest in various issues (or one's projections about the future or aversion to risk) without also presenting even a weak argument for truthtelling with respect to one's reservation price.

Finally, one should understand that a bargainer's self-interest is never promoted by disclosure for its own sake. Rather, what is in the bargainer's self-interest is discovering truthful information about the other side's interests and situation. Thus, what is true in distributive bargaining is also true where there are opportunities for integrative bargaining; the best possible position is to secure perfect information about the other side's position while disclosing nothing at all about one's own. Disclosure is rational and in a bargainer's self-interest only insofar as it may be essential to securing the information she needs. If she can secure that information without disclosure, whether through research or simply by getting the other side to spill the beans over drinks, there is no case for openness and truthtelling. Moreover, as is also the case with distributive bargaining, if she can induce the other side to disclose because they wrongly think she is doing the same, it cannot be argued that her immediate, individual, and pecuniary self-interest would be advanced by a policy of openness and truthtelling.

* * *

Russell Korobkin,[*] *A Positive Theory of Legal Negotiation*
88 GEO. L.J. 1789, 1789-92 (2000)[**]

* * *

In recent years, scholars have made two attempts to categorize more systematically the wide range of negotiation tactics, providing a theoretical overlay to the nuts-and-bolts, tactical view of the negotiating process. The first classifies negotiating tactics as either "cooperative" or "competitive" in style. For example, a competitive negotiator makes extreme opening demands, asking for far more than she actually hopes to receive. A cooperative negotiator, in contrast, makes more modest and realistic opening demands. The competitive/cooperative dichotomy can be useful to the negotiator because it helps him to identify different options whenever tactical choices present themselves. To use the same example, when a negotiator is called on to make an opening demand, keeping the competitive/ cooperative dichotomy in mind might help him to generate more aggressive and more friendly options than would otherwise come to mind.

The utility of the dichotomy is limited, however, because it does not imply any descriptive theory of negotiators' goals — what negotiators actually use competitive or cooperative tactics for. Neither competition nor cooperation is a goal in itself, and most scholars who employ this dichotomy even claim that neither approach is intrinsically more useful in helping the negotiator to achieve the ultimate — if unhelpfully vague — holy grail of negotiating "success." The cooperative/competitive dichotomy can help negotiators identify options when they come to a choice-point in the maze of the negotiation, but the dichotomy cannot help them better judge which direction to choose.

Contemporary negotiation theory more often relies on a second dichotomy between "distributive" and "integrative" negotiating approaches. Accord-

---

[*] Russell Korobkin is Professor of Law, University of California Los Angeles. In this article, he argues that all negotiator activities have as their goal either defining the bargaining range or dividing the existing surplus between the parties.

ing to this categorization, negotiators use distributive tactics to "claim value" — that is, to capture the fixed gains in trade created by the agreement for himself or for his client. In contrast, negotiators use integrative tactics to "create value" — that is, identify tradeoffs and options that will simultaneously make both parties better off. The distribute/integrative dichotomy is a far more useful heuristic than the competitive/cooperative dichotomy because the former describes goals to which negotiators gear their tactical choices. Although useful, this categorization is not the only way to view the tactics of negotiation systematically — the cathedral, of course, appears differently in different light — and it may not be the most useful.

One problem with this categorization is that all negotiated agreements "create value" in the sense that both parties are made better off than they would be if they filed to reach agreement. Because even distributive bargaining thus leads to "integrative" agreements, the distinction between the new categories in tenuous. Integrative techniques my be differentiated from distributive ones as allowing negotiators to create even more efficient agreements than would otherwise be possible by redefining the subject matter of the negotiation. For example, if a new car dealer is willing to offer a buyer a larger "trade-in" credit than the buyers' used are is worth to him, the parties can create value by changing the negotiation from one for a "new car" to one for a "new car plus trade-in." But this value-added definition leads to a second problem with the integrative/distributive dichotomy: integrative bargaining merely combines two or more opportunities for distributive bargaining — buyer and seller now negotiate the price of the new car and the trade-in simultaneously. While this. . . . technique is useful, elevating integrative bargaining to the same theoretical plane as distributive bargaining oversells the importance of the former. Finally, opportunities for such value-added integrative bargaining are probably fewer in legal negotiation than in other contexts because the subject matter of legal negotiations is often clear to both parties and money is often of substantial concern to both.

This article presents a new dichotomy. . . . This "zone definition/surplus allocation" dichotomy provides a complete description of the negotiating process. . . .

First negotiators attempt to define the bargaining zone — the distance between the reservation points (or "walkaway" points) of the two parties — in the manner most advantageous to their respective clients. I call this activity "zone definition." Exploring alternatives to agreement, questioning, persuading, misleading, committing to positions, and redefining the negotiation's subject matter are all tactical tools used in zone definition. Because transactions are economically rational — in the sense that reaching agreement is better than not reaching agreement for both parties — only at points within the bargaining zone, zone definition can be understood as an inherently economic activity.

Second, negotiators attempt to convince their opponent to agree to a single "deal point" within the bargaining zone. I call this activity "surplus allocation." Surplus allocation effectively divides the cooperative surplus that the parties create by reaching an agreement. For both parties, transacting at any point within the bargaining zone is more desirable than not reaching agreement, but each knows that the same is true for the other. Once the bargaining zone is established, there is no economically obvious way for the parties to select a deal point. As a result, surplus allocation usually requires that negotiators appeal to community norms of either procedural or substantive fairness. Consequently, surplus allocation can be understood as an inherently social activity.

Negotiating tactics that can be classified as "competitive" or "cooperative," or as "distributive" or "integrative," also fit into the zone definition/surplus allocation dichotomy, but they are organized differently under the new dichotomy than they are under the existing frameworks. Both zone definition and surplus allocation can be achieved by competitive or cooperative tactics. While surplus allocation is a distributive exercise, zone definition can be achieved with both integrative and distributive tactics.

* * *

Anne Lytle, Jeanne M. Brett & Debra L. Shapiro,[*] *The Strategic Use of Interests, Rights, and Power to Resolve Disputes*
15 NEGOT. J. 31, 33-34, 38-49 (1999)[**]

Interests, Rights, and Power: Three Approaches for Resolving Disputes

According to Ury, Brett, and Goldberg (1993), disputants can choose to focus on several different approaches to negotiate: interests, rights, or power. Focusing on interests means that the parties try to learn each other's underlying needs, desires, and concerns, and find ways of reconciling them in the construction of an agreement. A focus on interests provides the opportunity for learning about the parties' common concerns, priorities, and preferences, which are necessary for the construction of an integrative, or a mutually beneficial agreement that creates value for the parties. Focusing on rights means that parties try to determine how to resolve the dispute by applying some standard of fairness, contract, or law. A rights focus is likely

[*] Anne L. Lytle is Senior Lecturer, Organisational Behaviour at the Australian Graduate School of Management, University of New South Wales. Jeanne M. Brett is DeWitt W. Buchanan, Jr. Distinguished Professor of Dispute Resolution and Organizations at the J. L. Kellogg Graduate School of Management, Northwestern University. Debra L. Shapiro is Clarice Smith Professor of Management & Organization at University of Maryland. In this article they describe how parties use both distributive and integrative approaches in the course of a single negotiation in order to achieve their goals.

partner's prior act, pervades negotiations. Yet, if negotiators are cycling between interests, rights, and power, how much reciprocity is going on in these negotiations?

Reciprocity of Interests, Rights, and Power

The literature on reciprocity of communications during negotiations asserts that a variety of different types of communications, including cooperative, distributive, procedural, and affective are reciprocated. In other words, negotiators tend to reciprocate each type of communication previously spoken by their partners. This literature suggests that interests, rights, and power communications will be similarly reciprocated. However, because we found a significant degree of cycling between interests, rights, and power, we wondered whether reciprocity coexists with the movement among negotiation strategies.

Our results indicate that although there was a significant amount of movement between strategies, a reciprocal response was in fact the most likely response to communication involving interests, rights, or power. No other response was as likely as a reciprocal response, and the reciprocal response occurred with a greater than chance probability. Interests were reciprocated 42 percent of the time, rights 22 percent, and power 27 percent. Proposals for settlement were reciprocated 43 percent of the time, and general facts about the situation 55 percent. These reciprocity percentages are all significantly different from the base rate level of chance reciprocity, which is 10 percent for each category.

Reciprocity of rights and power communications, although significant, occurred less frequently than reciprocity of interests, facts, and proposals. This finding led us to investigate the implications of reciprocating rights and power communications. The negotiation literature suggests that when rights and power communications are reciprocated the negotiation may enter a negative conflict spiral and the outcome may be in jeopardy.

Reciprocity and Dispute Outcomes in Cases Involving Rights and Power

Ury, Brett, and Goldberg suggest that the process of determining who is right or has more power results in a competition between parties over who will prevail. This claim is generally supported by research reporting that the higher the overall frequencies of arguments, personal attacks, threats, and demands, the more likely that outcomes will be one-sided or distributive. Parties may argue about who is right or wrong under the contract or the law and who is more powerful without addressing the underlying reasons why the dispute has happened in the first place. Compared to a power approach, we believe a rights focus may be somewhat less damaging to the relationship if the dispute is taken out of the parties' control and decided by a court or a third party. Power approaches, on the other hand, may be more contentious if there is direct interaction, and may create new disputes and leave open opportunities for revenge. Both of these approaches, however, may have high costs in time, effort, and money, and leave little opportunity to address the causes of the dispute or to create mutually beneficial solutions.

* * *

Strategic Implications for Negotiations

Our data-based exploration of the interests, rights, and power strategies resolving disputes provides a number of insights into contentious negotiations. First, our research affirms that negotiators use a variety of different approaches during dispute resolution negotiations. One approach is interest-based, but negotiators may spend substantial time discussing facts, making proposals, and posturing with respect to rights and power. Using these different approaches strategically, particularly confronting rights and power strategies when they are used against you, is an important negotiation skill. Second, our findings with respect to reciprocity help to explain why it is so difficult to keep a negotiation focused on interests if the other party uses rights or power. While reciprocity can help to keep parties focused on interests, it can also draw parties into conflict spirals. Knowing how to manage reciprocity so as to sustain your negotiation strategy regardless of the other party's approach is another important negotiation skill. Third, the one-sidedness of distributive outcomes is affected by reciprocity of rights and power communications. Therefore, strategies for refocusing the negotiation away from rights and power are important negotiation skills.

In the remaining sections of this essay, we focus on strategies for managing dispute resolution negotiations and offer practical recommendations to negotiators concerning: which strategy to use when beginning negotiations; how to deflect rights-and-power strategies and refocus the negotiation on interests; when to use rights-and-power strategies; and how to implement rights-and-power strategies effectively.

Starting the Negotiation

There is no one "best way" to approach a dispute. How you begin a dispute resolution negotiation should be a strategic choice based on a careful analysis of the parties, their goals, and the situation. Before going to the negotiation table, it is important to evaluate the pros and cons of beginning with facts of the case, rights, power, or interests against the unique features of each dispute situation.

Facts. Beginning the negotiation by discussing facts helps delineate the area of dispute: what parties agree about and what they do not. In some cases, discussing the facts can be constructive in discovering what the situation is and what the problems are or even identifying what a potential solution might be.

Negotiators may find that there are no facts in dispute, but that the interpretation of the contract or the law is in dispute. In such cases, seeking advice from third parties or legal experts to clarify how a court would interpret the contract and law may give parties a realistic assessment of the rights context of their dispute and provide impetus for settlement.

Alternately, the parties may find that they do not agree on the facts. * * * Unless one party can provide the other with new, credible information supporting that party's interpretation of the facts, the dispute over the facts is likely to spiral into a he said/she said situation, which is unlikely to result in any sort of solution to the dispute.

Rights. Opening the negotiation by presenting an interpretation of the rights framework of the dispute, if you believe that it is in your favor, is a strong offensive opening. A rights opening lets the other party know that you think you should prevail in the dispute and why. * * * Of course, had the other party already accepted this interpretation of the rights framework, there would likely be no dispute to resolve.

Such an opening, we believe, may encourage a reciprocal defensive response presenting an alternative interpretation of the rights framework. * * * The parties may then engage in a series of rights-based communications, each trying to convince the other that its interpretation is correct and the other side's is incorrect. Without an independent interpretation of the disputed rights framework, the parties are likely to have difficulty reaching agreement, unless one capitulates on the rights question, or both turn away from trying to resolve the rights dispute.

Power. Opening the negotiation by discussing your power to coerce the other party to concede may result in a short negotiation, if your power is credible and the other negotiator concedes. * * *

The other negotiator, however, may understand that carrying out a threat requires an expenditure of resources. Knowing that you would rather not have to act on your threat to use power, the other negotiator may call your bluff and walk away, leaving you in the position to act on your threat or lose face, neither of which is a desirable option. Given human nature, the more likely response of the other negotiator is to counter-threaten, generating an escalation of conflict and commitment to disputing.

Interests. We see few risks in opening negotiations by focusing on the other party's interests, asking questions, and giving a little information about your own interests. An interests approach is particularly appropriate if the other party is thought to be generally cooperative and you are aware of a possible solution that might be acceptable to both parties. * * *

By strategically reciprocating information-sharing, negotiators should be able to move from sharing interests to sharing interests-based proposals to settlement. Those interests-based proposals will contain elements that are both integrative . . . and distributive. . . . It may be possible to resolve the dispute without ever resolving who was right and who was wrong under standards of fairness, contract, or law or who has the greatest power to harm the other.

The risks in opening a negotiation with an interests approach are that you send a message that you are seeking settlement, and even might share a little confidential information to try to get settlement negotiations moving. These seem to us to be minimal risks. Sending a message that you are seeking settlement does not reveal your bottom-line settlement terms. Sharing a little information about your own interests does not mean you reveal all your interests and priorities to the other party without receiving information in return. Effective negotiation requires balancing cooperative and competitive (or individualistic) orientations. Our recommendation to open negotiations by focusing on interests is geared to give the cooperative orientation a chance.

Breaking the Spiral of Reciprocity

A negotiator may sometimes feel trapped in the throes of a conflict spiral, where the negotiation has deteriorated into a back-and-forth battle over facts, rights, or power statements with little chance of progressing to a more productive exchange. There are several options to break the bonds of reciprocity and move the negotiation toward a more effective interests-based discussion.

Do Not Reciprocate. A negotiator can simply refuse to reciprocate communications involving facts, rights, or power, and instead ask an interests-based question. A number of theorists and commentators also recommend not reciprocating rights or power.

When dealing with some insensitive negotiators, it may take several redirections of communications over facts, rights, or power before the other party realizes that you want an interests-based conversation. To the critics who say that refusing to reciprocate rights and power threats sends a message of weakness, we would point out that, by refocusing the negotiations on interests, we are not advocating that negotiators make concessions substantively or strategically. Indeed, by refusing to be drawn into a strategy that will not further his or her interest, the negotiator has strongly defended the preferred interest-based approach to negotiations.

* * *

Do Not Make Unilateral Concessions. Osgood suggests a unilateral strategy called "GRIT," or Graduated and Reciprocated Initiatives in Tension Reduction, for breaking out of a conflict spiral. This strategy proposes offering a concession to the other party, announcing that this concession is intended to break the escalation, inviting the other party to reciprocate the concession, and then making the unilateral concession.

We found that making unilateral concessions was not effective for refocusing negotiations in our study. Concessions were not as effective in refocusing negotiations from rights and power (60 percent refocus) as were other noncontentious communications (77 percent refocus). In negotiations that have not reached impasse, making concessions may actually encourage, rather than stop, a conflict spiral. The unilateral concession may be seen as a reward for contentious behavior, and therefore encourage the repetition of such behavior in the hopes of accruing more concessions.

Combining Types of Communications. Although not reciprocating rights-and-power communications was an effective way to break the bonds of reciprocity, research suggests that reciprocating may be instinctive. Lerner explains: "We all recognize intellectually that repeating our ineffective efforts achieves nothing and can even make things worse. Yet, oddly enough, most of us continue to do *more of the same*, especially under stress." Many negotiators with whom we have discussed the nonreciprocating strategy are uncomfortable with it, because they believe that it conveys a message of weakness.

We thought it might be possible to reciprocate a rights-or-power communication and also change the focus away from rights or power by combining it, for example, with an interests-based question or a proposal for settlement. In the context of labor negotiations, Walton, Cutcher-Gershenfeld and McKersie suggest that managers combine "forcing" (distributive tactics and threats) with "fostering" (integrative tactics and information sharing) strategies to achieve better negotiated outcomes. Putnam points out that negotiators often mix cooperative and competitive negotiation orientations in the same statement, creating equivocal messages about their intentions. * * * Given the seemingly natural tendency to reciprocate especially negative behaviors, sending a combined communication at least gives the negotiator a choice of what to reciprocate. So, too, an opening toward interests may be more appreciated and therefore more likely to be reciprocated when it is associated with power.

* * *

Label the Process. Several commentators have suggested that recognizing or labeling a tactic as ineffective can neutralize or refocus negotiations. This suggestion is supported by our results. We found that process-labeling statements were relatively infrequent responses to rights-and-power communications, but were quite effective when they were used, refocusing the other negotiator 82 percent of the time. * * *

When to Use Rights or Power in Negotiations

Maintaining a primary focus on interests, in our view, will in most cases result in a satisfying, mutually beneficial outcome that has the potential to resolve the underlying causes of the dispute. This preference for an interests-based strategy, however, does not mean that negotiators should never use rights or power in negotiation. When and how to effectively use rights or power is a strategic decision that needs to be based on an analysis of the specific dispute situation.

One time to use rights or power is when the other party refuses to come to the negotiating table, despite significant efforts to encourage that party to do so. In such a situation, no negotiation is taking place, and little is lost by threatening action based on rights or power. Perhaps the threat will convey to the other party the severity of the situation. * * *

Another time to use rights or power is when negotiations have broken down, interests-based negotiation is exhausted, and parties are at an impasse. A credible threat, especially if combined with an interests-based proposal for resolution, may restart the negotiations. As in the previous situation, since negotiations are hopelessly stalled, not much is lost in threatening action based on rights or power. Disputants should be sure, however, that they have truly engaged in an interests-based approach and that they are not moving to rights or power prematurely. The other side, for example, might see no reason to make serious steps toward agreement if you have not shared interests and formulated specific requests or steps toward progress. Focusing on discussion of details, asking specific questions, and making very specific requests can sometimes avert an evolution towards rights or power.

Alternately, we found in our study that negotiators used rights and power most often two times in negotiations: at the beginning, and in the third quarter. Rights and power communications early in the negotiation may not always be intended as threats, but merely as information. But, consider what information such statements convey. * * * [For example] "I've discussed the case with my attorney, who tells me the contract is in my favor, I'm not afraid to go to court." If you know that the other party does not agree with your interpretation of the rights base of the dispute, why risk directing the focus of negotiations to these disputed rights? It may be a better strategy to hold this information back to be used (if necessary) later in the negotiation.

Rights-and-power communications used in the third quarter of the negotiations may be attempts to influence the distributive outcome of the negotiation. * * *

In both of these examples, the threatening information is credible and serves an informational purpose. In the third quarter example, however, the threat has an additional function of turning down a proposal, underscoring the unacceptability of the offer. Using threats in the third quarter of the negotiation to try to claim more value from an agreement that both parties realize is acceptable may be a risky undertaking. Clearly, some of the third quarter threats in our study were of this nature. Conceding to a threat involves loss of face, and sometimes a negotiator will prefer to walk away from an acceptable settlement rather than to concede further and lose face. If a negotiator does choose to make threats for this purpose, it may be strategic to combine these threats with some sort of positive, interests-based incentive for the other side in order to help them save face.

The Effective Implementation of Rights and Power Strategies

Although the decision about when to use rights and power strategies is an important one, how these strategies are implemented determines their success in transforming the negotiation back to a productive interaction and effectively meeting your interests. Rights-and-power communications are implicit or explicit threats. They state what the negotiator's views are of his or her alternatives to settlement. Using threats effectively means getting the other party to the negotiating table, and once there, getting an acceptable agreement. Effective threats are specific and credible, focus on harming high-priority interests, and leave a pathway back to interests.

Credibility. First, threats based on rights or power must be credible. The other party must believe that you are able and willing to actually carry out your strategy. Credibility is increased by specifying a number of key details about when, where, how, and by whom this strategy will be carried out, as well as by demonstrating that you are prepared to begin the implementation. * * * A detailed, well-constructed threat, whether rights or power-based, is much more convincing when the initiator expresses what will be done to implement the threat rather than communicates some vague actions stemming from a fleeting emotional state.

Harming High-Priority Interests. Second, threats based on rights or power must be carefully focused on the other party's high-priority interests. If they are not, there will be little incentive to comply with the threat. This focus should be something that either the person or the company really does not want to happen, or conversely, something that they do not want to "give up." The object of the threat must be something that really makes the person want to comply with your demands. Depending on levels of personal power and connection, it might be better to focus on the company's interests than those of a specific individual. This is because the company may choose to sacrifice the individual doing the negotiating if things get out of control. On the other hand, if the individual is an integral part of the organization, then that individual's interests can also be a focus.

* * *

Leave a Pathway Back to Interests. Most importantly, a pathway must be left for the other party to turn off the threat. In other words, there must be some way for the other party to save face and reopen the negotiations and avoid the threat. If you do not provide some way to turn off the threat, you force yourself to have to implement the threat. Once you put your threat into action, you often lose your power and any ability to influence the other party to meet your demands. A good way to turn off a threat is to combine the threatening rights-or-power communications with an interests-based proposal that indicates not only what you need in order to reach agreement, but also something positive that you are willing to do in order to reach agreement.

A threat typically defines a *negative* consequence: "I will take you to court" or "I will inform my colleagues in the printing industry about my negative experiences with your product and with your company." If you threaten, but add "if you can agree to (meet my demands in the specified way by the specified time), then I will help you to publicize your product" or "we will work together to develop a product to make your company profitable again." The other party may have a positive incentive to meet your demands and to turn off your threat.

If You Act on a Threat, You Lose Your Power. It is imperative to remember that once you carry through with your threat, you frequently lose your source of power. You may have already harmed the other negotiator's interests to such an extent that he or she has little ability or reason to come back to interests and meet your demands. * * *

Usually, the point of making a threat is actually *not* to follow through with it. You do not want to have to implement your threat. You want the other party to meet your interests and turn off the threat. Any time you make a threat, however, you must be aware that the possibility exists of having to actually implement the threat. Therefore, think carefully before framing your threat. You must be willing to suffer the consequences.

In sum, a good way to implement either rights-or-power strategies is to follow this sequence: State (1) the specific, detailed demand that you are making and the deadline by which it must be satisfied; (2) the specific, detailed, credible threat (rights or power-based) that harms the other side's underlying interests; and (3) the specific, detailed positive consequence that will follow if the demand is met by the deadline.

Conclusions

In difficult negotiations that have the potential to evolve into conflict spirals, trying to focus exclusively on interests is not always an effective strategy. We propose that it is necessary to be well-versed in interests, rights, and power approaches to dispute resolution negotiations and to know how to move effectively among these three strategies during the course of a negotiation.

Our study affirms that dispute resolution negotiations do cycle through interests, rights, and power strategies. Reciprocity can direct a negotiation toward interests, or toward a rights or power-based conflict spiral, and hence, a one-sided distributive outcome that leaves significant joint value on the table. Yet, even though the allure of reciprocity is strong, we found that negotiators can deflect rights and power strategies and refocus disputes by: (1) not reciprocating rights and power communications and responding with a noncontentious communication; (2) not making unilateral concessions and thereby not reinforcing contentious strategies; (3) combining reciprocity of a rights-or-power communications with a noncontentious communication; and (4) labeling the process as ineffective and calling for a different approach to the negotiation.

But even these steps may not be enough to ensure successful resolution of difficult disputes. One must also evaluate the pros and cons of beginning negotiations with different strategies as well as the conditions which can for a change in strategy. Furthermore, the negotiator who lacks the skills to implement interests, rights, and power strategies to their maximum potential risks losing the advantages that each strategy has to offer, and perhaps ending up worse off than before the negotiations began.

Robert J. Condlin,[*] *Bargaining in the Dark: The Normative Incoherence of Lawyer Dispute Bargaining Role* 51 MD. L. REV. 1, 50-66 (1992)[**]

* * *

D. Coordinated Bargaining

The question of whether rational bargainers should choose competitive or cooperative strategies has been a subject of study in the game theoretic branch of mathematical science since the 1950s. Recent work in perhaps the most well-known part of this subject, that based on the formal problem of the "prisoner's dilemma," lends support to the conclusion that, under conditions approximated in legal dispute settlement, cooperation is the strategy of choice for bargainers interested in distributing resources efficiently and maximizing individual return. This work to a large extent corroborates the claims of cordial, principled, and problem-solving bargaining, and when combined with them makes a more powerful case for the efficacy of the cooperative approach. To appreciate the full force of the argument for the legal bargainer's practical need to cooperate, therefore, it is necessary to understand the lessons of this recent work.

The prisoner's dilemma is a game between two players, descriptively named *A* and *B*, each of whom is faced with a choice of two strategies, cooperate or defect. The game board is a four-box matrix (see below) consisting of different payoffs for each of the four pairs of strategies for playing the game. In the most basic form of the game, the players are allowed only to choose a strategy and may not discuss their choices with the other player, either before or after playing.

---

[*] Robert J. Condlin is Professor at University of Maryland School of Law. In this excerpt he describes a computer tournament held to determine the winning strategy in a prisoners' dilemma game, and its implications for negotiations.

PRISONER'S DILEMMA MATRIX

PLAYER *B*

		COOPERATE	DEFECT
PLAYER *A*	COOPERATE	3 3	5 0
	DEFECT	0 5	1 1

Player *A*'s payoff is given in the lower left hand corner of each quadrant, and Player *B*'s in the upper right hand corner. If *A* defects while *B* cooperates, *A* successfully double-crosses *B*. This is the best *A* can do and the worst *B* can do, so *A* gets a payoff of 5 and *B* gets 0. Conversely, if *A* cooperates and *B* defects, the northeast quadrant, then *A* gets 0 and *B* gets 5. If both players cooperate, each gets 3, if both defect, each gets 1. *A*'s preferred ordering of the quadrants is southwest, northwest, southeast, northeast, and *B*'s preferred ordering is northeast, northwest, southeast, southwest.

The numbers are not important in themselves. That is, it does not matter that the payoff increments are 5, 3, 1, and 0. They could be any set of *T, S, R*, and *P* that satisfy the following conditions:

(1) $T > R > P > S$

(2) $(T + S) / 2 < R$

That is, T, the temptation to defect (the five payoff), must be greater than R, the reward for mutual cooperation (the three payoff), which in turn must be greater than P, the punishment for mutual defection (the one payoff), which in turn must be greater than S, the sucker's return for unilateral cooperation (the zero payoff). The second condition simply says that mutual cooperation is better than the average of the other two, so that if bargainers are playing several repetitions of the game they cannot improve on cooperation by taking turns suckering each other (which itself is a form of cooperation).

Game theorists have been intrigued by this paradox: both players prefer mutual cooperation, the three-three square, to mutual defection, the one-one square, but if both are rational they will find themselves, to their infinite frustration, trapped in the one-one square. Why is that? Look at the problem first from A's point of view. A reasons: "B can either cooperate or defect. If B cooperates, I should defect because then I get 5 instead of 3. If B defects, I should also defect, because then I get 1 instead of 0. No matter what B does I am better off defecting than cooperating." B of course reasons in the same way, so both players defect and end up in the one-one square.

One might argue that A and B, recognizing their dilemma, should make a leap of faith and trust each other to decide unilaterally to cooperate. But just as A (or B) says to herself, "well maybe I should cooperate and gamble that B will cooperate as well," she realizes two things. First, if B is rational she will defect, and second, even if B wants to cooperate she will have to count on the fact that A is rational and will defect. A defects, therefore, and acts out the logic of the prisoner's dilemma. It is difficult to produce a cooperative outcome when rational behavior points in the opposite direction.

There is a wealth of literature on playing the game, but relatively little about how to play it well. Nonetheless, certain conclusions emerge. First, there is no optimum universal strategy, that is, no strategy that is better than all others under all circumstances. How one plays depends upon with whom one is playing. Second, there is no way out of the dilemma if there is only one play to the game because a player is trapped in the southeast corner if she is going to be rational. If the game is played many times over, though, without a fixed ending point (the so-called iterated prisoner's dilemma), players can use the future ability to cooperate or defect as a kind of carrot and stick to coordinate choices and to develop a pattern of mutual cooperation. The interesting question, then, is how one plays the iterated prisoner's dilemma so that such a pattern develops.

In an interesting and clever experiment, Robert Axelrod took up this question. He invited game theory professionals from all over the world, including people who had published articles on the prisoner's dilemma, to submit computer programs for playing a round robin, iterated version of the game, in effect to participate in a prisoner's dilemma game tournament. Each program would play every other program, a clone of itself, and a random (i.e., coinflipping) program, two hundred times. Fourteen teams participated, with programs ranging from the very simple to the moderately complex. When the tournament was over, the simplest program, called "tit for tat," had won. Tit for tat cooperated on the first play of the game, and mimicked its opponent on each successive play, so that if the other player defected, tit for tat punished it on the next play by also defecting; if the other player cooperated, tit for tat rewarded that move on the next play by also cooperating. At the end of two hundred rounds, tit for tat had cleaned up.

Now it is at least peculiar that a program which cannot, by definition, win any single play of the game, can win the tournament. Compare tit for tat, for example, with the equally simple "Always Defect." Always Defect never loses (i.e., never gets zero, the S payoff) in head-to-head play. The worst it can do is tie (i.e., get one, or the P payoff) if the other party also always defects. If the other cooperates on even one move, Always Defect is five points up. Always Defect never loses and sometimes wins, tit for tat never wins, and yet tit for tat eventually drives Always Defect out of the bargaining universe. How does this happen? The answer, when one thinks about it, is obvious. Tit for tat collects "threes," the reward for mutual cooperation, in many instances where Always Defect, and defecting strategies generally, collect "ones," the punishment for mutual defection. Over the long haul, the difference between three and one, multiplied many times, adds up. By eliciting sustained cooperation from a wider range of strategies, tit for tat makes up in the aggregate what it loses in some particular plays of the game. Like the professional golfer who always finishes second, it leads the money list at the end of the year.

After the first tournament, Axelrod invited a larger list of players to submit programs for a second tournament. In this tournament, there were sixty-two entries from six countries, people of all ages and levels of expertise, and from eight different academic disciplines. All of the entrants were familiar with the results of the first round, and yet tit for tat won again. Tit for tat was still able to evoke cooperation when other more sophisticated programs were not, even after these other programs saw tit for tat operate. Axelrod traced tit for tat's robustness to four qualities that other programs did not share in the same measure. Tit for tat (and successful strategies generally) succeeded because it was nice, provocable, forgiving, and transparent. It was nice in that it was never the first to defect; provocable in that it did not let a defection go unpunished; forgiving in that it punished each defection only once; and transparent in that its playing patterns were easy to figure out, so that opponents did not see it as defecting randomly or behaving obscurely, and thus they were not suspicious of it. The combination of initial trust in the opponent (never be the first to defect), a capacity for certain but restrained retaliation for transgressions (defect once and then forgive), and clarity of purpose (be transparent), accounted for tit for tat's success.

Axelrod then ran a series of hypothetical replays of the tournament in which the environment of each replay was determined by the results of the previous one. A program's score indicated its fitness, and fitness determined the number of progeny the program had in the next round. As the tournament progressed through generation after generation, the environment gradually changed. At the beginning, poor programs and good programs were equally represented, but as time passed, the poorer ones dropped out and the good ones flourished. The rank order of the good programs changed, however, because goodness was no longer measured against the same universe. Programs whose success came from interaction with other good programs continued to succeed. But programs that won because they were able to exploit dumb programs found their base of support eroding as dumb programs were gradually squeezed out, and eventually they suffered the same fate.

Tit for tat fared spectacularly well in this "ecological tournament." After a thousand generations, its rate of growth was greater than that of any other program, even though it did not outscore a single one of its rivals in any of its encounters. Tit for tat succeeded because it was able to elicit cooperation from the greatest number of other players. Axelrod concluded that tit for tat was able to do this because

> other rules anticipate [its] presence and are designed to do well with it. Doing well with [tit for tat] requires cooperating with it, and this in turn helps [tit for tat]. Even rules . . . that were designed to see what they could get away with, quickly apologize to [tit for tat]. Any rule which tries to take advantage of [tit for tat] will simply hurt itself. [It] benefits from its own nonexploitability. . . .

On the basis of the ecological tournament, Axelrod offered preliminary answers to three questions about the evolution of cooperative bargaining norms that had long troubled bargaining theorists. The first asks how cooperation gets started in an environment of unconditional defection. The answer is through the invasion of small clusters of conditionally cooperating bargainers. In Axelrod's words, "mutual cooperation can emerge in a world of egoists without central control by starting with a cluster of individuals who rely on reciprocity." Small clusters of cooperators can propagate even in a hostile environment, provided that they defend themselves in tit for tat- like fashion. Programs that are just nice (i.e., complete pacifists), on the other hand, will not survive. The second question concerns robustness: What strategy does well in a shifting and unpredictable environment? The answer is that any strategy with the traits of niceness, provocability, forgiveness, and transparency will do so. Such strategies, once established, tend to flourish in an ecologically evolving world. And the final question is about stability: Can cooperation protect itself from invasion? The ecological tournament proves that it can, that once cooperation establishes itself, it is permanent. As Axelrod puts it, "[t]he gear wheels of social evolution have a ratchet."

* * *

If prisoner's dilemma analysis has implications for legal dispute settlement, one still must be clear about the extent of those implications. In a one-time negotiation (with no prospect of the bargainers meeting again), Axelrod's conclusions are of limited use. Tit for tat is a strategy for repeat bargaining and it can do no better than a "good" result in any single encounter. Just as the power of tit for tat is not apparent until one looks at its results over time, so too the argument for bargaining cooperatively is not convincing until it is applied to a bargaining career. A lifetime of negotiation is, in a significant sense, like a long-playing, iterated prisoner's dilemma game tournament. Individual negotiations are separate plays of the game, and negotiator histories, known through direct experience and reputation, are records of the patterns of play. Unlike bargaining in a single encounter (where an opening or random defection may determine outcome), over the course of a career, bargaining in a cooperative manner will pile up hundreds of "threes," the reward for mutual cooperation, which will cancel out the occasional "zeros" suffered at the hands of others who always or randomly defect. The argument that one should cooperate, therefore, applies only to strategies for bargaining relationships in which there is reason to believe that the parties will bargain again, in person or through the proxy of their reputations in the bargaining community. In such relationships, achieving a "tie," or never losing by more than one move, is like always finishing second. It returns more in the end than competitive strategies that produce occasional victories, but that more often produce middling deadlocks and mutual defeats.

* * *

Successful bargainers, then, live in and contribute to a world of other successful bargainers. They try only for their fair share of bargained-for resources, and they work hard to insure that others, including adversaries, get their deserved shares as well. For them, doing well is a group phenomenon in which the real returns come over time.

But so it is clear, bargaining cooperatively does not mean being a patsy, splitting the difference, or giving away the store. Cooperative bargainers are as aggressive and energetic as their adversarial counterparts in the pursuit of strong claims, even to the point of demanding most of the bargaining pot when the strength of a client's case warrants it. The extent to which a strategy is cooperative is determined not by looking at the outcome it produces, but at the manner in which it proceeds. Cooperative bargainers are those who do not unilaterally defect on adversaries not known to be competitors, and unless provoked, do not defect at all. That is, they do not conceal information the other side has a right to know, nor advance false arguments on the hope that they will be believed. They do not use leverage or make demands that cannot be justified on some substantive ground, nor otherwise betray reasonable adversary expectations about cooperative behavior based on the bargainers' past histories (or, when that evidence is too thin, based on community standards of fair bargaining practice). When these ground rules are followed, bargaining outcome becomes a function of the substantive strength of the parties' respective claims and the bargainers' skill and persuasiveness in arguing for them. Cooperative bargaining sometimes produces even distributions and sometimes rewards one side more than the other; what happens in any particular case depends on the relative strength of the parties' respective claims. One thing is clear, however: being cooperative is not just another way of saying divide everything in half.

* * *

Ronald J. Gilson & Robert H. Mnookin,[*]
Disputing Through Agents: Cooperation and Conflict Between Lawyers in Litigation
94 COLUM. L. REV. 509, 550-54 (1994)[**]

* * *

A. Cooperation and the Norms of Professional Conduct

Traditional norms of professional conduct are insistently client-centered. As in other professional relationships, the lawyer's technical skills and regulatory monopoly provide both a means to advance the client's interest in a specialized environment and a facade behind which the lawyer can favor herself at the client's expense. Professional responsibility, like other forms of fiduciary obligation, seeks to disarm that conflict by imposing a duty of loyalty that privileges the client's interest over that of the lawyer. In the litigation context, the client's preferred position is given shape through the norm of zealous advocacy: the lawyer must vigorously assert the client's interests; the final authority on important issues of strategy rests with the client; and the client may discharge his lawyer at will, but the lawyer has only limited ability to withdraw from representation. To paraphrase the punch line of a particularly unpleasant lawyer joke, there are few things that a lawyer can decline to do.

This picture of client-centered advocacy presents a serious problem for the lawyer seeking to establish or maintain a reputation for cooperation. The zealous advocacy model views litigation from the client's perspective: as a one-round game. But in establishing and maintaining the reputation necessary to facilitate cooperation between clients, a lawyer necessarily plays a multi-round game for different clients. The lawyer may have to forgo litigation tactics that are both lawful and in the client's best interest in a particular lawsuit to allow the lawyer effectively to commit other clients to cooperate in other lawsuits. More concretely, if the payoff structure in a lawsuit takes the form of a prisoner's dilemma, the lawyer may best serve the client's interests by mid-stream defection, even though the lawyer thereby destroys her privately and socially valuable reputation for cooperation. Is zealous advocacy therefore inconsistent with reputation-based cooperation? Can a lawyer decline to defect even if defection is otherwise lawful? Can she withdraw if the client insists on defection? Can the lawyer and client agree at the outset of the representation that the lawyer will adopt a cooperative

---

[*] Ronald J. Gilson is Charles J. Meyers Professor of Law and Business at Stanford Law School. Robert H. Mnookin is Samuel Williston Professor of Law at Harvard University. Their article looks at lawyers' conflicting incentives to cooperate and to compete with litigation adversaries.

[**] Copyright © 1994 Columbia Law Review. Reprinted with permission.

rather than a zealous advocacy litigation style? Each of these questions raises important issues of professional responsibility. Our goal here is not to resolve those issues — we leave that task to another round — but to highlight the potential of professional norms to be a barrier to commitments to cooperate.

To see the impact of professional rules of conduct, suppose that in the pre-litigation game a client and her opponent both choose lawyers with reputations for cooperation. The client disturbs the cooperative equilibrium, however, by a subsequent decision to defect at a crucial stage in the litigation. For example, the two lawyers may be engaged in voluntary information exchange rather than adversarial formal discovery, with the implicit understanding that material information will not be withheld. The client then instructs its lawyer to withhold an important document. If the other side discovers the defection the lawyer predictably loses her reputation for cooperation. What can the lawyer do within the limits of the rules of professional conduct to save her reputation? Keep in mind that if the answer is nothing, more is lost than just the particular lawyer's reputation. Because the client's initial selection of a cooperative lawyer will no longer bind the client to a cooperative strategy, the parties can no longer reach a cooperative equilibrium. The cooperative lawyer has three possible responses, each of which poses a significant issue of professional conduct.

Most directly, the lawyer simply might decline to follow the client's instruction. The client is then put to a choice: either continue with the cooperative strategy or discharge the lawyer. Either outcome would protect the lawyer's cooperative reputation. This happy outcome, however, poses significant problems of professional responsibility. So long as the client's direction is not illegal, there is substantial support for the proposition that the choice of strategy belongs exclusively to the client. Thus, the client's instruction to defect puts the lawyer, not the client, to a choice: obeisance or withdrawal. However, withdrawal is available only if the circumstances satisfy the preconditions to the ethical termination of the representation. This shift in the locus of the decision is crucial because the client's right to discharge the lawyer is unqualified while the lawyer's right to withdraw is significantly restricted. The lawyer cannot avoid these restrictions by forcing the client to choose between following the cooperative strategy and discharging her.

A less drastic response by the lawyer would also save her reputation; however, it is also problematic under professional responsibility rules. The potential for defection results from the lawyer's reputation for cooperation. Her very retention implicitly represents that she will not behave strategically in exchanging voluntary disclosures. Only because the other counsel relies on the implicit representation can defection benefit the client and damage the reputation of the cooperating lawyer. In this situation, the lawyer can protect her reputation while still following the letter, if not the spirit, of the client's directions by generally disclosing to opposing counsel that continued reliance on the lawyer's reputation in this case would not be appropriate. For example, one lawyer who found himself in this situation recounted that he dealt with the problem by simply saying "en garde" to opposing counsel. The message imbedded in the phrase was that opposing counsel should protect himself, that cooperative rules did not apply, and that subsequent adversarial behavior, because not unexpected, would not be a reputational breach. Here again, however, the lawyer's effort to preserve his reputation poses issues of professional conduct. As we have seen, the client has a strong claim to the ultimate authority on issues of strategy. Moreover, a lawyer is obliged to protect a client's confidences. The lawyer's clever disclosure of the new rules of engagement, which renders the strategy, and the client's authority, less effective, plausibly conflicts with the professional norms that allocate strategic discretion to the client and that create the lawyer's obligation to maintain client confidences.

That leaves the lawyer with but a single response in the face of client direction to defect — withdrawal. But it is not clear that the ethical norms allow withdrawal under these circumstances. Under the Model Code of Professional Responsibility (Model Code), a lawyer can withdraw from representation in this situation only if the client "[i]nsists that the lawyer pursue a course of conduct that is illegal or that is prohibited under the Disciplinary Rules." The Model Rules of Professional Conduct (Model Rules) generally provide the lawyer with a broader withdrawal right, but there is substantial ambiguity concerning its application in our circumstance. Model Rule 1.16(b)(3) allows the lawyer to withdraw, even if doing so has a material adverse effect on the client, if "a client insists upon pursuing an objective that the lawyer considers repugnant or imprudent." The Model Rules, however, distinguish between objectives and means. Our situation clearly concerns a strategy — a means not an objective. Thus, the Model Rule would also not allow withdrawal.

* * *

James A. Rosenstein,[*] *Ten Obstacles to a Negotiated Agreement and How to Overcome Them*
44 PRAC. LAW. 47, 60-64 (1998)[**]

* * *

Identifying Potential Obstacles to Agreement

1. Have all parties whose input to the process is essential to its success been identified and brought into the negotiations? [The Missing Party Obstacle]

---

[*] James A. Rosenstein is Principal of the Philadelphia law firm, Rosenstein Associates. His article offers practical suggestions for dealing with the tension between distributive and integrative approaches to negotiation.

[**] Copyright © 1998 James A. Rosenstein. Reprinted with permission.

2. Are there issues of concern to a party that have not surfaced in the negotiations but which must be addressed if a successful conclusion is to be achieved? [The Hidden Agenda Obstacle]

3. Do the negotiators have a clear understanding of all of the interests of their clients that they are trying to advance or protect and the relative importance of those interests to their clients? [The Unstated Assumption Obstacle]

4. Have the negotiators effectively analyzed the issues (including how they may be interrelated) and thought creatively about solutions? Have they established their own best alternative to a negotiated agreement in light of those interests? [The Inadequate Analysis Obstacle]

5. Do the parties in fact share one or more common objectives, and if so, has that information been communicated to all of them? [The Inadequate Disclosure Obstacle]

6. Are some or all of the parties utilizing negotiating tactics that tend to drive the parties apart rather than bringing them closer together? [The Incredible Position Obstacle]

7. Is there a wide disparity in the relative importance of the issues to be negotiated? [The Trying To Run Before Learning How To Walk Obstacle]

8. Are the parties so overwhelmed with the magnitude or complexity of the issues they must address that they appear to be paralyzed, and thus unable to start meaningful negotiations? [The Biting Off More Than You Can Chew Obstacle]

9. Are there psychological or emotional factors (such as distrust, fear, and feelings of inadequacy) that inhibit the ability of the parties to consider the issues reasonably objectively? [The Sloped Playing Field Obstacle]

10. Do the parties approach the negotiations as a way to find "win-win" solutions or do they see one party necessarily losing if the other wins? [The Need To Save Face Obstacle]

Actions To Overcome or Prevent Obstacles

Type of Obstacle	Corrective Actions	Preventive Actions
1. The Missing Party	The parties must determine whether they have included all stakeholders whose interests could be significantly affected by the results of the negotiations and whose cooperation is needed to effectuate the decisions made in the negotiations. Any such essential party should be brought into the process as soon as possible after determining that its input is needed.	In the early stages of negotiations, look carefully at the issues, brainstorm how they could be addressed, identify all parties whose input would be required if any proposed plan of action were to be followed, and involve those parties in the negotiations (or at least those aspects of the negotiations where their input is likely to be needed).
2. The Hidden Agenda	If a negotiator suspects that either her client or another party has a hidden agenda that threatens the successful conclusion of their negotiations, the negotiator should endeavor to identify that issue so that a decision can be made regarding what should be disclosed to the other party and when that disclosure should occur.	As early as possible in the negotiations, the parties should be encouraged to identify fully all of the respective interests they need to advance or protect in the negotiations or that would be affected by the outcome of the negotiations. (Although these interests should be disclosed, it should not be necessary for any party to disclose to the other, at least in the early stages of the negotiations, the relative importance they ascribe to each of these interests.)

3. The Unstated Assumption	As soon as one party suspects that another party hasn't disclosed an underlying assumption that could threaten the success of the negotiations, a strong effort should be made to uncover the unstated assumption and (if it does exist) to determine jointly whether it is feasible to continue the negotiations and (if so) what changes in assumption will be required.	Each negotiation team should conduct a thorough analysis of their interests before progressing far into the negotiations. This analysis should include reaching agreement with the client on a negotiation strategy, evaluation of the likely interests and strategies of the other parties, when various information should be disclosed to the other parties, and the client's BATNA.
4. The Inadequate Analysis	A party that has not followed the preventative recommendations under 2 and 3 above, and discovers in the course of negotiation that it has not done its homework will be faced with the dilemma of whether to bow out of the negotiations because it is uncertain if the risks of continuing are affordable or whether to undertake the necessary BATNA analysis on a hurried and pressured basis. The result of a BATNA analysis might be to enable the party to continue to negotiate but it could also result in terminating negotiations because the party's BATNA is preferable. Of course, a party's credibility with the others would be severely damaged by such a withdrawal or even by last minute scrambling that causes substantial changes in its negotiating position.	Each of the parties should take the preventative action recommended in 2 and 3 above. In addition, each party must continue to analyze new information, as it is learned in the process of the negotiations, to determine whether changes in the original negotiation strategy are called for.

5. The Inadequate Disclosure	If it becomes apparent that a party does not share even one negotiation objective with the other parties, it would be wise to replace the dissident party with one who does share at least one objective, or (if this is not possible) all parties should cut their losses and terminate the negotiations.	If each party has thoroughly identified its interests (see 2 and 3 above) they should ascertain from the other parties if they all want to achieve a common objective through the negotiations. If there is no such common objective, it might be prudent to discontinue the negotiations and devote your energies to pursuits that are likely to be more fruitful.
6. The Incredible Position	One response to the assertion of an extreme position that has frequently proven to be effective is to clearly reject the proposal while pressing the proposer to explain in detail how he arrived at his position. When this is done, the extreme position often becomes untenable.	Taking the preventative actions recommended in 2, 3 and 4 above should minimize the risk that one or more of the parties will adopt a bargaining position that brings into question whether they are negotiating in good faith.
7. Trying to Run Before Learning How to Walk	Whenever it becomes apparent that the parties are unwilling to address an issue, it should be temporarily put aside in favor of more tractable ones. When the non-deferred issues have all been successfully addressed, the parties should then attempt to reach closure on the more difficult issues, or (if this continues to be unachievable) they must determine whether they can postpone addressing them.	Taking the preventative actions recommended in 2, 3 and 4 above should minimize the likelihood that the parties will try to run before they learn how to walk, with respect to these negotiations.

8. Biting Off More than You Can Chew	Problems that appear intractable because they involve a complex set of interrelated issues may best be tackled by focusing on their components, arriving at tentative resolutions of each one. It may be necessary to change a tentative resolution if analysis of other aspects of the overall problem raises new concerns not previously considered.	Taking the preventative actions recommended in 2, 3 and 4 above should minimize the likelihood that the parties' approach to the negotiations will flounder because they tried to bite off more than they could chew.
9. The Sloped Playing Field	If the negotiations appear to be breaking down for this reason, a strategy must be quickly determined and implemented in order to maintain or restore mutual trust and confidence. In many instances, this will necessitate the intervention of a skilled neutral facilitator.	As soon as it appears that one or more of the parties is displaying signs of distrust, fear, inadequacy, or the like that could significantly affect their decisionmaking, it is in the best interests of all of the parties that this concern be addressed promptly. Doing so may require any combination of (1) identifying and addressing the source of these feelings, (2) strengthening the negotiating team for the party having those feelings, and (3) using a neutral facilitator to help the parties establish the necessary comfort level.

10. The Need to Save Face	A party who rejects an otherwise reasonable proposal merely because he perceives that he will lose face as a result of agreeing to it can frequently be won over either by an additional concession from the other party or by being convinced that the proposal will actually be face-saving rather than face-losing.	Negotiators who strive to find win-win solutions are seldom faced with an opposing party who resists an otherwise reasonable proposal merely because of a perception that it will cause him to lose face.

Chapter 5
PSYCHOLOGICAL ASPECTS OF NEGOTIATION

Although you may be studying negotiation for the first time as you read this book, you have been negotiating since earliest childhood — learning, through interactions with caregivers and, later, peers, how to get your needs met. Anyone who has dealt with a two-year-old knows the power of the word "no" to alter the dynamics of parent-child relations and to require creative problem-solving to avert a costly stalemate between the negotiating parties. Children negotiate with siblings and peers about what television show to watch and what games to play; they negotiate with parents and teachers about what they eat and when they go to sleep and how much time they spend doing math or reading. Even if the rule in your family was "whatever Mom or Dad says goes," that is itself a significant lesson about the role of power in negotiation. Faced with such a display of parental authority, you probably also learned how to gain leverage and to neutralize that power — for example, by forming coalitions with siblings to bend the rules or by appealing to whichever parent was perceived as softer on a particular issue.

As an adult, you have been involved in many more obvious negotiations, with housemates, partners, co-workers, bosses, and professors. The significance of this lifelong involvement in negotiation is twofold. First, it gives you a wealth of experience to draw on in conducting legal negotiations. Second, it means that you already have many well-established patterns of negotiation behavior that you may never have given much thought. Since you do have a background in negotiation — an advantage you probably did not have when you began studying torts or intellectual property law — you can build on what you already know in developing your skills as a legal negotiator. At the same time, you will only be able to change the way you negotiate by becoming aware of the habits you have developed over the years and evaluating their effectiveness in professional negotiations.

A. TRANSFERENCE: THE POWER OF THE PAST

Your past experience has created certain expectations about relationships between people and, in particular, about what happens when people's wishes and needs conflict. You will carry those expectations into every negotiation. They will influence how you perceive the other parties to the negotiation, how you act in relation to them, and how you react to the level of conflict between you. What psychologists call transference — the tendency to attribute to people you meet characteristics of important people in your past — is ubiquitous in human interactions. One way to understand it is as an attempt to make the strange familiar. Whether your transference reaction to a person is positive or negative, it at least puts him in a known category. There is a certain comfort in that — even if the expectation that gets set up, for example, is that the person across the table will be dismissive and self-absorbed like your older sister.

Transference operates largely outside of awareness: it is usually unconscious and is just "there" in your response to people you encounter. It affects negotiations just as it does every other interaction between people. You may trust the smiling older man across the table more than you should because he reminds you of a favorite uncle, or you may take an immediate dislike to the man your brother's age who is actually prepared to offer you a very favorable deal. Indeed, any strong reaction to a negotiation counterpart, whether positive or negative, may be a useful clue to the effects of transference. On the one hand, if the other person really is dismissive and self-absorbed like your sister, you will likely find her more difficult to deal with than someone else might, given that emotional connection. On the other hand, awareness of transference should also help you to monitor your assumptions about the meaning of another person's behavior. Often, what you read into a situation is just that, something that your pre-existing expectations tell you is happening, rather than an accurate assessment of what is actually going on. When you have a strong reaction to someone you are negotiating with, try taking a step back from the process, mentally or literally, by taking a break, to think about what other experiences might be contributing to your reaction. Doing so will help you remain focused on the task at hand and able to use your experience productively. The articles below by Nelken and Watson discuss the impact of transference and other unconscious psychological processes on negotiations.

B. THE IMPORTANCE OF SELF-OBSERVATION

Putting your past experience to use requires thinking about negotiations — whether about what movie to see with friends or who does the dinner dishes or when an important project will be turned in — *as* negotiations. If you apply the concepts discussed in earlier chapters, would you describe a particular interaction as a distributive or an integrative bargaining situation? What led you to see it that way initially? Did your views change over time? How did your relationship with the other party affect the negotiation and how was the relationship affected by it? What would you do differently today? Most important, what patterns do you see in the ways that you have approached negotiations in the past? If you think carefully about these questions, you will learn some things about the kind of negotiator you are — your characteristic strengths and weaknesses — that will help you decide what skills you need to develop next.

As a lawyer, you will be negotiating on behalf of others and getting paid for it. If you are usually inclined to go along with others rather than to risk open conflict by stating your views, you may find yourself giving in too quickly in legal negotiations in order to smooth over differences, at considerable cost to some clients. Conversely, if you insist on getting your own way most of the time, you may take a competitive posture in negotiations even when your client would benefit from a more conciliatory stance. No single approach to negotiations is best for all situations. Part of improving your skills as a negotiator is developing a variety of approaches that you can use, depending on the context, the parties, and the subject matter being negotiated.

You will negotiate with many different people over time, but you will have to deal with yourself every time you negotiate. The more you can develop your capacity for self-observation as a negotiator, the more your approach will become the result of thoughtful understanding of yourself and the process, rather than of unexamined reaction to what others do and say. Keeping a journal in which you reflect on what went well and not so well in negotiations, and on how you felt about what was going on, will enable you to see how you improve over time, and what difficulties persist. What upset you about the other party's way of talking to you? What was happening when you started to feel tense and pressured to reach a resolution? Were the parties talking to each other or past each other? While thinking negotiations over after the fact is a useful learning tool, writing about them encourages more thorough analysis. A permanent record allows you to review problem areas and to note abilities that may not be obvious to you in any single negotiation. It also makes it easier for you to begin to recognize the negotiation patterns you have already established, based on your experiences with conflict since childhood.

Keeping a journal will help you to learn from others as you reflect on their styles and how they affected you. Every negotiator has different skills. Seeing an effective demonstration of an approach that you have never tried or never succeeded at using can help you get out of the box of your own characteristic way of doing things. By analyzing what the other person did and what worked about it, you will be able to make it your own and to incorporate it into your growing set of skills.

C. DEALING WITH FEELINGS

In order to develop flexibility in negotiating, however, you must first become aware of how you already do negotiate. To gain that awareness, you have to pay attention not only to how you typically act in negotiations, but also to how you feel, particularly about the interpersonal conflict that is an inherent part of them. Just as it is difficult to represent clients adequately without understanding both the content of their problems and their feelings about those problems, it is important in learning how to negotiate well to develop a capacity for self-reflection that will allow you to know as much as possible about yourself as a negotiator. Under the stress of negotiations, you are likely to fall back on familiar patterns, for better or worse. If you can be honest with yourself about what excites you, scares you, worries you, pleases you or enrages you in negotiations, you will be less likely to be tripped up by these strong emotions. You will also be better able to choose how you actually behave in the process, rather than simply reacting reflexively. The article below by Adler and his co-authors discusses ways of dealing with two common emotions, anger and fear, in the negotiation context.

Analyzing past negotiations, as well as current ones, will help you identify issues and situations that are particularly loaded for you and that call for careful thought and preparation to deal with appropriately. Suppose you know that you get angry when you feel that your good will is called into question. If you reflexively lose your temper, you may end up derailing the process unnecessarily. If you can learn to step back instead and to listen carefully before reacting, you may conclude that you were mistaken or that you can find a more constructive way to respond. Analyzing your negotiations will also help you see what you do well as a negotiator and give you the confidence to rely on those strengths as you develop your skills. For example, if others generally listen to what you have to say and take you at your word, that will be a great asset in legal negotiations and will give you credibility that others may have difficulty establishing.

D. THE NEGOTIATION CONTEXT

At every stage of a negotiation, the parties affect and are affected by each other. You can plan what you will do first in a negotiation; but after that, what you do or say — and what an impartial outside observer would advise you to do or say — depends to some extent on how the other party responds and what form the negotiation begins to take as a result. The relationship between negotiators is co-created, even in a purely distributive bargaining situation where it is the adversarial one of *caveat emptor*. To negotiate effectively, you have to be both flexible and attentive to the negotiation context as it develops. You also have to be prepared to help shape the negotiators' relationship in a way that serves your client's goals.

Just as you will react to others based on your past experience, they will react similarly to you. What appears to be irrational behavior in negotiation, when not simply calculated for effect, is often the result of unconscious assumptions by the negotiators about each other and the situation. An opponent who bristles at everything you say may be responding less to what you are actually saying than to his own internal conflicts. Based on his understanding, he may be behaving quite sensibly. But if his behavior has little to do with the present reality of the situation, the result may be that the negotiation is derailed or ends in stalemate unless you can help alter the dynamics between you.

In *Getting Past No*, excerpted in Chapter Three, Ury notes that most people respond to a perceived attack by retaliating, or by giving in, or by breaking off contact. Instead, he encourages a negotiator in that situation to "go to the balcony": to step back and think about the process as objectively as possible, rather than simply reacting. If you can observe what is happening and avoid taking it personally, you will not lose sight of your own goals. You may also be able to address the problem in a productive way that gets the negotiation back on track. Many negotiations fail, not because there is no actual zone of agreement between the parties, but because the parties get caught up in their own, transference-laden, (mis)perceptions of the situation. Sorting out what you are contributing to a difficult negotiation and what your counterpart is contributing is not easy in the heat of the moment. Learning to step back from the fray enough to permit your observing capacities to function makes it more likely that you will be able to do so and to maintain or restore your joint focus on a task.

E. COGNITIVE/SOCIAL PSYCHOLOGICAL RESEARCH

In addition to what you can learn from analyzing your own past and current negotiations, there is an extensive literature in cognitive and social psychology that examines negotiation behavior in experimental situations and describes patterns common to many negotiators. Cognitive psychologists start from the premise that people are fundamentally rational beings who seek rational ends. Many of the studies examine the ways in which people nonetheless negotiate in predictably irrational ways. The assumption is that such irrational behavior results from errors in information processing, insufficient information, biases, and the like.

Among the many important findings in this literature, some of the most striking are summarized in the articles below by Mnookin, Bazerman, Thompson and DeHarpport, and Birke and Fox. Mnookin discusses the work of Kahneman and Tversky on framing effects — the tendency to accept an offer when it is presented as a gain and to reject it when it is presented as a loss, even if the actual payoff is the same in both cases — and loss aversion — the willingness to risk more to avoid a loss than to insure a like gain. He also describes Ross's studies of "reactive devaluation" — discounting the value of an offer made by an opponent, when the same offer would be considered attractive if made by an ally or a neutral third party. Bazerman explores the "winner's curse" — a variant of reactive devaluation in which a negotiator regrets having made a certain offer if the offer is readily accepted by the other party; negotiator overconfidence; and the non-rational escalation of conflict in the face of sunk costs.

Another related concept discussed by Thompson and DeHarpport and Bazerman is the "fixed pie" perception that leads negotiators to assume that their interests conflict and that a gain for one must mean a loss for the other. Thompson and DeHarpport suggests that this perception, like many others, is reinforced by the predisposition to pay attention to information that confirms, rather than disconfirms, your expectations. Birke and Fox describe several variants of this perspective bias, as well as other common biases in judgment and decision-making that affect legal negotiators: the availability heuristic — the tendency to be overly influenced by vivid examples, such as widely reported high jury verdicts; the psychology of value and framing; and the psychology of social influence.

Taken together, these articles illustrate the myriad ways in which people resist information that does not fit with their preconceptions. They also show how ingrained, in American culture at least, beliefs about the importance of competition and winning are. When you read these articles and think back over your own negotiations, you will probably recognize many instances in which you fell into the "cognitive traps" described. You may also learn from them ways of framing proposals in negotiations that will make them more likely to be accepted by the other side. Perhaps surprisingly, you will probably not become immune to repeating the irrational behaviors the authors describe. One puzzle researchers have found is that people tend to continue acting irrationally even when they understand at a conscious, rational level the cognitive errors involved. An answer to that puzzle may have to be sought at the unconscious level, where motivations are both more complex and more obscure, as the discussion above about transference suggests.

In addition to the psychological aspects of negotiation discussed here, culture and gender are often important variables in the negotiation context. The next chapter explores how culture and gender affect participants' experience of legal negotiations.

Melissa L. Nelken,[*] *Negotiation and Psychoanalysis: If I'd Wanted to Learn About Feelings, I Wouldn't Have Gone to Law School*
46 J. LEGAL EDUC. 420 (1996)[**]

I first became interested in the relationship between psychoanalysis and negotiation fifteen years ago, when I began teaching lawyers and law students negotiation skills. Most of the books on legal negotiation at the time focused on the bag-of-tricks approach to successful negotiation: the top ten ways to outwit your adversary. As I began to think about different approaches, one thing that consistently struck me was that when I gave a negotiation problem to a pair of students — a set of facts regarding a law-

---

[*] Melissa L. Nelken is Professor of Law at University of California, Hastings College of the Law and faculty chair of its Center for Negotiation and Dispute Resolution. Her article discusses unconscious processes in negotiation and the importance of self observation in developing negotiation skills.

[**] Copyright © 1996 Journal of Legal Education. Reprinted with permission.

suit or a business deal — the results of the negotiations based on those facts varied widely from pair to pair. If there was a $50,000 range within which settlement was possible under the instructions, there would be settlements throughout the range. Each pair of students would have reached a mutually satisfactory end point that was clearly dictated only partially by the information they had received from me.

Some of the differences could be explained by some students' learning the top ten list better than others: if you reveal your bottom line to your opponent, it will be difficult to settle much above it. But, having said that, I began to wonder why some people *do* consistently reveal their bottom line, or do the spiritual equivalent; why others routinely mow down their opponents in single-minded pursuit of the last possible dollar; and why still others pursue a collaborative approach that benefits both parties. How, in other words, do people help and hinder themselves in the process of negotiating? How might it be possible to help people become more aware of what they're doing, more able to choose how to respond in a specific situation? Psychoanalysis has been central to my thinking about these questions and to the way I have come to understand the negotiation process.

The Psychoanalytic Viewpoint and the Legal Viewpoint

Psychoanalysis focuses on mental processes that are unconscious: the wishes, fears, beliefs, and defenses that motivate our actions without our being aware of them. It asserts that our conscious stance in the world results from a complex internal process, going back to earliest childhood, that involves compromises among conflicting feelings. Indeed, we all develop mechanisms for remaining unaware of many of our conflicts, and much of psychoanalysis as a therapy is taken up with exploring and understanding these so-called resistances. The influence of our primary caretakers affects our sense of who we are and who we should be, by way of our identifications with them. In addition, our feelings — positive and negative — about important figures in our past are readily transferred to the present, where they inevitably color, and sometimes dominate, our reactions to those we encounter in daily life. Ambiguity, ambivalence, and overdetermination are central to psychoanalytic thinking: we don't resolve conflicts so much as learn more and more about their multiple facets and ramifications. The value of the analytic process for the individual lies in a growing capacity for self-observation and the concomitant ability to make choices about behaviors that had previously seemed immutable.

Law, by contrast, is aggressively rational, linear, and goal-oriented. Law, many lawyers say, is based on facts, not feelings; it is logical; and success is measured by whether you win or lose in court or by the dollar amount of settlements. Lawyers must *act* on behalf of their clients, and there is a premium on reaching sound decisions quickly. In law school, students are taught that how they feel about the cases they read is irrelevant; what matters is the soundness of their logic. Unlike medicine, for example, law is still taught largely as an exercise in abstraction, based on case reports and analysis of judicial opinions.

Resistance to the human dimension of the lawyer's work is built into most law training. Few law students have any contact with actual clients in a clinical setting before graduation; and even courses that simulate aspects of law practice other than trials — such as interviewing, counseling, and negotiation — are relatively uncommon. As a result, many new lawyers are unprepared to deal with the actual people who become their clients and have little idea how to translate classroom theory into practice. Indeed, since the profession idealizes the lawyer as the amoral agent of her client's ends — having no wishes, hopes, or fears of her own — the impact of the lawyer's personal conflicts on her ability to function in her professional role is officially denied and is seen as a failing, rather than as a vehicle for learning.

A Psychoanalytic Approach to Negotiation

Introducing psychoanalytic ideas in a legal setting poses a challenge, then, to the received wisdom of the lawyer. As one student said to me many years ago: "If I'd wanted to learn about feelings, I wouldn't have gone to law school." Her comment reflected not only personal discomfort with the inquiry I was encouraging, but also a sense that such an inquiry was out of place in legal education. Yet the process of lawyering, as distinct from legal theory, inevitably involves the lawyer deeply in the hopes, fears, and conflicts of her clients; and these inevitably arouse responses in the lawyer, no matter how much the professional ideal would have us believe otherwise. In addition, in representing her clients, the lawyer has no choice but to be who she is: her own conflicts, and attitudes toward conflict, will inform every task she undertakes on a client's behalf.

Negotiation, for example, is at the heart of what lawyers do. Since more than 90 percent of civil lawsuits never go to trial, even those lawyers who handle lawsuits and not business deals spend a significant amount of time negotiating — not just details like the timing of discovery but the ultimate resolution of the dispute itself. Lawyers tend to think that they will some-how be able to stay out of the way when they negotiate, that the process will go on outside of them. In fact, most are unaware of the extent to which their own needs and conflicts enter into the negotiation process. Everyone has heard stories of lawyers so competitive that they poison deals that could have been made to the benefit of their clients; there are also lawyers whose need to accommodate those they negotiate with leads them to give away the store, to the detriment of their clients. Without some degree of self-under-standing, then, some attention to feelings, lawyers run the risk of missing much that is central to competent representation.

Approaching negotiation psychoanalytically, I try to acquaint lawyers with the idea of unconscious mental processes and the influence of such processes over them, illuminating the internal and interpersonal dynamics at work in all negotiations. Beyond questions of conscious style and strategy, every negotiator apprehends what is at stake in a negotiation and what is going on between the parties to it in terms of internally motivated expectations about human relationships. As one woman said, "I always enter negotiations thinking that the other side is in a better position and that I am at their mercy." By developing a capacity for such self-observation, a negotiator becomes more aware of the dynamics of negotiation, of how her and her opponent's responses to each other and to the conflict embodied in the negotiation affect what both of them do and say on behalf of their clients. This increased self-awareness enables her to make choices about how to handle the negotiation that would not otherwise be open: to behave, in fact, more rationally, more like the ideal lawyer. For example, she might recognize that her insecurity about a particular negotiation stems from her own conflicts about aggression or from her reactions — most notably, transferences — to her opponent. That realization may enable her to prepare for and to conduct the negotiation differently, with less chance of falling into counterproductive behaviors.

An understanding of the interpersonal dynamics of conflict has benefits as well for the lawyer-client relationship, since clients inevitably suffer when their lawyers insist on divorcing the professional encounter from the emotional underpinnings of the dispute involved. Client dissatisfaction with legal representation often results from the lawyer's inability to see the client's emotional self as anything but an impediment to sensible, rational management of the legal problem the client brings. A lawyer who has developed some understanding of her own internal conflicts will be better able to tolerate the client's feelings and to incorporate them with the legal facts in seeking a satisfactory resolution of a particular dispute.

The Power of Assumptions

One of the things that happen when two lawyers sit down to negotiate is that they tend to make certain assumptions about each other, even if they have never met. Even if they do not meet, but talk on the telephone, they make assumptions, and their assumptions can determine what happens in the negotiation. For example, I sometimes begin a negotiation seminar with some variation on the prisoner's dilemma game. In the original version, two prisoners who are not permitted to communicate are encouraged to incriminate each other. If neither one does so, both will go free; if both do, both will spend a short period in jail. If only one of them incriminates the other, the one who is incriminated goes to jail for a long time and the other is released. Enlightened self-interest calls for a strategy of silent cooperation here; but how is it to be achieved?

If one asks the participants how they decide what to do under these circumstances, the most common response will be couched in terms of the negotiator's expectation of what the other side would do: "I wanted to say nothing (the cooperative bid) but I thought he would try to trick me, so I had to incriminate him." From a psychoanalytic point of view, we might say that the wish to take advantage of the other is denied and projected; the speaker then sees himself as ratting on his fellow criminal only in self-defense. Imagine the speaker's surprise when his opponent attributes a similar motive to him! Putting the two sides in separate rooms, so that the parties do not even know who their opponents are, highlights the issue of where they get their presumed knowledge about each other.

Since a course in negotiation is no place to go into the determinants of a person's projections, of what use is it to a negotiator to know that they occur? First and foremost, it makes the negotiator aware that she may be under the sway of powerful assumptions about her opponent which may not be accurate and which warrant further checking. The woman quoted above who always went into negotiations thinking that her opponents had the upper hand went on to say, "What I need to realize is that they wouldn't be across the table from me if they didn't have some desire to settle. Keeping this in mind helps me not to enter on the defensive."

The lesson is not quickly learned, by any means. We all trust the accuracy of the lens through which we view the world, and it is only through repeated confrontation with its distortions that we begin to question it. Nonetheless, when a negotiator begins to ask herself whether or not a certain conviction she has about her opponents might be internally generated, she becomes more attuned to seeking information from the other side to test the accuracy of her perceptions. Since bargaining for information is at the heart of negotiation, realizing that there are powerful internal forces motivating one's perception of the other actors in a negotiation opens up the whole question of what *other* assumptions — about the strength or weakness of each side's case, about what is important or unimportant to the other side — are being treated as if they were facts. Increased efforts to test reality accurately by gathering information from the other side, rather than working from internally generated assumptions, reduce the anxiety inherent in the negotiation process. Such efforts also produce better — because more reality-based — outcomes.

In addition, when someone realizes how many different meanings can be read into the simple choices involved in a game like the prisoner's dilemma, she begins to think more carefully about *the* meaning she tends to attribute to another's words, and even to her own. When she tries to explain how it is that incriminating the opponent in the first round of a multiround prisoner's dilemma game did not mean that she was not interested in cooperating in the future, she begins to wonder why she had to say "Let's cooperate" in such a convoluted way. What often emerges is a recognition of underlying anxieties about opening with an optimistic bid — such as fearing being taken advantage of or being perceived as weak. When these anxieties can be acknowledged and explored, it becomes possible to choose not to act on them. But without encouragement to look beyond the available rationalizations for her conduct, a negotiator is likely to persist in counterproductive behavior, even in the face of a conscious awareness that cooperation is essential to success in this game.

Once I broach the idea that one's own internal reality — the assumptions, anxieties, and conflicts that are part of who one is — has a lot to do with what happens when one negotiates, those who don't reject the notion out of hand tend to be intrigued. Law students are interested because they often feel stifled by the narrowly rational atmosphere of law school; and lawyers who have practiced for any length of time have usually found that in the heat of negotiations what continues to trip them up is an inability to respond flexibly and to grasp the dynamics of a situation. As one man commented, "It is particularly hard for us as law students to learn to negotiate effectively, because to do so we necessarily have to unlearn our reliance on rules."

Without the formality of courtroom procedures, lawyers are left to their own devices in negotiations, and they learn quickly that their personal reputations will be affected by how they conduct themselves: "I had the idea that these negotiation problems were *games* we were to play-act — unreal, theoretical problems like the rest of what I analyze, criticize, or play out in my other classes. How naive and ridiculous for me not to know that every action I take in class has some real-life impact." It soon becomes clear that, in order to understand the process as it unfolds, they need to call on many skills beyond the logical analysis and forceful argumentation in which they have been so thoroughly trained.

Learning What You Already Know

Unlike most of what gets taught in law school, negotiation is not actually a new subject to anyone. Everyone negotiates all the time — with family, friends, coworkers, teachers, anyone with whom there is a conflict or a possibility for joint action. This means that someone who thinks she is learning about negotiation for the first time as a lawyer actually has a lifetime of experience in the subject to draw on — or to stumble over. Identifications with parents and other significant people have a powerful impact on how people negotiate, as they do on every other aspect of their lives; and transference reactions are intensified by the level of conflict and anxiety inherent in a negotiation.

Thinking about how her approach to negotiation as well as her negotiation style have been shaped by past experiences helps a lawyer to organize her present experience in a way that maximizes the possibilities for learning. Since she herself is the one negotiator she can't walk away from, the more she can become aware of what motivates her own behavior in negotiations, the more able she will be to step back in the heat of the moment and to reflect on whether what is happening really serves the interests of her client. Along the way, she will also gain considerable skill in reading what is going on in her opponents.

One way to get people to utilize what they already know about negotiation but are largely unaware of — to make it available to them as they make choices in legal negotiations — is to have them keep journals, in which they reflect on what takes place during negotiations and also explore experiences that they have never thought of before as negotiations. Writing about the negotiation styles in their families of origin, they begin to see where they got some of their ideas about what you should or should not do in a negotiation, what works and what doesn't, and how power is manifested or disguised in the process.

Looking at current negotiations in their lives outside class, both personal and professional, they begin to see certain patterns in the way they approach conflict, based on these family models, and certain situations that are particularly anxiety-producing for them. One woman wrote that although her Korean-born parents think she is "too American" to understand the unspoken messages that characterize their speech, she finds that her own negotiating style suffers from the same cultural indirectness: "I also skirt around saying what I really want and hope that the opposing negotiator understands what I want through some cosmic energy transference." A man who described his father as harsh, both intellectually and physically, said, "Now, I realize I remove myself from situations that remind me of negotiations with my father. I anticipate hostility sometimes where there is no danger of it arising. This sometimes leads me to make concessions to assure that the danger level is never reached."

As in psychoanalysis, making connections of this sort is only a first step toward actually being able to behave differently in the heat of negotiation. But by linking up what happens in negotiation with what happens in the rest of life, lawyers begin to think more about what part they play in what happens to them (and to their clients) at the negotiating table. And, of course, the same lessons are borne in on them time and again as they negotiate against different people, so they can confirm their initial insights and begin to work them through. As one woman commented, "I have always known I have a temper that surprises people when it finally shows up and a sharp tongue, and that I avoid conflict like the plague, but I never thought of these things as being part of my 'negotiation style' or things that will show up in my business life as well. Since they will indeed, however, I am glad to know about them but frustrated by how hard it will probably be to change them."

The Professional Ideal

In addition to the personal issues that arise in the negotiation process, every lawyer confronts the idealization in American legal culture of an aggressive, competitive stance towards others, based on the adversary model of the courtroom. As society's hired guns, lawyers are supposed to shoot first and ask questions later. Indeed, many highly competitive people are attracted to law and to the tangible evidence of "winning" it provides in terms of courtroom victories and megadeals. Those who are able to identify with the adversarial role often behave more aggressively in their professional capacity than they do in their personal lives. They are rewarded and reinforced by the professional ideal and are often quite unable to see its drawbacks and limitations — for example, in situations where a long-term relationship is more important than a short-term victory.

For many others the overriding competitive ethos produces considerable conflict, however much it may unconsciously be part of what attracts them to the profession; and it confronts them every time they negotiate. For example, one woman spoke of the "shame" attached to being other than a competitive negotiator. Thinking about the sources of that shame in the professional ideal, as well as in the more personal meanings it has, allows people to evaluate the strengths and weaknesses of the ways they *do* approach negotiations, and to consider that any single focus — whether it is on winning or on maintaining a relationship with the opponent — will be inappropriate in some situations and appropriate in others. One woman expressed her dilemma this way: "I think I will have to realize that people's feelings, and personal relations, while important, should not always be so paramount to me that I give away the store, especially in a legal negotiation setting. I don't want to be a negotiator who crumbles when someone is tough or stubborn. I would like to use my strengths — reasonableness, perceptiveness, and willingness to discuss things — to overcome the weaknesses associated with being an other-directed person in the realm of legal negotiations."

The importance of cultural sensitivity in what is rapidly becoming a global economy underscores the need to rethink the emphasis in American law on competitive behavior as the royal road to success in negotiation. The competitive ideal can be puzzlingly remote to those who have been brought up in a different mold. A woman whose Buddhist family had escaped to the United States after years in prison and refugee camps in Southeast Asia was viewed as unusually competitive and aggressive by her family's standards — "the nail that sticks out," as they put it. Reflecting on her negotiation experiences over the course of a semester, however, she saw herself in a quite different light: "This is the first time that I come to face how different I am from the others. My assumptions about people, my values, the way I deal with conflict, how I get what I want and how I treat others and want to be treated, all these I discover are not exactly in line with most of my classmates. These differences are all the product of the way I was brought up."

The "shame" of not being singlemindedly competitive will in fact prove to be a strength in many negotiations, including those with people whose cultural values are different from ours. An aggressive, competitive lawyer can quickly find himself facing a stone wall rather than a deal if he overlooks the importance of allowing his counterpart to save face, for example, in the course of a negotiation.

The Benefits of Thinking Analytically

Although the exploration of such sensitive topics is often difficult — I have occasionally had students tell me that they simply could not write on a particular topic, or talk about it in class — most people find that their increased understanding of what goes on *in them* during a negotiation has tangible benefits in terms of the results they achieve. One man wrote, "I now see that all that is subjective and emotional about a negotiation is an integral part of it, and that I ignore the 'subcurrents' at my peril. I also see that personal wants and needs are less likely to take on the force of compulsions, or work against me in unpredictable ways, if I am aware of them." The more people are able to make sense of their experience of a negotiation, the less it feels like something that just happens to them. As they develop a capacity for self-observation, they are more able to stop and think about what is happening and to modify their behavior accordingly. One student, for example, realized that saying no to a proposal in negotiation was unthinkable to her because she grew up with a father who always said, "When I say jump, your only question should be 'How high?'" As she began to learn that she could be assertive without disrupting all possibility of communication, she became a much more effective negotiator. She also became able to make conscious use of her attunement to the needs of others in productive ways, such as to build consensus in a group negotiation setting.

The best tribute to this approach that I have received came from a woman who wrote at the end of a semester: "I don't think my strengths and weaknesses have changed much at all, but I am better able to recognize them when they appear, to see what they are and, in tranquility, to see where they come from. This skill has been much improved over the last fifteen weeks, and I think it's a highly valuable one. So I guess I do have one more arrow in my quiver — the strength of dealing with my own worst enemy." In the long run, skills acquired through such self-observation take a negotiator further than any top ten list ever will. Although learning about feelings is hard and unfamiliar work, especially for lawyers, the potential benefits — to the lawyers themselves and the clients they serve — make it a critical addition to our ways of thinking about and teaching negotiation.

Robert H. Mnookin, Scott R. Peppet & Andrew S. Tulumello,* *The Tension Between Empathy and Assertiveness*
12 NEGOT. J. 217, 217-26 (1996)**

In our view, negotiation — whether between labor and management, state and state, or neighbor and neighbor — characteristically involves the management of three different tensions. These tensions are to some extent inescapable, and understanding them is an indispensable first step to their successful management.

The first involves a tension between efficiency and distribution. Lax and Sebenius have described the dilemma that a negotiator faces between "cooperative moves to create value and competitive moves to claim it." An individual negotiator is primarily concerned with the size of her slice of the pie, and with the size of the pie as a whole only to the extent it enlarges her slice. There is often a tension, therefore, between a negotiator's moves that facilitate enlarging the pie and those intended to secure a favorable distribution.

The second tension is widespread and exists whenever a negotiator acts on behalf of another person or entity — in other words, whenever a negotiation involves an "agent" representing a "principal." Examples include a lawyer negotiating on behalf of a client; a manager negotiating on behalf of a public company; a union representative negotiating for workers; or a diplomat representing a national government. Tension arises in this type of negotiating relationship because agents have interests of their own. Managers, diplomats, and lawyers worry about their organizations or clients. An agent's interests may align with those of the principal to a greater or lesser degree, but they rarely align completely. This divergence of interests creates a tension between principal and agent.

The third tension — and the subject of this article — deals with an interpersonal aspect of negotiation: how should a negotiator approach his or her dealings with another? We propose that negotiation behavior can be conceptualized along two dimensions — *assertiveness* and *empathy*. By assertiveness, we mean the capacity to express and advocate for one's own interests. By empathy, we mean the capacity to demonstrate an accurate, nonjudgmental understanding of another person's concerns and perspective.

---

* Robert H. Mnookin is Samuel Williston Professor of Law at Harvard University. Scott R. Peppet is Associate Professor at University of Colorado School of Law. Andrew S. Tulumello is an attorney in private practice. Their article examines the importance both of taking in what the other side says in a negotiation and of being firm in representing your own client's point of view.

Empathy and assertiveness are in "tension" because many negotiators implicitly assume that these two sets of skills represent polar opposites along a single continuum and that each is incompatible with the other. Some worry for example, that to listen or empathize too much signals weakness or agreement; they perceive empathy to be incompatible with assertion. Others are concerned that if they advocate too strongly they will upset or anger their counterpart; they believe that assertion undermines empathy. Many negotiators fall somewhere in between. Not needing to dominate but preferring not to surrender control, they are unsure how much to assert. Or, open to understanding the other side but also wanting to secure the best possible outcome, they do not know how much to empathize. In short, many negotiators feel stuck. We propose that empathy and assertiveness do not represent polar opposites along a single dimension and that rather they should be conceptualized as two independent dimensions of negotiation behavior. We hope to demonstrate that the most effective negotiators develop strengths along both dimensions.

* * *

Empathy

For purposes of negotiation, we define empathy as the process of demonstrating an accurate, nonjudgmental understanding of the other side's needs, interests, and positions. There are two components to this definition. The first involves a skill psychologists call *perspective-taking* — trying to see the world through the other negotiator's eyes. The second is the nonjudgmental *expression* of the other person's viewpoint in a way that is open to correction. In crafting this definition, we have found useful the work of Carl Rogers. Rogers described empathy as:

> [E]ntering the private perceptual world of the other and becoming thoroughly at home in it. It involves being sensitive . . . to the changing felt meanings which flow in this other person. . . . It means temporarily living in his/her life, moving about in it delicately without making judgments, sensing meanings of which he/she is acutely aware. . . . It includes communicating your sensings of his/her world as you look with fresh and unfrightened eyes at elements of which the individual is fearful. It means frequently checking with him/her as to the accuracy of your sensings, and being guided by the responses you receive. . . . To be with another in this way means that for the time being you lay aside the views and values you hold for yourself in order to enter into another world without prejudice.

For Rogers, empathy involved the process of "nonjudgmentally entering another's perceptual world." For us, it also involves the active expression of this understanding of the other side.

Defined in this way, empathy requires neither sympathy nor agreement. Sympathy is "feeling for" someone — it refers to an affective response to the other person's predicament. For us, empathy does not require people to have sympathy for others' plight. Instead, we see empathy as "a value-neutral mode of observation," a journey in which we explore and describe another's perceptual world without commitment. Empathizing with someone, therefore, does not mean sympathizing with, agreeing with, or even necessarily liking the other side. Instead, it simply requires the expression of how the world looks to that person.

The benefits of empathy relate to the integrative and distributive aspects of bargaining. Consider first the potential benefits of understanding (but not yet demonstrating) the other side's viewpoint. Skilled negotiators often can "see through" another person's statements to find hidden interests or feelings, even when they are inchoate in the other's mind. Perspective-taking thus facilitates value-creation by enabling a negotiator to craft arguments, proposals, or trade-offs that reflect another's interests and that may create the basis for trade.

Perspective-taking also facilitates distributive moves. To the extent we understand another negotiator, we will better predict their goals, expectations, and strategic choices. This enables good perspective-takers to gain a strategic advantage — analogous, perhaps, to playing a game of chess with advance knowledge of the other side's moves. It may also mean that good perspective-takers will more easily see through bluffing or other gambits based on artifice. Research confirms that negotiators with higher perspective-taking ability negotiate agreements of higher value than those with lower perspective-taking ability.

The capacity to *demonstrate* our understanding of the other side's viewpoint — to reflect back how they see the world — confers additional benefits. Negotiators in both personal and business disputes typically have a deep need to tell their story and to feel that it has been understood. Meeting this need, therefore, can dramatically shift the tone of a relationship. The burgeoning literature on interpersonal communication celebrates this possibility. As Nichols writes, ". . . when . . . feelings take shape in words that are shared and come back clarified, the result is a reassuring sense of being understood and a grateful feeling of shared humanness with the one who understands." The subtext to good empathy is concern and respect, which diffuses hostility, anger and mistrust, especially where these emotions stem from feeling unappreciated or exploited.

Another important benefit of expressing our understanding is that this process may help correct interpersonal misperceptions. Many scholars have documented the mistakes in person-perception that beset most negotiations; such mistakes are perhaps the foremost contributors to negotiation and relationship breakdown. Negotiators, for example, often make various attributional errors — that is, they attribute to their counterparts incorrect or exaggerated intentions or characteristics based on limited information. If, for example, our counterpart is late to a meeting, we tend to assume that he either intended to make us wait or that he his chronically tardy, even to lead to a distributive agreement — one in which there is a winner and a loser, or a compromise that does not realize potential integrative gains. Focusing on power means that parties try to coerce each other into making concessions that each would not otherwise do. A power focus also usually leads to a distributive agreement, and potentially can result in a desire for revenge or the creation of future disputes.

Figure 1

Three Approaches to Resolving Disputes

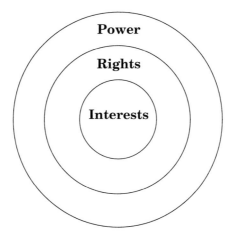

The interrelationship between these three approaches is illustrated in Figure 1 as three concentric circles, with reconciliation of interests occurring within the contexts of the parties' rights and power, and determination of rights occurring within the context of parties' power to abide by the determination. Ury et al. argue that all three elements exist within a single dispute and that, while negotiating, parties may choose to focus on interests, rights, or power as well as cycle among these three approaches. In other words, interests, rights and power provide three different strategic alternatives for negotiating the resolution of disputes. The extent to which parties utilize all three approaches within a single negotiation is one of the questions addressed by our research.

* * *

Consistent with Ury, Brett, and Goldberg, we found that most negotiators cycled through all three approaches during their negotiations. Across the 25 negotiations that we studied, however, we found more emphasis on rights and power in the first and third quarters than in the second and fourth quarters of negotiation. Our finding that there were different strategies used by each negotiator in the same negotiation led us to another level of inquiry. There is substantial research indicating that reciprocity, or the greater than base-rate probability that an act will be conditional on the though we may be meeting him for the first time. In either case, we have formed an attribution or judgment that may prove unnecessarily counter-productive.

By expressing our understanding, we can correct — or at least test — our attributions about others. By journeying into their shoes, we collect new information and new clues as to their motivation that may help us to revise our earlier assessments. In a sense, empathy requires us to roll back our judgments into questions or tentatively-held assumptions until we have more complete information.

Finally, empathy inspires openness in others and may itself be persua-sive. A disparate series of studies supports this conclusion. Research on role reversal — whereby one person attempts to articulate her counter-part's views in the first person voice — shows that accurate role reversal defuses others' adherence to initial negotiating positions and increases their willingness to compromise. Similarly, message analysis research indicates that two-sided messages, which describe the other's viewpoint before one's own, are more effective than one-sided messages.

Assertiveness

By assertiveness, we mean the ability to express and advocate for one's own needs, interest, and positions. The underlying skills include identifying one's own interests, speaking (making arguments, explaining), and even lis-tening. Assertiveness also presupposes the self-esteem or belief that one's interests are valid and that it is legitimate to satisfy them. Assertiveness training, for example, involves developing self-respect and self-confidence as much as learning discrete speaking or advocacy skills.

We can relate the benefits of assertiveness to the integrative and dis-tributive aspects of bargaining. It is well established that assertion confers distributive benefits — assertive negotiators tend to get more of what they want. Less well understood is the role assertion plays in value-creation. Assertiveness contributes to value-creation because it is through direct expression of each side's interests that joint gains may be discovered. Asser-tion may be relatively easy in commercial negotiations between strangers, but can be more difficult where conflict arises in the context of a long-term relationship. If one or both parties fails to assert their interests, both may suffer because value may be left on the table.

Assertiveness may also facilitate successful working relationships. Assertive negotiators who voice and advocate for their needs experience less fear of exploitation than those who do not. The assertive negotiator con-fronts relationship difficulties as they occur — rather than permitting them to fester — thereby initiating interpersonal adjustments that make long-term cooperation possible. Finally assertive behavior may promote self-respect. Assertiveness-training guides emphasize this possibility. As one proclaims, "the extent to which you assert yourself determines your self-esteem." Negotiators improve their outcomes if they are satisfied with both their substantive agreement and personal performance.

Are Empathy and Assertiveness Incompatible?

Students often ask whether it is possible to be both highly assertive and highly empathetic. Many implicitly assume that the behaviors associated with each are essentially incompatible, and that in a negotiation they must choose a single point on an axis on which empathy and assertiveness are opposite poles. . . . This often leads to paralysis, confusion, or frustration, as students try to decide what relative priority to attach to these two desirable sets of skills.

We suggest that empathy and assertiveness are not opposites, but instead two independent dimensions of negotiation behavior. . . . Rather than there being an inevitable trade-off between them, we propose that a negotiator can exhibit high levels of both. Indeed, psychologists have found that adding an empathetic component to an assertive message improves competence and likability ratings while maintaining ratings of effectiveness. A combination of empathy and assertiveness is more persuasive than assertive advocacy alone.

Negotiation Styles: Competing, Accommodating, and Avoiding

Our claim that empathy and assertiveness represent different dimensions can be illuminated by considering three common negotiation "styles." These are *competing, accommodating* and *avoiding*, each of which represents a different suboptimal combination of empathy and assertiveness. There is a considerable literature, of course, related to these three categories, and scholars disagree over what exactly these categories describe, using such words as *styles, strategies, intentions, behaviors, modes* and *orientations*. There is certainly no consensus about their meaning. Our purpose here is not to settle these debates about definitions, but instead to use these categories as heuristics that highlight the utility of our empathy-assertiveness framework. The two-dimensional framework [is] illustrated in Figure 3, which measures empathy along the vertical axis and assertiveness along the horizontal axis.

Figure 3

Negotiation Styles

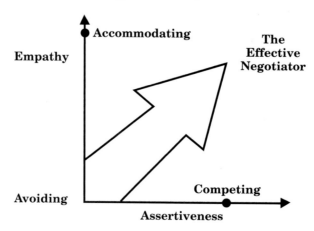

Competing

A competitive style consists of substantial assertion but little empathy. A competitor wants to experience "winning" and enjoys feeling purposeful and in control. Competitive negotiators exude eagerness, enthusiasm, and impatience. Because conflict does not make them feel uncomfortable, they enjoy being partisans. Competitive negotiators typically seek to control the agenda and frame the issues. They can stake out an ambitious position and stick to it, and they fight back in the face of bullying or intimidation.

The advantages of this style flow directly from this characterization. Competitors are not afraid to articulate and push for their point of view. With respect to distributive bargaining, they fight hard to get the biggest slice of any pie.

But this tendency also has disadvantages. Competitive negotiators risk provoking the other side and incur a high risk of escalation or stalemate. In addition, because competitive negotiators are often not good listeners, they have difficulty developing collaborative relationships that allow both sides to explore value-creating opportunities. They may also pay a high price in their relationships, as others, perceiving them as arrogant, untrustworthy, or controlling, avoid them. We have found that competitors can be surprised by the resentment they engender, as they see their behavior as simply part of the negotiation game.

Competitive negotiators also tend to be hard on themselves. They feel responsible when agreements turn our poorly. Their competitive buttons often get pushed, and they may regret or feel embarrassed by their loss of self-control. Finding it difficult to participate in a team or to delegate responsibility, competitors may feel disconnected from their colleagues.

Accommodating

Accommodating consists of substantial empathy but little assertion. An accommodator prizes good relationships and wants to feel liked. Accommodators exude concern, compassion, and understanding. Concerned that conflict will disrupt relationships, they negotiate in "smoothing" ways to resolve differences quickly. Accommodators typically listen well and are quick to second-guess their own interests.

This style has straightforward advantages. Negotiators concerned with good relationships on balance probably do have better relationships, or at least fewer relationships marked by open conflict. Because they listen well, others may see them as trustworthy. Similarly, they are adept at creating a less stressful atmosphere for the negotiation.

One disadvantage of this tendency is that it can be exploited. Hard bargainers may extract concessions by implicitly or explicitly threatening to disrupt or terminate the relationship. Another disadvantage may be that accommodators pay insufficient attention to the substance of the dispute because they are unduly concerned about disturbing a relationship. Accommodators, therefore, can feel frustrated dealing with both substantive and interpersonal issues.

Avoiding

An avoiding style consists of low levels of empathy and assertiveness. Avoiders believe that conflict is unproductive, and they feel uncomfortable with explicit, especially emotional, disagreement. When faced with conflict, avoiders disengage. They tend not to seek control of the agenda or to frame the issues. Rather, they deflect efforts to focus on solutions, appearing detached, unenthusiastic, or uninterested.

At times, avoidance can have substantial advantages. Some disputes are successfully avoided. In other cases, avoiders may create a "chasing" dynamic in which the other side does all the work (arranging the negotiation, establishing the agenda, making proposals). Because they appear aloof, avoiders can have more persuasive impact when they do speak up. In addition, their reserve and cool-headedness makes it difficult for others to know their true interests and intentions.

The greatest disadvantage of this tendency is that avoiders miss opportunities to use conflict to solve problems. Avoiders often disengage without knowing whether obscured interests might make joint gains possible — they rarely have the experience of walking away from an apparent conflict feeling better off. Even when they do negotiate, avoiders leave value on the table because they refrain from asserting their own interests or flushing out the other side's. Avoiders fare poorly in the distributive aspects of bargaining.

Like competitors, avoiders also have a difficult time sustaining strong working relationships. Others see them as apathetic or indifferent. Avoiders may well have a rich internal life, but because they do not express and share their feelings, they can feel misunderstood or overlooked. Some avoiders feel stress from internalizing conflict and concealing their emotions.

Interactions

We have found that these styles interact with one another in fairly predictable patterns, and now offer a brief overview of how each style is likely to interact with the others. These sketches are, of course, oversimplified, but even as caricatures they may be helpful in diagnosing and anticipating the problems that arise when negotiators with different or similar styles meet.

The case of two competitors. They will produce an energetic negotiation — making offers and counteroffers, arguments and counterarguments. They may relish the strategic dance of bargaining for the sheer fun of it. However, because both are primarily focused on "winning," they are likely to reach a stalemate, neither negotiator listening to the other. The challenge for the two competitors, therefore, is to find ways of trading control and to frame "compromises" in terms digestible to the other side.

By contrast, when a competitor meets an avoider, a different problem arises. Avoiders have a knack for driving competitors crazy. By refusing to engage, they exploit the competitor's need to control. Frustrated competitors may offer concessions to induce avoiders to come to the table. Alternatively, competitors might alienate avoiders by coming on too strong. Thus, the challenge for competitors is to manage their need for control and their comfort with open conflict in a way that is safe for avoiders to engage. By improving their assertiveness skills, avoiders may learn to engage with competitors without feeling bullied or intimidated.

For the accommodator, negotiating with a competitor can be a nightmare. Savvy competitors can exploit the accommodator's desire to preserve the relationship and to minimize disagreements. Because accommodators often make substantive concessions to solve conflicts quickly, they could improve their performance by developing assertiveness skills to match their refined sense of empathy.

Finally, when two accommodators negotiate, the risk is that neither will work hard enough on the substance of the problem. Both will be attentive to the other's relationship needs, but neither may focus sufficient attention on important distributive issues or adequately probe the other side's interests so as to exploit value-creating opportunities.

The Effective Negotiator

Each of these problematic interactions highlights the importance of being able to both empathize and assert as needed in a given negotiation. If both negotiators can skillfully empathize and assert, the pair can work toward a beneficial solution that exploits the opportunities for value-creation and manages distributive issues.

Even if one's counterpart is *not* so skilled, however, we believe that a negotiator is most effective if she leads the way by successfully combining empathy and assertiveness. The normative task is to manage the tension between empathy and assertiveness by moving to the "northeast" on our graph (see Figure 3), and by helping design a process that permits the other side to do so as well. This often means agreeing to listen and empathize for a period on the condition that the other side agrees to try to do so later in the negotiation, and also discussing explicitly that a demonstrated understanding of the other's views should not be interpreted as agreement. In this way, a negotiation can sometimes evolve toward problem-solving even if it begins less productively.

In all events, our claim is that the effective negotiator should be able to draw upon his own well-developed empathy and assertiveness skills no matter what the orientation of the other side.

Barriers to Empathy and Assertiveness

Although both empathy and assertiveness produce substantial benefits in negotiation, comparatively few negotiators have well developed skills along both dimensions. Why is this so?

First, developing these skills often requires changing ingrained habits. Over time, people may develop certain tendencies when faced with conflict. Changing habits is always difficult and it may be especially so when change is perceived as jeopardizing the benefits (identified above) associated with a negotiation style. Second, many negotiators exaggerate the potentially harmful consequences of exercising new skills. For example, a competitive negotiator may worry that empathy will be perceived as weakness. She may also fear that if she really understands the other side she might no longer be able to assert her own interests forcefully. Analogous concerns may prevent accommodating negotiators from becoming more assertive. A negotiator may fear that assertive behavior will necessarily jeopardize a valued relationship. Some associate assertiveness with rude and distastefully aggressive behavior.

Thus, because of habits, fears, and erroneous assumptions, negotiators may find it difficult to be both highly assertive and highly empathetic. Our experience in teaching negotiation, however, is that students can overcome these barriers and broaden their repertoire of negotiation skills.

* * *

Andrew S. Watson,[*] *Mediation and Negotiation: Learning to Deal With Psychological Responses*
18 U. MICH. J.L. REFORM 293, 296-303 (1985)[**]

* * *

II. LAWYER AS NEGOTIATOR — PSYCHOLOGICAL TENSIONS

* * *

A lawyer's view of the ethical duty to "zealously represent his client" will vary greatly according to the psychological conflicts the lawyer has about the negotiation process. This conflict has little to do with the *content* of the negotiation; rather, it relates to the internal, psychological process that negotiation activities trigger.

* * *

The process of negotiation is full of vigorous interchanges, many of which are likely, sooner or later, to stimulate aggressive impulses. This elicitation of aggression is commonplace. An opponent's aggressive response "legitimates" an aggressive reaction. An opponent's passive response, on the other hand, may also stimulate aggressiveness; an activity-oriented attorney may have difficulty coping with inactivity. Aggression, a heavily conflicted emotion for many, is an emotion to which lawyers have a special sensitivity. The combination of a particular person's capacity to be passive with the negotiation process's requirement of extensive listening, can draw forth sufficient aggression to insure that unconscious "defense mechanisms" emerge, preventing rational responses to some of the important elements of the negotiation and precluding effectiveness. Although such aggressive behavior will be masked by various "explanations," the real reason will be unexpressed concerns over hurting and being hurt. The result will be a stalemate.

Attitudes towards "maleness" and "femaleness" will inevitably emerge in the negotiation process, regardless of the gender of the participants. Each of us has deep, unconscious, images of what we must do to be male or female. We wish to behave in ways consistent with the image we seek to project and avoid actions resembling the behavior of the opposite gender. Because little human behavior is biologically gender-linked, humans may select from a broad range of available behaviors; these behaviors are, however, socially gender-linked. This discontinuity between a broader biological and a narrower social range of behaviors can be a source of great

---

[*] Andrew S. Watson was a psychoanalyst and Professor of Law at University of Michigan Law School who co-taught classes on negotiation. His article deals with psychological tensions commonly encountered in negotiation.

personal discomfort and, more importantly, highly complicated, individual defensive actions that interfere with the negotiation process.

* * *

In the last analysis, the psychological dynamics of the negotiator are highly personal qualities. A skilled and thoughtful lawyer will "keep book" on his opponents and attempt to define and understand them in these psychological terms. Individual negotiators' attributes are finite in number, and their constancy and continuity will enable counsel to use them to predict an opponent's tactics and strategies. Lawyers follow this practice, for example, when they engage in "judge shopping."

Experienced negotiators acknowledge the wisdom of one person conducting the active discussion to keep the line of argument on track. One non-speaking team member can observe the non-verbal behaviors of the opponents and ponder their underlying implications. Often non-active members of a negotiating team broadcast vivid messages that powerfully communicate the team's intentions. When you discover a large stock of supplies behind one part of your opponent's lines, you may deduce that something important is scheduled to happen there.

A negotiator must constantly address the ubiquitous question of veracity, his own and his opponent's. At first glance, determining what is a lie appears to be a simple task; it turns out to be a complicated matter about which much controversy exists in negotiation circles. It is my own impression that lawyers are inclined to over-diagnose lying and to include a variety of psychological distortions within its ambit; this makes lying a very difficult problem to which lawyers must respond. It is probably best to reserve the term *lie* for those distortions made deliberately to mislead. A good negotiator, after clarifying and narrowing his definitions, should try to understand how he *feels* about lying. A powerful reaction to somebody else's lies suggests great concern over one's own honesty, and grappling with that kind of issue is always the first order of business in dealing with any psychological response. In general, we are more frightened of our own impulses and feelings when we don't understand them. We handle impulses and feelings better when we know what they are and why we are afraid of them. We are then in a position to test our real vulnerabilities and take concrete measures to protect ourselves.

It behooves working professionals to ground all standards, including those related to lying, on more rational bases than unexamined moral interdiction. Lying can be so advantageous superficially that some basis should be established for *not* doing it. The obvious reason is that others' knowledge of one's lying leads to a loss of credibility which, for a working professional, can only have destructive results. I would like to suggest a second reason. Even if others do not learn about a lie, the negotiator who lies knows that the lie occurred and must then recognize that others may successfully lie to him. This induces a paranoid attitude, a psychological burden that can never be totally put aside. The long-term costs of lying imply a cost-benefit analysis supporting the old admonition to do unto others as you would have them do unto you.

* * *

Negotiators will profit from knowledge of their own prejudices. I do not even argue about whether prejudices exist; I acknowledge that debate occurs about the extent and nature of prejudices. Erikson notes that any well-reared child knows that everything that he learns in his own environment is Good/Right/Nice and everything outside his own surroundings is Bad/Evil/Not Nice. Everyone carries these values out of childhood into adolescence, when a wider sociability diminishes prejudgment as individuals learn to question their own archaic presumptions. Bluntly stated, prejudices exist. Although they may assume myriad subtle forms shaped by culture and family idiosyncrasies, all prejudices stand as "Truths." The important question is whether they have been reevaluated, understood, and reintegrated in the thinking and decision-making of the adult individual.

III. TRANSFERENCE PATTERNS

Another important organizing principle, transference, and its counterpart in the observer, countertransference, assist psychiatrists in understanding human behavior. Transference and countertransference are patterned behaviors that are substantially predictive of an individual's response to the multitude of stimuli from the external world. A transference response to a person is defined as

> [T]he fusion of unreal attributes which the observer believes to be present in the observed, with those which are in fact present. The unreal attributes consist of "projections," which derive from some superficial likeness to an important person from the past such as a parent. The observer then treats the new person as *if* they were the original model. The part qualities are seen as the whole.

Among the several definitions of transference, this one is somewhat controversial but, I believe, the most useful because it identifies and points the way for the intellectual procedures necessary to use the definition effectively.

These transference patterns reveal individual attitudes and feelings. They also may lead individuals to stereotype the observed behavior of others. Information about transference patterns can be elicited in some types of interviews. This information in turn allows conclusions to be drawn about individuals' behaviors.

The learned behavior that psychiatrists call *character* is adaptive in nature and relates to transference. This psychological rather than moral character constitutes the complex set of behaviors by means of which a person is recognized. It consists of the automated, adaptational response patterns allowed by the individual's culture and adopted by the individual, even though they may sometimes cause distress in others. Some response patterns express compromise behaviors. For example, a brash, assertive, humorous speech pattern may allow an individual to express thinly disguised aggression. The same things said "with a straight face" would enmesh a person in deep social difficulty but said in "jest," the comments are acceptable — they are in character.

In accord with the proposition to know thyself, a lawyer should be aware of how her/his character looks and feels to others. "What do they encounter when they deal with me?" While a lawyer can do little to change this character, the individual can, like a good poker player, cut losses or bet good cards aggressively. This accords with the admonition to avoid a losing battle or, if you must fight, to lose as cheaply as possible. Know your character assets and use them skillfully, even as you avoid the kinds of encounters with which you have difficulty. Let your partner handle those.

Similarly, your opponent's character qualities must be assayed. If he is a blustery, macho type, it will not do to collide with him and stimulate his fulminating masculine assertiveness. What might he do with a "soft," "yielding," non-aggressive person? Will he quiet down? It's worth an experiment, because .jousting requires two parties. Such a pairing may force the negotiation into a more rational channel, allowing progress to occur.

How may a lawyer handle his opponent's character? First, learn to "diagnose" his behavior. One requisite assumption is that the observed character traits are purposeful. To determine the purpose one must, to use Reik's felicitous expression, "listen with the third ear." For example: "Why does my opponent verbally beat upon me in such a way that I become angry and resistive to everything he says or does? Does my opponent have some need to fail at this procedure by alienating me? Does he hope to make me angry and irrational?" Or: "Why do all of my opponent's comments always sound as if they are subtly granting me permission for my moves? Do they need to feel always in control to be comfortable?"

I have been noting character-based behaviors of which the actor may have been completely oblivious and therefore unaware of the problems the behaviors caused in the negotiation setting. Sometimes the knowledge that such behaviors occur without malice, i.e., without "mens rea," helps one to cope with an unpleasant encounter. In some situations, knowledge is power.

* * *

Max H. Bazerman,[*] *Negotiator Judgment: A Critical Look at the Rationality Assumption*
27 Am. Behav. Sci. 211, 215-24 (1983)[**]

* * *

THE MYTHICAL FIXED-PIE OF NEGOTIATIONS

Integrative agreements are nonobvious solutions to conflict that reconcile the parties' interests and yield a higher joint benefit than a simple compromise could create. To illustrate, consider the compromise between two sisters who fought over an orange (Follett, 1940). The two sisters agreed to split the orange in half, allowing one sister to use her portion for juice and the other sister to use the peel of her half for a cake. The two parties in this conflict overlooked the *integrative* agreement of giving one sister all the juice and the other sister all the peel.

Walton and McKersie suggested two directly opposing models of the bargaining process. The distributive model views negotiation as a procedure for dividing a fixed-pie of resources, or, "How much of the orange does each sister receive?" According to this model, what one side gains, the other side loses. A number of situations are accurately depicted by the distributive model. If you were to purchase a commodity in a resort location with cash (with no other purchases from the seller possible), the negotiation for the amount of cash that you pay would be depicted by the distributive model. In contrast, Walton and McKersie's integrative bargaining model views negotiation as a means by which parties can make trade-offs or jointly solve problems to the mutual benefit of both parties, or, "How can the orange be divided to maximize the joint benefit of the two sisters?" According to this model, the two parties' success at joint problem-solving will determine the size of the pie of resources to be distributed. As we describe below, the integrative model describes far more negotiations than most people realize.

The fixed-pie assumption of the distributive model represents a fundamental bias in human judgment. That is, negotiators have a systematic intuitive bias that distorts their behavior: they assume that their interests directly conflict with the other party's interests. The fundamental assumption of a fixed-pie probably results from a competitive society that creates the belief in a win-lose situation. This win-lose orientation is manifested objectively in our society in athletic competition, admission to academic programs, industrial promotion systems, and so on. Individuals tend to generalize from these objective win-lose situations and apply their experi-

---

[*] Max H. Bazerman is Jesse Isidor Straus Professor at Harvard University Business School. His article looks at some common irrational beliefs about negotiation.

ence to situations that are not objectively fixed-pies. Faced with a mixed-motive situation requiring both cooperation and competition, it is the competitive aspect that becomes salient — resulting in a win-lose orientation and a distributive approach to bargaining. This in turn results in the development of a strategy for obtaining the largest share possible of the perceived fixed-pie. Such a focus inhibits the creativity and problem-solving necessary for the development of integrative solutions.

The pervasiveness of the fixed-pie perception, as well as the importance of integrative bargaining, can be seen in the recent housing market. When interest rates first shot above 12% in 1979, the housing market came to a dead stop. Sellers continued to expect the value of their property to increase. Buyers, however, could not afford the monthly payments on houses they aspired to own, due to the drastically higher interest rates. Viewing the problem as a distributive one, buyers could not afford the prices sellers were demanding. This fixed-pie assumption (which was prevalent throughout the industry) led to the conclusion that transactions would not occur until seller resistance points decreased, buyer resistance points increased, and/or interest rates came down. However, once the real estate industry started to view real estate transactions integratively, some relief was provided. Specifically, sellers cared a great deal about price — partly to justify their past investment. Buyers cared about finding some way to afford a house they aspired to own — perhaps their first house. The integrative solutions were the wide variety of creative financing developments (e.g., seller financing) of the early 1980's, which allowed sellers an artificially high price in exchange for favorable financing assistance to the buyer. Creative financing integrated the interests of buyers and sellers, rescuing an entire industry from our common fix-pie assumptions.

The above arguments suggest that while some fixed-pies exist objectively, most resolutions depend on finding favorable trade-offs between negotiators, trade-offs that necessitate eliminating our intuitive fixed-pie assumptions. Winkelgren suggests that we often limit our finding creative solutions by making false assumptions. The fixed-pie perception is a fundamentally false assumption that hinders finding creative (integrative) solutions. A fundamental task in training negotiators lies in identifying and eliminating this false assumption, and institutionalizing the creative process of integrative bargaining.

* * *

THE NONRATIONAL ESCALATION OF CONFLICT

* * *

It is easy to see the process of nonrational escalation of commitment unfold in a number of actual conflict situations. The negotiation process commonly leads both sides initially to make extreme demands. The escalation literature predicts that if negotiators become committed to their initial public statements, they will nonrationally adopt a nonconcessionary stance.

Further, if both sides incur losses as a result of lack of agreement (e.g., a strike), their commitment to their positions is expected to increase, and their willingness to change to a different course of action (i.e., compromise) is expected to decrease. The more a negotiator believes there is "too much invested to quit," the more likely he or she is to be intransigent.

An understanding of escalation can be very helpful to a negotiator in understanding the behavior of the opponent. When will the other party really hold out? The escalation literature predicts that the other side will really hold out when it has "too much invested" in its position to give in. This suggests that there are systematic clues as to when you can threaten your opponent and win, and when the threat will receive an active response, due to your opponent's prior public commitment to a course of action. Strategically, then, a negotiator should avoid inducing the opponent to make statements or to behave in any way that would create the illusion of having invested too much to quit.

* * *

A number of principles have been identified . . . concerning the avoidance of escalation in general. Many of these can be applied to negotiators:

Continually evaluate the cost and benefits of maintaining a conflict in its current form. When competition exists, we often lose perspective of our goals and instead seek victory over the opponent. Forced consideration of the costs and benefits of escalating the conflict encourages rationality — that is, following the course of action that will best achieve the objectives.

Be aware of the nonrational tendency to escalate commitment to a previous course of action. Escalation often takes the form of creeping incrementalism — "We need to strike for only one more week to get the company to give in." The strongest safeguard against this pattern of escalation is awareness. People who are trained to recognize escalatory situations are less likely to become entrapped.

Recognize sunk costs. Accountants and economists teach the principle that irrelevant historical costs should not be considered in a decision. Most of us, however, intuitively and inappropriately include sunk costs in evaluating courses of action. Instead, alternative courses of action should be evaluated in terms of *future* costs and benefits.

Be aware of the tendency to try to justify past actions. A primary explanation for why people escalate commitment to a course of action involves our need cognitively to justify past actions. That is, escalation of commitment to a strike can be seen as a psychological attempt to make the original decision to strike appear rational. The importance of this principle is strengthened when the constituency is monitoring the negotiator's success.

NEGOTIATOR OVERCONFIDENCE

Consider the following scenario:

You are an advisor to a major-league baseball player. In baseball, a system exists for the resolution of compensation conflicts that calls for a player and a team who do not agree to submit final offers to an arbitrator. Using final offer arbitration, the arbitrator must accept one position or the other, not a compromise. Thus, the challenge for each side is to come just a little closer to the arbitrator's perception of the appropriate compensation package than the opposition. In this case, your best intuitive estimate of the final offer that the team will submit is a package worth $200,000 per year. You believe that an appropriate wage is $400,000 per year but estimate the arbitrator's opinion to be $300,000 per year. What final offer do you propose?

This scenario represents a common cognitive trap for negotiators. Individuals are systematically overconfident in estimating the position of a neutral third party and in estimating the likelihood that a third party will accept their position. In the baseball example, if the arbitrator's true assessment of the appropriate wage is $250,000, and you believe it to be $300,000, you are likely to submit an inappropriately high offer and overestimate the likelihood that the offer will be accepted. Consequently, the overconfidence bias is likely to lead the advisor to believe that less compromise is necessary than a more objective analysis would suggest.

* * *

Research demonstrates that negotiators tend to be overconfident that their positions will prevail if they do not "give in." Neale and Bazerman show that negotiators consistently overestimate the probability, under final offer arbitration, that their final offer will be accepted. That is, while only 50% of all final offers can be accepted, the average subject estimated that there was a much higher probability that his or her offer would be accepted. If we consider a final offer as a judgment as to how much compromise is necessary to win the arbitration, it is easy to argue that when a negotiator is overconfident that a particular position will be accepted, the incentive to compromise is reduced. If a more accurate assessment is made, the negotiator is likely to be more uncertain and uncomfortable about the probability of success. One strategy to reduce this uncertainty is to compromise further.

Interestingly, individuals and organizations become aware of their overconfidence over time. When final offer arbitration was first introduced into baseball, the final offers of the two parties involved in any arbitration were drastically disparate, largely due to their overconfidence. Baseball negotiators have since learned that they fare better by coming closer to an objective analysis of the arbitrator's position. This is demonstrated by the fact that over the years final offers of competing parties converged dramatically.

* * *

THE WINNER'S CURSE

Imagine that you are in a foreign country. You meet a merchant who is selling a very attractive gem. You have bought a few gems in your life but are far from being an expert. After some discussion, you make the merchant an offer that you believe (but are uncertain) is on the low side. He quickly accepts, and the transaction is completed. How do you feel? Most people would feel uneasy with the purchase after the quick acceptance. Yet, why would you voluntarily make an offer that you would not want accepted?

To understand this quandary, consider the experimental work of Bazerman and Samuelson. The problem we posed to Boston University M.B.A. students can be summarized as follows:

> The subject is to play the role of the acquirer in a potential corporate takeover. The subject's firm (the acquirer) is considering making an offer to buy out another firm (the target). However, the acquirer is uncertain about the ultimate value of the target firm. It only knows its value under current management is between $0 and $100 per share, with all values equally likely. Since the firm is expected to be worth 50% more under the acquirer's management than under the current ownership, it appears to make sense for a transaction to take place. While the acquirer does not know the actual value of the firm, the target knows its current worth exactly. The target can be expected to accept any offer that is profitable to its shareholders. In this exercise, what price per share should the acquirer offer for the target?

The problem is analytically simple (as will be demonstrated shortly) yet intuitively perplexing. The dominant response was between $50 and $75 (90 out of 123 responses). How is this $50 to $75 decision reached? One common, naive explanation is that, on average, the firm will be worth $50 to the target and $75 to the acquirer; consequently, a transaction in this range will, on average, be profitable to both parties.

Now consider the logical process that a normative response would generate in evaluating the decision to make an offer of $60 per share (a value suggested naively to be "mutually acceptable"):

> If I offer $60 per share, the offer will be accepted 60% of the time — whenever the firm is worth between $0 and $60 to the target. Since all values are equally likely, the firm will, on average, be worth $30 per share to the target when the target accepts the offer. Since the value of the firm is worth 50% more to the acquirer, the average value of the firm to the acquirer when the target accepts a $60 per share offer will be $45 per share, resulting in a loss of $15 per share ($45 - $60).

Consequently, a $60 per share offer is ill-considered. It is easy to see that the same kind of reasoning applies to *any* positive offer. On the average, the acquirer obtains a company worth 25% less than the price it pays. Thus, the best the acquirer can do is not to make an offer ($0 per share). Even though in all circumstances the firm is worth more to the acquirer than to the target, any offer leads to a negative expected return to the acquirer. The source of this paradox lies in the target's accepting the acquirer's offer when the acquirer least wants the firm — when it is a "lemon." Unfortunately, only 9 of 123 subjects correctly offered $0 per share.

Most individuals have the analytical ability to follow the logic that the optimal offer is $0 per share (no offer). Yet without assistance, most individuals would make a positive offer (typically between $50 and $75 per share). Thus, individuals systematically exclude information from their decision processes that they have the ability to include. They fail to realize that their expected return is *conditional* on an acceptance by the other party, and that an acceptance is most likely to occur when it is least desirable to the negotiator making the offer.

The key feature of the "winner's curse" in the bargaining context is that one side has much better information than the other side. Though we are all familiar with the slogan "buyer beware," our intuition seems to have difficulty putting this idea into practice when asymmetric information exists. Most people realize that when they buy a commodity they know little about, their uncertainty increases. The evidence presented here indicates that against an informed opponent, their expected return from the transaction may decrease dramatically. Practically, the evidence suggests that people undervalue the importance of accurate information in making transactions. They undervalue a mechanic's evaluation of a used car, a house inspector's assessment of a house, or an independent jeweler's assessment of a coveted gem. Thus, the knowledgeable gem merchant will accept your offer selectively, taking the offer when the gem is probably worth less than your estimate. To protect yourself, you need to develop or borrow the expertise to balance the quality of information.

* * *

Leigh Thompson & Terri DeHarpport,[*]
Social Judgment, Feedback, and Interpersonal Learning in Negotiation
58 ORG. BEHAV. & HUM. DECISION PROC. 327, 341-42 (1994)[**]

* * *

A key factor that leads to inefficient performance in negotiation is the fixed-pie perception, or the belief that the opponent's interests are completely opposed to one's own. Perhaps the most remarkable finding attesting to the tenacity of the fixed-pie perception was the observation that even some negotiators who were provided with full feedback about the other person's interests failed to report noticing the critical aspect of the diagnostic information — namely, that their opponent had different priorities. This was found even though negotiators were prompted to carefully consider the information. Why is the fixed-pie perception so tenacious?

According to the cognitive approach heuristic[***] information processing principles promote the endurance of fixed-pie perceptions. Heuristic information processes operate at the level of attention, encoding, memory, and judgment. People attend to information that is consistent rather than inconsistent or irrelevant to their expectations. This suggests that in negotiation, people will be more likely to attend to information and notice behaviors that are consistent with their fixed-pie perception. People encode or interpret information in a manner that is consistent with their expectancies and ignore or misconstrue information that is inconsistent or irrelevant with respect to their expectancies. Thus, negotiators are likely to interpret their opponent's behaviors in a manner that is consistent with their fixed-pie perception. Information that is consistent with one's expectations is more likely to be recalled because people may use their existing schemas and stereotypes to infer what they cannot remember. Further, information that is encoded in a well-developed schema provides more associative paths that can be searched during recall. Finally, people's judgments are strongly influenced by confirmatory information processing. That is, people will seek information in a biased and selective manner that confirms, rather than disconfirms, their expectancies. Thus, a number of basic information processes promote the fixed-pie perception in negotiation. In addition to these basic cognitive, information-processing principles, a number of higher level cognitive factors may also operate in a manner that instantiates and maintains

---

[*] Leigh Thompson is J. Jay Gerber Distinguished Professor of Dispute Resolution & Organizations at Kellogg Graduate School of Management, Northwestern University. Terri DeHarpport was a doctoral candidate at the Kellogg School of Management at the time this article was written. This excerpt focuses on cognitive errors in negotiation.

[**] Copyright © 1994 by Academic Press. Reprinted by permission of Elsevier.

[***] "Heuristics" are persuasive, although not logically compelling, explanations. [Ed.]

the fixed-pie perception. For example, cognitive balance principles suggest that people will be likely to bring their perceptions of their opponent's interests in line with their perception of the opponent as an adversary. Together then, a number of basic cognitive processes appear to operate to maintain negotiators' fixed-pie perceptions.

* * *

Robert H. Mnookin,[*] *Why Negotiations Fail: An Exploration of Barriers to the Resolution of Conflict*
8 OHIO ST. J. ON DISP. RESOL. 235, 243-47 (1993)[**]

* * *

C. Cognitive Barriers.

The third barrier is a by-product of the way the human mind processes information, deals with risks and uncertainties, and makes inferences and judgments. Research by cognitive psychologists during the last fifteen years suggests several ways in which human reasoning often departs from that suggested by theories of rational judgment and decision making. Daniel Kahneman and Amos Tversky have done research on a number of cognitive biases that are relevant to negotiation. This evening, I would like to focus on two aspects of their work: those relating to loss aversion and framing effects.

Suppose everyone attending this evening's lecture is offered the following happy choice: At the end of my lecture you can exit at the north end of the hall or the south end. If you choose the north exit, you will be handed an envelope in which there will be a crisp new twenty dollar bill. Instead, if you choose the south exit, you will be given a sealed envelope randomly pulled from a bin. One quarter of these envelopes contain a $100 bill, but three quarters are empty. In other words, you can have a sure gain of $20 if you go out the north door, or you can instead gamble by choosing the south door where you will have a 25% chance of winning $100 and a 75% chance of winning nothing. Which would you choose? A great deal of experimental work suggests that the overwhelming majority of you would choose the sure gain of $20, even though the "expected value" of the second alternative, $25, is slightly more. This is a well known phenomenon called "risk aversion." The principle is that most people will take a sure thing over a gamble, even where the gamble may have a somewhat higher "expected" payoff.

[*] Robert H. Mnookin is the Samuel Williston Professor of Law at Harvard University. This article reviews several aspects of psychological research on negotiation.

Daniel Kahneman and Amos Tversky have advanced our understanding of behavior under uncertainty with a remarkable discovery. They suggest that, in order to avoid what would otherwise be a sure loss, many people will gamble, even if the expected loss from the gamble is larger. Their basic idea can be illustrated by changing my hypothetical. Although you didn't know this when you were invited to this lecture, it is not free. At the end of the lecture, the doors are going to be locked. If you go out the north door, you'll be required to *pay* $20 as an exit fee. If you go out the south door, you'll participate in a lottery by drawing an envelope. Three quarters of the time you're going to be let out for free, but one quarter of the time you're going to be required to pay $100. Rest assured all the money is going to the Dean's fund — a very good cause. What do you choose? There's a great deal of empirical research, based on the initial work of Kahneman and Tversky, suggesting that the majority of this audience would choose the south exit — i.e., most of you would gamble to avoid having to lose $20 for sure. Kahneman and Tversky call this "loss aversion."

Now think of these two examples together. Risk aversion suggests that most of you would not gamble for a gain, even though the expected value of $25 exceeds the sure thing of $20. On the other hand, most of you would gamble to avoid a sure loss, even though, on the average, the loss of going out the south door is higher. Experimental evidence suggests that the proportion of people who will gamble to avoid a loss is much greater than those who would gamble to realize a gain.

Loss aversion can act as a cognitive barrier to the negotiated resolution of conflict for a variety of reasons. For example, both sides may fight on in a dispute in the hope that they may avoid any losses, even though the continuation of the dispute involves a gamble in which the loss may end up being far greater. Loss aversion may explain Lyndon Johnson's decision, in 1965, to commit additional troops to Vietnam as an attempt to avoid the sure loss attendant to withdrawal, and as a gamble that there might be some way in the future to avoid any loss at all. Similarly, negotiators may, in some circumstances, be adverse to offering a concession in circumstances where they view the concession as a sure loss. Indeed, the notion of rights or entitlements may be associated with a more extreme form of loss aversion that Kahneman and Tversky call "enhanced loss aversion," because losses "compounded by outrage are much less acceptable than losses that are caused by misfortune or by legitimate actions of others."

One of the most striking features of loss aversion is that whether something is viewed as a gain or loss — and what kind of gain or loss it is considered — depends upon a reference point, and the choice of a reference point is sometimes manipulable. Once again, a simple example suggested by Kahneman and Tversky, can illustrate.

Suppose you and a friend decide to go to Cleveland for a big night out on the town. You've made reservations at an elegant restaurant that will cost

$100 a couple. In addition, you've bought two superb seats — at $50 each — to hear the Cleveland orchestra. You set off for Cleveland, thinking you have your symphony tickets and $100, but no credit cards.

Imagine that you park your car in Cleveland and make a horrifying discovery — you've lost the tickets. Assume that you cannot be admitted to the symphony without tickets. Also imagine that someone is standing in front of the Symphony Hall offering to sell two tickets for $100. You have a choice. You can use the $100 you intended for the fancy dinner to buy the tickets to hear the concert, or you can skip the concert and simply go to dinner. What would you do?

Consider a second hypothetical. After you park your car, you look in your wallet and you realize to your horror that the $100 is gone, but the tickets are there. In front of the Symphony Hall is a person holding a small sign indicating she would like to buy two tickets for $100. What do you do? Do you sell the tickets and go to dinner? Or do you instead skip dinner and simply go to the concert?

Experimental research suggests that in the first example many more people will skip the symphony and simply go out to dinner, while in the second example, the proportions are nearly reversed; most people would skip dinner and go to the concert. The way we keep our mental accounts is such that, in the first instance, to buy the tickets a second time would somehow be to overspend our ticket budget. And, yet, an economist would point out that the two situations are essentially identical because there is a ready and efficient market in which you can convert tickets to money or money to tickets.

The purpose of the hypotheticals is to suggest that whether or not an event is framed as a loss can often affect behavior. This powerful idea concerning "framing" has important implications for the resolution of disputes. . . .

D. "Reactive Devaluation" of Compromises and Concessions.

The final barrier I wish to discuss is "reactive devaluation," and is an example of a social/psychological barrier that arises from the dynamics of the negotiation process and the inferences that negotiators draw from their interactions. My Stanford colleague, psychology Professor Lee Ross, and his students have done experimental work to suggest that, especially between adversaries, when one side offers a particular concession or proposes a particular exchange of compromises, the other side may diminish the attractiveness of that offer or proposed exchange simply because it originated with a perceived opponent. The basic notion is a familiar one, especially for lawyers. How often have you had a client indicate to you in the midst of litigation, "If only we could settle this case for $7,000. I'd love to put this whole matter behind me." Lo and behold, the next day, the other side's attorney calls and offers to settle for $7,000. You excitedly call your client and say, "Guess what — the other side has just offered to settle this case for

$7,000." You expect to hear jubilation on the other end of the phone, but instead there is silence. Finally, your client says, "Obviously they must know something we don't know. If $7,000 is a good settlement for them, it can't be a good settlement for us."

Both in laboratory and field settings, Ross and his colleagues have marshaled interesting evidence for "reactive devaluation." They have demonstrated both that a given compromise proposal is rated less positively when proposed by someone on the other side than when proposed by a neutral or an ally. They also demonstrated that a concession that is actually offered is rated lower than a concession that is withheld, and that a compromise is rated less highly after it has been put on the table by the other side than it was beforehand.

An example which should provide the flavor of this research is the work of Ross and his colleagues. One study took place in the context of a campus-wide controversy at Stanford over university investment policy concerning companies that did business with South Africa. Ross and his colleagues asked Stanford students to consider two compromise proposals. One proposal, termed the "specific divestment plan," entailed immediate Stanford divestment from corporations doing business with the South African military or police. The other, so-called "deadline plan," proposed to create a committee of students and trustees to monitor investment responsibility, with the promise of total divestment two years down the road if the committee was not satisfied with the rate of progress shown in dismantling the apartheid system in South Africa.

The experiment went as follows: one group of randomly assigned students was told that the University planned to undertake specific divestment, another group was told that the University planned to undertake the deadline plan, the remainder were given no specific reason to believe that the university was considering the immediate adoption of either alternative. The students were asked which plan they preferred. Students tended to denigrate whichever of the two compromise proposals the trustees had been said to offer, and to prefer the alternative proposal. When told that Stanford was allegedly ready to implement the deadline plan, 85% of the respondents ranked specific divestment as the preferred move. By contrast, when the university purportedly was going to pursue specific divestment, 60% rated that plan worse than the deadline plan.

Ross has described a range of cognitive and motivational processes that may account for the reactive devaluation phenomenon. Whatever its roots, reactive devaluation certainly can act as a barrier to the efficient resolution of conflict. It suggests that the exchange of proposed concessions and compromises between adversaries can be very problematic. When one side unilaterally offers a concession that it believes the other side should value and the other side reacts by devaluing the offer, this can obviously make resolution difficult. The recipient of a unilateral concession is apt to believe that her adversary has given up nothing of real value and may therefore resist any notion that she should offer something of real value in exchange. On the other hand, the failure to respond may simply confirm the suspicions of the original offeror, who will believe that her adversary is proceeding in bad faith and is being strategic.

* * *

Robert S. Adler, Benson Rosen & Elliot M. Silverstein,[*] *Emotions in Negotiation: How to Manage Fear and Anger*
14 NEGOT. J. 161, 167-77 (1998)[**]

* * *

Positive and Negative Aspects of Emotions in Negotiations

Among other things, the art of negotiation lies in discerning and working out differences between the parties. At times the differences may provoke substantial conflict, leading to emotional outbursts and heated discussions. Many people find exhilaration in the adrenaline "rush" that occurs during such moments, but an equal or greater number react to conflict by dreading and avoiding it. These varying reactions suggest that emotions function both in positive and negative ways. In fact, we believe that emotions play a variety of roles, some at times overwhelming and some often quite subtle.

The rich variety of functions precludes any easy generalization about emotions' role in negotiations. Those who would eliminate emotions in negotiation wrongly focus only on the negatives, missing the critical nature of emotion — after all, emotions are what give vitality to the values and goals that negotiators bring to the table. One need only ponder briefly to see the many positives of emotions in negotiations. If we do not care about what we seek, we become indifferent, and therefore ineffective, bargainers. Emotions give us our values and motivate us to pursue them. Moreover, the emotions that we display help us signal the other party about our intentions and give us critical feedback about the other side's mood and willingness to agree.

Because we realize that the other side may scrutinize us for signs of fear or excessive eagerness, we try to subdue the outward manifestation of these

[*] Robert S. Adler is Professor and Benson Rosen is Robert March and Mildred Borden Hanes Professor at Kenan-Flagler Business School, University of North Carolina at Chapel Hill. Elliot M. Silverstein was Director of Psychology at Dorothea Dix Hospital, Raleigh, North Carolina and Adjunct Professor at University of North Carolina School of Law when this article was published. Their article discusses how to deal with strong emotions during negotiations.

feelings so that we will not be taken advantage of. At times, we all admire the person who can maintain an impassive "poker face" in a negotiation, thwarting attempts to read his or her feelings about specific proposals. Similarly, those who can communicate confidence despite their inner quakes also inspire our admiration. On the other hand, the opposite approach can also be powerful. Extravagant displays of anger or irrational outbursts can sometimes be effective in breaking an impasse or intimidating an opponent. A "madman's advantage" can be produced by such displays, which can greatly increase a bargainer's power at critical moments in a negotiation.

Of course, not all emotions involved in a negotiation result in or carry positive feelings. Where one party believes that the other side cannot be trusted, tries to overreach, or unreasonably rejects a fair offer, he or she may experience frustration, anger, fear, or sadness. In these instances, emotions can get out of hand and thwart agreement. At the extreme, intense anger can result in violence, broken friendships, and festering anger. Intense fear can produce equally unacceptable outcomes; fearful negotiators leave themselves open to intimidation, exploitation, and capitulation.

Fear and Anger in Negotiations: Some Cautious Advice

Undoubtedly the two most intense emotions that confront negotiators are fear and anger. Anger can flash white-hot at a moment's notice and fear can reduce one to paralysis. Although other emotions arise during the course of a negotiation, our experience strongly suggests that the two that affect negotiations most often and most dramatically are fear and anger. Accordingly, we focus on them with the hope that addressing them can also provide insight into dealing with other emotions.

We caution those who would rely on our advice to remember Augustus Caesar's admonition to "hasten slowly." No general principle works effectively in all circumstances and with all people. In some situations, in fact, the best course of action may well be to do the opposite of what we counsel. Because of the complexity of life and human interaction, the only rule that works in all instances is "it depends." Accordingly, an ability to read the situation at the moment helps enormously. Nonetheless, based on years of practice and confirmed by a number of studies, we believe that, in most situations, what we recommend will help negotiators deal with highly emotional settings.

Anger in Negotiations

Two millennia ago, poet and satirist Horace wrote *Ira furor brevis est* — anger is a short madness. When we become truly furious, we may act in an utterly irrational way for a period of time. Although a temper tantrum may relieve pent-up feelings for a moment, we often find regret and negative recriminations following such displays. On this point, Queen Elizabeth I reportedly observed, "anger makes dull men witty, but it also keeps them poor."

Anger springs from many sources. On one hand, it may arise from the perception that someone has violated written or unwritten rules of behavior. In chimpanzee society, De Waal notes that members of a group exhibit what he terms *moralistic aggression*, that is, chimps perceived as stingy and unsharing are more likely to be attacked and refused favors than those that act in a more generous spirit. On a human level, someone who rudely breaks in line or who recklessly cuts us off in traffic will likely ignite fires of indignation if we are the victims of these transgressions.

Anger also arises when one encounters snubs, rudeness, or anything that provokes a feeling of being unfairly diminished — we get angry because we feel vulnerable and exposed. In similar fashion, shame may trigger anger. If our egos are bruised in a manner that makes us feel small, we react defensively, and often in anger. The evolutionary basis for anger seems clear: anger motivates us to retaliate when we are attacked and to defend ourselves against those whom we believe are doing us harm. As with other emotions, what one feels at any given moment is both physical and situational. Fear may prompt a chimpanzee to flee from a more powerful lion, but anger will drive it to lash out at a weaker chimp who snatches a piece of food that it was about to eat.

In the negotiation context, a host of factors can contribute to anger and aggression. Citing a variety of studies, Barry and Oliver suggest the following examples where these negative emotions can arise in dyadic negotiations: where bargainers are accountable to angry constituents; where bargainers face time pressures; where they perceive the situation as win-lose with divergent goals between the parties; or, generally, where the parties are otherwise unconcerned with protecting a working relationship. In a study of anger in mergers and acquisitions, Daly found the following types of behavior likely to trigger anger: misrepresentation; making excessive demands; overstepping one's authority; showing personal animosity; questioning a representative's authority to negotiate; seeking to undermine a representative's authority by "going over his head"; and dwelling on unimportant details.

There are occasions when anger, legitimately expressed, can play a positive role in producing an agreement — for example, when it helps persuade others because it demonstrates intensity and sincerity of a position. On the other hand, this emotion often injects a sour note into the proceeding, impeding agreement. Anger does so in at least three ways: it clouds our objectivity because we lose trust in the other side; it narrows our focus from broader topics to the anger-producing behavior; and it misdirects our goals from reaching agreement to retaliating against the offender.

Anger not only carries a high potential for disrupting negotiations, it also can present serious health risks. When we become angry, the stress hormones, adrenaline and cortisol, surge, raising heart rate and blood pressure, and triggering cells to issue heart-threatening fat and cholesterol into the bloodstream. A substantial number of large-scale longitudinal studies have shown a significantly increased risk for heart disease among those found to have high hostility levels.

As we indicated previously, negotiators can take steps to control the excesses of anger and to manage it to productive ends. What follows is a series of observations and recommendations for doing so.

Dealing With Your Anger

The critical need for self-awareness. Virtually all researchers and commentators on emotions and negotiations insist that the first step necessary in controlling anger is self-awareness. If we cannot sense when our anger has been aroused, we will miss an opportunity to control it. Anger typically has physical manifestations, such as a rapid heartbeat, muscle tensing, increased sweating, or flushed face.

In a quiet moment, one should reflect on the warning signs that indicate the onset of one's anger. We need to know how quickly we anger and how soon we get over it. If need be, one should consult with friends and family to see whether one exhibits any warning signs that a tantrum is imminent. The earlier that anger can be sensed, the more likely it is to be controlled. One also needs to determine how visibly one displays anger. Some people quickly lose their temper in extremely obvious ways. Others smolder but show few external signs that they are angry. Showing anger is not always bad, but the trick is to do so only when it serves a strategic purpose.

Determine situations that trigger inappropriate anger. In some cases, anger is an appropriate response to a provocative situation. At other times, we may instantly, and inappropriately, ignite in circumstances that most other bargainers would not find provocative. For example, some people react furiously to meetings that start a few minutes late. Others become livid at real or imagined slights to their dignity. Anger at these moments generally serves no useful purpose. Determining those things that trigger inappropriate anger may permit us to take steps to avoid them or to take preventive measures to control anger.

Decide whether to display anger. Recognizing how and why our anger arises does not mean that we should always avoid angry feelings or never display anger. But, if one can recognize the onset of anger, one can decide how best to deal with it. In some cases, we should reveal our feelings. For example, if a fellow negotiator has just falsely accused us of lying, we might want to demonstrate extreme displeasure in a way that persuades the other side that such charges are false and will not be tolerated. The trick is to do so in a manner that makes the point, but does not undermine the negotiation. This requires a careful assessment of the circumstances and of our opponent's reaction to our anger, and a measured approach to expressing our feelings.

Behavioral techniques to reduce anger. In some cases, one may feel anger but realize that it is inappropriate to the setting. For example, if our anger stems from outside circumstances or if displaying anger will undermine our goals in a negotiation, we should do our best to bring such feelings under control. Experts suggest a variety of behavioral techniques that can work, including:

- call a temporary halt to the negotiation to cool off;
- count backwards from 10 to 1;
- go to the restroom;
- get a drink of water or soda;
- tense and untense your leg muscles under the table;
- begin writing points that you wish to discuss later in the negotiation (this will help you stay organized and will give you some time to cool off);
- consciously try to take deep breaths in a silent manner;
- think about a scene from your past in which you were relaxed;
- imagine the source of your anger in a setting where he or she is getting his or her just deserts;
- exercise vigorously prior to and after a challenging negotiation.

Studies show that "cooling-off" periods, although one of the most commonly employed and successful methods of lessening angry moods, will not work if that time is spent re-living the anger-triggering moment and wallowing in the perceived outrage. What is needed, instead, is time spent focusing on other matters or reassessing the situation to realize the inappropriateness of an angry outburst. Studies also show that it is possible to use a so-called "freeze-frame" approach in which negotiators shift their attention from angry thoughts by recalling a pleasant experience to focus on calming their heartbeats until they feel a "calm, anchored sensation" in the chest. This technique moderates the heart and nervous system.

Express anger and disappointment effectively. In addition to the behavioral techniques for dealing with the physical and emotional aspects of anger, we need ways to communicate our displeasure and convey our concerns. Accusing an opponent of improper behavior rarely moves a negotiation forward and typically sets it back when he or she reacts in a predictably defensive manner. Instead, we need to be assertive without provoking or escalating deal-killing emotions in the other side. Among the approaches for doing so are the following:

- explain the behavior that upsets you in specific and objective terms;
- describe your feelings about what bothers you;
- try to get your opponent to view the matter from your perspective;

- do not accuse your opponent of misbehavior;

- show respect for your opponent:

- apologize for any misunderstanding that your own behavior might have caused if that will help move the discussion without making you appear weak.

Avoid "negotiator's bias." Most negotiators view themselves as fair and honest. Yet, we often fall into a perception trap in which we, without justification, view opponents whom we know nothing about as hostile. Why is this? Negotiation is a process that obviously involves conflict and competition, which call for intense "thrust-and-parry" skills. Accordingly, wary negotiators will approach bargaining with caution and trepidation. Although being on-guard makes perfect sense, research suggests that we have an unconscious tendency to carry a "negotiator's bias" into bargaining sessions; that is, we view our opponents as competitive while viewing ourselves as noncompetitive and cooperative. Moreover, when disagreements arise in negotiations, each party tends to view his or her behavior as relatively innocent while seeing the opponent as intentionally harmful, hostile, or aggressive. To say the least, the tendency to jump to such negative, and often unwarranted, conclusions explains why emotions can become instantly heated. Avoiding hasty judgments about our opponents' intentions requires realistic, clear thinking.

Try to promote trust. Trust is a key underpinning of successful negotiations. If negotiators cannot trust each other, then every issue requires verification and each agreement necessitates iron-clad guarantees. Anger, expressed inappropriately, can destroy trust. To promote good feelings and trust, various commentators recommend "positive-framing" approaches that promote the sense that our opponents have gained concessions from us rather than that we have handed them favorable terms that cost us little and about which we care little. In fact, research suggests that the most effective concessions that one can make are those that reduce or eliminate an opponent's losses; the least effective are those that somewhat improve gains already made by the other side.

Finally, to no one's surprise, humor, especially when directed at ourselves, helps create a particularly warm atmosphere for a negotiation. As Henry Ward Beecher wrote, "good humor makes all things tolerable." For most people, ill feelings and good humor cannot coexist.

Dealing With Your Opponent's Anger

Just as we need to develop a good instinct for determining when we become angry; we also need to be able to read our opponents' moods, particularly those involving frustration and anger. Here are some techniques that may be useful:

Defuse heated emotional buildups. Every good negotiator seeks to remain alert to the mood of a negotiation at all times. One should always seek to monitor opponents for anger. If one senses a rising temper on the other side, it may help to ask directly: "Mary, is something bothering you?" or "Tom, did my comment about the necessity of meeting deadlines disturb you? or "Regina, you look angry. Are you?"

Assess the significance of angry displays. When an opponent erupts in anger, one should assess as carefully as possible the significance of the anger. Does it seem calculated? Can the person regain composure? In some cases, the other side may try to convey anger as a strategic maneuver to dislodge us from a firmly-held position. Dealing with such an approach calls for a different response then dealing with a truly lost temper. Trying to placate someone who is using anger strategically to gain concessions may well lead us to make overly generous offers.

Address an opponent's anger. In some cases, you may need to say something like "Irv, I'm sure you're going to rethink the comments you've just made. I hope that you realize they were inappropriate. In the meantime, you've made me angry, so I need a break before we resume bargaining." It rarely hurts to acknowledge an opponent's anger even when one disagrees that it is justified. In some cases, an apology — even one felt to be undeserved — will help smooth the course of a negotiation. You should not apologize, however, in a way that leads an opponent to conclude that you have conceded a point that remains in dispute or that you are a weak negotiator. Thus, instead of offering a personal apology, you can — as easily and as effectively — simply apologize for the "bad situation."

Respond to anger in strategic ways. In some cases, the only appropriate response to a lost temper is to lose yours as well. Responding in kind, however, is usually not effective. Instead, think strategically. Temper losses often put the angry person at a disadvantage and the nimble negotiator can advance his or her position decisively. If you need a break to avoid losing your temper, take one. If not, you can wait silently for the angry person to become contrite and to make concessions. Sometimes a modest concession on your part immediately after an outburst by your opponent will elicit a much larger one from him or her.

Help an angry opponent save face. Perhaps the biggest deal breaker in negotiations is "face loss." Where parties feel they will lose face if they agree to an opponent's demands, they are likely to derail the negotiation even if it is not in their interest to do so. So critical is "face" to a negotiation that parties will hold to untenable positions that will cost them money or even provoke wars — Schoonmaker cites the example of two Latin American countries that fought a war because of angry feelings over a soccer match. Accordingly, one should always try to help an angry opponent save face especially if lost face is what triggered the outburst in the first place. A friendly, reassuring (but not patronizing) approach may work wonders in these situations.

Involve a mediator when you anticipate anger. If you believe that a strong potential for destructive anger exists in a particular negotiation, enlist the aid of a mediator or someone whose presence will act as a calming influence to the process.

Fear In Negotiation

Without doubt, fear is a pivotal emotion. At extreme levels, fear mobilizes all of the body's resources to escape physical harm; at lesser intensities, it leads us to worry about looming problems or pending concerns. Worry serves a vital function when it is contained properly — it leads us to plan ways to deal with our daily challenges. For example, worries about an exam will prompt us to study to ensure a satisfactory performance.

The neural pathways that trigger a fear reaction are well developed and strong. Recent studies that trace neural pathways of animals conditioned to fear brief electrical shocks have provided a large body of data about fear responses. The data strongly suggest heavy involvement of the amygdala in assessing danger and triggering fear responses. A critical insight derived from various studies is that trauma experienced at young ages — from one to three — may have particularly powerful and lasting effects because they are retained as emotional memories in the amygdala, but not as conscious declarative memories because the brain's hippocampus (where conscious memories are stored) may not have matured to the level where it can retain such memories. Thus, we may react with dread to stimuli that provoke emotional memories, but not be able to explain the source of the fears.

Fear in negotiations arises in a variety of circumstances. If we face an aggressive opponent, if we bargain without adequate preparation, if we sense that our opponent has superior bargaining power, if we feel insecure about our ability as a negotiator, we may experience moderate to extreme levels of fear. In extreme cases, we may simply fear the physical manifes- tations of fear itself — sweaty palms, shaky legs, queasy stomach, thump- ing heartbeat, trembling muscles, and even disrupted vision. This so-called "fear of fear" syndrome can be particularly debilitating because those who suffer it will seek to avoid stressful situations, even those in which they oth- erwise might have the power to produce favorable outcomes for themselves.

Dealing With Your Fear

Know your warning signs. As with anger, you should learn to sense when you begin to experience fear or anxiety. The body's reaction to fear is dif- ferent from that of anger. With anger, for example, blood flows to the hands, making it easier to strike an opponent. With fear, blood rushes to the large skeletal muscles, such as the legs, making it easier to flee. In metaphorical terms, our blood "boils" when we experience anger, but it "runs cold" when we are frightened.

Understand that fear is often a normal reaction. When you face a chal- lenging situation, scientific research suggests you will often experience a quickened heart rate, a rise in blood pressure, stomach turbulence, muscle tension and a heightened awareness. Although most of us welcome the heightened awareness, we find the other physical manifestations of fear to be quite unpleasant. Most successful people, especially athletes, learn to harness the symptoms of fear to improve their performances. Trying to ignore your feelings can be dangerous — you may suddenly freeze or "choke" if you are feeling tense due to fear. The key is to channel the feelings into effective responses and to minimize the disruptive effects of fear.

Determine how visibly you display fear. Displaying fear is rarely helpful in a negotiation. Accordingly, it is useful to get a sense of how you look when you are fearful. One of the quickest giveaways of fear is a cracking voice. An inability to make eye contact is another easily detected mannerism of fear. If your voice feels likely not to hold, make sure that you have a glass of water nearby. A quick gulp followed by clearing your voice usually puts things in order. Speaking slowly in the bottom ranges of your voice, from as low in your diaphragm as you can manage also helps.

Determine situations that trigger fear. Determine whether your fear relates to the situation in which you must act or to the person with whom you must interact. If you suspect that you will be fearful during a negotiation, redouble your preparations. For most of us, a planned-for contingency is rarely as frightening as an unplanned-for emergency.

Behavioral techniques to reduce feelings of fear. Most of the behavioral techniques that dispel anger also work in reducing fear. For example, calling a temporary halt to the negotiation to regain your composure or going to the restroom are as effective in dealing with fear as they are in reducing anger. Two slightly different approaches from those recommended for anger control are to:

- think about a scene from your past in which you were confident and in control; and

- imagine the source of your fear in a setting where you control them or where they look ridiculous and weak.

Careful preparation reduces fear. Preparation for a negotiation involves researching the problem and developing a strategy. Few things dispel fear more effectively than careful preparation. Sometimes a rehearsal of the negotiation helps build confidence. Researching your opponent may also help. Negotiators who have prepared carefully and who know their "bottom line" or their "walk away" points are much less likely to be cowed or tricked in a negotiation. To the extent that you know your goals and strategy and stick to them, you will probably be able to control your fears. In all instances, keep your goals clearly in mind.

Act confident even if you do not feel so. Although there are probably occasions where showing anger makes sense in a negotiation, it is difficult to imagine instances in which showing fear strengthens one's hand. Accordingly, to the extent possible, try to project an appearance of confidence. In fact, researchers suggest that it is possible to increase feelings of confidence by focusing our thoughts on our strengths, and by substituting positive self-statements for fearful thoughts. Because perceptions play such a large role in negotiation, one should work hard at developing a confident demeanor and by backing it up with a positive attitude in approaching a negotiation.

Avoid quick agreements motivated by fear. If you are on the verge of agreeing to a deal that makes you feel uncomfortable, indicate that you need to consult with a superior or that you feel a need to think over the matter.

Try to reduce your stress level. If you are someone who feels anxiety more than you would like to or who constantly loses control when you are fearful or anxious, stress experts indicate that there are steps you can take to reduce anxiety. You should consider the following steps:

- short-term cognitive behavior therapy that teaches you to recognize and reduce inappropriate anxiety;

- relaxation therapy that teaches you simple steps to follow for avoiding anxiety;

- talk about feelings of anxiety with friends and family (if they will listen with sympathy);

- try to develop coping strategies by noting which personal techniques help reduce your anxiety;

- exercise on a regular basis;

- exercise vigorously before or after stressful situations; and

- discuss anti-anxiety drugs with your physician.

Dealing With Your Opponent's Fear

Monitor all negotiations for emotional buildups. Every good negotiator seeks to remain alert to the mood of a negotiation at all times. You should always seek to monitor your opponent for fear.

Show flexibility in how you react to your opponent's fear. In some cases, your opponent's fear can open the way for a settlement that is strongly in your favor. In others, fear may hinder agreement if your opponent becomes immobilized, loses the ability to bargain thoughtfully, or explodes in anger. Also, if you plan to enter into a long-term relationship with your opponent, you may wish to go out of your way to dispel his or her fears.

Where helpful, share your fears and anxieties with your opponent. Empathizing with your opponent by describing your own fears in similar situations may help dispel your opponent's fears. Of course, one should avoid providing an opponent with ammunition to be used against him or her at a future time. Sometimes, however, sharing vulnerabilities promotes trust in ways that no other approach can do.

Help your fearful opponent save face. Again, where parties feel they will lose face if they agree to an opponent's demands, they are likely to derail the negotiation even if it is not in their interest to do so.

* * *

Richard Birke & Craig R. Fox,[*] *Psychological Principles in Negotiating Civil Settlements*
4 HARV. NEGOT. L. REV. 1 (1999)[**]

Fewer than five percent of all civil cases filed will result in a verdict; most of the rest will be resolved by negotiation between attorneys. Even in the fraction of cases that go to trial, lawyers negotiate such important matters as discovery schedules, dates for depositions, court appearances, and stipulations that limit the number and complexity on contested issues.

Although lawyers, like most other professionals, typically believe that consistent, reasoned, objective, and rational decisionmaking characterizes their negotiations, an abundance of evidence suggests that this belief is misplaced. Research in the past few decades has documented pervasive psychological biases in the judgment and decisionmaking of a wide array of professionals and laypersons. For example, people tend to seek information that confirms their prior beliefs, and also tend to ignore or derogate information that refutes those beliefs. In the practice of law, such biases can act as barriers to mutually beneficial settlements.

* * *

When judging the value of a case, lawyers naturally look for information concerning the past resolution of similar disputes. The greater the number of comparable cases, the more precisely the outcome of the present case can be estimated. Routine tort cases are reported in many jurisdictions, and it is a relatively simple research matter to determine the expected jury award in a given location for, say, a "slip and fall" at a commercial establishment, assuming there are no unusual circumstances. An insurance dispute over the lost value of a home damaged by fire is similarly easy to determine, because comparable homes can be appraised or the costs of rebuilding can be assessed.

---

[*] Richard Birke is Associate Professor, Willamette University College of Law. Craig R. Fox is Associate Professor, UCLA Anderson School of Management. Their article reviews numerous studies in the psychology literature relevant to legal negotiations.

Of course, there are sometimes unique circumstances that make a given dispute much more difficult to value. For example, if the person who slipped and fell was a member of the Olympic skating team, or if the destroyed home was a rare example of a celebrated architect's work, the values would be much more difficult to estimate with precision. We believe that such unusual cases are, by definition, relatively rare.

Memorable cases will naturally spring to the lawyer's mind when she is considering the value of a case in the same topical area. Likewise, if the case at hand is superficially similar to a high-profile case, the lawyer may use the latter as a basis for judging the former. Trouble arises when these salient, related cases distort the lawyer's appraisal of the case at bar.

1. Psychology Relating to Preliminary Valuation: The Availability and Anchoring Heuristics

Consider the following question: are there more male or female lawyers in America? To answer this question with complete accuracy would require demographic professional data. However, people render judgments on such matters all the time based on their own experience and intuition. In this case, for example, most people consult their memory and conclude that because it is easier to recall examples of male lawyers than female lawyers, the former are probably more common than the latter. They are using a mental short cut or *heuristic* to solve the problem. In this case, people automatically assume that when it is easier to recall examples of something, it tends to be more common. In the example of male and female attorneys, such reasoning provides the correct answer.

Now consider a different question: are there more murders or suicides each year in America? If you answered "murders," you might be surprised to learn that, in fact, suicides are much more common. In this second instance, the "availability heuristic" fails because one's memories do not reflect a representative sampling of what exists in the world. Memories are often biased by vivid, extreme events that tend to receive extensive media coverage. Movies, television dramas, and news reports tend to make murder seem much more common than suicide.

There are many instances of such distortions. For example, people typically think that there is a higher percentage of African-American citizens in Los Angeles than African-American officers on the L.A. police force, that a higher proportion of top Hollywood actors than U.S. Congressmen are homosexual, and that it rains more in Seattle than it does in Northern Georgia. None of these apparent "facts" is true, but because it is easier to conjure images of African-American Los Angelinos than it is to conjure images of African-American L.A. police officers, openly gay actors than openly gay politicians, and rainy scenes of Seattle than rainy scenes of Georgia, most people automatically deem the former more common than the latter.

Media reporting facilitates availability distortions of legal matters as well. When people think of a tort case in contemporary society, they are likely to think of McDonald's coffee or Dow Corning breast implants. When thinking of a murder trial, O. J. Simpson may come to mind first. When thinking of sexual harassment suits, the case involving Paula Jones and President Clinton comes to mind, and then perhaps the cases involving Anita Hill and Clarence Thomas, Baker & McKenzie, Mitsubishi, and former Senator Packwood. Although people may be aware that these cases are atypical, their sensational portrayal by the media renders them readily available to memory. In fact, these cases are newsworthy precisely because they are not typical. However, when making predictions, people often fail to compensate for the gap between what is memorable and what is typical. If a lawyer knows that the upper end of jury awards in sexual harassment claims is 7.2 million dollars, she may realize that her case is worth less, but the fact that it is so easy to recall such notable cases as Baker & McKenzie makes an extreme award seem possible.

This bias may be reinforced by a second psychological phenomenon: the tendency to anchor on a salient number and make insufficient adjustments in response to individuating details of the case at hand. For example, if a recent court award for a similar case comes to mind, people may be unduly influenced by this value in their assessment of the present case. Research shows that even when a focal number is not particularly relevant, it can exert a bias on judgment under uncertainty. For example, in one study, participants were asked to judge the percentage of African countries that were members of the United Nations. Before participants gave their answer, the experimenter spun a wheel to determine a threshold percentage. Despite the fact that the focal number was absolutely irrelevant to the issue, the number had a dramatic influence on respondents' estimates. When the wheel landed on the number ten, the median estimate of African countries in the United Nations was twenty-five percent; however, when the wheel landed on the number sixty-five, the median estimate was forty-five percent.

People are especially susceptible to anchoring bias when they have little relevant experience or knowledge. However, expertise alone fails to provide protection from this tendency. In one study, several experienced real estate brokers were asked to provide information they used to appraise a piece of residential real estate and to estimate how accurately agents could appraise its value when given that information. The brokers responded that the information should support an agent's estimate within five percent of the true value. Other groups of agents were given packets of information on a home that included a bogus listing price that was eleven percent above the true listing price or eleven percent below the true listing price. These two groups were asked to estimate the appraised value of the home. Although the agents explicitly denied that listing price affected their appraisals significantly, the manipulation of the bogus listing price led to a substantial difference in these values between the groups.

* * *

Throughout the course of representation, civil litigators devote most of their billable hours to gathering information. During the early stages, most of this information gathering is aimed at assessing the strength of their clients' cases. Such information generally includes client interviews, review of documents, depositions, and investigation of additional sources found through the discovery process. It is imperative for those in the business of lawyering to assess a great deal of information of uncertain probative value in order to anticipate what a client might be entitled to if she went to court. These assessments help the lawyer determine what a good settlement goal might be.

In most arenas there is not an objective means for weighing evidence. Reasonable lawyers disagree about the predicted effect that certain testimonial or physical evidence might have on a jury. Even if opposing attorneys agreed that evidence was favorable to one side, they might disagree about the extent to which it supports that side.

In addition, weight must be assigned to the presentation of evidence. A skillful presenter can highlight nuances and combine strands of evidence in ways that make a finder of fact more likely to reach a favorable conclusion than would be the case were the evidence presented in a random order or in a drab manner. And, of course, a judge may exclude evidence or alter its presentation.

Whenever the attorney evaluates any facet of a case, she does so through the lens of her own biased perspective, which may distort her assessment of the case as a whole. Indeed, this bias way result in a grossly self-interested view that precludes a settlement that might occur if both sides were more objective.

A lawyer is likely to be biased in two related ways. First, despite the fact that she has not yet heard from the other side, she is likely to evaluate the strength of the case as more favorable to her client than would a neutral party with access to both sides' information and arguments. Second, she is likely to be overconfident in her assessment of her likelihood of prevailing and likewise overestimate her ability to influence the final outcome.

1. Psychological Biases

a. Perspective Biases

In general, people have great difficulty divorcing themselves from their idiosyncratic role sufficiently to take an objective view of disputes in which they are involved. In one study, researchers provided four groups of respondents with summary information pertaining to legal disputes. In the partisan conditions, respondents were given background information and either the plaintiffs or the defendant's arguments, but not both. In the neutral conditions, respondents were given either background information only or background information and both the plaintiffs and defendant's arguments. Participants in all conditions were asked to predict how many of twenty jurors would find for the plaintiff. Participants in the plaintiff condition predicted that a significantly higher proportion of jurors would find for the plaintiff than did participants in the defendant condition, despite the fact that both sides were aware that they were not provided with the other side's arguments. Participants in the neutral conditions (background only, or background and both sides' arguments) had a more balanced view than did participants in either of the partisan conditions.

* * *

Overconfidence stems, in part, from pervasive biases in the ways people pursue and evaluate evidence. Psychological studies have shown that people are more likely to seek information that confirms rather than discredits their hypotheses, and they tend to assimilate data in ways that are consistent with their prior views. In discovery, for example, attorneys are more likely to seek information that supports their viewpoint than they are to seek information that supports their opponents' cases. They work on "their side" of a case, and tend to construe the information that they find in a way that confirms their pre-existing beliefs about their odds of prevailing.

A second positive illusion is people's tendency to overestimate their ability to control outcomes that are determined by factors outside of their control. In one classic study by psychologist Ellen Langer, subjects bet more on a game of pure chance when they competed against a shy, awkward, poorly dressed individual than when they competed against a confident, outgoing, well-dressed person. In a second study, subjects were offered one-dollar tickets to an office lottery. Each ticket consisted of two pictures of a famous football player, one of which was put into the box from which the winning ticket would be drawn. When participants were asked later at what price they would be willing to sell their ticket, those who had chosen the ticket for themselves demanded $6.87 on average, whereas those who had been assigned a ticket at random demanded only $1.96 on average.

* * *

A third variety of positive illusion is the tendency to hold overly positive views of one's own attributes and motives. For example, most people think that they are more intelligent and fair minded than average. Ninety-four percent of university professors believe that they do a better job than their colleagues. More to the point, most negotiators believe themselves to be more flexible, more purposeful, more fair, more competent, more honest, and more cooperative than their counterparts.

In a negotiation, this self-enhancing bias may lead an attorney to believe that she should hold out for a favorable settlement, because she is a more skilled attorney. Although skill among attorneys varies and it is rational to take skill into account when evaluating the worth of a case, lawyers at all skill levels are very likely to overestimate their abilities relative to those of their peers. This self-confidence may prove to be an effective bargaining tool to the extent that it sends a signal to her counterpart that the attorney is committed to seeing the case through to trial if necessary. However, if both sides overestimate their chances of prevailing in court, this bias will lead to excessive and costly discovery and litigation.

* * *

2. Remediation

What can be done to circumvent these biases? Research suggests that egocentric biases may be very difficult to eliminate. It may be useful to actively anticipate arguments in favor of the opponent's case, but at least one study suggests that this tactic is not sufficient — perhaps because advocates easily generate counter arguments. However, this same study showed that egocentric bias was significantly mitigated when participants were asked to explicitly list weaknesses in their own case. Hence, to achieve a more balanced view of one's prospects, it is essential to make a concerted and sincere effort to play devil's advocate. . . .

* * *

1. Psychology of Biased Assimilation

As mentioned earlier, people generally seek evidence that would confirm initial hypotheses, to a greater extent than they seek "disconfirming" evidence. In addition, we previously reviewed evidence that attorneys tend to predict trial outcomes in an egocentric manner. It is also true that partisans tend to evaluate and assimilate information they receive in a way that is biased in favor of their own position. In one influential experiment, Lord, Ross and Lepper presented proponents and opponents of capital punishment with details of two studies, one supporting its effectiveness as a deterrent and a second providing evidence against its effectiveness as a deterrent. Participants on average rated the study that supported their view to be logically superior to the study that contradicted their view. Furthermore, after reading both studies, participants felt more strongly about their previously held views. Hence, mixed evidence widened the gap between groups, polarizing rather than reconciling beliefs.

Fox and Babcock found a similar effect in a study that simulated a civil lawsuit over a real-estate transaction. Participants were assigned at random to opposing roles in the dispute, which was modeled after a real case. After reading identical background information, both sides displayed an egocentric bias, tending to predict that a neutral judge would decide in their favor. Participants in both groups next read identical packets containing discovery information, including letters exchanged between the principals, relevant documents, and deposition excerpts. After reading this packet, both sides became more biased in favor of their own position. The larger the disparity between the predictions for an opposing pair, the longer (and more expensive) the simulated litigation between the pair tended to be. More information caused partisans to become more entrenched, disparities between valuations to grow, and costs of disputing to rise.

* * *

Despite the fact that much of law school classroom discussion focuses on notions of justice and equity, there is no consensus in the legal community about what fairness means or how it should be determined. In practice, some of the most arduous legal battles involve competing norms of fairness. Is equal distribution of rewards fair in a situation in which business partners did an unequal share of the work? What if one partner contributed more physical capital and the other contributed more intellectual capital?

In some practice areas, and in some jurisdictions, precedents exist that favor a particular norm of fairness over others. However, in the privately ordered world of settlement negotiations and contract interpretation, the norms are no better defined than in the world at large, and lawyers are not trained to be better judges of fairness than are architects, dentists, musicians, or chefs.

1. Psychology of Fairness

a. Self-Interested Choice of Norms

The most common norms of distribution that are invoked in negotiation include equality, egalitarianism, equity, need, and past practice or precedent. The aforementioned egocentric bias phenomenon suggests that people tend to define what is fair in a self-interested manner. For example, people in positions of high power tend to favor distributions based on equity norms, whereas those in positions of lower power favor equality norms. In one study, researchers instructed pairs of people to complete a work task in which they received feedback on their performance. When participants outperformed strangers, they were more likely to divide compensation according to an equity norm, giving more to themselves; however, when the stranger outperformed them, participants tended to favor an equality norm, splitting the money evenly.

b. Relative Versus Absolute Payoffs

The rational model traditionally assumes that people act as if they are striving to maximize their own outcomes, without regard to the outcomes of others. In reality, negotiators are sensitive not only to their own payoff, but also to the relative payoff to their counterparts. In one study, participants' satisfaction with a negotiated outcome was affected more strongly by their counterparts' relative payoffs than by their own absolute payoffs. For instance, subjects on average reported more satisfaction with an outcome that imposed a loss of $600 to themselves but a loss of $900 to their counterparts, compared to an outcome that offered a gain of $600 to themselves but a gain of $900 to their counterparts.

Empirical studies suggest that people are neither as selfish nor as forgiving as classical economic theory predicts. In one study, researchers asked subjects to play a so-called "dictator" game in which they could split twenty dollars with an anonymous other person in one of two ways: either keep ten dollars and give ten dollars, or keep eighteen dollars and give two dollars. Contrary to the strategy suggested by a purely rational model, seventy-six percent of subjects chose to split the money evenly. Moreover, a second group of subjects were willing to forgo gains in order to punish greedy players: seventy-four percent preferred to receive five dollars and give five dollars to a person who had split the original twenty dollars evenly rather than receive six dollars and give six dollars to a person who had taken eighteen of the original twenty dollars. Another notable study involved an "ultimatum game" in which a first player made an offer to divide $100, and a second player decided whether to accept or reject that distribution. If the second player accepted, the money was divided according to the first player's suggested split; if the second player rejected, neither player received any money. Contrary to the rational model, first players demanded, on average, less than seventy percent of the prize, and as many as twenty percent of second players rejected positive offers that allocated most of the prize to their counterparts. Again, participants in ultimatum games are often willing to hurt themselves in order to punish others who they believe have behaved unfairly. . . .

* * *

The foregoing studies suggest that most people are more sensitive to how fairly they have been treated than to how they have fared in objective terms, that reasonable people differ on what they see as fair in a given situation, and that people tend to evaluate fairness in a self-interested manner. Moreover, people are often willing to harm themselves in order to punish those who they perceive to be acting unfairly. Hence, in negotiation, it is critical to consider fairness carefully and avoid if at all possible the *perception* that one is acting unfairly. In fact, it may be easier to get one's counterpart to agree to appropriate standards for determining what is fair than it is to get her to agree on specific terms of a settlement.

* * *

* * * In general, it is important that one's counterpart is not made to feel they are "losing" relative to what you are receiving, what others are receiving, or what they have received in the past.

Question 7: Should I make the first offer, and if so, what should it be?

* * *

1. Psychological Considerations

There is little empirical research on the question of whether it is best to make the first offer. Two psychological phenomena may be relevant. In situations where one's counterpart has only a vague sense of what is reasonable (e.g., because there is little or no judicial precedent), making the first offer may afford an opportunity to exploit the aforementioned anchoring bias, and draw the counterpart into an order of magnitude that is more favorable to the offeror before the counterpart makes an offer that anchors both parties in a range that favors him. On the other hand, a pervasive norm that governs negotiation behavior is that of reciprocity, according to which one should reciprocate concessions made by others. In fact, distributive negotiations typically settle roughly midway between the opening offers to the extent that this midpoint is feasible for both sides. Hence, making the second offer can afford the negotiator an opportunity to define where that midpoint lies. In general, whether one makes the first offer in order to exploit anchoring, or makes the second offer in order to leave room for concessions and exploit reciprocity, it is good strategy to make as extreme an opening offer as can be gotten away with, but not so extreme that the offeror appears to be negotiating in bad faith.

* * *

Traditional economic analysis suggests that people should be sensitive to the impact of offers on final states of wealth, and that the particulars of how those offers are communicated should not matter. Empirical studies of attorneys suggest that describing an offer in terms of gains versus losses can affect a lawyer's willingness to accept the offer. Certainly, lawyers choose words carefully, and this tendency extends to the crafting and communication of offers. However, for the most part, attorneys use this skill to avoid admitting or denying liability, or to avoid the accidental creation of exploitable weaknesses in their cases. Less thought goes into the question of how to frame an offer so that it is most likely to be accepted.

1. The Psychology of Value and Framing

Behavioral decision theorists have documented systematic violations of the standard economic assumption that people evaluate options in terms of their impact on one's final state of wealth. In particular, *prospect theory* assumes that people adapt to their present state of wealth and are sensitive to changes with respect to that endowment.

Second, people exhibit diminishing sensitivity to increasing gains and losses. For example, increasing an award from zero to $1000 is more pleasurable than increasing an award from $1000 to $2000; increasing an award from $2000 to $3000 is even less pleasurable, and so forth. Similarly, increasing a payment from zero to $1000 is more painful than increasing a payment from $1000 to $2000, and so on. One key implication of this pattern is that people's willingness to take risks differs for losses versus gains. For example, because $1000 is more than half as attractive as $2000, people typically prefer to receive $1,000 for sure than face a fifty-fifty chance of receiving $2,000 or nothing (i.e., they are "risk-averse" for medium probability gains). In contrast, because losing $1000 is more than half as painful as losing $2000, people typically prefer to risk a 50-50 chance of losing $2,000 or losing nothing to losing $1,000 for sure (i.e., they are "risk-seeking" for medium probability losses).

Third, prospect theory asserts that losses have more impact on choices than do equivalent gains. For example, most people do not think that a fifty percent chance of gaining $100 is sufficient to compensate a fifty percent chance of losing $100. In fact, people typically require a 50% chance of gaining as much as $200 or $300 to offset a 50% chance of losing $100.

Taken together, the way in which a problem is framed in terms of losses or gains can have a substantial impact on behavior in negotiations. First, loss aversion contributes to a bias in favor of the status quo because relative disadvantages of alternative outcomes loom larger than relative advantages. Hence, negotiators are often reluctant to make the tradeoffs necessary for them to achieve joint gains. To illustrate, consider the case of two partners in a failing consulting firm. The joint office space and secretarial support costs are unduly burdensome, and each could operate productively out of their homes with minimal overhead costs. If they could divide their territory and agree not to compete, each could have a profitable career — but each would have to agree to give up half the firm's client base. Each partner may view the territory they retain as a gain that doesn't compensate adequately for the territory they must relinquish. Yet failure to make such a split consigns them to continuation in a losing venture.

Second, both loss aversion and the pattern of risk seeking for losses may lead to more aggressive bargaining when the task is viewed as minimizing losses rather than maximizing gains. Indeed, in laboratory studies, negotiators whose payoffs are framed in terms of gains (e.g., they were instructed to maximize revenues) tended to be more risk-averse than those whose payoffs are framed in terms of losses (e.g., they were instructed to minimize costs): the first group tended to be more concessionary but completed more transactions. Recently, Professor Rachlinski documented greater willingness to accept settlement offers in legal contexts when the offer is perceived as a gain compared to when it is perceived as a loss.

Third, the attractiveness of potential agreements may be influenced by the way in which gains and losses are packaged and described. In particular, if a negotiator wants to present a proposal in its best possible light to a counterpart, he or she should attempt to integrate each aspect of the agreement on which the counterpart stands to lose (in order to exploit the fact that people experience diminishing sensitivity to each additional loss) and segregate each aspect of the agreement on which the counterpart stands to gain (in order to avoid the tendency of people to experience diminishing sensitivity to each additional gain). For instance, in the partnership dissolution example, it would be most effective to describe the territory forgone as a single unit (e.g., "everything west of highway 6 is mine") and the territory obtained in component parts (e.g., "and you will have the Heights neighborhood, the eastern section of downtown, everything north of there to the river, South Village, etc."), and least effective to describe the territory foregone in component parts (e.g., "I keep the west side of downtown, the riverfront, North village, and everything between downtown and Ballard Square. . .") and the territory obtained as a single unit (e.g., "everything east of highway 6 is yours").

* * *

Negotiation is, in part, a game of mutual influence. Many attorneys are naturally gifted in the art of social influence while others are less comfortable with this dimension of lawyering. We believe that the study of social influence tactics can help attorneys protect themselves against exploitation.

1. Psychology of Social Influence

A vast literature in social psychology examines how individuals persuade others to accede to their requests. Psychologist Robert Cialdini organizes the literature into six pervasive principles of social influence that we describe below. Cialdini observed these tactics in his study of salespeople, fund-raisers, advertisers, and other professionals. We believe that these principles apply with equal force to negotiations of civil settlements by attorneys.

a. Reciprocation

One should repay, in kind, what another person has provided. Even uninvited favors and gifts leave people with a sense of indebtedness that they feel they must reciprocate. In negotiation, there is a strong norm that a party should respond to each concession that his or her counterpart makes with a concession of his or her own, even if the initial offer was rather extreme.

The tendency to reciprocate is not in itself problematic, but when one side reciprocates relatively trivial concessions with meaningful concessions, such as a significant reduction in what was already a reasonable request, she may be committing a negotiation error. A skillful negotiator knows that people tend to reciprocate acts of kindness, even when the original kindness is uninvited and of no value to the recipient. Lawyers bargain over both substantive and logistical matters, such as discovery schedules, stipulations, deposition schedules, compliance with orders, and the possible settlement of the action. They rarely get everything they want, and the result of these interactions generally involves some degree of compromise from both sides. Occasionally, a logistical concession from one attorney may elicit a substantive concession from opposing counsel.

Two suggestions are in order. First, . . . the lawyer should make an optimistic first offer in order to leave room for concessions that will be expected by the other side (in response to concessions that they will make). Second, it is important to resist the temptation to reciprocate meaningless or negligible concessions.

b. Commitment and Consistency

Once a person makes a choice or takes a stand, she encounters personal and interpersonal pressure to behave consistently with that commitment. There are at least three manifestations of this principle in negotiation. First, a public commitment to a statement of principles, an aspiration, or a criterion of fairness is difficult to abnegate at a later time. Second, after a negotiator gets her "foot in the door" by having her counterpart accede to a small initial request, later cooperation becomes more likely. Third, after investing significant time and energy into crafting a tentative agreement, negotiators are more likely to give in to last-minute requests by their counterparts.

* * *

It is quite common for negotiators to force end-game concessions. For instance, when a real estate deal is near consummation, it is common for sellers and mortgage companies to reveal myriad small costs that were not discussed earlier. Lawyers may try at the last moment to tack on attorney's fees and court costs to a settlement. Provided that these costs are small relative to settlement amounts, the recipient of such a request may feel that it is better to concede rather than to scuttle the whole deal and "go back to square one." Again, one useful means to defend against such exploitation is to decide in advance on a reservation price and to resist temptations to back off of this value unless additional information justifies doing so.

* * *

c. Social Proof

People view a behavior as correct in a given situation to the degree that they see others performing it. The reactions of others thus serves as "proof" that the behavior is appropriate. For example, canned laughter has been shown to elicit more laughter in audiences and cause them to rate material as funnier than they do in its absence. In general, people are more likely to follow the behavior of others when the situation is unclear or ambiguous or when people are unsure of themselves. Moreover, people are more likely to follow the example of others whom they perceive to be similar to themselves. Senior lawyers in large firms inculcate junior associates into practice, in part, by modeling a great many behavioral characteristics that are not necessarily effective, but which are nonetheless deeply ingrained. When and where to meet for negotiations, how to dress for work, and how to interview clients are all matters that are typically transmitted uncritically from one generation of firm lawyers to the next.

In settlement negotiations, lawyers can exploit past precedents and examples of other litigants who have accepted similar terms in attempts to gain compliance. In order to defend against such tactics, we encourage lawyers to seek out for themselves information concerning comparable cases and values in order to effectively evaluate the case at bar.

* * *

d. Liking

People prefer to say yes to others they know and like. Several factors promote liking: physical attractiveness, similarity, compliments, cooperation, and familiarity. Contrary to the popular belief that a successful negotiator ruthlessly intimidates and exploits her counterparts, a positive relationship can be more effective for achieving mutually beneficial and equitable outcomes. Moreover, leading economists have argued that cooperation and honesty tend to promote long-term success in bargaining. And studies of lawyers negotiating prove that those who are cooperative (a trait that engenders liking) are rated as more effective, on average, than lawyers who are not.

* * *

e. Authority

People are more likely to accede to the request of a perceived authority figure. The best known illustration of this principle is Milgram's work, which demonstrated the willingness of ordinary people to administer what they thought were dangerous levels of electrical shocks to a person with an alleged heart condition merely because an "experimenter" in a white laboratory coat insisted that "the experiment requires that [they] continue." Equally sobering is the demonstration by Hofling and his colleagues in which a researcher identified himself over the phone as a hospital physician and asked hospital nurses to administer a dangerous dose of an unauthorized drug to a specific patient; in this case 95 percent of the nurses attempted to comply. Not only do titles tend to promote compliance and deference, but so do uniforms and other trappings, such as fancy automobiles. Certainly, most trial attorneys will agree that the judge's physically elevated status and somber, traditional robe reinforce a courtroom hierarchy in which the judge enjoys the greatest status. Even a retired judge or a sufficiently senior partner may lend an air of authority to a position or an offer, as might a "home turf" advantage.

* * *

f. Scarcity

Opportunities often seem more valuable when they are less available. According to psychological reactance theory, when people are proscribed from making a certain choice, they desire that choice more and work harder to obtain it. This is the principle underlying the success of the ubiquitous "limited time offer" in consumer advertising. Threats to freedom can take the form of time limits, supply limits, and competition. In negotiation, these tactics can be a particularly effective means of gaining compliance. Savvy negotiators can dramatize their alternatives by entertaining competing bids, or they can strategically impose artificial time limits for negotiation.

* * *

Chapter 6

CULTURE AND GENDER IN NEGOTIATION

Teaching about the impact of culture and gender on negotiation is one of the most challenging aspects of a negotiation class. We are each immersed in our own version of both culture and gender, and what psychologist Lee Ross has called "naïve realism" — each individual's belief that he or she sees the world as it really is — makes it difficult to get much useful perspective on these subjects. The cultural emphasis in the United States on political correctness often makes it difficult to discuss if, how, and why men and women differ in their attitudes toward negotiation or in their performance as negotiators. Similarly, efforts to illuminate cultural differences all too readily result in superficial stereotypes of little use to a thoughtful negotiator in an increasingly global business/legal environment.

The aim of this chapter is not to provide answers about how (or if) culture and gender impact negotiation style and performance, but to raise questions and present different points of view on these topics, with the hope that the articles will stimulate discussion and an interest in becoming better acquainted with, and examining, your own personal theories on these subjects.

A. CULTURE

The chapter starts with culture, because culture is the water in which we swim, including when we negotiate. According to Avruch in Chapter One, "culture refers to the socially transmitted values, beliefs and symbols that are more or less shared by members of a social group." As Americans and as lawyers or lawyers to be, you partake of both national and professional cultures that affect how you understand and perform the task of resolving disputes through negotiation. Indeed, the approach to negotiation taught in this book, and in most law school negotiation courses around the country today, is an outgrowth of — and, to some extent, a reaction against — an American legal culture shaped by the case law method of teaching and an adversary system of dispute resolution by third-party adjudication.

1. Culture is Always Plural

It is important to consider the cultural underpinnings of American legal negotiation styles and theory as diversity among lawyers and globalization of markets increase. These changes make it more likely than ever that you will find yourself negotiating with people whose basic assumptions about conflict and appropriate methods of conflict resolution are quite different from your own. At the same time, reducing these differences to a single dimension, for example by describing "Japanese" or "Latin American" negotiating styles, sacrifices the true complexity of the matter. Nationality is only one aspect of a person's cultural identification: as Avruch points out in his article below on culture and teaching negotiation, "for a given individual, culture always comes in the plural." Your culture is *simultaneously* national, ethnic, religious, familial, professional, etc — and which of these predominates depends largely on the context in which you find yourself. At the same time, the interweaving of your cultures is not always harmonious: many law students struggle, for example, with discrepancies between what they see as the demands of legal professional culture and the cultural expectations and behaviors that they bring to the law school experience.

2. Cultural Assumptions in Negotiation

The individualistic assumptions that permeate negotiations in a European American context are hardly universal. As Markus and Lin discuss in their article below, other cultures do not view conflict as a confrontation between independent agents who assert themselves and their rights and who press to win out over others. Many Asian cultures, for example, put far more emphasis on relational aspects of dealing with conflict and on the importance of restoring group harmony. In Markus and Lin's view, even integrative approaches to bargaining — often considered to be an antidote to the forcing, self-centered quality of adversarial distributive negotiation — reflect the individualistic assumptions of European American culture and its emphasis on rationality, direct expression of personal wishes and needs, and abstract principles.

How, then, can you develop an understanding of others' cultural perspectives and conduct negotiations with them in a way that is sensitive to what matters to them, a way that is *not* the equivalent of speaking English louder and louder in order to make them understand? Docherty's discussion suggests that to get beyond the common heuristics for learning about culture — culture as iceberg or cultural patterns — you need to engage in "symmetrical anthropology," seeking to surface your own cultural assumptions about negotiation while trying to learn about others'. What are the metaphors that you (and they) find compelling, or confusing? What are your shared and differing expectations about how the process should unfold? The challenges you face in an unfamiliar cultural context are similar to those discussed in Chapter Two on the importance of testing your assumptions in any negotiation by bargaining for information. Rather than simply filling in the blanks for yourself to make a coherent picture of the situation, you need to explore where you and your counterpart may see things differently, even if you appear to be speaking the same language. This is difficult enough in a negotiation with another American lawyer. Negotiating with someone from another culture calls into question even more basic assumptions and requires attention to aspects of the setting and nuances of tone and meaning that are usually taken for granted.

3. Attitudes Toward Time

One aspect of cultural difference frequently noted has to do with attitudes toward time: what it means to be "on time" for scheduled meetings; whether or not time spent getting to know the other negotiators is considered central to the process; to what extent past and future events are relevant to the current negotiations between the parties. To understand how important sensitivity to time issues is in cross-cultural negotiations, think about how you feel if someone arrives twenty minutes after the time appointed for a meeting. Do you consider the time set merely a guideline, or is it a commitment? What assumptions do you make about the person who shows up well after the agreed time? A negative reaction to such "lateness" in a culture that is not wedded to punctuality can sour negotiations before they begin, when greater cultural awareness would have let you know that it is not a comment on your or your client's importance, but merely customary.

Ours is a culture in which "time is money." Americans often treat negotiations as something to be gotten through quickly, by "cutting to the chase," rather than as an opportunity to establish a relationship that will develop and bring benefits to both parties over time. Where we might see others as "wasting" time in small talk when negotiations begin, they may see us as brusque and indifferent to the personal connections on which business relations are built in their culture.

Because we are each so embedded in our own culture's sense of time, it takes effort to adjust to another culture's rhythms and its sense of the proper bounds of any negotiation in terms of past and future. In the world of the one-shot deal, yesterday and tomorrow do not have much meaning. Yet those who see any given negotiation as part of a larger web of relationship may consider both past and future to be integral aspects of the matter under discussion; and you will be hard pressed to negotiate well unless you appreciate this aspect of your counterpart's time horizon.

4. You Have Culture, Too

It is probably impossible to extract yourself sufficiently from the cultures in which you are embedded to see them as only *a* way of construing the world and human relations. However, as Avruch also suggests below, it is useful as a start to recognize that *you* have culture, too. Your attitudes toward conflict and your approach to conflict situations like negotiation are powerfully influenced by your intersecting cultural identifications. It is precisely those aspects of your own culture that you accept most unquestioningly — indeed are largely unaware of — that are most culture-bound, whether the relevant culture is ethnic, national, familial, professional, religious or some combination of these. This point is echoed in the article by McDonald, who describes what he calls the "U.S. negotiating style," based on his decades of experience as a diplomat in the international arena. To what extent does his characterization of the strengths and weaknesses of this style ring true for you?

5. Cross-Cultural Negotiation Styles

The final article in this section, by Salacuse, serves as a bridge between the materials on culture and those on gender. Salacuse reports on a survey of negotiators from many different countries about their negotiating styles. One striking finding is that in some areas where there were *national* differences in style, the responses also demonstrate *professional* similarities, that is, members of a given professional subculture respond similarly, even though their national cultures are different. In addition, there are also variations in the responses of men and women to some of the questions. While these gender differences might lend support to the idea that men and women approach negotiation differently, the gender differences were not uniform from country to country (Spanish women, for example, were much more likely than American women to see negotiation as a win-lose proposition) — suggesting that the contours of gender, too, may be culture specific.

B. GENDER

As discussed in Chapter One, the legal culture in which American negotiation theory and teaching has developed is one dominated by the case law method and the adversary system. And, until relatively recently, that legal culture has been predominantly male. It is perhaps not surprising then, that American legal culture has long privileged purportedly "masculine" characteristics such as rationality, competition, self-assertion, and decisiveness as central to negotiation success. With the increased number of women entering the profession over the last 30 years, there has been growing interest in learning to what extent, if any, the attributes mentioned above are distinctly male and whether they do, in fact, lead to greater negotiation success. During this same period, new theories of integrative negotiation have also posited the importance of other, communication and relationship building skills to successful negotiation.

1. Theories of Gender Difference

The effects of gender on negotiation outcomes have been studied from many different angles, and, as Menkel-Meadow discusses below, there are a number of theories about what gives rise to supposed gender differences. Some theorists argue that they result from the differing socialization of boys and girls as they grow up: the "gender-appropriate" behaviors that they are taught, explicitly and implicitly. Others contend that they result largely from differences in situational power between men and women in the world. A third view posits that gender interacts with other characteristics like status (or race, or class, or occupation) to create observed differences. Finally, researchers in social psychology have demonstrated that the expectations of *others* can operate powerfully to bring about what is perceived as gender-appropriate behavior.

Each of these theories has its proponents and its detractors, and there is a rich research, as well as theoretical, literature that seeks to explore the complex social and psychological underpinnings of these various points of view. Some aspects of the research literature are discussed below, and you will certainly have many opportunities to test out various theories in the course of your learning about negotiation, as well as in your work as a negotiator.

2. Gender Difference in Negotiations

The article below by Greenhalgh and Gilkey discusses some of the literature on male-female differences in negotiation and reports results from their own experimental study. Based on their research, the authors emphasize that what they describe as "masculine" and "feminine" orientations in negotiation do not correspond strictly to biological sex, but refer only to clusters of traits that are often found together in both male and female negotiators. Clear differences are hard to point to, because socialization in childhood leads to differing expectations about appropriate sex roles — for example, from dominating and aggressive to nurturing for men. Here, too, unconscious factors undoubtedly play a role: the process of identification with important adults in early life further complicates the picture. A female negotiator who as a child identified with her father, or with "masculine" attributes of her mother, may exhibit typically "masculine" tendencies such as focusing on logic and power and being intent on winning her position in negotiations.

My own research on over 700 law students' negotiation styles, excerpted below, found that men and women see themselves as having different styles — with men tending to be more competitive and women tending to be both more collaborative and more accommodating in their approach. Since these findings are based on self-report, it is difficult to know whether they reflect actual differences in practice or merely the respondents' self-image as negotiators. Even if the reported style differences are accurate, it is not clear whether they lead to better outcomes for men or for women when they negotiate.

Although some studies have found that men do better than women, especially in distributive bargaining situations, Craver's and Barnes's research on negotiation performance in a law school negotiation course does not support this conclusion. Their article below discusses both some of the pervasive stereotypes about gender effects in negotiation and the results of the authors' analysis of the classroom performance of over 600 negotiation students. In a study published the same year involving 163 students in a first-year lawyering program, Farber and Rickenberg reached similar results using a single negotiation problem. They also found, however, that the women in their study evaluated their abilities lower than the men did — although the women's actual outcomes in the negotiation did not differ significantly from the men's! Their data did not enable them to say whether this latter finding resulted from men's overconfidence as negotiators, women's under-confidence, or both; but other research on gender stereotypes may illuminate some sources of men's and women's differing expectations in negotiations.

3. The Impact of Gender Stereotypes

Social psychologists have done extensive research on the ways that stereotypes can affect behavior. Kray and her co-authors in the articles that follow have studied how gender stereotypes can be confirmed or disconfirmed under experimental conditions. Building on the work of social psychologist Claude Steele and others, they look at the impact of what is called "stereotype threat." As defined by Steele,[1] stereotype threat occurs when a person has identified with a particular activity or field of study (such as math or science — and law? — for women), despite whatever societal obstacles there may be to pursuing it:

> It is the social-psychological threat that arises when one is in a situation of doing something for which a negative stereotype about one's group applies. This predicament threatens one with being negatively stereotyped, with being judged or treated stereotypically, or with the prospect of conforming to the stereotype. Called *stereotype threat*, it is a situational threat — a threat in the air — that, in general form, can affect the members of any group about whom a negative stereotype exists.

Examining stereotype threat in the context of negotiation, Kray and her co-authors, in the first paper excerpted below, found that when women and men were given a negotiation task and told that it was purely for learning

---

[1] Claude M. Steele, *A Threat in the Air*, 52 AM. PSYCHOLOGIST 613, 613-29 (1997).

purposes, they performed equally well. However, when they were told that
the task was for diagnostic purposes — to assess negotiating skills at the
beginning of a negotiation course — the women did worse than the men.
Even if the women did not believe that the stereotypes about women negotiators applied to them, they were aware of those stereotypes and were
affected by them. Apparently, the mention of the diagnostic nature of the
task was sufficient to trigger stereotype threat in the women: they expected
to do worse than the men in the negotiation; made less optimistic opening
offers (an often reliable predictor of final results); and ultimately reached
less favorable outcomes overall. In addition, while the women's performance
was adversely affected by stereotype threat, the men's performance was
enhanced by the positive stereotypes they carried about effective negotiators.

Interestingly, though, when the stereotype was made *explicit* by telling
the participants that the "most effective negotiators are rational and
assertive rather than being emotional, passive, and overly accommodating," the women's performance improved. They responded to the explicit
activation of the stereotype by making *more* optimistic opening offers and
tended to achieve better results than the men in mixed-gender negotiations. Kray labeled this phenomenon *stereotype reactance*, arguing that
when the stereotype is made explicit, women dissociate themselves from
stereotypically feminine behaviors and behave more in line with the characteristics explicitly described as effective.

In a later study, also excerpted below, Kray and her co-authors looked further at how negotiation performance is tied to gender stereotypes and the
ways in which those stereotypes are activated. This research shows that
both men and women are attuned to stereotypes and alter their behavior in
accordance with the particular content of an explicit positive stereotype.
Both male and female subjects behaved more cooperatively and had higher
joint gains when told that effective negotiators acted in stereotypically feminine ways ("have a keen ability to express their thoughts verbally, good listening skills, and insight into the other negotiator's feelings"). When
masculine stereotypes were linked with effectiveness, however, both men
and women leveraged their power to achieve more one-sided gains.

Gender stereotypes may be most powerful when people negotiate on their
own behalf. Babcock's 2002 study[2] of graduating masters' degree students
at Carnegie Mellon University showed that men's starting salaries were 7.6
percent higher on average than women's. When the researcher tried to
understand where this difference came from, she discovered that 93% of the
women had accepted the first salary offer made by their employer, while 57%
of the men had negotiated for more money. Almost all (7.4%) of the differ-

---

2 Linda Babcock, Do Graduate Students Negotiate Their Job Offers? 1-2 (Carnegie Mellon
University) (unpublished report, cited in LINDA BABCOCK & SARA LASCHEVER, WOMEN DON'T ASK
(2003)).

ence between the men's and women's average starting salaries resulted from the increased offers received by those who negotiated for a higher salary! By contrast, other recent research indicates that negotiators behave differently when they act on behalf of others, as lawyers generally do for clients; and that women and men are likely to have similar pre-negotiation expectations in these circumstances. When identified with the professional role and culture of lawyers — and seeking to further someone else's aims — women may be more comfortable setting and working towards high goals in negotiation.

The cultural and gender issues discussed here apply, of course, not only to negotiations between lawyers, but also to the many negotiations that occur between lawyers and their clients. The following chapter examines some of those negotiations, as well as other facets of the lawyer-client relationship.

Kevin Avruch,[*] *Culture and Negotiation Pedagogy*
16 Negot. J. 377 (2000)[**]

Of the three concepts in the title of this essay — culture, negotiation, and pedagogy — I want to direct most of my remarks to the first. My presumption is that negotiation pedagogy concerned in any way with culture, in the end, can only be as good as the concept of culture it draws upon. And so far, the picture does not look very encouraging.

This is so for two reasons. First — although the situation is improving — students of negotiation (as analysts and practitioners) have generally paid scant attention to cultural issues. Early classics in the field whether oriented analytically (*e.g., The Art and Science of Negotiation* [Raiffa 1982]), or toward practice, simply neglected to mention culture. In its first edition, the best-selling *Getting to YES*, the epitome of negotiation practice for many folks today, mentioned culture not at all. A second edition added a section addressing ten questions people asked about the first edition, rather like a rabbinical responsa, and here culture is lumped, in a single question along with personality and gender. Readers of the second edition of *Getting to YES* are warned to look out for culture but not to stereotype (good advice!). And a comprehensive review of mainly experimental research on negotiation devotes barely two (out of about 200) pages to culture, in a concluding section called "prospects for further research." This small proportion, I'm afraid,

---

[*] Kevin Avruch is Professor of Anthropology at George Mason University and Associate Director of the Institute for Conflict Analysis and Resolution, which is based at the University. His article addresses the largely unexamined role of culture in negotiation theory and practice in the United States.

[**] Copyright © 2000 Negotiation Journal. Reprinted with permission of Blackwell Publishing, Inc. and the Program on Negotiation at Harvard Law School.

reflects accurately the amount of substantive work on culture done by experimentalists, at least through the early 1990s.

The second reason for not being encouraged by the treatment of culture in works on negotiation reflects the defective way in which the idea usually has been conceptualized. I say this with humility. Culture is, as Raymond Williams remarks, "one of the two or three most complicated words in the English language." And even those of us who spend a lot of time trying to think seriously about culture often get discouraged by the baggage, conceptual as well as political, carried along with it.

Despairing conceptually (postmodernists condemn it as "totalizing"), some want to drop the term "culture" entirely in favor of related ideas: *discourse* or perhaps *episteme* as understood by Foucault, or *habitus* by Bourdieu, or *worldview*, to name a few. As for its political encumbrances (postmodernists here damn it as "neocolonialist"), think of how culture has been used strategically by some actors in the human rights debate — counter-(neo)colonialist — as a way of defending their practices when criticized by "the West." Now the usefulness of culture as a social science idea is threatened by its having been taken over by the political actors it is meant to explain.

The defects I have in mind are different ones, however, though they are in some ways reactions to how complicated the concept actually is. First, culture is *reduced*, turned for example into a label, a handy name for persons aggregated in some social, often national, sometimes ethnic group — and used to distinguish this group from other aggregates. Secondly, culture is *essentialized*, shorn of all processual or emergent qualities, made unitary and freed from inner dissensions: reified, homogenized, and frozen spuriously in synchronic stasis.

In either case, the conception of culture thus brought to bear is an exceedingly *thin* one. In return for thinness, however, researchers in this tradition get something they can use: a *variable*. As a label for certain kinds of social groups in their normative aspects, culture is thus reduced by simple nominalization; essentialized, it is amenable to scaling. Either way, we can, without too much difficulty, "count" it.

What Culture Is Not

But what is it, precisely, that we end up counting? The notion of culture that predominates in much work on negotiation typically relies on recycling remnants of what used to be "national character" studies in the 1950s and 1960s. This is perhaps exemplified nowadays in work dealing with "national negotiating styles." Such a notion of culture is based upon at least six mutually related ideas, ways of conceiving culture that are inadequate. Peter Black and I have discussed these ideas at length elsewhere. Briefly, they are as follows:

1. Culture is homogenous. This presumes that cultures are free of dissensions, of internal contradictions or paradoxes such that culture provides unambiguous behavioral instructions for individuals.

2. Culture is a thing. Reified, culture is presumed to act independent of individual agency. As in Samuel Huntington's scheme, cultures "clash" with one another across static geopolitical landscapes in Spenglerian epics.

3. Culture is uniformly distributed among members of a group. This inadequate idea is what makes nominalizing culture — turning it into a label — possible. Like "national character," it fits the requirements of work that stresses the "national negotiating styles" approach. Intracultural variation, if ever noted, whether at the individual or group level, is dismissed as "deviance."

4. An individual possesses but a single culture. Usually the "culture" here is national or ethnic. The individual is simply and monolithically Mexican, Moroccan, Moluccan. Once again, the effect is to make culture a synonym for group identity. When predominantly identified with national or ethnic groupings, moreover, this inadequacy makes it more difficult for researchers to think productively about other "vessels" filled by cultural content: professions or occupations, or organizations and institutions, for example. It also tends to "freeze" culture in a single sociological category, at the expense of recognizing situational or contextual factors — think of the important research on "boundary roles" or negotiating definitions of the situation, that could benefit from a nuanced cultural perspective.

5. Culture is custom. Here, culture is virtually synonymous with "tradition," customary ways of behaving. It is thus reduced to a sort of surface-level etiquette. Cultural variation becomes, as Peter Black once put it, merely a matter of "differential etiquette."

6. Culture is timeless. In this contrast, a changeless quality is imputed to culture, especially to so-called traditional cultures. We speak here, for example, of the "Arab mind" as though a unitary cognizing element has come down to us from Muhammad's Mecca. Or, "Be careful," the neophyte heading off to Beijing on a mission is told: "The Chinese have been negotiating for a thousand years." (One wonders if the adviser has any particular Chinese in mind.)

I hasten to add that these inadequate ideas about culture are at least deployed by those researchers in negotiation who count (or count on) culture at all. In other approaches, as noted earlier, culture is rendered so thinly as to come out all but invisible, as in *Getting to YES's* first edition or *The Art and Science of Negotiation.*

What would explain this invisibility? First, there are the cloaking potentialities of power. Many researchers and instructors coming to negotiation from realist or neorealist positions within the field of International Relations (IR) assume the state is an independent unitary actor in an anarchic international environment where power ultimately trumps everything else — and what constitutes "power" is self-evident and acultural. Secondly — and this realist IR shares with much of the social psychology of negotiation — there are the overriding presumptions of rational choice theory, also cloaking culture, that guide researchers' thinking, modeling, and gaming. States, like individuals, are presumed to act in ways that strive "rationally" to maximize universally held and self-evident material interests, or utilities like security.

Among others, one question raised by this notion would focus on the nature of utilities. In a sense, we can know about them only after the players have chosen them — behavioral choice then determines cognitive preferences (and the tautology is complete). We can assume a universal set of preferences, but explaining the choices of some other players who appear to have other preferences — those in other cultures, for instance — becomes problematic. Or, we can admit that utilities can vary with context (culture), thus admitting cultural preferences into the model but preserving its essential character of rational choice. This is the usual tack taken by those who see culture operating only at level of "values" in a conflict or negotiation. But including "values" does not address the generally attenuated psychology presumed by rational choice, nor does it give to context the full weight of its potential constitutive influence on defining the situation — on players' cognitions and affect.

Comaroff and Roberts, looking at dispute resolution among the Tswana, point to the dilemma here: "[Once the dispute] process is linked with utility — whether utility be conceived in terms of the universalist maximization of interest or the pursuit of indigenous values — it is a short step to treating sociocultural context as 'given' and its relationship to the dispute as unproblematic." Elsewhere Wildavsky has made a similar point, arguing for the cultural variability of interests rather than assuming their universality. And perhaps most interesting, Ross has pointed out that from "within" a given cultural context — say, our own — culturally constituted affective "motives" can appear identical to rationally chosen "interests." That is, when interests are shared *intra*culturally, "they certainly operate like motives, offering a readily available account of why people behave as they do." It is only "when we consider cross-cultural encounters [that], the difference between interests and motives is more significant." Sometimes in such intercultural encounters, in fact, *we* may have difficulty even interpreting *their* (apparent) motives as *rational* interests at all. Serious misunderstandings may result when the culturally constituted motives of one party do not match the assumed universal interests posited by the other.

One upshot of this culturalist approach is not to deny the relevance or usefulness of rational choice theory, but to see it as a culturally constituted ethnopsychology, explanatorily relevant for particular actors in specific domains, situations, or cultural settings — all to be ascertained empirically. Until this is recognized, national choice theorists will naturally "cloak" culture, rendering it wholly invisible or relevant only at the level of values.

In addition to the seductions of power and the power of rational choice theory, there is another reason for culture's neglect in much research on negotiation, and this is especially germane pedagogically as it reflects the special role played by *practice* in negotiation scholarship. As Sara Cobb remarks, negotiation is a field particularly occupied by scholar-practition-ers. Faculty "who teach and conduct research on negotiation are often them-selves skilled practitioners. Additionally, the questions that drive research bubble up from dilemmas in practice." To my mind, this insight is key. All too often, the "theory" of negotiation propounded by experienced practi-tioners derives strongly from their experience and practice. Here I hold to the proposition that *where practice is situated, there is theory derived.*

And for negotiation — as, indeed, for conflict resolution in general — the practice overwhelmingly has been culturally situated within a North American, male, white, and middle-class world. There are political, as well as conceptual or pedagogical, corollaries to this proposition. For once the folk practice of a particular cultural world — ours — gets enshrined as experts' "theory," then, in intercultural encounters, it may be exported or imposed on our interlocutors with a total lack of self-consciousness about the "home-court" advantages that we gain by insisting that our model be followed. In short, by suppressing the cultural dimension, including the epistemological implications of *situated practice*, we run the risk of losing at the same time a way to get at the asymmetries of power in intercultural negotiations in the real world.

Some Thoughts on What Culture Is

Thus far I have dwelt mostly on what culture, in my view, is not: an homogenous, essentialized, uniformly distributed, customary, timeless, and stable thing. I shall now say a few words about how, in contrast, I concep-tualize culture, and then some words on how I approach teaching it to stu-dents of conflict resolution.

Following Schwartz, I see culture as consisting of the "derivatives of experience, more or less organized, learned or created by the individuals of a population, including those images or encodements and their interpreta-tions (meanings) transmitted from past generations, or contemporaries, or formed by individuals themselves." In the main, this is a symbolic (stress-ing interpretation and meaning) and cognitivist definition, stressing images or encodements that others have called schemas or cognitive representa-tions.

But note that such schemas are not just handed down unchanged and authoritatively by generations past: some are created afresh by individuals, and all derive ultimately from experience in and of the world — from social practice. Moreover, the definition must be expanded to maintain that these images and encodements are not uniformly distributed in a population; they are differentially distributed both sociologically (i.e., in terms of class, gender, ethnicity, occupation, region, etc.) and psychologically (in terms of their differential psychodynamic internalization — their affective and motivational "loading" — by specific persons).

Because "culture" now consists of numerous schemas derived from diverse experience and distributed across complex social and psychological landscapes, one is led immediately to understand that, for a given individual culture always comes in the plural. It is unlikely that a single cultural descriptor can authoritatively characterize an individual across all contexts or situations. This is one reason why the "national negotiating styles" literature is so unsatisfactory to some negotiation researchers. As is well known, sometimes scientists, engineers, or military officers from different "cultures" can communicate more easily with one another "across" the negotiating table than they can with those on their own team, who may share national but not the negotiation-relevant professional "images and encodements." (And even the assumed sharing of "national" culture, given sociological and psychological distributional complexities, can be all too easily overestimated, as well.)

Some Thoughts on Teaching About Culture

Finally, with respect to negotiation, how do I teach students using this conceptualization of culture?

First, I do not teach that culture is another "variable" that can be arrayed alongside age, income, or passport nationality. Nor is culture another independent causal vector in schematic models of negotiation. Culture is context, not cause. It is, speaking metaphorically, the "lens" through which causes are refracted.

Secondly, I am mistrustful of simulations wherein students are expected to "play" the roles of cultural others, particularly in negotiations involving so-called deep-rooted or protracted identity conflicts. Even for teaching purposes, if one wants to simulate an Israeli-Palestinian negotiation, go to Israelis and Palestinians to do it. I have a healthy respect for the definition of the situation to affect role players' behavior — a cursory consideration of Milgram or Zimbardo's work, on obedience to authority and guard-prisoner roles, if nothing else, commands this respect. But intercultural negotiations, especially around affectively-loaded identity issues, are simply not modeled well by outsiders in semiscripted roleplays.

Third, although students expect to jump right into problems of "negotiating with other cultures," I never begin by teaching about intercultural negotiation — even from first-rate books like Raymond Cohen's *Negotiating Across Cultures*. Cohen's book comes very near the end of the course. Instead, I begin with two or three substantive ethnographies, or cultural accounts, of particular cultures, preferably those that also stress social conflict and conflict resolution. In my opinion, students should first grapple with understanding what negotiation or conflict resolution "looks like" inside "a" culture, before they can move to the complications of cross- or intercultural negotiation or conflict resolution.

Two books I have used for years to illustrate conflict resolution within particular cultures are Carol Greenhouse's *Praying for Justice* and Lawrence Rosen's *Bargaining for Reality*. Greenhouse's book focuses on the culture of Southern Baptists in a suburb of Atlanta (who are conflict-avoiders); Rosen's on Moroccans in the city of Sefrou (for whom nearly everything social is "negotiable"). I use these works to set out what a good cultural analysis looks like, how it is done, as well as its limitations (e.g., causality, as mentioned earlier). I also use them to show why culture analysis that depends completely on "counting" culture is deficient.

Take a "trait" like "individualism," usually counterposed to "collectivism" in scores of aggregating cultural accounts — Geert Hofstede's for example. Both the American, Protestant folks of Greenhouse's account and the Moroccan, Sunni Muslims of Rosen's, can be characterized as "individualistic." But aside from what Wittgenstein called "family resemblance," this individualism, as historically derived, phenomenologically experienced, and socially deployed by Baptists and Muslims, looks very different in the two contexts — and both are different from the individualism of Hobbes or Adam Smith. When students grapple with deconstructing "individualism" in different cultural settings, most come away with less faith in the predictive power (a few, even in the validity) of aggregating cultural accounts.

And fourth and finally, I have to remind some of my students that they — we — "have culture" as well. Culture is not just something possessed by the others — the ethnics, the third-worlders, the clients of the World Bank and the IMF, the objects of our humanitarian peacekeeping interventions. Cultural analysis is always reflexive. Sometimes I can even get some of them to see the cultural underpinnings of such expert theories as rational choice or principled negotiation.

Hazel Rose Markus & Leah R. Lin,[*]
Conflictways: Cultural Diversity in the Meanings and Practices of Conflict
in CULTURAL DIVIDES (Deborah A. Prentice & Dale T. Miller eds., 1999)[**]

* * *

This chapter focuses on what we call *conflictways* — differences in the meanings and practices of conflict. We describe a cultural psychological approach to conflict and review some research analyzing the understandings and practices of conflict observed in four overlapping yet still somewhat different cultural contexts: European American, Asian American, Mexican American, and African American.

* * *

Conflictways vary dramatically among cultural contexts — contexts specified by ethnicity, religion, gender, social class, educational background, age, or region of the country or world. These variations are not merely differences in how to think about conflict *after* behavior has occurred. Instead, conflictways are fully active in the *constitution* of behavior. Is silence acquiescence or passive aggressiveness? Is a joke a provocation or play? Conflictways are implicated in these responses and are thus an important means by which people engage in and experience their social worlds.

Conflictways include the invisible, tacit, and commonsense understandings that people have about themselves and their worlds, including what is right and wrong, how to proceed, whom to turn to, and what to expect. One of the most important tacit understandings, and one that may be particularly significant for an analysis of conflict, is the view of what it means to be a "good" or "proper" person. In many cultural contexts, the individual is parsed and understood not as a separate or distinct entity, as in the United States, but instead as an interdependent member of a given social unit. Each cultural context's conception of self and its relation to others is an integral part of understanding cultural differences regarding conflict. Two distinct conceptions will be discussed in the following sections.

Conflict in Individualist Worlds

The empirical and theoretical analysis of conflict has been pursued largely within a Western context, and particularly a mainstream American context. If it is the case that the cultural pervades and cannot be sepa-

---

[*] Hazel Rose Markus is Davis-Brack Professor in Behavioral Sciences at Stanford University. Leah R. Lin was a doctoral candidate in social psychology at Stanford University when this article was published. Their article addresses approaches to conflict in different cultural settings.

[**] Copyright © 1999 Russell Sage Foundation. Reprinted with permission.

rated from the psychological, then many of social psychology's "basic" understandings of conflict carry Western or European American assumptions about the nature of the individual, the group, and social behavior. * * * The focus in such a view is on the autonomous individual rather than on the social unit of which the individual is a part.

* * *

The cultural model of the independent person that prevails in North America and is reflected in the "rational actor" of game theory, the "reasonable person" of the legal system, and the "authentic self" of most psychological theorizing defines certain features as natural, necessary, and good: (1) that the individual is a stable, autonomous, "free" entity; (2) that he or she possesses a set of characteristic, identifying, and self-defining attributes — preferences, motives, goals, attitudes, beliefs, and abilities — that are the primary forces that enable, guide, or constrain behavior; (3) that individuals take action that is oriented toward the expression of their opinions and beliefs, the realization of their rights, and the achievement of their own goals; and (4) that the individual often regards relationships as competing with personal needs and considers the expectations of others and obligations to others as interfering with personal goals.

* * *

The assumptions of individualism have direct consequences for the sources, meanings, and practices of conflict. Within a world organized according to the tenets of individualism and animated by the web of associated understandings and practices, any perceived constraint on individual freedom is likely to pose immediate problems and require a response. Typically the most appropriate response in a conflict situation involves a direct or honest expression of one's ideas. Indeed, it is sometimes the individualist's moral imperative, the sign that one is being a "good" person, to disagree with and remain unmoved by the influence of others. The right to disagree, typically manifested by a direct statement of one's own views, can create social difficulties, but it is understood and experienced as a birthright. Further, an individualist perspective, which often tends toward mechanical and determinist understandings of the world, is also likely to assume that there is, in a given conflict situation, a right or a wrong way, that there is one truth — such that A and not-A cannot both be true — and that sufficient debate, argumentation, and application of "reason" will reveal *the* truth.

Conflict in Interdependent Worlds

Regardless of a person's particular set of sociocultural niches within the United States, anyone living in this country is exposed to and lives within institutions — the legal system, the political system, the media — that are founded on and operate within an individualist framework of ideas and practices. Yet individualist notions of personhood are neither the "natural" way nor the only way to think about what it means "to be." In fact, most of the world's diverse cultural systems do not represent the person and the social world in this way at all. And even within the United States, many people also participate in cultural contexts that are not primarily rooted in individualist assumptions.

Interdependent views of personhood not only differ quite dramatically in their particulars but assume that what is obvious and "natural" is that the self is a *relational* entity. The self, from this perspective, is understood as fundamentally interdependent with others. The self cannot be separated from others and the surrounding social context and is typically not seen as "possessing" enduring, trans-situational qualities or attributes of its own in isolation from its relationships and contexts. In fact, understanding other notions of personhood requires dissolving the boundary between self and others or self and society that is such an obvious starting point in many European American and also some North American and European formulations.

In the models of the self that are prevalent in many of the cultures of the world — including China, Japan, Korea, and South Asia as well as those of Africa, much of the Middle East, and Central and South America — the person is inherently and fundamentally connected to others. These cultural models of the person place greater stress than individualist models on social and relational concepts such as empathy, reciprocity, belongingness, kinship, hierarchy, loyalty, honor, respect, politeness, and social obligation. Typically in those cultural contexts, social relationships, roles, norms, and group solidarity are more fundamental to social behavior than self-expression. Although the individual is certainly aware of his or her own desires and interests, he or she is expected to meet others' expectations and work for the good of the dyad, the group, the institution, or the nation. Being a good or respectable person derives from active engagement in the social roles that configure social life and harmonious participation in honorable social relations.

More specifically, the cultural model of the interdependent person defines certain features as natural, necessary and good, including the idea that a person (1) is a flexible, connected entity who is bound to others; (2) participates in a set of relationships, groups, and institutions that are the primary forces that enable, guide, or constrain actions; (3) conforms to relational norms and responds to group goals by seeking consensus and compromise; and (4) often regards personal beliefs and needs as secondary to norms and relationships. * * *

As with individualism, these ideas about relationality and interdependence have multiple sources and are mutually reinforcing. In many East Asian cultures, interdependent views have arisen from several overlapping religious and philosophical traditions. Buddhism, for example, asserts that people and the world must be considered in relative rather than absolute terms. Change is seen as fundamental to reality. Inconsistency and contradiction are to be expected, while the notion of a person as a consistent or unchanging entity is viewed as misleading, if not wrong-headed. Buddhism also encourages empathy and compassion for others with whom we are interdependent. Confucianism and Buddhism both emphasize harmony, selflessness, and subordination of the individual's own interests to the interests of a larger group. Confucianism also highlights the cultivation of the person into a proper social being, the importance of the social order, ind the restoration of harmony through compromise. And Taoism contributes an appreciation of the value in living in the correct way.

* * *

With different conceptualizations of the social world come different metaphors and understandings of conflict. According to ethnographic studies in Central and South America — regions of the world also characterized by more interdependent models of the person — conflict is often believed to result from tangled interpersonal nets or webs. Lederbach, in his analysis of Costa Rica, for example, finds that people often describe themselves as "trapped inside" a conflict and that the goal is to manage an "exit" through talk or dialogue. The role of a third person, who will connect individuals and maintain the integrity of the interpersonal web in the conflict, is critical. In contemporary Hawaiian culture, conflict is typically described as resulting from "blocked pathways" in the channels of "flowing affect" that connect people to one another. Conflict is represented as entanglements or relationships that "all jam up," and resolution often involves a respected elder who facilitates the disentanglement. This facilitation includes a number of components, such as confession, apology, forgiveness, and release, that are not commonly invoked in more independent perspectives on conflict.

* * *

Interdependent constructions of the world have powerful consequences for the analysis and practice of conflict. From an interdependent perspective, the underlying goal of social behavior is not the preservation and manifestation of individual rights and attributes, but rather the preservation of relationships. For example, it is better to endure the suffering associated with being wronged than to disrupt harmony by complaining. Thus, interdependent conflictways include strategies that emphasize indirectness rather than direct confrontation, the use of mediators or arbitrators, reliance on apology and forgiveness, and avoidance techniques like waiting, withdrawing, and even false promising. In a conflict, one should engage others, persuade them, and draw out their cooperation. Often the goal is to avoid hostility or the outbreak of confrontation because of the fear of damaging the relationship or producing lingering animosity.

Wall and Blum, in a fascinating study of community mediation in the People's Republic of China, report that in contrast to the United States, conflict mediation is a fact of everyday life in China, where there are over one million mediators. Mediators are present in good times and bad, and they make societal harmony their objective. Mediation in China proceeds very differently than it does in the United States, where mediators help the parties hammer out an agreement that protects the individual interests of both parties. First, in China the mediator's knowledge of the disputants is thought to be an asset, unlike the neutrality that is considered essential in the United States. Mediation is regarded as a responsibility to the community rather than to the individual; the community has a right to be safe, educated, employed, and at peace. Mediation is not voluntary, and the mediators, not the disputing parties, initiate the process. Finally, in the United States disputing parties expect personal satisfaction from mediation, while in China the parties may expect only that the dispute will be temporarily managed and some interpersonal harmony restored.

* * *

Conflictways in European American Contexts: Individual Rights and Autonomy

The meaning of conflict in many European American contexts, and particularly Anglo-American cultural contexts, reflects a view of the person as an autonomous entity who possesses individual rights and is motivated by a configuration of internal or personal values and goals. In European American cultural contexts, individuals are expected to express their *own* beliefs and pursue their *own* goals; it is their duty to do so because their ideas and attitudes literally define the self. Indeed, behavior is a reflection or expression of individual beliefs and goals. Within this cultural context, people defend conflict as perceived incompatibility in individuals' beliefs about an issue, or incompatibility in the accomplishment of their goals. These lay definitions are consistent with the mainstream social psychological view that conflict arises when incompatible activities occur, and that this incompatibility reflects differences in individuals' ideas, values, and goals.

European American conceptions of conflict are predicated on a notion of the person as an agentic performer of individual actions rather than a responsive being situated in and actively adjusting to a network of relationships. In contrast with the prevalent ideas and practices of Asian American, African American, and Mexican American contexts, conflict in European American contexts is not considered the product of the ongoing process of being in relationship with others. Conflict arises when the activities of two individuals interfere with one another. Thus, conflict emerges from incidental situations rather than as an inevitable consequence of relationality. For people with bounded, individualist selves, conflict with others can be self-defining or identity-promoting. It brings into sharp relief their own desires, preferences, and goals and provides the opportunity to verify or express them.

The paradigmatic expression of the European American perspective on conflict is articulated in Fisher, Ury, and Patton's best-selling handbook of negotiation strategy, *Getting to YES: Negotiating Agreement Without Giving In*. Even the title of this media sensation suggests that the goal of European

Americans in conflict (consistent with the independent view of self) is to arrive at a solution without compromising personal integrity or making concessions. Careful observers of European American conflict, Fisher and his colleagues note that people in this cultural context tend to confront others directly while stridently promulgating a particular position that outlines the actions that they would be willing or unwilling to take. The authors of *Getting to YES* are critical of this positional bargaining strategy because it commits participants to unwise agreements, entails lengthy negotiations, and jeopardizes the long-term relationship between the parties. Nevertheless, the alternative strategy they offer also bears the unique stamp of the European American view of conflict: (1) separate the people from the problem; (2) focus on interests, not positions; (3) generate a variety of possibilities before deciding what to do; and (4) insist that the result be based on some objective standard.

First, by advising negotiators to distinguish the people from the problem, Fisher and his colleagues assume that the content of conflict may be extracted from the relationship between the participants (a peculiar idea in Chinese contexts). Moreover, they assume that this separation facilitates the reconciliation of problematic issues that are inherently extra-relational. They warn that in a positional bargaining situation, "the parties' relationship tends to become entangled with their discussions of substance." A common European American view is that the substance of a conflict lies in the different positions advocated by the participants. Instead, Fisher and his colleagues argue, in their discussion of their second tip, that the substance is the participants' individual interests. Although the authors try to revise the prevailing European American view of conflict, they view "interests" as a manifestation of a set of needs, desires, concerns, and fears that are internal to the person. Again, their suggested revision of European American conflictways is itself a reflection of that cultural view of the person.

In their resolution-oriented strategy, Fisher, Ury, and Patton also recommend that negotiators generate multiple solutions to the problem. They go so far as to suggest that these solutions be designed to maximize mutual gain. This advice appears to be at odds with the European American preference for single solutions and individual interests. However, ultimately the suggestion is directed toward a particularly European American goal: to identify and decide on a single, binding agreement. Although these authors advise negotiators to brainstorm many possible solutions, all but one of these are to be cast aside once a decision has been made. This decision is considered a primary and enduring outcome of the conflict rather than a transitory agreement that remains open to subsequent negotiation. Furthermore, they recommend that negotiators base their decision on "objective" criteria. "Logical" appeals to principles of fairness, efficiency, or scientific merit, they contend, eliminate competition between individual wills. This view presumes that the relational aspect of a conflict is inevitably a competition between independent agents, and that abstract principles can circumvent this supposedly counterproductive form of relationality to reveal an objectively correct solution.

* * *

The norms that regulate conflict resolution prescribe rational debate, confrontation with the other, direct expression of opinions, and quick decisiveness. In the European American conception, rational debate between spokespeople for different positions facilitates an objectively reasonable resolution to a conflict. Direct, honest statements of opinion permit the parties to confront the problem. Emotional expression is considered a distraction from the rational debate and an obstacle to conflict resolution.

The desirable mode of behavior during a conflict is detached, cool, quiet, and without affect. Kochman suggests that because the white middle-class European American mode of discussion or debate is supposed to be dispassionate and impersonal, any display of affect is thought to be dysfunctional, not legitimate, and a sign of weakness. According to Kochman, the idea of rational debate is that the merits of an idea are intrinsic to the idea itself. How much a person cares about the idea and is willing to defend it are irrelevant; it is right or wrong, true or false. In fact, displaying an emotional attachment for one's positions or ideas is believed to be in bad form. The ideas should stand and speak for themselves independent of the people who hold or express them. Rational debate or conflict is thought to proceed best with an air of neutrality or impersonality.

Although the European American approach to conflict is so widely shared and sustained by members of this cultural group that it goes unexamined and uncontested, it can contrast dramatically with the approaches adopted by other groups who engage in mainstream contexts but who also have significant experience in social contexts configured differently. Exploring these differences reveals the particular challenges of intercultural conflict . . . in the Unites [sic] States.

Conflictways in Asian American Contexts: Giving Face and Avoiding Confrontation

Although Asian Americans construct ways of life and ethnic identities that distinguish them from Asians who live in Asia, some features of the cultural experience of this group overlap with that of Asians abroad, particularly since most immigration from Asia has occurred in the second half of the twentieth century. Oyserman and Sakamoto suggest that many contemporary Asian Americans are constructing complex identities that embrace some aspects of American traditions of individualism while still retaining many interdependent meanings and practices. Characterizations of conflict in Asian cultures can then be used to make some initial inferences about Asian American conceptions of conflict, although it is immediately evident that these practices may change in important ways as they come in contact with European American practices.

Analogous to the connection in a European American context between the meaning of conflict and an independent conception of self, the meaning of conflict for Asians reflects an interdependent view of the person. In Asian cultures, the self is defined in relationship to others and is viewed as part of a larger social unit. Conflict then is a disturbance or disharmony in the relationship between individuals. This disharmony may arise from disagreement about an issue, or even incompatible activities of the sort that are problematic in European American contexts. However, in Asian cultures, conflict is at heart relational rather than activity-oriented. * * *

Cultures that foster an interdependent view of self embed individuals in networks of relationships that are expected to endure across a lifetime. For conflict, the implications of this social system are threefold. First, the appropriate management of conflict is an important priority because the consequences of conflict are likely to persist over time. Second, the time available for reestablishing relational harmony is extensive because the relationship will continue to exist, even if in disharmony. Third, conflict is an inevitable part of relationships since they endure over such a long time. * * * From this perspective, once individuals have built a long-term relationship with one another, conflict is an irrepressible, nonpathological, perhaps necessary component of their relationship.

The enduring quality of many relationships in Asian cultures gives rise to the codification and institutionalization of procedures for managing conflicts. While people in European American contexts often seek conflict avoidance or resolution, Asian approaches aim for management or control of the conflict. These procedures recognize the differences between the participants and attempt to minimize the negative consequences of the differences prior to confrontation. As noted by Tu Mu, a Chinese poet of the T'ang dynasty, "He who excels at resolving difficulties does so before they arise."

In Japan conflict management is represented by the metaphor of nemawashi, or root binding. Binding the roots of a tree before transplanting it is thought to facilitate its growth following the transition. Analogously, in conflict situations, laying an interpersonal groundwork of discussion and consensus-building activities before taking action that addresses the conflict is thought to help reestablish harmony among the participants and prevent loss of face. Cohen suggests that informal contact in these contexts allows one to negotiate without negotiating.

Nemawashi is commonly accomplished by the use of three procedures. First, face-to-face talks among pairs of participants allow them to survey the conflict and persuade others that an appropriate action can be found. Second, in the ringi procedure, the participants circulate a written copy of a proposed action for endorsement. The circulation of the document serves to disseminate information about the action to those involved in the negotiation ahead of time and make participants aware of the emerging consensus.

Third, neutral go-betweens may speak to individuals on both sides of a conflict to arrange its management.

The clusters of behaviors associated with nemawashi illustrate the operation of several norms for conflict that uniquely characterize the Asian approach. Indirectness of expression, avoidance of confrontation, and group decision-making are fundamental to nemawashi. Whereas people who live in European American contexts often prefer rational or logical debate, people in East Asian cultures favor indirect communication that uses ambiguity and imprecision to circumvent confrontation and delay commitment to any single proposal. This conflict management process is time-consuming compared with European American conflict resolution, but it focuses on cultivating flexibility and a willingness to adapt or adjust to a variety of situations. The deliberative pace allows participants to consider multiple alternatives and arrive at a consensual decision that is designed to ensure that none of the participants loses face in overt competition with another. In European American contexts, once a decision is made it is often viewed as a final resolution of the problem. However, in Asian contexts, even following complicated procedures like those associated with nemawashi, the emerging decision is subject to revision in order to accommodate subsequent changes in events.

Beyond nemawashi strategies of management, Lebra suggests that the Japanese have developed considerable cultural expertise in enacting strategies that do not allow confrontation to develop, perhaps as a consequence of their interest and focus on sociality and the maintenance of relationships. Besides strategies of anticipatory management (arranging circumstances to avoid situations that typically give rise to conflict), Japanese contexts are characterized by the use of (1) negative communication — when A is angry with B, he does not confront but avoids contact or refuses to respond; (2) situational code switching — parties in conflict stay away from each other, but behave in a situationally appropriate manner when they do come into contact; (3) triadic management — when a confrontation is threatened between A and B, a third party is asked to mediate the communication; (4) displacement — making a protest in the name of another, revealing frustration to a close other who is not the source of the conflict, or criticizing a less powerful person who is not directly involved; and (5) self-aggression — protesting by exaggerated compliance or obedience, and acceptance instead of rejection of an undesirable plan.

Lebra stresses that conflict management from the Japanese perspective does not mean conflict *resolution*. In fact, the strategies that she describes may intensify the awareness of conflict. People participating in cultural systems that foster and promote interdependence will interfere with one another frequently, and because of the ever-present possibility of conflict, practices of nonconfrontation and harmony will be well elaborated. Cultural virtuosity with respect to the maintenance and promotion of harmony requires a nuanced understanding of conflict and, Lebra argues, a view of harmony models and conflict models as not mutually exclusive.

All of the well-known strategies for conflict management in Japanese cultural contexts are readily comprehensible from a European American perspective; some, such as triadic management and displacement, are quite common. Yet the idea of managing conflict by trying to prevent it is much less well developed in mainstream settings. From a European American point of view, conflict, although it can be negative in its consequences, is not altogether negative or undesirable. From the interdependent perspective, avoiding conflict, even if doing so entails acceptance or "giving in," is critical and identity-promoting. When selves are defined relationally or through interdependence, disturbing or destroying the relationship threatens self. In interdependent cultural contexts, it is critical to honor the opponent's face or to give face. "Face entails the presentation of a civilized front to another individual within the webs of interconnected relationships in a particular culture. . . . Face is a claimed sense of self-respect in an interactive situation." Once face has been taken away, it has to be given back by one's opponent; it cannot be restored in other ways. Ting-Toomey and Cole, in delineating problems of intercultural contact, note that while negotiators from interdependent contexts are often particularly concerned with honoring face, negotiators participating in independent worlds are often most adept at threatening face.

A variety of studies and anecdotal reports from European Americans doing business in China also suggest that people in Chinese cultural contexts are likely to be very attuned to the threat or presence of interpersonal conflict. Leung, in a comparison of conflict resolution styles of Hong Kong Chinese students and American students, reports that the modes of conflict resolution preferred by Chinese students were those assumed most likely to reduce animosity. Furthermore, informal procedures like mediation and bargaining were also preferred to explicitly confrontational procedures. In a similar study by Trubisky, Ting-Toomey, and Lin comparing Taiwanese and American students, the Taiwanese students favored the use of styles identified as "obliging" and "avoiding," "integrating," and "compromising." * * * On the other hand, European Americans may understand indirectness as a lack of honesty or weakness in one's convictions rather than as a strategy for conflict management and consensus building.

* * *

Asian Americans in Asian cultural contexts are likely to avoid a direct expression of their own ideas and may refrain from putting their own positions directly on the table. The Asian American's ties to cultural contexts that claim that "the mouth is the source of misfortune" and "heaven moves without a single word" are likely to encourage both a wariness for whatever their opponents are saying on the surface and a search for the meanings behind the words. While European Americans will often assume it is the speaker's responsibility to say specifically what is on his or her mind, Asian Americans may believe they should not communicate their ideas or opinions too explicitly, especially to outgroup members; doing so might be perceived as rude and disruptive.

* * *

European Americans also report difficulties understanding some Chinese practices not only because the Chinese use more indirect methods of communication but also because they appear to hold very different notions of what a contract signifies. For European Americans, a contract represents the end of a negotiation, whereas in many Chinese contexts it is only the beginning. For example, Chinese negotiators may ask for special considerations that seem to change the terms of the agreement after the contract has been signed. For the Chinese, the contract establishes a relationship, and a relationship partner can be counted on for extra consideration or special favors. The management of conflict in Asian cultures is an ongoing process in a changing world. In addition to attempting to identify solutions that would restore group harmony, conflict management is itself a harmonizing process that strengthens the social connections between group members as it simultaneously strengthens independent identities, which are rooted in relationships.

Conflictways in Mexican American Contexts: Respect and Mutual Positive Feelings

Characterizing conflict from Mexican American perspectives is perhaps even more difficult than characterizing it from an Asian American perspective. Conflict in Mexican culture, and in Latin American cultural systems more broadly, has received only meager attention in the social sciences. The work that is available, however, suggests that a variety of values and practices remain important for people who have participated in Mexican cultural contexts even when they are quite fully engaged in American mainstream contexts. Most important, in contexts that are primarily Mexican and Mexican American the individual is viewed within a hierarchical system of relationships. One key quality for being a worthy or honorable person in this system is *simpatia*, or the ability to both respect and share others' feelings.

In many Hispanic and Latin American cultural contexts, a person who behaves properly, and thus is esteemed and fulfilled, is one who knows how to judge a social situation and engage in an appropriate level of relatedness, showing the proper courtesy and decorum depending on age, sex, and social status. The capacity to honor others, fulfill one's obligations, and give respect while maintaining respect, or the positive evaluation of others, is critical to a good standing in the community and to survival within that community. A resolution that ensures an individual's autonomy or guarantees individual rights is often less important in a conflict than resolution that is appropriate to the particular setting and maintains or restores an individual's pride and honor.

Compared to many European American contexts, in Mexican American contexts a great emphasis is placed on interpersonal reality and the maintenance of harmony in interpersonal relationships. A recent study compared the preferences of Mexican Americans and European Americans for different work situations. Given a choice, Mexican Americans preferred the work situation in which coworkers spend time getting to know each other and establishing relationships with one another before beginning to work. European Americans were more likely to choose the situation in which people cut to the chase and begin working almost immediately, believing that one should not waste time on social trivialities and that results are more important than relationships.

* * *

Greenfield and Suzuki point out that many Mexican Americans and Latinos are raised to respect elders and accept their opinions without question. The emphasis in institutional settings like schools on the value of logical or rational argumentation may well be at odds with practices of respect. These authors report on a study of conferences between immigrant Latino parents and elementary school teachers in which the teacher criticized every child for a failure to express his or her views in class. As with schools, workplace settings that require individual assertiveness and the direct expression of one's opinions may be difficult to negotiate for those who have engaged primarily in Mexican contexts. Culturally mandated politeness or respect may be interpreted by supervisors or coworkers, not as deference or respect for authority, but as passivity or apathy.

In Mexican American cultural contexts, the extended family provides a primary social network for self-definition. However, the metaphor of the family may also serve as a model for work relationships. A manager may be treated as the head of a family that includes workers in the position of children. Both familial and work relationships are regulated by the concept of respeto, a representation of the status differences between individuals. Loosely translated as "respect," respeto refers to the relational status of individuals with differential power, based on differences in position, age, or influence.

* * * The notion of respeto and the behaviors attendant to it are means by which people in predominantly Mexican American cultural contexts understand and maintain interpersonal bonds. The primary importance of managing harmonious if unequal relationships in Mexican American cultural contexts is reflected in this approach to conflict.

Conceiving conflict as a disharmony in a relationship, people living in Mexican American contexts may avoid conflict by using a number of strategies. One is to facilitate cooperation, which may circumscribe many conflict situations. Kagan and Madsden found that Mexican American children were more likely to cooperate with peers than were European American children, who were more likely to compete than their Mexican American counterparts. Another strategy for avoiding conflict is to control one's negative emotions. McGinn, Harburg, and Ginsburg found that when European American and Mexican men were presented with hypothetical situations that held potential for conflict with a friend, the Mexican respondents were more likely than the European Americans to report that they would try to avoid negative emotions like anger and irritation. A third strategy for avoiding conflict is to provide information that maintains the relationship between individuals even if the information is misleading about extra-relational realities. For instance, requests may receive responses that are compliant in rhetoric but not in action. The respondent's goal may be to manage the relationship by agreeing to the request rather than risk destabilizing the interaction with a refusal. As Cohen notes, in some difficult situations "truth is not imperative when a lie avoids unpleasantness."

When these avoidance strategies fail and conflict seems inevitable, confrontational discussions occur in Mexican American contexts. However, within these confrontations, Mexican American cultural norms may maximize the possibility of reestablishing harmony. For women, this means expressing concern for the relationship and the other person. For men, it means talking to reach a mutual understanding. The final goal of conflict in Mexican American contexts is often a mutual coordination of feelings rather than a formal agreement or the resolution of an issue. A successful outcome is associated with positive engagement in interpersonal relationships.

Conflictways in African American Contexts: Advocacy and Confrontation

Analyzing African American conflict meanings and practices is a particularly complex and potentially controversial endeavor. Conceptions of self in African American contexts reflect mainstream models of the autonomous agentic self, but they also reflect interdependent understandings of group identity and belongingness. African American contexts are often described as reflecting a communalism in which group concerns can transcend individual concerns more easily than is the case in primarily European American contexts. Moreover, in many African American settings a clear emphasis is placed on unity, cooperative effort, and collective responsibility. This type of interdependence may be a legacy of African notions of personhood and/or a continuing legacy of involuntary immigration, slavery, discrimination, poverty, and minority status, or some combination of all of these.

Somewhat in contrast to Asian American contexts, in African American contexts, people live within social contexts of friends and extended family but relate to these contexts in terms of separate individuals with unique thoughts and feelings. From this perspective, the self is publicly represented by the expression of these thoughts and feelings to others. The self is co-constructed by the individual and the social group as individuals direct their expressions toward relational others and the others respond to these expressions.

Kochman, in one of the few direct comparisons of some European American and African American behavioral styles, observes that in public debate or argument the "black mode," as he calls it, is often animated, interpersonal, emotional, and confrontational. In many African American cultural contexts, being animated or energetic is entirely appropriate in a dispute or conflict. In fact, discussions that are devoid of affect or dynamic opposition are unlikely to be taken seriously or regarded as significant. In an analysis of "black talk," Smitherman suggests that African American communication often requires a dialogue or a dynamic exchange between A and B, not A lecturing B. Moreover, because it is not universally held that emotion makes an argument less cogent, African Americans sometimes view efforts by European Americans to set aside feelings as unrealistic, illogical, or even politically devious. And indeed, in conflicts between blacks and whites, whites often observe that the level of black affect or anger was inappropriate and thus perceive the argument as illegitimate.

In African American cultural contexts, the meaning of conflict may be simultaneously individual and relational. Understood as a lack of agreement between individuals, African American notions of conflict sometimes imply that individuals have differing points of view but emphasize the discrepancy in participants' positions rather than focusing on the consequences of the discrepancy. In contrast, more European American definitions of conflict often focus largely on consequences, that is, the interference of incompatible beliefs or goals in individual activity.

Although the relational aspect of the African American conceptions of conflict seems similar to Asian concepts of disharmony, the approaches to conflict tied to these meanings are divergent. Unlike people in Asian American contexts, people in African American contexts may confront others about points of disagreement. However, the ensuing discourse is not intended to be a "rational" consideration of the issue with the goal of achieving "objectivity," as argument is constructed in many European American contexts. In African American cultural contexts, the participants in a conflict are often expected to formulate personal positions on an issue and present those positions as advocates. Emotional investment in the position is viewed as a measure of commitment rather than as an impediment to reasoning. Combining argumentation, emotion, and metaphor, African American approaches to conflict may be viewed as participation in a joint performance governed by its own cultural logic and rhythm. This style of conflict may reflect the cultural value placed on movement, expressive individualism, and affect in many African American contexts.

One goal of conflict in African American contexts is to work toward resolving the problem that initially caused the disagreement by representing personal views in an impassioned confrontation. However, unlike European American practices, resolution depends on the compelling presentation of arguments rather than attempts to appeal to some objective truth. By forcefully but credibly making a case for their own point of view, people engaged in African American contexts in conflict may persuade others of their position and thereby reestablish interpersonal harmony.

Researchers note that within some African American contexts, there is a distinct concern with expressive individualism and with the cultivation of spontaneity and unique self-expression in ways that can diverge from European American emphases on uniqueness. Although believing oneself to be distinct and better than one's peers is also common in many European American cultural contexts, directly showing off or calling attention to the self is often discouraged. By contrast, according to Kochman, in some African American cultural contexts behavior labeled as "stylin' out," "showboating," or "grandstanding" can be viewed positively.

As is true in many cultural contexts that emphasize interdependence, in many African American cultural contexts it is assumed that people cannot be separated from their positions, and disputes are cast as a contest between individuals rather than between opposing ideas. Once construed as a contest, Kochman argues, "attention is also paid to performance, for winning the contest requires that one outperform one's opponents: outthink, outtalk, and outstyle them. It means being concerned with art as well as argument." Kochman also notes a difference in ideas about entering a discussion or debate. Observing the differences between white and black gatherings, he notes that in the former the general rule seems to be that people speak in the order in which they are recognized. In black gatherings, he observes, the floor is often given to the person who feels his or her point is most pressing.

* * *

Jayne Seminare Docherty,[*] *Culture and Negotiation: Symmetrical Anthropology for Negotiators*
87 MARQ. L. REV. 711, 712-22 (2004)[**]

* * *

One commonly used heuristic device for thinking about culture is the iceberg. This model begins with the empirical observation that cultures differ in terms of normative behaviors and other traits, but assumes that these are like the tip of an iceberg. There is much more to culture under the surface of what we can readily observe. Above the surface we find behaviors,

---

[*] Jayne Seminare Docherty is Associate Professor of Conflict Studies, Eastern Mennonite University. Her article deals with ways to understand culture — one's own and others'.

artifacts and institutions. Just below the surface we find norms, beliefs, values and attitudes. A sensitive observer can "uncover" these and become more knowledgeable about a culture. The deepest level is all but invisible even to members of a cultural group. It contains the deepest assumptions about the world, the sense-making and meaning-making schemas and symbols, the beliefs about what is real in the world, and beliefs about how individuals experience the world. This is a useful model, but it is also misleading. It does not reflect the dynamic quality of cultures, which are far from frozen. It also implies that all of the individuals in a given iceberg (culture) share that culture evenly; this is never the case.

* * *

A more sophisticated approach to culture in negotiation involves identifying patterns or types of cultures by studying a large group of cultures. Instead of getting inside of a specific culture to understand it, this approach stands outside of cultures and looks for patterns or cultural styles. These are often presented as a list of dichotomous characteristics including: high context/low context; individualism/ collectivism; and egalitarian/hierarchical. A high-context culture often relies on indirect communication, because the participants are expected to understand the complex meaning of relatively small non-verbal gestures. A low-context culture will tend to rely on direct statements and formal, clear ratification of written negotiated agreements. Negotiators from individualist cultures may worry less about preserving relationships than negotiators from collectivist cultures. And, negotiators from egalitarian cultures are likely to be less concerned about issues of rank and privilege than negotiators from hierarchical cultures.

* * *

The goal in identifying types of cultures or developing cultural profiles is to alert negotiators to communication patterns and to provide cautionary advice about how to communicate in a particular cultural context or with someone from a particular culture. This way of thinking about culture is more useful for negotiators than lists of traits as long as they recognize the following: these dichotomies are actually continua; within cultures, changes in context (e.g., family versus business setting) will lead people to locate in different places along the continua; there are subcultural variations within any culture; and not all individuals carry their culture in exactly the same way.

* * *

It is critically important to remember that our own cultures are largely invisible to us; they are simply our "common sense" understandings of the world. Hence, "conflict is, at essence, the construction of a special type of reality. Most of the time we assume and take for granted that we share a single reality with others, but we do not." We see culture when we are forced to recognize that not everyone experiences and lives in the world the way we do. Perhaps we experience "language shock" when we recognize that someone may be speaking the same language, but we are not sure they live on the same planet we do. Or, we may encounter someone whose "moral order" — their "pattern of . . . compulsions and permissions to act in certain ways and [their] prohibitions against acting in other ways" — differs from our own. In negotiations, these moments of shock and surprise may occur around issues of risk because risk is very much a cultural construct. We may also experience surprise when people use the same language, even the same metaphors, but we discover that their shared language is actually covering over profound differences in their sense of reality. What *we* assume is negotiable may not be negotiable to another person and vice versa.

* * *

In France, there is a serious conflict over new government rules against wearing religious symbols in school. French officials have said this prohibits Muslim girls from wearing head coverings to school. Convening a negotiation in this case might be impossible because for many of the Muslim students this is a non-negotiable issue. Furthermore, the French officials may be reluctant to confer authority on religious leaders by engaging imams in a negotiation process. Each side brings a culture to this encounter that makes convening a negotiation difficult or perhaps impossible.

Culture frames our responses to conflict by giving us cognitive and affective frameworks for interpreting the behavior and motives of others and ourselves. Most negotiation models assume that "each individual human being pursues his or her personal values and self-interest, typically in the context of — and against others — rationally pursuing their own self-interest and their personal values." But this is not the only way to think about human beings and their motives. Some cultures may assume that human beings are inherently relational beings who seek to preserve their relationships even if it "costs" them something. Or a culture may assert that protecting traditions is the most important imperative for all members of the community.

When we encounter cultural differences about when and how to negotiate, we can focus on what the other person is doing "wrong" compared to us. This approach does, in fact, appear in many negotiation books and articles. If we look closely, we can see that the implicit, sometimes explicit, question is "how do we get the X (fill in the name of another culture of group) to negotiate 'properly'?" Most commonly, this appears in the form of a question about how we get these other people to negotiate "rationally," with no recognition that rationality is culturally constructed.

Or, instead of focusing on what is wrong with the other culture, we can become adept at a form of "symmetrical anthropology" that is "capable of confronting not beliefs that do not touch us directly — we are always critical enough of them — but the true knowledge to which we adhere totally. We can subject our own culture(s) to the same scrutiny we apply to the culture(s) of others. That means we will need to become critically aware of our own assumptions about negotiation. What does it mean to say "get beneath positions to interests?" Does everyone share the assumptions about human nature and social relationships on which this approach to finding a "win-win" solution rests?

V. TEACHING CULTURAL SKILLS TO NEGOTIATORS

So, how do negotiators learn to become "symmetrical anthropologists" in cross cultural settings? How do they learn to read the culture of their interlocutors and heighten their awareness of their own culture? First, they broaden their expectations about negotiation behavior. They do not always assume the other party is a cost-benefit calculator who is motivated only, or even primarily, by self-interest. They recognize that the reasons individuals choose one action over another are complex and that they are shaped by context. In a car dealership, I might be a rational actor trying to maximize my own benefit. But in a divorce, I might be operating with much more complicated motives and much different sets of moral imperatives and prohibitions.

* * *

One way into culture is through worldviews, or more accurately, through the worldviewing process that every human being engages in every day. . . . Our own worldviewing (and our own worldviews) are largely invisible to us unless we bump up against a worldview other than our own or we confront a new experience for which we do not have easy answers. Every individual and every society engages in worldviewing — which is not a conscious, rational, intellectual activity, but a largely unconscious process of ordering the world and giving it meaning. A useful way to think about and get hold of a worldview (our own or someone else's) is to think of people as answering the following five questions at an unconscious level as they move through their daily lives:

- What is real?

- How is the real organized?

- What is valuable about those things (or people or institutions or traditions, etc.) that are real?

- How do we know about what is real?

- How should I (or we) act (or not act)?

People are not able to answer these questions directly, but their answers "leak out" in their language, in their actions, and in their institutions — in their culture. So, if we hold these questions in mind while we are listening to a party in a conflict tell his story, we can learn to hear his worldview. From that we know what matters to him, what he thinks he can and cannot do, what he values, and what kinds of knowledge he will accept or reject. These are all factors that will motivate him in a conflict.

* * *

Metaphors are another window onto culture. "Metaphors link two concepts together by employing familiar entities or systems to give shape to unfamiliar entities or systems. By drawing an analogy between the (relatively) known and the (relatively) unknown, metaphors guide perception, action, and reasoning." It makes a difference whether we call the forest a farm or a wilderness. We will advocate for different policies and take different actions depending on which metaphor we validate. When someone uses a metaphor — particularly if it resonates with others or it brings a negative response from others — we can gently probe for more information. Metaphor interviewing — taking someone's own metaphor or a metaphor used by another party and asking the interviewee to expand on the metaphor — elicits stories that are rich in worldviewing information.

* * *

Social scripts are also a window into culture. A script is "a commonly assumed temporal ordering for some kind of event, for example, 'a meal in a restaurant', 'trip to the beach.'" Formal education is a widely shared life experience, but the script for "participating in a class" varies considerably depending on cultural context. As an undergraduate I enrolled in many small classes. The script for attending class involved rigorous preparation before class, vigorous discussion and debate during the class, and a sense of intellectual equality — ideas were judged on their merit, not on whether they came from the professor or the students. When I went to Scotland for graduate school, I discovered that the script for attending class involved sitting quietly and taking notes while the professor lectured. Years later, when teaching in South Carolina in a conflict resolution program, I created a script for attending class that required active participation in a wide variety of activities including discussions, role plays, listening to and responding to short lectures, group work, and brainstorming.

* * *

Every culture, and every individual, carries a script — or more likely a set of scripts — for negotiation. We may see one script applying to family negotiations and another script applying to business negotiations. Whatever script or scripts we have to work with creates a range of choices for our own actions and a set of expectations about the other party's behaviors. It is precisely when these scripts clash that we think there is a "cultural issue" or a "cultural problem" in a negotiation. The good thing about scripts is that they can be flexible. We can improvise new scripts, and in fact, we do that when we try to find ways to negotiate in cross-cultural settings. Or, at least we do that if we do not treat culture asymmetrically by assuming the real problem is to get the other person to take a "proper" role in our script.

* * *

John W. McDonald,* *An American's View of the U.S. Negotiating Style*

AM. DIPLOMACY (2001), http://www.americandiplomacy.org**

After reviewing my own experience of forty years as an American diplomat and international negotiator, I have developed my own personal definition of a U.S. negotiating style. This definition bears in mind that any style of negotiation is tempered and influenced by the personality and the ability of the individual negotiator, as well as the cultural, political, emotional, and physical situations surrounding the negotiations. In fact, the cases in this issue suggest strongly that many factors, in addition to style, are at work in shaping the process and outcome of international negotiations, including tactics strategy, the structure of the negotiations, and external influences, to name a few.

I believe the following characteristics, both positive and negative, taken collectively, define a U.S. negotiating style.

Impatient — We are the most impatient people in the world. This characteristic is carried over into our negotiating style to such an extent that the rest of the world recognizes this trait in our negotiators and takes advantage of it at every opportunity. Impatience is such an ingrained, subconscious tendency in most Americans that they don't even realize the rest of the world marches to the tune of a different drummer. Different perceptions time cause many misunderstandings during negotiations.

Arrogant — Most other peoples believe that we are the most arrogant, or certainly one of the most arrogant, nations in the world. Our superpower is certainly a part of this image. This power-based arrogance is often projected by our negotiators across the conference table at international gatherings. Often such arrogance is seen by others as our second nature. We seem to project the belief that we are superior to other peoples because we have led the world for fifty years and know that we are best in everything we do. Many Americans are actually surprised when they are accused by non Americans of possessing this characteristic and frequently take exception to this criticism, thereby making matters worse.

Listening — We are not good listeners. This goes hand in hand with impatience and arrogance. Because we have not developed good listening skills, which require patience, we are assumed to be superficial and uninterested in other points of view, and therefore arrogant.

---

* Ambassador McDonald retired from the U.S. Foreign Service in 1987 after 40 years as a diplomat. His article addresses common perceptions of Americans as negotiators. American Diplomacy is an online newsletter available at *www.americandiplomacy.org.*

** Copyright © 2001 American Diplomacy. Reprinted by permission.

Insular — Most Americans have limited experience with regard to other cultures. This shortcoming can often lead to mistakes, misunderstandings and subsequent embarrassment on the part of the Americans. Such restricted experience often leads to a feeling of insecurity on the part of the Americans and may result in their making a limited outreach towards other delegates. Rarely is this misinterpreted by others as shyness, but rather as a lack of interest. It may also be considered to be part of an American superiority complex.

Legalistic — The majority of American negotiators are lawyers. This means that they are intelligent, hardworking, adversarial, usually dedicated to the task at hand, and legalistic. Legalistic, in this context, means concerned with detail. We are less interested in general principles, or with the larger picture, and are more interested in the fine print of the agreement. It also means that when an agreement is reached, we consider it final. It is not subject to being reopened or renegotiated. Because our law schools teach students to go out and win, we are trained in the win-lose concept of negotiations: I win - you lose. International negotiations today are more and more frequently based on a consensus building approach or win-win philosophy.

Naive — Our insular attitude, and sometimes our appearance, can give the impression that we are naive, are easy marks for the skilled negotiator and are someone to be taken advantage of. This can actually happen to a newcomer to the international negotiating arena, but the impression is usually incorrect and not long lasting. In fact, the characteristics of naiveté can be turned around, to the advantage of the American negotiator.

Friendly — We are recognized as being friendly, out-going, and having a sense of humor. This trait is particularly important. Being friendly helps to build a sense of trust among negotiators. Having a sense of humor, at the right time, is essential because it can be used to break tension and often helps to move a difficult negotiating process along, towards a satisfactory conclusion.

Fair — We are perceived as believing in fair play and honesty. This characteristic is widely recognized throughout the international community, and respected.

Flexible — U.S. negotiators have more authority to make decisions during negotiations than most other delegations. This means that they can often make decisions on the spot, at the conference table. This flexibility is due to the fact that good negotiator is trusted by his headquarters. He has also built some negotiating flexibility into the U.S. position, before leaving for the conference. In addition, U.S. delegations are larger than most other delegations because they include subject matter experts, who often have the answers to substantive questions at their fingertips. This enables the United States to project a positive image and to adapt the U.S. position more quickly and more easily than other delegations in order to meet a new situation or a particular issue that has just arisen.

Risk Takers — More so than most, U.S. negotiators are risk takers. They are often prepared to put forward new and innovative ideas, suggestions for compromise, even specific language that can move the conference towards agreement. This is often done without prior approval from headquarters and represents the risk the head of delegation is prepared to take, in order to reach consensus. This trait is widely recognized and highly respected by other delegations.

Pragmatic — The U.S. point of view is usually a practical, pragmatic one. We are rarely interested in high-flown rhetoric, long, flowery speeches or a dogmatic, ideological point of view. We want to get on with discussing the substance of the issues on the agenda and try to reach some practical conclusion about the matter at hand.

Preparation — We are usually the best prepared delegation at the conference table. We go to extraordinary lengths, often starting many months in advance of a conference, to prepared [sic] position papers, briefing books, and background documentation. The U.S. delegation attempts to anticipate every issue that might arise during the negotiations and develop a response to that situation, ready to be used at the conference. All position papers prepared for intergovernmental negotiations are approved in advance by each agency in the executive branch that has an interest in that subject. This is time and effort well spent and is reflected repeatedly in the final positive results of the negotiations.

Cooperative — Americans are cooperative. They are aware of the importance of interagency coordination in the development of U.S. positions papers. At the conference itself they recognize the necessity for working and cooperating with other delegations, the conference secretariat, the press, nongovernmental organization representatives, and the private business sector. They also recognize the authority of the head of their delegation and acknowledge the importance of the delegation's need to speak with one voice on an issue.

I believe that a combination of these characteristics can be found in all of the American delegates who represent the United States Government at the one thousand annual, international, intergovernmental conferences the United States attends. There may be other traits which could be added to the list of attributes defining a U.S. negotiating style. It is clear, however, that the positive characteristics outweigh the negative ones. With awareness, training, skill, and study, the negative traits can be changed and corrected. When this is achieved, our negotiators will be more effective and be viewed by the rest of the world with even greater esteem and respect.

Jeswald W. Salacuse,[*] *Ten Ways that Culture Affects Negotiating Style: Some Survey Results*
14 NEGOT. J. 221, 222-28, 231-33, 236-38 (1998)[**]

* * *

Based on a review of the literature as well as interviews with practitioners, the author, in an earlier work identified ten factors in the negotiation process that seem to be influenced by a person's culture. Cultural responses to each of these negotiation factors appear to vary between two polar extremes. The ten negotiating factors and the range of possible cultural responses to each are illustrated in Figure 1. These factors (with their polar extremes) are:

1. negotiating goals (contract or relationship?);

2. attitudes to the negotiating process (win/win or win/lose?);

3. personal styles (formal or informal?);

4. styles of communication (direct or indirect?);

5. time sensitivity (high or low?);

6. emotionalism (high or low?);

7. agreement form (specific or general?);

8. agreement building process (bottom up or top down?);

9. negotiating team organization (one leader or consensus?); and

10. risk taking (high or low?).

* * *

In order to test this approach to understanding negotiating style, the author translated the matrix into a survey questionnaire and administered it to over 370 business executives, lawyers, and graduate students (many of whom had substantial work experience) from all continents at various sites in North America, Latin America, and Europe over a period of four years.

* * *

. . . Ultimately, the survey study considered responses of persons from twelve countries. The nationalities and number of respondents in each group were as follows: the United States (41); the United Kingdom (17);

---

[*] Jeswald W. Salacuse is Henry J. Braker Professor of Commercial Law at the Fletcher School, Tufts University. His article looks at culture in terms of national, professional, and gender differences among negotiators.

France (10); Germany (11); Spain (19); Mexico (12); Argentina (26); Brazil (9); Nigeria (15); India (9); China (11); and Japan (11).

Since professional or occupational background also constitutes a type of subculture that may influence negotiating style, the survey data also examined correlations between professional background and responses with regard to the ten negotiation factors. Here the study examined the completed questionnaires of all respondents except for nine which were either illegible or blank with respect to occupation. Thus 301 responses were examined with respect to occupation, and they were organized into eight occupational groupings. The groupings and the number of persons in each were as follows: law (103); management and marketing (59); engineering (31); the military (5); accounting and finance (21); diplomacy and public service [on the assumption that government employees share a common public sector culture] (14); teaching (21); and students (47). Responses were also tabulated with respect to gender.

In general, the survey revealed significant correlations between the respondents' assessment of certain traits of their negotiating styles on the one hand and their national cultures and professional backgrounds on the other. However, one should read the survey results with several caveats. First, the answers that the respondents gave reflected only how they saw themselves (or would like others to see them) rather than their negotiating styles and behavior in actual negotiations. One can only interpret the survey results as indicating a limited predisposition of individuals from particular cultures toward certain factors affecting the negotiation process.

Second, style in a given negotiation may be influenced by numerous factors besides culture, including personality, bureaucracy, business experience, and the nature of the transactions under negotiation. For example, an executive who is predisposed to approach a business negotiation as a problem-solving, integrative process may behave in a distributive, confrontational way when faced with a hostile counterpart at the negotiating table.

Third, all the respondents spoke English, completed the survey in English, had substantial international experience, and were participating in graduate university education or advanced executive seminars, also conducted in the English language. As a result, they may not be representative of most persons from their respective cultures. On the other hand, they are fairly representative of executives and officials who conduct international negotiations on behalf of organizations.

Fourth, the meaning of key terms in the survey — such as direct, indirect, risk, general, and specific — were not strictly defined but instead were interpreted by each respondent according to his or her own subjective view, a factor obviously influenced by culture.

Fifth, the size of the respondent group was limited; consequently, one should be cautious about drawing inferences from the survey that apply to whole cultures. Finally, although nationality and culture are not the same thing and several different cultures may sometimes be found in a single country; the questionnaire, which only asked the respondents to indicate their nationality, did not take account of this phenomenon.

Negotiating Goal: Contract or Relationship?

Different cultures may view the very purpose of a business negotiation differently. For many American executives, the goal of a negotiation, first and foremost, is to arrive at a signed contract between the parties. Americans consider a signed contract as a definitive set of rights and duties that strictly binds the two sides and determines their interaction thereafter.

Japanese, Chinese, and other cultural groups in Asia, it is said, often consider that the goal of a negotiation is not a signed contract, but the creation of a relationship between the two sides. Although the written contact describes the relationship, the essence of the deal is the relationship itself.

As a group, the respondents in this survey were fairly evenly divided on this question, with 54 percent viewing contract as a negotiating goal and 46 percent indicating that pursuing relationship was the goal. Similarly, while males had a slight preference for contract (57.3 percent) and females for relationship (52.5 percent), the difference was not significant, and certainly not as significant as the literature on gender might lead one to believe.

On the other hand, the survey results revealed significant differences both among cultures and professions on this question. Thus, with respect to national cultures, only 26 percent of the Spanish respondents claimed that their primary goal in a negotiation was a relationship compared to 66 percent of the Indians. On the other hand, the preference for a relationship was not as pronounced among the Chinese (54.5 percent) as one might have expected from the literature, and the Japanese appeared almost evenly divided on the question as did the Americans. Table I summarizes the survey results on this issue.

Table 1

Negotiating Goal: Contract or Relationship?

	Spain	France	Brazil	Japan	USA	Germany	U.K.	Nigeria	Argentina	China	Mexico	India
Contract (%):	74	70	67	55	54	54	47	47	46	45	42	33

An analysis of responses on the basis of occupational background also revealed significant variations. For example, while 71 percent of the lawyers favored contract as a negotiating goal, 61 percent of those with management or marketing experience preferred relationships. Table 2 summarizes the results.

Table 2

Occupations and Negotiating Goal: Contract or Relationship?

	Law	Military	Engineering	Diplomacy/ Public Sector	Student	Accounting/ Finance	Teacher	Management/ Marketing
Contract (%):	71	60	52	50	49	43	43	39

Although for the group as a whole, the responses by males and females did not reveal significant differences, one did find substantial variations between genders within certain cultures. Thus, whereas 66.7 percent of U.S. male respondents chose contract as a negotiating goal, 71.4 percent of the U.S. female respondents opted for relationship — a finding supported by American studies on the impact of gender on negotiation. On the other hand, 75 percent of French females and 66.7 percent of Spanish women chose contract — data suggesting that gender roles in negotiation may be more influenced by culture than biology

Negotiating Attitude: Win-Lose or Win-Win?

* * *

Among all respondents in the survey, approximately one-third claimed to see negotiations as win-lose, while two thirds saw it as win-win. Gender appeared to have no influence on responses, for the distribution among men and among women was essentially the same — one-third of the male respondents and one-third of the female respondents considered negotiation to be a win-lose process.

On the other hand, the survey revealed wide differences among the cultures represented in the survey on this question. Whereas 100 percent of the Japanese viewed negotiation as a win-win process, only 36.8 percent of the Spanish were so inclined. The Chinese and Indians, the other two Asian cultures represented in the survey, also claimed that negotiation for them was win-win, and the French, alone among Europeans, took a similarly pronounced position on the question. Table 3 summarizes the results.

Table 3

Negotiating Attitude: Win-Win or Win-Lose?

	Japan	China	Argentina	France	India	USA	U.K.	Mexico	Germany	Nigeria	Brazil	Spain
Win-Win (%):	100	82	81	80	78	71	59	50	55	47	44	37

An analysis of the responses by profession also found significant variations. Whereas only 14 percent of diplomats/public service personnel and 18 percent of management and marketing persons considered negotiations to be a win-lose process, 42 percent of the lawyers, 43 percent of the students, and 40 percent of the military held this view. Table 4 summarizes the results with respect to occupational background.

Table 4

Occupations and Negotiating Attitude: Win-Win or Win-Lose?

	Diplomacy/ Public Sector	Management/ Marketing	Accounting/ Finance	Teacher	Engineering	Student	Law	Military
Win-Win (%):	86	81	76	71	71	43	42	40

Although the responses of males and females as a whole tended to be similar, the survey revealed significant differences according to gender within specific cultures. Thus while only 20 percent of U.S. female respondents saw negotiation as a win-lose process, 50 percent of Spanish female respondents took this view.

* * *

Emotionalism: High or Low?

Accounts of negotiating behavior in other cultures almost always point to a particular group's tendency or lack thereof to display emotions. According to the stereotype, Latin Americans show their emotions at the negotiating table, while Japanese and many other Asians hide their feelings. Obviously, individual personality plays a role here. There are passive Latins and hot-headed Japanese. Nonetheless, various cultures have different rules as to the appropriateness and form of displaying emotions, and these rules are brought to the negotiating table as well.

Among all respondents, 65 percent claimed to tend toward high emotionalism while 35 percent indicated a tendency to low emotionalism. Roughly, the same distribution was to be found among male and female respondents. Professional groups revealed a similar distribution, except for teachers, 90 percent of whom saw themselves tending toward high emotionalism.

The various cultures surveyed indicated greater variations. The Latin Americans and the Spanish were the cultural groups that ranked themselves highest with respect to emotionalism in a clearly statistically significant fashion. Among Europeans, the Germans and English ranked as least emotional, while among Asians the Japanese held that position, but to a lesser degree than the two European groups. Table 9 summarizes the results with regard to emotionalism.

Table 9

Emotionalism: High or Low?

	Brazil	Argentina	Mexico	Spain	China	USA	Nigeria	France	India	Japan	U.K.	Germany
High (%):	89	85	83	79	73	74	60	60	56	55	47	36

Form of Agreement: General or Specific?

Cultural factors may also influence the form of the written agreement that parties try to make. Generally, Americans prefer detailed contracts that attempt to anticipate all possible circumstances and eventualities, no matter how unlikely. Why? Because the "deal" is the contract itself, and one must refer to the contract to handle new situations that may arise in the future. Other cultural groups, such as the Chinese, prefer a contract in the form of general principles rather than detailed rules. Why? Because, it is claimed, the essence of the deal is the relationship between the parties. If unexpected circumstances arise, the parties should look to their relationship, not the details of the contract, to solve the problem.

Among all respondents in the survey, 78 percent preferred specific agreements while only 22 percent preferred general agreements. Male and female participants responded in approximately the same proportions. The survey found that a majority of respondents in each cultural group preferred specific agreements over general agreements. This result may be attributable in part to the relatively large number of lawyers among the respondents, as well as to the fact that multinational corporate practice favors specific agreements and many of the respondents, regardless of nationality, had experience with such firms. The survey responses on this point may have been a case where professional or organizational culture dominated over national cultural traits.

On the other hand, the degree of intensity of responses on the question varied considerably among cultural groups. While only 11 percent of the British favored general agreements, 45.5 percent of the Japanese and of the Germans claimed to do so. Table 10 sets out the survey results with respect to agreement form.

Table 10

Agreement Form: General or Specific?

	Japan	Germany	India	France	China	Argentina	Brazil	USA	Nigeria	Mexico	Spain	U.K.
Specific (%):	46	45	44	30	27	27	22	22	20	17	16	11

Occupational groups demonstrated wider variations, a factor which supports the notion that professional culture may dominate national culture on this question. For example, while 100 percent of the respondents with military backgrounds preferred specific agreements, only 64 percent of management and marketing persons and of diplomats and civil servants had a similar inclination. Table 11 summarizes the data with respect to occupations on this question.

Table 11

Occupations and Agreement Form: General or Specific?

	Military	Student	Accounting/ Finance	Law	Engineering	Teacher	Diplomacy/ Public Sector	Management/ Marketing
Specific (%):	100	92	86	84	74	71	64	64

* * *

Risk Taking: High or Low?

Research indicates that certain cultures are more risk averse than others. In deal making, the culture of the negotiators can affect the willingness of one side to take "risks" in a negotiation — to divulge information, try new approaches, or tolerate uncertainties in a proposed course of action.

Among all respondents, approximately 70 percent claimed a tendency toward risk taking while only 30 percent characterized themselves as low risk takers. Here too, the distribution among men and women was similar and tended to follow that of all respondents as a group. However, among cultures, the responses to this question showed significant variations. The Japanese are said to be highly risk-averse in negotiations, and this tendency was affirmed by the survey which found Japanese respondents to be the most risk-averse of the twelve cultures. Americans in the survey, by comparison, considered themselves to be risk takers, but an even higher percentage of French, British, and Indians claimed to be risk takers. Table 16 summarizes the survey results with respect to risk.

Table 16

Risk Taking: High or Low?

	France	India	U.K.	China	USA	Nigeria	Argentina	Germany	Brazil	Mexico	Spain	Japan
High (%):	90	89	88	82	78	73	73	72	56	50	47	18

The survey also found significant differences among professional groups. For example, whereas 100 percent of the military respondents considered themselves to be high risk takers in negotiations, only 36 percent of the diplomats and civil servants characterized themselves similarly. Table 17 summarizes survey responses on the question of risk taking.

Table 17

Occupations and Risk Taking: High or Low?

	Military	Accounting/ Finance	Engineering	Management/ Marketing	Student	Teacher	Law	Diplomacy/ Private Sector
High (%):	100	81	77	75	72	67	66	36

Generally, males by a large majority within each cultural group considered themselves high risk takers, with the exception of the Japanese (12.5 percent), Spanish (39 percent) and Mexicans (44 percent). Female respondents who registered higher percentages of risk taking than males from the same culture were U.S. women (86 percent), Spanish women (67 percent) and Mexican women (67 percent).

Conclusion

The limited survey reported here confirms what numerous other studies, relying principally on a methodology based on observations and interviews, have also found: that culture can influence the way in which persons perceive and approach certain key elements in the negotiating process. A knowledge of these cultural differences may help negotiators to better understand and interpret their counterpart's negotiating behavior and to find ways to bridge gaps created by cultural differences.

Equally important, the survey suggests that professional and occupational culture may be as important as national culture in shaping a person's negotiating style and attitudes toward the negotiation process. If true, this finding has at least two important implications. First, both scholars and practitioners need to take into account professional culture, as well as national culture, in their studies and analysis of the impact of culture on negotiating behavior. Second, when faced with a cultural difference at the negotiating table, negotiators from different cultures but similar occupational or professional backgrounds might seek to rely on the elements of their professional culture in trying to bridge the cultural gap between them.

Carrie Menkel-Meadow,[*] Teaching about Gender and Negotiation: Sex, Truths, and Videotape
16 NEGOT. J. 347, 362-64 (2000)[**]

* * *

The effects of gender as a "variable" in negotiation practice have themselves been theorized, and students of negotiation should be aware of both the theory and the empirical tests of those theories. Sources of presumed gender differences in negotiation are now analyzed in at least four basic categories. The most conventional and standard explanation for gender differences in negotiation behavior is *socialization*: Men and women are simply socialized in different ways and to value things differently, which produces different expectations, behaviors, perceptions, outcomes, and levels of satisfaction in negotiation. So, as the standard story goes, men are more competitive, assertive, direct, have higher expectations, achieve more for themselves (and their clients in agent situations), but may also be more stubborn, less creative and problem solving and less focused on relationship while more focused on task and self. Women are accommodating, fear competition, have excessive concern for the other, but are better listeners, seek integrative and fair solutions and are most comfortable when negotiating with other women. Though the socialization theory is prevalent and basic (and actually "covers" for the even more basic — biological determinism — which no one seriously argues for in our field anymore), it actually has not been tested. If gender socialization is the crucial variable, then we should look at differences based on actual socialization practices. After a reading of portions of Carol Gilligan's *In a Different Voice* in my negotiation classes, I always ask students to reflect on and report on their own socialization experiences. What we learn is that, like most conceptions of gender as a category, gender socialization is itself a dynamic and changing process. Women have

* Carrie Menkel-Meadow is A.B. Chettle, Jr. Professor of Law, Dispute Resolution and Civil Procedure, Georgetown University Law Center. Her article discusses various theories of gender difference.

** Copyright © 2000 Negotiation Journal. Reprinted by permission of Blackwell Publishing, Inc. and the Program on Negotiation at Harvard Law School.

now participated in team sports, men have taken dance classes, both boys and girls have been reared by single mothers, with or without siblings, children have been reared by substitute parents when both parents are working, so that conventional and gendered patterns of socialization may be breaking down somewhat. To fully test socialization theories, negotiators would have to be sorted by different socialization practices (across genders) and then we could see if gender differences in negotiation still persisted.

A more common explanation for gender difference is that of *situational power* (or social structure or "place" as Deborah Kolb calls it). Since women have less access to power and the powerful are more efficacious in negotiation, then power, not gender, determines negotiation outcomes. To the extent that women achieve positions of power, they too will exhibit the characteristics of powerful and efficacious negotiators (whether from a competitive or an integrative perspective). Status or power, then, is the real variable. And, since gender is merely correlated with low power or low status, findings of gender differences are artifacts of a different variable relationship.

Others argue that gender and status operate in an *additive* model that can produce more complex dynamics in assessing negotiating behavior. Women in positions of high power will exhibit different negotiating behaviors and achieve different outcomes than men in high-power settings, and women and men with little power likewise behave differently. One study, for example, found that women in some lower-power settings are, in fact, the most stubborn and competitive of negotiators, particularly when confronted by negotiation partners who are high-power males. Low-power males were more inclined to withdraw. To this so-called "additive" model, I would add the notion of "gender plus" (or gender minus), that is, gender as a demographic characteristic that interacts not only with power and status, but also with other demographic characteristics of the negotiators. As dimensions separate from "power" crudely defined, race, ethnicity, class, occupation, familial status, and other sociological statuses will interact differentially with gender to produce different negotiation expectations, goals, and behaviors. Ian Ayres' studies of negotiations in the car purchasing arena, for example, found that black females were the most disadvantaged in the prices demanded of them. This *gender plus* theory, then, acknowledges that gender is a separate prism through which other demographic factors may be "refracted" — each negotiator brings an "intersectionality" of a variety of personal characteristics which may affect perceptions and expectations of the other and may constrain the negotiation repertoires available for any negotiator.

Finally, a more modern theory which seeks to beg the question of essentialist or innate differences suggests that perhaps others' stereotypic *expectations* of gender-conforming behaviors will produce such behaviors or at least influence behavioral choices and outcomes. This last theory is often the most sophisticated at recognizing that negotiations are interactive, and thus different behaviors and outcomes may depend on whether the negotiation pair is same sex or mixed sex and may depend on the size and uniformity of gender composition of each negotiation team. To the extent that how one behaves in a negotiation is interdependent with the other negotiators' behavior (whether in a dyadic or multiparty negotiation), "gendered" behavior will be socially constructed from the interaction of the expectations, choices, and behaviors that each party "enacts" in relation to the perceptions, behaviors, and assumed assumptions of the others. The "gendered" quality of negotiation behavior may shift from moment to moment as participants "enact" behaviors, confront them, respond to them, ignore them, shift them, or engage in any number of infinitely complicated maneuvers around or through gender stereotyping. Thus, negotiation behaviors may be a particularly rich, albeit difficult, environment in which to test the "post-modern" and ever-changing enactments of self and other through the "constructed" and interpretative moves of "the negotiation dance."

* * *

Leonard Greenhalgh & Roderick W. Gilkey,[*]
Our Game, Your Rules: Developing Effective Negotiating Approaches
in NOT AS FAR AS YOU THINK: THE REALITIES OF WORKING WOMEN 135, 137-42 (Lynda L. Moore ed., 1986)[**]

* * *

Backgrounds

One of the most important factors affecting your approach to negotiation is your time perspective. If you view a negotiation as a single event, you will tend to focus on your immediate gain and probably will not make sacrifices in order to preserve and improve your relationship with the other person. This is known as an *episodic orientation*: you see the negotiation as a single episode whereby the history and future of your relationship with the other person are largely irrelevant. The contrasting time perspective is known as a *continuous orientation*. With such a perspective, you pay attention to the long-term relationship between you and the other person. The present negotiation is one event in a stream of interactions. Therefore, the history and future of the relationship are important — perhaps more important than immediate gain. Thus it is natural to expect that differences in time perspective will lead to differences in negotiating behavior. An episodic orientation should be associated with a competitive approach ("I need to

---

[*] Leonard Greenhalgh is Professor at Tuck School of Business, Dartmouth College. Roderick W. Gilkey is Associate Professor of Psychiatry at Emory University School of Medicine. Their article discusses socially constructed masculine and feminine approaches to negotiation.

[**] Copyright © 1986. Reprinted with permission of Lynda L. Moore.

come out ahead in this deal, and it's going to be at your expense"), whereas a continuous orientation should be associated with a more cooperative approach ("Let's find a way to meet both our needs").

Negotiators' different personalities are likely to affect whether they tend to perceive a bargaining situation as more episodic or more continuous. In particular, such differences in time perspective seem to result from a more fundamental difference in men's and women's orientations toward interpersonal relationships. This difference has been noted in a number of studies that have concluded that women tend to be concerned with their need to get along with others, cooperativeness, and fairness to both parties; men, by contrast, are concerned with their own interests, competing, and avoiding being controlled or dominated by others.

One researcher attributes these contrasting orientations to differences in early developmental experiences. Females develop their sex-role identity from an interaction *with* the mother that emphasizes interdependence, whereas males establish their sex-role identity through separation and individuation *from* their mothers. These differing experiences produce fundamental sex differences later in life that lead women to define themselves *in relation* to others and men in *contrast* to others.

A related factor is the difference in the way boys and girls approach games. Boys are brought up to play competitive games, in which the objective is to beat the opponent. It is acceptable to gloat about victory and deride the loser. Girls play games that focus less on winning and losing. In fact, if their games are progressing in such a way that someone is going to feel bad, girls are likely to stop the game or change the rules: girls don't sacrifice relationships in order to win games.

Carol Gilligan, in her now-classic book *In a Different Voice*, examines the consequences of such basic differences when those individuals become older children. She notes that the greater emphasis on interdependence and mutuality in women's development accounts for the difference between the sexes in their perspective on moral dilemmas: women tend to emphasize their long-term responsibilities and men their immediate rights.

Gilligan cites as an example the case of two eleven-year-old children, a boy and a girl, who respond to questions about a moral dilemma. The boy, Jake, uses deductive logic to deal with what he sees as a conflict over rights and principles among three people, and he describes the solution that would quickly resolve the issues. The response of the girl, Amy, seems less clear and more equivocal. It is tempting to view Amy's response as being logically inferior to and less morally mature than Jake's, but on closer examination it becomes clear that she is viewing the conflict in very different terms. For her, the problem is one of trying to resolve a human-relations issue through ongoing personal communication. Jake, by contrast, views it as a conflict over rights that can be resolved through a morally informed legal system (the set of rules by which the "game" is played). Amy's response is actually based on a relatively sophisticated analysis of interpersonal dynamics. Her response calls for an ongoing series of interactions concerned more with preserving the relationships between conflicting parties than with deciding the parties' rights in the immediate situation.

Support for Gilligan's point of view can be found in studies that investigate the motivation of individuals to determine how they relate to other people. For example, some researchers have found a difference between boys and girls in the kinds of achievement toward which they aspire. Boys primarily strive to achieve success and therefore are more task-oriented; girls strive primarily to achieve praise and therefore are more relationship-oriented. Other studies have shown a tendency for males to be more competitive and women more cooperative in their interpersonal interactions. Still other studies have examined whether males and females want different things from their jobs. Those studies examine the view that women tend to be more concerned with interpersonal relationships in the work environment, whereas men appear to be more concerned with such factors as the opportunity for advancement (winning) and greater responsibility and influence (dominance).

One difficulty in conducting these studies is that women react to the experimental situation itself. A group of studies suggests that females appear to be more sensitive than males to a number of interpersonal cues that can influence their responses to the experiments. Such cues include the sex of the experimenter, whether communication is controlled or free in the experiment, and whether fairness issues are involved in the conflict. These factors tend to affect women more than men and may indeed explain why research findings have been inconsistent.

Thus some of the traits that tend to characterize women make it difficult for researchers to identify male-female differences accurately. Taken as a whole, the diverse studies of gender differences show some general tendencies but are inconsistent in their specific conclusions. The inconsistencies are understandable when one takes into account that the behavior of adult negotiators is a function not only of biological sex but also of the effects of developmental experiences. The different childhood socialization experiences of males and females can result in different sex-role orientations, ranging from strongly masculine to strongly feminine. A strongly masculine person is concerned with power and prefers to dominate others rather than be dominated by them; a strongly feminine person is less concerned with dominance and more concerned with nurturance. Masculinity-femininity, however, does not correspond exactly to biological sex. Some boys are raised to have predominantly feminine orientations, and some girls are raised to have predominantly masculine orientations. All people fall on a continuum between these two extremes. Because sex role is expected to have greater effect on negotiating behavior, sex role rather than biological sex is used in the research reported here and in the discussion that follows.

The Study

Having come this far in researching the literature, we were confident that there were masculine-feminine differences in negotiating approaches. As social scientists, however, we realized that our past observations could simply be hunches, that the studies we had read reported some inconsistencies, and that no one had yet directly studied masculine-feminine differences of adult negotiators. The burden of proof was on us to show that such differences really exist.

We decided to study masculine-feminine differences in a controlled, laboratory setting. Instead of observing everyday negotiations, we simulated the situations under controlled conditions and had young professionals role-play the negotiations. There was enough flexibility in the role instructions to allow masculine-feminine differences to emerge as expected. The use of a laboratory study had two advantages over observing naturally occurring negotiations: First, it allowed us to eliminate most extraneous factors that could contaminate the results; second, it would allow other researchers to replicate our study, thereby adding to its scientific value.

The results of the study proved consistent with what we had hypothesized. Several differences between masculine and feminine negotiators emerged and are summarized in table 9-1. The most basic finding was that feminine negotiators tend to visualize the long-term relationship between the people involved when they think about negotiations. Their masculine counterparts tend to visualize a sporting event in which the other person is an opponent who has to be beaten.

Table 9-1

Summary of the Different Tendencies of
Masculine and Feminine Negotiators

Masculine Tendencies	*Feminine Tendencies*
Visualize a one-shot deal	Visualize the present transaction as one event in a long-term relationship.
Seek a sports-type victory	Seek mutual gain
Emphasize rules-of-the-game, precedents, and power positions	Emphasize fairness
Explain logic of their position	Inquire about other's needs and make personal appeals
Conceal or misrepresent their own needs	Be up front about their own needs
Speak in a dominating or controlling manner	Use "powerless" speech
Be intransigent about their position, perhaps trying to conceal their rigid stance	Be willing to compromise
Interrupt and deceive the other party	Avoid tactics that might jeopardize the long-term relationship

Consistent with this basic difference in orientation, feminine negotiators were likely to be more empathic: that is, they had a natural tendency to try to see the situation from the other person's point of view. This put them in a position to meet mutual needs, which is an ideal outcome of negotiations when there is an ongoing relationship. Furthermore, in the absence of an urgency to "win," feminine negotiators sought fairness and were willing to compromise to achieve a fair outcome.

Finally, the feminine negotiators' concern with the long-term relationship seems to lead them to avoid using tactics that might jeopardize that relationship. Thus we found that feminine negotiators were less likely to deceive the other person. Ironically, the stereotypical view of women's and men's relative trustworthiness is just the opposite. When social psychologists ask people whether women or men are more likely to use underhanded tactics, most people choose women as the less trustworthy. Our research shows that, in fact, women are likely to be more trustworthy than men.

* * *

Melissa L. Nelken,[*] *The Myth of the Gladiator and Law Students' Negotiation Styles*
7 Cardozo J. Conflict Resol. 1, 4-12, 15-17 (2005)[**]

* * *

The negotiation styles included in the TKI [Thomas-Kilmann Conflict Mode Instrument] involve differing mixes of assertive and cooperative behavior.* * *

Competing: In many ways, students who are strong in competing fit the stereotype of lawyers generally. They are assertive, self-centered, focused, and determined to "win." The war and sports metaphors frequently used to describe legal negotiations fit competitors well because they tend to think of negotiations as a battle of wits or a game, and they are not afraid of rough play. These characteristics serve them well in situations in which the relationship between the parties is of little importance, such as a personal injury suit between strangers. As with the other categories though, the problems created by a competing style are often the mirror-image of its strengths: competitors may be so focused on the bottom line and so intent on "beating" the other party that they miss opportunities for joint gain. They tend to have a "fixed pie" mentality, seeking to claim the largest share of the pie rather than trying to enlarge the pie for everyone. When an ongoing relationship is important to the parties, a competing stance can lead to hard feelings and the sacrifice of long-term potential for short-term gain. Competitors may also be so goal-oriented that they miss some of the subtle, nonverbal signals that can provide valuable information to a negotiator.

Collaborating: A collaborating style combines a strong sense of one's own interests with a concern for the other party's interests. Collaborators want to get the best possible deal for everyone involved. They are prepared to spend time and energy getting everyone's interests on the table and exploring different solutions to see which combination of options works best. They are creative, open to new ideas, and not wedded to their own agenda. In many situations, a collaborative style focused on creating value can lead to novel solutions that leave both parties better off than they would otherwise be, such as settling costly and protracted contract litigation by renegotiating the terms of the parties' business relationship and starting over. In some situations, though, the search for the optimal result may entail more time and effort than the dispute or the relationship between the parties requires. Where time is truly of the essence, a collaborative style is more likely to exacerbate a problem than to resolve it since collaborators are seldom satisfied until they have examined a wide array of options.

---

[*] Melissa Nelken is Professor of Law, University of California, Hastings College of the Law, and Faculty Chair of its Center for Negotiation and Dispute Resolution. Her article discusses negotiation styles of law students.

[**] Copyright © 2005 Cardozo Journal of Conflict Resolution. Reprinted by permission.

Compromising: A compromising style, like a collaborative one, combines both assertiveness and cooperation. Compromisers see themselves as fair, reasonable, easy to deal with, and prepared to give and take in the course of negotiating. They are the classic "split the difference" closers in a negotiation, valuing efficiency and timesaving over detailed bargaining about every issue and every dollar at stake. The risk for the compromiser (and her clients) is that the emphasis on being, and being perceived as, fair and reasonable may lead to concessions on issues that are important or that could have been resolved more favorably if the negotiator had been less quick to compromise. Thus, the most common negative cited by students who are strong compromisers is that they get less for their clients than they could have.

Avoiding: Answers such as "I feel that differences are not always worth worrying about" on the TKI characterize an avoiding style. Avoiders are unlikely to fan the flames of a dispute and generally believe that many problems will go away if left alone. They "don't sweat the small stuff" and prefer not to get involved in protracted negotiations over details. Law students often react negatively to being categorized as conflict avoiders, perhaps because they believe that you have to love conflict to be a good lawyer. In fact, an avoiding style can be powerful, at least when you have some leverage in a negotiation. The other party has to figure out a way to engage the avoider, and this often takes the form of unilateral concessions to get the negotiation moving. However, when a negotiator lacks leverage, there is always the risk that the problem will only get worse the longer she ignores it; and avoiders sometimes end up making concessions simply in order to bring a negotiation to a close.

Accommodating: An accommodator is more focused on others' needs than on her own needs. Accommodators are good at building and maintaining relationships, and they are willing to do much of the work necessary to keep relationships going. Accommodators are skilled at reading inconspicuous signals that reveal other parties' interests and concerns. In a negotiation where the relationship between the parties is important, a lawyer with an accommodating style will be sensitive to the nuances of the other party's situation and will make sure that its needs are taken into account in developing proposals for resolving the conflict. Where the parties' needs are not overlapping, however, the accommodator's focus on what the other side wants may leave her client open to exploitation, especially at the hands of a negotiator who is focused only on her own client's goals. Over time, accommodators can become resentful when their concern for the other party is not reciprocated. Students with an accommodating style often expect to find the world of legal negotiation a rough place and they approach it with trepidation.

IS THERE A "BEST" LEGAL NEGOTIATION STYLE?

Obviously, none of the above styles is appropriate for all negotiations; there is no one best style. A competing style can turn a potential long-term business relationship into nothing more than a short-term deal that will never be renewed. An accommodating style, especially in a one-shot negotiation like a personal injury suit, might lead to an unfavorable settlement for the accommodating lawyer's client. A collaborative approach, when a quick resolution is important, may waste precious time, energy, and money. A skillful negotiator, then, always has to consider the subject matter of the negotiation, the situation of the parties, and the styles of the other negotiators in deciding what negotiation style is most likely to further her client's goals in a particular instance. Flexibility is the key to success in a variety of negotiations, and the TKI results can help beginning and experienced negotiators pinpoint the characteristics that they need to hone and develop in order to become more effective.

Fortunately, most people who take the TKI are not pure types: even those who score particularly high (ninetieth percentile and above) in one category have some traits that fall in the other styles. Many people tend to be evenly spread among the categories, with a high score (seventy-fifth percentile and above) in one or another style, and some have similar scores in all five categories. The usefulness of the TKI, and of the categories it defines, is not so much to pigeonhole people as to make them aware that they have *multiple* ways of approaching conflict situations, and that they can choose among them. A person's style is not uniform. It can and should be varied to adapt to the subject matter, the context, and the other parties in different negotiations.

Some people do have a well-defined preference for one style, as measured by a high score in one TKI category. They may find it difficult to shift gears and adopt another style. For such people, the TKI highlights a default style that is likely to control unless they devote considerable thought and planning to using other approaches. Even when they do so, a strong default style is likely to reassert itself if the going gets tough and the negotiator starts to feel insecure or thwarted in achieving her goals. When the default style is strongly competitive, accommodating or avoiding (the unmixed TKI styles), it can be particularly difficult to incorporate mitigating characteristics of the other styles in a stressful situation. Since negotiating skill requires comfort and facility in employing the full range of styles described by the TKI, one challenge in teaching negotiation is to help students explore the possibilities of their underdeveloped styles.

WHAT STYLES DO LAW STUDENTS USE?

The TKI was originally graphed in relation to the scores of a group of mid-level managers in the 1970s, and the chart in the published test booklet reflects the scores of that group. Since that time, the TKI has been widely used and its categories are the basis for the discussion of negotiation styles in a recent book by Professor G. Richard Shell of the Wharton School at the University of Pennsylvania. Professor Shell has also published his own TKI chart, based on the scores of 1682 participants in executive education programs. Both sources look at bargaining styles of business executives, rather than those of lawyers or law students. It has not been clear how relevant their results are for negotiators in another field.

Do different professions draw people with markedly different negotiation styles? Are law students, for example, more competitive on average than business people? Do male and female students have different styles? Does the experience in law school affect students' negotiation styles? Without a body of data that allows comparisons, it has not been possible to know how, if at all, law students differ from the other groups studied. To answer these and other questions, I have been collecting data from negotiation and mediation classes at Hastings for several years, and systematically over the last two academic years from Hastings, Boalt, and Stanford law schools . . . [for] a [total] sample of 754 students. . . .

* * *

. . . To look at characteristics of law school negotiation students as a group, it is easier to read a simple chart that shows the mean score in each category (Figure 2). The most salient finding here is that the negotiation students in the law school sample, like lawyers in the earlier Williams and Schneider studies, are more likely to seek compromise (the mean score is 7.5) than to use any other negotiating style (the remaining four categories are clustered around a score of +/- 5.5). Law students actually use a competing style marginally *less* frequently than any of the others.

* * *

MALE-FEMALE DIFFERENCES IN NEGOTIATION STYLE

When the negotiation student sample is broken down by gender (Figure 4), the main differences are in the competing and accommodating categories. There, the results are consistent with the social stereotype that women focus more on building and maintaining relationships than men do. The female mean for competing (self-assertion) is lower than that for males (5.1 versus 5.8) and the female mean for accommodating (concern for others) is higher than the male mean (5.8 versus 5.1). These differences in means are statistically significant (the p-value for competing is .02 and the p-value for accommodating is .0001).

* * *

Craver's 1990 study of the impact of gender on negotiation outcomes concluded that there were no statistically significant differences in negotiation *performance* between male and female law students, despite pervasive stereotypes that women are socialized to be less competitive than men and are thus less likely to prevail in the world of legal negotiations. Putting his results together with my data suggests that on average, there may be some significant differences in *style* between men and women. However, overall, these style differences will not lead to significant differences in negotiation results. While the female mean for competing in Figure 4 is lower than the male mean, the female means for both collaborating and compromising, involving a *combination* of assertiveness and concern for others, are higher (5.9 versus 5.6 on collaborating and 7.6 versus 7.3 on compromising), though the differences in these means are not statistically significant. Although a competitive approach will sometimes lead to the greatest gain in a negotiation, in other circumstances a focus on both parties' needs will actually yield better results. The emphasis in negotiation teaching over the last twenty years on integrative/problem-solving bargaining and communication skills has shown that there is much more to successful negotiating than single-minded value claiming. As more and more lawyers enter practice with training in negotiation, and the experience of attending law school with equal numbers of women and men, the stereotypes Professor Craver sought to dispel in his study may begin to wither away of their own accord.

* * *

The TKI was designed to be context-neutral in order to reduce social desirability bias, or the tendency to give what is thought to be the "right" answer about how to handle a particular conflict situation. I am not aware of any studies that explore what contexts test takers actually imagined in responding to the TKI, or how their responses varied with the imagined context. I usually ask students to choose the response that they feel is most characteristic of them, without regard to a particular context, since that response is likely to be the default mode used in a moment of stress or uncertainty.

What happens, though, to negotiation style when a person is immersed in a new culture, such as law school, where she is expected to adopt a new social role as a member of the legal profession? To examine the impact of law school on students' negotiation styles, I administered the TKI to a group of first-year students in the third week of the fall semester and also to a group of third-year students (30 percent of whom had taken a negotiation course) during the spring semester.

Based on these groups, it appears that the law school experience may change students' approaches to conflict, to some extent in ways that the stereotypes about lawyers would predict. First-year students were *less* competitive and *more* accommodating than third-year students (4.9 versus 5.4 for competing; 6.0 versus 5.4 for accommodating). These differences may be attributable to a number of factors, including experiencing the case method of instruction, with its reliance on litigated cases; the importance of competitively-earned grades for job placement; and the power of role expectations regarding "lawyer-like" conduct as "hard" rather than "soft."

Interestingly, the first-year students were also *less* collaborative than the third-years (5.5 versus 5.8). Although the difference between the two groups on collaborating (.3) was smaller than on either competing (.5) or accommodating (.6), it may suggest that winning is not the *only* goal emphasized during law school training. Perhaps with more emphasis in various courses on group projects (rather than on individual achievement), as well as more wide-spread teaching of specific problem-solving skills, law schools might increase the degree to which they train future lawyers to be truly effective negotiators.

CONCLUSION

The competitive/adversarial lawyer stereotype of popular culture is not borne out by studies of either lawyers or law students. The data discussed above on negotiation styles of law students demonstrate that they are most likely to use a compromising style in dealing with conflict. In this respect, they resemble the lawyers in earlier studies that showed the predominance of cooperative/problem-solving behavior in actual legal negotiations. Since the earlier studies also demonstrated that problem-solvers are far more likely than adversarial types to be perceived as effective negotiators, we have to wonder whether, in this age of ADR and the vanishing trial, we are successfully preparing our students for the real-life demands of law practice by maintaining our litigation-oriented curriculum.

One result of the law school experience appears to be an increase in students' competitive behavior and a decrease in their willingness to accommodate others in conflict situations. By focusing legal education almost exclusively on litigated cases, we succeed in teaching students the law, and how the common law develops; but these cases model only an adversarial approach to resolving disputes. Reliance on the case method risks failing to teach students a myriad of other skills, like communication, facilitation, and problem-solving skills, that are essential to the effective practice of law. Negotiation is at the heart of what lawyers do, whether they are transactional lawyers or litigators. Training effective negotiators and dispute resolvers requires building on the strengths our students bring in the arts of compromise, rather than continuing to exalt an adversary ideal that often fails to serve the interests of their future clients.

Figure 2. Mean TKI Scores of Law School
Negotiation Students (n=754)

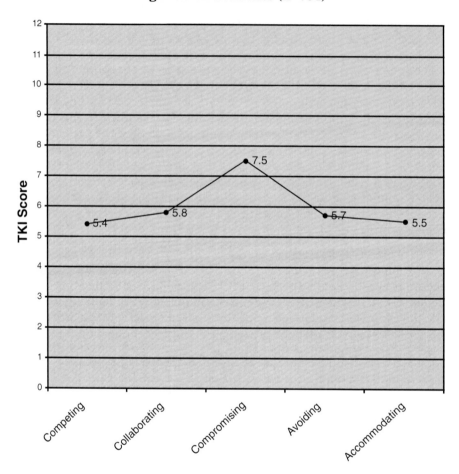

Negotiation Style

Figure 4. Mean TKI Scores of Male (n=291) and Female (n=463) Law School Negotiation Students

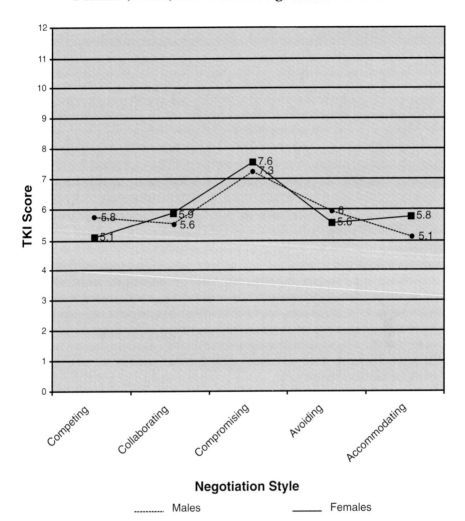

Negotiation Style

---------- Males _____ Females

Charles B. Craver & David W. Barnes,[*] *Gender, Risk Taking, and Negotiation Performance*
5 MICH. J. GENDER & L. 299, 309-21, 347 (1999)[**]

* * *

II. Real And Perceived Gender Differences

Many people believe that men and women behave in stereotypically different ways when they interact. Various traits are attributed to males, with other characteristics being attributed to females. While some of these gender-based differences may reflect real — i.e., empirically demonstrated — behavioral traits, others are merely perceived differences that have no scientifically established bases. Nonetheless, whether these differences are real or imagined, they may influence the way in which men and women interact when they negotiate, because the participants expect these factors to affect their dealings.

Men are thought to be rational and logical, while women are considered emotional and intuitive. Men are expected to emphasize objective fact, while women focus more on relationships. As a result, men are considered more likely to define issues in abstract terms and to resolve them through the application of reasoning based on justice and rights. Men are thought more likely to rely on theoretical legal principles than are women.

Men are expected to be dominant and authoritative, while women are viewed as passive and submissive. Research shows when the sexes interact, men tend to speak for longer periods of time and to interrupt more frequently than women. Men usually exert more control over the subjects being discussed; they employ more direct language, while women tend to exhibit tentative and deferential speech patterns. During conversations, women tend to adopt physical alignments that are cohesive and supportive of other group members, and they are inclined to make more eye contact than their male cohorts. The masculine tendency to dominate male-female interactions could provide men with an inherent advantage during negotiations, by enabling them to control the agenda and direct the substantive discussions. . . .

* * *

Male and female self-concepts are affected by the stereotypical ways in which others evaluate their performances. Men who perform masculine tasks no more proficiently than women tend to be given higher evaluations

---

[*] Charles B. Craver is the Freda H. Alverson Professor of Law, George Washington University School of Law and David W. Barnes is Distinguished Research Professor of Law, Seton Hall University. Their article summarizes the literature on gender differences in negotiation and presents the results of their research on the subject.

than the equally performing women. When men are successful, their performance tends to be attributed to intrinsic factors such as intelligence and hard work. When women are successful, however, their performance is likely to be attributed to extrinsic variables such as luck or the actions of others. This enhances male self-confidence by permitting them to receive credit for their accomplishments, and it undermines the confidence of successful women by attributing the reasons for their accomplishments to external considerations.

When men and women encounter competition, they may behave differently. Various scholars have suggested that "women are more likely [than men] to avoid competitive situations, less likely to acknowledge competitive wishes, and not likely to do as well [as men] in competition." Many women are apprehensive regarding the negative consequences they associate with competitive achievement. "Again and again women report the feeling that a successful woman alienates herself from both women and men." Gender-based differences in competitive behavior may be attributable to different acculturation processes for boys and girls. Parents have tended to be more protective of their daughters than of their sons. Boys have traditionally been exposed to competitive situations at an early age. They have been encouraged to participate earnestly in little league baseball, basketball, football, soccer, and other competitive athletic endeavors. These activities introduce boys to the "thrill of victory and the agony of defeat" during their formative years. "Traditional girls' games like jump rope and hopscotch are turn-taking games, where competition is indirect since one person's success does not necessarily signify another's failure." Even though it is true that federal and state civil rights enactments have required educational institutions to provide female students with athletic opportunities equal to those available to male students, the percentage of women participating in overtly competitive sports continues to lag behind the percentage of men. Furthermore, at the little league and junior high school levels, the principal objective of boys' sports is victory, while the primary goal of girls' sports is often the chance to participate. While directly competitive games teach boys how to resolve the disputes that inevitably arise during those encounters, girls rarely have the opportunity to learn such informal conflict resolution skills. By adulthood, men are much more likely to have become accustomed to the rigors of overt competition and familiar with the application of societal rules to resolve intercompetitor controversies.

Competitive games teach boys that it is more enjoyable to win than to lose. They usually receive parental — particularly paternal — approval when they prevail. They learn that a positive mental attitude is likely to enhance their probability of success. It is thus not surprising that college men generally exude greater confidence in problem-solving situations than college women. Men expect to achieve more advantageous results than women in similar situations. This factor suggests that college males would be more successful than college females in competitive interactions, such as those involving negotiation simulations. Those individuals who begin bargaining encounters with greater confidence and higher aspiration levels tend to attain more favorable agreements. They undermine opponent expectations and cause less confident adversaries to reassess their situations in ways that benefit the more confident participants.

In competitive settings, males are generally expected to behave more aggressively than females. Boys usually receive parental approval for aggressive and competitive tendencies, while girls are encouraged to be passive and dependent. During interpersonal transactions, men are more likely to employ "highly intense language" to persuade others, and they tend to be more effective when using this approach. Women, on the other hand, are more likely to use less intense language during persuasive encounters, and they are inclined to be more effective behaving in this manner. During conversations, men tend to downplay their doubts, while women are likely to downplay their certainty, enabling male speakers to exude a greater degree of confidence in what they are saying. Females tend to employ language containing more disclaimers (e.g., "you know," "it seems to me") than males, which may be perceived by their listeners as indications of reduced confidence levels. Women are more likely than men to use more indirect language during conversations, which may be perceived as a sign of uncertainty, while men tend to make more direct statements, which enhances the appearance of male assertiveness. When women eschew traditionally feminine conduct and behave in a stereotypically masculine fashion, they are usually not rewarded. They are instead criticized for deviating from conventional male-female role expectations.

The competitive performance double standard adversely affects female students in other aspects of their law school and professional experiences. In their study of law students at the University of Pennsylvania, Lani Guinier, Michelle Fine, and Jane Balin found that students who openly demonstrate their intellectual capabilities through regular class participation are characterized differently by other students based on their gender. While male participants are given negative labels, these tend to be of a gender-neutral variety (e.g., "asshole"). Their female cohorts, however, are often given labels that directly relate to their femininity (e.g., "man-hating lesbian" or "feminazi dyke"). Women who act forcefully or competitively in professional settings may encounter similar challenges to their femininity. This disparate treatment of women may reflect male discomfort with women who behave in an unexpectedly "masculine" manner. It also places women in an unfair position and may be deliberately designed by dominant males to undermine female confidence and diminish their law school and professional achievements.

Men in the Legal Negotiating class have occasionally indicated that they are particularly uncomfortable when female opponents obtain extremely beneficial results from them. A few have even indicated that they would prefer the consequences associated with nonsettlements to the possible embarrassment of "losing" to female opponents. While male students almost never apologize for their successes, a number of female class members indicate discomfort with their achievements and apologize to opponents whom they have out-performed. Even female students tend to be more critical of women who attain exceptional bargaining results than they are of male classmates who achieve equally advantageous negotiation terms.

When men negotiate, they generally endeavor to maximize their own side's return, while women are inclined to emphasize the maintenance of relationships. This phenomenon may explain why women tend to employ more accommodating strategies than men when resolving conflicts. One scholar writes, "Women seem more likely to prefer less adversarial methods of resolving disputes that do not harm the other side — relying on methods of problem solving and reconciliation rather than aggressive posturing. . . ." This more accommodating style may be especially beneficial when long-term relationships are involved, because of its capacity to enhance business relationships over prolonged periods.

When men and women negotiate, they often have different expectations regarding the results they would prefer to achieve. Men tend to expect "equitable" bargaining distributions, while women tend to believe in "equal" exchanges. These predispositional differences may induce female negotiators to accept equal negotiating results despite their possession of superior relative bargaining strength, while male bargainers seek equitable exchanges that reflect relevant power imbalances. Their egalitarian propensity could disadvantage women who hesitate to use favorable power imbalances to obtain more beneficial results for their sides. This factor would be particularly important with respect to bargaining interactions that are primarily distributional in nature, such as those involving monetary exchanges.

A recent study by Professor Ayres has indicated that car dealers tend to treat male and female, and Caucasian-American and African-American, customers differently when they negotiate car prices. Salespeople give male buyers more favorable opening offers and more generous final offers than female customers under identical circumstances, and they favor Caucasian-American buyers over African-American customers. Final offers given to African-American females averaged almost $900 more in dealer profit than those given to Caucasian-American males. These differences may reflect opportunistic car salesperson behavior designed to take advantage of what are stereotypically perceived to be less proficient and less empowered female/minority bargainers, or they may reflect salesperson fears of being out-negotiated by female or minority customers.

Empirical evidence indicates that women are not as effective when employing deceptive tactics as their male cohorts. Studies have shown that men are more comfortable in situations in which they are expected to dissemble, and they find it easier to behave in a Machiavellian manner. Women are inclined to be more trusting than men, and they tend to be less forgiving of deceitful behavior than their male cohorts. These factors should further benefit male negotiators, because individuals involved in legal negotiations are usually endeavoring to mislead their opponents.

On the one hand the negotiator must be fair and truthful; on the other he must mislead his opponent. Like the poker player, a negotiator hopes that his opponent will overestimate the value of his hand. Like the poker player, in a variety of ways he must facilitate his opponent's inaccurate assessment. The critical difference between those who are successful negotiators and those who are not lies in this capacity both to mislead and not to be misled.

Despite the various factors that would support the theory that more competitive male negotiators should achieve more beneficial results than female negotiators, empirical studies involving competitive interactions do not consistently substantiate this supposition. Psychologists attempting to measure male-female differences during competitive encounters have most frequently employed variations on the "Prisoner's Dilemma" exercise. The Prisoner's Dilemma archetype entails two criminal suspects who are caught and separately interrogated by the police, who lack clear evidence of their guilt. If one confesses, he will receive a light sentence, while his partner will be given a lengthy term of imprisonment. If both confess, they each receive intermediate terms, while if neither confesses, they both receive lighter terms.

If the stereotypical belief that men are more competitive than women is correct, one might reasonably expect men to behave more competitively when they participate in the Prisoner's Dilemma game. Men would be more likely to establish higher aspiration levels and would endeavor to take advantage of the perceived feminine tendency to be more accommodating. Various Prisoner's Dilemma studies have, however, discerned few or no gender differences. In one compilation of numerous Prisoner's Dilemma studies, many of the cited studies found no statistically significant gender differences with respect to competitive tendencies; of those experiments that did discern different behavior, some found males to be more competitive, and some found females to be more competitive. Almost identical findings were obtained with respect to cooperative behavior. Most studies discovered no difference based upon participant gender, while others obtained mixed results.

Various factors might explain why the anticipated gender differences did not materialize. In their study, Grant and Sermat found that women could be both more cooperative and more competitive, without being submissive. Furthermore, when men and women interact in competitive environments, men occasionally make the mistake of assuming that the women will not be as competitive, and these males behave less competitively. Men who modify their conduct based on this stereotype merely provide the female participants with an inherent advantage. In addition, women who encounter men in competitive environments often work more diligently to achieve optimal results. "It is as if the men [are] 'brought down' by the women and the women [are] 'brought up' by the men."

Other important gender differences occur when men and women interact in competitive settings. Although women have been found to employ "less powerful language when they are in less powerful roles," they use equally forceful language when they occupy positions of equality with men. During most of the Prisoner's Dilemma studies, the male and female participants were placed in positions of relative equality.

Another factor that may explain the lack of gender differences is the impact of educational attainment. . . . Highly educated professionals exhibit a similar trend, with women adopting more masculine styles of communication. These findings would suggest that if professionals are trained in mediation or negotiation skills, gender-based communication differences would be minimized. This would not, however, guarantee that male and female subjects would be viewed identically even when they behaved similarly. Male-female stereotypes could still cause some observers to perceive women participants as less controlling and less influential than male participants, even in circumstances in which the women were objectively exhibiting dominant behavior.

One might reasonably expect gender-based communication stereotypes to place women at a disadvantage when facing legal negotiation exercises in the classroom. They would be likely to be perceived as less dominant and less forceful, and they would be expected to be less logical and more emotional. Nonetheless, two significant factors counterbalance these stereotypes. First, the advanced education possessed by law students and the specific training received in a legal negotiation course would minimize gender-based communication differentials. Second, the female negotiators may benefit from the established fact that women are typically more sensitive to nonverbal messages than their male cohorts. Since a significant amount of critical communication during interpersonal transactions is nonverbal, the enhanced ability of female negotiators to decode such signals could offset any disadvantage associated with latent stereotyping.

* * *

Read together, our findings suggest that while women and men may not perform identically in negotiation settings, there is no factual basis for assuming that women are weaker or less capable negotiators. Our results directly challenge beliefs about women suggesting that female negotiators are likely to perform less proficiently than their male peers. These stereotypical perceptions have undoubtedly disadvantaged women in numerous academic and professional settings, including those seeking entry level associate positions and female associates seeking entrance to firm partnerships. We hope that legal professionals who hold gender-based beliefs such as those we have discussed will reevaluate their expectations in a manner that will diminish — if not entirely eliminate — subtle biases against women attorneys.

Sandra R. Farber & Monica Rickenberg,[*] *Under-Confident Women and Over-Confident Men: Gender and Sense of Competence in a Simulated Negotiation*
11 YALE J.L. & FEMINISM 271, 291-93 (1999)[**]

* * *

We asked students to rate themselves on eight abilities.[3] Overall women rated their abilities lower than did men. Of the eight individual abilities, the largest differences were in men's and women's ratings of their ability to work with numbers and to bluff.

Using the Bem Sex Role Inventory as a guideline we grouped the ability items into "masculine" and "feminine" composites.[70] We found that men rated themselves higher on the "masculine" abilities than women. We found no gender difference in students' ratings of their "feminine" abilities. This finding is consistent with research indicating that women's confidence has lagged behind men's in traditionally masculine areas but was equivalent in traditionally feminine domains.

* * *

The gender gap in students' perceptions of their competence was not borne out by any corresponding difference in their achievements. Women and men achieved comparable outcomes in the negotiation; we found no significant gender differences in the raw or normalized outcome data. This result was consistent among students in the Workways sections and the others, and among students assigned to represent the homeowner and the contractor. There were no gender differences in the settling points that students constructed. Also, there was no relationship between the outcomes that students achieved and their satisfaction with either their overall performance in the negotiation or with the outcomes.

In juxtaposing these actual outcomes with the gender gap in students' assessments of abilities, our data do not enable us to determine whether men overestimated their competence and performance, women underestimated their competence and performance, or both. A lack of realism in either direction poses problems. Those who approach the task with an excess of confidence may happily settle on an initially appealing plan with-

---

[*] Sandra Farber was an instructor in the Lawyering Program at NYU School of Law when this article was written. Monica Rickenberg, Esq. is the Restorative Justice Coordinator at the Westchester Mediation Center of CLUSTER, Inc. in Yonkers, NY.

[**] Copyright © 1999 Yale J.L. & Feminism. Reprinted by permission.

[3] (1) to listen to and pick up on others' concerns; (2) to work with numbers; (3) to present the law effectively; (4) to bluff; (5) to argue persuasively; (6) to develop rapport with colleagues; (7) to think on your feet; (8) to present a compelling story. [Editor's note.]

[70] "We calculated the 'masculine' composite as an average of the following abilities: working with numbers, bluffing, and thinking on one's feet. What we termed the 'feminine' composite was an average of the abilities to listen to others' concerns and to develop rapport. Our identification of certain abilities as stereotypically 'masculine' and others as stereotypically 'feminine' is in accord with research on gender stereotypes." [authors' note]

out considering a full range of options and therefore fail to choose the most advantageous route, or they may set their sights unrealistically high and therefore be unable to reach an agreement. On the other hand, those who have an unjustifiably low view of their competence might set unnecessarily low goals, be too quick to make concessions, or unwittingly communicate their lack of confidence to clients or opponents.

* * *

Laura J. Kray, Leigh Thompson & Adam Galinksy,[*]
Battle of the Sexes: Gender Stereotype Confirmation and Reactance in Negotiation
80 J. Pers. & Soc. Psychol. 942, 943-46, 948-50 (2001)[**]

* * *

Gender Stereotype Confirmation in Negotiation

Raiffa identified the following traits as characterizing effective negotiators: assertive, rational, decisive, constructive, and intelligent. In contrast, ineffective negotiators are regarded to be weak, emotional, irrational, and too conciliatory. Many of the traits that characterize effective negotiators are perceived to be masculine in nature, and many of the traits of ineffective negotiators are perceived to be feminine.

We hypothesize that men and women perceive a correlation, or mapping, between negotiator stereotypes and classic gender stereotypes. Evidence that modern sexism is subtle and covert leads us to believe that this mapping process is not necessarily explicit, but rather implicit. Further, this mapping process serves to generate a causal mental model in terms of how gender affects negotiation performance. The hypothesized process is similar to what Hamilton and Rose demonstrated with illusory correlation. In these studies, they observed a cognitive bias in how people process stereotype-consistent and inconsistent traits regarding occupations. In fact, the perceived correlation between traits and occupations is more congruent with existing stereotypic beliefs than is the actual correlation.

To determine the effect of stereotypes on the ability of men and women to claim resources, the interpersonal nature of negotiation requires that we consider the effect of stereotype activation for each gender separately. With this in mind, a key characteristic of mixed gender negotiations is the recog-

---

[*] Laura J. Kray is Associate Professor, Haas School of Business, University of California Berkeley. Leigh Thompson is the J. Jay Gerber Distinguished Professor of Dispute Resolution & Organizations, Kellogg School of Management, Northwestern University. Adam Galinksy is Associate Professor of Management & Organizations, Kellogg School of Management, Northwestern University. This article explores the impact of stereotype threat and stereotype reactance on mixed-gender negotiations.

nition that the negative gender stereotype vis-á-vis women in negotiation
has a complementary component: Men enjoy what we call a *positive stereotype advantage* in the negotiation domain. Below we elaborate on our
hypotheses regarding stereotype activation for each gender in negotiations.

The Effect of Stereotype Activation on Women

In a recent series of investigations, Steele tested a theory of stereotype
threat. According to Steele, *stereotype threat* is concern and anxiety over confirming, as self-characteristic, a negative stereotype about one's group. In
fact, the mere knowledge that a negative stereotype exists about a social
group (such as intellectual ability for African American individuals or math
performance for women) can negatively affect the performance of members
of those groups on stereotype-relevant tasks. At a cognitive level, stereotypical attributes are connected to a person's behavioral repertoire, which
is why the mere mention of a stereotype can lead to the enactment of stereotype-consistent behaviors. Further, it is not necessary that the person
believe the stereotype for their behavior to be negatively affected. In fact the
most advanced members of groups (e.g., female math majors, African Americans at elite schools) tend to be the most adversely affected in their performances by stereotype threat. Concern over confirming the stereotype
produces anxiety and reduces performance, and, thus, the person unwittingly confirms the stereotype.

We predicted that when women are made implicitly aware of traditional
gender stereotypes, they behave in ways to confirm the female stereotype
during a negotiation. We expect that women are reminded of gender stereotypes and experience a heightened concern for confirming the stereotype
when they highly identify with a particular domain and perceive a task as
diagnostic of their ability in this domain. It is under these conditions that
women are most susceptible to stereotype threat. Simply, we expected that,
by being primed about the negative gender stereotype, women may suffer
from negative arousal and fear of confirming the stereotype, which hinders their performance at the negotiation task. A decrease in performance
is expected to occur when the relationship between gender and negotiation
success has been subtly primed because a woman's cognitive-behavioral
defense systems have not been adequately summoned to react against it,
and instead, ineffective behaviors are primed that do not serve her well at
the bargaining table.

The Effect of Stereotype Activation on Men

We expect a negative female response to a gender stereotype prime to be
complemented with men confirming the male stereotype. Just as negative
stereotypes can impair performance, stereotypes can increase performance.
For instance, Spencer, Steele, and Quinn recently examined the effect of a
pervasive stereotype — that women are worse than men at solving difficult
math problems — on math performance. Men outperformed women only
when they were told that gender differences had been shown to exist (with

no mention of gender stereotypes). Moreover, men who were told that gender differences exist performed better than men who were told no gender differences exist. The results of this experiment suggest that positive stereotypes can boost performance.

Along similar lines, Stone, Lynch, Sjomeling, and Darley found that performance can be influenced by framing a task as relevant to either a positive or a negative stereotype about one's social group. Caucasians are presumed to be superior to African Americans on intellectual tasks, but inferior on athletic tasks. Stone et al. framed performance on a golf task to be dependent on either intellectual attributes or on athletic attributes. When framed as an intellectual task, Caucasians outperformed African Americans. When framed as an athletic task, African Americans outperformed Caucasians. Like men in the Spencer et al. experiment, positive stereotypes can have a facilitative effect on performance.

Following this logic, we expected that when a man is primed with information that the stereotype for his gender can be an advantage in an important situation, this may lead him to perform better than he otherwise would. Stereotyping has been linked to power, such that high-power individuals are more likely to hold stereotyped views of low-power individuals than vice versa. Building on this finding, we expected men to perceive greater power in negotiations when a gender stereotype has been primed than when it has not. We expected that men are aware of the same gender stereotypes as women, and this awareness is heightened when a task is perceived as diagnostic of ability. When reminded of the diagnosticity of a negotiation, that it reveals inherent ability differences, men are expected to experience a boost in their perceived ability to succeed. Armed with this surplus of confidence, men should be more capable of asserting their power in the negotiation, and we expected that this would ultimately serve men's interests in terms of bargaining effectiveness.

* * *

The purpose of this experiment was to examine stereotype threat processes when men and women negotiate with each other. To test Steele's theory in the negotiation context, we engaged participants who highly identified with the domain: students enrolled in a highly competitive MBA program at a top business school in which the negotiations course was the most popular elective in the school. On the basis of Steele's theory of stereotype threat, we expected a gender difference in negotiation performance to emerge only under threatening conditions — when the negotiation was perceived as highly diagnostic of ability and gender stereotypes were linked to negotiation success. Consistent with this hypothesis, men and women did not differ when the negotiation was billed as merely a learning tool that was not diagnostic of ability, but significant differences between the sexes did emerge when the negotiation was perceived to reflect ability and future success.

To examine the underlying processes leading to this performance differential, we asked participants to indicate their performance expectations after being exposed to the diagnosticity manipulation, but before beginning the negotiation. As expected, the mere mention of the diagnosticity of the negotiation affected how well men and women thought they would do relative to one another. In other words, women in the diagnostic condition thought they would do worse than men would. In contrast, there was a trend for men to expect to do even better under diagnostic conditions than nondiagnostic conditions. This pattern also emerged on the extremity of the first offers that the negotiators made. Extremity of first offers is often predictive of actual outcomes in distributive negotiations and has been linked to performance expectations. Expecting to get less (or more) of the pie can lead to less (or more) extreme first offers and ultimately to worse (or better) outcomes. Merely mentioning that a task with gender-linked expectations was diagnostic of ability, without mentioning social categories or even stereotypical traits, affected both expectations for performance and actual negotiation outcomes.

* * *

Stereotype Reactance

Psychological reactance theory states that when people perceive a threat to their freedom, they react by asserting their freedom more forcefully than they would otherwise. In one demonstration of psychological reactance theory, people in a parking lot who were getting into their cars were slower when they knew someone was waiting for their parking spot than when no one was waiting; this effect was magnified when the person waiting honked to speed them along.

Stereotype reactance in women. We theorized that psychological reactance also operates when people perceive limitations to their ability to perform. Negative stereotypes held by others are one obvious limitation that could affect performance for members of social groups (e.g., women and African Americans). We expected reactance to occur when an individual was explicitly told that his or her social category was a liability for an important task, such as a negotiation. We hypothesized that, when women are explicitly threatened (i.e., made aware of the correspondence between the stereotypes of women and ineffective negotiators), they react by engaging in behaviors that are counter to those prescribed by the stereotype. We call this *stereotype reactance* and distinguish it from stereotype confirmation.

The key difference in terms of whether women are expected to confirm or react against a gender stereotype in negotiations is whether the stereotype is activated implicitly (below a perceivers' conscious awareness) or explicitly (obvious to the perceiver). The implicit priming of knowledge structures produces assimilation effects, or judgments and behaviors that become more consistent with the activated knowledge structure than they would otherwise. For example, people primed with the stereotype of "hooligans" subsequently performed less well on a general knowledge scale compared with when they were primed with the stereotype of university professors. Assimilation effects depend on participants not noticing a connection between the priming task and the judgment task.

Conversely, explicit priming, which occurs when a person's attention is blatantly drawn to the activated knowledge structure, produces a contrast effect (or reactance), whereby judgments and behaviors become less consistent with the activated knowledge structure than they would otherwise. When people are blatantly and explicitly primed, they perceive the primed construct to be a biasing influence, and to correct for this undesired influence on thought and deed, they attempt to overcompensate for the biasing influence. For example, if a person reads a description about a prototypical elderly person, then the perceiver is later likely to walk more quickly down a corridor, a behavior in contrast to the elderly stereotype, than if they had not read the first description, presumably because people attempt to counter the influence of the prime by dissociating their judgments and behavior from the implications of the activated knowledge structure. However, if the elderly stereotype were more subtly primed, we would expect an assimilation effect, or behaviors more consistent with the stereotype.

Positive-stereotype disadvantage in men. When a person is explicitly told that his or her social category provides an advantage, such as the case with men and negotiation ability, we expect that this explicit recognition of their superiority can have a detrimental effect on that person's performance — resulting in a disadvantage. This hypothesis grows out of an abundant literature on "choking under pressure" that suggests that having "the home team advantage" can actually be a disadvantage in competitive situations that are relevant to one's self-identity.

Similarly, when men fear that their unexceptional math ability will be exposed in a test designed to identify the highest achievers, their performance suffers. Thus, the positive stereotype becomes a burden, increasing anxiety and decreasing performance. Each of these psychological responses leads us to predict a seemingly ironic outcome for men — a performance decrement — when they are explicitly told that their gender grants them a certain advantage in mixed-gender negotiations.

Our predictions represent a significant departure from Steele's theory of stereotype vulnerability. When gender stereotypes are subtly and implicitly invoked, we expect stereotype confirmation, but our model predicts the opposite when it comes to explicit primes. When performance is perceived by women to be highly relevant to their identity, and they are explicitly told that a social category to which they belong will hinder their ability to succeed, we expect them to dissociate from the traditional female stereotype and engage in behaviors that are less consistent with the stereotype relative to when the stereotype is implicitly activated. Likewise, men's concern for disconfirming their advantageous position may be heightened under these circumstances, leading to inferior performance.

* * *

This experiment demonstrates that the mode by which a stereotype is activated impacts the effect it has on individuals. It is under conditions that would seem to be the most disadvantageous — when women are explicitly reminded of negative gender expectations and stereotypes in a situation that is challenging and competitive — that outcomes lean toward women relative to their male negotiating partners. Men, on the other hand, were less successful in negotiating when their gender advantage was made explicit.

The effect of the mode of stereotype activation was evident from the moment that negotiators made their opening offers to one another. Previous research has established that the extremity of opening offers is highly related to ultimate negotiation outcomes, and this study replicates this effect. Because opening offers generally mark the beginning of two negotiators' interactions together, it seems likely that these opening offers were almost entirely determined by each negotiator's level of mental preparedness. When negative gender stereotypes were explicitly endorsed, women entered the negotiation more aggressively than when the stereotype was implicitly endorsed — and the path analysis we conducted suggests that this level of assertiveness appears to have largely determined the agreement ultimately reached between male and female negotiators.

Within the context of negotiations, the balance of power in terms of negotiated outcomes appears to be in favor of men when gender stereotypes are subtly activated without any mention of gender. However, when these same stereotypes are activated and explicitly endorsed as pertaining to gender, negotiation agreements tended to favor the female negotiator. This finding is consistent with our argument that the implicit activation of stereotypes leads to assimilation effects, or judgments and behaviors that are more consistent with the activated knowledge structure than they would otherwise be, whereas the explicit activation of stereotypes produces a contrast effect (or reactance), whereby judgments and behaviors are less consistent with the activated knowledge structure than they would otherwise be.

* * *

Laura J. Kray, Jochen Reb, Adam D. Galinsky & Leigh Thompson,[*] *Stereotype Reactance at the Bargaining Table*

30 PERS. & SOC. PSYCHOL. BULL. 399, 400-01, 408-09 (2004)[**]

* * *

Stereotype threat describes the concern a person feels about confirming, as self-characteristic, a negative stereotype about one's group. This threat becomes reality because concern over confirming the stereotype produces anxiety, lowers expectations, and reduces performance; thus, it unwittingly confirms the stereotype. Kray and colleagues found that simply describing a negotiation as diagnostic of ability was enough to produce a male advantage at the bargaining table.

Because many of the traits associated with effective negotiators are stereotypically masculine in nature, subtly activating the masculine stereotype tends to lead to outcomes that confirm the stereotype of male dominance at the bargaining table; that is, when people are told that effective negotiators are rational, assertive, unemotional, and have a high regard for their own interests (stereotypically masculine traits), male negotiators have an advantage over female negotiators. Despite the fact that gender was not mentioned in connection with these traits, the resulting difference in aspirations, opening offers, and profits across gender was significant.

The male advantage can be reversed when men and women are told that stereotypically feminine traits are important determinants of negotiation success. Proclaiming that effective negotiators "express their thoughts verbally, have good listening skills, and possess insight into the other negotiator's feelings" leads to a female advantage at the bargaining table. More specifically, Kray, Galinsky, and Thompson found that subtly linking these stereotypically feminine traits with effective negotiating led women to have higher aspirations, make more aggressive opening offers, and negotiate more profitable agreements for themselves than did men.

These findings suggest that stereotype threat processes apply to both men and women in negotiations; implicitly activating negative stereotypes about one's group leads to decrements in performance for the stereotyped

---

* Laura J. Kray is Associate Professor, Haas School of Business, University of California Berkeley. Jochen Reb is Assistant Professor of Organizational Behavior, Singapore Management University. Adam D. Galinsky is Associate Professor of Management & Organizations, Kellogg School of Management, Northwestern University. Leigh Thompson is Jay Gerber Distinguished Professor of Dispute Resolution & Organizations, Kellogg School of Management, Northwestern University. Their article discusses how explicit stereotype activation affects both men and women in negotiations.

group. In general, stereotype threat appears not to be limited to traditionally disadvantaged groups; when traits that are stereotypically connected to a target's social category are linked to negative performance expectations in a domain, the target will tend to feel stereotype threat and confirm the stereotype. The above pattern is consistent with assimilation effects, whereby the implicit and subtle activation of a stereotype tends to lead to behaviors that are consistent with the stereotype. These findings suggest that the linkage between stereotype activation and performance depends on the content of the activated stereotype, that is, whether the activated traits suggest a masculine or feminine advantage.

But stereotype activation does not always lead to the assimilation effects characteristic of stereotype threat. Kray et al. also demonstrated that explicitly and blatantly acknowledging that the association between stereotypically masculine traits and effective negotiating is linked to gender differences can ironically produce a female advantage at the bargaining table in mixed-gender dyads. Kray et al. argued that the explicit activation of the gender stereotype was perceived as a limit to the female negotiator's freedom and ability to perform, thereby invoking stereotype reactance. Kray et al. defined stereotype reactance as the tendency to behave in a manner inconsistent with a stereotype. Explicitly activating a negative stereotype resulted in stereotype reactance. This finding is consistent with previous research regarding contrast effects: When a perceiver's attention is blatantly drawn to the link between a stereotype and a social category, it can produce behaviors that are inconsistent with the stereotype. It appears that the manner in which stereotypes are activated determines whether they create an assimilation effect (stereotype threat) versus a contrast effect (stereotype reactance), which suggests that the linkage between stereotype activation and performance depends on the manner in which stereotypes are activated.

Building on results from previous research on stereotype reactance, we contend that the explicit activation of a gender stereotype leads negotiators to engage in behaviors consistent with the content of the activated positive stereotype. In an effort to avoid being pigeon-holed, the negotiator disadvantaged by the stereotype may engage in counterstereotypic behaviors. By realizing that the stereotypical perception of their ability is invalid, negotiators who are the target of a negative stereotype may adjust their goals and strategies accordingly. For example, Kray et al. found that the explicit activation of the masculine stereotype led female negotiators to identify with stereotypically masculine (counterstereotypic) traits as their key strengths and disidentify with stereotypically feminine traits. Furthermore, explicit masculine stereotype activation led women to set higher aspirations than implicit masculine stereotype activation.

This finding supports the notion that the explicit activation of the masculine stereotype focuses attention toward one's strengths and power in the negotiation. Reactance processes likely result from stereotypically disadvantaged negotiators' awareness that the stereotypical perception of their ability is invalid in the current context, that both negotiators are actually on a level playing field, or that they themselves hold a power-based advantage. If our understanding of the process through which reactance occurs is accurate, then it suggests that negotiators should only react when they possess sufficient power in the situation to stand their ground at the bargaining table. . . .

* * *

The purpose of the current set of experiments was to gain a deeper understanding of how the explicit linkage of gender to performance affects negotiating behavior. The current experiments suggest that performance is intimately linked to the content of gender stereotypes and the manner in which they are activated. Of importance for understanding gender differences in negotiations as a situational phenomenon, this research shows that both men and women are sensitive to the content of an activated stereotype and adjust their behaviors accordingly.

We hypothesized that the explicit activation of gender stereotypes leads negotiators to engage in behaviors consistent with the content of the activated positive stereotype; for the disadvantaged negotiator, this leads to counterstereotypic behaviors. Because focusing on power is stereotypically masculine, we expected agreements to reflect a greater power struggle after the explicit activation of masculine stereotypes. Consistent with this hypothesis, the explicit activation of masculine stereotypes led to more one-sided outcomes in favor of the high-power negotiator (Experiment 1). This was true for men and women alike. When the traits that were linked to effective negotiations were stereotypically feminine, evidence of a heightened power struggle after explicitly mentioning gender was absent. Instead, negotiators seemed to act in accordance with the feminine stereotype and behaved more cooperatively, with the explicit activation of feminine stereotypes leading to higher joint pay-offs (Experiment 2). In total, this set of results suggests that the manner in which stereotypes are activated affects the salience of viable alternatives to the current negotiation and the degree to which those alternatives determine the division of resources.

This research advances our understanding of the process through which stereotype reactance works. Kray et al. defined stereotype reactance as the tendency to behave in a manner inconsistent with a stereotype. This definition suggests that when the stereotype is explicitly activated, the negotiator subjected to the limiting stereotype will engage in counterstereotypic behaviors. We found evidence of this process across two experiments. Because the content of the masculine stereotype is related to aggressiveness, concern with one's own interests, and overall competitiveness, to react against the stereotype is to claim and secure a profitable division of the pie. In contrast, the feminine stereotype includes attributes related to insight and concern for the other side, such that reacting against the stereotype involves creating and expanding the pie.

By manipulating the relative power of the negotiators, we also investigated the limits of stereotype reactance. In both experiments, a power asymmetry was made salient and negotiators with more power claimed the lion's share of resources for themselves. Power is indeed a crucial predictor of negotiated outcomes. In the first experiment, however, when the masculine stereotype was explicitly activated, low-power women did not reverse the gender gap and achieve superior outcomes. This finding suggests that reacting against the masculine stereotype and achieving an advantage at the distributive bargaining table only occurs when the stereotypically disadvantaged negotiator is not also crippled by tangible power deficiencies. Although necessary for overcoming power deficiencies, engaging in counterstereotypic behaviors does not appear to be sufficient for reversing the gender gap.

Thus, the explicit activation of stereotypes does not automatically lead to a reversal of the gender gap in negotiations but does so only in contexts in which the stereotyped negotiator possesses some initial power and leverage in the negotiation. Blatantly telling women that they lack the attributes necessary to prevail at the distributive bargaining table produces stereotype threat in the absence of power and stereotype reactance when sufficient power is possessed. On a practical note, these findings suggest that an effective way of circumventing the negative consequences of stereotypes is to increase more objective sources of power. If the power of the stereotyped person is weak, an explicit confrontation with the stereotype is even more threatening and results in greater performance decrements than the implicit activation of the stereotype. Female stereotype threat can only become stereotype reactance when sufficient power is possessed.

Our understanding of performance differences as resulting from contextual factors is consistent with previous theorizing regarding stereotype threat. Work on stereotype threat suggests that differences between social groups in stereotype-relevant performance domains are not the product of inherent, invariant deficiencies of a group but that underperformance by stereotyped groups is a situational phenomenon. When individuals fear that their performance may confirm a negative stereotype about their social group, they tend to live down to the negative expectations and show performance decrements. These effects can occur for men and women; for Caucasians, African Americans, Latinos, and Asians; and even for social class. These findings demonstrate clearly that stereotype threat is not limited to one stereotyped group but occurs whenever negative performance expectations exist for a social group that are based on the possession of stereotypical traits.

This research also enriches our understanding of how power affects negotiation agreements. How negotiators responded to the salient power asymmetry that existed in both experiments depended on the manner in which stereotypical traits were linked to performance. We have argued that the explicit activation of stereotypes increases behaviors that are consistent with the positive traits linked to performance. Depending on the content of the stereotype, power asymmetries were either emphasized or deemphasized in the negotiation. When masculine traits were explicitly linked to performance, the negotiation process became more competitive and the negotiator with the power advantage prevailed to a larger extent than when masculinity was implicitly connected to performance. When feminine traits were explicitly linked to performance, power asymmetries were not emphasized; instead, agreements became more integrative in comparison to when femininity was only implicitly linked to performance. Research suggests that degree to which power is attended to and exercised depends on the negotiation context.

* * *

Chapter 7

THE LAWYER-CLIENT RELATIONSHIP

When lawyers negotiate in their professional capacity, they do so on behalf of clients, yet clients are all but invisible in most books on negotiation. The lawyer is commonly assumed to know what the client wants, and the only question addressed is how to get it from the other side. In fact, the relationship between lawyer and client is multilayered and itself evolves through a complex process of interpersonal negotiation during the course of representation. In order to do a good job for clients, a lawyer has to develop a thorough understanding of the client's situation and needs. Skill as a negotiator begins with skill in working with the clients who hire you to negotiate for them. This chapter addresses some of the challenges in learning to work well with clients and some of the conflicts that develop for lawyers when they represent clients in negotiations.

A. INTERVIEWING AND COUNSELING CLIENTS

Many law schools now offer courses in interviewing and counseling, and such a course is a valuable adjunct to a course on negotiation. Developing the skills needed to gather information from clients — both about the subject matter of your representation and about the client's priorities in having that representation carried out — is essential. In addition, learning how to help a client sort through the options for resolution in order to choose the outcome that most closely fits his needs is a valuable, and often neglected, aspect of legal representation. To negotiate on behalf of a client, you have to have a thorough understanding of his point of view on the matter being negotiated. If you want to explore possible integrative solutions, you need to know the client's priorities well enough to know what particular options might work for him. For example, if your client needs money quickly, it will do no good for you to pursue a negotiated deal involving postponement of payments. Too often, lawyers and other professionals assume that they know what the client wants or that they can decide what is in the client's best interest. What they are really doing is substituting their own views for those of the client, often based on a paternalistic attitude of superior professional competence.

1. Obstacles to Understanding

We all tend to believe that other people think like we do and assume that our own decisions and choices have a certain inexorable logic to them. Becoming aware of that bias can help to overcome one of the obstacles to listening well to clients. Remaining open to what may be a very different point of view, both about the subject at hand and about desirable resolutions to a given dispute, is critical. For example, the client may be anxious to preserve a relationship with the other party, while you see mainly an opportunity for a distributive "win" in a negotiation. Or in a lawsuit, the client may so much want an opportunity to make her case at trial that she is not prepared to accept even a generous settlement offer.

How do you find out what a client actually wants out of a given negotiation? First of all, you have to recognize the things that make it difficult for you to listen to your client: your own preconceptions about the client or the case; your own expectations of yourself in your role as lawyer; and so on. Benjamin in the selection below calls these the "defenses and values" that every interviewer brings to the interview situation. If you believe that your job as a lawyer is to control the interaction between you and your client, or that you are only earning your keep if you are doing the talking, you will have a hard time even hearing what is on the client's mind. If you have pigeonholed the client or the client's case as belonging to a certain type, you may interpret whatever you hear in accordance with those expectations and ignore potentially important information that does not fit with them. While it is not possible to do away entirely with such defenses and values, if you are aware of them and can monitor their influence during an interview, they will be less likely to block communication between you and your client

2. Obstacles to Communication

Of course, the client brings her own set of defenses and values to the interview as well — both in terms of dealing with people in positions of authority such as lawyers, and in relation to the conflict or dispute that brings her to your office in the first place. She may fear that you will think badly of her if she is candid about what led her to consult you, or she may try to avoid revealing information that she believes will be harmful to her case. If you insist on controlling the interview, the client may feel that she cannot say what is most pressing from her point of view and that she is being asked instead about things that do not matter. In addition, recalling traumatic events is painful, and a client who feels that she is not being heard will have increased difficulty revealing details of her experience. Since clients often feel that they should defer to a lawyer and avoid saying anything that might shock or embarrass her, the conversation can be quite constrained if you are not alert to the ways in which the client finds the encounter personally threatening.

3. Overcoming Communication Barriers

To overcome these barriers, you must keep in mind that what is routine for you may not be so for the client. In order to encourage the client's participation, you must be prepared to explain why it is important to gather certain information in detail and how it will assist the client's case. You must also be able to listen empathetically — to put yourself in your client's shoes in order to understand not only what happened, but also what it means to the client. People are usually upset and confused when they consult lawyers, and they are likely to have conflicting feelings about the subject of the consultation. If the client's business partnership is faltering, does he experience it as a personal failure or as due to external factors, or (more likely) both?

Lawyers often consider themselves better equipped by their training to provide technical solutions to clients' problems, rather than to sort through their feelings with them. Ignoring those feelings, though, can be costly both in terms of client satisfaction with the outcome and in terms of the time it takes to achieve a negotiated result. Without a full understanding of the client's perspective, you will not be able to help the client come up with appropriate solutions. A client whose underlying concerns have not been attended to may balk when a settlement is proposed. The business partner in the preceding example might be fed up with the irresponsible behavior of his partner and at the same time might want to find some way to salvage the business and the relationship, if possible. Whatever his legal rights may be with respect to dissolving the partnership, your representation will not be adequate unless you can make room for him to consider a variety of other options that address his multiple concerns.

B. ACTIVE LISTENING

Making room for the client involves, first of all, the lawyer's ability to put aside her own beliefs and preconceptions about the situation enough to attend, in a non-judgmental way, to what the client has to say. By asking open-ended questions ("Tell me about what happened;" "What would you like to see come out of this?") and listening carefully to the answers, you can avoid narrowing the focus of the interview before you even knows what the client's perspective is. You have to gather details and seek legally relevant information, but if you insist on getting just the facts and ignoring everything else, you may miss the forest for the trees.

The ability to listen is often undervalued in law school, with its emphasis on oral argument and Socratic dialogue. In an interview situation, however, it can make the difference between a passive client, who speaks only in response to questions that the lawyer thinks to ask, and a client who conveys both the substance of the problem and the complex emotions that underlie the bare facts. Emotions matter: they will have a lot to do with how you should proceed. Given the facts, does the client want vengeance, or reconciliation, or a quick resolution that will allow him to move on, or any number of other possible solutions? To create an atmosphere that minimizes the barriers to communication between lawyer and client, you must be able to attend both to the feelings expressed and to the content of the client's problem. When you do, you will be able to demonstrate your active understanding of what you have heard by paraphrasing it to the client. The client will then know that you grasp the situation as he perceives it.

1. Listening Well

Active listening requires practice, and it is hard work. It involves taking in what the other person is saying and then letting them know that you "get" their experience of the situation ("As I understand what you're saying, you feel let down and angry at your partner's getting involved in outside activities at such a critical time for your business, and you also feel that she is essential to its success"). Such listening is difficult, and legal training has traditionally put a premium on talking well, not on listening well. In many circumstances, people tend to focus more on their planned response than on what someone else is saying to them. Also clients, like other people, are often not aware of how they feel or try to keep their feelings in check when talking to a stranger. To listen well, you have to look for clues in the way that a client says things, in his body language, and in what he leaves unsaid. You do not have to be a mind reader to do this: emotions are so powerful that people leak clues all the time. As Sigmund Freud, the founder of psychoanalysis, noted almost 100 years ago about his early efforts to understand the meaning of his patients' symptoms:

> When I set myself the task of bringing to light what human beings keep hidden within them. . .by observing what they say and what they show, I thought the task was a harder one than it really is. He that has eyes to see and ears to hear may convince himself that no mortal can keep a secret. If his lips are silent, he chatters with his finger-tips; betrayal oozes out of him at every pore. [1]

Freud's insight was echoed by Charlene Barshefsky, the former United States representative in charge of China trade negotiations. Talking about the importance of watching your counterpart in negotiations, she said, "the body always speaks well before the mouth ever opens."[2] Mixed motives and conflicting feelings are universal human characteristics, however much the law seeks to contain and channel them with its emphasis on rationality. If you develop the skill of watching as you listen to clients, you will pick up useful information that their words alone do not convey, and you will be bet-

---

[1] Sigmund Freud, 7 Standard Edition of the Complete Psychological Works of Sigmund Freud 77-78 (James Strachey trans., The Hogarth Press 1953) (1905).

[2] Eric Schmitt, *Questions for Charlene Barshefsky*, N.Y. Times, Oct. 1, 2000, (Magazine), at 21.

ter able to represent their interests in all their complexity. It goes without saying that this skill will also stand you in good stead when you negotiate with others on their behalf, as Barshefsky confirms.

2. Using Client Feedback

Listening actively means that you try to attend to more than just your client's words. But how are you to know when you are really following him and when you are reading things into what he says that are inaccurate? When you paraphrase what you hear to the client, it gives him the opportunity to refine or correct your understanding in response. As he does so, he also reflects on both the facts and the feelings behind them, and he may achieve a better understanding of his own situation and of himself in it. The experience of being understood — indeed, the experience of someone *trying* to understand — is not that common for anyone. When you listen actively to a client, it usually enables him to express himself more freely, increasing the flow of information. The quality of the information you receive also improves through this feedback process, and you will end up with a fuller picture of both the problem and of the client.

C. THE FRAMEWORK FOR NEGOTIATIONS

Once you have gained a sense of the client's perspective on the problem through open-ended questions and active listening, you can ask more focused follow-up questions to develop the legal framework necessary for addressing it. In preparation for negotiations, Menkel-Meadow proposes developing the following inventory of client needs during the interview process:[3]

---

[3] *See* Carrie Menkel-Meadow, *Toward Another View of Legal Negotiations: The Structure of Problem-Solving*, 31 UCLA L. REV. 754, 804 (1984).

	Now (Short Run)	Later (Long Run)	Manifest (Articulated)	Latent (Unstated)
Economic (including Transaction Costs)				
Legal				
Social (Relationships)				
Psychological (Feelings) (Risk Aversion)				
Ethical/Moral (Fairness)				

Through a back and forth process of questioning, active listening, and clarification of needs, you and your client can develop a consensual, rounded picture of the client's problem and his feelings about it that allows you to move forward in planning what action to take.

Such a plan is not fixed for all time, of course; and subsequent events, including the response of other parties to your initial overtures, will require adaptation and reconsideration by lawyer and client. Although most discussions of legal interviewing and counseling focus on the early stages of the lawyer-client relationship, the article below by Gifford extends the client-centered counseling concept to negotiations and proposes a model for ongoing consultation between lawyer and client during the negotiation process. In contrast to a more traditional approach, in which the lawyer conducts negotiations on her own and presents only the final settlement proposal to the client, Gifford argues that the uncertainties characterizing negotiations warrant continuing client involvement as negotiations progress.

Although lawyers negotiate for clients in many contexts, litigation presents special difficulties for a client-centered approach to representation. Just as a surgeon may be predisposed to advise surgery, litigators may be inclined to see filing suit as the optimal solution to a client's problem, even if only for the negotiation advantage it might confer. Goodpaster's article below discusses the role and biases of the litigator-negotiator. He examines the various ways that initiating litigation tends to mold and shape disputes, as well as to limit the possibilities for creative resolution outside the adversary system, regardless of the client's desires.

D. HOW INVOLVED SHOULD THE CLIENT BE?

In an early study of lawyers and clients, excerpted below, Rosenthal distinguishes between traditional and participatory models of lawyer-client decision making. The client-centered approach to legal interviewing discussed above aims to move away from the traditional view that the lawyer-client relationship involves an authoritative expert and a passive recipient of that expert's legal assistance. It proposes a more collaborative model in which both parties take an active role. The advent of managed care in medicine has accelerated such a shift in the relationship between doctor and patient, as patients have become more proactive in seeking the care they need and deciding what treatment regimens to follow. Among lawyers, the traditional model still has considerable vitality, for many of the reasons cited by Rosenthal over thirty years ago. First of all, lawyers make the rules. Although the ethics codes exalt the notion of loyalty to clients as part of the duty owed by an agent to a principal, the lawyer is presumed to know best when it comes to carrying out the client's business. Second, the traditional division of labor between lawyer and client obscures the extent to which conflicts between them are inherent aspects of their relationship.

In general under the ethical rules, the client determines the ends of the representation and the lawyer determines the means (See Chapter Eight, Model Rule 1.2 and EC 7-7 in the Model Code). In the negotiation context, this means that the client has the final say about whether to accept a settlement proposal, but not about how to conduct the negotiations themselves. The traditional concept of lawyer control over the means of accomplishing the client's goals results in the client's business being carried out largely in the client's absence, without consultation about the methods used. Yet, as we have seen, how negotiations are handled can have significant repercussions for clients, especially when there is an ongoing relationship between the parties. An overly aggressive lawyer can poison future prospects in such a situation, and the parties' relationship may be of paramount importance to the client. Similarly, a distributive versus an integrative negotiation orientation can affect the substantive results achieved. A client's input on how to conduct negotiations, even if the client is not an experienced negotiator, may reflect an informed understanding of the parties and the dispute. A more participatory approach to legal representation makes room for discussions of how means and ends interact in negotiation and of the client's interest in making sure that the means employed meet his long-term as well as his short-term goals.

E. CONFLICTS BETWEEN LAWYER AND CLIENT

Since a lawyer earns her living by representing clients, it is inevitable that her interests will not always be aligned with the client's. A lawyer on contingent fee will often be better off settling early for less money and moving on to the next case, while her client may prefer to hold out for a larger settlement offer. A lawyer paid at an hourly rate has an incentive to prolong the representation to increase her fee. Beyond these conflicting financial interests, there are issues of reputation and overall effectiveness as a negotiator that work against the ideal of zealous advocacy on behalf of each and every client, as discussed in the articles by Gilson and Mnookin in Chapter Four and by Condlin in Chapter Eight. A lawyer cannot afford to treat every client's case as if it were the only case she has, even though that is what the ethical rules contemplate. Whatever other justifications are put forward, the fact that the lawyer works largely in the client's absence and controls the means by which the client's ends are carried out thus serves the lawyer's self-interest. The lawyer needs the client in order to have a practice, but the client never knows just how loyal the lawyer is because of these countervailing forces.

The power dynamic between lawyer and client is a product of their mutual independence and interdependence; and it produces uneasiness for both. One thing that makes a realistic assessment of the relationship difficult is that it would require straight talk between lawyer and client about its limitations. Clients would have to recognize that the lawyer is unlikely to accomplish everything they want, and lawyers would have to acknowledge the conflicting loyalties that ethical rules cannot eradicate. In the absence of such a candid discussion, as the second excerpt from Rosenthal's book describes, what often transpires is some indirect form of client "management" in the name of serving the client's interests.

Building on Rosenthal's work, Felstiner and Sarat have examined empirically the ways that lawyers and clients negotiate reality in their relationship and how they influence and are influenced by each other in carrying out their respective roles. Interestingly, much of what they call negotiation takes place non-verbally, that is, neither party to the relationship openly acknowledges the inherent tension between them or explicitly addresses how they might deal with it in the context of ongoing representation. Instead, both lawyer and client engage in a potentially counter-productive process of manipulating the other in various ways — lawyers, for example, by using what the authors call "law talk" to gain the upper hand over clients and clients by holding back information that could make the lawyer's job easier. This tacit bargain between lawyer and client to avoid open discord helps to explain why lawyers often feel uncomfortable having their clients present during negotiations. Not only are they concerned that the client might disrupt their negotiation strategy by revealing information or making concessions too readily, but also that the client might object to the extent to which the lawyer is prepared to compromise in order to reach a resolution. The article by Rhode brings a feminist perspective to the question of power dynamics between lawyers and clients, especially traditional, authoritarian male lawyers and female clients. All of these authors address ethical dilemmas that characterize the lawyer-client relationship. The next chapter focuses on these and other ethical issues in negotiation.

DOUGLAS E. ROSENTHAL,[*]
LAWYER AND CLIENT: WHO'S IN CHARGE?
13-23 (1974)[**]

* * *

How Active Should Clients Be in Trying to Understand Their Problem and in Trying to Influence its Solution?

According to the traditional theory the client who is passive, follows instructions, and trusts the professional without criticism, with few questions or requests, is preferable and will do better than the difficult client who is critical and questioning. It is of paramount importance that the interaction between client and professional be stable and free of conflict. This stability requirement is one of the justifications cited for demanding complete client confidence in the professional consultant. Without such confidence the client may disrupt the consultation and undercut the effectiveness of the professional's service. It has been argued by Moore and Tumin that client trust in unvarying professional competence and the certainty of a good outcome is necessary whether or not trust actually is warranted. This assumes, gratuitously, that the public can be kept in the dark if it turns out that professional performance is in reality poor. . . . The less cynical view is that most professional performance is in reality of sufficient competence to justify public trust.

The participatory theory promotes an active strategy assuming that it is primarily the client's own responsibility to grapple with the problem. Instead of delegating responsibility to the professional and leaving the decisions to him while being kept only minimally informed, the participating client seeks information to help him define his problem and what he wants to accomplish, rather than waiting to be told how to proceed. Periodically he reviews and reevaluates the steps already taken, and the professional's performance by questioning and by appraising the consistency and accuracy of the professional's answers. He is aware that there are open choices to be made in solving his problem and expects to have his concerns reflected in the choices made.

* * *

The passive client's delegation of responsibility and control detaches him from the problem solving process. Only repeated or dramatic evidence of professional nonperformance or misconduct leads to an active reevaluation of the delegation — and the decision whether or not to fire the first professional and delegate responsibility to a second one.

---

[*] Douglas E. Rosenthal is a partner in the law firm of Constantine Cannon in Washington, D.C. This excerpt from his book focuses on the differences between a traditional and a participatory model of lawyer-client relationships.

[**] Copyright © 1974 Russell Sage Foundation. Reprinted with permission.

Of course, the active strategy is costly. From the client, it demands energy, intelligence, and judgment. From the professional it demands patience and tolerance built on recognition of an obligation to earn the client's cooperation. The passive strategy makes fewer demands on both parties, but if the professional in fact makes a mistake, it may not be noticed in time to be corrected.

* * *

Do Client Problems Have a Single Best Routine and Technical Solution Accessible to Lay Understanding?

A majority of claimants in the client sample reacted to the threatening uncertainties raised by their claims by looking to their lawyer for authoritative direction. An outgoing retired rabbi interviewed said, for example, "If the lawyer is competent, he knows with certainty what can be done with the law." The rabbi is expressing the idea that most of the uncertainty, the openness of problems in which there is no unvarying set of circumstances to be dealt with in a standardized way and involving disparate personal values (that may dictate contrary choices) has been largely removed from the law. . . .

* * *

But actually, in his research into matrimonial cases O'Gorman found the client's own uncertain feelings made things unusually open, unstructured and nonroutine for a legal problem. A variation of this belief in certainty concedes that uncertain knowledge and open choices are difficulties in the professions, but only in those fields which are at the "creative frontiers" of new and changing knowledge. By implication while, say, outer-space law is an atmosphere incognita, much less is uncertain within the terrain of well-established legal knowledge of a field such as torts.

The participatory theory stresses the uncertainty of the criteria and procedures of professional practice, the dependence of a best course of action on what is important to the client as much as on some objectively right remedy.

* * *

If professional problems are essentially closed as traditionalists claim, client delegation is more justifiable. However, if they are essentially open, client delegation limits the client's justifiable influence over the critical choices to be made. Similarly, if professional problems are essentially capable of routinization and the accurate prediction of various outcomes, the client is best served by putting himself in the hands of the professional who has mastered the standard responses. However, if they are in important ways nonroutinized, unpredictable problems, the client has a greater stake in seeing that his individual needs are being met.

The traditional theory rests heavily on the need for trust because it is believed that lay clients do not have and cannot feasibly obtain sufficient knowledge for even partial self-diagnosis and remedy.

* * *

Participationists are suspicious about the professionals wittingly or unwittingly maintaining client uncertainty and client feelings of incompetence as a means of increasing their own indispensability — their power over the client. For example, Davis has discussed the behavior of doctors who did not want to have to meet the demands for time, effort, and involvement which they felt a sample of Baltimore parents would make if they knew that their children almost certainly faced permanent crippling by polio. To avoid these demands, and thus better control the interaction with the parents, they told the anxious parents that the outcome of the polio was still in doubt — that it was too early to think about the possibilities of permanent impairment.

Many traditionalists would not deny that professionals frequently avoid informing their clients, but they feel that most clients prefer it this way. As they see it, clients want simple, reassuring answers. They are afraid of knowing too much lest some news be bad news.

* * *

The participationist counters that people have a greater capacity for confronting reality than they are given credit for — especially when the risks of avoiding reality are made clear to them.

The traditional model assigns the determination of how much information the client should be given about his problem and the possible ways of dealing with it to the discretion of each professional. The professional's judgment may be based on a case-by-case assessment of what each client wants to hear, how much trouble the client is likely to make for the professional in added demands, how much time and energy it is worth spending on the case, how easy it is to communicate with the client, and related factors.

A participatory view of the problem-solving relationship gives explicit and extensive disclosure a central place. Since it is the client who will have to live with the outcome, he should be informed about the risks and benefits of alternative courses of action even if the choice is obvious to the professional and even if the client does not fully comprehend what he is being told. It is not enough to leave the amount of disclosure to the discretion of the professional. The client should be entitled to this information as a matter of course. This information will not only provide psychological reassurance, but will provide a basis for the client's appraisal of the professional's competence to help him. Furthermore, it can be used as a means for sharing decision responsibility with the client. Full disclosure will facilitate the client's ratification of the action taken, thus minimizing the grounds for subsequent client grievances. The discipline of having to hear and understand the information will help the client to feel less estranged from the profession and professional jargon.

* * *

Do Professionals Give Disinterested Service?

The concept of disinterested service is a hallmark of the traditional model. The competent professional is able to see what is in the best interests of his client — and to make those interests his own. Disinterested service has two elements. Simultaneously, the professional must free himself from self-interested temptations that conflict with the client's cause; and he must strongly defend the client against outside interests that threaten him. Neutral detachment is not enough.

* * *

Critics of the traditional theory find it serving an important ideological function for the professional: to justify his freedom from criticism and control. The theory encourages both popular respect for the professions and practitioner self-respect: public relations and self-esteem. Participationists are suspicious that traditionalists may be engaging in self-delusive propaganda more than in realistic analysis. They feel traditionalists give insufficient attention to the possibility of the professional's bias in determining the client's interest. This is a major concern of psychoanalytic theory in the analyst-patient relationship. It is referred to as the twin problems of transference and countertransference. Somewhat simplified, transference is the patient's reacting to the professional based on attitudes learned in dealing with other persons who were important in his past. Superficial similarities between the professional and these earlier persons influence, without his awareness, the patient's behavior in the interaction. By uncovering these attitudes and behavior patterns, and by making the patient recognize them for what they are, the analysis is advanced. Countertransference is the same process with the roles reversed — the professional's unconscious needs which are triggered by the client and by having to deal with him. Even psychoanalysts who have experienced a long and intensive training analysis (aimed at making them sufficiently self-aware to help others effectively) experience countertransference toward their patients. The point relevant to a participatory theory is that the professional has self-interests, of which he himself may be unaware, that may compete with the objective interests of his clients. Without sufficient self-awareness, the professional is not likely to be disinterested. Traditionalists doubt that these unconscious needs play a significantly negative part in interaction between mature adults over nonpsychiatric "technical" matters.

The issue of disinterested service is allied closely with the nature of client problems. If problems are largely open questions with risks and benefits that depend greatly upon the client's subjective ideas and feelings, the client himself can be assumed to know best his own interest. If client problems are largely closed questions with reasonably predictable outcomes that can be weighed according to widely shared criteria of value, and if this weighing process demands largely noncommunicable specialized knowledge, the competent professional can be assumed to know best the client's interest. The further issue is whether or not the competent professional can sufficiently free himself from the competing claims of self, family, colleagues, and other clients to pursue the client's interest, however identified. The traditionalist says yes; the participationist is skeptical.

Alfred Benjamin,[*] *Communication and Facilitation* in THE HELPING INTERVIEW 165-72, 193-200 (4th ed. 1987)[**]

In this chapter we shall discuss communication. . . . In a sense we have been discussing it right along. Without communication there would be no interview. However, as we well know, there are interviews — even helping interviews — in which the communication is far from optimal. The interviewer's goal is to facilitate communication, but obstacles that impede, distort, or complicate it often arise. There are, obviously, various factors that can help or hinder communication. I have already stated some and hinted at others. I intend here to arrange these factors within a framework that may render them more meaningful. Like much else in this book, such an approach is not original with me. However, I find it congenial, clear, and simple. It has worked better for me than any other framework I have tried; pragmatically speaking, I have found it to be true. This framework includes two basic concepts: defenses and values.

Defenses and Values

The less defensive we as therapists or interviewers can become, the more we shall help our clients discard their defenses. Communication between us will improve as a consequence. The more we become aware of what our values are and the less we need to impose them on the client, the more we may help him become aware of his own values and retain, adapt, or reject them as he sees fit. Knowing my own values, I can state them. If I can accept them as a changing part of my changing self, I may be able to accept his as a changing part of his changing self. Some of these values of mine may remain constant for me, and some may for him; but I shall not be afraid to expose mine, nor shall I fear being exposed to his. He, in turn, may learn not to fear exposing his values or being exposed to mine because he will know that he is not being threatened. In such an atmosphere he may learn to describe his values without fear of being judged. He will not need

---

[*] Alfred Benjamin was a psychotherapist. This excerpt discusses obstacles to open communication between interviewers and clients.

[**] Copyright © 1987 by Houghton Mifflin Company. Adapted by permission.

to defend because he will not feel attacked. Perceiving no necessity to adjust to the interviewer's values, he may discover those he really believes in.

Some time ago I spoke with a young man who, looking back upon his school years, had this to say about one of his teachers:

> "He was my teacher for three years in junior high school, and I gave him hell. I was a devil then and hated the guy. That's what I thought then, but it wasn't only hate. He didn't let me get away with a thing in class, and lots of times he'd keep me in after school to talk things over. He told me exactly how he felt, and I remember I told him lots of things. . . . I don't know why exactly. . . I think, because I trusted him. Now that I think of it, that teacher never told me he was right and I was wrong. He said there were things I was doing he couldn't allow, or something like that, and he told me why. I told him how I felt about the kids in the class and how boring school was. He listened to it. We never got to see eye to eye on lots of things, but we knew where we stood. I know now that I learned more from him in those talks than I did during four years in high school. I didn't know it then, but he taught me to think and to see what I was doing. After a while he had enough, I guess, and I don't blame him. He gave me up for lost, I suppose, and he'll never know how much he helped me. It took me years to find it out."

Whenever the interviewer says directly or indirectly to the client, "You may not say this" she is using her value system to block communication. Whenever she states or implies, "I can't listen to this," she is telling the client not to communicate, to be ashamed of himself, to keep silent. If the interviewer will not listen, who will? Whenever the client says to himself, "I can't come out with this" or "She won't want to hear this," obstacles to good communication exist. They may be largely of his own making, but they may also reflect the interviewer's behavior. It is quite another matter if the client can say to himself, "I know she won't like hearing this one bit, but I also know she can take it." We can never be certain, of course, just how the client perceives us, whom he sees in us, or of whom we remind him. The only choice open to us, it would seem, is to be as genuinely ourselves as possible and to behave as nondefensively as possible in the hope that eventually he will see us as we are.

Rogers has pointed out that our own need to evaluate, to confirm, or to deny constitutes a major obstacle to good communication. I am convinced that this is so. For example, if, when the client tells me that everyone at the meeting turned against him, I show interest in how he perceived the situation, I shall be opening the gates to communication. On the other hand, if I tell him that it surely wasn't so terrible, that he is exaggerating, or that he was probably at fault if people turned against him, I shall be closing those gates. In the former case my response will lead him to explore the situation as it appears to him. I may then be able to help him examine it further and clarify his role as well as his perceptions of others and theirs of him. In the latter case, my reply tells him in essence that he has misjudged the situation and that the fault may well have been his. He may consequently feel the necessity to defend himself against my judgment and thus fail to come to grips with the situation itself.

To take another example, if the interviewee tells me she liked a certain book and I tell her I did not, she will either refrain from examining just what she liked about the book or feel the need to defend her liking it. On the other hand, if I exhibit an interest in her view, she may feel encouraged to discuss the book and explore what she liked about it. Consequently, she may begin to learn something about herself, her likes and dislikes, her values. Having been respectfully listened to, she may wish to hear my views because she has become genuinely interested in my values — but as mine, not hers. Our respective values may or may not be modified as a result, but at least we shall have learned how we both feel about the book.

Communication is not essentially better if I simply agree with the client when she states that she likes a certain novel. We have really described nothing and learned nothing about each other's values. We do not know, in other words, what led each one to like the same book. One may have liked it because of the plot; the other because of the vivid characterization. Reasons for liking the same thing can be very diverse. Regarding communication, the fact of our mutual liking is far less significant than the fact that we have been enabled to express the reasons for it.

There exists a real possibility that as the result of such mutual describing, the perception of one or both partners will undergo change. For some people this offers a challenge; they regard it as a part of growing. For others it spells danger; for them change is threatening, and they cannot allow communication to be clear and direct. They will obstinately defend themselves against change. Their values will prove a reliable shield in warding off the threat.

Many therapists and interviewers who have learned not to fear revealing themselves have discovered that clients absorb this lesson from their example. The therapist can allow herself to describe how she perceives the client's behavior without making the latter feel that he is being evaluated or categorized. The therapist may say, for example: "I feel bored with that old story" or "The way you talk about it makes me feel that there is more to it than that" or "I feel slightly annoyed by those smiles; I wonder how you really and truly feel about me" or "I feel that you want me to tell you what is right for you, but I can't."

Authority as a Defense

At times the therapist or any interviewer employs his authority as a defense, a barricade. "Teachers are never wrong," "The doctor knows best," and "Adults have more experience" are often convenient defenses. They won't solve the problem confronting the client but serve to protect the interviewer from "attack" in the form of an honest search by the client, a real coping with his situation. Confronted by a facade of superiority, the client must defend himself as best he can. If he perceives it as the expression of the interviewer's values, he may either submit or emerge with a shield to defend his own values. Two formidable obstacles to communication will then prevail: the interviewer's use of authority and the client's use of weapons to combat it.

I am not suggesting that our role — our function in society and in the life of the client — has no relation to authority; it has. The issue is how we apply that authority in the helping interview and to what ends. While the interview is proceeding, are we indicating, implying, or stating "This is not to be discussed," "That is a professional secret," "You'll just have to take my word for it," "I know best," "This is final; there is nothing to add"? When the client is confronted with such attitudes, it is not surprising if she feels that she is being hemmed in and treated like an object. She may submit, learning thereby to depend on authority. She may rebel, resorting to a defense of her own. What will be absent is a free, open expression and exchange of ideas and feelings. Communication will have been obstructed.

The alternative is an atmosphere in which a sense of equality prevails — not equality of knowledge, experience, or professional skill, naturally, but equality of worth and dignity, with each human being fully respecting the other. Here no defensive shield is available to us, the interviewer; we are vulnerable. With nowhere to hide, we may come to light as a real person trying to help another real person. The client will soon discover that we are neither all powerful, all-wise, nor the embodiment of human virtue. The sooner he does, the better for him and our relationship. Seeing that we are not a closed book, he may permit himself to turn the pages of his own. He will find that the shields he brought with him as a result of habit and experience are not needed here. Since he will be confronting a true other, he will find that he can express his true self. For him, too, there will be no place to hide, but he will not be alone. Another will be there as he begins to cope with his own self.

Do we really possess the answers? Are we certain we are right? Are our conclusions necessarily correct just because they are ours? In an atmosphere in which equal meets equal our certainty may well have to give way to a mutual attitude of "Let's see" or "Let's try." This may be no more than provisional, but it will be understood by both, hence meaningful to both. Deprived of defensive shields, we have no alternative but to be flexible, to look at and respond to all aspects of a given situation. We may help the client reach a decision. We may even be making it for her in a manner of speaking. But whatever we do, we shall be doing it with her, not to her. She will consider herself as an equal, allowing herself to take from us what she chooses and to reject what is not for her.

* * *

Judging as a Defense

A final defense must be mentioned: judging the client. It, too, constitutes an obstacle to open communication in that it encourages us to rationalize our behavior rather than come to grips with it. We judge the client to be "uncooperative," "a troublemaker" "aggressive," "submissive," "eccentric," and so forth. Consequently, we see her as such, and, more often than not, she will tend to see herself as such. But is this her real self, all of it or even a part? Or is this our perception of her, our perception at a given time and place and under given circumstances? Are we perhaps in error? Even if we are right, if we have "judged" her correctly, have we "judged" ourselves as well? May she not be acting this way because of us — because of her perception of us or her reaction to our perception of her?

Students who are attempting to listen to their taped interviews as non-defensively as possible often wonder whether they have judged the client correctly or whether their judging was meaningful at all. Clients as well, hearing their own tapes, frequently begin to wonder if they have perceived the interviewer correctly and judged her fairly. It is amazing how much closer to each other the two partners in an interview can draw when they both remove their defensive armor. Then real coping occurs; and arguing, so frequently found in interviews, tends to disappear. By arguing I do not mean honest disagreement or an open clash of values. I mean misunderstandings, confusion, trying to get the upper hand, making a point regardless of whether it is being listened to, saying something for the record and not to the other.

I have found that the more obstacles to communication there are, the more arguing shows up. This should not surprise us, for arguing is bound to result from these obstacles. Each side holds for dear life to its own; it is give or take, not give and take. Gradually the interview comes to a halt. The session isn't really over, but it seems as if nothing more can be said or done. Client and interviewer appear to be saying to each other: "This arguing isn't getting us anywhere so we may just as well stop. You can't listen to me, and I can't listen to you, so what's the use." It is useless, in fact. But even at this point if we can be honest enough to realize what has been going on and to express it, we may yet save the situation. "We've been kind of yelling at each other, and now it looks as if there is nothing more to say. I suppose we've gotten things off our chests, but I'm not sure whether we've gotten across to each other. Frankly, as the argument got hotter and hotter, I heard less and less of what you were saying; and I suppose it was the same with you. Why don't we just assume we've made a bad job of it and try again?"

* * *

Dealing with Obstacles

There are ways — such as checking notes, listening to tapes, and discussing interviews with professional persons — whereby one can discover to what extent communication obstacles are present. These self-imposed tests and tasks, so to speak, are not foolproof. In any case, it is undoubtedly valid to say that communication obstacles exist to some degree in every interview. Our goal, as I perceive it, is not to eliminate them altogether, for our inability to achieve this might lead us to despair. It is, rather, to become aware of our behavior in interviews, to see where we may be creating obstacles, and to try to reduce these as much as possible, all the while recognizing that we remain humanly fallible. The five ways of reducing obstacles I am about to discuss have helped me and a good many of my students.

Talking Too Much or Too Little

If you tend to talk as much or even more than the client, chances are that you are blocking communication from her to you. It is quite likely that you are acting as an authority, as the superior in the interview who must be respectfully listened to, and that the client perceives you in this way. You may be lecturing the client and not becoming sufficiently aware of her internal frame of reference while causing her to become too much aware of yours.

Should you find yourself talking very little — about 10 percent or less of the total talk — you may wish to look into this. Are there many pauses, awkward silences? Do you say so little because you are reluctant to get in the client's way but find that in holding back you are getting in his way nonetheless? Do the two of you seem comfortable with the fact that you are talking so little, or does the atmosphere seem unnatural and tense to you both? If you find that the little you say enables the client to release feelings and express ideas and at the same time enables you to go along with him, you may have achieved good rapport. The amount of talk is but one indication of what goes on in the interview and must be seen within the context of the entire process.

Cutting Off

Do you tend to let the client finish what he has to say, or do you often finish it for him and reply to that? Do you tend to interrupt him because you are quick to catch his intent and become impatient? Believing that you have heard many times in the past what he is now saying, do you become bored and cut him off? After your interruptions, what happens to the flow of the interview? An interruption creates a major communication obstacle. It cuts short communication that is actually taking place. Our motives may be the best: to show that we understand so well that we can finish the client's sentence for him, to demonstrate our interest by interjecting questions. Motives notwithstanding, we are actually choking off what is coming our way, although we may sincerely believe ourselves to be encouraging further flow.

At times interruptions lead to a form of duet; both partners are talking at once — the one continuing with what she was saying when interrupted and the other continuing to interrupt her. When we realize what is happening, we can probably do nothing better than stop and, if necessary, state openly what has occurred. But this explanation should be very brief lest it become, in turn, an interference. "Sorry, go ahead" may suffice. At times the client, well trained to look up to "authority," may stop in her tracks as soon as we open our mouth. Here we may have to say more: "Sorry I cut you off. I was too quick on the trigger. Please go ahead; I'll have my say when you're through."

We must become especially aware of interruptions by the client. These may well indicate that we have not understood him aright, that he has decided to add or amend, or that, for one reason or another, he finds it difficult to continue listening to us. Remarks such as "I'm talking now, so please listen" or "I've done you the courtesy of listening to you, so now please do me the courtesy of listening to me" usually add insult to injury. The helping interview is not an exercise in manners except insofar as we wish to use it to teach manners. Whatever the case, if the client interrupts us and we wish to remove communication obstacles to the greatest extent possible, sensitivity on our part to what is going on may assist us to find the causes. If we really wish to hear the client, the best thing is to stop and listen. There will always be time for us to have our say. Our need to talk, unfortunately, is often greater than our ability to listen. This is a very human failing, but since it creates obstacles to communication, it should be overcome.

Responses

Am I responding to what the client has expressed or to what, in my opinion, she should have expressed? In other words, am I responding to her needs or to my own? Do my responses enable her to express herself further? Are my responses clear? Am I getting across to her? Do my responses constitute additional obstacles to those she is already facing? In short, are my responses a help or a hindrance to the flow of her talk? We shall consider this aspect more fully in the next chapter.

Forces and Facets

Any topic discussed in an interview usually has several facets. Do I assist the client to see, discuss, and cope with as many of these as possible? When a course of action is being considered, normally certain forces push the client in one direction, and other forces pull him in another. This pushing and pulling may be going on simultaneously. Am I helping the client to explore all the aspects of his conflict, or does my behavior impede his doing so? Do I place obstacles in the way of his exploring his own life space and perceptual field? We cannot always answer these difficult questions, but the posing of them itself may remove impediments to communication.

A Helpful Communication Test

In his well-known article "Dealing with Breakdowns in Communication — Interpersonal and Intergroup," written in 1951, Rogers (1961, ch. 17) referred to an interesting communication test that has since been frequently employed in human relations training and in various classroom situations. The test is challenging and difficult, but I have found that people value the learning experience involved and derive genuine satisfaction from it. Two or more persons are asked to discuss a topic on which they hold differing views. Each is allowed to say whatever he likes under one condition: before voicing his views, he must restate the ideas and feelings expressed by the person who spoke immediately preceding him and do so to that person's satisfaction. The assumption is that if I can tell you what you said and felt, then I heard and understood you. If I cannot, either I placed obstacles in the way or you did not make yourself sufficiently clear. Thus the test motivates the speaker to clarify his thinking and the listener to concentrate on what is being said rather than on the reply he is about to make.

The higher feelings rise in the discussion, obviously the harder it is to obey the rule. At times tempers reach such a high pitch that a moderator is required. As each participant speaks, the neutral restates to that participant's satisfaction what she has said and felt before the next participant is allowed to speak.

In the helping interview we may not always wish to restate the thoughts and feelings expressed by the client, but if we are able to recapture his message to us in this manner, it will show that minimal communication obstacles are present. In other words, if I can provide an atmosphere in which you can release your feelings and ideas without interference from mine and if I can recognize these ideas and feelings as yours, showing you that I have heard, understood, and accepted them as yours, chances are that we are truly communicating and that obstacles are at a minimum. Furthermore, in such an atmosphere you will be receptive to the ideas and feelings I communicate to you. Thus the result will be a genuine interview.

When the Client Won't Talk

Interviewing does not consist of talk alone; there is nonverbal communication as well. However, if there is no talk at all, there may be no interview at all. I am often asked, "What should I do if the client won't talk or won't continue to talk?" I am certain that in most instances the client will talk if really given the opportunity. I once met a young woman who wished to discuss her relationship with her husband. She insisted that he was the "silent type" and hardly ever spoke. We agreed that the three of us would meet. The husband talked — at least he attempted to — but each time he started, his wife would interrupt. Perceiving this, I could not help but smile. The young woman understood the smile and made a supreme effort to allow him to talk. When I last heard from her, she good-humoredly volunteered the information that her husband was no longer the silent type and that she had learned a great deal about her own behavior.

It is not always as simple as this, I admit, but if the client is interested in the interview, he will usually talk if we let him or encourage him a bit.

On the other hand, he may not have wanted the interview and may feel pushed into it by others, perhaps by ourselves. In that case it may be preferable for us to indicate that we understand and accept his reluctance, and then refrain from pushing him further. If and when he becomes ready, or "motivated," he will return and he will talk. Should he not return, it will not be because we consciously made the experience a threatening and unpleasant one. Not everyone wishes to be helped and not everyone can be helped in the helping interview. To have a sincere offer of help rejected is painful, but we must learn to accept this. We may even eventually learn to accept the fact that in situations in which we have "failed," another can succeed.

But what if the client won't continue to talk? Here I am assuming that communication has taken place, that contact has been established. If the client then stops, perhaps she has finished. Or maybe we have thrown obstacles into her path, the kind discussed above. Or perhaps the client has come up against obstacles in herself that hinder her from going further. The response to the ensuing silence will depend upon the interviewer's perception of what is happening. I can only suggest possible ways to reopen communication.

"Is there anything else you wish to say?" (Client shakes his head.) "All right, I'd just like to make one more comment. . . ."

"I see you find it difficult to continue. I wonder if your silence is connected with anything I've said."

"I don't quite know what to make of this silence. Perhaps there is something you find difficult to put into words."

"The last time we hit a silence like this, you said it was because of something I had done. How about this time?"

Preoccupation with Self

A basic factor in communication relates more to the therapist's behavior than to the client's. As the interview proceeds, you, the therapist, may be asking yourself what to say or do next. This concern with your own role may so absorb your attention that you will not be genuinely listening to the client. You will be preoccupied with that small voice inside that insists on knowing how to act next. This inner voice constitutes a clear obstacle to communication. It is not to be confused with the other inner voice that brings you closer to the world of the client — that "third ear" with which you suddenly understand something haltingly expressed. The voice that insists on knowing what to do next is a block between you and your partner in the interview. It is concerned more with you than with him, more with the impression you will make on him that with the impressions he might make on you if you were listening and trying to understand with him.

Should you, then, not be concerned with what your are to do or say? Naturally you must be, but not consciously while the client is expressing herself. When you really listen, almost inevitably a moment's silence will intervene between the client's pausing and your carrying on. Whatever you say or do next will be unpremeditated. It may not be polished or carefully thought through, but it will be genuine. It will come forth spontaneously as the result of your having truly listened. At any rate, you will not have planned your action at the expense of having lost track of the client. You will not sound like the "ideal" therapist, but you may well sound like yourself. The ideal therapist does not exist, but you do; and if the client can sense the genuine, unplanned, spontaneous you, she will have an experience rare in our society. She might even dare to learn from this experience.

On the other hand, should the client sense that we are occupied not with what he is saying but with our eventual response to it, this could be very harmful to the relationship between us. He might imbibe from this a lesson I doubt we wish him to learn: in the interview the important thing is not to be listened to but to be responded to. Were he to act on this conclusion, he would not listen to us either but instead would plan his responses. Perhaps this sounds absurd, but I have known it to happen.

When not stemming merely from lack of experience, this preoccupation with self, I fear, has deep roots somewhere else. We are concerned with how we shall appear instead of being satisfied with what we are. We are concerned with demonstrating our role rather than revealing ourself; with being perceived as superior rather than behaving as an equal; with presenting a show of authority rather than letting our authority — if it exists at all — come through naturally in the ongoing exchange of ideas and feelings.

I reiterate my conviction that the therapist's preoccupation with self at the expense of the client creates a serious obstacle to interpersonal communication. If we can accept ourselves as fallible, we shall err less. If we can learn to rely on our spontaneity, sensitivity, and basic common sense, we shall listen better and understand more. Our behavior influences that of the client more than we know. Behaving openly ourselves, we shall encourage him to do likewise.

* * *

Donald G. Gifford,[*] *The Synthesis of Legal Counseling and Negotiation Models: Preserving Client-Centered Advocacy in the Negotiation Context*
34 UCLA L. REV. 811, 844-50, 855-62 (1987)[**]

* * *

A. Prenegotiation Counseling Conference

Prior to negotiations with the other party, the lawyer should engage in a significant counseling session with the client. The substance of this conference should include four separate topics. First, the lawyer and client should analyze, with all available information, both the client's Best Alternative to a Negotiated Agreement (BATNA) and the likely outcome and consequences of the negotiation alternative. Second, they should discuss the negotiation "strategy," and the possible consequences of its choice for the client and his problem. Third, the lawyer and client should explore integrative solutions which would meet both the client's and the other party's needs. Finally, they should decide how much negotiating "authority" the client should grant the lawyer; this decision should consider the implications for both the negotiation process itself and the client's involvement.

Lawyers usually negotiate with the other party's attorney without a substantial prenegotiation conference. Often they only ask the question: "Do you want me to see what I can get for you by talking to the other side?" or enter negotiations without the client's express approval. This approach is ill-advised for the reasons discussed below.

The lawyer should provide the client with a realistic description of the client's BATNA and the prospects for a satisfactory negotiated result at the earliest possible time. This lessens the likelihood that after negotiations, the lawyer and client will have vastly different opinions on the advisability of accepting or rejecting the settlement offer. Lawyers often quite naturally postpone bad news until the last possible moment, and, as a result, they allow their clients to entertain unrealistically optimistic expectations until the negotiations conclude. Reality then intrudes when the lawyer believes settlement is justified, and the client dismisses this option because he still possesses unrealistic expectations about what will happen at trial or about the viability of his other nonlitigation BATNA.

Additionally a substantial prenegotiation counseling session is necessary because the lawyer may be better able to evaluate objectively the negotiated and nonnegotiated alternatives prior to a negotiation session than

---

   * Donald G. Gifford is Edward M. Robertson Professor of Law at the University of Maryland School of Law. His article looks at ways to involve clients more in negotiation decision making.

afterwards. Admittedly, her evaluation may suffer somewhat since less information is available. After the lawyer negotiates, however, it is difficult for her to avoid having her own ideas about the best options for the client. When she describes the negotiated and nonnegotiated alternatives to the client during the postnegotiation counseling conference, her own preferences will likely color, consciously or unconsciously, her descriptions of the options. An initial comprehensive description of the legal consequences of the alternatives to a negotiated agreement dissuades, and possibly prevents, the lawyer from biasing her description of those alternatives after negotiations. Her prenegotiation assessment thus assures the objectivity of her postnegotiation analysis.

As previously noted, any discussion prior to the negotiations of the likely settlement outcome and alternatives is tentative. The lawyer, therefore, should emphasize this when talking with the client. Lawyers typically begin negotiating prior to completing their own investigation of facts, legal research, and discovery. In addition, the lawyer is unaware initially of how the other side views the case and of additional information that will be gleaned during the negotiation process. When the lawyer's evaluation of the case changes during negotiations, however, she should be able to justify during the postnegotiation counseling session how the new information changed her valuation.

The second issue to be discussed during the prenegotiation conference is which negotiation strategy best serves the client's interests. As previously mentioned, the Model Rules of Professional Conduct require the attorney to consult her client regarding the "means" of representation; this requirement suggests that the attorney should consult with the client regarding the negotiation strategy she intends to use. Some clients will decline any interest in their lawyers' negotiating tactics, but each client should reach this decision only after the lawyer outlines how negotiation tactics can affect the client. In particular, the lawyer and client should explore the implications of the lawyer's intended negotiation strategy on future relationships between her client and the other party. If the parties have a continuing relationship, a noncompetitive negotiation strategy is usually preferred. The competitive strategy often generates distrust and ill-will and may alienate other lawyers and invite retaliation for violating fairness norms. On the other hand, some clients prefer the competitive strategy in negotiating with a party with whom they have a continuing relationship, because it establishes a strong bargaining image and discourages future attempts at exploitation by the other party. Because clients have different concerns about how their lawyer's negotiating behavior affects their own relationships with other parties, their input should be solicited prior to the negotiations.

The lawyer and the client also should consider the lawyer's authority to enter into an agreement binding on the client. The type of authority a client delegates to the lawyer ranges from unlimited authority, which gives the lawyer *carte blanche* to enter into an agreement on behalf of the client, to "open authority," which authorizes the lawyer to negotiate, but does not give her any authority to enter into a binding agreement. The type of authority affects both the negotiation process and the prospects for a client-centered counseling process. In simulated experiments, social scientists have found that representatives who are accountable to clients (have limited authority) are more likely to be "tough" and to use competitive tactics under most circumstances. Attorneys merely nominally accountable to the client, whose authority is limited only within the broadest parameters, however, tend to negotiate less vigorously than if they had unlimited authority. One experienced negotiator told Professor Raiffa about his frustrations in negotiating when his client has a very liberal "bottom line": "It's difficult to exaggerate with an innocent face when you know quite well that the numbers say otherwise." In a context in which the lawyer intends to engage in problem-solving bargaining, a grant of unlimited authority gives her greater flexibility to consider integrative proposals and invent solutions for the parties' problems.

Even though granting the lawyer broad authority facilitates cooperative and problem-solving negotiations, a more restricted grant also has distinct advantages. . . . Restricting the lawyer's authority to enter into a binding agreement also aids client-centered advocacy because the client retains greater control over his attorney's conduct during the negotiation. A series of incrementally increasing grants of authority over the course of the negotiation guarantees that the attorney must consult regularly with the client. Presumably, lawyers preface such requests for additional authority with reports on the current status of the negotiations, and thus keep the client better informed about the negotiations and more directly involved in them.

The lawyer and client also should consider together whether they can devise solutions that satisfy the underlying interests of both the client and the other party. The proponents of problem-solving bargaining, including Fisher and Ury and Menkel-Meadow, previously have recognized the ways in which effective client counseling contributes to successful negotiations, at least in the context of the problem-solving approach they advocate. Because problem-solving negotiation stresses creative solutions that satisfy the parties' underlying needs, Menkel-Meadow emphasizes that the lawyer and client should identify the client's needs, look for nonlegal solutions, and ascertain the client's values and preferences regarding potential solutions. The "crux" of the problem-solving negotiation strategy, according to Menkel-Meadow, is the counseling process preceding the negotiation itself. During these planning sessions, lawyer and client should develop proposed solutions to the problem[s] facing the parties, which then will be considered with the other party's lawyer during negotiations.

Both Menkel-Meadow and Fisher and Ury recommend the technique of brainstorming during the counseling sessions. As previously described, "brainstorming" is designed to produce as many potential solutions to the problem as possible. The participants in a brainstorming session are encouraged to articulate whatever possible solutions come to mind, regardless of how ridiculous or nonviable they initially appear. The lawyer and client suspend critical evaluation and judgment until all possible proposals have been listed, and only then do they consciously and systematically consider the viability of each option and its advantages and disadvantages. This technique reduces the possibility that a viable option will not be considered because the participants have excluded it as a result of intuitive or subconscious prejudices that are not valid when carefully considered. Brainstorming also counteracts the tendency of many lawyers to be overly critical and to seek only the "best answer" to a problem as a result of their personalities or their legal training.

Brainstorming prior to the negotiations significantly contributes to both client-centered counseling and negotiation results. Brainstorming actively involves the client in the negotiation process, builds rapport, and often provides the client with a more realistic picture of the difficulties to be faced during the negotiation. Brainstorming with the client also increases the likelihood that negotiations will yield desirable results. Clients, particularly those engaged in businesses or other specialized activities, frequently know more about their problems and possible solutions than do the lawyers. In addition, several individuals brainstorming about a problem tend to generate more potential solutions than only two negotiators, and thus they increase the likelihood of finding a solution that satisfies the underlying needs of both parties.

* * *

C. Client-Counseling Conferences During the Course of the Negotiations

The lawyer should confer often with her client during the course of the negotiations, preferably after each contact with the other lawyer. Frequent client contacts between negotiation sessions facilitate both client-centered advocacy and negotiation results which maximize the interests of the parties.

In many instances, these client conferences may be brief and conducted either on the telephone or in writing. The lawyer, at a minimum, should inform the client about any negotiation proposal made by either party that conceivably could lead to agreement. In a distributive bargaining context, the lawyer should relate the last offer made by both parties; in the problem-solving context, she should describe any proposed solutions to the parties' problems which are arguably viable. The lawyer also should inform the client about any new material facts learned during the negotiations. Finally, she should share with the client whatever she discovered during the negotiations about how the other values the issues at stake. As previously discussed, early in a negotiation the client only vaguely understands how the other party views the situation. The lawyer, therefore, needs to correct any earlier errors in diagnosing the problem or assessing the other party.

During the next segment of an intranegotiation counseling conference with the client, the lawyer should determine how the information gained during the negotiation process affects the client's assessment of his alternatives to a negotiated agreement. In a multiple issue negotiation, she also should explore whether the client has changed his relative priorities among the various issues. Traditional negotiation models fail to recognize that clients legitimately may change their minimum disposition points during the negotiations; when confronted with new information, the client may reassess his bottom line and his priorities among the issues. Similarly, in negotiations offering significant problem-solving opportunities, the lawyer frequently becomes aware of additional potential solutions during the negotiation sessions which she previously had not considered. Conversely, the negotiations many times demonstrate that some options, which were regarded as feasible during prenegotiation counseling conferences, are either unfeasible or unacceptable to the other party.

Once the negotiations begin, it is particularly important for the lawyer and the client to discuss the client's relative preference among the issues. One problem-solving bargaining technique, "log-rolling," consists of one party conceding on some issues while the other party concedes on others. To the extent that the parties place differing emphasis on the various issues, log-rolling increases the joint benefit to the parties beyond what would be accomplished if each party conceded an equivalent amount on each individual issue. To be effective, log-rolling requires that the lawyers clearly understand their clients' "preference-sets" for the multiple issues at stake in a negotiation. The client frequently finds it impossible to decide, prior to the negotiations, which issue he is willing to concede; such choices often must wait until after he knows which issues the other party values most highly. Professor Druckman has developed a bi-directional model of bargaining that describes negotiation movement as a response to inputs from both the other party and one's client. According to Druckman, the *timing* of a concession or other adjustment to a proposal is most often a response to the other side's negotiating behavior, while the *choice* of which issue to concede, and the *amount* of the concession are determined by the client.

* * *

When the lawyer and the client confer regularly before the negotiations begin and between negotiation sessions, the client is better informed about the substance of the negotiations and more accustomed to participating in the decision-making process. By the time of the postnegotiation conference, the client already should be aware of his nonsettlement alternatives, because his lawyer has discussed these with him prior to the negotiations and kept him informed during the negotiations of any new information affecting his BATNA. Further, because the lawyer constantly updated the client on the actual content of the negotiations, the client has become gradually aware of the substance of the negotiated option.

The client's greater understanding of the alternatives available to him, prior to the postnegotiation counseling conference, favorably affects the counseling conference and makes the client-centered decisionmaking more feasible. First, the amount of new information the lawyer must convey to the client regarding the available alternatives and the consequences of each option is considerably less, because of the client's familiarity with most of this information. Conversely, the lawyer enters the conference more knowledgeable about the client's attitudes and preferences regarding the various options. Thus, the postcounseling conference is likely to be less unwieldy, since the lawyer and client can consider much of the information regarding the alternatives and the client's preferences by summarizing earlier discussions. With less new information to be considered, a somewhat less structured and more informal format than the one Binder and Price outlined probably can be used.

The second advantage of the ongoing counseling process is that it is less likely the lawyer and client will disagree vehemently and unexpectedly about the relative desirability of the remaining alternatives. As previously discussed, the lawyer's comprehensive discussion with the client prior to the negotiations about the client's BATNA serves as a check on the lawyer's tendency to present the BATNA in a biased manner after negotiations in order to substantiate her own opinion that one alternative is preferable. More importantly, however, ongoing counseling makes it less likely the client will form unrealistic expectations about the results of either the negotiation or the alternatives to negotiations. With the traditional counseling model, a client frequently strongly objects to both the negotiated settlement and the BATNA because the lawyer failed to foster realistic expectations in her client. Ongoing negotiation counseling means that the client's unrealistic expectations will be challenged and adjusted incrementally during the negotiation process itself and will not be abruptly destroyed during a power struggle between lawyer and client following negotiations. Clients no longer will be confronted unexpectedly following negotiations with what Binder and Price call a "lose-lose" choice; lawyers will not need to lower dramatically the expectations of their clients in order to bring them face-to-face with the choice realistically available to them — their involvement in the negotiation process itself will have accomplished that.

Finally, counseling sessions with the client during the negotiation process contribute to client-centered advocacy by building a relationship with the lawyer in which the client actively participates in the decisionmaking process. This experience, combined with the client's greater understanding of the available alternatives and their consequences, lessens the inherent power differential between the client and the "professional" or "expert" lawyer. The client's experience as an active participant during the negotiation process more likely will result in true client-centered advocacy than more subtle techniques, such as allowing the client to choose which alternative should be discussed first so that the lawyer's sequencing of alternatives does not implicitly suggest the lawyer's preference. This is not to say such a technique is not beneficial, but only that its use probably has a fairly marginal impact on the allocation of authority between lawyer and client when compared with a continuing relationship in which authority is shared.

Regular consultation with the client during negotiations also reduces the risks inherent in having the lawyer make recommendations during the postnegotiation counseling conference. This is a controversial suggestion, because Binder and Price suggest that lawyers should avoid answering a client's request for advice. Yet, as previously discussed, lawyers frequently make recommendations. Advice from the lawyer is less troubling when the client and lawyer already have established a pattern of client-centered counseling during negotiations. If the lawyer's prior counseling contacts with the client suggest that the client is an "independent decisionmaker," instead of a passive client who believes his role is to do what the lawyer recommends, then the lawyer's advice probably will not impair the client's ability to make his own decisions. The lawyer certainly should not hesitate to point out an inconsistency between the client's tentative decision and his previously expressed preferences or values. These inconsistencies more often will be apparent to the lawyer following an ongoing process of negotiation counseling, because she will have appreciably greater awareness of the client's preferences. Finally, because the client has known his lawyer's analysis of the available alternatives for a longer period of time, the client is better able himself to evaluate this information and advice carefully. With more time to consider the lawyer's analysis away from her office, the client finds it easier to disagree with her recommendation and to reject it when appropriate. Thus, if the lawyer explains the choices available to the client at the earliest possible time and otherwise demystifies the negotiation process, the client is empowered to make his own decisions.

* * *

Gary Goodpaster,[*] *Lawsuits as Negotiations*
8 NEGOT. J. 221, 223-24, 227-28 (1992)[**]

* * *

The litigator-negotiator's role. Lawyers obviously play an important role in transforming grievances, claims, or disputes into lawsuits and in channeling clients into litigated, as opposed to negotiated, dispute resolution. This is not to say that lawyers will inevitably advise clients to sue, even when they appear to have a good and litigable claim. Yet lawyers often do move clients toward litigation. A lawyer may assess the situation as one

---

[*] Gary Goodpaster is Professor Emeritus at University of California, Davis School of Law. His article discusses how lawsuits are used strategically to accomplish negotiation goals.

requiring litigation, not seeing nonlitigious ways to get good results. In many cases, lawyers instinctively or calculatedly advise litigation as a way to get, and leverage, an ultimate negotiated solution.

Lawyer-client relationships in lawsuits. Filing a lawsuit takes away much of the parties' power to decide the shape and content of their dispute. Instead, it devolves that power on legal professionals who, using system resources, translate that dispute into a strictly enforced adversary contest. Over time, the demands of the adversary trial process, the advocacy ethos that encourages and justifies taking extreme positions, and the momentum of invested emotion and contest may work progressively to polarize the parties' attitudes. These factors will certainly shape the parties' perceptions of the situation. Finally, the adversary contest itself will exclude the principals from a continued active role in resolving their own dispute.

Clients vary in their degree of sophistication in dealing with lawyers and handling involvements in lawsuits. Lawyers differ in their approaches to clients and in the ways in which they manage or relate to them. In a lawsuit, the lawyer is a representative or agent who occupies the boundary role position. That is, while nominally only a client's agent, the lawyer is the major actor in advancing and managing the litigation. The lawyer is thus in a position to assess it, to make predictions regarding it, and to compare litigated, as against negotiated, result potentials. The roles lawyers have in shaping, managing, and assessing the possible outcomes of lawsuits, and their ability to shape their clients' perceptions of the litigation, give them considerable situational power — one might even say, depending on the client, virtual dominance — over their clients regarding settlement.

The litigator-negotiator's bias. The lawyer's status as legal representative also predisposes her in her approach to dispute resolution. Often, accountability to another leads one to greater advocacy than is the case when acting for oneself. The lawyer who represents a client is accountable to the client, and the client will evaluate the lawyer's performance. Strengthening this effect in the lawyer-client relationship is the lawyer's ethical obligation to devote herself single-mindedly to the client's interests. Furthermore, lawyer-client meetings, where the two discuss lawsuit progress, are also likely to increase pressure for lawyer loyalty, commitment, and advocacy. Finally, litigation is itself a competitive contest. As a lawsuit progresses, the other side will present its point of view oppositionally. Inevitably, this will incline all parties, clients as well as lawyers, to view themselves as engaged in a combat or battle. Thus, in addition to the parties' possible initial competitive stances, the litigation process itself generates increasing, competitive impetus, what we might call competitive "lock-in" effects.

* * *

As parties progress through the litigation process toward trial, they can assess their case from time to time. Their perceptions of case merit and value can change as they gather further information, assess probable witnesses, and receive favorable and unfavorable court rulings on motions and requests. Because case prognosis changes as these various events occur, the parties may not have strong incentives to consider settlement discussions until faced with the prospect of immediate trial. As a result, many cases do not take assessable shape until fairly late in the litigation process.

In the discovery process available in American litigation, the litigating parties can force one another to disclose information. This imposes a cost, but also could facilitate settlement negotiations. It may be a lack of information or a misperception of provable facts that causes parties to make unrealistic claims or have unrealistic expectations. Nevertheless, because discovery takes time and is the subject of adversarial combat, the process — in cases of any complexity at all — usually works against settlement efforts. Obtaining full discovery may take years, and many lawyers, hoping to find some valuable information or simply acting cautiously, will defer serious settlement discussion until discovery is complete. This is particularly true when the lawyer is also busy with other cases, and does not have, or take, the time to assess the settlement suitability of pending litigation. In addition, litigants often contest discovery adversarially, and that psychologically reinforces adversariness as a dispute resolution mode. The costs that discovery imposes on the parties also constitute an increased investment in a litigated solution.

Of course, at the end of the discovery process, each party should have fairly full information about the other's case. This information is most useful to lawyers in assessing the viability and value of a case. Such information can stimulate productive settlement discussions, but can also limit settlement possibilities. This is because litigators shape the case adversarially; the information the lawyers acquire is, for the most part, only relevant to the issues framed in the suit. Other information useful to fashioning a creative settlement (for example, information regarding party interests not directly or immediately implicated in the suit) will not likely be there. Unless all concerned make special efforts, this means that lawsuit settlement negotiations, whenever they occur, will tend to follow competitive-compromise, rather than problem-solving, bargaining models.

* * *

DOUGLAS E. ROSENTHAL,[*]
LAWYER AND CLIENT: WHO'S IN CHARGE?
109-13 (1974)[**]

* * *

[One] option for the attorney to maximize his returns involves manipulating the client. Erving Goffman has been a prime mover in getting social scientists to look at the often subtle and easily missed mechanisms of control that one person uses to manage his relationship with another. One skill that distinguishes between successful and less successful lawyers is their mastery of the "art of impression management," an art Goffman has explored in much of his work. A lawyer with impression management skills is able to use his authoritative position as expert and helper to manage the professional relationship with his client virtually as he sees fit. Several different lawyer management styles have been noted in past research. There is a dominating aggressive pattern of lawyer behavior toward clients and a more permissive, conciliatory style. Some lawyers direct more of their attention to research and analysis, preferring to deal with the client's problem as a technical matter. Others are drawn more to dealing with the client's view of his problem and prefer to adopt a counseling rather than a technical orientation. Still others are primarily interested in making money and make no bones about this to the client. What has not been sufficiently stressed in past research is that the good lawyers have mastered a repertory of these styles and can shift from one to another as they choose. One lawyer interviewee, who has done graduate work in sociology, said that this is the important insight he was afraid would not receive sufficient attention in the present analysis. He put the matter succinctly:

> A main difference between a good attorney and a poor attorney is the number of roles and the sensitivity in determining which lawyer role to play in which situation, that a lawyer has at his command.

A good lawyer manages not only his client, but also the insurance adjuster, the judge, and the jury. His clients admire him, adjusters and judges respect him, and juries believe him. Qualities that impress some of these people in some situations are not the same ones that work in other settings.

When faced with an economic interest that competes with the client's, most attorneys employ the device of preparing the client to accept less than he anticipates and persuading him that it is in his best interest to do so — "cooling the client out." Cooling the client out is not per se good or bad. Most lawyers justify the practice because, they claim, most clients expect to

---

[*] Douglas E. Rosenthal is a partner in the law firm of Constantine Cannon in Washington, D.C. This excerpt examines how lawyers "manage" their clients in the course of legal representation.

become rich out of their claims. Where this unrealistic expectation is indeed held, the client must be disabused to forestall inevitable disappointment. However, interviews indicate that some clients have lost the "pot of gold" mentality by the time they reach the lawyer. For many of them, being cooled out by their attorney is less justifiable as a reality principle. Instead, it makes sense only as a way to make the case disposition economically feasible for the attorney. If the lawyer can convince the client that holding out for a trial or pretrial last-ditch settlement offer is dangerous, he can manage the client into an early discounted settlement. This may well be the main reason why a majority of clients receive a smaller recovery than the panel evaluation of their case worth.

In a few instances, cooling out the client is a breach of legal ethics. One specific limitation on a lawyer's impression management is the principle that a case may not be settled without the client's informed consent. A lawyer is also obligated to disclose, immediately, every settlement offer made by the insurer. Nevertheless, a few attorneys have conceded that they regularly make unethical misrepresentations to discourage a client's inclination to feel that his lawyer didn't get enough money for him. One admitted,

> Theoretically, it's unethical not to report accurately negotiations with an insurer to the client. But you can't, and no lawyer does. You tell him about it in such a way that he is prepared to be satisfied. Say the other side offers $5,000. You tell the client that they offered $3,000. He'll say, "That's no good." You agree and say, casually, that you will try to get $4,500 out of them which would be fine. He's still not so happy, but reluctantly agrees. Two days later you call him back with the "good news" that you got him more than he expected, $5,000. Now the client is prepared to be happy. You know what is a good settlement and what he should take. If it is necessary to lie and cheat him to get him to accept what's good for him you do it.

* * *

. . . . The inexorability of the economic conflict of interest between lawyer and client in so many cases, raises a serious question about the appropriateness of the traditional ideal that an ethical and competent lawyer can and will make the client's interest his own. Goffman puts the matter as follows:

> Performers often foster the impression that they have ideal motives . . . and ideal qualifications for the role and that it was not necessary for them to suffer any indignities, insults, and humiliations, or make any tacitly understood "deals" in order to acquire the role. . . . Reinforcing these ideal impressions there is a kind of "rhetoric of training" whereby . . . licensing bodies require practitioners to absorb a mystical range and period of training, in part to maintain a monopoly, but in part to foster the impression that the licensed

practitioner is someone who has been reconstituted by his learning experience and is now set apart from other men.

. . . . The nature of the legal problems with which the attorney grapples are uncertain and costly. Error is not always avoidable. Yet the traditional model dictates, and most lawyers and clients accept the dictum, that the lawyer should appear to be a rock of informed judgment, knowing with technical precision the client's true interest and being free from human pressures to compromise that interest. To play the part within the design of the traditional model, to make a living yet keep clients content, the lawyer must engage in impression management generally, and especially in client cool out. As Victor Thompson notes,

> The greater the discrepancy between the self-image projected, on the one hand, and reality, on the other, the greater the load placed upon sheer play acting.

[Another] option for resolving the conflict between the lawyer's and client's interest is to bring the specific conflict issues up for discussion and negotiation between the two parties. . . . One of the actions distinguishing some participating from nonparticipating clients is that they tend not to wait for the lawyer to raise these issues. Instead, they themselves spot one or more of them — the extent of the fee, the amount of emotional support to be given, the relative merits of delay — and bring them into the open for joint discussion.

Obviously lawyers find it easier to perform their roles by trying to maintain as much control as possible over all aspects of the way a claim is conducted. The less flexible persist in this behavior even when it antagonizes the client. . . . The few very skilled lawyers . . . tactically relinquish some control by disclosure and compromise with respect to a few issues without, however, relinquishing their considerable overall control of case strategy. Lawyers acknowledge the obligation of explaining details of a case to the client — in the abstract. Of the lawyers responding to a question about whether or not they recognize any such obligation, 62 percent (28 of 45) responded, "yes, without qualification." However, when given a list of specific open issues that might possibly be disclosed to the client and discussed with him, a majority favored disclosure only with respect to two: the need to hire an expert witness and the final settlement terms. Less than 20 percent favored discussing with the client when to begin suit, how much to sue for, in which court to sue, whether or not to seek a jury trial, or at what level to set the initial settlement demand.

* * *

William L. F. Felstiner & Austin Sarat,[*] *Enactments of Power: Negotiating Reality and Responsibility in Lawyer-Client Interactions*
77 CORNELL L. REV. 1447, 1454-68 (1992)[**]

* * *

Two things should be noted about conventional views of power in lawyer-client relationships. First, these views are basically structural: they suggest that power varies by status, economic resources, field of law, or the vagaries of particular clients. Second, they treat power as a "thing" possessed at one time or another by one of the parties to a lawyer-client relationship. As we see it, power in lawyer-client interactions is less stable, predictable, and clear-cut than the conventional view holds. Power is not a "thing" to be possessed; it is continuously enacted and re-enacted, constituted and reconstituted. The enactments and constitution are subtle and shifting; they can be observed only through close attention to the microdynamics of individual lawyer-client encounters.

II

ENACTMENTS OF POWER IN DIVORCE CASES

In the divorce lawyer's office two worlds come together: the legal world for which the lawyer speaks and to which he provides access and the social world of the client, beset with urgent emotional demands, complex and changing relationships, and unmet financial needs. Just as the legal world appears arcane and ritualized to the uninitiated, the world of the client is one to which the lawyer has access in only a limited, very mediated way. When lawyer and client interact, each confronts, in the world the other inhabits, something new and opaque, yet something of indisputable relevance to their relationship.

To each, the hidden world of the other becomes known mostly through reciprocal accounts. This means that lawyer-client interaction is a process of story-telling and interrogation in which lawyer and client seek to produce for each other a satisfying rendition of her distinctive world. What each accepts as "real" in these accounts is negotiated, implicitly as well as explicitly, and frequently transformed over the course of their interaction. Negotiating a version that overlaps and is treated as a joint product is essential if lawyers and clients are to construct a mutually tolerable story that is likely to be persuasive to the other side or to a judge.

---

[*] William L. F. Felstiner is Professor in the Law and Society Program at the University of California, Santa Barbara. Austin Sarat is William Nelson Cromwell Professor of Jurisprudence and Political Science at Amherst College. Their article is an empirical study of the ways lawyers and clients negotiate their relationship and the division of power between them.

[**] Copyright © 1992 Cornell Law Review. Reprinted with permission.

Making a landfall in the treacherous waters of each other's world can be a threatening experience for both lawyers and clients. In the world of law, unknown rules and people operating in forbidding surroundings and through alien processes can influence or decide matters of great moment to clients: child custody, the rights of a non-custodial parent, the disposition of the family home, the division of property and income. In the social world of the client, the lawyer's professional skills may be severely tested by the client's guilt about marriage failure, unresolved feelings for the spouse, continuing and often irritating disputes over children and money, or by a new relationship whose relevance to the divorce may not be acknowledged. Even when the lawyer tries to keep it at bay, the social world of the client is continually present.

For both lawyer and client the stakes are high in what the other knows and reveals. While the client must rely on the lawyer's legal experience, the lawyer is largely dependent on the client's interpretations of her social world. For both, motives, goals and data may be suppressed by plan or inadvertence. Each may consciously adopt a narrative style and rules of relevance that limit what the other can assimilate. They may each say both more and less than they intend as they explain what they want the other to know.

Although lawyers and clients are highly dependent on each other, the stories they tell about their interactions are tales of suspicion and doubt. Clients are suspicious about the depth of commitment lawyers bring to their cases and their own ability to control the content and timing of their lawyers' actions. They worry about lawyers who are too busy to attend fully to the idiosyncrasies of their cases, and about divided loyalties, competence, judgment and personality. Lawyers, on the other hand, are concerned because they have to deal with and depend on people who are likely to be emotionally agitated, in the midst of a profound personal crisis, ambivalent about divorce, determined to hurt their spouse, and misguided about what they can expect from the divorce process.

These concerns lead to responses that themselves produce secondary problems. Lawyers worried about the emotional instability of their clients often appear hyper-rational, detached, disloyal, and callous. Clients, put off and alienated by such appearances, appear even more unstable and unpredictable to their lawyers. Lawyers worry about distortions introduced into client accounts and attempt to test client stories without expressing overt skepticism.

. . . . In the standard analysis of the profession, lawyers are presented either as agents moving tactically toward their clients' clearly expressed goals, as principals paternalistically operating in accordance with their sense of the clients' best interests, or as opportunists using the clients' cases to work out their own agendas. Given these very different images of lawyers, it is natural to pose Rosenthal's well-known question, "Who's In

Charge?" However, asking "who's in charge" implies both that a single, stable answer can be provided, and that the possessor of power can be clearly identified.

We think that neither is the case. Both lawyers and clients are sometimes frustrated by feelings of powerlessness in dealing with the other, and such feelings must be taken seriously. Often no one may be in charge. Interactions between lawyers and clients involve as much drift and uncertainty as they do direction and clarity of purpose. It may be difficult, at any one moment, to determine who, if anyone, is defining the objectives, determining strategy, or devising tactics.

Power in lawyer-client relationships would not be so ambiguous if it were just an attribute of position, or if it could be captured by attending simply to offices, roles and forms. Whether in lawyer-client interactions or elsewhere, however, power does not exist outside of particular social interactions. It is always generated from the inside in a continuing series of situated assertions and rejoinders, by claims and responses to those claims, and by particular gestures and the resistance those gestures provoke. It is not like a tool sitting on a shelf, waiting to be picked up and applied to the task at hand. Power, rather, is enacted and constituted moment-by-moment. It is seen in indirect moves and sleights-of-hand, in ruptures and ellipses, and in what is left unsaid and unacknowledged as well as in forceful, continuous and overt assertion.

Power is continuously produced in the regular and apparently uneventful routines and practices that comprise most social interactions. But it is also conditioned by the cultural resources that particular lawyers and clients bring to their relationships. Even when it seems robust and irresistible, power may be fragile and contested. Each of the social interactions through which power is constituted has its own distinctive history and its own particular future. In this sense power is always created anew and, like any newborn, its progress and outcome is uncertain.

The malleability of power, however, does not mean that the respective positions of lawyer and client are decided by a coin toss, or that they are open to limitless development at the start of every session. Lawyer-client interaction always occurs in the space of law. For the lawyer, this means that interaction takes place in a familiar space, a space of privilege. The books on the lawyer's shelves are books the lawyer has read or knows how to read; the language spoken is a language in which lawyers are trained and with which they are comfortable; the rituals performed give special place to the lawyer even as they are forbidding and unwelcoming to the uninitiated.

* * *

III

ENACTMENTS OF POWER AND THE NEGOTIATION OF REALITY

In the world of no-fault divorce, the legal process formally has limited functions — dividing assets and future income, fixing custody and visitation, and, occasionally, protecting physical safety and property. Lawyers must understand their client's objectives concerning these issues. But determination of clients' interests is a known quagmire. Clients may not know what they want or may not want what they ought to want. They may change their minds in unpredictable ways, or they may not change their minds when they ought to do so. Clients may be insufficiently self-conscious, or plagued by false consciousness. Moreover, they may find it difficult to distinguish between lawyers who are trying to impose their vision of client needs on clients and lawyers who are trying to get clients to share a vision of those needs that is not controlled by the power of the lawyer's professional position.

When it comes to defining goals, lawyers generally are permissive. That is, they are intensely concerned that the client adopt "reasonable" goals, but within the rather broad parameters of that notion, lawyers are not directive. For divorce lawyers and their clients, the realm of "reality" is the realm of the possible. Within that realm, the final choice is generally left to the client. However, before that choice can be made, considerable energy is devoted to the construction of a mutually acceptable account of the reality of divorce. Defining and identifying "realistic" goals, and orienting and reconciling clients to the world of the legally possible, occurs during complex negotiations in which struggle, if not overt conflict, is frequent.

The mutual construction of reality takes two forms in divorce cases. On the one hand, lawyer and client may develop, over time, a set of goals and tactics that capitalize on the lawyer's knowledge of the legal world and the client's knowledge of her own social world. The final version of what is real is not dictated by one or the other, but built by them together without the need for either to alter the other's view in many important respects. On the other hand, lawyer and client may not see reality in converging terms and each may seek to defend and/or advance his particular vision. Developing a mutually satisfying sense of what reasonably can be expected or achieved is at the heart of the complex lawyer-client interactions we observed. Yet that sense is not so concrete and tangible that, once achieved, it can be taken for granted and easily maintained. It is always in danger of slipping away as events from the client's social world intrude into the deliberations, and as lawyer and client together gather information about the goals, expectations and strategies of their adversaries.

In examining the ongoing and fragile negotiation of reality between lawyers and clients, we focus first on the factors that "distort" reality for lawyers and clients, and then on the strategies and tactics employed to promote particular versions of reality. Clients, of course, have greater difficulty than lawyers in becoming oriented to the world of the legally possible. Some of the difficulty is obvious. Emotionally off-balance, angry, depressed, anxious or agitated, they may have trouble understanding what they are told, believing the information that they get and focusing on the alternatives that are presented to them. They may be impelled to strike at or "pay back" their spouse in ways that are inconsistent with reality and even, by altering the posture of the other side, make their goals more difficult to attain.

Second, clients may expect more of the legal system than it can deliver under even the best of circumstances. Unrealistic expectations may range from saving the marriage to transforming the spouse, but they are most likely to be centered on financial affairs. Clients tend to reason up from needs, rather than down from resources, and they have great difficulty in dealing with the gap between the two. Additionally, clients are slow to realize that many legal entitlements are not self-executing. The judge at the hearing on temporary support may say that the client is entitled to $100 a week, but that does not guarantee that the client will receive anything. Many clients are naive about their own financial needs, and may have to be patiently educated by their lawyers. Some clients have difficulty grasping the limits of what is possible because they cannot believe that the law actually is as it actually is. Finally, clients are slow to understand the costs of achieving their objectives. Vindication, the last dollar of support, meticulous estimates of property value, a neat and precise division of property, a visitation scheme that covers a very wide range of contingencies, and equitable arrangements that govern the future as well as the present may be theoretically possible, but even approximations require extensive services that middle-class clients generally cannot afford.

Lawyers, of course, are less encumbered on the legal side in developing a view of reality in particular cases. Nevertheless, it is not all clear sailing for them. There are, for instance, three kinds of information problems. In order to form a view of the possible they may need to know things that clients sometimes cannot tell them. These include client goals as well as things that clients sometimes will not tell them, such as their feelings. In addition, there are things that clients sometimes try to tell lawyers that lawyers do not recognize or understand. For example, in a case that we previously analyzed at some length, the client could not decide whether she wanted to settle or litigate, and could not make the lawyer understand that she had great difficulty in negotiating a settlement with her spouse because she could not trust him to fulfill any commitments that he made.

It would, however, be a mistake when thinking about divorce cases to assume that clients are emotional cripples and that the personalities, problems and politics of lawyers do not interfere with their ability to define reality and/or respond to their clients' definitions. Lawyers may not be astute, attentive or experienced enough to catch the client's message. In addition, they may be so overworked or so worn down by practice that they do not have the patience or stamina to negotiate effectively with their clients.

However serious the distortions in the lawyer's grasp of the legally possible, the difficulties they face in determining social reality, in determining what is socially possible, are more serious. The lawyer's ability to interpret the social world of the client depends on the raw information they receive from clients, the interpretations that clients present, and the interpretations or re-interpretations that lawyers themselves make. All of these steps are complicated and pose difficulties for lawyers. Occasionally, information is presented without an overt interpretation. For example, a client may simply state, "He did not give me money for tuition." More often, however, the information the client does provide is reconstituted through the client's experience and perception of self into highly interpreted material: "He had no interest at all in furthering my education." Often the client's presentations are influenced by emotional and financial stakes, or are incomplete or conflicted. The nature of client communications means that lawyers must continually sift through and evaluate the social world presented by the client in order to reconstruct a picture of the world that they can effectively use in promoting the client's interests. In this effort they may, from time to time, be assisted by information that comes from other sources, such as opposing counsel or relevant documents. For the most part, however, lawyers must depend on their own experience and judgment.

Lawyers use an array of strategies to try to persuade their clients to adopt a particular definition of reality. Of course, their knowledge of legal rules and process, and the information that they have about specific players, such as other lawyers, judges and mediators, provide powerful arguments. Unless they have been through the process before, clients' only sources of information about the nature and limits of divorce law are their own lawyer and anecdotes related by their family and friends. In addition to their feel for the legal system and for the *dramatis personae*, lawyers, particularly specialists in family law, benefit from their experiences in prior cases. Having "heard it all before," they frequently interpret the behavior of the spouse and his or her lawyer with some accuracy, looking beyond words and positions articulated to more fundamental concerns.

Still, many divorce lawyers use their knowledge and experience in a manipulative way. The most common technique is to engage in what we call "law talk." Law talk consists of the conversations that lawyers and clients have about the legal system, legal process, rules, hearings, trials, judges, other lawyers and the other lawyer in the case. In general, we have found law talk to be a form of cynical realism through which the legal system and its actors are trashed on various accounts, frequently in an exaggerated fashion. The purpose of this rhetorical style is usually to convince the client that the legal process is risky business, that legal justice is different from social justice, and that clients can only achieve reasonable certainty at a reasonable cost, and maintain some control over a divorce, by negotiating a settlement with the other side.

Even when it takes the form of hyperbole, law talk is not commonly introduced into lawyer-client conversations in an aggressive way. Lawyers often join with their clients' positions and appear, at least initially, to be sympathetic. They introduce their clients to reality by invoking their own understanding of legal norms and their own expectations about what courts would do were they to go before a judge. Clients are told that it does not make sense to "insist on something that is far out of line from what a court would do."

Lawyers use delay and circular conversation to convey messages about what is legally realistic. They engage in a form of passive resistance, maintaining the form of the agency relationship while subtly altering its substance. Rarely are expectations overtly branded as unrealistic in a judgmental sense; instead, most lawyers patiently, but insistently, remind their clients of the constraints that the law imposes on both of them, that is, of law's definition of reality.

The behavior of clients mirrors that of their lawyers. Expectations about lawyer performance are generally not made explicit. Clients rarely specify what they want their lawyers to do or how they want their lawyers to behave. In fact, one of the chief difficulties with which lawyers and clients must contend is their mutual aversion to confrontation. In the face of continued client demands for the unreasonable, lawyers restate technical or strategic difficulties, try to recast reasonable goals into acceptable outcomes, or simply change the subject. They do not, however, directly tell their clients that they are being unreasonable.

In the face of lawyers' insistence that they accommodate themselves to the reality of what the law allows, clients generally persist, at least initially, in expounding their needs, explaining their notions of justice, or reiterating their objectives. But rarely do they insist that their lawyer make a particular demand, argue a particular position, or even endorse their view. Where dissatisfaction is great, the usual client response is exit rather than voice.

Although law talk is the divorce lawyer's basic device in efforts to reorient her clients' views of reality, others include rhetorical flourishes, technical language and role manipulation. Perhaps proceeding from experience in the law school classroom, some lawyers conjure up a "parade of horribles." In this scenario, clients are informed that if they continue to seek one goal or another, they will suffer a series of negative consequences of continuing and mounting severity. Alternatively, lawyers tell stories about other clients who have persisted in similar courses of action, pursued understandable but unrealistic objectives, and suffered disastrous results.

While technical language is rarely used as a strategy to confuse a client or make him feel dependent on professional expertise, clients report to us that it has this effect nonetheless. Some lawyers invest, or try to invest, their views with added persuasive authority by puffing up their status in the legal community. They cast themselves as the "dean" of the divorce bar, or as one of its most experienced and astute practitioners, or as an insider with special access to the judge and other functionaries. * * *

Clients are more limited in the resources that they can mobilize to persuade lawyers to accept their view of reality. Their inherent advantage is their knowledge of their spouse and generally superior ability to estimate the spouse's reaction to offers or demands. Lawyers are sensitive to this comparative advantage and often try to exploit it. * * *

In addition to deploying their knowledge of their own social world, clients frequently assert their views, or resist their lawyers', through repetition and denial. Lawyers may talk about the unreasonable or the unobtainable, they may predict this or that outcome, but clients need not, and frequently do not, acquiesce. Rather, clients may become quiet or change the subject, only to reintroduce the same topic later. What may seem to the observer to be wasted motion and circularity, may really be a tactic in an ongoing negotiation. Finally, clients on occasion fight back by withholding information, sometimes explicitly, sometimes not. They use this tactic when they want to exclude the lawyer from some field of inquiry, often because they consider an issue out of bounds or would be embarrassed by some disclosure.

The negotiation of reality between lawyer and client is time-consuming and repetitive, yet often incomplete or unclear in its results. Whose definition of reality prevails is often impossible to determine. Even as decisions are made and documents are filed, how those decisions and documents relate to lawyer-client conversations about goals and expectations can be mysterious. It is, however, precisely by attending to this mystery that one can understand enactments of power and tactics of resistance.

IV

ENACTMENTS OF POWER AND THE NEGOTIATION
OF RESPONSIBILITY

Unlike the effort to define reasonable and attainable goals, the task of securing the client's objectives initially appears to be neither opaque nor ambiguous. The steps that must be taken to get on with the case are routine. Particular, well-defined procedural requirements must be satisfied to secure various kinds of court assistance. Knowing and executing the necessary steps are conventionally regarded as the lawyer's responsibility. Many involve details of procedure beyond the experience of even the most sophisticated client. Most of the remaining steps involve various kinds of negotiations with the other side. Where the lawyer believes tasks are more easily or more cheaply carried out by the client himself, such an assignment ought to be straightforward. Some activities are clearly the exclusive preserve of the lawyer — preparing the pleadings, conducting hearings and trials, for example. However, other aspects of divorce that can be shared or assigned to the client often are not.

In general, lawyers try to maintain control over negotiations with the other side, except in discussions about personal property. They do this by insisting that these negotiations take place on a lawyer-to-lawyer basis. To lawyers, these professional exchanges are a core element of legal services in divorce, an arena in which their professional experience and competence are more nearly actualized than in helping clients comprehend the legal process or figure out their financial prospects. Nevertheless, some clients, perhaps fearful that their interests will not be adequately represented, want to negotiate directly with their spouse.

But whatever the explicit assignments of responsibility, divorce cases are not self-executing. It is not always clear what needs to be done, who is going to do it, and who is responsible for assuring that it gets done. Either lawyer or client might not take the steps that they ought to take, have agreed to take, or been urged to take. In this context, enactments of power, either in assuming or assigning responsibility, are, like those in the negotiation of reality, often unclear or confused.

One reason legal action in divorce does not proceed in a clear and orderly way is simply that individual and organizational agendas are beyond the control of any single party to the case. However, the divorces that we observed suggest that the fundamental reason cases do not proceed steadily or smoothly is that lawyers and clients on the *same* side encounter, from each other, various levels of procrastination, vacillation, disapproval, withdrawal, repression, and information problems that delay, distort and jeopardize what they are trying to accomplish. These moves involve indirect enactments of power and indirect tactics of resistance. Rarely do lawyers or clients acknowledge that they are not going to do what they said they would do, or that they are repressing their inclination to say something they are not going to say. The effect of these covert enactments of power becomes manifest only after a price has been paid, and these enactments are more powerful on that account.

One of the surprising aspects of the lawyer-client relationship in divorce proceedings is the rarity of the imperative mode. Put quite starkly, clients almost never say to their lawyers something on the order of "I am the client, I am paying the bill, now do this." This finding is not a comment about a form of speech. It is not that clients just find a more diplomatic way of issuing a command. Rather, in the face of disagreement, clients do not assert their prerogative to tell the lawyer what to do. Such a finding would not be so remarkable if the professional in question possessed scientific or technological expertise, such that a lay person would be out of order were he to issue commands against the professional's technical judgment. However, in the context of divorce, many of the judgments over which conflicts occur do not reflect technical considerations; rather, they are questions of timing, motive and interpretation for which the lawyer may have no comparative advantage. Indeed, insofar as the resolution of those questions depends upon a feel for the behavior of the spouse, the client's qualifications may well be superior.

Lawyers are no more inclined to command than are their clients. They may urge, cajole, flatter, use rhetorical tricks, provide unqualified or contingent advice, predict harm, discomfort, frustration or catastrophe, but they almost never say, "I am the professional, I am the expert, now do this." Furthermore, although lawyers frequently fail to act, they rarely invoke their knowledge and experience as grounds for refusing to act.

The avoidance of imperative modes suggests that the expressive forms used are intuitively sound. Both lawyers and clients apparently recognize that, were they to behave as if they were hierarchically empowered, they would undermine the legitimacy of what is generally considered to be a cooperative enterprise. But sound as the conventional forms may be for defining the limits of overt power, an unwillingness to issue commands opens a wide territory for subtle and latent maneuver.

* * *

Deborah L. Rhode,[*] *Gender and Professional Roles*
63 FORDHAM L. REV. 39, 49-53 (1994)[**]

* * *

B. *Lawyer-Client Relationships*

Feminists' second line of challenge to conventional professional structures involves their power dynamics. Lawyer-client relationships frequently display patterns of dominance that ill-serve broader societal interests.

The problems often start in law school. Conventional classroom hierarchies encourage extremes of both unreflective passivity and aggressive competition. The structure of professorial control over the content and evaluation of learning processes discourages independent thought and encourages participation designed more to impress than inform. All too often, the "search for knowledge" becomes a scramble for status that undermines broader educational objectives. Authoritarian structures and inadequate clinical and seminar opportunities shortchange capacities that feminists believe should be central to professional practice. Certain skills, such as collaboration, empathetic listening, and ethically reflective decision making, call for more interactive, egalitarian teaching formats.

The patterns of dominance reinforced in legal education are replicated in later workplace relationships, particularly those involving subordinate

---

[*] Deborah L. Rhode is Ernest W. McFarland Professor at Stanford Law School. This excerpt discusses the adverse effects of professional dominance on the lawyer-client relationship.

[**] Copyright © 1994 Fordham Law Review. Reprinted with permission.

groups. Authoritarian, paternalistic interactions between lawyers and clients often obscure the needs that prompted professional consultation in the first instance. One study involving low-income legal aid clients found that lawyers frequently interrupted and attempted to control the topic in over ninety percent of their comments. Yet professionals who constantly redirect the conversation of those they purport to serve cannot effectively connect their skills to real human needs. Nor can such strategies enable individuals to assess and assert their own best interests. Empirical research consistently indicates that clients who actively participate in decision-making do better and have greater satisfaction than those who do not.

The adverse effects of professional dominance are compounded by other status inequalities such as class, race, ethnicity, and gender. The most egregious cases of manipulating, circumventing, or simply overlooking client objectives have involved subordinate groups. Women's experiences in divorce proceedings offer a case in point. Legal aid lawyers frequently have refused to handle such proceedings on the ground that they present no pressing need or important law reform issues even though clients give high priority to these cases.

Even for middle and upper-income parties, a mismatch persists between what many women seek and what many attorneys supply. Empirical studies reveal participants occupied with two different divorces: lawyers with the financial and legal consequences of separation, and clients with the social and emotional ones. Attorneys receive little training in how to respond to individuals in stress, and often end up talking past the concerns that are most central to the parties. The problem is apparent in many dialogues recorded in recent research on divorce practice. For example:

> Client: There was harassment and verbal degradation. No interest at all in my furthering my education. None whatsoever. Sexual harassment. If there was ever any time when I did not want or need sex, I was subject to, you know, these long verbal whiplashings. Then the Bible would be put out on the counter with passages underlined as to what a poor wife I was. Just constant harassment from him.

> Lawyer: Mmn uh.

> Client: [I] could lock myself in the bathroom and he would break in. And I was just to listen, whether I wanted to or not. . . . There was no escaping him, short of getting in a car and driving away. But then he would stand outside in the driveway and yell, anyhow. *The man was not well.*

> Lawyer: Okay. Now how about any courses you took?

Clients are like performers playing before bored, but dutiful legal audiences; lawyers do not "interrupt the aria, but [they do not] applaud much either for fear of an encore." As a result, the process becomes for many clients "at best a distraction and at worst an additional trauma." While lawyers cannot substitute for trained therapists, neither can they function effectively as legal advisors without adequate skills in empathetic listening.

Attorneys accustomed to dominating clients' decision-making for "their own good" may too readily replicate those patterns when it serves practitioners' own interests. One of the most obvious examples involves lawyer-client sexual relationships. Although the extent of the practice is difficult to measure, almost a third of surveyed attorneys are aware of one or more such relationships. Research involving a variety of professions finds that such sexual intimacy puts clients at substantial risk. These relationships are likely to compromise independent judgment by both parties. Attorneys who want to prolong or terminate sexual intimacy may skew their legal advice accordingly. And clients who are involved in such relationships do not always feel able to challenge the quality of assistance provided, the strategies proposed, or the fees requested. Nor is intimacy wholly consensual if parties fear that rebuffing their lawyer would adversely affect their legal representation or impose the expense and delay of hiring other counsel.

Although almost three-quarters of surveyed lawyers acknowledge that sexual involvement with clients causes problems, no state imposes a categorical prohibition, and only a few address the issue explicitly. Many practitioners oppose bar regulation on the ground that it would interfere with lawyers' privacy and associational rights, create "oppressive bureaucracies," discourage relationships that promote "fervent[ ]" advocacy, and force single lawyers to "revert to celibacy."

A widespread view is that attorneys "should be able to sort out their sexual activities without any advice from the state bar."

On some level, most feminists would agree. Attorneys should. But as a review of recently reported cases makes clear, too many lawyers need better advice from somewhere, and they aren't getting it from courts or disciplinary authorities. Sanctions and reporting structures are far from adequate. More bright line rules are necessary, preferably ones prohibiting such involvement. Other professions have implemented such prohibitions without the dire consequences that opponents have invoked. At the very least, if a client complains, the burden should fall on the attorney to prove that the sexual relationship was consensual and that professional services were not adversely affected.

* * *

Chapter 8

ETHICAL ISSUES IN NEGOTIATION

Every state except California (which has its own code of ethics) has adopted some version of the American Bar Association's Model Rules of Professional Conduct or its Model Code of Professional Responsibility. These rules govern all aspects of legal practice, including negotiation on behalf of clients. Despite the fact that negotiation is a central activity for most lawyers — whether it involves negotiating the timing or location of a deposition, the terms of a contract, or the settlement of a lawsuit — the ethical rules have little to say about appropriate negotiation behavior. Indeed, when negotiation is mentioned specifically in the rules, it is to point out that a different — and *lower* — ethical standard applies to negotiation than to other lawyer activities. For example, Model Rule 4.1(a) prohibits a lawyer from "knowingly" making "a false statement of material fact or law to a third person." Comment 2 to that rule, however, states that "estimates of price or value placed on the subject of a transaction" are not considered to be statements of material fact "under generally accepted conventions in negotiation" — thus leaving room for all manner of puffing and bluffing designed to mislead an opponent.

The generality of the ethical rules and the fact that negotiations typically take place in private, without oversight by either the public or any judicial officer, means that there is little effective monitoring of negotiation behavior and that information about individual negotiators is largely shared on an informal basis. Lawyers are expected to be rational, analytic, and dispassionate in handling cases. As we have seen, however, negotiations involve interpersonal conflict, and negotiators usually lack critical information about the other side's true situation and needs. In the face of such uncertainty and tension, self-protective behavior is common. The negotiator who does not simply give in to the other side to escape conflict may be sorely tempted to stretch the bounds of the ethical rules to gain her footing in the process.

A. THE USE OF DECEPTION

A central issue in negotiation ethics is whether the deceptive techniques common in distributive bargaining — for example, concealing and minimizing your willingness and authority to settle, making false demands, or low-balling — are appropriate in legal negotiations. Some authors, such as White in the article that follows, insist that such tactics are fundamental to negotiation itself and therefore cannot be considered unethical when used by lawyers. Further, his argument goes, the ethical duty of zealous advocacy *requires* that lawyers use such tactics in pursuit of their clients' goals. By contrast, the late Judge Rubin argued that, as professionals, lawyers should be held to a higher standard than that of the bazaar or the used car lot. In the article below, Rubin proposes that the rules of legal ethics should not tolerate negotiation conduct designed to mislead and confuse the other side.

These debates go far beyond the subject of negotiation, since they involve both the nature of law as a profession and the extent to which aspirations for professional conduct can or should be translated into ethical rules binding on all lawyers. At the same time, they have a concrete practical importance for the negotiator. Most negotiations have distributive aspects; and every negotiator has to decide for herself, within the broad outlines of the ethical rules, how far she is willing to engage in deception on behalf of her clients in order to maximize gain. On the one hand, if you are authorized to settle for $50,000 and you say so explicitly, you have to consider whether you are advocating sufficiently vigorously for your client. On the other hand, if your authority is $50,000 and you lead the other side to believe that your client will not accept anything less than $150,000, you have to ask whether it is ethical to do so. If you decide that it is, as the comment to Model Rule 4.1, above, suggests, then you have to decide which of the means you could use to create that belief — bluffing, evasion, deflection, outright lying — are themselves ethical.

Although affirmative lies about material facts or law are clearly prohibited under the ethical rules, lying can be effective, at least if it is not discovered. Given the uncertainties of the negotiation situation, rationalizations — and potential rewards — for lying abound, and lawyers often justify it as a preemptive necessity ("Sally hit me, so I hit her first"). The waffling in the rules about what constitutes a material fact in negotiation — illustrated by Comment 2 to Model Rule 4.1, noted above — and about what constitutes misrepresentation encourages such rationalizations. A lawyer has no duty to volunteer relevant facts to the other side, and under Comment 1 to Model Rule 4.1, incorporating or affirming a statement by someone else that a lawyer knows to be false is not unequivocally rejected as unethical misrepresentation ("A misrepresentation *can* occur if . . ."). For example, many lawyers would consider it ethical to say "Smith's deposition solidly supports our position that your client was speeding," even when they know that Smith has since changed his story.

Model Rule 4.1 evidences the profession's profound ambivalence toward categorically rejecting deceptive tactics that can bring great advantage to one's client, while often being virtually undetectable by the other side. The most recent revision of Comment 1 to Model Rule 4.1 broadened the definition of misrepresentations by adding that they "can also occur by partially true but misleading statements or omissions that are the equivalent of affirmative false statements;" but it is not clear just what additional conduct is prohibited by this language. Many authors, including Wetlaufer in the excerpt below, have noted both the individual and social costs of routine use of deception: the corrosive effects of lying on the liar herself and on the system that countenances it, even in the name of duty to clients.

Another point of view about deception, illustrated by the article by Hartwell, suggests that context is crucial to experiencing deception in negotiation as ethical or unethical. A lawyer engaged in a competitive negotiation to purchase goods, Hartwell argues, does not expect the other side to be forthcoming or even straightforward about its selling price or its interest in making a deal. The puffing and bluffing that occur in such negotiations do not surprise or upset the participants. What is perceived as unethical, he maintains, is a deception of context: for example, when someone engaged in an apparently integrative negotiation makes false demands in order to improve the outcome for his client.

B. THE ZEALOUS ADVOCATE AND THE ADVISOR

Although much questionable negotiation behavior is justified on the basis of the ethical duty of zealous advocacy contained in Canon 7 of the Model Code ("A lawyer should represent a client zealously within the bounds of the law"), both the Model Code and the Model Rules recognize that lawyers act as advisors to clients as well as advocates for them. Model Rule 2.1 deals with the often-ignored function of the lawyer as counselor and acknowledges the propriety of a lawyer's advice "refer[ring] not only to law, but to other considerations such as moral, economic, social, and political factors, that may be relevant to the client's situation." A lawyer does not have to stand by silently, no matter what ends a client seeks, nor is she limited to giving purely technical advice.

Indeed, a lawyer who takes the counseling function seriously may find herself faced with fewer ethical dilemmas during negotiations. In her role as the client's advisor, she can point out ethically questionable ramifications of certain courses of action and recommend alternatives. She and her client can consider important factors other than the bottom line before entering into negotiations and can develop their strategy in light of them. By keeping the client informed and involved while negotiations are underway, the lawyer can raise new issues and seek the client's approval in an ongoing fashion, as the article by Gifford in the preceding chapter suggests. Of course, the client may also insist that his lawyer proceed in a manner that the lawyer disapproves. In such a situation, the lawyer's options for withdrawal are themselves limited by the ethical rules (*see* Model Rule 1.16 below), as the article by Gilson and Mnookin in Chapter Four discusses.

C. ROLE MORALITY AND PERSONAL MORALITY

The lawyer's role as representative of her clients is often said to require an amoral stance that may differ considerably from what the lawyer would consider appropriate in her personal life. Beyond formal rules, then, each lawyer also has to decide what she is morally prepared to do for her clients, given that she is acting in a representative capacity. The client is entitled to competent representation; and the lawyer must be able to function competently without being compromised by her own internal conflict about her role. Yet many lawyers do not feel comfortable with purely instrumental ethics: if it gets you what your client wants, it is ethical, as long as it is not specifically prohibited by the rules. Such an approach ignores any claims that society may have about how its business gets carried out and leaves the individual lawyer in the dubious role of the classic "hired gun" for the client. The personal toll of accepting such a role uncritically was satirized 150 years ago by Charles Dickens, writing about the unending case of Jarndyce and Jarndyce in the novel *Bleak House*:

> How many people out of the suit, Jarndyce and Jarndyce has stretched forth its unwholesome hand to spoil and corrupt, would be a very wide question . . . . In trickery, evasion, procrastination, spoliation, botheration, under false pretences of all sorts, there are influences that can never come to good . . . . The receiver in the cause has acquired a goodly sum of money by it, but has acquired too a distrust of his own mother, and a contempt of his own kind . . . . Shirking and sharking, in all their many varieties, have been sown broadcast by the ill-fated cause; and even those who have contemplated its history from the outermost circle of such evil, have been insensibly tempted into a loose way of letting bad things alone to take their own bad course, and a loose belief that if the world go wrong, it was, in some offhand manner, never meant to go right.

In the article excerpted below, Rhode discusses the feminist critique of the traditional utilitarian and rights-based justifications for lawyers' role morality. She argues instead for direct moral accountability for professional actions, based on the realities of social and economic relations rather than on abstract ethical precepts. The article by Lax and Sebenius suggests some non-instrumental ways of thinking about ethically questionable tactics in negotiation, including such tests as whether you can look yourself in the mirror afterward or would be willing to have your family or friends know what you did. To what extent are the tests proposed by these authors appropriate for a lawyer acting as a client's agent? Must a lawyer lead a double ethical life, or else eschew serving in a representative capacity?

D. DIFFERING ETHICAL STANDARDS

Even within a single legal community, different lawyers will have different standards for acceptable negotiation behavior. These standards derive from the negotiation culture in which they grew up — in the family and among peers — as well as from the professional culture adopted in law school and law practice. In my negotiation classes there are often fierce debates about the limits of "ethical" puffing and bluffing in legal negotiations; about what constitutes a lie; and about whether lying on behalf of a client is ever justifiable. If someone says in response to a settlement proposal, "I can't do that," is it a lie if the proposal is within his authority, but is less than he thinks he can get for his clients? Or is it the other lawyer's job to probe the meaning of "can't" ("not acceptable" versus "not possible")? Is it ethical to tout the virtues of your client's property and to seek a substantially higher price than you have been offered for it by a dealer? The range of what is considered acceptable or necessary behavior in negotiation is broad, especially as the profession becomes more diverse and practice becomes more global. Individual and cultural factors affect both negotiating style and views of ethically appropriate negotiation conduct, as the articles by Markus and Lin and by Avruch in Chapter Six discuss. The rules of ethics, because of their generality, do little to advance uniform standards even for all American lawyers.

E. LAWYER-CLIENT ETHICAL DILEMMAS

Aside from concerns about the ethics of certain kinds of statements or omissions, there are more general ethical issues that confront lawyers when they negotiate. Even if a lawyer's clients are not "repeat players" in the legal system, the lawyer herself is. She has colleagues, and most likely friends, among her fellow lawyers. She deals with these lawyers more regularly than she does with any individual client, especially if she is in a specialized field such as criminal or securities law. Inevitably, there will be some conflict between her efforts to negotiate any given case effectively and her personal interest in maintaining productive and amicable relations with other lawyers. If she pushes too hard for a particular disposition, will the prosecutor make her pay for it in the next case? Should she agree to settlement terms proposed by her opponent because she knows that next month she will be asking him for similar treatment on behalf of a different client? What if she has just been referred an important case by the opposing lawyer's firm? The excerpt below from Lowenthal's article discusses the ethical conflicts created by continuing relationships among negotiators.

Such conflicts pit the lawyer's long-term interest in professional reputation and efficacy against any particular client's short-term interest in maximizing gain in the current transaction or dispute. In the excerpt that follows, Condlin discusses how this inherent principal-agent conflict leads to unproductive behavior, including the ritualized aggression that characterizes many legal negotiations. This aggression often serves to mask an underlying, and sometimes unacknowledged, need to maintain long-term effectiveness as a negotiator by cooperating with the other side. Nonetheless, it is questionable whether making such trade-offs among clients, much less acting so as to preserve relationships with other lawyers, meets the standards of devotion to the individual client's cause that the ethical rules contemplate. The article by Gilson and Mnookin in Chapter Four also addresses the pressures on lawyers to negotiate cooperatively.

Just as the reality of a lawyer's professional and social connections with other lawyers is bound to create some ethical conflicts, the realities of law practice will create others. Under the ethical rules, the decision to settle is left squarely to the client (Model Rule 1.2(a); Model Code, EC 7-7). Unless sophisticated, however, a client is likely to be influenced by his lawyer's views on the advisability of settlement. The lawyer's own circumstances, in turn, are likely to color her advice: how much time she has available to pursue the case; how likely she is to be compensated adequately for her time if she does continue; how interesting she finds the case. The lawyer's personal cost benefit analysis may bias her presentation of the facts in discussing settlement with the client. If she pessimistically assesses the likelihood of a better outcome at trial, she lowers the client's expectations and gains his agreement to settle now. Or, she may try to increase the chances of his agreeing by presenting an "offer" of $40,000 when she actually has an offer of $47,000. When she later comes back with "more," the client is prepared to accept his good fortune and settle. By such maneuvers, a lawyer attempts to satisfy her own conflicting interests, while maintaining the client's good will. The client makes the decision, but the lawyer has stacked the deck.

Although the rules of ethics emphasize the centrality of the lawyer's duty to her client, they cannot do away with such conflicts of interest as they pertain to negotiation or to other aspects of law practice. The lawyer who is aware that her own interests can potentially interfere with her advocacy for clients will be better prepared to think through these conflicts and to keep her ethical obligations clearly in mind when negotiating.

F. RECOGNIZING ETHICAL DANGER POINTS

Wherever a given negotiator draws the line for herself between ethical and unethical conduct, she needs to become aware of what sorts of situations or interactions with other negotiators are likely to trigger crossing that line. One obvious and common source of such ethical lapses is inadequate preparation for negotiations, which can lead to lying in order to save face when caught off guard. Inexperienced negotiators often lie out of desperation, and such lies can be avoided by careful pre-negotiation planning. If you have thought through the weaknesses of your case and how to address them if they come up in the negotiation, you are less likely to feel on the spot and to lie or otherwise act unethically in response.

Pressure from a client or senior partner to obtain a specific result in a negotiation can produce similar behavior, as can the negotiator's own exaggerated expectations of herself or her strong reaction to the personality or conduct of the other negotiator. Such external or internal pressures to succeed in negotiations, perhaps beyond what is realistically possible, are not as easy to alleviate as is lack of preparation. To mitigate their impact, you have to make use of self-reflection and learn to recognize the signs that such factors are at work and may affect how you behave in the heat of negotiations. What are the consequences you anticipate if you do not accomplish the desired result? How realistic are they? What alternatives do you have to behaving unethically? By acknowledging the pressures you feel to act unethically, you will be more able to step back when they assert themselves. Doing so will allow you to find more productive ways to respond to those pressures than by saying or doing something you will later regard as improper.

Alvin B. Rubin,[*] *A Causerie on Lawyers' Ethics in Negotiation*
35 LA. L. REV. 577 (1975)[**]

* * *

Although less than one fourth of the lawyers in practice today devote a majority of their time to litigation, and most spend none at all in the traditional courtroom, there are few lawyers who do not negotiate regularly, indeed daily, in their practice. Some lawyers who handle little conventional litigation persist in saying that they do not act as negotiators. If there are a few at the bar who do not, they are *rarae aves*. Patent lawyers, tax counselors and securities specialists and all those who perform the myriad tasks of office law practice may not dicker about the value of a case — though some assuredly do; but they constantly negotiate the settlement of disputed items.

Neither the Code of Professional Responsibility nor most of the writings about lawyers' ethics specifically mention any precepts that apply to this aspect of the profession. The few references to the lawyer's conduct in settlement negotiations relate to obtaining client approval and disclosing potentially conflicting interests. It is scant comfort to observe here, as apologists for the profession usually do, that lawyers are as honest as other men. If it is an inevitable professional duty that they negotiate, then as professionals they can be expected to observe something more than the morality of the marketplace.

* * *

---

[*] Alvin B. Rubin was United States District Judge for the Eastern District of Louisiana at the time he wrote this article. From 1977 until his death in 1991, he was on the United States Circuit Court of Appeals for the Fifth Circuit. His article argues for a heightened standard of ethics for lawyers as a professional obligation.

[**] Copyright © 1975 Louisiana Law Review. Reprinted with permission.

There are a few rules designed to apply to other relationships that touch peripherally the area we are discussing. A lawyer shall not:

- knowingly make a false statement of law or fact.

- participate in the creation or preservation of evidence when he knows or it is obvious that the evidence is false.

- counsel or assist his client in conduct that the lawyer knows to be illegal or fraudulent, or

- knowingly engage in *other illegal conduct* or conduct contrary to a Disciplinary Rule.

- conceal or knowingly fail to disclose that which he is *required by law* to reveal.

In addition, he "should be temperate and dignified and . . . refrain from all illegal and morally reprehensible conduct." The lawyer is admonished "to treat with consideration all persons involved in the legal process and to avoid the infliction of needless harm."

Taken together, these rules, interpreted in the light of that old but ever useful candle, *ejusdem generis*, imply that a lawyer shall not himself engage in illegal conduct, since the meaning of assisting a client in fraudulent conduct is later indicated by the proscription of *other* illegal conduct. As we perceive, the lawyer is forbidden to make a false statement of law or fact *knowingly*. But nowhere is it ordained that the lawyer owes any general duty of candor or fairness to members of the bar or to laymen with whom he may deal as a negotiator, or of honesty or of good faith insofar as that term denotes generally scrupulous activity.

Is the lawyer-negotiator entitled, like Metternich, to depend on "cunning, precise calculation, and a willingness to employ whatever means justify the end of policy?" Few are so bold as to say so. Yet some whose personal integrity and reputation are scrupulous have instructed students in negotiating tactics that appear tacitly to countenance that kind of conduct. In fairness it must be added that they say they do not "endorse the *propriety*" of this kind of conduct and indeed even indicate "grave reservations" about such behavior; however, this sort of generalized disclaimer of sponsorship hardly appears forceful enough when the tactics suggested include:

- Use two negotiators who play different roles. (Illustrated by the "Mutt and Jeff" police technique; "Two lawyers for the same side feign an internal dispute. . . .")

- Be tough — especially against a patsy.

- Appear irrational when it seems helpful.

- Raise some of your demands as the negotiations progress.

- *Claim* that you do not have authority to compromise. (Emphasis supplied.)

- After agreement has been reached, have your client reject it and raise his demands."

Another text used in training young lawyers commendably counsels sincerity, capability, preparation, courage and flexibility. But it also suggests "a sound set of tools or tactics and the know-how to use (or not to use) them." One such tactic is, "Make false demands, bluffs, threats; even use irrationality."

Occasionally, an experienced legal practitioner comments on the strain the custom of the profession puts on conscience. An anonymous but reputedly experienced Delaware lawyer is quoted as saying, "The practice of tax law these days requires the constant taking of antiemetics."

* * *

Honesty, as the oath administered to witnesses makes clear, implies not only telling literal truth but also disclosing the whole truth. The lawyer has no ethical duty to disclose information to an adversary that may be harmful to his client's cause; most lawyers shrink from the notion that morality requires a standard more demanding than duty to clients. EC 4-5 prohibits a lawyer from using information acquired in the representation of a client to the client's disadvantage, and this, together with the partisan nature of the lawyer's employment, indicates to the practitioner that nondisclosure is both a duty to the client and consistent with ethical norms.

While the lawyer who appears in court is said to owe a duty to disclose relevant legal authorities even if they harm his client's position, he need not disclose, and indeed most would say that he must conceal, evidence damaging to the client's cause. This fine analysis of what a lawyer should reveal to the judge in court doubtless inspired the observation by the Italian jurist, Piero Calamandrei, who, in his celebrated *Eulogy of Judges*, asked:

> Why is it that when a judge meets a lawyer in a tram or in a cafe and converses with him, even if they discuss a pending case, the judge is more disposed to believe what the lawyer says than if he said the same thing in court during the trial? Why is there greater confidence and spiritual unity between man and man than between judge and lawyer?

Let us consider the proper role for a lawyer engaged in negotiations when he knows that the opposing side, whether as a result of poor legal representation or otherwise, is assuming a state of affairs that is incorrect. Hypothesize: *L.*, a lawyer, is negotiating the sale of his client's business to another businessman, who is likewise represented by counsel. Balance sheets and profit and loss statements prepared one month ago have been supplied. In the last month, sales have fallen dramatically. Counsel for the potential buyer has made no inquiry about current sales. Does *L* have a duty to disclose the change in sales volume?

Some lawyers say, "I would notify my client and advise him that *he* has a duty to disclose," not because of ethical considerations but because the client's failure to do so might render the transaction voidable if completed. If the client refused to sanction disclosure, some of these lawyers would withdraw from representing him *in this matter* on ethical grounds. As a practical matter, (i.e., to induce the client to accept their advice) they say, in consulting with the client, the lawyer is obliged to present the problem as one of possible fraud in the transaction rather than of lawyers' ethics.

In typical law school fashion, let us consider another hypothet. *L*, the lawyer is representing *C*, a client, in a suit for personal injuries. There have been active settlement negotiations with *LD*, the defendant's lawyer. The physician who has been treating *C* rendered a written report, containing a prognosis stating that it is unlikely that *C* can return to work at his former occupation. This has been furnished to *LD*. *L* learns from *C* that he has consulted another doctor, who has given him a new medication. *C* states that he is now feeling fine and thinks he can return to work, but he is reluctant to do so until the case is settled or tried. The next day *L* and *LD* again discuss settlement. Does *L* have a duty either to guard his client's secret or to make a full disclosure? Does he satisfy or violate either duty if, instead of mentioning *C's* revelation he suggests that *D* require a new medical examination?

Some lawyers avoid this problem by saying that it is inconceivable that a competent *LD* would not ask again about *C's* health. But if the question as to whether *L* should be frank is persistently presented, few lawyers can assure that they would disclose the true facts.

Lawyers whose primary practice is corporate tend to distinguish the two hypothets, finding a duty to disclose the downturn in earnings but not the improvement in health. They may explain the difference by resorting to a discussion of the lower standards (expectations?) of the bar when engaged in personal injury litigation. "That's why I stay away from that kind of work," one lawyer said. The esteem of a lawyer for his own profession must be scant if he can rationalize the subclassifications this distinction implies. Yet this kind of gradation of professional ethics appears to permeate the bar.

* * *

The professional literature contains many instances indicating that, in the general opinion of the bar, there is no requirement that the lawyer disclose unfavorable evidence in the usual litigious situation. The *racontes* of lawyers and judges with their peers are full of tales of how the other side failed to ask the one key question that would have revealed the truth and changed the result, or how one side cleverly avoided producing the critical document or the key witness whom the adversary had not discovered. The feeling that, in an adversary encounter, each side should develop its own case helps to insulate counsel from considering it a duty to disclose information unknown to the other side. Judge Marvin Frankel, an experienced and perceptive observer of the profession, comments, "Within these unconfining limits [of the Code] advocates freely employ time-honored tricks and stratagems to block or distort the truth."

The United States Supreme Court has developed a rule that requires the disclosure by the prosecutor in a criminal case of evidence favorable to the accused. But this is a duty owed by the government as a matter of due process, not a duty of the prosecutor as a lawyer. In all other respects in criminal cases, and in almost every aspect of the trial of civil cases, client loyalty appears to insulate the lawyer's conscience. Making fidelity to client the ultimate loyalty and the client himself the authority served appears to sanction the abdication of personal ethical responsibility, a kind of behavior described by psychologist Stanley Milgrim in *Obedience to Authority*. He discusses a series of experiments in which people are induced to inflict apparent physical pain on another person because someone in authority orders it. The lawyer permits obedience to the client's interest to provide the moral authority as well as the rationalized justification for his conduct.

Do the lawyer's ethics protest more strongly against giving false information? DR 7-102(A)(5), already quoted, forbids the lawyer to "knowingly make" a false statement of law or fact. Most lawyers say it would be improper to prepare a false document to deceive an adversary or to make a factual statement known to be untrue with the intention of deceiving him. But almost every lawyer can recount repeated instances where an adversary of reasonable repute dealt with facts in such an imaginative or hyperbolic way as to make them appear to be different from what he knew they were.

Interesting answers are obtained if lawyers are asked whether it is proper to make false statements that concern negotiating strategy rather than the facts in litigation. Counsel for a plaintiff appears quite comfortable in stating, when representing a plaintiff, "My client won't take a penny less than $25,000," when in fact he knows that the client will happily settle for less; counsel for the defendant appears to have no qualms in representing that he has no authority to settle, or that a given figure exceeds his authority, when these are untrue statements. Many say that, as a matter of strategy, when they attend a pre-trial conference with a judge known to press settlements, they disclaim any settlement authority both to the judge and adversary although in fact they do have settlement instructions; estimable members of the bar support the thesis that a lawyer may not misrepresent a fact in controversy but may misrepresent matters that pertain to his authority or negotiating strategy because this is expected by the adversary.

To most practitioners it appears that anything sanctioned by the rules of the game is appropriate. From this point of view, negotiations are merely, as the social scientists have viewed it, a form of game; observance of the

expected rules, not professional ethics, is the guiding precept. But games-
manship is not ethics.

* * *

A different distinction is drawn by Calamandrei:

> The difference between the true lawyer and those men who consider
> the law merely a trade is that the latter seek to find ways to permit
> their clients to violate the moral standards of society without over-
> stepping the letter of the law, while the former look for principles
> which will persuade their clients to keep within the limits of the
> spirit of the law in common moral standards.

The courts have seldom had occasion to consider these ethical problems,
for disciplinary proceedings have rarely been invoked on any charge of misconduct in the area. But where settlements have in fact been made when one
party acted on the basis of a factual error known to the other and this error
induced the compromise, courts have set releases aside on the basis of mistake, or, in some cases, fraud.

* * *

A lawyer should not be restrained only by the legal inhibitions on his
client. He enjoys a monopoly on the practice of law protected by sanctions
against unauthorized practice. Through a subpart of the profession, lawyer-
educators, the lawyer controls access to legal education. He licenses practitioners by exacting bar examinations. He controls access to the courts
save in those limited instances when a litigant may appear *pro se*, and then
he aptly characterizes this litigant as being his own lawyer, hence having a
fool for his client.

The monopoly on the practice of law does not arise from the presumed
advantages of an attorney's education or social status: it stems from the concept that, as professionals, lawyers serve society's interests by participating
in the process of achieving the just termination of disputes. That an adversary system is the basic means to this end does not crown it with supreme
value. It is means, not end.

If he is a professional and not merely a hired, albeit skilled hand, the
lawyer is not free to do anything his client might do in the same circumstances. The corollary of that proposition does set a minimum standard: the
lawyer must be at least as candid and honest as his client would be required
to be. The agent of the client, that is, his attorney-at-law, must not perpetrate the kind of fraud or deception that would vitiate a bargain if practiced
by his principal. Beyond that, the profession should embrace an affirmative
ethical standard for attorneys' professional relationships with courts, other
lawyers and the public: *The lawyer must act honestly and in good faith.*
Another lawyer, or a layman, who deals with a lawyer should not need to
exercise the same degree of caution that he would if trading for reputedly

antique copper jugs in an oriental bazaar. It is inherent in the concept of an ethic, as a principle of good conduct, that it is morally binding on the conscience of the professional, and not merely a rule of the game adopted because other players observe (or fail to adopt) the same rule. Good conduct exacts more than mere convenience. It is not sufficient to call on personal self-interest; this is the standard created by the thesis that the same adversary met today may be faced again tomorrow, and one had best not prejudice that future engagement.

* * *

While it might strain present concepts of the role of the lawyer in an adversary system, surely the professional standards must ultimately impose upon him a duty not to accept an unconscionable deal. While some difficulty in line-drawing is inevitable when such a distinction is sought to be made, there must be a point at which the lawyer cannot ethically accept an arrangement that is completely unfair to the other side, be that opponent a patsy or a tax collector. So I posit a second precept: *The lawyer may not accept a result that is unconscionably unfair to the other party.*

A settlement that is unconscionable may result from a variety of circumstances. There may be a vast difference in the bargaining power of the principals so that, regardless of the adequacy of representation by counsel, one party may simply not be able to withstand the expense and bear the delay and uncertainty inherent in a protracted suit. There may be a vast difference in the bargaining skill of counsel so that one is able to manipulate the other virtually at will despite the fact that their framed certificates of admission to the bar contain the same words.

The unconscionable result in these circumstances is in part created by the relative power, knowledge and skill of the principals and their negotiators. While it is the unconscionable result that is to be avoided, the question of whether the result is indeed intolerable depends in part on examination of the relative status of the parties. The imposition of a duty to tell the truth and to bargain in good faith would reduce their relative inequality, and tend to produce negotiation results that are within relatively tolerable bounds.

But part of the test must be in result alone: whether the lesion is so unbearable that it represents a sacrifice of value that an ethical person cannot in conscience impose upon another. The civil law has long had a principle that a sale of land would be set aside if made for less than half its value, regardless of circumstance. This doctrine, called lesion beyond moiety, looks purely to result. If the professional ethic is *caveat negotiator*, then we could not tolerate such a burden. But there certainly comes a time when a deal is too good to be true, where what has been accomplished passes the line of simply-a-good-deal and becomes a cheat.

The lawyer should not be free to negotiate an unconscionable result, however pleasing to his client, merely because it is possible, any more than he is free to do other reprobated acts. He is not to commit perjury or pay a bribe or give advice about how to commit embezzlement. These examples refer to advice concerning illegal conduct, but we do already, in at least some instances, accept the principle that some acts are proscribed though not criminal: the lawyer is forbidden to testify as a witness in his client's cause, or to assert a defense merely to harass his opponent; he is enjoined to point out to his client "those factors that may lead to a decision that is morally just." Whether a mode of conduct available to the lawyer is illegal or merely or unconscionably unfair, the attorney must refuse to participate. This duty of fairness is one owed to the profession and to society; it must supersede any duty owed to the client.

* * *

James J. White,[*] *Machiavelli and the Bar: Ethical Limitations on Lying in Negotiation*
1980 AM. B. FOUND. RESOL. J. 926[**]

* * *

The difficulty of proposing acceptable rules concerning truthfulness in negotiation is presented by several circumstances. First, negotiation is non-public behavior. If one negotiator lies to another, only by happenstance will the other discover the lie. If the settlement is concluded by negotiation, there will be no trial, no public testimony by conflicting witnesses, and thus no opportunity to examine the truthfulness of assertions made during the negotiation. Consequently, in negotiation, more than in other contexts, ethical norms can probably be violated with greater confidence that there will be no discovery and punishment. Whether one is likely to be caught for violating an ethical standard says nothing about the merit of the standard. However, if the low probability of punishment means that many lawyers will violate the standard, the standard becomes even more difficult for the honest lawyer to follow, for by doing so he may be forfeiting a significant advantage for his client to others who do not follow the rules.

* * *

. . . On the one hand the negotiator must be fair and truthful; on the other he must mislead his opponent. Like the poker player, a negotiator hopes that his opponent will overestimate the value of his hand. Like the poker player, in a variety of ways he must facilitate his opponent's inaccurate assessment. The critical difference between those who are successful negotiators and those who are not lies in this capacity both to mislead and not to be misled.

---

[*] James J. White is Robert A. Sullivan Professor at University of Michigan Law School. His article examines the role of deception in legal negotiations and appropriate ethical limits on it.

[**] Copyright © 1980 American Bar Foundation. Reprinted with permission.

Some experienced negotiators will deny the accuracy of this assertion, but they will be wrong. I submit that a careful examination of the behavior of even the most forthright, honest, and trustworthy negotiators will show them actively engaged in misleading their opponents about their true positions. That is true of both the plaintiff and the defendant in a lawsuit. It is true of both labor and management in a collective bargaining agreement. It is true as well of both the buyer and the seller in a wide variety of sales transactions. To conceal one's true position, to mislead an opponent about one's true settling point, is the essence of negotiation.

Of course there are limits on acceptable deceptive behavior in negotiation, but there is the paradox. How can one be "fair" but also mislead? Can we ask the negotiator to mislead, but fairly, like the soldier who must kill, but humanely?

* * *

Pious and generalized assertions that the negotiator must be "honest" or that the lawyer must use "candor" are not helpful. They are at too high a level of generality, and they fail to appreciate the fact that truth and truthful behavior at one time in one set of circumstances with one set of negotiators may be untruthful in another circumstance with other negotiators. There is no general principle waiting somewhere to be discovered as Judge Alvin B. Rubin seems to suggest in his article on lawyer's ethics. Rather, mostly we are doing what he says we are not doing, namely, hunting for the rules of the game as the game is played in that particular circumstance.

The definition of truth is in part a function of the substance of the negotiation. Because of the policies that lie behind the securities and exchange laws and the demands that Congress has made that information be provided to those who buy and sell, one suspects that lawyers engaged in SEC work have a higher standard of truthfulness than do those whose agreements and negotiations will not affect public buying and selling of assets. Conversely, where the thing to be bought and sold is in fact a lawsuit in which two professional traders conclude the deal, truth means something else. Here truth and candor call for a smaller amount of disclosure, permit greater distortion, and allow the other professional to suffer from his own ignorance and sloth in a way that would not be acceptable in the SEC case. In his article Rubin recognizes that there are such different perceptions among members of the bar engaged in different kinds of practice, and he suggests that there should not be such differences. Why not? Why is it so clear that one's responsibility for truth ought not be a function of the policy, the consequences, and the skill and expectations of the opponent?

Apart from the kinds of differences in truthfulness and candor which arise from the subject matter of the negotiation, one suspects that there are other differences attributable to regional and ethnic differences among negotiators. Although I have only anecdotal data to support this idea, it seems plausible that one's expectation concerning truth and candor might be different in a small, homogeneous community from what it would be in a large, heterogeneous community of lawyers. For one thing, all of the lawyers in the small and homogeneous community will share a common ethnic and environmental background. Each will have been subjected to the same kind of training about what kinds of lies are appropriate and what are not appropriate.

Moreover, the costs of conformity to ethical norms are less in a small community. Because the community is small, it will be easy to know those who do not conform to the standards and to protect oneself against that small number. Conversely, in the large and heterogeneous community, one will not have confidence either about the norms that have been learned by the opposing negotiator or about his conformance to those norms.

* * *

Five Cases

Although it is not necessary to draft such a set of rules, it is probably important to give more than the simple disclaimer about the impossibility of defining the appropriate limits of puffing. . . . To test these limits, consider five cases. Easiest is the question that arises when one misrepresents his true opinion about the meaning of a case or a statute. Presumably such a misrepresentation is accepted lawyer behavior both in and out of court and is not intended to be precluded by the requirement that the lawyer be "truthful." In writing his briefs, arguing his case, and attempting to persuade the opposing party in negotiation, it is the lawyer's right and probably his responsibility to argue for plausible interpretations of cases and statutes which favor his client's interest, even in circumstances where privately he has advised his client that those are not his true interpretations of the cases and statutes.

A second form of distortion . . . is distortion concerning the value of one's case or of the other subject matter involved in the negotiation. Thus the Comments make explicit reference to "puffery." Presumably they are attempting to draw the same line that one draws in commercial law between express warranties and "mere puffing" under section 2-313 of the Uniform Commercial Code. While this line is not easy to draw, it generally means that the seller of a product has the right to make general statements concerning the value of his product without having the law treat those statements as warranties and without having liability if they turn out to be inaccurate estimates of the value. As the statements descend toward greater and greater particularity, as the ignorance of the person receiving the statements increases, the courts are likely to find them to be not puffing but express warranties. By the same token a lawyer could make assertions about his case or about the subject matter of his negotiation in general terms, and if those proved to be inaccurate, they would not be a violation of the ethical standards. Presumably such statements are not violations of the ethical standards even when they conflict with the lawyer's dispassionate analysis of the value of his case.

A third case is related to puffing but different from it. This is the use of the so-called false demand. It is a standard negotiating technique in collective bargaining negotiation and in some other multiple-issue negotiations for one side to include a series of demands about which it cares little or not at all. The purpose of including these demands is to increase one's supply of negotiating currency. One hopes to convince the other party that one or more of these false demands is important and thus successfully to trade it for some significant concession. The assertion of and argument for a false demand involves the same kind of distortion that is involved in puffing or in arguing the merits of cases or statutes that are not really controlling. The proponent of a false demand implicitly or explicitly states his interest in the demand and his estimation of it. Such behavior is untruthful in the broadest sense; yet at least in collective bargaining negotiation its use is a standard part of the process and is not thought to be inappropriate by any experienced bargainer.

Two final examples may be more troublesome. The first involves the response of a lawyer to a question from the other side. Assume that the defendant has instructed his lawyer to accept any settlement offer under $100,000. Having received that instruction, how does the defendant's lawyer respond to the plaintiff's question, "I think $90,000 will settle this case. Will your client give $90,000?" Do you see the dilemma that question poses for the defense lawyer? It calls for information that would not have to be disclosed. A truthful answer to it concludes the negotiation and dashes any possibility of negotiating a lower settlement even in circumstances in which the plaintiff might be willing to accept half of $90,000. Even a moment's hesitation in response to the question may be a nonverbal communication to a clever plaintiff's lawyer that the defendant has given such authority. Yet a negative response is a lie.

It is no answer that a clever lawyer will answer all questions about authority by refusing to answer them, nor is it an answer that some lawyers will be clever enough to tell their clients not to grant them authority to accept a given sum until the final stages in negotiation. Most of us are not that careful or that clever. Few will routinely refuse to answer such questions in cases in which the client has granted a much lower limit than that discussed by the other party, for in that case an honest answer about the absence of authority is a quick and effective method of changing the opponent's settling point, and it is one that few of us will forego when our authority is far below that requested by the other party. Thus despite the fact that a clever negotiator can avoid having to lie or to reveal his settling point, many lawyers, perhaps most, will sometime be forced by such a question either to lie or to reveal that they have been granted such authority by saying so or by their silence in response to a direct question. Is it fair to lie in such a case?

Before one examines the possible justifications for a lie in that circumstance, consider a final example recently suggested to me by a lawyer in practice. There the lawyer represented three persons who had been charged with shoplifting. Having satisfied himself that there was no significant conflict of interest, the defense lawyer told the prosecutor that two of the three would plead guilty only if the case was dismissed against the third. Previously those two had told the defense counsel that they would plead guilty irrespective of what the third did, and the third had said that he wished to go to trial unless the charges were dropped. Thus the defense lawyer lied to the prosecutor by stating that the two would plead only if the third were allowed to go free. Can the lie be justified in this case?

How does one distinguish the cases where truthfulness is not required and those where it is required? Why do the first three cases seem easy? I suggest they are easy cases because the rules of the game are explicit and well developed in those areas. Everyone expects a lawyer to distort the value of his own case, of his own facts and arguments, and to deprecate those of his opponent. No one is surprised by that, and the system accepts and expects that behavior. To a lesser extent the same is true of the false demand procedure in labor-management negotiations where the ploy is sufficiently widely used to be explicitly identified in the literature. A layman might say that this behavior falls within the ambit of "exaggeration," a form of behavior that while not necessarily respected is not regarded as morally reprehensible in our society.

The last two cases are more difficult. In one the lawyer lies about his authority; in the other he lies about the intention of his clients. It would be more difficult to justify the lies in those cases by arguing that the rules of the game explicitly permit that sort of behavior. Some might say that the rules of the game provide for such distortion, but I suspect that many lawyers would say that such lies are out of bounds and are not part of the rules of the game. Can the lie about authority be justified on the ground that the question itself was improper? Put another way, if I have a right to keep certain information to myself, and if any behavior but a lie will reveal that information to the other side, am I justified in lying? I think not. Particularly in the case in which there are other avenues open to the respondent, should we not ask him to take those avenues? That is, the careful negotiator here can turn aside all such questions and by doing so avoid any inference from his failure to answer such questions.

What makes the last case a close one? Conceivably it is the idea that one accused by the state is entitled to greater leeway in making his case. Possibly one can argue that there is no injury to the state when such a person, particularly an innocent person, goes free. Is it conceivable that the act can be justified on the ground that it is part of the game in this context, that prosecutors as well as defense lawyers routinely misstate what they, their witnesses, and their clients can and will do? None of these arguments seems persuasive. Justice is not served by freeing a guilty person. The system does not necessarily achieve better results by trading two guilty pleas for a dismissal. Perhaps its justification has its roots in the same idea that formerly held that a misrepresentation of one's state of mind was not actionable for it was not a misrepresentation of fact.

In a sense rules governing these cases may simply arise from a recognition by the law of its limited power to shape human behavior. By tolerating exaggeration and puffing in the sales transaction, by refusing to make misstatement of one's intention actionable, the law may simply have recognized the bounds of its control over human behavior. Having said that, one is still left with the question, Are the lies permissible in the last two cases? My general conclusion is that they are not, but I am not nearly as comfortable with that conclusion as I am with the conclusion about the first three cases.

Taken together, the five foregoing cases show me that we do not and cannot intend that a negotiator be "truthful" in the broadest sense of that term. At the minimum we allow him some deviation from truthfulness in asserting his true opinion about cases, statutes, or the value of the subject of the negotiation in other respects. In addition some of us are likely to allow him to lie in response to certain questions that are regarded as out of bounds, and possibly to lie in circumstances where his interest is great and the injury seems small. It would be unfortunate, therefore, for the rule that requires "fairness" to be interpreted to require that a negotiator be truthful in every respect and in all of his dealings. It should be read to allow at least those kinds of untruthfulness that are implicitly and explicitly recognized as acceptable in his forum, a forum defined both by the subject matter and by the participants.

* * *

Conclusion

To draft effective legislation is difficult; to draft effective ethical rules is close to impossible. Such drafters must walk the narrow line between being too general and too specific. If their rules are too general, they will have no influence on any behavior and give little guidance even to those who wish to follow the rules. If they are too specific, they omit certain areas or conflict with appropriate rules for problems not foreseen but apparently covered.

There are other, more formidable obstacles. These drafters are essentially powerless. They draft the rules, but the American Bar Association must pass them, and the rules must then be adopted by various courts or other agencies in the states. Finally the enforcement of the rules is left to a hodgepodge of bar committees and grievance agencies of varied will and capacity. Thus the drafters are far removed from and have little control over those who ultimately will enact and enforce the rules. For that reason, even more than most legislators, drafters of ethical rules have limited power to influence behavior. This weakness presents a final dilemma and one they have not always faced as well as they should, namely, to make the appropriate trade-off between what is "right" and what can be done. To enact stern and righteous rules in Chicago will not fool the people in Keokuk. The public will not believe them, and the bar will not follow them. What level of violation of the rules can the bar accept without the rules as a whole becoming a mockery? I do not know and the drafters can only guess. Because of the danger presented if the norms are widely and routinely violated, the drafters should err on the conservative side and must sometimes reject better and more desirable rules for poorer ones simply because the violation of the higher standard would cast all the rules in doubt.

Gerald B. Wetlaufer,[*]
The Ethics of Lying in Negotiations
75 IOWA L. REV. 1219, 1224-32 (1990)[**]

* * *

B. The Types of Lies That Might Be Told in Negotiations

There are a variety of lies that one might tell in order to secure an advantage in a negotiation. Initially, of course, we might lie about the nature, history, characteristics or value of the property which is the subject of the negotiation, whether it be a lawsuit, an automobile or a piece of land. We might also lie about the possible consequences of some decision that might be made by the person with whom we arc negotiating. Lies of this kind include false promises, false threats, and false predictions related to the value of the property which is the subject of the negotiation. We might also lie about our own or our client's opinions, characteristics, authority, interests and priorities, reservation price, or alternatives to agreement. These lies operate to misrepresent our willingness to settle, the price above which we will not buy (or below which we will not sell), our client's insistence on custody, the presence or activities of competing bidders, or our availability and readiness for trial. This category also includes various supposedly white lies and lies to save face.

C. The Effects That Lies May Have

The lies that we tell in the course of negotiations may have a number of different effects on the negotiation, on the parties, and on the larger community. While most of these lies are calculated to disadvantage the other party, there are some that, at least in theory, are not. Those that do not threaten such disadvantage are pure "white" lies. They are said to be harmless, to grease the wheels of discourse, and to increase the likelihood that the parties will move quickly toward a mutually beneficial agreement.

---

[*] Gerald B. Wetlaufer is Professor at University of Iowa College of Law. His article discusses the incentives to lie in negotiation and the relevant ethical limitations on lying.

The broader and more important category of lies, though, is comprised of those "distributive" lies by which the liar seeks to capture an advantage over the other party. These include, among others, the lies — like those involving one's reservation price — that Professor White has identified as the measure of a negotiator's effectiveness. To illustrate the effect of these lies, let us assume that Mr. Seller is negotiating to sell a factory and that his reservation price is $900,000. Below that price, he is better off keeping the plant. After an extensive search, he has identified one, and only one, prospective purchaser. Her name is Ms. Buyer. Mr. Seller has estimated that her reservation price, the price above which she will not buy, is $1,200,000. Though he has no way of knowing for sure, you and I know that this estimate is exactly right. Mr. Seller's objective is to sell at the highest possible price, even if it means lying. In the course of several hours of bargaining, Mr. Seller has, through an outright lie about a competing bid, persuaded Ms. Buyer that he will not sell the property for anything less than $1,100,000, a figure that is $200,000 above his actual reservation price. The bargaining continues and eventually they split the difference between Mr. Seller's *perceived* reservation price ($1,100,000) and Ms. Buyer's *actual* reservation price ($1,200,000). With a price of $1,150,000, Ms. Buyer is happy because she believes she has captured exactly half of the available surplus. Mr. Seller is ecstatic, believing (correctly) that he has captured $250,000 of the $300,000 surplus and that his "winning margin" of $200,000 is attributable solely to his skills as a liar. Other distributive lies, such as lies about the mileage of a used car, may operate in slightly different ways, sometimes by altering the other party's assessment of its own reservation price. What these lies all have in common is that, if they are successful, the liar becomes richer in the degree to which the victim becomes poorer.

Distributive lies are not, however, always successful. There are, in fact, three ways they can misfire and cause injury to the *liar*. First, distributive lies may fail to deceive, either because they are never believed or because they are believed but then discovered. Lies that fail in this way may cause such damage to the relationship between the negotiators that the intended victim will be unwilling or unable to enter into what would otherwise be a shift in bargaining power *away* from the liar and in favor of the intended victim. They may have adverse effects on the liar's credibility and effectiveness both in the remainder of the negotiation at hand and in future negotiations with this and other adversaries. They may also provoke defensive or retaliatory lying.

Distributive lies also may cause injury to the liar, and to the liar's victim, when they deceive the victim and thereby block the parties from reaching a beneficial agreement that otherwise would have been available. Assume for instance that Ms. Buyer is negotiating over the price of a car and that her reservation price is such that she will not pay more than $10,000. Further, she has estimated that Mr. Seller's reservation price is such that he will not accept less than $8,500. Ms. Buyer has, by lying, persuaded Mr. Seller that her reservation price is $9,000-$1,000 less than her actual reservation price. Her belief is that there is a $1,500 in surplus to be distributed between the parties, that she will by her lie capture $1,000 of that surplus, and that she will then perhaps "split the difference" with regard to the remaining $500. Unfortunately, Ms. Buyer has misjudged Mr. Seller's reservation price. Instead of the $8,500 that she had estimated, Mr. Steller's reservation price is actually $9,300. There is still a $700 range, $9,300 to $10,000, within which an agreement would leave *both* parties better off than they would be without an agreement. But having committed herself to her false reservation price ($9,000), Ms. Buyer may now be unwilling or unable to make an offer *higher* than that amount. Consequently, the deal may be lost and her all-too-successful distributive lie will have deprived the liar and her victim of $700.

A nominally successful lie can also cause injury to the liar and the victim by causing them to reach an agreement that is less beneficial than it might otherwise have been. This contention requires an understanding of the concept of "integrative" or "win-win" bargaining. Integrative bargaining has the effect not of dividing the pie, but of making it larger. A textbook example might involve two brothers who are haggling over an orange. An evenhanded distributive outcome could be reached by cutting the orange through the middle and giving one half to each brother. Further exploration, however, might reveal an opportunity for integrative bargaining. One brother, it turns out, wants to peel the orange and eat the fruit; the other hates eating oranges but needs the rind for garnishing his cake. By discovering this information and dividing the orange differently — all the fruit to one, the entire rind to the other — we can move from a 50-50 outcome to, in this case, a 100-100 result.

Integrative bargaining has several characteristics that bear upon the problem of lying in negotiations. First, opportunities for integrative bargaining are not always present — and when they are, we almost never know it. Second, even when there are integrative opportunities to expand the pie, the pie will almost always, eventually, need to be divided. That division will be an occasion for distributive, win-lose bargaining. What complicates matters is that, while lying may be the watchword in distributive bargaining, full and truthful disclosure is the key to identifying and exploiting opportunities for integrative bargaining. Thus certain kinds of lies, told to secure distributive (pie-splitting) advantages, may make it impossible for the parties to discover and exploit the integrative (pie-expanding) opportunities that may be available. For example, lies about our interest or priorities can *simultaneously* win the liar a larger share of the pie *and* blind both parties to those avenues by which the pie might have been expanded. In this way, a successful distributive lie may injure both the liar and his victim by causing them to reach an agreement that is less productive of *total* profit than might, but for the lie, have been the case.

Lying in negotiations may also cause injuries that are more general and far-reaching than the immediate effects upon the parties to the negotiation.

Lies that are discovered may, for instance, cause persons other than the liar to engage in defensive lying either later in that same negotiation or in *other* negotiations. Such lies can diminish the level of trust and increase the frequency with which additional lies are told. As public trust declines, so does our ability to engage in effective communications and to make and exchange credible commitments, including the promises that underlie contracts. As these capacities decline, so does the efficiency with which we are, all of us, able to conduct our affairs. These discovered lies may, in addition, diminish the possibilities of ethical restraint, community and reciprocity.

Moreover, lies that are successful and undiscovered may lead to further lies by lowering the liar's barriers against lying and by empowering, at least in the mind of the liar, some justification for lying that is, on the merits, insufficient. As those justifications are empowered, the barriers against lying fall still further. Otherwise successful lies may also affect the liar's self-image and sense of personal integrity, as well as his trust in others. Thus, undiscovered lies, like discovered lies, may have adverse effects on a community's capacity for trust, efficiency, ethics, and reciprocity.

In the end, lying in negotiations can produce a wide range of possible effects. While the distribution of these effects is anything but symmetrical, they include both costs and benefits. Two things, though, are clear. The most important is that we cannot say as a general matter that honesty is the best policy for individual negotiators to pursue if by "best" we mean most effective or most profitable. In those bargaining situations which are at least in part distributive, a category which includes virtually all negotiations, lying is a coherent and often effective strategy. In those same circumstances, a policy of never lying may place a negotiator at a systematic and sometimes overwhelming disadvantage. Moreover, there are any number of lies, including those involving reservation prices and opinions, that are both useful and virtually undiscoverable. Accordingly, if the policy we pursue is one of honesty, we must do so for reasons other than profit and effectiveness. The second point is that one who lies in negotiations is in a position to capture almost all of the benefits of lying while suffering only a small portion of the costs and that, in the language of the economists, this state of affairs will lead, almost automatically, to an overproduction of lies.

D. *The Circumstances in Which the Negotiator Must Decide Whether to Lie*

The circumstances in which we negotiate are highly conducive to lying. The heart of the problem is that, in ways that have just been seen, lying can be highly effective. Lying offers significant distributive advantages to the liar and the incentive to lie is therefore great. Moreover, because we understand that our adversary is under that same incentive to lie, we are highly attentive to the possibility that we are being conned and are predisposed to assume the worst.

This situation is made worse by the importance we assign to these particular distributive advantages. At stake is the distribution of scarce and highly valued resources and opportunities. We are engaged in a negotiation precisely because we care about the distribution of those resources. We care because of our individualistic interests, ambitions, and desires. We may care still more because we are negotiating not just for ourselves but also for others. Those others may include clients, employers, partners, employees, and families. Some of these others may pay our salaries. All share, to some degree, in the results we produce. The presence of these others buttresses our desire to win, strengthens the temptation to lie, and permits us to invoke a series of arguments according to which those lies might be permissible because of our duties to others. The stakes are also raised by the presence of audiences and by the high value we lawyers place on our reputation with those audiences, specifically our reputation for instrumental effectiveness and for a kind of invulnerability to being victimized by other people's lies.

If the predicament is difficult because lying is effective and the stakes are high, it is made still more so by the gross imperfection of our information and the biases that are likely to effect [*sic*] our perception and our judgment. The first problem we face is that we generally do not know whether our adversary is lying to us. Except for those rare occasions when an ace falls from a sleeve and the lie is clearly revealed, we have only intuitions and imperfect judgments on which to rely. These estimates are difficult because, even within a single community, the relevant practices of negotiators will vary widely. Many will define their objective in such a way that the ethics of lying are irrelevant. Others will define their objective in a way that takes account of ethics, but will then embrace an extraordinarily wide range of beliefs as to when it is ethically permissible to lie. Most of the time we do not know how our adversary defines her objective and even if we knew she defined it in a way that took account of ethics, we would not know her views on the ethics of lying.

This absence of relevant information is then compounded by the systematic biases that are likely to affect our perceptions and assessments, biases that enhance the probability that we will lie. We are predisposed to believe that our cause is just; to assume the worst with regard to our adversary's character, motives and conduct; and to accept the sufficiency of the justifications we give ourselves for the lies we tell. While this is particularly true in the contentious realm of litigation, it is also likely to be true, in some degree, across the entire range of negotiations. We are predisposed to understate the frequency and overstate the legitimacy of the lies we tell, and to do exactly the opposite with regard to the frequency and legitimacy of our adversary's lies.

* * *

Deborah L. Rhode,[*] *Gender and Professional Roles*
63 FORDHAM L. REV. 39, 45-49 (1994)[**]

* * *

A. Role Morality Reconsidered

The mayor and Montaigne have always been two people, clearly separated. . . . An honest man is not responsible for the vices or the stupidity of his calling. . . .

During the early 1930s, anthropologist Ralph Linton introduced the term "role" into the social science literature to describe rights and duties belonging to a particular status. Ethical theorists have borrowed the term to differentiate role morality and personal or ordinary morality. The conventional assumption, captured by Montaigne, is that individuals holding certain occupational positions assume ethical obligations that may diverge in significant ways from those acceptable within society generally. The theory is that some institutions can function effectively only if participants adjust their sense of moral responsibility in light of particular institutional needs.

Conventional accounts of professional ethics rest on related premises about professional roles. The prevailing assumption is that individuals' ability to assert legal rights rests on having lawyers who defend, not judge, their clients. Fulfilling professional responsibilities may require actions that run counter to individuals' personal moral values.

From a feminist perspective, this traditional concept of role-differentiated morality is unsatisfying in several respects. At the most fundamental level, feminists join other critics in questioning the distinction between ordinary morality and role morality. As they note, "no one is ever an abstract moral agent." Individuals always function within relationships and make ethical choices in view of their particular responsibilities as parents, friends, spouses, employees, and so forth. If, as feminists have long insisted, the personal is political, it is also professional. Both role morality and ordinary morality assume that individuals "in different circumstances and with different abilities have different obligations."

A related criticism is that traditional concepts of role do not advance analysis about what those different obligations demand. All too often, individuals deny personal accountability for professional acts on the ground that they are just "doing their jobs." Yet this strategy attempts to avoid responsibility even as it is exercised. The choice to defer to role is itself a moral choice and needs to be justified as such. Conventional approaches to professional ethics fail to provide adequate justifications. By encouraging

---

[*] Deborah L. Rhode is Ernest W. McFarland Professor at Stanford University Law School. This excerpt focuses on feminist critiques of traditional conceptions of lawyers' role morality.

deference to abstract role-based norms, these approaches devalue the contextual and relational dimensions that are central to feminist theory and that should be central to ethical analysis. The result is to impoverish both personal and professional identity.

Conventional understandings of role morality for lawyers illustrate what is lost under these traditional conceptions of professional ethics. To understand what feminists find problematic about current ethical norms, it is helpful first to review the obligations that those norms entail. In general, attorneys are expected to act as neutral partisans who should represent their clients zealously within the bounds of the law regardless of their own views concerning the justness of the cause. Although lawyers may not assist fraudulent, harassing, or illegal conduct, they are given wide latitude to protect client interests at the expense of broader societal concerns. For example, they may present evidence that they reasonably believe to be inaccurate or misleading as long as they do not know it to be false; they may withhold material information in civil cases that the other side fails to discover; they may invoke technical defenses to defeat rightful claims; and they may remain silent about a client's prior wrongful conduct even when disclosure would prevent substantial financial harm or physical risk to innocent parties.

The rationale for this morally neutral partisanship rests on two primary lines of argument. The first invokes utilitarian, instrumental reasoning. It assumes that the most effective way to achieve justice is through the competitive clash of two zealous adversaries, and that their effectiveness depends on trusting relationships with clients. On this view, an adversarial system will function fairly only if individuals have full confidence in the loyalty and confidentiality of their advocates.

From feminists' standpoint, this conventional justification for the partisanship role is too abstract and acontextual to yield morally satisfying outcomes. The assumption that truth or fairness necessarily results from adversarial clashes is neither self-evident nor supported by empirical evidence. It is not the way most professions or most legal systems pursue knowledge. Moreover, the conventional paradigm presupposes a fair contest between combatants with roughly equal resources, capacities, and incentives. Such equality is all too infrequent in a social order that tolerates vast disparities in wealth, renders most legal proceedings enormously expensive, and allocates civil legal assistance largely through market mechanisms.

In response to such criticisms, defenders of partisan norms rely on an alternative rights-based justification. On this view, respect for clients' individual autonomy implies respect for their legal entitlements and requires undivided loyalty from their legal advisors. By absolving attorneys from accountability for their clients' acts, the traditional advocacy role encourages representation of those most vulnerable to public prejudice and state oppression. The promise of non-judgmental advocacy also encourages legal consultation by those most in need of ethical counseling. Any alternative system, it is argued, would threaten rule by an oligarchy of lawyers.

Feminists join other critics in raising two central objections to this rights-based defense of neutral partisanship. The first is that it collapses legal and moral entitlements. It assumes that society benefits by allowing clients to pursue whatever objectives the law permits. Yet conduct that is antithetical to the public interest in general or to subordinate groups in particular sometimes remains legal. For example, prohibitions may appear too difficult or costly to enforce, or decision makers may be uninformed, overworked, or vulnerable to interest-group pressures. In such contexts, lawyers may have no particular moral expertise, but they at least have a more disinterested perspective than clients on the ethical dimensions of certain practices. For attorneys to accept moral responsibility is not necessarily to impose it. Unless the lawyer is the last in town (or the functional equivalent for indigent clients), his or her refusal of the neutral partisan role does not preempt representation. It simply imposes on clients the psychological and financial cost of finding alternative counsel.

A second problem with rights-based justifications for partisanship is that they fail to explain why rights of clients should trump those of all other individuals whose interests are inadequately represented. For feminists, that failure is most apparent when it threatens the welfare of disadvantaged groups including women, or of especially vulnerable third parties, such as children in divorce cases and consumers of hazardous products. In such circumstances, partisanship on behalf of organizational profits inadequately serves values of individual autonomy. Case histories of the Dalkon Shield and asbestos litigation, as well as less politicized financial scandals, illustrate the human misery and social costs that can accompany unqualified advocacy.

Finally, the submersion of self into role carries a price not only for the public in general, but for lawyers in particular. The detachment of personal and professional ethics often

> encourages an uncritical, uncommitted state of mind, or worse a deep moral skepticism. . . . In a large portion of his daily experience, in which [a lawyer] is acting regularly in the moral arena, he is alienated from his own moral feelings and attitudes and indeed from his moral personality as a whole. . . .

> The social costs of cutting off professional deliberation and action from their sources in ordinary moral experience are even more troubling. First, cut off from sound moral judgment, the lawyer's ability to do his job well — to . . . effectively advise his clients — is likely to be seriously affected. . . .

* * *

[M]ost importantly, when professional action is estranged from ordinary moral experience, the lawyer's sensitivity to the moral costs in both ordinary and extraordinary situations tends to atrophy. The ideal of neutrality permits, indeed requires, that the lawyer regard his professional activities and their consequences from the point of view of the uninvolved spectator.

From most feminists' perspective, a preferable alternative would break down the boundary between personal and professional ethics. In essence, lawyers should accept direct moral accountability for their professional acts. Attorneys' decisions should not depend on a reflexive retreat into role; rather, individuals need to consider how the purposes of that role can best be served within a particular context. In some instances, those purposes call for deference to collectively determined legal and ethical rules. But such deference is justifiable only if the rules themselves allow room to take account of all the morally relevant factors in a given situation. So, for example, lawyers need to evaluate the rationale for zealous partisanship not by reference to some abstract model of an equal adversarial contest before a neutral tribunal. Instead, they need to consider a realistic social and economic landscape in which legal rights and resources may be unevenly distributed, applicable laws may be unjustly skewed, and the vast majority of cases settle without ever reaching an impartial decision maker.

Oscar Wilde once reminded us that to be virtuous according to common conventions of behavior was not necessarily demanding. All it required was a certain reflexive timidity and lack of imaginative thought. To have moral character is something else again, and we need to recognize the difference.

* * *

David A. Lax & James K. Sebenius,[*] *Three Ethical Issues in Negotiation*
2 NEGOT. J. 363, 363-68 (1986)[**]

The agent for a small grain seller reported the following telephone conversation, concerning a disagreement over grain contracted to be sold to General Mills:

> We're General Mills; and if you don't deliver this grain to us, why we'll have a battery of lawyers in there tomorrow morning to visit you, and then we are going to the North Dakota Public Service

---

[*] David A. Lax is a principal in Lax Sebenius LLC and co-head of Summa Capital Management. James K. Sebenius is Gordon Donaldson Professor at Harvard University Business School. Their article looks at negotiation ethics from the viewpoint of tactical choices, distributional fairness, and effects on third parties.

[**] Copyright © 1986 Negotiation Journal. Reprinted with permission of Blackwell Publishing, Inc. and the Program on Negotiation at Harvard Law School.

[Commission]; we're going to the Minneapolis Grain Exchange and we're going to the people in Montana and there will be no more Muschler Grain Company. We're going to take your license.

Tactics mainly intended to permit one party [to] claim value at another's expense inescapably raise hard ethical issues. How should one evaluate moves that stake out positions, threaten another with walkout or worse, misrepresent values or beliefs, hold another person's wants hostage to claim value at that person's expense, or offer an "elegant" solution of undeniable joint benefit but constructed so that one side will get the lion's share?

One approach to these questions is denial, to believe, pretend, or wish that conflict and questions of dividing the pie have no part in negotiation and hence such tactical choices are falsely posed: "If one really understood that the whole process was effective communication and joint problem solving, one could dispense with any unpleasant-seeming tactics, except to think about responding to their use by nasty opponents." However, denying that conflict over process and results is an essential part of negotiation is badly flawed conceptually. Or, one can admit that there are hard ethical questions but deny they are relevant, as suggested by the following advice from a handbook on business negotiation:

> Many negotiators fail to understand the nature of negotiation and so find themselves attempting to reconcile conflicts between the requirements of negotiation and their own senses of personal integrity. An individual who confuses private ethics with business morality does not make an effective negotiator. A negotiator must learn to be objective in his negotiations and to subordinate his own personal sense of ethics to the prime purpose of securing the best deal possible for his principals.

Just as we are uncomfortable denying the reality of conflict in bargaining in order to evade ethical issues, it is scarcely more satisfying to admit that ethical issues exist but, following the author of the above remark, simply to assert that they are irrelevant. Instead, we find at least two kinds of reasons to be concerned with ethical issues in negotiation.

Many people want to be "ethical" for *intrinsic* reasons — apart from the effect of such choices on future encounters. Why? Variously, because it simply feels better, because one ascribes an independent value to acting "ethically," because it may be psychologically healthier, because certain principles of good behavior are taken as moral or religious absolutes, or for other reasons. Yet it is often hard in negotiation to decide what actions fit these criteria, especially when values or principles appear to conflict.

Ethical behavior may also have *instrumental* value. One hears that "it pays to be ethical" or "sound ethics is good business," meaning that if a negotiator calculates correctly, taking into account the current and long-run costs of overly shrewd behavior, profits and benefits will be higher. The eighteenth century diplomat Francois de CalliPres (1716) made a more expansive version of this point:

> It is a capital error, which prevails widely; that a clever negotiator must be a master of the art of deceit. . . . No doubt the art of lying has been practiced with success in diplomacy; but unlike that honesty which here as elsewhere is the best policy, a lie always leaves a drop of poison behind, and even the most dazzling diplomatic success gained by dishonesty stands on an insecure foundation, for it awakes in the defeated party a sense of aggravation, a desire for vengeance, and a hatred which must always be a menace to his foe . . . the negotiator will perhaps bear in mind that he will be engaged throughout life upon affairs of diplomacy and that it is therefore his interest to establish a reputation for plain and fair dealing . . . [which] will give him a great advantage in other enterprises on which he embarks in the future.

Of course, such justifications of ethics in terms of *prudence* rely on the calculation of its benefits turning out the right way: "Cast thy bread upon the waters," the Bible says, "and it shall return to thee after many days." The harder case, however, is when ethical behavior does *not* seem to pay — even after correctly factoring in the long-term costs of reputation, credibility, how others may react, and any ill social effects. Then one is back to intrinsic justifications.

Assuming, however, that ethical issues *are* relevant to bargaining, for whatever reasons, three characteristic areas strike us as especially useful to discuss: the appropriateness of certain tactics, the distribution among the bargainers of value created by agreement, and the possible effects of negotiation on those not at the table (externalities). Without elaborating the philosophical frameworks within which such questions can be more fully addressed, we offer some thoughts on making these kinds of inescapable ethical choices.

1. Tactical Choice

The essence of much bargaining involves changing another's perceptions of where in fact one would settle. Several kinds of tactics can lead to impressions that are at variance with the truth about one's position: persuasive rationales, commitments, references to other no-agreement alternatives, calculated patterns of concessions, failures to correct misperceptions, and the like. These tactics are tempting for obvious reasons: one side may claim value by causing the other to misperceive the range of potentially acceptable agreements. And both sides are generally in this same boat.

Such misrepresentations about each side's real interests and the set of possible bargaining outcomes should be distinguished from misrepresentations about certain aspects of the substance of the negotiation (e.g., whether the car has known difficulties that will require repair, whether the firm being acquired has important undiscussed liabilities, and so on). This latter category of tactics, which we might dub "malign persuasion," more frequently fails tests of ethical appropriateness. Consider two such tests.

Are the "Rules" Known and Accepted by All Sides?

Some people take the symmetry of the bargaining situation to ease the difficulty of ethical choice. The British statesman, Henry Taylor, is reported to have said that "falsehood ceases to be falsehood when it is understood on all sides that the truth is not expected to be spoken." In other words, if these tactics are mutually accepted as within the "rules of the game," there is no problem. A good analogy can be found in a game of poker: Bluffing is expected and thus permissible, while drawing a gun or kicking over the table are not. Yet often, the line is harder to draw.

For instance, a foreigner in Hong Kong may be aware that at least some tailors bargain routinely, but still be unsure whether a particular one — who insists he has fixed prices — is "just bargaining." Yet that tailor may reap considerable advantage if in fact he bargains but is persuasive that he does not. It is often self-servingly easy for the deceiver to assume that others know and accept the rules. And a worse problem is posed if many situations are often not even recognized as negotiation, when in fact they exhibit its essential characteristics (interdependence, some perceived conflict, opportunistic potential, the possibility of explicit or tacit agreement on joint action). When, as is often the case in organizational life, such less acknowledged negotiation occurs, then how can any "rules" of the game meet the mutual "awareness and acceptance of the rules" test?

Can the Situation Be Freely Entered and Left?

Ethicist Sissela Bok adds another criterion: For lying to be appropriate, not only must the rules be well-understood, but the participants must be able freely to enter *and* leave the situation. Thus to the extent that mutually expected, ritual flattery or a work of fiction involve "lying," there is little problem. To make an analogy between deception and violence: though a boxing match, which can involve rough moves, meets this criterion, a duel, from which exit may be impossible, does not.

Yet this standard may be too high. Bargaining situations — formal and informal, tacit and explicit — are far more widespread than many people realize. In fact, a good case can be made that bargaining pervades life inside and outside of organizations, making continual free entry and exit impractical. So if bargaining will go on and people will necessarily be involved in it, something else is required.

Other Helpful Questions

When it is unclear whether a particular tactic is ethically appropriate, we find that a number of other questions — beyond whether others know and accept it or may leave — can illuminate the choice. Consider several such questions:

Self-image. Peter Drucker asks a basic question: When you look at your-self in the mirror the next morning, will you like the person you see? And there are many such useful queries about self-image, which are intended to clarify the appropriateness of the choice itself and not to ask about the possible consequences (firing, ostracism, etc.) to you of different parties being aware of your actions: Would you be comfortable if your co-workers, colleagues, and friends were aware that you had used a particular tactic? Your spouse, children, or parents? If it came out on the front page of the *New York Times* or the *Wall Street Journal*? If it became known in ten years? Twenty? In the history books?

Reciprocity. Does it accord with the Golden Rule? How would you feel if someone did it to you? To a younger colleague? A respected mentor? A mem-ber of your family? (Of course, saying that you would mind very much if it were done to another need not imply that the tactic is unethical; that per-son may not be in your situation or have your experience — but figuring out the reason you would be bothered can give a clue to the ethics of the choice.)

Advising Others. Would you be comfortable advising another to use this tactic? Instructing your agent to use it? How about if such advice became known?

Designing the System. Imagine that you were completely outside the set-ting in which the tactic might be used, but that you were responsible for designing the situation itself: the number of people present, their stakes, the conventions governing their encounters, the range of' permissible action, and so on. The wrinkle is that you would be assigned a role in that setting, *but* you would not know in advance the identity of the person whose role you would assume. Would you build in the possibility for the kind of tactics you are now trying to evaluate? A simpler version of this test is to ask how you would rule on this tactic if you were an arbitrator, or perhaps an elder, in a small society.

Social Result. What if everybody bargained this way? Would the result-ing society be desirable? These questions may not have obvious answers. For example, hard, individual competition may seem dehumanizing. Yet many argue that, precisely because competition is encouraged, standards of living rise in free-market societies and some forms of excellence flourish.

Alternative Tactics. Are there alternative tactics available that have fewer ethical ambiguities or costs? Call the whole issue be avoided by following a different tack, even at small cost elsewhere?

Taking a Broader View. In agonizing over a tactic — for instance, whether to shade values — it is often worth stepping back to take a broad perspec-tive.

First, there is a powerful tendency for people to focus on conflict, see a "zero sum" world, and primarily aim to enlarge their individual shares. Such an emphasis on "claiming" is common yet it can stunt creativity and often cause significant joint gains to go unrealized. In such cases, does the real problem lie in the ethical judgment call about a tactic intended to claim value, or is it a disproportionate focus on claiming itself? If it is the latter, the more fruitful question may be how to make the other face of' negotiation — moves jointly to "create value" — more salient.

Second, does the type of situation itself generate powerful tendencies toward the questionable tactics involved? Is it an industry in which "favors" to public officials are an "expected" means for winning good contracts? If so, evaluating the acceptability of a given move may be less important than deciding (1) whether to leave the situation that inherently poses such choices, or (2) which actions could alter, even slightly, the prevalence of the questionable practices.

2. Distributional Fairness

One reason that a tactical choice can be uncomfortable is its potential effect on the distribution of value created by agreement. If a "shrewd" move allows a large firm to squeeze a small merchant unmercifully or an experienced negotiator to walk away with all the profit in dealings with a novice, something may seem wrong. Even when the nature of the tactics is not in question, the "fairness" of the outcome may be.

This difficulty is inherent in negotiation: Since there is a bargaining set of many potential agreements that are better for each person than his or her respective alternatives to agreement, the value created by agreement must necessarily be apportioned. Ultimately, when all joint gains have been discovered and common value created, more value for one party means less for another. But just where should the value split be? This, of course, is the age-old problem of "distributive justice," of what a just distribution of rewards and risks in a society should be. In the same way that this is a thorny, unresolved problem at the social level, so it is for individual negotiators — even when less well-recognized. And this is why the problem is so hard, and does not admit easy answers.

A classic problem among game theorists involves trying to develop fair criteria to arbitrate the division of $200 between two people. An obvious norm involves an even split, $100 for each. But what if one is rich and the other poor? More for the poor man, right? "Not at all!" protests the rich woman, "you must look at *after-tax* revenue, even if you want a little more to end up going to the poor man. Moreover, you should really try to equalize the amount of good done for each of us — in which case $20 to him will improve his life much more than $180 will mine. Or look at it the other way: Ask who can better afford to *lose* what amounts — and he can afford to lose $5 about as much as I can $195. Besides, he is a wino and completely on his own. I will sign this pledge to give the money to Mother Teresa, who will use it to help dozens of poor people in India. After all, that poor man *was* rich just two weeks ago, when he was convicted of fraud and had all his money confiscated to pay back his victims."

Who "should" get what in a negotiated agreement? The preceding tongue-in check discussion should not obscure the importance of distributional questions; certainly negotiators argue for this solution or that on the basis of "fairness" all the time. But the rich woman's objections should underscore how fragile and divisive conceptions of equity may be. One person's fairness may be another's outrage.

And fairness not only applies to the process of bargaining but also to its underlying structure. Think of the wage "bargaining" between an illegal alien and her work supervisor who can have her deported at a moment's notice. Is such a situation so loaded against one of the participants that the results are virtually certain to be "unfairly" distributed?

Many times, by contrast, we will be comfortable answering that we do *not* care about the actual result, only that the process was within normal bounds, that the participants [were] intelligent and well-informed enough, and that no one outside the negotiation was harmed by the accord.

3. Externalities

A third broad question involving others who are not at the bargaining table deserves some mention. If the Teamsters Union, major trucking firms, and a "captive" Interstate Commerce Commission informally bargained and agreed on higher rates, what about the interests of the unrepresented public? How do the children's' interests figure into a divorce settlement hammered out by two adversarial lawyers who only know that each parent wants custody? Or, suppose that a commission negotiates and decides to raise *current* Social Security benefits dramatically but pay for them by issuing very long-term bonds, the bulk of whose burden will fall on the *next* two generations?

It is often easy to "solve" the negotiation problem for those in the room at the expense of those who are not. If such parties cannot take part directly, one way to "internalize" this "externality" is to keep their interests in mind or to invite the participation or observation of those who can represent their interests, if only indirectly. Deciding that the process could be improved this way may not be too hard, though the mechanics of representation can be trickier. Yet, even with "proper" representation, what about the actual outcome? We are back to questions akin to those in the last section on distribution.

There is another, more subtle, external effect of the way in which ethical questions in bargaining are resolved. It involves the spillover of the way one person bargains into the pattern of dealings of' others. Over time, each of us comes to hold assumptions about what is likely and appropriate in bargaining interactions. Each tactical choice shapes these expectations and reverberates throughout the circles we inhabit. And many people lament that the state of dealings in business and government is such that behavior we might prefer to avoid becomes almost irresistible, since others are doing it and overly idealistic actions could be very costly.

* * *

Gary T. Lowenthal,[*] *A General Theory of Negotiation Process, Strategy and Behavior*
31 U. KAN. L. REV. 69, 105-08 (1982)[**]

* * *

1. The Relationship Between the Negotiators Themselves

Anticipation of a continuing relationship between negotiators, independent of a particular transaction they are negotiating, affects their strategies in dealing with one another. For example, experiments conducted by researchers at the University of Chicago in the 1960's indicated that when friends negotiate with one another, they tend to seek equitable outcomes. Summarizing the correlation between a continuing friendship and bargaining strategy, the experimenters noted:

> Wise persons . . . do not treat every encounter like a used-car transaction where they never expect to see the other again; friends, instead, also take care that the other obtains an outcome sufficiently rewarding so that he is willing to interact again.

The logic of this analysis applies to continuing professional relationships as well as personal relationships. Plea negotiations between a prosecutor and a public defender assigned to handle all the cases for indigent defendants in a particular court illustrate this principle. In seeking a favorable plea bargain for a specific client, a conscientious defense lawyer often attempts to persuade the prosecutor of weaknesses in the government's case, and emphasizes salient points concerning the defendant's age, prior criminal record, attitude, family background, employment, efforts toward rehabilitation, and minimal culpability for the charged offense. Successful negotiation depends in part on convincing the prosecutor to exercise discretion in treating a defendant more leniently than others charged with the same or equally serious offenses. A lawyer's credibility in making representations that a client is entitled to special consideration is diluted, however, by the frequency that the lawyer must make such arguments on behalf of other clients. As a result, the defender's competitive drive to persuade the prosecutor to reassess an initial evaluation of a case is tempered by the defense lawyer's obligation to make similar arguments on behalf of other

---

[*] Gary T. Lowenthal is Professor at Arizona State University Sandra Day O'Connor College of Law. This excerpt focuses on the ethical dilemmas created by the relationships between negotiators.

[**] Copyright © 1982 Kansas Law Review. Reprinted with permission.

clients whose cases are assigned to the same court and prosecutor. Strongly worded arguments are reserved for the truly exceptional case.

Negotiation behavior is similar in other contexts. Walton and McKersie noted, for example, that collective bargaining parties often seek conciliatory solutions to impasses when they anticipate that they will be dealing with one another almost continuously in administering the contract, handling grievances, and resolving periodic disputes not covered by the agreement. Similarly, a seller who knows that she may conduct future business with a particular buyer may be inclined to employ collaborative strategies in negotiating a "fair" price, rather than hard-sell techniques designed to maximize the seller's profit on the individual transaction. Bluffing, concealment of authority to compromise, and commitment strategies are more likely to be used in situations in which the seller has no expectation of future transactions with the buyer. Indeed, anticipation of a continuing relationship with the other party in any negotiation may be the greatest deterrent against . . . "feigned collaboration". . . .

Continuing professional relationships between lawyer-negotiators may cause the most serious ethical problems associated with bargaining, since an individual clients' interests may be sacrificed for those of other clients or for the lawyer's desire to get along with other members of the bar. For example, counsel for a party in a civil action may be less inclined to file a series of pretrial motions and written interrogatories for the purpose of gaining leverage in settlement negotiations if the law firm representing the adverse party is in a position to reciprocate with similar tactics in other cases. The public defender, who tempers plea bargaining arguments to preserve credibility and fails to push cases to the brink of trial to extract better deals, also illustrates this problem. Collaborative strategies may be chosen over competitive alternatives to enhance a lawyer's long range negotiation effectiveness, rather than the gain of the client in the instant case.

Although neither the Model Code of Professional Responsibility nor the Model Rules of Professional Conduct address this issue specifically in the context of negotiation, both take the position that a lawyer should *never* compromise the legitimate interest of a client for either the lawyer's own personal interest or the interests of any other clients. Instead, lawyers are expected to decline employment that may result in conflicting client interests, withdraw from representing clients whose interests conflict with those of other clients, or obtain the informed consent of all affected clients. The underlying premise of these rules is that "[l]oyalty is an essential element in the lawyer's relationship to a client. The lawyer must be free of other responsibilities that would significantly inhibit giving advice or assistance to the client."

Such laudatory principles are unassailable in the abstract, but impractical in many contexts. Can a public defender fight tooth and nail for every competitive bargaining advantage for *every* client, repeatedly using threats and statements of inflexible commitment, while still maintaining credibility? Moreover, withdrawal may not be a realistic alternative when the conflict of interest is an inherent tension affecting every client represented by a negotiator with a high volume, specialized practice. Informed consent also can be unrealistic, since not many clients are likely to agree to counsel's failure to use applicable competitive tactics in order to maintain credibility in future negotiations on behalf of other — unnamed — clients. In the end, lawyers must — and inevitably do — balance individual client interests in seeking competitive advantage in negotiations.

* * *

Robert J. Condlin,[*] *Bargaining in the Dark: The Normative Incoherence of Lawyer Dispute Bargaining Role*
51 MD. L. REV. 1, 78-80, 84-86 (1992)[**]

* * *

IV. The Bargainer's Dilemma

Practical bargaining is cooperative bargaining. Clients do better, at least clients in the aggregate, when represented by lawyers who bargain cooperatively and are known to do so. Nevertheless, a particular client, valuing her own immediate return in an individual case more highly than the interests of clients in the aggregate (which may include the particular client's own future interests), may seek to trade on rather than contribute to her lawyer's history of cooperating. She may instruct the lawyer to defect when the adversary cooperates, and may ground this instruction on the lawyer's ethical obligations to be deferential and competent. This places the lawyer in a bind. Does she bargain ethically or practically? Does she reject the instruction and preserve her reputation for cooperating, so that she can secure better settlements, on average, for all of her clients, including those in the future? Or does she follow her client's instruction, exploit the adversary's reasonable but, as it will turn out, unwarranted cooperation, and plant the seeds of future retaliation?

The dilemma is serious, not necessarily because it is widespread — it may or may not be — but because lawyers seem to assume that it is the paradigm case. They see the defecting client as every client, and feel the pressure to bargain competitively across the board. Clients do not correct the assumption, some perhaps because they agree with it, others perhaps because they do not know that it has been made, and still others perhaps because they see

---

[*] Robert J. Condlin is Professor at University of Maryland School of Law. This excerpt examines how the ethical mandate of zealous representation is transformed by the need for cooperation to resolve disputes.

[**] Copyright © 1992 Robert J. Condlin. Reprinted with permission.

legal representation as a technical process in which following the lawyer's lead is the proper (and safest) course. Whatever the reasons, the view that clients invariably want to compete has developed a life of its own, and is now treated as received wisdom in large parts of the profession. Lawyers trapped in this view, as well as those representing clients who truly want to defect, need a reply to the client's argument from deference and competence.

* * *

Seemingly trapped in a no-win situation, lawyers have made an interesting and clever, albeit probably unself-conscious, adaptation. Lawyer bargaining is not just adversarial; it is also stylized. It is adversarial because it is made up, in the main, of aggressive communication maneuvers such as argument, challenge, and demand. It is stylized because this aggressive maneuvering is carried out in a slightly exaggerated, somewhat predictable, and essentially impersonal fashion. Both dimensions are important to wriggling out of the dilemma of lawyer bargaining role. The adversarial part allows lawyers to believe that they have fought hard for their clients, and in the process that they have been deferential to client wishes and diligent in their pursuit. The stylized part allows them to preserve bargaining relationships with other lawyers by signaling, through a set of rhetorical conventions, that the aggressiveness is not personal, but is just part of the lawyer act. Behavior that is both adversarial and stylized is a lawyer's way of being (or believing she has been) both ethical and practical, of protecting her reputation for cooperating, while at the same time arguing zealously for the interests of her clients. It is an effort to walk a line between the important but conflicting normative pulls of bargaining's ethical and practical sides, complying minimally with each and not openly violating either.

In a sense, of course, stylized aggressiveness is not a successful response to the dilemma of bargaining role. It often routinizes client interests and thus is not diligent, while at the same time it frequently offends other lawyers and thus is not cooperative. This objection misses the point, however. There is often no way to be both diligent and cooperative, to be practically effective and ethically scrupulous, at least in the hardest of cases. Yet lawyers need to be practical to prosper and want to be ethical to make prosperity palatable. They need to reconcile bargaining's confused normative universe, or at least appear to do so, and stylized adversarial advocacy is simply the best of a bad lot of present options for allowing them to believe this has been done.

The understandable, if ultimately mistaken, wish to be true to all facets of a complex and sometimes contradictory bargaining role is a less exciting explanation of competitive lawyer bargaining behavior than explanations based on the legal profession's deeply rooted and pathological need to fight, or a failure of technique, but most reality is more mundane than the most exciting stories that are told about it. Lawyers know how to cooperate (the existence of private dispute settlement in a system of adversary advocacy is proof of that), but they are unclear about the extent to which they are permitted to do so consistently with their other important role-related obligations. . . .

* * *

Steven Hartwell,[*] *Understanding and Dealing with Deception in Legal Negotiation*
6 OHIO ST. J. DISP. RESOL. 171, 182-92 (1991)[**]

* * *

B. Negotiation Contexts

"Negotiation" is the name of a context and, as well, the name of a set of contexts. When two opposing attorneys meet on the courthouse steps just before trial, the environment cues them that what they say in the next few minutes should be interpreted as within the context "negotiation." Only a naive attorney would interpret the greetings, inquiries about parking problems, and other such topics as merely conversation within the context of polite social intercourse. Negotiation, however, is a complex context containing within it several different contexts. The meaning of certain words or gestures in one of these contexts may differ from their meaning in another context. The context of a "courthouse steps" negotiation differs from the collegial "office" context of negotiating among one's peers within a law firm or law school faculty. The contextual interpretation of "deception" in one such context may differ from the contextual interpretation in another. Environmental cues and the language employed guide us in the appropriate interpretation of deceptive language and conduct. In order to understand better how these deceptions are interpreted, we need to review briefly the three major contexts that constitute most negotiations.

Professor Thomas Gifford has recently offered a comprehensive typology of negotiation contexts. His typology identifies three explicit contexts: competition, cooperation and integration (often called "collaboration"). The first context, competition, is marked by high demands, limited disclosure of information, threats, apparent commitments to positions, and deception. Asserted opening demands, bottom lines, constraints on authority to bargain, the identity of one's principal, and the seriousness of threats should all be taken as potentially deceptive. For example, a statement by one negotiator that "One million dollars is the least we will accept to settle this case" should, given a competitive context, be interpreted as a high demand

---

[*] Steven Hartwell is Professor at University of San Diego School of Law. His article discusses the importance of negotiation context in determining whether deception is perceived as ethical or unethical.

and a probable deception. The opponent would undoubtedly err if he were to interpret this statement as a candid offer.

The characteristic pattern that identifies the second context, cooperation, is the pattern of alternating and sequential concessions directed toward a compromise. Each party typically opens with offers that are less than what they expect at a final settlement. Given the above statement in a cooperative context, the opponent should interpret it as a signal inviting a counter-offer with the expectation that the opponent will then make a lesser demand. The speaker does not intend to deceive as he might in a competitive context, but intends that the statement encourage a sequence of concessions in which he himself intends continued participation. Plea bargaining between experienced prosecutors and defense counsel typically follows a cooperative context.

With the third context, integration, the negotiators engage in problem solving to satisfy their common interests. Given the "one million dollar" statement, the opponent should interpret it as candid, and designed to help both negotiators resolve their common problem. The two negotiators may have, for example, two million dollars to resolve a certain problem. The speaker does not intend to deceive or to induce a counter-offer. Integration differs from cooperation in several respects. Cooperation typically presumes a zero-sum situation in which your gain is my loss. The pattern of sequential concessions is intended to reach a fair division of a fixed pie. Integration typically presumes a non-zero sum situation, that is, a situation in which the pie can be made larger or in which the parties can abandon the original pie and, by working together, construct a new and tastier pie.

C. Deception of Context

A major thesis of this paper is that the kind of deception that threatens a negotiation is a deception *about* a context and not a deception *within* a context. As long as each negotiator accurately identifies the negotiation strategy (that is, the negotiation context) of the other, and appropriately anticipates the kind of candidness and deception which that negotiation context entails, deception will not derail the negotiation. If, for example, both negotiators knowingly employ a competitive context, then each will interpret the other's statements as presumptively deceptive. A negotiator who understands the negotiation context as competitive cannot rationally walk out of a competitive negotiation in a rage over a deception. Similarly, if both negotiators knowingly engage in a integratively-contexted negotiation, neither should ever intentionally deceive the other because it is not in their own self-interests to do so. However, negotiations are complex events and negotiators sometimes misread the context of a negotiation and consequently misinterpret the language of their opponents. At other times, negotiators act irrationally by refusing to recognize a patently obvious context, a type of negotiation pathology explained in Part IV.

1. Why We React More Strongly to Deception of Context. Good reasons compel negotiators to react more strongly to deception about a context than to deception within a context. Deception about context is potentially much more harmful than deception within a context. To be deceived about a context is to misinterpret every piece of information within that context. Consider the feeling of discovering that a person whom we thought to be a friend (that is, a person within a "friend context") has, from the very beginning, been a false friend. This sudden realization means that we have misunderstood everything this person has said to us. We have been deceived not once but numerous times. We may feel painfully humiliated. The difference between deception within a context and deception about a context is the difference between merely falling short and betrayal, between Peter and Judas.

2. Embarrassment and Shame. We intuitively express the difference between deception within a context and deception about a context with the social concepts of embarrassment and shame. Embarrassment is always context dependent. What is embarrassing in one context (belching in the faculty dining room, a deception in an integrative negotiation context) may not be embarrassing somewhere else (belching at home in front of one's long suffering family, a deception in a competitive negotiation context). Embarrassment is a negotiator's typical reaction to being caught in an inadvertent deception within a context that does not permit deception, such as a deception within an integrative context. Someone is embarrassed because he has not acted consistently with the context he wishes to project. The deceiver's embarrassment (flushed face, stammering) signals his opponent that he did not mean to deceive (that is, that he momentarily and inadvertently slipped from his role as an integrative negotiator). Sometimes negotiators are embarrassed when they discover they have been deceived because the deception indicates that they have not been the astute, sophisticated negotiators they thought themselves to be.

3. Shame. In contrast to embarrassment, shame typically entails intentional deception *about* a context. Shame is not being the person one claims to be in some fundamental way. Shame entails the violation of some general principle of civil conduct. To be a false friend and betray another is shameful.

IV. CLINICAL TEACHING ABOUT DECEPTION

A. The Danger Point in Negotiating

The first step in teaching students how to handle deception is to alert them to the danger point in negotiating, that is, the point at which contexts change during a negotiation. As Professor Gifford points out, negotiators frequently use more than one strategy (more than one context) in a single negotiation. A common contextual sequence in a zero-sum negotiation, for example, is from competition to cooperation. The negotiators compete until they become exhausted and call a truce. They then proceed cooperatively, making sequential, reciprocal concessions. The most dangerous point in such a negotiation, the point when context deception is most likely to occur, is the transition point between contexts. After an hour of competitive bashing, negotiator A makes a gesture of conciliation consistent with his decision to change the negotiation context to cooperation. Negotiator B interprets this gesture as just another competitive gimmick. She pretends to go along with what she perceives as his continuing competitive game plan and then zaps him with a deception. Upon his discovery of the deception, he is outraged. She perceives his outrage as just one more competitive tactic. The viability of the negotiation is now imperiled.

* * *

The major problem dedicated cooperators encounter is learning to read context rather than content. By reading context, I mean the ability to recognize the negotiation situation as competitive, cooperative, or integrative from cues apart from what the opponent says. Generally speaking, all zero-sum negotiations should be understood as potentially competitive. Dedicated cooperators wish even zero-sum negotiations to be only cooperative. They grasp at the first cooperative-appearing straw that blows their way. When an opposing competitive negotiator states that he is going to proceed cooperatively. . . , the dedicated cooperator mistakenly believes this content (the statement of cooperation), rather than the context (a competitive zero-sum negotiation). Typically, competitive negotiators employ a cooperative strategy only in a zero-sum negotiation when they get desperate. Dedicated cooperators must learn to wait them out.

Dedicated competitors who negotiate with dedicated cooperators face a different task. Competitors run the risk of so enraging deceived cooperators that they will refuse to negotiate further, thereby increasing everyone's transaction costs. Once again, the problem is a misreading of context. Just as the dedicated cooperator prefers cooperation and presumes others also do, the dedicated competitor prefers competition and presumes that others do as well. When a dedicated cooperator responds in anger to a competitor's deceptive tactic, the competitor reads the anger as merely a tactic within a competitive strategy. Dedicated competitors also infuriate their opponents by treating all negotiations as if they were zero-sum. They often fail to take advantage of the extra profit available to both parties through collaboration in integrative negotiations.

Once either the deceived cooperator or the deceiving competitor understands what has happened, she needs to take corrective action. Assuming the competitor wants the negotiation to continue, she needs to apologize (act "embarrassed") and make a cooperative gesture. She must understand that the outraged cooperator may have interpreted her competitive ploy as a shamefully immoral act.

The outraged cooperator has the more difficult task of convincing the competitor that the cooperator has reasonably interpreted the competitor's conduct as a contextual statement promising cooperation. The obvious problem is that the competitor will interpret the cooperator's outrage as merely a competitor's ploy. Hence, the cooperator has to make a very strong "context statement." That is, the cooperator has to do something that clearly signals that his outrage is about the deception of context and not about a deception within a context of competition. Because context cues come primarily from the environment surrounding the dialogue, the cooperator needs to change the environment dramatically. One way to change the environment is to refuse to continue negotiating. I believe that it is sometimes more effective to break the negotiation entirely and to stage a walk-out. I instruct students in my Legal Negotiation course who perceive themselves as dedicated cooperators to walk out at least once during the semester. Many who do engineer a walk-out report a sense of liberation.

* * *

SELECTED PROVISIONS

ABA MODEL RULES OF PROFESSIONAL CONDUCT (2006)[*]

RULE 1.2 SCOPE OF REPRESENTATION AND ALLOCATION OF AUTHORITY BETWEEN CLIENT AND LAWYER

(a) **Subject to paragraphs (c) and (d), a lawyer shall abide by a client's decisions concerning the objectives of representation and, as required by Rule 1.4, shall consult with the client as to the means by which they are to be pursued. A lawyer may take such action on behalf of the client as is impliedly authorized to carry out the representation. A lawyer shall abide by a client's decision whether to settle a matter. In a criminal case, the lawyer shall abide by the client's decision, after consultation with the lawyer, as to a plea to be entered, whether to waive jury trial and whether the client will testify.**

(b) **A lawyer's representation of a client, including representation by appointment, does not constitute an endorsement of the client's political, economic, social or moral views or activities.**

(c) **A lawyer may limit the scope of the representation if the limitation is reasonable under the circumstances and the client gives informed consent.**

(d) **A lawyer shall not counsel a client to engage, or assist a client, in conduct that the lawyer knows is criminal or fraudulent, but**

a lawyer may discuss the legal consequences of any proposed course of conduct with a client and may counsel or assist a client to make a good faith effort to determine the validity, scope, meaning or application of the law.

Comment

Allocation of Authority between Client and Lawyer

[1] Paragraph (a) confers upon the client the ultimate authority to determine the purposes to be served by legal representation, within the limits imposed by law and the lawyer's professional obligations. The decisions specified in paragraph (a), such as whether to settle a civil matter, must also be made by the client. See Rule 1.4(a)(1) for the lawyer's duty to communicate with the client about such decisions. With respect to the means by which the client's objectives are to be pursued, the lawyer shall consult with the client as required by Rule 1.4(a)(2) and may take such action as is impliedly authorized to carry out the representation.

[2] On occasion, however, a lawyer and a client may disagree about the means to be used to accomplish the client's objectives. Clients normally defer to the special knowledge and skill of their lawyer with respect to the means to be used to accomplish their objectives, particularly with respect to technical, legal and tactical matters. Conversely, lawyers usually defer to the client regarding such questions as the expense to be incurred and concern for third persons who might be adversely affected. Because of the varied nature of the matters about which a lawyer and client might disagree and because the actions in question may implicate the interests of a tribunal or other persons, this Rule does not prescribe how such disagreements are to be resolved. Other law, however, may be applicable and should be consulted by the lawyer. The lawyer should also consult with the client and seek a mutually acceptable resolution of the disagreement. If such efforts are unavailing and the lawyer has a fundamental disagreement with the client, the lawyer may withdraw from the representation. See Rule 1.16(b)(4). Conversely, the client may resolve the disagreement by discharging the lawyer. See Rule 1.16(a)(3).

[3] At the outset of a representation, the client may authorize the lawyer to take specific action on the client's behalf without further consultation. Absent a material change in circumstances and subject to Rule 1.4, a lawyer may rely on such an advance authorization. The client may, however, revoke such authority at any time.

* * *

Criminal, Fraudulent and Prohibited Transactions

[9] Paragraph (d) prohibits a lawyer from knowingly counseling or assisting a client to commit a crime or fraud. This prohibition, however, does

not preclude the lawyer from giving an honest opinion about the actual consequences that appear likely to result from a client's conduct. Nor does the fact that a client uses advice in a course of action that is criminal or fraudulent of itself make a lawyer a party to the course of action. There is a critical distinction between presenting an analysis of legal aspects of questionable conduct and recommending the means by which a crime or fraud might be committed with impunity.

* * *

RULE 1.16 DECLINING OR TERMINATING REPRESENTATION

(a) Except as stated in paragraph (c), a lawyer shall not represent a client or, where representation has commenced, shall withdraw from the representation of a client if:

(1) the representation will result in violation of the rules of professional conduct or other law;

* * *

(b) Except as stated in paragraph (c), a lawyer may withdraw from representing a client if:

(1) withdrawal can be accomplished without material adverse effect on the interests of the client;

(2) the client persists in a course of action involving the lawyer's services that the lawyer reasonably believes is criminal or fraudulent;

(3) the client has used the lawyer's services to perpetrate a crime or fraud;

(4) the client insists upon taking action that the lawyer considers repugnant or with which the lawyer has a fundamental disagreement;

* * *

(7) other good cause for withdrawal exists.

* * *

Comment

[1] A lawyer should not accept representation in a matter unless it can be performed competently, promptly, without improper conflict of interest and to completion. Ordinarily, a representation in a matter is completed when the agreed-upon assistance has been concluded. See Rules 1.2(c) and 6.5. See also Rule 1.3, Comment [4].

Mandatory Withdrawal

[2] A lawyer ordinarily must decline or withdraw from representation if the client demands that the lawyer engage in conduct that is illegal or violates the Rules of Professional Conduct or other law. The lawyer is not obliged to decline or withdraw simply because the client suggests such a course of conduct; a client may make such a suggestion in the hope that a lawyer will not be constrained by a professional obligation.

* * *

Optional Withdrawal

[7] A lawyer may withdraw from representation in some circumstances. The lawyer has the option to withdraw if it can be accomplished without material adverse effect on the client's interests. Withdrawal is also justified if the client persists in a course of action that the lawyer reasonably believes is criminal or fraudulent, for a lawyer is not required to be associated with such conduct even if the lawyer does not further it. Withdrawal is also permitted if the lawyer's services were misused in the past even if that would materially prejudice the client. The lawyer may also withdraw where the client insists on taking action that the lawyer considers repugnant or with which the lawyer has a fundamental disagreement.

* * *

RULE 2.1 ADVISOR

In representing a client, a lawyer shall exercise independent professional judgment and render candid advice. In rendering advice, a lawyer may refer not only to law but to other considerations such as moral, economic, social and political factors, that may be relevant to the client's situation.

Comment

Scope of Advice

(1) A client is entitled to straightforward advice expressing the lawyer's honest assessment. Legal advice often involves unpleasant facts and alternatives that a client may be disinclined to confront. In presenting advice, a lawyer endeavors to sustain the client's morale and may put advice in as acceptable a form as honesty permits. However, a lawyer should not be deterred from giving candid advice by the prospect that the advice will be unpalatable to the client.

(2) Advice couched in narrowly legal terms may be of little value to a client, especially where practical considerations, such as cost or effects on other people, are predominant. Purely technical legal advice, therefore, can sometimes be inadequate. It is proper for a lawyer to refer to rele-

vant moral and ethical considerations in giving advice. Although a lawyer is not a moral advisor as such, moral and ethical considerations impinge upon most legal questions and may decisively influence how the law will be applied.

(3) A client may expressly or impliedly ask the lawyer for purely technical advice. When such a request is made by a client experienced in legal matters, the lawyer may accept it at face value. When such a request is made by a client inexperienced in legal matters, however, the lawyer's responsibility as advisor may include indicating that more may be involved than strictly legal considerations.

(4) Matters that go beyond strictly legal questions may also be in the domain of another profession. Family matters can involve problems within the professional competence of psychiatry, clinical psychology or social work; business matters can involve problems within the competence of the accounting profession or of financial specialists. Where consultation with a professional in another field is itself something a competent lawyer would recommend, the lawyer should make such a recommendation. At the same time, a lawyer's advice at its best often consists of recommending a course of action in the face of conflicting recommendations of experts.

Offering Advice

(5) In general, a lawyer is not expected to give advice until asked by the client. However, when a lawyer knows that a client proposes a course of action that is likely to result in substantial adverse legal consequences to the client, duty to the client under Rule 1.4 may require that the lawyer act if the client's course of action is related to the representation. A lawyer ordinarily has no duty to initiate investigation of a client's affairs or to give advice that the client has indicated is unwanted, but a lawyer may initiate advice to a client when doing so appears to be in the client's interest.

RULE 4.1 TRUTHFULNESS IN STATEMENTS TO OTHERS

In the course of representing a client a lawyer shall not knowingly:

(a) make a false statement of material fact or law to a third person; or

(b) fail to disclose a material fact to a third person when disclosure is necessary to avoid assisting a criminal or fraudulent act by a client, unless disclosure is prohibited by Rule 1.6.

Comment

Misrepresentation

(1) A lawyer is required to be truthful when dealing with others on a client's behalf, but generally has no affirmative duty to inform an opposing

party of relevant facts. A misrepresentation can occur if the lawyer incorporates or affirms a statement of another person that the lawyer knows is false. Misrepresentations can also occur by partially true but misleading statements or omissions that are the equivalent of affirmative false statements. For dishonest conduct that does not amount to a false statement or for misrepresentations by a lawyer other than in the course of representing a client, see Rule 8.4.

Statements of Fact

(2) This Rule refers to statements of fact. Whether a particular statement should be regarded as one of fact can depend on the circumstances. Under generally accepted conventions in negotiation, certain types of statements ordinarily are not taken as statements of material fact. Estimates of price or value placed on the subject of a transaction and a party's intentions as to an acceptable settlement of a claim are in this category, and so is the existence of an undisclosed principal except where nondisclosure of the principal would constitute fraud. Lawyers should be mindful of their obligations under applicable law to avoid criminal and tortious misrepresentation.

Fraud by Client

(3) Under Rule 1.2(d), a lawyer is prohibited from counseling or assisting a client in conduct that the lawyer knows is criminal or fraudulent. Paragraph (b) states a specific application of the principle set forth in Rule 1.2(d) and addresses the situation where a client's crime or fraud takes the form of a lie or misrepresentation. Ordinarily, a lawyer can avoid assisting a client's crime or fraud by withdrawing from the representation. Sometimes it may be necessary for the lawyer to give notice of the fact of withdrawal and to disaffirm an opinion, document, affirmation or the like. In extreme cases, substantive law may require a lawyer to disclose information relating to the representation to avoid being deemed to have assisted the client's crime or fraud. If the lawyer can avoid assisting a client's crime or fraud only by disclosing this information, then under paragraph (b) the lawyer is required to do so, unless the disclosure is prohibited by Rule 1.6.

SELECTED PROVISIONS

ABA MODEL CODE OF PROFESSIONAL RESPONSIBILITY (1981)*

CANON 7

A Lawyer Should Represent A Client Zealously Within The Bounds Of The Law

ETHICAL CONSIDERATIONS

EC 7-1

The duty of a lawyer, both to his client and to the legal system, is to represent his client zealously within the bounds of the law, which includes Disciplinary Rules and enforceable professional regulations. . . .

* * *

EC 7-7

In certain areas of legal representation not affecting the merits of the cause or substantially prejudicing the rights of a client, a lawyer is entitled to make decisions on his own. But otherwise the authority to make decisions is exclusively that of the client and, if made within the framework of the law, such decisions are binding on his lawyer. As typical examples in civil cases, it is for the client to decide whether he will accept a settlement offer or whether he will waive his right to plead an affirmative defense. A defense lawyer in a criminal case has the duty to advise his client fully on whether a particular plea to a charge appears to be desirable and as to the prospects of success on appeal, but it is for the client to decide what plea should be entered and whether an appeal should be taken.

* * *

EC 7-8

A lawyer should exert his best efforts to insure that decisions of his client are made only after the client has been informed of relevant considerations. A lawyer ought to initiate this decision-making process if the client does not do so. Advice of a lawyer to his client need not be confined to purely legal considerations. A lawyer should advise his client of the possible effect of each legal alternative. A lawyer should bring to bear upon this decision-making process the fullness of his experience as well as his objective viewpoint. In assisting his client to reach a proper decision, it is often desirable for a lawyer to point out those factors which may lead to a decision that is morally just as well as legally permissible. He may emphasize the possibility of harsh consequences that might result from assertion of legally permissible positions. In the final analysis, however, the lawyer should always remember that the decision whether to forego legally available objectives or methods because of non-legal factors is ultimately for the client and not for himself. In the event that the client in a non-adjudicatory matter insists upon a course of conduct that is contrary to the judgment and advice of the lawyer but not prohibited by Disciplinary Rules, the lawyer may withdraw from the employment.

EC 7-9

In the exercise of his professional judgement on those decisions which are for his determination in the handling of a legal matter, a lawyer should always act in a manner consistent with the best interests of his client. However, when an action in the best interest of his client seems to him to be unjust, he may ask his client for permission to forego such action.

EC 7-10

The duty of a lawyer to represent his client with zeal does not militate against his concurrent obligation to treat with consideration all persons involved in the legal process and to avoid the infliction of needless harm.

* * *

EC 7-21

The civil adjudicative process is primarily designed for the settlement of disputes between parties, while the criminal process is designed for the protection of society as a whole. Threatening to use, or using, the criminal process to coerce adjustment of private civil claims or controversies is a subversion of that process, further, the person against whom the criminal process is so misused may be deterred from asserting his legal rights and thus the usefulness of the civil process in settling private disputes is impaired. . . .

* * *

EC 7-23

. . . .The adversary system contemplates that each lawyer will present and argue the existing law in the light most favorable to his client. Where a lawyer knows of legal authority in the controlling jurisdiction directly adverse to the position of his client, he should inform the tribunal of its existence unless his adversary has done so; but, having made such disclosure, he may challenge its soundness in whole or in part.

* * *

DR 7-102 Representing A Client Within The Bounds Of The Law

(A) In his representation of a client, a lawyer shall not:

(1) File a suit, assert a position, conduct a defense, delay a trial, or take other action on behalf of his client when he knows or when

it is obvious that such action would serve merely to harass or maliciously injure another.

(2) Knowingly advance a claim or defense that is unwarranted under existing law, except that he may advance such claim or defense if it can be supported by good faith argument for an extension, modification, or reversal of existing law.

(3) Conceal or knowingly fail to disclose that which he is required by law to reveal.

* * *

(5) Knowingly make a false statement of law or fact.

(6) Participate in the creation or preservation of evidence when he knows or it is obvious that the evidence is false.

* * *

DR 7-105 Threatening Criminal Prosecution

(A) A lawyer shall not present, participate in presenting, or threaten to present criminal charges solely to obtain advantage in a civil matter.

* * *

Chapter 9

MEDIATION: FACILITATED NEGOTIATION

By this point, you have already become familiar with some of the many ways in which negotiations can go wrong. A party's fear of losing face makes him stubbornly refuse an advantageous offer. A lawyer's aggressive behavior leads to a stalemate instead of an agreement. Negotiators reach an agreement, but both sides are dissatisfied and feel that they left money on the table. In all these situations, there was a valuable deal to be made, but the negotiating parties did not manage to make it. Their emotions got the better of them, or they overestimated the other side's need to settle, or they lacked critical information that would have helped them reach a positive outcome. Such deadlocks occur every day, as even a cursory glance at the daily newspaper will tell you, in every negotiation arena from the tense political discussions between Israelis and Palestinians to the most mundane disputes between neighbors about barking dogs or loud music.

A. BRINGING IN A THIRD PARTY

Many of the techniques recommended in earlier chapters are designed to avoid such unproductive results by improving communication and information flow between negotiators. Sometimes, though, the parties or their lawyers are so entrenched in their positions or the issues that separate them are so complex or heated that further progress becomes impossible. At this point, they may decide to call in a third party to diagnose the problem and to help them resolve their dispute. The most formal version of this kind of help, of course, involves hiring a lawyer to file suit and having the matter resolved by a judge or jury. Another, less formal, type of adjudication is arbitration, in which a third party hears evidence from lawyers for both sides and renders a decision. But what if the parties themselves want to retain control over the outcome, yet still feel that negotiations are stuck and that they are unable to move forward on their own? Would a neutral outsider be able to help them resolve their dispute, without taking decision-making power away from them? Just as you may have observed others negotiating and been able to offer feedback that helped their negotiations go more smoothly, a mediator serves the formal function of facilitating negotiations between parties, with or without the participation of their lawyers.

A mediator, unlike a judge or an arbitrator, has no decision-making power: she cannot render a verdict or make an award. The parties themselves must agree to any resolution of their conflict. Mediation is often particularly attractive when there is a long-term relationship that gives the parties a stake in working out a mutually satisfactory agreement. They may expect to continue dealing with each other in the future, like parents mediating child custody and other aspects of divorce, or they may not, like business partners seeking an amicable dissolution rather than a court battle. Even when there is no long-term relationship, as in much mediation conducted through courts' alternative dispute resolution programs, parties often find mediation attractive because it permits creative solutions that are not limited to what a court could order one or the other to do. In addition, mediation offers the parties in a litigated case an opportunity to participate directly in the settlement process. Until that point, the case will usually have been handled exclusively by their lawyers.

B. HOW MEDIATION WORKS

A central aspect of the mediator's job is to focus on the negotiating process between the parties: to improve their ability to communicate clearly and constructively with each other; to help them explore options they may not have considered previously or not have considered seriously; and to reduce the interpersonal tensions that often lead to stalemates in negotiation. As a neutral with no stake in the outcome of the dispute, the mediator is in a good position to see the ways that the parties' behavior works against reaching a satisfactory resolution and to help them take a more productive approach to their conflict. The fact that she has no decision-making power does not mean that she is without authority altogether in the parties' eyes. Her presence alone, as an outsider to the conflict, will often promote the parties' renewed efforts to reach agreement. In addition, her process expertise will enable her to assist them in moving past the point at which they became stuck on their own. Finally, if she has expertise in the subject matter of the dispute or obtains private information by meeting separately with the parties, she may offer her own evaluation of their substantive proposals and make recommendations about settlement.

1. The Mediator's Presence

How does the mediator's presence help? A person who is locked in a dispute and unable to walk away tends to see the other party as the problem, rather than as part of a solution to the problem. Having reached a stalemate, both sides are likely to feel embattled and at risk. The presence of a third party can mitigate the mutual attribution of blame and allow the parties to focus discussion on the substance of their conflict and on their present and future needs, rather than on perceived wrongs in the past. Whatever she may lack in legal power to resolve disputes, the mediator has a certain transference authority by virtue of being called in as a potential peacemaker. Being an outsider, she also has a wider perspective on the parties' situation, and her neutrality reinforces their battered hopes for a fair resolution. As long as the mediator does not get drawn into the conflict between them, her involvement reinforces in a concrete way the idea that a middle ground can exist between the parties' initially polarized points of view. Simply by being there, she symbolizes the possibility of finding a zone of agreement.

2. Facilitating the Process

A mediator's process skills are important because negotiating parties have usually become defensive and stopped listening to each other by the time they call in a third party. By practicing active listening, the mediator demonstrates good communication skills and models a more effective way for the parties to explore their differences. Active listening also helps her clarify the parties' individual perceptions of the obstacles to resolution. She will attempt to restate one party's point of view in a way that allows the other party to take it in and consider it. Often, the parties can hear things more easily coming from the mediator than from each other, both because of the way she frames what she says and because she is not perceived as having a vested interest in a particular point of view. Mediation may succeed in part because reactive devaluation (see the article by Mnookin in Chapter Five) is less likely to occur when the mediator presents a settlement proposal rather than one of the parties. As communication improves, the parties' resistance to each other diminishes, and the possibility of their reaching agreement increases.

3. Evaluating Substantive Issues

Some mediators focus not only on the process issues of how the parties talk and listen to each other, but also on the substance of their conflict. The mediator may actively seek to craft an acceptable resolution, using either the parties' proposals or her own. She will base her suggestions on information learned during private caucuses with the individual parties, held after the parties meet together in joint session. Although strictly speaking she has no decision-making power, a practitioner of so-called "evaluative" mediation will often work hard to move the parties toward an agreement that she believes is in their mutual interest. If the parties are involved in litigation, the mediator may well be an experienced lawyer who will give her evaluation of how a judge or jury is likely to perceive the case, who is likely to prevail in court, and what the verdict might be. When pre-trial mediation is mandated by statute or court rule for litigated cases, careful evaluation by the mediator often makes it possible for the parties to settle the case before trial, even if they do not reach resolution during the mediation itself.

C. FACILITATION OR EVALUATION?

Within the mediation community, there is considerable debate about the appropriate scope of the mediator's role. Some believe that it should be limited to process issues, that the function of the mediator is to facilitate interpersonal communication by modeling and encouraging active listening between the parties, clarifying their needs and interests, and helping them explore potential options for agreement. Mediators who subscribe to a purely facilitative model of mediation often will not meet separately with the parties, but conduct all discussions jointly. Their rationale is that one of the purposes of mediation is to empower the parties, rather than to rely on the supposed wisdom and decisional expertise of an outsider. In this view, separate caucuses are counterproductive because they invest the mediator, rather than the parties, with secret knowledge and, hence, power over the outcome. Some advocates of this approach to mediation maintain that the experience can do far more than resolve individual disputes: it can also transform the parties involved. The article below by Bush proposes that mediation can influence both how the parties approach one another thereafter and how they deal with different, unrelated conflicts in their lives.

Others see the mediator as having a result-oriented, evaluative function. In this view, mediation is a form of shuttle diplomacy, in which the mediator caucuses with each party after an initial joint session. On the basis of what she learns from these individual discussions, the mediator can then craft a proposal for resolution which she expects both parties will be able to accept. While the mediator cannot impose a decision on the parties, once she obtains private information from them, she is the only one in the room who knows with any certainty where the zone of agreement lies. This gives her the power that goes with being the "one who knows", and thus gives her proposals substantial weight. Many so-called "muscle" mediators feel that this is exactly what parties are paying them for: to use their substantive expertise and the confidential information they acquire to come up with acceptable proposals for resolving the parties' dispute. It is perhaps not surprising that retired judges, many of whom are among the most sought-after mediators, often fall into this category. Their past experience gives added weight to their recommendations, especially in litigated cases, and they readily take a decisive role in the process.

Some mediators strike a middle ground between the extremes of purely facilitative and strongly evaluative approaches to mediation. These mediators have a facilitative style that is designed to improve communication and to involve the parties actively in the process, both in joint sessions and in private caucuses. At the same time, they use their substantive expertise to ask the participants pertinent questions about the strengths and weaknesses of their cases. Being familiar with relevant jury verdicts, these mediators can act as a sounding board for litigants about the costs and benefits of proceeding to trial. In addition, they know how deals are constructed in their field and can be sure that the parties consider all relevant facets of a potential agreement, without ever telling the parties how they should resolve the matter at hand.

In the article that follows, Lowry argues there is really no such thing as *non*-evaluative mediation. Everything a mediator does or says in the course of a mediation is based on her evaluations of the situation: how else would she decide whether to speak or to be silent, or when to hold a private caucus, or what to say or not to say to the participants? Evaluation, in the sense of exercising judgment, is essential to the process of trying to help the parties. Lowry urges that the focus needs to be on when and how the mediator evaluates and on the primary goal of fostering the parties' capacity to negotiate with each other. That some mediators go so far as to urge a particular outcome, however, may mean that the process no longer feels very different from adjudication. Indeed, as lawyers take part in mediation more frequently, both as mediators and as representatives of their clients, it is perhaps not surprising that mediation starts to resemble the adjudicative processes that lawyers are most familiar with. In litigated cases, where lawyers are routinely present in mediation sessions and the alternative to a mediated resolution is trial, the influence of the adversary system is likely to be even greater.

D. MEDIATOR TRAINING

Unlike law or psychotherapy, the practice of mediation is not restricted to those who have certain degrees and a special state license. While mediators come from varied backgrounds, many of them are lawyers or psychotherapists by training. They have developed mediation skills either on their own in the course of their practices or have learned them through continuing education or private mediation training programs. The field has become more professionalized in recent years. Specialized organizations, such as for family law mediators, are being incorporated into more general ones, for dispute resolution professionals of all types. These organizations promulgate standards of training and practice for their members and also serve an educational and informational function as the field matures. Nonetheless, there are still not significant legal barriers to someone's holding herself out as a mediator and seeking clients, with or without formal mediation training.

Many lawyers who are drawn to mediation have mixed practices, sometimes representing clients and sometimes acting as neutrals. Others do mediation exclusively, or combine it with an arbitration practice, often after a number of years' work in traditional adversary representation. The growth of both private and court-annexed alternative dispute resolution programs in the last twenty-five years has made it more important for all lawyers to familiarize themselves with mediation, since they may well end up representing clients before a mediator. In addition, these programs have increased the demand for law-trained mediators, making mediation more viable as a career option for interested lawyers.

E. THE ROLE OF LAWYERS IN MEDIATION

At this point, you may be wondering how lawyers come into the picture in mediation, if its purpose is to leave decision-making in the hands of the parties. Depending on the circumstances, lawyers may play one or more roles in the process. First, they can work as mediators. While the adversary model that dominates legal education is not conducive to acting in a facilitative role, as the first Riskin article below discusses, lawyers are in some ways well suited to be mediators. A lawyer-mediator does not represent either party in the traditional sense. However, her substantive expertise and the fact that formal legal proceedings are often seen as the primary alternative to a consensual resolution enable her to provide disputing parties with a realistic sense of what they will face if they don't come to agreement on their own. In addition, many courts have made mediation available, on a voluntary or mandatory basis, to litigants. As a result, the demand for mediators with litigation experience has increased. Parties who are already involved in a lawsuit are that much closer to having a judicial resolution imposed on them, and they often want an expert evaluation of how the court is likely to rule.

Although listening skills of the sort emphasized in this book are hardly a staple of the law school curriculum, many lawyers find that they are essential in the practice of law and work to develop them. Depending on their own personalities and those of the parties, as well as the nature of the dispute, lawyer-mediators may take a primarily facilitative or a primarily evaluative stance, or move from one to the other, as the second Riskin article below describes. For many litigators, working as a mediator offers a welcome opportunity to put their legal skills to work in bringing parties together, rather than acting solely as an advocate for one side in an adversarial situation.

Another way that lawyers get involved in mediation is as the representative of one of the parties. When litigation is pending, represented parties may hire a mediator privately or may participate in a court-annexed mediation program. Lawyers routinely accompany their clients to such mediations, as well as prepare both their clients and themselves for the presentations they will make there. It is often difficult for lawyers to make the shift from one-on-one negotiations with an adversary to negotiations in the presence of a mediator — and of the lawyers' own clients. In order to do a good job as a *mediation* advocate, a litigator has to adapt her courtroom style to the more informal, consensus-seeking atmosphere of mediation, as well as to make room for the active participation of her client in the process. Knowing something in advance about the context of mediation can help you adjust your negotiation style to that situation. The article below by Arnold addresses some of the difficulties that lawyers face in making that transition. In addition, given the wide variety of approaches used by mediators, from the purely facilitative to the strongly evaluative, it is important to consider what kind of mediator you and your client are choosing if you do opt for mediation, as the second Riskin article illustrates.

A lawyer may also act as an advisor to a party engaged in mediation. In a divorce situation or a business dispute, for example, the parties may try to resolve as many issues as possible in a private mediation. The mediator, who may or may not be a lawyer, may take a purely facilitative approach, attempting to help the parties work out an arrangement that both parties feel is fair. When the parties have developed a workable proposal through mediation, the mediator will often suggest that they take it to their individual lawyers to get the benefit of a legal opinion on the agreement. When advising clients in this context, a lawyer has to take into account not only her client's legal entitlements, but also his motivation to reach an agreement through mediation that works for both parties, even if it is not something that a court could order. A lawyer who has a strong rights perspective may have difficulty appreciating that a client might prefer an agreement that gives him less in some respects than the law allows, but more in others than the law is capable of enforcing. For example, a divorcing couple might come up with a flexible arrangement for financial support that will allow them both to complete further education over time, rather than being locked into a fixed formula that will make it difficult for either of them to achieve those goals. As long as the client understands the ramifications of the mediated agreement after discussion with his lawyer and appreciates the alternatives, the lawyer-advisor has fulfilled her limited role in this context.

F. THINKING LIKE A MEDIATOR

Studying mediation in the context of a course on negotiation can help you learn when calling in a third party may be appropriate and useful in the course of representing clients. In addition, thinking about what a mediator does and about how mediation works can help you identify and change counterproductive behaviors in negotiation before they escalate to the point that outside assistance becomes necessary. Although as an advocate participating in a negotiation you cannot be neutral, you can think about how the situation might look to an impartial observer. When you confront obstacles to agreement, taking this kind of perspective may allow you to consider your own role in creating the obstacles, as well as the other party's, and make room for altering your approach. As the first Riskin article below discusses, imagining yourself in the third chair may be a difficult mental exercise, given the focus in law school on argument and confrontation. Learning to do it well, however, will help you to become a better negotiator, as well as a better advocate for clients in a mediation setting.

Leonard L. Riskin,[*] *Mediation and Lawyers*
43 OHIO ST. L.J. 29, 43-48 (1982)[**]

* * *

A. *The Lawyer's Standard Philosophical Map*

E. F. Schumacher begins his *Guide for the Perplexed* with the following story:

> On a visit to Leningrad some years ago, I consulted a map . . . but I could not make it out. From where I stood, I could see several enormous churches, yet there was no trace of them on my map. When finally an interpreter came to help me, he said: "We don't show churches on our maps." Contradicting him, I pointed to one that was very clearly marked. "That is a museum," he said, "not what we call a 'living church.' It is only the 'living churches' we don't show."

> It then occurred to me that this was not the first time I had been given a map which failed to show many things I could see right in front of my eyes. All through school and university I had been given maps of life and knowledge on which there was hardly a trace of many of the things that I most cared about and that seemed to me to be of the greatest possible importance to the conduct of my life.

The philosophical map employed by most practicing lawyers and law teachers, and displayed to the law student — which I will call the lawyer's standard philosophical map — differs radically from that which a mediator must use. What appears on this map is determined largely by the power of two assumptions about matters that lawyers handle: (1) that disputants are adversaries — i.e., if one wins, the others must lose — and (2) that disputes may be resolved through application, by a third party, of some general rule of law. These assumptions, plainly, are polar opposites of those which underlie mediation: (1) that all parties can benefit through a creative solution to which each agrees; and (2) that the situation is unique and therefore not to be governed by any general principle except to the extent that the parties accept it.

The two assumptions of the lawyer's philosophical map (adversariness of parties and rule-solubility of dispute), along with the real demands of the adversary system and the expectations of many clients, tend to exclude mediation from most lawyers' repertoires. They also blind lawyers to other kinds of information that are essential for a mediator to see, primarily by

---

[*] Leonard L. Riskin is Chesterfield Smith Professor of Law at the University of Florida College of Law. In this article he contrasts the lawyer's traditional mind set to that required of a mediator.

[**] Copyright © 1982 Ohio State Law Journal. Reprinted with permission.

riveting the lawyers' attention upon things that they must see in order to carry out their functions. The mediator must, for instance, be aware of the many interconnections between and among disputants and others, and of the qualities of these connections; he must be sensitive to emotional needs of all parties and recognize the importance of yearnings for mutual respect, equality, security, and other such non-material interests as may be present.

On the lawyer's standard philosophical map, however, the client's situation is seen optimistically; many links are not printed. The duty to represent the client zealously within the bounds of the law discourages concern with both the opponents' situation and the overall social effect of a given result.

Moreover, on the lawyer's standard philosophical map, quantities are bright and large while qualities appear dimly or not at all. When one party wins, in this vision, usually the other party loses, and, most often, the victory is reduced to a money judgment. This "reduction" of nonmaterial values — such as honor, respect, dignity, security, and love — to amounts of money, can have one of two effects. In some cases, these values are excluded from the decision makers' considerations, and thus from the consciousness of the lawyers, as irrelevant. In others, they are present but transmuted into something else — a justification for money damages. Much like the church that was allowed to appear on the map of Leningrad only because it was a museum, these interests — which may in fact be the principal motivations for a lawsuit — are recognizable in the legal dispute primarily to the extent that they have monetary value or fit into a clause of a rule governing liability.

The rule orientation also determines what appears on the map. The lawyer's standard world view is based upon a cognitive and rational outlook. Lawyers are trained to put people and events into categories that are legally meaningful, to think in terms of rights and duties established by rules, to focus on acts more than persons. This view requires a strong development of cognitive capabilities, which is often attended by the under-cultivation of emotional faculties. This combination of capacities joins with the practice of either reducing most nonmaterial values to amounts of money or sweeping them under the carpet, to restrict many lawyers' abilities to recognize the value of mediation or to serve as mediators.

The lawyer's standard philosophical map is useful primarily where the assumptions upon which it is based — adversariness and amenability to solution by a general rule imposed by a third party — are valid. But when mediation is appropriate, these assumptions do not fit. The problem is that many lawyers, because of their philosophical maps, tend to suppose that these assumptions are germane in nearly any situation that they confront as lawyers. The map, and the litigation paradigm on which it is based, has a power all out of proportion to its utility. Many lawyers, therefore, tend not to recognize mediation as a viable means of reaching a solution; and worse, they see the kinds of unique solutions that mediation can produce as threatening to the best interests of their clients.

"One of the central difficulties of our legal system," says John Ayer, "is its capacity to be deaf to the counsel of ordinary good sense." A law school classroom incident shows how quickly this deafness afflicts students — usually without anyone's [*sic*] noticing. Professor Kenney Hegland writes:

> In my first year Contracts class, I wished to review various doctrines we had recently studied. I put the following:

> In a long term installment contract, Seller promises Buyer to deliver widgets at the rate of 1,000 a month. The first two deliveries are perfect. However, in the third month Seller delivers only 999 widgets. Buyer becomes so incensed with this that he rejects the delivery, cancels the remaining deliveries and refuses to pay for the widgets already delivered. After stating the problem, I asked "If you were Seller, what would you say?" What I was looking for was a discussion of the various common law theories which would force the buyer to pay for the widgets delivered and those which would throw buyer into breach for cancelling the remaining deliveries. In short, I wanted the class to come up with the legal doctrines which would allow Seller to crush Buyer.

> After asking the question, I looked around the room for a volunteer. As is so often the case with the first year students, I found that they were all either writing in their notebooks or inspecting their shoes. There was, however, one eager face, that of an eight year old son of one of my students. It seems that he was suffering through Contracts due to his mother's sin of failing to find a sitter. Suddenly he raised his hand. Such behavior, even from an eight year old, must be rewarded.

> "OK," I said, "What would you say if you were the seller?"

> "I'd say 'I'm sorry'."

I do not mean to imply that all lawyers see only what is displayed on the lawyer's standard philosophical map. The chart I have drawn exaggerates certain tendencies in the way many lawyers think. Any good lawyer will be alert to a range of nonmaterial values, emotional considerations, and interconnections. Many lawyers have "empathic, conciliatory" personalities that may incline them to work often in a mediative way. And other lawyers, though they may be more competitive, would recognize the value of mediation to their clients. I do submit, however, that most lawyers, most of the time, use this chart to navigate.

One reason for the dominance of this map is that it may be congruent with the personalities of most lawyers, who may be drawn to the law because of this map and the ability to control that it gives them. There are other reasons, though, for its strength, and some of these impress the map's contours on the minds of even the most conciliatory attorneys. First, it is consistent with the expectations of most clients. Second, it is very often functionally effective in achieving the kinds of results generally expected from a "victory" in the adversary system. Third, it generally redounds to the economic benefit of lawyers, and often of clients. Fourth, it gives the appearance of clarifying the law and making it predictable. Fifth, it accords with widely-shared assumptions that we will achieve the best society by giving individual self-interest full expression.

A final, and dominant, source of the popularity of the standard map is legal education, which is thoroughly pervaded by this vision. Nearly all courses at most law schools are presented from the viewpoint of the practicing attorney who is working in an adversary system of act-oriented rules, a context that he accepts. There is, to be sure, scattered attention to the lawyer as planner, policy maker, and public servant, but ninety percent of what goes on in law school is based upon a model of a lawyer working in or against a background of litigation of disputes that can be resolved by the application of a rule by a third party. The teachers were trained with this model in mind. The students bring a rough image with them; it gets sharpened quickly. This model defines and limits the likely career possibilities envisioned by most law students.

The adversary, rule/act perspective infuses not just the subject matter but also the educational process. Combined with the case method of instruction, it has a constricting effect. As David Smith has written:

> In some respects, the case method contains within it the same infirmities inherent in the adversary process. In the same way that the adversary process shapes, determines and excludes evidence on the basis of whether it is 'relevant' to the hearing, the case reveals only those facts that shed light on the principle of law being exposed. And just as the adversary process excludes evidence which might be critical in exposing the more significant social problem underlying the particular symptomatic problem before the court, so the case typically excludes evidence of social problems that go beyond the narrow issue with which the case is concerned.

This distinctive point of view colors many interpersonal relationships, too. The student must compete not just with his professors but with his classmates as well. Law schools have institutionalized the battle of wits.

* * *

Robert A. Baruch Bush,[*] *"What Do We Need a Mediator For?": Mediation's "Value-Added" for Negotiators*
12 Ohio St. J. on Disp. Resol. 1, 5-23, 27-29 (1996)[**]

* * *

As a former student of mine argued to me when we met at a conference in a state that had recently adopted court-ordered mediation:

> I enjoyed learning about mediation in law school. But now that I'm in the world of practice, I frankly don't see the point. I work for a major civil litigation firm, and almost all the cases we handle settle before trial — and they always have — whether or not there's a mediator involved. So what does having a mediator add? As far as I'm concerned, it's just another hoop you have to jump through and an additional expense. Tell me, am I missing something?

Before trying to answer the questions posed by my student . . . , it is important to note that these questions themselves show an intuitive clarity about mediation's "place" in the dispute resolution universe that some scholars might envy. Many dispute resolution scholars, including myself, have presented and analyzed mediation as "an alternative to adjudication." In fact, we are now coming to see that this comparative framework is itself misconceived. The "standard" method of case disposition, to which mediation or any other alterative process should be compared, is not adjudication or trial at all, but rather *settlement* — either by direct party negotiations or, where parties have lawyers, by negotiation between lawyers. A solid body of research tells us that throughout the country the vast majority of disputes are settled before a legal claim is ever filed; and of those cases that are brought to court, the large majority end in a negotiated settlement of some kind, and fewer than 10% are adjudicated to a verdict. Given this context, if a process is being proposed as an "alternative" method of resolution, to what should it be compared?

The answer, clearly, is that it should he compared to the standard method of resolution, not to an exceptional method used in a tiny fraction of cases. Viewed in proper perspective, mediation and other third-party processes are alternatives not to court, but to unassisted settlement efforts, including party-to-party, lawyer-to-party and lawyer-to-lawyer negotiation. Thus, the relevant question to be asked and answered about mediation is: How does it compare to, and what advantages does it have over, the negotiation process in its various configurations?

---

[*] Robert A. Baruch Bush is Harry H. Rains Distinguished Professor at Hofstra University School of Law. His article focuses on the significance of participation and communication to parties involved in mediation.

* * *

One theme that the negotiation scholars have developed is the "barriers" concept. That is, they suggest that the most important factors in explaining failed negotiations are two kinds of "informational barriers" that impede negotiations and agreement. These barriers arise from structural and perceptual dynamics inherent in the negotiation process itself, and in this sense they represent "bugs" in the process that can undermine it despite the parties' skills and their desire to reach a settlement.

* * *

The first kind are described as "strategic barriers." These arise because each negotiator usually holds certain private information, and each has a strategic incentive to hide this information or even mislead the other side about it, in order to win a larger share of the stakes. Even though this kind of strategic concealment will probably result in sub-optimal outcomes, it is often quite rational, because openness and honesty could mean both giving up one's own advantage and creating one for an opponent who is ready and willing to exploit it.

Looking at it differently, parties are (rightly) suspicious of each other in bargaining, and therefore not likely to put full and honest information on the table. Since everyone knows this is so, no one can rely upon the information put forth by the other. Thus, the barrier created by strategic behavior is informational poverty and unreliability. There is not enough reliable information on the table to enable the parties to identify possibilities for mutually beneficial exchange, and there is no way to improve the informational environment as long as strategic incentives exist. As a result, deals are not made, or the deals that are made are sub-optimal.

C. Cognitive Barriers

A second kind of informational barrier also arises, which impedes the use of whatever information parties do manage to put forth (despite strategic incentives), because of what negotiation scholars call "cognitive biases." The insight here is based on psychological research showing that, in the cognitive processes by which people assimilate information, there are regular and identifiable "departures from rationality" that lead to distortion and misinterpretation of the information received. Negotiation scholars have shown that the same cognitive biases that operate elsewhere also affect the negotiation process.

As an example, consider "loss aversion": In making decisions, individuals tend to give prospective losses more significance than prospective gains of actually equivalent value. Therefore, if taking an action would involve both getting something and giving something up, the object gained will seem less valuable than the object given, even if it is actually of equal or somewhat greater worth — because people tend to "feel the pain" of a loss more than they "feel the pleasure" of a gain. The action may therefore not be taken, despite its rational desirability, due to the cognitive distortion of value. In negotiation, loss aversion results in the reluctance of negotiators to make "trade-offs," even when an objective comparison shows that each side would gain more than it is giving up in the trade.

The barrier created by this and other cognitive biases is informational distortion. Even the information that is revealed by the parties gets distorted as it is received and processed. Because of cognitive biases, each party is incapable of reading the information provided by the other side — including offers and demands — accurately and objectively. Therefore, each is likely to analyze this information with a false and distorted perspective that, once again, leads them to miss opportunities for deals entirely, or make deals that fail to realize all possible joint gains.

Together, strategic and cognitive barriers help explain why reaching negotiated agreement is difficult, no matter how skillful the negotiators. Impasses and sub-optimal bargains result because of decisions that are made with inadequate and unreliable information, which is further distorted through biased interpretive processes. And the strategic incentives and cognitive biases responsible for these informational barriers are very difficult for the parties themselves to change or transcend.

* * *

What is the value-added of mediation to negotiators; what does the mediator add or facilitate that the parties could not accomplish on their own? The study of strategic and cognitive barriers suggests a powerful answer. First, *mediators can help parties put more information on the table and ensure that it is more reliable* and less suspect than would be the case if the parties negotiated alone. As a result, parties can enrich their informational environment, gain greater clarity and then go ahead as they would in negotiation and make decisions for themselves — but on an improved information base. Second, *mediators can help parties perceive each other* — including past and present actions, attitudes, motivations and positions — *more fully and accurately* than they would if left to themselves. The parties can thus avoid responses in negotiation that are based upon false assumptions about one another stemming from cognitive biases. The implication of the theory is that, with better information and less interpretive distortion (i.e., with the barriers lowered) settlements will be reached more often and on terms that come closer to optimality.

* * *

The new and broader question is: What are parties looking for, in general, when they are considering whether to bring an intervenor into their conflict? Even more broadly, what do parties most desire in a conflict handling process with or without an intervenor? Or, to relate the broad question to our subject of mediation, what features do parties value in conflict handling processes that mediation can uniquely offer?

* * *

In looking for answers to this second set of questions, I want to point to another part of the literature of the field — the scholarship on party attitudes toward dispute resolution processes. There is a rich literature on this subject, including studies of party satisfaction with mediation and other processes, as well as research that tries to identify what *leads to* party satisfaction — what effects and features of processes parties value most. In numerous studies, researchers have interviewed and surveyed parties who have participated in different processes to determine levels of party satisfaction, rates of compliance with agreements or decisions and other post-process attitudes and effects.

* * *

A. Evaluation Studies

The first studies are evaluation studies of mediation itself, in which follow-up questions are asked of parties to elicit the reasons for their high satisfaction and compliance levels. Some of the most frequently given reasons are the following: mediation enabled the parties to deal with the issues they themselves felt important; it allowed them to present their views fully and gave them a sense of having been beard; it helped them to understand each other. Significantly, these and other commonly cited reasons relate to how the process worked rather than the outcome it produced. Parties report high satisfaction levels with mediation, and for similar reasons, even in cases where no settlement was reached, and even when the parties "did worse" in mediation than they might have done in court — suggesting that settlement production per se, and even quality of outcome, are not what parties find most valuable about mediation.

B. Procedural Justice Studies

The second group of studies is associated with "procedural justice" theory. These studies use various research techniques to measure attitudes about consensual processes like negotiation, mediation and nonbinding arbitration, by comparison to impositional procedures like adjudication or binding arbitration, in real and hypothetical situations. Their findings show that *parties usually prefer the consensual processes, even where the outcomes they receive in these processes are unfavorable.* Moreover, the main reason for this preference is the value that disputants place on "process control," a term that includes both the opportunity for meaningful participation in determining the outcome of the procedure (whatever it may ultimately be) and the opportunity for full self-expression. Consensual processes like mediation and negotiation offer a greater degree of process control, and hence they are seen by parties as "subjectively fairer" and are preferred, regardless of whether they ultimately lead to favorable outcomes. In other words, procedural justice research shows that parties care as much about how dispute resolution is conducted as they do about what outcome results; and consensual processes provide the "how" that parties value most.

C. The Common Answer

Thus, when we examine why mediation generates high levels of party satisfaction and compliance, by comparison to court hearings, two distinct kinds of research — evaluation and procedural justice studies — tell us the same thing: Parties' favorable attitudes toward mediation stem largely from *how* the process works, and two features in particular are responsible. Those features are: (1) the greater degree of participation in decisionmaking that parties experience in mediation; and (2) the fuller opportunity to express themselves and communicate their views, both to the neutral and to each other, that they experience in the process. Because of these features, parties find mediation highly valuable, even when no settlement is reached, and even when a mediated settlement embodies a less favorable outcome than they could have obtained in court.

There is thus a substantial body of research that answers our question about what parties value in dispute resolution processes. The most remarkable thing is what the answer is *not*. Despite what we might have thought, parties do not place the most value on the fact that a process provides expediency, efficiency or finality of resolution. Not even the likelihood of a favorable substantive outcome is considered most important. Rather, an equally, if not even more highly, valued feature is "procedural justice or fairness," which in practice means the greatest possible opportunity for *participation* in determining outcome (as opposed to assurance of a favorable outcome), and for self-expression and communication.

* * *

[In a study of court-order mediation,] lawyers valued mediation over unassisted negotiation because they found that:

- it structures the negotiation process in ways that lead to increased information becoming available to the negotiators, so that attorneys can better advise clients about what to do;

- it increases clients' sense of participation in and control over their case, which is frequently attenuated in lawyer-lawyer negotiation; and

- it "provides a setting for communication between the parties that settlement [negotiation] does not, a setting in which parties can and do discuss and explain needs and problems and express anger and disappointment . . . , not just exchange demands and positions," in which clients can feel that "another person has heard their side of the story[,] that the other side . . . has heard their side" and in which "[suspicions and] misconceptions that clients tend to have about the other side" are cleared up.

With these findings in mind, recall what the party satisfaction and procedural justice literature has shown about why disputants prefer consensual processes over impositional ones: the former offer greater opportunities for *participation* and *communication*. Both mediation and negotiation are preferred over court for this reason. Here is the point: the lawyered mediation study shows that disputants find mediation "an improvement on negotiation" *for the very same reason*. That is, although both negotiation and mediation involve more and better party participation and communication than court proceedings, mediation provides even greater levels of both of these desired features than negotiation — and thus adds value to the negotiation process. This same conclusion can be reached by a theoretical analysis, but the concrete findings of the lawyered mediation study make it very clear. They confirm that just as the party-attitude research explains why parties prefer both negotiation and mediation to trial, it also explains why parties will value mediation over unassisted negotiation; because mediation offers more of the "process control" that parties value in consensual processes generally.

* * *

Now I want to throw a different light on the picture presented today, by reframing somewhat the conclusions reached thus far. Suppose we put the question that we have been examining in a slightly different form, by asking: What is the most important product or effect that mediation *uniquely* offers, *as an alternative to negotiation*, that parties to conflict in fact value? Based on the material reviewed today, it is clear that the answer is not greater speed, lesser cost, increased likelihood of settlement or even improved quality of outcome.

Instead, we can say that the most important product that mediation provides (that other negotiation alternatives do not) is *a twofold, qualitative improvement* over the way the negotiation process works when unassisted. One dimension of this improvement is an *increased level of party participation in and control over decisions* made in the process. This includes, for each party, greater ability to acquire and exchange information and to analyze it accurately, as well as greater direct involvement in decisionmaking when lawyers or other agents are involved. The result is a qualitatively different deliberation and decisionmaking process, which enables parties to accept or reject terms of agreement with clarity, as they see fit, and thus to effectuate their desires in conflict situations more fully.

Along with others, I have described this as the "value of self-determination" in mediation. People value the experience of self-determination. They believe they know what is best for themselves and they want the opportunity to effectuate it, in conflict as in other aspects of their lives. The evidence presented today shows that mediation provides that opportunity, to an even greater degree than negotiation.

The second way in which mediation improves negotiation is by *improving the character and quality of the communication that occurs between the parties* as human beings during the process. This includes an increased opportunity to present and receive a broad range of messages — verbal and non-verbal, rational and emotional — and, even more importantly, the reduction of all kinds of distortion and misunderstanding that otherwise tend to skew the interpretations that parties place on each other's statements and actions. In simple terms, conflict leads disputants to demonize each other, and mediation "de-demonizes" people to one another. Again, the evidence presented today suggests that parties value this "product" highly.

People do not want to be regarded by each other, or even to regard each other, as demonic and ill-intentioned, and to relate to each other on the basis of such mutual negative characterization. Mediation enables them to deal with a conflict without doing so, and even to find more positive ways of regarding each other, despite serious disagreement. * * *

Leonard L. Riskin,* *Mediator Orientations, Strategies and Techniques*
12 ALTERNATIVES TO HIGH COST LITIG. 111 (1994)**

Almost every conversation about "mediation" suffers from ambiguity. People have disparate visions of what mediation is or should be. Yet we lack a comprehensive system for describing these visions. This causes confusion when people try to choose between mediation and another process or grapple with how to train, evaluate, regulate, or select mediators.

I propose a system for classifying mediator orientations. Such a system can help parties select a mediator and deal with the thorny issue of whether the mediator should have subject-matter expertise. The classification system starts with two principal questions: 1. Does the mediator tend to define problems narrowly or broadly? 2. Does the mediator think she should evaluate — make assessments or predictions or proposals for agreements — or facilitate the parties' negotiation without evaluating?

The answers reflect the mediator's beliefs about the nature and scope of mediation and her assumptions about the parties expectations.

Problem Definition

Mediators with a narrow focus assume that the parties have come to them for help in solving a technical problem. The parties have defined this problem in advance through the positions they have asserted in negotiations

---

* Leonard L. Riskin is Chesterfield Smith Professor of Law at the University of Florida College of Law. In this article he describes some of the major differences in mediators' approaches to their task.

** Copyright © 1994 CPR Institute for Dispute Resolution, 366 Madison Avenue, New York, NY 10017-3122; (212) 949-6490. The CPR Institute is a non-profit initiative of 500 general counsel of major corporations, leading law firms and prominent legal academics whose mission is to install alternative dispute resolution (ADR) into the main-stream of legal practice. Reprinted with permission.

or pleadings. Often it involves a question such as, "Who pays how much to whom?" or "Who can use such-and-such property?" As framed, these questions rest on "win-lose" (or "distributive") assumptions. In other words, the participants must divide a limited resource; whatever one gains, the other must lose.

The likely court outcome — along with uncertainty, delay and expense — drives much of the mediation process. Parties, seeking a compromise, will bargain adversarially, emphasizing positions over interests.

A mediator who starts with a broad orientation, on the other hand, assumes that the parties can benefit if the mediation goes beyond the narrow issues that normally define legal disputes. Important interests often lie beneath the positions that the participants assert. Accordingly, the mediator should help the participants understand and fulfill those interests — at least if they wish to do so.

The Mediator's Role

The evaluative mediator assumes that the participants want and need the mediator to provide some direction as to the appropriate grounds for settlement — based on law, industry practice or technology. She also assumes that the mediator is qualified to give such direction by virtue of her experience, training and objectivity.

The facilitative mediator assumes the parties are intelligent, able to work with their counterparts, and capable of understanding their situations better than either their lawyers or the mediator. So the parties may develop better solutions than any that the mediator might create. For these reasons, the facilitative mediator assumes that his principal mission is to enhance and clarify communications between the parties in order to help them decide what to do.

The facilitative mediator believes it is inappropriate for the mediator to give his opinion, for at least two reasons. First, such opinions might impair the appearance of impartiality and thereby interfere with the mediator's ability to function. Second, the mediator might not know enough — about the details of the case or the relevant law, practices or technology — or give an informed opinion.

Each of the two principal questions — Does the mediator tend toward a narrow or broad focus? and Does the mediator favor an evaluative or facilitative role? — yield responses that fall along a continuum. Thus, a mediator's orientation will be more or less broad and more or less evaluative.

ROLE OF MEDIATOR

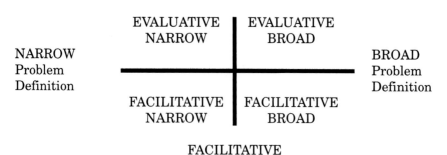

EVALUATIVE

	EVALUATIVE NARROW	EVALUATIVE BROAD	
NARROW Problem Definition			BROAD Problem Definition
	FACILITATIVE NARROW	FACILITATIVE BROAD	

FACILITATIVE

Strategies and Techniques Of Each Orientation

Each orientation derives from assumptions or beliefs about the mediator's role and about the appropriate focus of a mediation. A mediator employs strategies — plans — to conduct the mediation. And he uses techniques — particular moves or behaviors — to effectuate those strategies. Here are selected strategies and techniques that typify each mediation orientation.

Evaluative-Narrow

The principal strategy of the evaluative-narrow mediator is to help the parties understand the strengths and weaknesses of their positions and the likely outcome at trial. To accomplish this, the evaluative-narrow mediator typically will first carefully study relevant documents, such as pleadings, depositions, reports and mediation briefs. Then, in the mediation, she employs evaluative techniques, such as the following, which are listed from most to least evaluative:

- Urge parties to settle or to accept a particular settlement proposal or range.

- Propose position-based compromise agreements.

- Predict court (or administrative agency) dispositions.

- Try to persuade parties to accept mediator's assessments.

- Directly assess the strengths and weaknesses of each side's case (usually in private caucuses) and perhaps try to persuade the parties to accept the mediator's analysis.

Facilitative-Narrow

Like the evaluative-narrow, the facilitative-narrow mediator plans to help the participants become "realistic" about their litigation situations. But he employs different techniques. He does not use his own assessments, predictions or proposals. Nor does he apply pressure. Moreover, he probably will not request or study relevant documents, such as pleadings, depositions, reports, or mediation briefs. Instead, because he believes that the burden of decision should rest with the parties, the facilitative-narrow mediator might ask questions — generally in private caucuses — to help the participants understand both sides' legal positions and the consequences of non-settlement. Also in private caucuses, he helps each side assess proposals in light of the alternatives.

Here are examples of the types of questions the facilitative-narrow mediator might ask:

- What are the strengths and weakness of your case? Of the other side's case?

- What are the best, worst, and most likely outcomes of litigation? How did you make these assessments? Have you thought about [other issues]?

- How long will it take to get to trial? How long will the trial last?

- What will be the associated costs — in money, emotions, or reputation?

Evaluative-Broad

The evaluative-broad mediator also helps the parties understand their circumstances and options. However, she has a different notion of what this requires. So she emphasizes the parties' interests over their positions and proposes solutions designed to accommodate these interests. In addition, because the evaluative-broad mediator constructs the agreement, she emphasizes her own understanding of the circumstances at least as much as the parties.

Like the evaluative-narrow mediator, the evaluative-broad mediator is likely to request and study relevant documents, such as pleadings, depositions, and mediation briefs. In addition, she tries to uncover the parties' underlying interests by such methods as:

- Explaining that the goal of mediation can include addressing underlying interests.

- Encouraging the real parties, or knowledgeable representatives (with settlement authority) of corporations or other organizations to attend and participate in the mediation. For instance, the mediator might invite such individuals to make remarks after the lawyers present their opening statements, and she might include them in most settlement discussions.

- Asking about the participants' situations, plans, needs and interests.

- Speculating about underlying interests and asking for confirmation.

The evaluative-broad mediator also provides predictions, assessments and recommendations. But she emphasizes options that address underlying interests, rather than those that propose only compromise on narrow issues. In the mediation of a contract dispute between two corporations, for instance, while the facilitative-narrow mediator might propose a strictly monetary settlement, the evaluative-broad mediator might suggest new ways for the firms to collaborate (perhaps in addition to a monetary settlement).

Facilitative-Broad

The facilitative-broad mediator seeks to help the parties define, understand and resolve the problems they wish to address. She encourages them to consider underlying interests rather than positions and helps them generate and assess proposals designed to accommodate those interests. Specifically, she might:

- Encourage the parties to discuss underlying interests in joint sessions. To bring out such interests, she might use techniques such as those employed by the evaluative-broad mediator.

- Encourage and help the parties to develop their own proposals (jointly or alone) that would respond to underlying interests of both sides.

The facilitative-broad mediator does not provide assessments, predictions or proposals. However, to help the participants better understand their legal situations, she will likely allow the parties to present and discuss their legal arguments. In addition, she might ask questions such as those listed for the facilitative-narrow mediator and focus discussion on underlying interests.

In a broad mediation, however, legal argument generally occupies a lesser position than it does in a narrow one. And because he emphasizes the participants' role in defining the problems and in developing and evaluating proposals, the facilitative-broad mediator does not need to fully understand the legal posture of the case. Accordingly, he is less likely to request or study litigation documents, technical reports or mediation briefs.

However, the facilitative-broad mediator must be able to quickly grasp the legal and substantive issues and to respond to the dynamics of the situation. He needs to help the parties realistically evaluate proposals to determine whether they address the parties' underlying interests.

Mediator Techniques

Mediators usually have a predominant orientation, whether they know it or not, that is based on a combination of their personalities, experiences, education, and training. Thus, many retired judges, when they mediate, tend toward an evaluative-narrow orientation.

MEDIATOR TECHNIQUES

The following grid shows the principal techniques associated with each mediator orientation, arranged vertically with the most evaluative at the top and the most facilitative at the bottom. The horizontal axis shows the scope of problems to be addressed, from the narrowest issues to the broadest interests.

EVALUATIVE

Urges/pushes parties to accept narrow (position-based) settlement	**Urges/pushes parties** to accept broad (interest-based) settlement
Develops and proposes narrow (position-based) settlement	**Develops and proposes** broad (interest-based) settlement
Predicts court outcomes	**Predicts** impact (on interests) of not settling
Assesses strengths and weaknesses of legal claims	**Probes** parties' interests

NARROW   BROAD

Problem Definition	Litigation Issues	Other Distributive Issues	Business (Substantive) Issues	Business Interests	Personal Interests	Social Interests	Problem Definition

Helps parties evaluate proposals	**Helps parties** evaluate proposals
Helps parties develop narrow (position-based) proposals	**Helps parties** develop broad (interest-based) proposals
Asks parties about consequences of not settling	**Helps parties** develop options
Asks about likely court outcomes	**Helps parties** understand issues and interest
Asks about strengths and weaknesses of legal claims	**Focuses discussion** on underlying interests (business, personal, societal)

FACILITATIVE

Yet mediators do not always behave consistently with the predominant orientations they express. Some mediators lack a clear grasp of the essence of their own expressed orientation. It is also common for mediators to employ a strategy generally associated with an orientation other than their own. This might help them carry out a strategy associated with their predominant orientation. For example, a prominent facilitative-broad mediator who often conducts sessions with parties only — not their lawyers — routinely predicts judicial outcomes. But he also emphasizes the principles underlying the relevant rules of law. He then encourages the parties to develop a resolution that makes sense for them and meets their own sense of fairness; in essence, he evaluates in order to free the parties from the potentially narrowing effects of law.

In addition, many mediators will depart from their orientations to respond to the dynamics of the situation. A prominent evaluative-broad mediator, for instance, typically learns as much as he can about the case and the parties' circumstances and then develops a proposal, which he tries to persuade the parties to accept. If they do not accept the proposal, he becomes more facilitative.

Another example: an evaluative-narrow mediator may explore underlying interests (a technique normally associated with the broad orientations) after her accustomed narrow focus results in a deadlock. And a facilitative-broad mediator might use a mildly evaluative tactic as a last resort. For instance, he might toss out a figure that he thinks the parties might be willing to agree upon, while stating that the figure does not represent his prediction of what would happen in court.

Speaking generally, broad mediators, especially facilitative ones, are more willing and able to narrow the focus of a dispute than are narrow mediators willing and able to broaden their focus. Again speaking generally, evaluative-mediators are more willing to facilitate than facilitative mediators are to evaluate. However, many evaluative mediators lack facilitation skills.

Many effective mediators are versatile and can move from quadrant to quadrant (and within a quadrant), as the dynamics of the situation dictate, to help parties settle disputes.

Using the Grid to Select a Mediator

The grid should help disputants determine what kind of mediation they wish to undertake and what sort of mediator to seek. Here are some general points to keep in mind.

The parties' informed expectations about the problems to be addressed and what they need from a mediator should govern their mediator-selection process.

It is difficult, though, to develop informed expectations before the mediation starts. A party's strong belief that he wishes and needs only to address a distributive (win-lose) issue, for example, would incline him toward selecting a narrow mediator. An additional belief that he will need direction or some pressure, would suggest that he should lean toward an evaluative-narrow mediator.

Still, I would caution parties against feeling very confident in their initial assessments. Often the litigation process encourages a narrow perspective on the dispute. If litigation-oriented lawyers are selecting the mediator, they may be inclined toward a litigation-like outcome, which is best provided by an evaluative-narrow mediator (a category in which retired-judge mediators are heavily represented). Unless the lawyers are sophisticated about mediation, however, they might see only the virtues of this approach — its simplicity and efficiency — and not its potential drawbacks.

Such drawbacks include the risk that the evaluative-narrow approach could foreclose a creative, interest-based agreement. Similarly, a party originally inclined toward dealing collaboratively with underlying interests may learn during the mediation that the other side insists on a narrow approach and needs guidance from the mediator in order to reach resolution. For all these reasons, it may be wise to select a mediator whose background and experience make her versatile.

Subject-Matter Expertise

In selecting a mediator, what is the relevance of "subject-matter expertise?" The term could mean substantial understanding of either the law, customary practices, or technology associated with the dispute. In a patent infringement lawsuit, for instance, a mediator with subject-matter expertise could be familiar with the patent law or litigation, practices in the industry, or the relevant technology — or with all three of these areas.

The need for subject-matter expertise typically increases to the extent that the parties seek evaluations — assessments. predictions or proposals — from the mediator. The kind of subject-matter expertise needed depends on the kind of evaluation or direction the parties seek. If they want a prediction about what would happen in court, they need a mediator with a strong background in related litigation. If they want suggestions about how to structure future business relations, perhaps the mediator should understand the relevant industries. If they want to propose new government regulations (as in a regulatory negotiation), they might wish to retain a mediator who understands administrative law and procedure.

In contrast, to the extent that the parties feel capable of understanding their circumstances and developing potential solutions — singly, jointly or with assistance from outside experts — they might prefer a mediator with great skill in the mediation process, even if she lacks subject-matter expertise. In such circumstances, the mediator need only have a rough understanding of the relevant law, customs and technology. In fact, too much subject-matter expertise could incline some mediators toward a more evaluative role, and could thereby interfere with developing creative solutions.

Tom Arnold,[*] 20 Common Errors
in Mediation Advocacy
13 ALTERNATIVES TO HIGH COST LITIG. 69 (1995)[**]

Trial lawyers who are unaccustomed to being mediation advocates often miss important arguments. Here are 20 common errors, and ways to correct them.

Problem 1: Wrong client in the room

CEOs settle more cases than vice presidents, house counsel or other agents. Why? For one thing, they don't need to worry about criticism back at the office. Any lesser agent, even with explicit "authority," typically must please a constituency which was not a participant in the give and take of the mediation. That makes it hard to settle cases.

A client's personality also can be a factor. A "Rambo," who is aggressive, critical, unforgiving, or self-righteous doesn't tend to be conciliatory. The best peace-makers show creativity, and tolerance for the mistakes of others. Of course, it also helps to know the subject.

Problem 2: Wrong lawyer in the room

Many capable trial lawyers are so confident that they can persuade a jury of anything (after all, they've done it before), that they discount the importance of preserving relationships, as well as the exorbitant costs and emotional drain of litigation. They can smell a "win" in the court room, and so approach mediation with a measure of ambivalence.

Transaction lawyers, in contrast, tend to be better mediation counsel. At a minimum, parties should look for sensitive, flexible, understanding people who will do their homework, no matter their job experience. Good preparation makes for more and better settlements. A lawyer who won't prepare is the wrong lawyer.

Problem 3: Wrong mediator in the room

Some mediators are generous about lending their conference rooms but bring nothing to the table. Some of them determine their view of the case and urge the parties to accept that view without exploring likely win-win alternatives.

The best mediators can work within a range of styles that Leonard L. Riskin developed in a recent issue of Alternatives. . . . [T]hese styles fall

---

[*] Tom Arnold is Of Counsel with Howrey, LLP in Houston. In this article he discusses how trial lawyers need to adapt their advocacy techniques in a mediation setting.

along a continuum, from being totally facilitative, to offering an evaluation of the case. Ideally, mediators should fit the mediation style to the
case and the parties before them, often moving from style to style as a
mediation progresses.

Masters of the process can render valuable services whether or not they
have substantive expertise. When do the parties need an expert? When
they want an evaluative mediator, or someone who can cast meaningful
lights and shadows on the merits of the case and alternative settlements.

It may not always be possible to know and evaluate a mediator and fit the
choice of mediator to your case. But the wrong mediator may fail to get a settlement another mediator might have finessed.

Problem 4: Wrong case

Almost every type of case, from antitrust or patent infringement to unfair
competition and employment disputes, is a likely candidate for mediation.
Occasionally, cases don't fit the mold, not because of the substance of the
dispute, but because one or both parties want to set a precedent.

For example, a franchisor that needs a legal precedent construing a key
clause that is found in 3,000 franchise agreements might not want to submit the case to mediation. Likewise, an infringement suit early in the life of
an uncertain patent might be better resolved in court; getting the Federal
Circuit stamp of validity could generate industry respect not obtainable
from ADR.

Problem 5: Omitting client preparation

Lawyers should educate their clients about the process. Clients need to
know the answers to the types of questions the mediator is likely to ask. At
the same time, they need to understand that the other party (rather than
the mediator) should be the focus of each side's presentation.

In addition, lawyers should interview clients about the client's and the
adversary's "best alternative to negotiated agreement," and "worst alternative to negotiated agreement," terms coined by William Ury and Roger
Fisher in their book, Getting to YES. A party should accept any offer better
than his perceived BATNA and reject any offer seen as worse than his perceived WATNA. So the BATNAs and WATNAs are critical frames of reference for accepting offers and for determining what offers to propose to the
other parties. A weak or false understanding of either party's BATNA or
WATNA obstructs settlements and begets bad settlements.

Other topics to cover with the client:

- the difference between their interests and their legal positions;
- the variety of options that might settle the case;
- the strengths and weaknesses of their case;
- objective independent standards of evaluation;

- the importance of apology and empathy.

Problem 6: Not letting a client open for herself

At least as often as not, letting the properly coached client do most, or even all, of the opening and tell the story in her own words works much better than lengthy openings by the lawyer.

Problem 7: Addressing the mediator instead of the other side

Most lawyers open the mediation with a statement directed at the mediator, comparable to opening statements to a judge or jury. Highly adversarial in tone, it overlooks the interests of the other side that gave rise to the dispute.

Why is this strategy a mistake? The "judge or jury" you should be trying to persuade in a mediation is not the mediator, but the adversary. If you want to make the other party sympathetic to your cause, don't hurt him.

For the same reason, plenary sessions should demonstrate your client's humanity, respect, warmth, apologies and sympathy. Stay away from inflammatory issues, which are better addressed by the mediator in private caucuses with the other side.

Problem 8: Making the lawyer the center of the process

Unless the client is highly unappealing or inarticulate, the client should be the center of the process. The company representative for the other side may not have attended depositions, so is unaware of the impact your client could have on a judge or jury if the mediation fails. People pay more attention to appealing plaintiffs, so show them off.

Prepare the client to speak and be spoken to by the mediator and the adversary. He should be able to explain why he feels the way he does, why he is or is not responsible, and why any damages he caused are great or only peanuts. But he should also extend empathy to the other party.

Problem 9: Failure to use advocacy tools effectively

You'll want to prepare your materials for maximum persuasive impact. Exhibits, charts, and copies of relevant cases or contracts with key phrases highlighted can be valuable visual aids. A 90-second video showing key witnesses in depositions making important admissions, followed by a readable size copy of an important document with some relevant language underlined, can pack a punch.

Problem 10: Timing mistakes

Get and give critical discovery, but don't spend exorbitant time or sums in discovery and trial prep before seeking mediation.

Mediation can identify what's truly necessary discovery and avoid unnecessary discovery. One of my own war stories: With a mediation under way and both parties relying on their perception of the views of a certain vice president, I leaned over, picked up the phone, called the vice president, introduced myself as the mediator, and asked whether he could give us a deposition the following morning. "No," said he, "I've got a Board meeting at 10:00. "

"How about 7:30 a.m., with a one-hour limit?" I asked. "It really is pretty important that this decision not be delayed." The parties took the deposition and settled the case before the 10:00 board meeting.

Problem 11: Failure to listen to the other side

Many lawyers and clients seem incapable of giving open-minded attention to what the other side is saying. That could cost a settlement.

Problem 12: Failure to identify perceptions and motivations

Seek first to understand, only then to be understood. Messrs. Fisher and Ury suggest you brainstorm to determine the other party's motivations and perceptions. Prepare a chart summarizing how your adversary sees the issues.

Problem 13: Hurting, humiliating, threatening, or commanding

Don't poison the well from which you must drink to get a settlement. That means you don't hurt, humiliate or ridicule the other folks. Avoid pejoratives like "malingerer," "fraud," "cheat," "crook," or "liar." You can be strong on what your evidence will be and still be a decent human being.

All settlements are based upon trust to some degree. If you anger the other side, they won't trust you. This inhibits settlement.

The same can be said for threats, like a threat to get the other lawyer's license revoked for pursuing such a frivolous cause, or for his grossly inaccurate pleadings.

Ultimatums destroy the process, and destroy credibility. Yes, there is a time in mediation to walk out — whether or not you plan to return. But a series of ultimatums, or even one ultimatum, most often is very counterproductive.

Problem 14: The backwards step

A party who offered to pay $300,000 before the mediation, and comes to the mediation table willing to offer only $200,000, injures its own credibility and engenders bad feelings from the other side. Without some clear and dramatic reasons for the reduction in the offer, it can be hard to overcome the damage done.

The backwards step is a powerful card to play at the right time — a walk away without yet walking out. But powerful devices are also dangerous. There are few productive occasions to use this one, and they tend to come late in a mediation. A rule of thumb: unless you're an expert negotiator, don't do it.

Problem 15: Too many people

Advisors — people to whom the decision-maker must display respect and courtesy, people who feel that since they are there they must put in their two bits worth — all delay a mediation immeasurably. A caucus that with only one lawyer and vice president would take 20 minutes, with five people could take an hour and 20 minutes. What could have been a one-day mediation stretches to two or three.

This is one context in which I use the "one martini lunch." Once I think that everyone present understands all the issues, I will send principals who have been respectful out to negotiate alone. Most come back with an expression of oral settlement within three hours. Of course, the next step is to brush up on details they overlooked, draw up a written agreement and get it signed. But usually those finishing touches don't ruin the deal.

Problem 16: Closing too fast

A party who opens at $1 million, and moves immediately to $500,000, gives the impression of having more to give. Rightly or wrongly, the other side probably will not accept the $500,000 offer because they expect more give.

By contrast, moving from $1 million to $750,000, $600,000, $575,000, $560,000, $550,000, sends no message of yield below $500,000, and may induce a $500,000 proposal that can be accepted.

The "dance" is part of communication. Skip the dance, lose the communication, and risk losing settlement at your own figure.

Problem 17: Failure to truly close

Unless parties have strong reasons to "sleep on" their agreement, to further evaluate the deal, or to check on possibly forgotten details, it is better to get some sort of enforceable contract written and signed before the parties separate. Too often, when left to think overnight and draft tomorrow, the parties think of new ideas that delay or prevent closing.

Problem 18: Breaching a confidentiality

Sometimes parties to a mediation unthinkingly, or irresponsibly, disclose in open court information revealed confidentially in a mediation.

When information is highly sensitive, consider keeping it confidential with the mediator. Or if revealed to the adversary in a mediation where the case did not settle, consider moving before the trial begins for an order in limine to bind both sides to the confidentiality agreement.

Problem 19: Lack of patience and perseverance

The mediation "dance" takes time. Good mediation advocates have patience and perseverance.

Problem 20: Misunderstanding conflict

A dispute is a problem to be solved together, not a combat to be won. To prepare for mediation, rehearse answers to the following questions, which the mediator is likely to ask:

- How do you feel about this dispute? Or about the other party?

- What do you really want in the resolution of this dispute?

- What are your expectations from a trial? Are they realistic?

- What are the weaknesses in your case?

- What law or fact in your case would you like to change?

- What scares you most?

- What would it feel like to be in your adversary's shoes?

- What specific evidence do you have to support each element of your case?

- What will the jury charge and interrogatories probably be?

- What is the probability of a verdict your way on liability?

- What is the range of damages you think a jury would return in his case if it found liability?

- What are the likely settlement structures, from among the following possibilities: Terms, dollars, injunction, services, performance, product, recission, apology, costs, attorney fees, releases?

- What constituency pressures burden the other party? Which ones burden you?

L. Randolph Lowry,* *To Evaluate or Not: That is Not the Question!*
38 FAM. COURT REV. 48 (2000)**

One of the invigorating aspects of the mediation field is the spirit of debate that takes place regarding approaches to the mediation process. Notable in recent years has been the debate over "evaluation" — the mediator providing an opinion of the case or a perspective on a party's position, suggesting an appropriate outcome, or even predicting how a court might

---

* L. Randolph Lowry is Director, Straus Institute for Dispute Resolution at Pepperdine University School of Law. In this article he looks at the various forms that evaluation takes in mediation and how it can best be used to facilitate negotiation between the parties.

resolve the case. The debate is taking place in scholarly articles, as both academics and practitioners describe what should occur and what should not occur in mediation. It consumes conversations at professional conferences. It is the subject of lively discussion in academic classrooms. The dialogue separates those in the mediation community as they seek to define whether or not evaluation should be a part of the true mediation process.

Although definitions of evaluation may vary, evaluation is commonly thought to include a range of activities such as expressing an opinion about a party's case, recommending a resolution, or predicting the ultimate outcome if the case were to be resolved in another forum. Professor Leonard Riskin may be credited with crystallizing the debate through the publication of his 1996 article, "Understanding Mediators Orientations, Strategies, and Techniques: A Grid for the Perplexed." In it, he suggests that evaluation involves assessing the strengths and weaknesses of the parties' case, developing and proposing options to resolve the case, and predicting the outcome at trial if a dispute, not settled in mediation, is litigated.

As the sides of the debate have formed, there are those who view such activity as contrary to the essence of "pure" or "traditional" mediation. They would describe mediation as the facilitation of the parties' own negotiation conducted by a third party who is neutral regarding the outcome. As Professors Kimberlee Kovach and Lela Love contend,

> Mediators should encourage parties to evaluate suggested options and alternatives and the viability of potential agreements. Mediators also should encourage parties to get outside advice, opinions and evaluations from appropriate experts. But mediators should not do these things themselves. "Evaluative" mediation is an oxymoron.

Advocates on the other side contend that evaluation does not detract but rather contributes to the effective resolution of cases. Jonathan Marks, a highly successful mediator and cofounder of the dispute resolution firm Endispute, suggests,

> In my practice, these facilitative skills are often not enough to overcome all the barriers to a negotiated settlement. Faced with intractable differences of view about who is going to win and what constitutes "fair settlement" I think the mediator's responsibility is to firmly step over the threshold from facilitator to evaluator.

Both sides in the debate passionately defend their perspectives. Both sides probably have experiences that confirm their assumptions. Both sides are sincere in their commitment to serve well those in conflict. Those on both sides would claim the title "Mediator," believing it describes what they do.

Although the discussion is stimulating and it has focused needed attention on an important area, perhaps the question is wrong. In most mediation, it is not a question as to whether or not evaluation will take place. More accurately, it is a question of when and how evaluation takes place. That latter question is the subject of this article.

Let me attempt to state the case. First of all, at least on one level, all mediators are involved in evaluation — that sense of making judgments on the information presented. Evaluation, at least internally with the mediator, is central to the mediator's work. It is the basis on which decisions are made regarding the management of the process and the parties as well as the resolution of the problem.

Evaluation in the sense of making judgments on the dynamics of the negotiation is the necessary and preliminary activity to facilitating the mediation process. By definition, a facilitator, from the unique neutral vantage point, assesses the dynamics of communication and through a variety of techniques guides the dialogue toward resolution. Pursuing a particular description of past events, asking a variety of questions to encourage parties to consider elements of the case, probing to discover underlying interests, and encouraging the analysis of possible solutions all reflect evaluation, even if only internal to the mediator. The mediator as a facilitator evaluates the parties, their positions, their perspectives, and the barriers to their achieving resolution. If mediators did not evaluate, they simply could not use their office and the techniques of the mediation dynamic to move parties toward settlement.

My colleague, Professor Lela Love, in her thought-provoking article, "The Top Ten Reasons Why Mediators Should Not Evaluate," describes what mediators do. Her descriptions are accurate, at least as they relate to stereotypical views of those activities. She describes the work of mediators in the following way:

> Mediators push disputing parties to question their assumptions, reconsider their positions, and listen to each other's perspectives, stories and arguments. They urge the parties to consider relevant law, weigh their own values, principles and priorities, and develop an optimal outcome.

She concludes by saying, "In doing so, mediators facilitate evaluation by the parties."

I agree and will forcefully advocate for mediators doing those things. But I do have one question. How does the mediator decide to do them? For instance, why would a mediator push parties to question their assumptions? Why would a mediator push parties to reconsider their positions? Why would a mediator urge parties to consider relevant law? I think it is because the mediator, in most cases, has evaluated the circumstance and feels that by doing those things, movement toward settlement can occur.

Granted, it is not the same as evaluating the case on a purely numerical basis and declaring to the parties that in the mediator's mind the case is worth a certain number of dollars. Most of the "evaluative" mediators I know rarely, if ever, do that. They do exactly what Professor Love suggests mediators do — question assumptions, reconsider positions, and consider the law — and in doing so, the dollar value of the case is affected! One cannot be purely dispassionate and completely nonjudgmental, avoid conclusive thinking, and do the things she suggests a mediators does. Just because the evaluation on the part of the mediator might be more subtle or expressed in less direct ways does not mean it does not occur!

If one is willing to consider at least the mediator's internal evaluation, then the issue really confronting us in the debate is whether the door should be opened to reveal the evaluation that has taken place. Does the mediator suggest a reaction to evidence, a feeling about the case, an idea regarding what a settlement might look like? Does the mediator understand reality and test the parties' understanding of it? Does the mediator ask questions with the intention of affecting a party's perspective? My strong sense is that many mediators not only evaluate internally but also express some sense of that evaluation during the mediation process.

Admittedly, there are a variety of somewhat different ways for that expression to take place. The stereotype of a retired judge — turned mediator is one where the judge focuses narrowly on the issues at hand, listens to both sides, and drawing upon years of judicial experience, suggests to the parties what they ought to do to settle the case in explicit and specific terms. The mediator is not reluctant to address, from expertise, the strengths and weaknesses of the case. She is certain about her understanding and ability to predict the likely outcome in an adjudicatory forum. She believes her role is to be honest and direct and, drawing on years of experience, to get the case settled.

There are many reactions to that stereotypical picture. First, it might be suggested that such an approach takes away from the ability of the parties to come to their independent conclusions regarding the appropriate resolution for their case. The concern is that the parties may be influenced by the power of the mediator's position and, when encouraged to settle based upon the expressed evaluation of the neutral, may sometimes have a greater degree of dissatisfaction with both the result and the process.

Second, those observing that model of evaluation may recognize that the evaluation could be wrong. It is a particularly talented individual who can decide the objective value of a particular case when every study of which I am aware would suggest that, giving 10 case files to 10 experts, will probably result in not a consensus but a range of the "right" outcome. To be more specific, the evaluative mediator may simply be wrong in the substantive evaluation and that is a risk to the parties, a risk to the mediator's personal reputation, and a risk to the ultimate success of the process.

Third, that type of evaluation may bring to a close too quickly the mediation process. Even if the result is right, moving too quickly to the sense of clear evaluation may deprive the parties of the opportunity to fully share their story or describe their case. As my colleague, Professor Bryan Johnston, would conclude, "The right answer at the wrong time is the wrong answer." It may result in dissatisfaction with the dynamic and may decrease, in the parties' eyes, the uniqueness and value of the mediation moment.

Fourth, that type of evaluation may damage, perhaps beyond repair, the negotiation between the parties. If the core of the mediation is negotiation — a communication process used to put details together or resolve conflicts — then activities that would inhibit the communication process certainly have the potential to affect, negatively, the negotiation. An evaluation as described above could have such an impact if it encourages one side and discourages the other side in its evaluation of the case and results in less willingness to negotiate. Professor Dwight Golann summed it up when commenting in the context of a litigated case:

> An evaluation often effectively ends the negotiation process, once a neutral has opined about the "right" result in a case, it is very difficult for a defendant to offer more or a plaintiff to accept less than the evaluator's number.

Fifth, that type of evaluation may result in the conflict being too narrowly defined. Although some cases involve a simple, single money issue, many cases really reflect more complex, multifaceted conflicts. Gravitation to the purely legal issues and evaluating what is likely to occur in an adjudicatory forum may very well miss the opportunity mediation uniquely provides to surface, address, and resolve other important but less legal issues. The mindset of litigation defines what is "relevant" in that forum but perhaps not what could be relevant in the forum of mediation.

Sixth, allowing or encouraging evaluation necessitates that the role of the mediator be carried out by persons who have the requisite training for such evaluation — usually lawyers and judges. It is argued that if an opinion on a likely court outcome or the merits of a particular legal case are addressed in an evaluative way, only those who have substantive legal expertise will be in a position to do so. It is contended that such could be problematic or damaging to the field because it may incorporate into mediation an otherwise outside set of professional responsibilities, decrease the talent and diversity in the pool of mediators, and possibly transfer "pure" mediation into a more adversarial process. This same concern would probably be expressed concerning "experts" in defined fields such as construction defect or environmental mediation.

Seventh, that kind of evaluation confuses the role of the third party. Although some make substantial effort to clarify and seek specific permission from the parties to carry out the role of facilitator, if any evaluation then takes place, there may be substantial confusion in the minds of those participants. This is more likely when disputes involve parties less experienced in the process. Such parties hear the introductory comments about the facilitative nature of mediation and its attribute of allowing parties to control the process and the outcome, and then, sometime later, the same mediator suggests to the parties a predicted outcome if the case is resolved in another forum. If the groundwork for such activity is not painstakingly laid, parties are confused or even offended by the actions of the mediator and the process that has unfolded.

Eighth, and finally, the stereotypical evaluative management of the process really moves it to something that is more adjudicative in nature and in doing so diminishes the quality of both mediation and adjudicatory processes, of which there are many. The definitive line between the various processes is blurred. As Professor Lela Love appeals,

> We need a genuine alternative to the adversarial paradigm of disputants who fight and a neutral assesses. . . . We lose a great deal if mediation becomes a mere adjunct of the adversarial norm. Having mediators use evaluation as a technique to get movement takes us in that direction.

In response to the stereotypical activity and the variety of reactions to it, one must conclude that each does pose some risk to the settlement of a particular case; some risk to the process of mediation, including its reputation; and some risk to the particular mediators and parties involved in a specific case. The fact that there may be risk, however, may not be justification for ignoring a technique that might aid settlement. There is risk in not evaluating a dispute that could be settled but then turns into protracted, expensive, and harmful litigation. There is risk in allowing parties to settle a case in such a way that it does not comply with an outcome the court will require. There is risk in allowing inexperience to prevail over experience. The response to risk is not to try to eliminate it and in doing so diminish the tools available in case settlement but rather to do what many professionals are trained to do, and that is to intelligently, thoughtfully, and strategically manage appropriate risks. In the case of mediation, that would suggest managing the risk of evaluation.

In addition, while those responses might be made to more overt evaluation by the mediator, the mediation community must come to grips with the stark reality of the marketplace. That reality suggests that for a large number of lawyers and clients evaluation is exactly what they expect to be included in a mediation process. Retired judges and experienced litigators who offer specific evaluation as a normal and important part of the process are professionally and financially successful. They are regularly chosen voluntarily, and many of their practices are booming, because disputants and lawyers desire their understanding of the settlement context of a particular case. The JAMS/Endispute organization, one of the largest dispute resolution providers in the nation, is composed primarily of retired judges who, I think it is fair to say, would lean toward the evaluative side of the continuum. Income for the firm will exceed $50 million this year; the organization's 350 arbitrators resolve more than 20,000 cases a year in 30 offices across the country. The approach of those mediators might be offensive to some and, while their technique might not be included as a separate chapter in most mediation textbooks, it would be foolhardy to suggest that the form of dispute resolution they practice is not endorsed, embraced, and selected by the tens of thousands who are clients of the mediation process.

* * *

That being the case, with all of the arguments on both sides as to what is and what should be, I would propose that the question to evaluate or to not evaluate is not the question for many practitioners. The question is more likely when and how should a mediator evaluate? The following is an attempt to suggest times when such might be appropriate and approaches that might be helpful while clinging to and valuing greatly the dynamic of mediation as a continuing negotiation between the parties.

First, evaluation ought to take place at a time when its influence will be greatest. Evaluation is not a tool for the mediator to demonstrate the mediator's own competence, nor a challenge for the mediator to manipulate a case in such a way that it comes out as he or she designates. Rather, evaluation is a technique to move parties from positions they have taken that have resulted in impasse to a mutually agreeable position so a settlement then takes place. Evaluation ought to be saved for those moments where such movement is necessary for the process to be successful. That time might be during initial caucus when the evaluation is used to help parties frame what might be relevant and what might be irrelevant to a settlement, or it might be very late in the process as parties are trying to decide who gets how much of the last relatively small amount of value. An evaluation can help the parties move sufficiently so a settlement can occur. I cannot specify an exact time for evaluation, but it appears that timing is an important, perhaps critical, consideration.

Second, the style of evaluation may be critical. I am confident that if we were able to listen in on mediations around the country we would hear a tremendous range of techniques in expressing evaluation. There are those who, in almost a self-effacing way, suggest an extremely tentative perspective on a particular issue or outcome. On the other hand, there are those who, with a great deal of self-confidence and egocentric focus, express in a dogmatic and perhaps abrasive way their evaluation on how a particular issue should be resolved. Again, I remain perplexed because both of those camps seem to continue to be busy in the world of professionally retained mediators. Why some people would pay for an evaluation that is so tentative as to perhaps not influence the parties or why others would pay for mental abuse and embarrassment is beyond me, but individuals do so every single day as they choose, voluntarily, a particular approach to mediation that they believe will be helpful.

Third, it appears that the nature of the evaluation will be somewhat affected by the type of relationship the mediator wishes to establish with those involved in the mediation. There are those mediators who want to be liked, who want to be perceived as a colleague in the grand problem-solving process, and who, when having established excellent relationships with the parties, will then draw upon the great sense of trust and regard to provide an evaluative perspective. Alternatively, there are those individuals who could care less about their personal relationship with the parties at the table, who are more interested in putting a notch on their mediation success belt, and who cannot believe why parties would not call them back for another successful mediation session. Obviously, the kind of relationship one would want with the parties might influence the nature and approach to evaluation. Although such a relationship is important for some, it is less important for others.

Fourth, there may be a strong connection between the nature of evaluation and the type of claim that is the subject of the mediation process. For instance, a claim relating to something for which the alternative is extraordinarily clear may allow the mediator greater confidence and promote more willingness to be evaluative. In the family area, family mediators suggest that there are relatively few questions as to the preferences of the court on a number of items in a marriage dissolution case. If that is true, the mediator may be more willing to evaluate with a great deal of confidence in light of that context. On the other hand, there are cases for which there are no clear external alternatives, for instance, a management dispute between an employer and an employee within an organization, and thus, in that context, it is hard to draw upon the predictability of resolution in another forum. In essence, the basis for evaluation may simply not exist.

Fifth, the focus of evaluation should be carefully considered. Sometimes evaluation on the merits of a party's position or the likelihood of prevailing in an adversarial forum is needed to move people from the position they have taken. Sometimes the focus of evaluation is a numerical settlement value of the case at hand. Sometimes the actions, attitudes, and behavior of the parties need to be evaluated by a neutral third party. Sometimes, the evaluation is of the state of the negotiation and what it might take to move from impasse to resolution. This article does not advocate for any particular focus but rather recognizes that the focus of what is evaluated should be the subject of careful analysis and planning.

Sixth, and finally, the method of evaluation may make a difference as well. For instance, if the issue turns on the definition of appropriate damages in a simple personal injury case, one option would be for the mediator simply to state what the damages appear to be and be straightforward in the presentation. Such a mediator mediating a personal injury case might say, "I have seen these before, I know what this kind of case is going to be worth and I would urge you to settle it in the range of $18,000 to $20,000, which will mean you, plaintiff, need to lower your demand by $5,000." There is a simplicity that is attractive in such a statement. There is a sense of expertise. There is an expression of confidence that such expertise is right; that confidence may very well be influential in the consideration of a party's negotiating position.

An alternative would be to seek the arrival of the parties at the same place through a series of questions that in reality reflect evaluation but may seem to be more consistent with the mediation process and less onerous in their use. For instance, in the same personal injury case, one might ask plaintiff's counsel, "What is the jury verdict range for these kinds of cases?" "What is the settlement range for these types of injuries?" "Does the existence of this particular fact increase or decrease the likelihood of being at the top of that settlement range?" "If that fact puts this case at the bottom of the settlement range, does it not seem reasonable to lower your demand so that you are within an accepted range and therefore are attracting the insurance company to meet you there and settle the case?" Although perhaps not artfully illustrated, one can see the progression of those questions leading to a conclusion that the same movement might be made, based upon the mediator's understanding or, if you will, evaluation of the circumstance. Such questioning can be expressed in an almost indicting spirit, or it can be expressed in the spirit of one who is seeking to understand and massage the process in such a way that parties can come together. In any event, the mediator has never made a statement as to his or her opinion directly but has reflected it in the questions the mediator has asked.

Others may add to these ideas about the type and timing of evaluation, but I hope they illustrate a dimension of the conversation that may be missing. We can argue all day about whether or not evaluation should be a part of the mediation process and miss the reality that directly or indirectly it is a part of many successful and satisfying mediation sessions. More important than the argument about whether evaluation should occur may be the discussion of when and how evaluation might most appropriately be carried out. As those who are bold enough to sit at the end of the table realize, answering the right question will enhance the assistance provided to those who sit on the sides of the table.

Chapter 10

THE NEXT CHALLENGE: MULTIPARTY NEGOTIATION

So far, I have been discussing negotiation largely as an encounter between two parties, each with some interests that conflict with the other's — hence the need to negotiate — but also with some potential to further the other's interests — hence the value in negotiating. Multiparty (or multilateral or group) negotiations occur whenever three or more people try to reach a joint decision about an issue on which they have differing views. Such negotiations can be as simple as three friends deciding where to spend a beautiful Sunday afternoon. They can also be as multi-layered as, for example, the members of an environmental organization (a constituent group) deciding what instructions to give three people (their negotiating team) who will represent them in meetings with the city, developers, and concerned citizens (a multilateral negotiation) about a proposed waterfront project. In the second example, each step in the process involves a multiparty negotiation: the constituents must come to some agreement about what to tell their representatives; the members of the negotiating team must plan a joint strategy, based on their constituents' needs and goals; and the four "sides" represented at the bargaining table must explore the possibilities for an agreement among them that will satisfy all of their constituent groups. In large-scale international negotiations, each of the steps mentioned is multiplied many times over, with dozens of constituent groups lobbying large negotiation teams both before and during negotiations that may involve dozens of countries.

Although there is no way in a single chapter to deal with all the complexities of such aggregations of negotiators and parties, I hope to acquaint you here with some of the characteristics that distinguish them. I begin by looking at some of the dynamics at play in group decision making, then turn to a number of multiparty situations lawyers encounter in negotiations: the principal-agent relationship between lawyer and client; negotiating teams; and coalitions of individuals or groups. The introduction closes with a discussion of some procedural issues that arise in multiparty negotiations and some procedural tools that can help make those negotiations more manageable and more productive.

A. GROUP DYNAMICS

Human beings are social animals, yet their efforts to function in groups are often fraught with tension. The saying that "two's company and three's a crowd" indicates how conflicted people can feel about group life, even when the group is small. Anyone who has ever participated in a meeting knows only too well the many ways groups can be frustrating. One or two people may dominate, virtually excluding input from others; the meeting may be so unfocused that time is mostly wasted; someone's bad day may spill over into the meeting and derail the group's functioning; existing conflicts within the group may erupt and prevent productive work from getting done. Groups often seem both to want someone to take charge and to "make things happen," and at the same time to resist efforts to be led in any particular direction. The pressures in a group are both internal and specific to the group's members and external, to the extent that members are accountable to others (their constituencies) for group decisions.

1. Individual Needs and Group Tasks

Every person brings to a group his or her own psychology, history, and expectations about group life: in this sense the room is full even if there are only three or four individuals sitting around the table. In every group there are tensions between the individual needs and aims of the members and the task of the group as a whole. People are concerned about how they will be seen by others; whether the group will hear them out and value their contributions; whether they will be in control or be controlled; and whether the group will simply fail to cohere at all. Sorting out the individuals' needs for affiliation, domination, or reassurance may or may not further the group task, but these needs will be present nonetheless and will have to be addressed explicitly or implicitly as the group tries to make progress toward its goals. Efforts to ignore individuals or to rule them out of order will only inflame them; and groups must always contend with the conflict between members' dependency on the group for some desired result and their wish to be free of the group's authority.

One aspect of the difficulty that groups have in functioning effectively derives from the "naïve realism" mentioned in Chapter Six. We all walk around with the assumption that the world is the way we see it, that is, that our assumptions about the world are facts. Inevitably, members of a group will have different perspectives on many issues: this is one of the reasons for bringing a group together to address a complex problem. It means, though, that every effort at group decision-making is also a negotiation about the nature of reality: tension and frustration result in part from the clash of individual perspectives, and emotions can run high. Group members have to be prepared repeatedly to focus their attention back to the group task when disruptions occur. Pointing to gains made and to common goals yet to be reached can help counter the unraveling effect of discontented individuals on the group as a whole.

As a corollary of naïve realism, people tend to credit information that agrees with what they already believe more than information that challenges their beliefs. Cognitive psychologists call this the "confirmation bias," and it is an obstacle to making optimal use of the multiple points of view that group members bring to the table. It is difficult to assimilate all the information that flies around the room in a group situation, both about the emotional state of all the different actors and about their various views on the issues the group is negotiating. The sorts of cognitive traps that we are prone to fall into even in relatively simple decision-making contexts, discussed in Chapter Five, are all the more likely to catch us up in group situations, where it is harder to take in all the available information and uncertainties abound.

In addition, the decision rules adopted by the group may affect members' efforts to assimilate new information. If the final decision is up to a single group member, others will have less incentive to integrate unfamiliar information into their thinking and thus will be less able to contribute to group discussions. The article below by Brett discusses some of the ways that group process can encourage or discourage members' full use of the varied perspectives in the group.

2. Constituent Pressures

In addition to the challenges to task-oriented group functioning that individuals bring to the table, individual members of a negotiating group are often answerable to some constituency or client, itself either an individual or a group. Negotiation group members face the same basic challenge that individual negotiators do: how to achieve their goals through working with others. Even when members of a group are all on the same "side," for example, members of a litigation team in a lawsuit or representatives of different departments in a company engaged in a joint project, they may still face pressures from people not present in the room to accomplish goals that serve the interests of a particular constituency.

The challenges in keeping a client abreast of developments as negotiations proceed, discussed in Chapter Seven, are multiplied when you are involved in a multiparty negotiation or your client is a group rather than an individual. In the multiparty situation, it is difficult for any single negotiator to control the pace of the negotiation: there is always the risk of getting left out and left behind if you do not keep up with the group's discussions. You may have to make rapid decisions that have not been considered previously with your client, and the client may end up feeling that you have exceeded your authority. When the client is a group, latent or patent divisions within the group regarding the conduct of negotiations may surface when the members feel that they are left out of the loop as negotiations proceed. Managing your dealings with a group client while conducting external negotiations on their behalf can be daunting; and the first excerpt from Goodpaster below addresses some ways to deal with the complexities of constituent pressure in this situation.

B. PRINCIPAL-AGENT RELATIONSHIPS

As lawyers, your professional negotiations will be undertaken as agents of your clients. In that role, there are legal, ethical, and practical constraints on your freedom to negotiate as you see fit. In earlier chapters I noted some of the challenges that arise when the negotiator is an agent of the interested party, rather than the interested party herself. The introduction of lawyers, as discussed in Chapter Seven, immediately adds another layer to the two-party negotiation scenario: every lawyer must negotiate the relationship with his or her client and the scope of the lawyer's agency before negotiating on the client's behalf.

Thus, your negotiation with another party's lawyer (the external negotiation) is influenced by, and may influence, your negotiation with your principal (the internal negotiation). First, the laws of agency limit your authority to make binding commitments on behalf of your principal. In addition, both the rules of legal ethics and the realities of law practice, as discussed by Gilson and Mnookin in Chapter Four and by Lowenthal and Condlin in Chapter Eight, create tensions in handling a negotiation for any particular client. Whatever authority you negotiate with your client before meeting with other parties may also need to be re-examined in light of information gained during negotiations, both to keep your client fully informed and/or to alter your authority to reach a favorable settlement.

Even the simplest bilateral negotiation — where two lawyers act as agents for two individuals — is in a sense a multiparty negotiation; and the lawyers must manage both the internal and the external negotiations carefully. When the client is a group, such as a union or an environmental organization, the internal negotiation will be more complicated still, depending on the hierarchy within the group and the presence or absence of divisions within it that impact the conduct of external negotiations. For example, during the internal negotiation, you may need to help your constituents (the group members) reach some consensus about their goals before you can conduct an external negotiation on the group's behalf. The first excerpt below from Goodpaster discusses some of the ethical and strategic challenges faced by a negotiator representing a group client.

Awareness of and attention to the negotiations that occur away from the table are important not only to handle your own client's affairs ethically and effectively, but also to negotiate well with other parties. Your own client is often a good source of information about another client's priorities, and it can sometimes be useful to structure your proposals in light of those, even if that client's lawyer takes a different position. This is true in bilateral negotiations; and, as the number of parties at the table increases, it becomes more critical to think about the intraparty negotiations and constituent pressures that affect what all the negotiators do and say around the table as external negotiations progress. For example, behavior at the table that makes no sense in terms of what is happening among the negotiators may be understandable as the product of pressures from constituents to maintain a certain public stance. Progress in the negotiation may then depend on the negotiators' abilities to read between the lines, as it were, and to find possibilities of compromise in the face of adamantly proclaimed positions.

C. NEGOTIATING TEAMS

As a lawyer, you may represent only individual clients and conduct all negotiations for those clients on your own as, for example, traditional personal injury lawyers do. But for many lawyers, law practice involves working in teams, including conducting negotiations as part of a team of lawyers (and perhaps other experts) representing the same party.

1. Challenges of Teams

There are both challenges and benefits to working as part of a negotiating team, and it is important to consider carefully how to minimize the former and maximize the latter in order to warrant the extra expense of using a team to negotiate. In addition to expense, some of the challenges include getting all team members usefully involved in both pre-negotiation preparation and in the external negotiation itself, so that the team actually benefits from their ideas and expertise; managing the team process so that decision making within the team does not become overly cumbersome or fractious; and developing smooth team functioning during external negotiations, in order to forestall another party's attempts to split the team or to gain advantage from information "leakage" by team members.

Clear communication and extensive joint preparation are essential to deal with the challenges of negotiating as a team. The individual contributions of each member must be incorporated into an agreed upon set of goals and strategies that the whole team will pursue. The role of each team member during the negotiation needs to be spelled out in advance, and divisions within the team have to be addressed promptly so that the team does not fall apart from internal strain. Since it is never possible to anticipate just how a negotiation will develop, it is important for the team to plan for breaks during negotiations and to agree how to call for unplanned breaks when necessary. The more flexible the team can be during negotiations, the more likely it is to succeed; and that flexibility depends on the establishment of trust and confidence among team members during the entire process of preparing for and conducting negotiations.

Where team members represent different constituencies, for example, several unions preparing for joint negotiations with management, they must each seek the best deal possible for their constituents in the internal team negotiations, while at the same time trying to preserve sufficient common ground with the other unions to make joint action feasible in the external negotiation. The additional challenge of constituent pressure in such a situation increases the difficulty of creating an effective negotiation team.

2. Benefits of Teams

Students often chafe at the complications of working as a team and express a preference for going it alone in negotiations. The psychological demands of working in a group are complex, as the section above on group dynamics discusses. The benefits of teams, though, are significant: teams reach better results than solo negotiators, whether they are negotiating against other teams or against individuals. Teams have the advantage of different perspectives, different sorts of expertise and experience, and different personalities. Moreover, assigning members roles that call for varied skills —spokesperson, process manager, numbers person — optimizes their participation in the negotiation. A team can better manage the information overload that a complex multi-issue negotiation creates: assigning team members specific tasks during the negotiation allows them to focus on the information that is pertinent to their role. The article below by Sally and O'Connor highlights some of the advantages and drawbacks to negotiation teams.

D. COALITIONS

A negotiator always seeks to increase her client's ability to reach a favorable settlement, whether by improving the client's alternatives to the present deal, by changing the other party's perceptions of the value of this deal, or by other means. One of the strongest ways to alter the dynamics in a negotiation is by forming a coalition — that is, an agreement for joint action — with another party or parties. Coalitions can form among individuals within a group, among groups on the same side of a negotiation, or among groups or individuals on different sides of a negotiation.

1. Coalition Formation

In a multilateral negotiation, two parties that are too weak on their own to accomplish their goals may be able to do so if they agree to work together. If Alice's position in a negotiation has a value of 40 points, Becca's has 35, and Colin's has 25, none of them is in a position to determine the outcome alone; but a coalition of any two of them will dominate the third. Becca and Colin together will have more power than Alice does, and if either of them allies with Alice against the other, that coalition will prevail.

Which coalition is likely to form in this simplified example will depend on many factors, including the overlap in each possible pair's interests and the degree to which any potential partner is in a position to satisfy independent interests of the other. To the extent that any pair's interests are shared, they are natural allies and can improve their bargaining power by joining forces. To the extent that their interests diverge, however, they must be able to agree on trades or side payments that make it still worthwhile to band together. Since the three parties in the example above can gain dominance by allying with any of the other parties, there will also be competition among them to be in a coalition. In this way, a party like Colin, who is the weakest of the three on his own, may increase his power by getting Alice and Becca to vie with each other to form a coalition with him (of course, Colin must not overreach, since he could also end up alone, facing an alliance between Alice and Becca). As you can see, the choice of coalition partners and the nature of the agreement they reach is itself a potentially complicated side negotiation that may take place either before or during the primary negotiation for which the coalition is formed.

With perfect information, which of the three parties above ultimately form a coalition would depend largely on the extent of the parties' overlapping interests. A coalition built on shared interests is both less costly than one that requires complicated side payments and also less vulnerable to unraveling, since its members have similar goals in the negotiation. In addition, the cost and effort of forming a coalition may contribute to its stability because of the partners' psychological investment in the arrangement and their uncertainty about improving their situation by forming a different coalition.

It is important to plan carefully how to approach potential coalition partners in order to maximize your chances of success in recruiting them. If you have no direct connection to the person or group you want to ally yourself with, you will have to develop a strategy for reaching them through contacts you do have. This process of "mapping backward," as Sebenius[1] has called it, will help you figure out both whose support you most need and how to get it in the course of preparing for a particular negotiation.

As in other aspects of negotiation, however, parties seeking coalition partners seldom do have complete information about others' interests and preferences; and what looks like a good match initially may turn out otherwise as negotiations progress. When the foundation for a coalition is or becomes insecure, the coalition may be difficult to maintain over time; and this is one aspect of coalitional instability, discussed below. The second excerpt from Goodpaster addresses some of the problems that arise in coalition formation and coalition maintenance.

---

[1] *See* James K. Sebenius, *Mapping Backward: Negotiating in the Right Sequence*, 7 NEGOT. 3 (2004).

2. Tacit Coalitions

The discussion above about coalitions proceeded as if the issue in a multi-party context is which of the parties or groups at the negotiation table are going to form alliances to alter the balance of power, that is, as if "the" negotiation consisted of a fixed number of actors and issues. However, strangers to the negotiation may also become influential because of actions taken by those at the table. As described by Lax and Sebenius, the fluidity of what is at stake and who has a say in what happens can be significant in negotiations:

> The game is that which the parties act as if it is. There is no a priori reason why this or that issue should be included or why this party or that interest should be excluded. If the parties deal with a particular set of issues, alternatives to agreement, and possible agreements, then, those elements, in fact, make up part of the game.
>
> In particular, analytically interesting coalition dynamics often arise in such situations where the game cannot be considered well-specified in terms of the parties involved. . . . For example, a country may wish to enlist the aid or assistance of others in achieving a particular objective. The process of choosing, then approaching and persuading, others to go along . . . [is what] we call party arithmetic.[2]

One of the examples they give is of a mine threatened with nationalization. In order to increase its power in negotiations with the government, the mining company entered into long-term supply contracts with third parties and sold the collection rights on those contracts to banks and others. By so doing, the mining company effectively created a coalition with those other parties, which now had a significant economic interest in the mine's uninterrupted operation. The formation of this tacit coalition created additional pressure on the government not to take action that would cause the mine to shut down, thus giving the mining company more leverage in what was nominally a bilateral negotiation.

As the example above illustrates, it is important when contemplating coalition formation to look not only to the parties at the negotiation table as potential allies, but also to other actors who may be able to influence the positions taken by parties at the table. The wider the ramifications of decisions reached in a given negotiation, the more likely it is that "outsiders" can affect those decisions if their interests are drawn into the process.

---

[2] David Lax & James Sebenius, *Thinking Coalitionally: Party Arithmetic, Process Opportunism, and Strategic Sequencing, in* NEGOTIATION ANALYSIS 153, at 164 (Peyton H. Young ed., 1991).

3. Timing of Coalition Formation

Probably the single biggest mistake that inexperienced negotiators make with respect to coalition formation is to wait until formal negotiations begin to think about it or to do anything about it. In a multilateral negotiation, or even in a bilateral negotiation where outsiders may influence what happens at the negotiating table — as the mining company example above illustrates — an essential part of pre-negotiation preparation is to position yourself as advantageously as possible by considering how coalitions can increase your leverage at the bargaining table.

Talking to other parties early and persuading them of the value of a coalition before joint sessions begin gives you the opportunity to start a negotiation from a position of strength rather than having to try to create one as negotiations progress. The sooner opposing parties become aware of the strength of your position, the less likely they are to become entrenched in their own in a way that leads to fruitless escalation of conflict rather than to cost-saving compromise.

When you seek the support of outsiders to bolster your case, getting them involved early may completely alter the nature of the negotiations themselves. A small independent bookseller may fear being put out of business by a large chain store opening nearby, and it may not have any means of negotiating successfully on its own with either the city or the chain. If it can mobilize its customers and other citizens who favor maintaining local businesses to lobby on its behalf, however, their political pressure may lead the city to deny a development permit to the chain or persuade the chain to put its store in a less contested location.

4. Coalition Aims

Coalitions can be formed either to bring about some desired change, as when neighbors or neighborhood organizations join together to get a city to create traffic barriers on residential streets, or they can form to block undesirable changes, such as the routing of a new freeway through a residential area. In both cases, individuals are unlikely to have much power negotiating with City Hall, but a coalition of neighborhood residents (perhaps joined by environmental groups and cyclists) can have a significant impact. In other circumstances, the parties to a coalition may be unlikely partners, but still aligned on a particular issue, for example, an environmental group and a regional airport authority, both of which oppose the construction of a new airport in the area, albeit for very different reasons.

5. Coalition Instability

Although forming a coalition can be advantageous, changing circumstances or new information may alter the coalition's desirability or viability. The attraction of coalitions is that they give parties power that they would not otherwise have, and the risk is that they are often unstable, making that power uncertain. Information that was not available at the time a coalition formed may make maintaining the coalition undesirable for some. A counter-coalition may form that alters the dynamics within the original coalition. Another party may manage to entice away one or more members of a coalition by offering them something that the coalition cannot provide, or the coalition members' views of their own interests may change as negotiations proceed. The shifting allegiances that result as coalitions form, dissolve, and reform — and the reconfigurations of power that accompany these changes — are an important aspect of the complexity of multiparty negotiations.

E. PROCEDURAL ISSUES

Multilateral negotiations may proceed much like bilateral negotiations when the number of parties is small enough for them all to meet and discuss issues jointly. As the number of parties increases, however, procedural issues become salient and are themselves the subject of delicate negotiations among the parties. Who meets with whom, in what order, and to discuss what issues are all matters that have to be addressed before the substantive issues can be tackled efficiently and effectively. In addition, rules of decision have to be formulated, since in the multiparty situation, there is always the risk of an agreement being thwarted by one or more holdouts.

It is not an exaggeration to say that without careful attention to ground rules, many multilateral negotiations would simply break down before they got off the ground. Clear procedures, and a clear understanding and acceptance of those procedures among the parties, are an essential first step in any contentious negotiation; and any negotiation involving many parties and many disputed issues is likely to be contentious.

1. Dividing the Whole into Parts

Large-scale, multiparty, multi-issue negotiations require procedural mechanisms to break talks down into manageable pieces. Process agreements can help streamline what would otherwise be an unwieldy and inefficient attempt to have too many people discussing too many topics at once.

The parties may agree, for example, to create committees of the whole to hold talks on certain issues in order to gauge the extent of the parties' disagreements and/or to reach provisional agreements. Small groups work more effectively than large groups, and dividing up the work enables the parties to use people on their team in a more specialized way during preliminary discussions.

Of course, there must also be procedures for determining the membership on such committees and for deciding which issues can be addressed through these or other mechanisms. Without procedures in place to decide how and when topics will be considered, negotiators will waste time and the substantive work of the negotiation will not be done in a rational manner.

2. Rules of Decision

In a bilateral negotiation, a decision is reached when both parties signal their acceptance of a proposed deal; there is no possibility of a non-unanimous agreement. In a multiparty situation, a requirement of unanimity may make reaching agreement impossible. One party or another can always hold the rest hostage by refusing to go along at the last minute, demanding further concessions before signing on to a deal. Thus, an important procedural issue that has to be resolved early on in a multiparty negotiation is whether a unanimity rule will govern the outcome, or whether the parties will commit to accept something short of unanimous agreement.

An obvious alternative to unanimity is to reach a decision based on majority rule. That is how popular elections are typically decided. In other situations, where the parties interact closely all the time, a super majority, e.g., 2 to 1, may be used in order to be sure that the result satisfies most, if not all, of the parties involved. One drawback of both these rules is that they require voting and may lead to a divisive result based on winners and losers. In addition, such decisions may be inefficient, since they do not take into account differences in the strength of the parties' preferences on various issues or the possibility of joint gains through trades.

In order to mitigate the adversarial overtones of majority rule, while at the same time avoiding the problem of holdouts preventing an agreement being reached, many multiparty negotiations use a consensus model. An attempt is made, after analysis of issues, discussion, and refining and combining arguments and proposals, to reach a decision that all parties can live with. One advantage of a consensus model is that it may allow an agreement to be reached without parties having to take an explicit stand on a proposal through voting, where votes one way or another might be interpreted by constituents as disloyal. A disadvantage of consensus decision-making can be that the result does not optimize available trades among the parties and may instead be only minimally satisfying to all.

Of course, it is not easy even to reach consensus in particularly contentious negotiations. Mnookin[3] describes a variant of consensus decision making that George Mitchell used in Northern Ireland. When general consensus could not be reached, decisions could still be made if there was "sufficient consensus" on an issue. In that context, sufficient consensus meant that any agreement had to be supported by parties representing a majority of each of the religious communities, Catholic and Protestant; by the Irish and British governments; and by a numerical majority of all parties participating in the talks. The use of this model enabled the parties to reach agreements that might otherwise have been politically impossible for some of them to accept:

> In late July 1996, it looked as though the negotiation participants would not be able to agree on a set of ground rules before the August recess. Finally a delegate suggested that the delegates vote on each individual section of the proposed rules *and* on the rules as a whole. Those with objections could vote, if they so desired, against each of the individual rules, but then vote for the rules as a whole. That way, minority parties concerned with maintaining their reputations with their constituencies could appear as having voted overwhelmingly against the rules, while still enabling them to pass.

3. Use of Third-Party Neutrals

In addition to ground rules that establish the procedures to be used, the scope and scale of multiparty negotiations may also make the use of third party neutrals critical to successful resolution of the dispute. Such parties may be brought in at the beginning, or their assistance may be sought when negotiations reach a stalemate after the parties fail to communicate productively with each other.

Disinterested parties may be brought in to manage the process as well as to assist in reaching substantive agreements. There are many roles that such third parties can play, and complex negotiations may require the assistance of multiple neutrals. Where there is longstanding distrust among parties, use of a neutral may be essential to making progress in negotiations; and the status and legitimacy of the person acting in that role will affect her ability to function effectively.

Third parties may be used, among other things, to gather information to help the parties analyze their dispute before negotiations begin; to design a process for resolving the conflict; to improve the parties' communication with each other; to manage the negotiations themselves; to help the parties

---

[3] *See* Robert H. Mnookin, *Strategic Barriers to Dispute Resolution: A Comparison of Bilateral and Multilateral Negotiations*, 8 HARV. NEGOT. L. REV. 1, 20-21 (2003) (citing Daniel F. Curran & James K. Sebenius, *The Mediator as Coalition Builder: George Mitchell in Northern Ireland*, 8 J. INT'L NEGOT. 111 (2003)).

collect and analyze relevant data; to work with negotiating teams and constituents to maintain clear communication; and to provide a neutral space for meeting that is not identified with one party or another.[4] The person may be designated as chair, facilitator, or mediator. Whatever title the parties give the neutral, it is essential that they be clear what role or roles they want her to play and that she has the necessary qualifications for the job. The neutral's prominence may be important to her credibility going in, but a prominent person who lacks process skills is unlikely to be able to moderate heated party discussions on the strength of her reputation alone.

Jeanne M. Brett,[*] *Negotiating Group Decisions*
7 NEGOT. J. 291, 297-99 (1991)[**]

* * *

Ensuring that Available Information Is Considered by the Group

Two aspects of a group's process can increase or decrease the likelihood that available information and perspectives are considered by the group. These are "discussion norms" and "decision rules." Both affect not just how much gets said, but how well what is said is listened to.

Groups quickly develop norms — standards for what is and is not appropriate behavior — and operating procedures, for example, decision rules. Often, neither is discussed explicitly, but both emerge out of group interaction. Norms about discussion develop as group members are positively or negatively reinforced by others for what they say. For instance, group members can quickly stifle the creative exchange of ideas by pointing out their negative aspects. Sometimes a decision rule, such as consensus, is assumed by group members to be in effect and is never explicitly agreed to. Other groups end up discussing a decision rule — for example majority rule — only after it becomes clear that consensus cannot be achieved.

There is no reason why groups cannot agree to discussion norms and decision rules prior to beginning deliberations on the substantive aspects of the group task — it is just that they do not seem to do so naturally. In order to ensure that available information and perspectives are considered, groups need to adapt particular discussion norms and decision rules.

---

4 *See* SUSAN L. CARPENTER & W.J.D. KENNEDY, MANAGING PUBLIC DISPUTES 191-93 (2001).

[*] Jeanne M. Brett is the DeWitt W. Buchanan, Jr., Distinguished Professor of Dispute Resolution and Organizations; Director of Dispute Resolution Research Center, Kellogg School of Management, Northwestern University. The excerpt deals with procedures for improving group decision-making.

[**] Copyright © 1991 Negotiation Journal. Reprinted by permission of Blackwell Publishing, Inc. and the Program on Negotiation at Harvard Law School.

Perhaps the most important norm for a group to develop is tolerance for conflicting points of view. Many techniques to enact this norm are available. The MIS task force in our example used several different ones. They agreed that members could make no negative comments about ideas during the presentation and brainstorming stages of group decision making. They gave their group facilitator the responsibilities of eliciting participation from all members, enforcing the no-negative-comments rule, recording all ideas, and making sure that, as the group organized and refined ideas, none was lost. Janis suggests other techniques for ensuring an exchange of ideas, including assigning the same problem to multiple groups or splitting the group in half, assigning a group member to play the role of devil's advocate, and inviting outside experts to challenge group members' assumptions.

One of the biggest problems in fostering an open exchange of ideas is that interpersonal relations become emotionally charged, especially when a group is working under a tight deadline. Members become frustrated and tempers flair. If this situation persists, both creativity and motivation to complete the task will suffer. To counteract emotional tension, groups need to provide members with ways to vent emotion without creating emotional escalation throughout the group.

* * *

Too often, group members tear out of their offices to attend a group meeting with preparation limited to reading the agenda on the elevator. If they have considered anything in preparation for the meeting, they may have thought about their own positions on the issues to be resolved. The result is likely to be a conflict-filled meeting. . . . Thorough preparation for a group meeting involves knowing your own and estimating the other group members' positions, interests, and priorities on the issues. These are terms commonly used in negotiations. "Positions" are what group members want; "interests" are the reasons why. One way to think about interests is to consider what assumptions underlie a group member's position or what that person's hidden agenda might be. "Priorities" are the rankings of the issues on a group's agenda in terms of importance.

A technique for managing all this information is to make an issue-by-group-member matrix, fill in interests associated with each issue, and then rank order the issues for yourself and the other members of the group. A rule of thumb negotiators use is that if they cannot fill out the matrix, they do not know enough about the others attending the meeting and should postpone the meeting (or at least decision making) until they do.

Preparing for a meeting as though it were a negotiation is useful on a number of dimensions. First, it provides a structure for the group's discussion. Positions must be backed up with explanations that reveal interests and priorities. Once interests are revealed, creative solutions can sometimes be identified. Alternatively, solutions may be developed that mesh different members' priorities. Second, it encourages listening. Since all columns of the matrix but one are estimates, group discussion provides a good opportunity to test assumptions and update the matrix. The updated matrix may reveal new alternatives. Third, it helps group members develop a strategic plan for revealing their own interests and priorities. This third point requires a bit of explanation, since how much information to reveal about interests and priorities poses a major dilemma to the group member.

A group member's interests and priorities are his vulnerabilities. Once the group knows a member's interests and priorities, it can design an agreement that provides that member the very least acceptable to him — an agreement just a little better for him than the no-agreement alternative. There is no guarantee that the full sharing of interests associated with discussion leading to a second agreement will improve this member's situation. In contrast, when a group member's interests and priorities are not well known to the group, it is harder to design the first agreement at the edge of what is minimally acceptable. And, when the first agreement is very beneficial to a member, the second agreement must preserve that benefit. The dilemma is how much information to reveal and how quickly to reveal it. When trying to construct an agreement, it is always better to ask questions and learn more about others' interests and priorities than to reveal information about one's own. On the other hand, group members may expect reciprocal information sharing and be intolerant of those who do not participate. Looking at a matrix of issues, positions, interests, and priorities may help a group member plan a strategy for revealing information about himself contingent on the information being revealed by other group members.

The decision rule used by the group affects how many members' interests must be considered by the group before it can make a decision. The larger the number of members needed to make a decision, the longer will be the group's deliberations, the greater will be the number of alternatives that the group considers, and the higher will be the quality of the group's decision. Among the decision rules a group might use are dictatorship (one person decides), oligarchy (a few powerful people decide), simple majority (one more than half of the group), two-thirds majority, consensus (about a two-thirds majority, with the minority withdrawing their dissent), and unanimity (all group members decide).

* * *

. . . [T]he decision rule influences the approach taken to decision-making and the role and the power of dissent. Majority rules imply that the decision will be dominated by faction or coalition formation and that the views of the majority coalition will dominate group discussion. Consensus and unanimity rules imply that the decision will be made by joint problem solving and that the interests of all members will be considered. Put simply, the power of dissenters increases with the number of people necessary to make a decision.

* * *

Gary Goodpaster,[*]
Coalitions and Representative Bargaining
9 OHIO ST. J. ON DISP. RESOL. 243, 267-71 (1993-1994)[**]

* * *

B. *Representing Groups and Constituencies*

While all negotiators who represent other parties in a negotiation must face conflicts between a principal's expectations and the realities of the actual negotiation, additional problems arise when the principal is a group or a constituency. When the negotiator represents a group, her task may further be complicated by conflicts within it. The group may lack consensus on goals. Different persons or coalitions within it may have different priorities regarding goals or issues. Group members way disagree not only about goals, but also about strategy, tactics, and bargaining styles, and about the significance of developing particular relationships with the other side.

Indeed, the larger and the more heterogeneous the represented group, the more likely the group itself will be in conflict. Individuals comprising the group will have different interests and needs, and different perceptions of the bargaining situation. Subgroups, coalitions, or factions may also form. Whether the larger group is composed of relatively independent individuals, subgroups, or a combination of the two, these different actors will likely operate from different informational bases, different levels of intelligence and experience, and will interpret, assess, and value differently what is involved in the negotiation. In addition, the issues to be negotiated, as well as their possible outcomes, may have different impacts on individuals or subgroups, causing these actors to respond differently to various proposed negotiation outcomes.

Even where a group is unified on some issues when negotiation begins, consensus may dissolve as negotiation progresses and group members' perceptions of the issues and bargaining situation may change. The group may continue to lack consensus on issues unresolved within the group prior to negotiation. Other, unexpected issues may also arise during the course of the negotiation. Indeed, the very process of negotiation may stimulate members' awareness of such issues and create incentives to work them out. Thus, even while engaged in negotiations with others, a group may have to engage in its own internal negotiations. These negotiations will affect the agent at the table, and the agent may also participate in or even manage the internal negotiations.

The negotiator who represents a group is in a critical position. It is useful to think of the negotiator in such a situation as a political actor having

---

[*] Gary Goodpaster is Professor of Law Emeritus, University of California at Davis. This excerpt addresses some of the challenges of representing a group in negotiations.

[**] Copyright © 1993 Ohio State Journal on Dispute Resolution. Reprinted by permission.

to respond to the demands and expectations of a constituency. Where the group is unified, he will be subject to the group's substantive expectations regarding negotiation outcomes and its behavioral expectations regarding the manner in which he will carry out bargaining, the latter possibly enforced by group surveillance. Where the group is not unified, the negotiator, as the individual at a critical decision point, will be the target or focus of group members' influence attempts. On the other hand, the negotiator develops information during bargaining from which he can assess bargaining possibilities. He is in a privileged position vis-à-vis the group and can influence its decisions.

There are group politics that will arise in representative bargaining, and the negotiator will inevitably be involved. But the negotiator in such a situation is in a delicate political position, for he occupies two roles that are potentially in conflict. As a group representative, he has a proscribed (sic) role in which he is expected to be loyal to the group and to act according to instructions or only in ways that will further its defined interests. As a negotiator, he has the functional role of working with the other side's negotiator to craft a settlement. Because he is at the bargaining table, the negotiator will have a much more realistic sense of what is possible in the negotiation and how best to achieve it. Unfortunately, his assessment may be at odds with that of his constituency. If the group he represents takes a hard-bargaining approach and expects him to demonstrate his toughness and ability to deliver the results it expects, his flexibility to overtly undertake problem-solving or integrative bargaining is limited. Indeed, the need to impress his constituency, at least if it oversees his bargaining, may even constrain the negotiator's ability to develop a cooperative, friendly, and trusting relationship with the other side's negotiator. In such a situation, the negotiator is aware of the audience for which he must perform, even if it is not present. This pressured performance may interfere with what, in his judgment, constitutes the best way to bargain under the circumstances.

C. Working with Clients and Constituencies

Negotiators caught in such "boundary" role conflicts have a number of options regarding ways in which to proceed. Indeed, whether the negotiator represents a single client or a constituency, the problems her representative role presents are similar. The only significant difference arises from the fact of constituency politics. Plainly, the politics within the constituency, and the politics of working with, or on behalf of, a constituency, deeply affect the ways in which a negotiator goes about her work for a constituency. Nevertheless, because the two kinds of representation involve similar problems, I will treat them together, noting where necessary, unique problems involved in constituency representation.

Ideally, the negotiator working for a client or constituency needs its trust and confidence and its authority to operate freely and flexibly to craft the best possible agreement. But a negotiator will not always have that freedom of action. Her client or constituency may have its own confirmed views of what it desires and how to achieve these desires. Within a constituency, there may be factions or coalitions, and the reigning power may need to deliver certain results to retain its position. The constituency may view the negotiator as a mere agent of its will and not as an active player in determining what to seek in the negotiation.

What a negotiator can do in such circumstances is highly contingent on the character, unity, and sophistication of her client or constituency. Her freedom of action also depends on her skill, sophistication, and the nature of her working relationship with her principal. There are a number of general possibilities. When the principal's substantive expectations appear to be greater than the negotiator's considered judgment of what is possible from the negotiation, the negotiator can work, in advance of settlement, to reshape those expectations. The negotiator takes an active role in working with her client or constituency to create the substantive flexibility that she believes is needed to negotiate effectively.

To maximize negotiating room, the negotiator needs to educate her principal about the advantages and disadvantages of various ways of negotiating. In doing so, she should seek authority from the client to negotiate flexibly. If the principal gives the negotiator broad authority to negotiate as she deems appropriate, she obviously will have to work with the principal to discover its true interests in the negotiation, to anticipate the other side's interests, and to develop possible alternative solutions to the presented bargaining problem.

She can accomplish this by working with the client or constituency as it develops its substantive bargaining expectations and aspirations. If the party's views are already settled, she may have to educate it regarding bargaining possibilities and attempt to persuade it to revise its expectations. Working with a group is more difficult than working with an individual client because there are more persons involved, making group consensus harder to achieve, and once achieved, even harder to revise. Factions or coalitions within the group will also complicate the negotiator's task, and the negotiator may even have to negotiate alliances within the group that will enable the group to be effective in external negotiations.

The client or constituency, however, may have settled substantive expectations that the negotiator cannot alter prior to negotiation. If negotiation will not lead to results that satisfy these expectations, the negotiator may have to act in some way to alter her principal's expectations so that it will both accept the results and not blame her for failure. But that may be difficult. . . . Depending upon the trust vested in her, she might succeed in direct efforts to educate the principal about the realities of the situation. If the principal cannot be educated in this way, the negotiator may manipulate the bargaining so that the represented party has to confront the apparent realities of bargaining itself, and so force it to revise its expectations.

But a negotiator's client or constituency is likely to have not only expectations about substantive negotiation results, but also about the way in which the negotiator negotiates. In the case of a constituency, if it has no representatives at the table other than the negotiator, or does not otherwise in some way surveil her bargaining activities, she may appear to retain flexibility to bargain in whatever way she deems most useful. If the resulting proposed agreement does not better or meet her client's or constituency's substantive expectations concerning outcomes, she will have the problem of justifying or explaining the discrepancy. She will be in trouble if she bargained in unexpected ways. To gain flexibility, the negotiator can work to shape her principal's behavioral expectations about how she will bargain. The ideal way to do this would be to educate the principal regarding all the different bargaining strategies, particularly problem-solving, for it is the least widely understood bargaining strategy.

* * *

Gary Goodpaster,[*]
Coalitions and Representative Bargaining
9 OHIO ST. J. ON DISP. RESOL. 243, 255-58 (1993-1994)[**]

* * *

G. Real Coalitions

[Understanding the dynamics of coalition formation requires] consideration of such factors as personal interaction, investment in coalition-building, information availability and costs, loyalty, ideological compatibility of the participants, and perceived possibilities of future use of the developed relationship.

In real negotiations, parties may not be completely clear about their dependencies on one another. When they form coalitions, they cannot necessarily be certain about how their joined forces will change the configuration of their dependencies on the other parties to the negotiation. This is particularly true where the other parties may also ally as a responsive move. Furthermore, negotiating parties often value the same things differently. Parties' respective valuations may become clear only after they trade. Consequently, in forming an alliance, partners may not be able to determine in advance their respective shares of the distribution realizable if the alliance succeeds. This uncertainty is increased when the gains or receipts of coordinated action are themselves uncertain or variable or differentially attractive to coalition members.

---

[*] Gary Goodpaster is Professor of Law Emeritus, University of California at Davis. This excerpt discusses factors contributing to coalition stability and instability.

To illustrate this point, consider the coalition of nations that formed to fight the Persian Gulf War. At the initiation of the war, its outcome was uncertain. Even if the allying partners expected victory, none could predict how substantial a victory, its overall costs, or the costs each partner would experience. Coalition members also had different stakes in a successful outcome. The security of oil resources was a concern to many of the coalition members, but not to all members. Saudi Arabia hoped to retain its sovereignty and territorial integrity. Egypt and Syria were partially motivated by political considerations, and Egypt was also motivated by a loan-forgiveness side deal with the United States. Perhaps out of long-term strategic alliance considerations, Japan agreed to help pay for the war, despite the fact that it did not have significant oil security concerns

III. BUILDING AND SHAPING COALITIONS

A. Internal Coalition Negotiations

By joining a coalition, a party gains something it could not otherwise obtain, but it also pays a price. The ability of a potential coalition member to extract gain from joining a coalition turns on the question of how dependent the coalition is on that party to add to the bargaining power it needs to reach the desired results. What a party gains and what it pays therefore depend on its relative value to the coalition, and that in turn is partly a matter of what the other parties to a coalition bring to it. A party's value may also depend upon the role of non-coalition members. For example, if a countercoalition begins to form, an uncommitted party may find itself the object of a bidding war, and therefore will be highly valued. On the other hand, it might also be left out altogether as competing coalitions maneuver to enlist other players.

Coalition-building may be even more complicated, however, as coalition-builders may not fully know exactly what resources potential members might bring to the negotiation. As builders acquire information, they may shift their focus to other potential partners or change the proposed terms of the coalition. The external negotiation in which the coalition is involved may provide information that causes parties to revalue their own positions and the value of any coalition. Furthermore, potential members of a tentative coalition may not be able to finalize their shares of any coalition gains until the coalition concludes its external bargaining. Members' shares will depend upon what the coalition gains in the overall bargain, and that may depend on what the allies contribute at the very end of the bargaining. The contribution that any given coalition member makes to the overall result may not be known until the end of play. For example, the single vote that creates the majority necessary to pass legislation loses its determinative value when others join the majority just before the vote.

Coalitions can also impede efficient bargaining. Coalition partners may agree that any final external bargain must meet certain conditions. They may impose such conditions to insure that each partner gets what it wants out of the external negotiation. In doing so, coalitions may impose such constraints on their negotiator that he is unable to make the best possible tradeoffs.

B. *Coalitional Stability*

If coalition members are merely self-interested and opportunistic, then coalitions would appear to be volatile and unstable. Nonetheless, many coalitions remain intact for the duration of a negotiation or even longer. This might occur if coalition members had compatible interests, compatible ideologies, affectional ties, or other loyalties. Coalitions are also stable where members see potential future advantage from the present relationship. Thus, a member may forego short-term gain, or even suffer a loss, as a price of maintaining a relationship in anticipation of a possible long-term gain.

Even where such factors are not important, there is an additional reason for coalitional stability. Parties invest time, effort, and resources in creating coalitions and creating expectations. As they do, their positions and commitments may change because of the alliance. There are costs involved in forming coalitions, in breaking them, and in creating new coalitions. Such costs impede coalition restructuring.

Furthermore, coalitions often form under conditions of uncertainty with regard to results, the members' relative interests, and possible shares in results. By adding parties to a coalition, the predictions, evaluations, assessments, and guesses that form the bases of judgment during negotiation may be further complicated. These factors of uncertainty, investment, commitment, and information, and the added costs incurred in shifting alliances make coalitions more stable.

Where coalition parties are represented rather than individuals, coalition restructuring may be even less likely, for it is notoriously difficult to get organizations to change course. Depending on the organization's structure, the costs of providing information to relevant actors and getting their approvals can be quite high. For example, trade associations or unions cannot convene their memberships for each shift in coalition politics. One moves mountains, if at all, only rarely.

Depending on the nature of the coalition, and on the character of the negotiation in which it is involved, there may be some tendency toward what we might call "coalitional inertia." Even when coalition members have no pay-off reasons for staying in a coalition, other forces may incline them to remain. Although a coalition-member may not leave the coalition, it can certainly threaten to do so. A member can still use its position to bluff for a greater share of the payoff. Whether other coalition members will call the bluff or pay depends on how well they analyze the threatening member's actual position and alternatives.

* * *

David Sally & Kathleen O'Connor,[*] *Team Negotiations*
87 MARQ. L. REV 883, 884-90 (2004)[**]

* * *

Rather than send a solo negotiator to the table, decision makers may opt to pull together a team to hammer out the terms of a deal. Despite the costs of assigning a deal to a team, there are a number of reasons why this decision can make good sense. Negotiation is cognitively taxing. Parties must continually attend to both their own and the other side's interests and constraints as they work to agree on mutually beneficial terms. Teams allow for a division of labor and a combining of skill that means that N + 1 heads are better than one. On a related note, teams are likely to provide functional diversity that can pave the way to better deals. Composing a team that includes both process and content experts, strategic as well as tactical thinkers, number crunchers and smooth talkers allows for a range of skills that is likely to outmatch those of any single team member. For political reasons, too, there may be wisdom in picking teammates from different groups. For instance, a local union is likely to select representatives from each of several bargaining units to increase the chances that contract terms will be ratified by the units.

Still, it is not a foregone conclusion that teams should always be chosen over solo negotiators: there are some deep, dangerous pitfalls. Decades of study of groups and teams by social psychologists highlight a fundamental tension experienced by teammates — how to capitalize on the diverse abilities and opinions of members while at the same time acting as a cohesive unit. . . . Teamwork presents special challenges in coordination and motivation of members. For instance, groups, especially groups larger than four, can suffer from free rider problems. Rather than adding to the team, the cover provided by larger groups provides an opportunity for members to reduce their efforts rather than to fully participate in group decisions. Even for teammates who are motivated to work hard to serve the team, some aspects of the process may interfere with effective decision making. For instance, people working in teams tend to focus their discussion on facts and opinions that are held in common, leaving unique pieces of information or bits of data out of the conversation. When these bits of information are critical to the decision, the cost is a low-quality outcome. As groups gel and members come to value their cooperative relationships with each other, they can develop an intolerance to dissenting voices, even when those voices challenge the majority to consider more carefully their own judgments and

---

[*] David Sally is Visiting Associate Professor of Business Administration, Tuck School of Business at Dartmouth and Kathleen O'Connor is Associate Professor of Management and Organizations, Cornell University. Their article discusses the benefits and challenges of negotiating as a team.

interpretation of facts. Thus, while there are some advantages to convening a team to carry out work that could be done by a solo, teams need to work hard to ensure the full participation of their members.

Compared to the study of work groups and teams, the literature on negotiation teams is far smaller, making it difficult for scholars to offer many empirically derived recommendations to practitioners. However, one solution to the paucity of empirical evidence is to turn to the wealth of research on work teams for answers. Although this is a reasonable source for insights, it is critical to acknowledge how negotiating teams differ from other kinds of work teams. Social psychologists have made a distinction between purely cooperative teams and purely competitive groups. Cooperative teams have members who share the same motives and incentives and are focused on reaching a common goal. Competitive teams, including those involved in social dilemmas, are motivated to maximize their own gains irrespective of others' outcomes. Negotiating teams face a more complicated set of constraints. When they are working together to draft a plan or marshal support for a set of positions or arguments, members of negotiating teams are engaged in a cooperative task. Yet, if they represent groups with conflicting interests, they have incentives to improve their standing at the expense of their teammates. When the team sits down across the table from another team or solo, it is engaged in a mixed-motive task, one that requires the team both to cooperate to reach a mutually beneficial deal and to compete to get the best deal -possible for its side. We will consider these unique features of negotiating teams as we review the advantages and liabilities of teamwork at the bargaining table.

* * *

A common thread that connects the studies of negotiating teams is the clear advantage negotiating teams enjoy over solos. Without exception, teams reach deals of better quality than do their solo counterparts. This is true regardless of whether teams negotiate against other teams or against solos. Thus, it is the team itself that is driving the effect rather than the composition of the other side. There are a number of reasons for this benefit. First, as we noted earlier, negotiating is a complex cognitive task. With every offer and every answer to a question, negotiators are receiving information that may very well yield insights into the other side's priorities, interests, and alternatives. In addition to managing the interpretation of incoming information, negotiators also must craft counteroffers, generate questions, and decide whether and how to answer the other side's questions. Although this is quite a task for a solo negotiator, especially as the complexity of the issues grows and the stakes mount, teams have the option of breaking the task into component parts that can be designated to team members (roles include spokesperson, offer tracker, etc.). The extra memory capacity and parallel data processing offered by the linked minds of the team may be able to handle complex issues and interests that would overwhelm and "crash" a solo negotiator.

Second, there are tactics available to a team that cannot be implemented by an individual. The most outstanding example is the good cop/bad cop tactic. This tactic depends critically on having two different people perform each role in the proper order (bad cop, then good Cop). Another example is the use of an intentionally absent team member who is holding a key resource — projections, budgets, authorization, etc. Many solo negotiators use this tactic to transform their side into a team by claiming that any additional offer or concession will have to be approved by the boss.

Third, with the addition of each new member of the negotiating team, the collective network of colleagues and acquaintances around the team grows. The larger the network, the better the access the team has to information that can help it in its negotiation. For instance, team members may tap members into their expanded network to learn about the other side, its interests, its likely strategy, and its outside options. Furthermore, many studies document that when negotiators are able to develop trust, they are able to exchange the information necessary to reach high-quality deals. With more members at the table, teams have multiple opportunities either to rely on established relationships or to develop relationships that are likely to be helpful for establishing trust and, therefore, sharing honest and accurate information. That this is more than a theoretical possibility has been confirmed in a field study of labor negotiations.

Particularly when there is potential in the negotiation to make trades among issues or to introduce additional issues, creative thinking can hold the key to mutually beneficial deals. In some cases, the broader the range of talents on the team, the better able the team should be to generate creative solutions. Creativity is threatened when negotiators feel stressed. Thus, to the extent that team membership insulates negotiators from the pressures that solos experience, it is likely to mitigate the stress a negotiator might feel if she or he were handling the negotiation alone. One specific pressure is accountability, namely, representing an outside constituency at the bargaining table. Solo negotiators who are accountable often adopt a rather competitive stance in the negotiation that can limit their ability to build trust, exchange critical information, and keep focused on opportunities for joint gains. Teams, however, are insulated from these effects. Even when a team is accountable for its outcomes, the members experience lower accountability pressures than solos and, more importantly, respond less competitively to these pressures. Hence, they are better able to balance the need to get the most out of the deal with an interest in cooperating to ensure that a mutually beneficial deal is reached.

Thus far, we have emphasized the benefits that flow to negotiating teams. Yet, there are downsides to sending teams to the table. The first, and simplest, fact to point out is that teams are costly. Multiple people are being paid to do what one person could conceivably handle. There is a cost/benefit calculation that must ultimately buttress any decision to employ a negotiating team instead of a single bargainer. The same calculation is relevant in determining the size of the team: Each new member adds a layer of costs to the deal that will need to be recovered. Also, a member's efforts at this table limit his or her involvement [in] other productive tasks. Any decision about assigning teams or solos must include some estimate of the costs and a consideration of the likely payouts.

Teams may be self-managing, but they are rarely self-sufficient — an organizational structure and culture supporting teams is necessary to make them effective. One pitfall that decision makers need to avoid is the "manager's fallacy" — the belief that the key to effective teams is to simply put a group of bright people in a room together and stand back to watch the magic. Difficulties with coordination and motivation that plague some teams need to be understood and steps taken to avoid them before they sabotage any benefits the team could deliver. In fact, some of the good news about negotiating teams may fail to translate into high-quality deals as team size increases beyond the three members that are typically assembled in social psychologists' laboratories. Empirical research on teams and groups working on other kinds of tasks shows that the greater the number of team members, the more anonymous and less accountable any one member may feel. Some members may take this opportunity to scale back their efforts, creating a free-rider problem. Assigning people to specific roles and holding them accountable for fulfilling their roles as well as for the team's output is one way to combat this problem on large teams.

Team oversight might also be necessary to assure that the team is sufficiently heterogeneous. Because friendship networks are largely based on similarity, a team that arises spontaneously or endogenously across one person's network may be insufficiently diverse for the purpose at hand. As outlined above, many of the benefits of teams only occur if there are differences in perspectives, information, and histories.

In addition to increasing personnel costs and requiring an active supporting structure, negotiating teams are slow. Coordination becomes a bigger problem as more people are added to the team. Teams need to take steps to ensure that everyone understands his or her role as well as the strategy for the negotiation. It can be very helpful for the team to establish a mechanism for taking breaks during the negotiation. This can serve two purposes. First, it can help keep the team moving in the same direction as the negotiation unfolds, and second, it gives the teammates a chance to continue to provide unique insights and ideas that can be used to formulate new offers or to readjust strategy.

A lack of coordination can cause teams to fracture, a risk not faced by individual negotiators. As the size of the team grows or as team members become more heterogeneous, the potential for intra-team conflict increases. The intra-team negotiation might end in an impasse as a team struggles to integrate the interests, positions, opinions, and outside options of all its members. It is essential to recognize that this struggle is not all bad: In fact, many intra-team disputes do not block performance. Conflicts that are focused on the task at hand, disagreements over the best strategy, or hashing out whether one set of issues deserves more or less consideration can help the team sort out its priorities and come to a better outcome than would have been possible had the team avoided the conflict. However, when the conflict becomes personal, the performance of the team is likely to suffer. Teams need to make sure that their conflicts do not spill over and become personal. This vigilance creates yet another time expenditure for team above what solos will spend, especially during the critical preparation stage where teammates are getting to know each other and are working to pull together a plan for their negotiation.

The risks from intra-team division can also be limited if teams agree to internal decision-making rules before the negotiation begins. Even if conflicts among teammates over priorities were resolved originally, the team is likely to face considerable difficulties in deciding whether to accept a particular offer, risking impasses in the process. When anticipating difficulties in making decisions about finalizing deals, it would be helpful for teams to agree on a decision rule. Although unanimity is ideal for satisfying each teammate, the team may be best served by a majority decision rule that ensures that most parties get what they need from the deal.

* * *